AFRICA: TRIBAL LOCATIONS AND POLITICAL BOUNDARIES, 1964

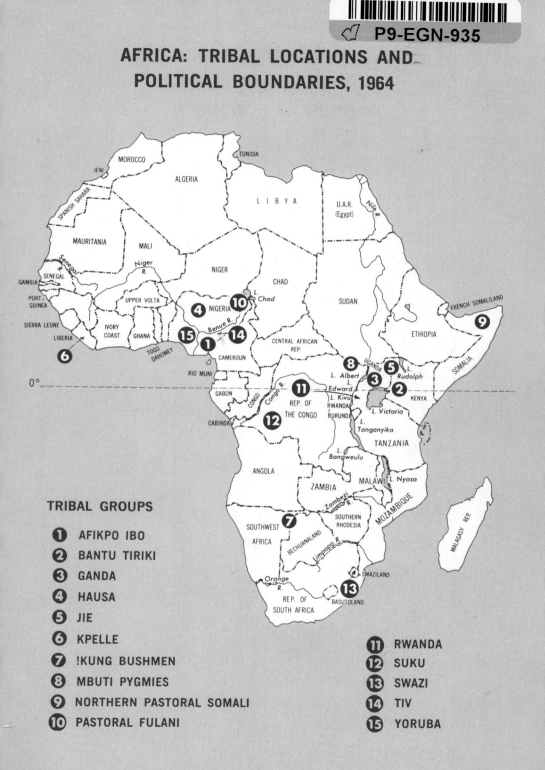

TRIBAL GROUPS

1. AFIKPO IBO
2. BANTU TIRIKI
3. GANDA
4. HAUSA
5. JIE
6. KPELLE
7. !KUNG BUSHMEN
8. MBUTI PYGMIES
9. NORTHERN PASTORAL SOMALI
10. PASTORAL FULANI
11. RWANDA
12. SUKU
13. SWAZI
14. TIV
15. YORUBA

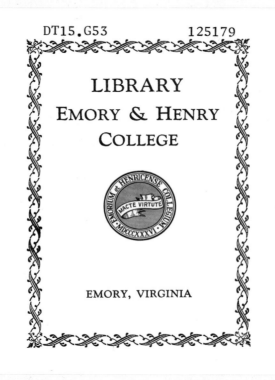

PEOPLES
OF AFRICA

PEOPLES

edited by JAMES L. GIBBS, JR.

UNIVERSITY OF MINNESOTA

OF AFRICA

Holt, Rinehart and Winston, Inc.

NEW YORK   CHICAGO

SAN FRANCISCO   TORONTO   LONDON

for James and Hortense

WHO EVER ENCOURAGED THEIR ERRANT SON

IN HIS URGE TO BECOME

A SILVERER OF THE MIRROR FOR MAN

PREFACE

For many years scholarly interest in the cultures of sub-Saharan Africa was confined largely to anthropologists and other specialists. These specialists have their own rich and varied technical literature on the subject. Today Africa has moved to the center of the world stage. The spotlight is on its peoples and their diverse life-ways, and African studies have assumed a position of curricular importance both here and abroad. Yet, there has been a lag in the provision of course materials on Africa for the student and the intelligent layman who seeks to acquire an adequate foundation in the subject—to go beyond the popularized, nontechnical literature—and move to deeper understanding and competence. *Peoples of Africa* was written primarily for the student who has had an introductory course in cultural or social anthropology or in sociology and is taking his first course dealing with the peoples and cultures of Africa. It should prove of interest to any serious reader concerned with emerging Africa.

All material for the book was newly written by contributors who were selected because of their intimate knowledge of one or more African societies and their demonstrated ability to put meaningful analyses of African societies and cultures into writing. Contributors who have already published full-length monographs on the culture they describe here have treated their material anew to meet the special purposes of the present volume. The aim has been to create a symposium consisting of well-rounded profiles representative of the peoples who live in Africa south of the Sahara Desert.

THE SAMPLE OF SOCIETIES The fifteen tribal groups described here are representative of the peoples of sub-Saharan Africa in five important aspects.

1. Among the tribal groups included are some living by each of the *major forms of subsistence* in sub-Saharan Africa: hoe agriculture, mixed farming, pastoralism, and foraging. The Afikpo Ibo, the Ganda, the Kpelle, the Suku, the Tiv, and the Yoruba are hoe agriculturalists. Mixed farming, where tillage and raising of small animals is supplemented by the keeping of large domestic animals, is practiced by the Bantu Tiriki, the Hausa, the Rwanda, and the Swazi. The Jie, the northern pastoral Somali, and the pastoral Fulani are pastoralists in whose lives farming plays virtually no role. Foraging (hunting and gathering) is the primary subsistence mode of the !Kung Bushmen and the Mbuti Pygmies.

2. Since the various modes of subsistence are associated with *different population sizes and related patterns of social and political organization*, these features are mirrored in the sample. The societies included range from the Mbuti Pygmies, a group of forty thousand, to the populous Hausa, Ibo, and Yoruba, each numbering over five million. The parallel levels of social organization vary from the band (of the !Kung Bushmen and the Mbuti Pygmies); to the middle range society (of the Afikpo Ibo, the Bantu Tiriki, the Jie, the Kpelle, the pastoral Fulani, the northern pastoral Somali and the Tiv); to the centralized state (of the Ganda, the Hausa, the Rwanda, the Suku, the Swazi and the Yoruba). The variation of social and political organization within each level is especially significant since it shows how the three structural principles of kinship, association, and territoriality may be combined. For example, the seven societies that have moderately or highly centralized traditional states differ greatly in their political structures because they vary in the way in which concentration of power is interwoven with the three basic structural principles. Additional diversity in sub-Saharan social forms is reflected in the kinship systems represented—patrilineal, matrilineal, and double descent systems—and in sodalities and associations, which include age groups, tribal fraternities, cult groups, mutual aid associations, craft organizations, and title-taking societies.

3. Each of the major sub-Saharan *culture areas and ecological zones* is represented. The major culture areas which, in the editor's view, best summarize the distribution of African cultures for the student new to African studies are those delineated by Melville J. Herskovits, most recently in 1962.[1] They are the Guinea Coast, represented by the Afikpo Ibo, the Kpelle, the Tiv, and the Yoruba; the Western Sudan, by the Hausa and the pastoral Fulani; the East Horn, by the northern pastoral Somali; the East African Cattle Area, by the Bantu Tiriki, the Ganda, the Jie, the Rwanda, and the Swazi; the Congo, by the Mbuti Pygmies and the Suku; the Khoisan, by the !Kung Bushmen; and the Eastern Sudan, which has not been included because, surprisingly enough, it has not been adequately studied. The central African area centering on the Congo Republic (Léopoldville), Southern Rhodesia, and Zambia is represented by only one society, the Suku, because tribal profiles of that region are already easily available.[2] The three major types of sub-Saharan habitat or vegetational zones—tropical forest, savanna, and desert—are also represented. The endpaper maps, which show the location of the various societies, indicate also major physical features, political boundaries, and vegetational zones as well as the Herskovits culture area boundaries.[3] This enables the reader to note

[1] Melville J. Herskovits, *The Human Factor in Changing Africa* (New York: Alfred A. Knopf, Inc., 1962).

[2] In *Seven Tribes of British Central Africa*, edited by Elizabeth Colson and Max Gluckman (Manchester, England: Manchester University Press, 1959).

[3] The culture areas are included by permission of Alfred A. Knopf, Inc.

the location of the societies and their relationship to the other features. The precise plotting of tribal locations allows the reader or instructor who wishes to use a more elaborate culture area scheme such as that of Murdock or Baumann and Westermann[4] to do so.

4. The five significant indigenous *racial stocks* of sub-Saharan Africa are sampled. Negroids are typified by the Afikpo Ibo, the Bantu Tiriki, the Ganda, the Hausa, the Kpelle, the Suku, the Swazi, the Tiv, the Yoruba and—in the view of most observers—the Hutu segment of the Rwanda. The Tutsi segment of the Rwanda belong to the Nilotic variant of the Negroid group, as do the Jie, who are sometimes referred to as "Nilo-Hamitic," which is not properly speaking a racial term but a cultural one. The highly unique Bushmanoids are represented by the !Kung Bushmen, and the equally distinctive Pygmoids by the Mbuti Pygmies and the Twa segment of the Rwanda. Finally, the pastoral Fulani and the northern pastoral Somali, the groups described here that most resemble the Caucasoids north of the Sahara, are classed either as Caucasized Negroids or Negroized Caucasoids.

5. Groups representative of each of the major sub-Saharan *language families* as delineated by Joseph Greenberg are included.[5] The Afro-Asiatic family is represented by the northern pastoral Somali (Cushitic branch) and by the Hausa (Chad subfamily); the Click (Khoisan) family, by the !Kung Bushmen; and the Macrosudanic family (Eastern Sudanic branch), by the Jie. Several branches and/or subfamilies of the far-flung Niger-Congo family are sampled. These include the Bantu languages (of the Central branch) spoken by the Bantu Tiriki, the Ganda, the Mbuti Pygmies, the Rwanda, the Suku, and the Swazi; another Central branch language spoken by the Tiv; the Kwa subfamily represented by the Afikpo Ibo and the Yoruba; the Mande subfamily represented by the Kpelle; and the West Atlantic subfamily represented by the pastoral Fulani.

Two further criteria were used in selecting tribal groups to be presented in this work. First, an attempt was made to include only groups among which *field research has been conducted recently*. With one exception, the field work upon which the papers in the book are based was carried out since 1950, with further research since 1960 in several cases. Secondly, the tribal groups selected, or their culture clusters, are *well represented in the literature on African societies*.[6] This means that the cultural configurations de-

[4] George P. Murdock, *Africa: Its Peoples and Their Culture History* (New York: McGraw-Hill, 1959) and H. Baumann and D. Westermann *Les peuples et les civilisations de l'Afrique* (Paris: Payot, 1957).

[5] Joseph Greenberg, *Studies in African Linguistic Classification* (New Haven: Compass Publishing Co., 1955). The 1955 names for language families were used because they have been widely adopted by Africanists, while later terms proposed by Greenberg and by others have been the subject of some controversy. (Cf. "Confusion in African Linguistic Classification" by Harold K. Schneider in *Current Anthropology*, Vol. 5, No. 1, 1964, pp. 56-57).

[6] This has influenced the tribal terminology chosen in one case. The Tiriki have

scribed here can be generalized to related peoples and that for each society included a wider and more specialized literature is available to the reader, as indicated in the bibliographies. This book is intended to serve as a bridge to such specialized literature within African studies,[7] whether it falls under the discipline of anthropology, geography, history, or political science.

THE CONTRIBUTIONS   Each of the contributions was written to a common outline prepared by the editor and reviewed by the contributors so that chapters would be basically comparable. However, the aim has been, insofar as is reasonable, to avoid any particular theoretical point of view and, to emphasize this goal, the studies are arranged alphabetically by the name of the tribal group and not by the culture area or subsistence mode.

Each chapter treats certain obvious factors such as location, physical type, language, habitat, economy, social and political organization, and religion. In addition, some topics not usually covered in brief cultural profiles are discussed. Among these are child training and socialization, patterns of formalized friendship, law, and social and economic change. Discussion of these topics should increase the usefulness of the volume for those interested in subjects such as culture and personality, ethno-law, and acculturation. Treatment of culture change is especially important because, increasingly, those who wish to learn about Africa are not anthropologists but political scientists, geographers, historians, missionaries, diplomatic and technical assistance personnel, and others, and they wish to know of change in African societies as well as traditional patterns. It is because of this that recent field work was stressed as a criterion in selecting societies to be presented. Because of limitations of space some topics could not be systematically treated, but the bibliographies accompanying each chapter will be useful to those who wish to delve further into a particular culture.

These studies are tribal descriptions prepared by the anthropologist who actually did the field work upon which the profile is based, and have the authenticity and vitality that come with such knowledge of a culture. Although each author organized his study around the common outline, he was free to let the field data and his own sense of the configuration of the culture, combined with his style of craftsmanship, shape his presentation. Similarly, the individual theoretical orientations of the authors are revealed in their writings—even though no central theoretical scheme is provided. These are a significant source of insight for the reader, for, as Paul Bohannan suggests in his study, an anthropologist's description of a culture is like a myth in that it is "a narrative that organizes data for some purpose."

---

been referred to as the *Bantu* Tiriki, even though the other Bantu-speaking societies have not been so designated, in order to stress the fact that the Abaluyia people to which they belong were formerly referred to as the Bantu of North Kavirondo.

[7] A useful complement to this book is a widely used collection of such professional papers, *Cultures and Societies of Africa* edited by Simon and Phoebe Ottenberg (New York: Random House, 1960).

A careful comparative reading of the formulations that the authors have written for the joint purpose offers documentation for the considerable body of common principles shared by all the social and behavioral sciences. At the same time the studies reflect the differences between the British "structural" school of African anthropology and the American approach, with which it has much in common but which is more "configurational." The analyses also portray varying time orientations some, more than others, being organized around the "diachronic" or historical model. Variations in the contributions also reflect differing richness of field data and the diverse research interests of the contributors. All the contributions offer valuable glimpses into the process of drawing inferences from data and "model building." Although it is not a major goal of the book, the volume is, incidentally, a study in the anthropological method.

THE INTRODUCTIONS Because general introductions to Africa's peoples and cultures[8] are already available to the student and the serious layman, this book contains only introductory comments to each chapter. These comments by the editor, intended mainly for the reader who is not using the book in connection with a formal course, stress the uniqueness of each culture and the study in which it is described. They suggest some of the features most significant about each culture from the point of view of African studies, especially anthropology. Where these features can be made clearer by drawing a parallel or pointing out a contrast with another culture represented here, this has been done.

The introductions are meant to be suggestive rather than exhaustive. Thus, the relationship between crops, land utilization, and political organization is discussed only in the introduction to the Ganda chapter, but the reader should not conclude that this relationship is without significance in other societies where it is less striking. The introductions are not intended to be summaries of the chapters. The significance of the particular cultural foci highlighted in the individual introductions will be most apparent to the reader only after he has acquired familiarity with the range and variety of the sub-Saharan cultures and societies by reading all the profiles. For example, the role of associations is especially crucial among the Ibo, and this role is, therefore, discussed in the introduction to that chapter. However, the reader should be acquainted with the role of associations in other societies in order best to understand their role in Afikpo. Such understanding is facilitated by the fact that each study describes all the features of the culture it summarizes.

The introductions and, of course, the chapters themselves provide a sense of the range of problems treated by Africanists and their relevance to

[8] Such introductions are "Africa and Its People," the introduction to the Ottenbergs' volume cited above; the Herskovits volume cited above; and Paul Bohannan's *Africa and Africans* [paperback; New York: Natural History Press (American Museum Science Books), 1964].

more general considerations in social science. By reading several relevant chapters the reader may deepen his understanding of some of the major problem areas of African studies such as the relationship between habitat and culture, variations in the form of the African kingdom and bureaucratic state, the economic and social uses of livestock, the economic and political impact of colonialism, variations in the types of associational groupings, and the syncretism of Islam and indigenous African religions.

ACKNOWLEDGMENTS   I would like to acknowledge with gratitude assistance that helped to make this book possible.

Paul Bohannan enthusiastically supported the original conception of the book and backed it with continuing interest and avuncular advice.

The contributors, widely dispersed, showed their devotion to African studies by cheerfully assuming a difficult writing assignment, by their promptness in meeting deadlines, and by their cooperation in working out editorial problems. I would also like to acknowledge their comments on the contributors' outline and the chapter introductions. Any flaws in the conception or organization of the book are mine, and I will welcome comments and criticisms from instructors, students, and other readers who use the book.

Publishers and scientific institutions have been generous in granting permission to reproduce previously published ethnographic material, maps, diagrams, and photographs. Daryll Forde, director of the International African Institute, has been particularly gracious. Some private individuals have kindly supplied photographs and permission to reproduce them. All such assistance is acknowledged with gratitude and specific acknowledgments are made in the first note in each chapter or in photographic captions. Except where otherwise noted, photographs were taken by the authors.

Several people have contributed to the preparation of the manuscript. Yvonne Foy, assistant librarian of the International African Institute, rendered special assistance. I am grateful to my colleagues E. Adamson Hoebel, for generous editorial comments and criticisms, and Robert F. Spencer, for helpful comments on the pronunciation guide. Rachel Bonney, Mary-Jean Marinan, and Audrey Vaale typed portions of the manuscript. James Sahlstrand and Wayne R. Lazorik helped prepare the photographs.

This volume could not have appeared without the constant and unselfish assistance of my wife, Jewelle Taylor Gibbs. She read the manuscript with meticulous care, assisted with preliminary copy editing, tended to numerous tedious details of its physical preparation, and made many helpful editorial suggestions. Above all, she was a source of encouragement and support over the four years in which the book was in preparation.

Minneapolis, Minnesota   James L. Gibbs, Jr.
November, 1964

CONTENTS

1

THE AFIKPO IBO
OF EASTERN NIGERIA

about the chapter

The Ibo, numbering some five million, are, like the Yoruba and Hausa, not only among the largest of Nigeria's ethnic groups, but among the largest tribal groups in Africa. Like the Yoruba, the Ibo consist of many "tribes" or peoples all speaking one language. They live in dispersed groups of villages and lack the cities and centralized kingdoms that characterize their Yoruba and Hausa neighbors. Anthropologists and political scientists have been intrigued to learn how a people as "progressive" and populous as the Ibo are socially integrated without reliance on centralized, bureaucratic political structures.

Ottenberg's recent research has shown that the absence of a complex, centralized kingdom need not imply structural or cultural simplicity. Her description of one of the Ibo peoples, the Afikpo, shows how the integration of Ibo society is achieved by the interplay of many elements, especially a strong development of associations—a culture trait that is characteristic of West Africa as a whole. Associations that play a part in integrating Afikpo society take many forms: age grades, a village men's society, title societies, and, most recently, improvement associations. Decision making, law enforcement, dispute settlement, and other political and social control functions are divided among several of these associational and kinship groups in such a way as to prevent the concentration of authority; a principle of checks and balances is at work.

The Afikpo Ibo, like the Suku, have a kinship system that serves

1

to resolve the contention of conflicting unilineal principles. Thus, the operation of interlocking factors is not limited to political organization; it is found also in the Afikpo double-descent kinship system. Double-descent systems are relatively rare in sub-Saharan Africa, so this chapter offers insight into the range of variation that occurs within African kinship systems.

Following a tradition that has deep roots in American anthropology, Ottenberg delineates Afikpo ethos in terms of a series of themes or postulates, some of which—such as a belief in male dominance—are common in African societies. She has traced the ways these themes are expressed and used in a number of social institutions. In performing their individual roles, Afikpo give expression to the common postulates and themes and form at the same time a network of social statuses. Ottenberg has shown both the vitality of Afikpo beliefs and behavior and the resulting structural configurations, demonstrating the compatibility of the "structural" and the "configurational" approach.

about the author

Phoebe Ottenberg, Extension Lecturer at the University of Washington, received her Ph.D. from Northwestern University in 1958, and has taught also at Macgregor College in Nigeria.

From 1951 to 1953 she did field research in Nigeria among the Afikpo Ibo as an Area Research Fellow of the Social Science Research Council and with a grant-in-aid from the African Studies Program of Northwestern University, and she did further research in Afikpo in 1959 and 1960. With her husband Simon Ottenberg, she is coeditor of *Cultures and Societies of Africa* (1960). Her writings include also "The Changing Economic Position of Women among the Afikpo Ibo" (1959) and (with Simon Ottenberg) "Afikpo Markets: 1900–1960" (1962).

PHOEBE OTTENBERG · *The Afikpo Ibo of Eastern Nigeria*[1]

INTRODUCTION

LOCATION · Reaching from delta swampland near the Gulf of Guinea northward through tropical rain forest to open grassland, from west of the Niger to the Cross River in the east, the Ibo peoples cover a major part of a thickly populated farming region of southeastern Nigeria.

LANGUAGE · The Ibo are not a single people but are made up of over two hundred groups or "tribes" totaling more than five million persons. Each group is a separate society consisting of from one to thirty or more villages or local communities, but the different "tribes" speak a common language, Ibo, one of the Kwa languages of the Niger-Congo family (Greenberg 1955:10), and share many features of custom and belief.

PHYSICAL APPEARANCE · The Ibo are Negro in physical type, with skin ranging from medium to dark brown, brown eyes, and black, curly hair. They are light in body build and generally short in stature, men averaging perhaps five feet four to five inches and women, five feet or less.

BACKGROUND · Before British occupation late in the nineteenth century and at the beginning of the twentieth century, many Ibo groups fought inter-tribal wars for the purpose of headhunting and obtaining captives to sell to slave traders. With European contact, education, and wider experience of the world about them, Ibo-speaking peoples have developed a new ethnic consciousness, a feeling of identity as Ibo, in relation to peoples of differing languages and backgrounds in the modern state in which they find themselves. The local groups have maintained their distinctive identities, however, and retain many of their traditional customs. It is one of the eastern Ibo groups, the Afikpo, that will be described here.

The origins of the Afikpo are obscure, and legends of the founding of

3

the different villages are of little help in solving the mystery other than by indicating that present-day Afikpo are descendants of several different peoples moving to the locality at various times in the past. One thing that is clear, however, is that there are strong ties with Aro Chuku, a village group forty miles to the south, which is the home of the Aro people and their famous oracle *ibini θkpabi*, known in English as the "Long Juju." Backed by the power of their oracle, which was greatly feared through eastern Nigeria, the Aro traveled throughout the area in precolonial times, setting up colonies among other Ibo peoples and conducting a lucrative trade in European goods from the coast and slaves from the hinterland.

Descendants of Aro colonists are a distinctive element of the Afikpo population today, and both Aro and non-Aro people in the villages worship local spirit shrines obtained from the parent shrine of *ibini θkpabi* at Aro Chuku. Evidence for considerable cultural intermixture other than that with the Aro is seen in the fact that, like some other eastern Ibo groups and non-Ibo peoples to the east of the Cross River,[2] Afikpo have double unilineal descent, rather than patrilineal descent, which is the rule for most Ibo groups including the Aro.

HABITAT AND CLIMATE · Afikpo is at the junction of two vegetation zones. To the north stretches rolling grassland—orchard bush dotted here and there with rock outcroppings, scrubby brush, and occasional groves and isolated giant trees that stand as remnants of the forest that once covered the area. To the south and eastward across the river is deciduous forest. The low flat country to the west is grassland that in the wet season becomes a swamp, studded with water lilies floating in the midst of rice fields. Though there are some oil palms in Afikpo, it is outside the so-called palm belt of the equatorial rain forest to the south.

Afikpo has well-defined climatic seasons, with rains from mid-May to October and a dry season from November to May. Of an average annual rainfall of 77 inches, about 60 fall during the climax period of May to October. There are occasional rains during the dry season, and severe electrical storms with high winds at the beginning and end of the rainy season.

SETTLEMENT PATTERN · The twenty-three villages of Afikpo lie clustered on and about a range of low sandstone hills running east-west some ninety miles north of the Gulf of Guinea. Several of the villages are built on a high bluff overlooking the west bank of the Cross River. Ranging from hamlets of a little more than a hundred persons to towns of more than two thousand, the Afikpo villages together form a village group,[3] with ties of kinship, custom, and a common government.

Some of the Afikpo villages are close together, whereas others are sep-

An Afikpo Compound Children returning to their homes in the compound in the late afternoon.

arated by a mile or more of bush. The villages are compact, each built around a central square (or two or more squares if the village is a large one), which is a clearing with a thatch-roofed mud resthouse of the village men's society and a large open space where meetings and ceremonies are held. Occasional large trees give patches of shade, and logs along the edges seat spectators at gatherings. Extending from a village, sometimes for several miles, is a wide band of farmland divided into six sections, one or two of which are cultivated each year while the others lie fallow. At the edge of the villages and along the roads and bush paths connecting them are scattered groves of oil and raffia palms. At the north edge of Afikpo, atop the highest hill, is the Government Station and Afikpo District Headquarters, former outpost of empire, now the buzzing center of local self-government.

Most villages are divided into wards, often called the upper and lower village in reflection of the topography, and each ward is divided into compounds. A compound is the home of a group of kinsmen and their wives, sometimes numbering several hundred persons, who live in houses crowded wall-to-wall along narrow alleyways, often on different ground levels with stairsteps or earthen ramps connecting the rows of houses. The entrance to a compound is usually through an ornamental gateway leading from the square. The back of the compound, at the edge of the village, is devoted to garden land where certain crops not planted on the farms are grown.

Ethos

Three values that dominate life in Afikpo, consciously expressed by the people and appearing again and again in various contexts in their activities, are the importance of strength, attachment to the land, and a sharp division between the sexes. These have their roots in precolonial days when life was indeed precarious, the land was almost the only source of subsistence, and sex polarity made for what was then the most efficient allocation of men's and women's resources and energy. Although a number of the outer aspects of life were greatly changed by the 1950s, the old values persisted, some in reinterpreted form.

A traditional expression of interest in physical strength that still continues is wrestling contests that take place among the men and boys, and to a limited extent among the girls, of Afikpo that give great prestige to the champion wrestlers. The idea of strength is also expressed in abstract form in the emphasis placed on individual achievement. In their admiration for the self-made man the Afikpo seemed to the fieldworkers to be 200 percent American. Great effort is exerted in the amassing of wealth toward conspicuous consumption, traditionally in the form of title-taking, that is, joining a title society by paying a high initiation fee and giving a series of feasts to the members, and in the form of second funerals. A second funeral is a ceremony performed in honor of a deceased parent, often years after his death, as a mark of respect for his spirit and a sign of achievement on the part of the funeral-giver. It commonly involves the sacrifice of a cow, or a cow and a horse in the preferred form of the ceremony, and a great expenditure in feasting the deceased's kinsmen and villagers.

Although the emphasis on individual achievement is very strong among the Afikpo, there is, paradoxically, an equally strong concern for group solidarity. Here, however, an individual's distinction is shared by his group, which often helps in his achievement by financial support and contributions to feasts, thereby enhancing the prestige of both individual and group.

Afikpo impress outsiders as self-assertive, verbal people, clear in their aspirations and explicit as to the role of others in helping or hindering them in achieving their goals. The Ibo people as a group are often described by non-Ibo as "pushing" or "aggressive," and it seems very possible that it is their concern for strength and achievement that lies behind these observations.

The Afikpo's attachment to the land is shown in many ways, but particularly by the feeling still held by many that farming is the best kind of work that one can do in life and by their keen devotion to their farms.

Relations between the sexes in Afikpo are marked by strong male domination, with an almost complete separation of daily activities of males and females, and this principle of division of the sexes is strictly observed from early childhood on. In precolonial days men's position of dominance carried with it the heavy responsibility of defense in warfare and controls over the land and the supernatural. Women were in a position of physical dependence on men, without whom they could not safely even go to the farms to tend their crops. Living was on a bare subsistence level, and there were none of the resources later acquired, such as new crops that increased the food supply and the opening up of market trade. Women's subjection to men was thus validated by men's responsibility for them, and although the economic picture had vastly changed by the 1950s, the basic values still obtained.

ECONOMY

CROPS AND DOMESTIC ANIMALS · The basis of the Afikpo economy is hoe farming. Traditionally both men and women earned their living by farming, and there were no full-time specialists. The major staple is the yam, several varieties of which are grown by men. Women's staples are cassava (manioc), coco yams, and ɛdo, a vine-borne, potatolike vegetable. "Small crops" also grown by women are maize, several types of beans, spinachlike leaves used in soup, fluted gourds, peanuts, okra, and tomatoes. Coconuts and fruits, such as oranges, mangoes, bananas, plantains, and papaya, grow in the villages and form a minor part of the diet. Rice farming was introduced about 1945 but by the early 1950s had not become a major activity.

Sheep, goats, chickens, and ducks are owned by both men and women. Afikpo once kept tsetse-resistant dwarf cattle, but these were outlawed because they broke into farm plots and trampled the crops. The maintenance of domestic animals is quite casual. They are kept in the houses at night to prevent theft, but during the day they fend for themselves. These animals are looked upon as a potential source of wealth, for they may be sold in the market, but little ritual or sentimental value is attached to them.

The Afikpo agricultural cycle is reflected in the names of the seasons. Okwu (heap), from about mid-February to May, is the season when the mounds in which the yams are grown are made and the yams are planted. Women's "small crops" are planted in and between the yam heaps after the yams are in the ground. From the time the last yams are planted, usually around mid-May, until the first yams are harvested for the New Yam Festival, ikeji (harvest yam), at the end of August, is θnwθ (famine). The season between the yam festival and mid-October is udumini (season of rain). During this time the yam harvest continues, and women's small crops except maize and peanuts are harvested. From about mid-October to February is ɔkɔci (there is no English equivalent), the time of ceremonials and rest from farmwork. Fallow bush is cut and burned at the end of ɔkɔci in preparation for heap-making and planting.

Harvesting Yams An elder harvests his first yam for the New Yam Festival. He holds a digging stick in his right hand. At left are yam vines; at lower right, cassava plants.

LAND TENURE · Since farmland is owned by groups of persons, not individuals, the right to use it derives from membership in the owning group. Because of the shortage of land in Afikpo, some individuals rent land from the people of neighboring village groups having land to spare. Farmland is also sometimes obtained on pledge by one group from the owning group in return for financial aid or some service rendered, such as support in a dispute. The bulk of farmland and groves of oil and raffia palms are owned by matrilineal descent groups, but some is owned by patrilineal groups, villages, and compounds. In addition, these trees and coconut palms growing in the villages may be individually owned by men but not women, for whom it is taboo to climb palm trees.

Land tenure is controlled by the men of the owning groups, and rights to use are allocated by the elders among them. With the exception of garden crops and some cassava, women grow their crops on the same land as their husbands' yams. Women have the right to use farmland of their matrilineal groupings, though access to it is usually obtained through their husbands, who approach the owning group to obtain such land on their wives' behalf. Husbands have rights to their wives' matrilineal farmland.

Since matrilineal groupings, which own the largest share of farmland, are not localized, the holdings of one matriclan may be scattered through the farmland of most of the Afikpo villages. The land farmed by one person is parceled into tiny plots, calculated in numbers of heaps, and may be located in the farmland sections of several different villages.

DIVISION OF LABOR · The basic unit of production is the household, consisting of a man and his wife, or wives, and unmarried children. In the polygynous family the household is divided into as many units as there are wives. For each unit the husband is responsible for supplying yams in season and meat or fish for feasts; the wife is responsible for the rest of the food supply.

There is explicit division of labor by sex. In farming, men clear the fields and make the heaps in which the yams are to be planted, though women and boys may help with this task. Men plant the yams and, after they have sprouted, tie the vines to poles to keep them off the ground. A wife hoes and weeds her husband's yam crop, and she is entirely responsible for her own crops. Men harvest the yams, and their wives and children carry them to the ɔba (yam barn), a series of high wood racks built in a grove outside each village.

Only men fish on the Cross River, but women fish in ponds and small streams in the bush. Women extract the oil from their husbands' palm fruits and are allowed to keep the kernels, which they sell for export or keep to use for skin lotion. Pots are made only by women who have been married.

In housebuilding, for the traditional wattle-and-daub, thatch-roofed houses, men build the bamboo frames. Women and children carry the earth and water for the mud walls. Men apply the mud to the frames and mold the earthen sleeping platforms inside the house. When the walls are dry, women smooth them outside and inside. Men make thatch, and boys attach it to the roof framework. In the newer mud-block houses men build the frames and mold the blocks; women carry the water to make the blocks and carry the blocks from where they are made to the building site.

Although age is not an important basis for labor division in daily tasks, there are certain duties that children perform. Within the different villages there are certain types of work and activities that are associated with the various categories of the Afikpo system of age groupings.

Afikpo have two types of cooperative work groups. The first, ozi ahɔ (work-everybody), is a men's group organized most commonly for house-building and sometimes for yam heap-making. The second type is ozuzu (committee), formed by young women on the basis of friendship for mutual help in weeding during a farm season. In addition to these voluntary groups the men's and women's age sets of a village may be called upon by the elders to perform tasks, such as building and repairing bush paths or clearing the village square.

Afikpo follow several occupations besides farming. In villages along the Cross River many men are full- or part-time fishermen. In the dry season, temporary communities of bamboo and palm-thatch shelters are built to house the fishermen and sometimes their families on the sand bars, where fish are smoked and sold to traders, who sell them locally and downstream.

Among women, particularly middle-aged and older, potmaking is a part-time occupation yielding an important source of income without which, many feel, they would be unable to feed themselves and their families.

Some men work part time as mat- and thatch-makers, and a few as woodcarvers. Traditionally the men of certain Afikpo patrilineages were blacksmiths, but this function has been taken over by men from communities to the north.

Occupations that have come with European contact are carpentry, tailoring, and tinsmithing. In the small district of shops and "bar and hotels" (taverns) that has grown up near the Government Station, a number of men have shops in which they make furniture and door and window frames, several tailor men's clothes to order for the growing number of men wearing European clothing, and a few make lamps and children's book boxes from kerosene tins and galvanized sheet zinc.

WAGE LABOR AND MARKETS · During the early 1950s a number of the young men of Afikpo worked in various cities of Nigeria and the British Cameroons. Most of them were men of some education, working as policemen, prison employees, clerical workers, laborers, and traders. The most common pattern was for them to return to Afikpo to marry and settle down.

In Afikpo there is a central market that meets every four days as well as several smaller markets, and Afikpo people trade also in the markets of neighboring village groups. A considerable number of young men, particularly those who have had a few years of schooling and reject farming as an occupation but are unable to qualify as clerks or teachers, are full-time traders in cloth, "articles" (sundries), and dried fish, buying their goods wholesale in cities and retailing them locally. Older men often go to market to sell surplus yams they have grown. In the early 1950s women sold pots and surplus farm products in Afikpo and nearby markets but did not follow trading as a full-time occupation. Market trade has shown a great increase since precolonial times and for many has become an important source of income for subsistence needs.

SOCIAL ORGANIZATION

Family and descent groups

DOUBLE DESCENT · The key to the understanding of Afikpo social organization is its double descent system, in which each individual is a member of groups tracing descent from a male founder through males and from a female founder through females. Thus, instead of being matrilineal or patrilineal, as is true of most African societies, Afikpo are both, and functions performed by descent groups are divided between the patrilineal and matrilineal groupings.

The basic descent groups are the patrilineal lineage (*umudi*) and the matrilineal clan (*ikwu*). There are about 150 such lineages and some 30 clans in the village group. The patrilineal lineage is the core of the group which, ideally, resides in one compound (*ɛzi*). It is therefore strongly localized. However, members of a matriclan do not live together in one locality, but are scattered through the Afikpo villages.[4]

The patrilineal lineage is generally divided into from two to four sub-lineages, Ndɛbu or Ndɛ (people), whose members are descended usually from sons of the lineage founder and are identified with a particular section of the compound. The matrilineal clan is divided into a large number of lineages, *ikwu era* (matriclan-breast), determined on a geographical basis, each composed of clan members living in neighboring villages. Because of the large size and the dispersed nature of the matriclan, with members some-times living a considerable distance from one another, the principle of sub-division into lineages is based on contiguity rather than on lineage segmen-tation—subdivision according to segments of the founder's family—as in the case of the patrilineage. In matters of everyday contacts and mutual support among members of a matrilineage, physical nearness is of more significance than closeness of kinship.

THE FAMILY   ·   The term "family," as used by English-speaking Afikpo (there is no Ibo word for "family"), may apply to several different groups. On the simplest level is the *elementary family,* composed of a father and a mother and their children, that is, the family in the usual Western sense of the word. But in Afikpo, where many men have more than one wife, there is also the *polygynous family,* made up of a father and his wives and all their children—father, mothers, and a group of full and half siblings. Residence is patrilocal; a girl goes to live with her husband when she marries, and sons, when they marry, do not traditionally leave home and set up domestic estab-lishments of their own. Therefore, in addition, there is the *extended family* (*umudi* or *Ndɛbu*): a father and his sons—or a group of brothers if the father is dead—their wives, sons, and unmarried daughters. The extended family usually has from about five to thirty members.

The extended family is, as a rule, housed in one section of the com-pound. Each married man has a house, as has each wife, where she lives with her children. In theory the houses of a family are close together, but in crowded compounds a family's houses may be spread about according to the availability of quarters as the family grows. A husband with a quarrel-some wife may arrange for her housing in a remote part of the compound away from the rest of the family.

Within the polygynous and extended families, patterns of authority are determined along lines of descent. The father in the polygynous family, or the eldest male who is sound of mind and body in the extended family, is its head. The head of the extended family looks after the members' welfare, and in the days of warfare he was responsible for their physical protection. He is supposed to see that the men and their wives receive sufficient farmland, to help the men in farming and undertakings such as trading, and to give his sons and younger brothers financial support in their first marriages. He advises family members and helps settle marital disputes that are brought to him, and he acts as a deputy for any of his brothers who live away from Afikpo.

In the polygynous family the ɔkpara (eldest son) of the father is in a position of special prestige and in adulthood will be expected to assume a position of leadership in the extended family and patrilineage. The eldest son of each co-wife is in adulthood concerned with the provision of matrilineal farmland for his brothers and sisters after they marry, and with the burial and funeral ceremonies of his mother. In addition, he acts as a helper and adviser of his sisters' sons.

Inheritance, like authority, follows descent lines, with emphasis on matrilineal ties. A man's house and the yams he has grown pass patrilineally to his sons; but most portable property, especially valuables (including money, which by the 1950s had become an important issue for most Afikpo), passes to male members of his matrilineage. A woman's property (her house is not her own, but belongs to her husband's patrilineal lineage) passes to her female matrilineal relatives. For both a man and a woman the division of property is supervised by the head or a male elder of the deceased's matrilineal lineage. Since British occupation there has been an increasing tendency for men to try to leave money to their sons rather than to their matrilineal kinsmen.

WIDER DESCENT GROUPS: THE PATRILINEAGE · In addition to the family groupings, the larger descent groups as a whole have an important significance in the lives of individuals. The patrilineal lineage, defined as a group of persons who can trace their descent through the male line to a known male ancestor, is usually of six to seven generations in depth and may vary in size from about a dozen to as many as five hundred members. It is known by the name of its founder, preceded by Ndɛ. Each lineage usually resides in one compound and has its own ancestral spirit shrine, ma obu (spirit-house), located in a men's resthouse (obu) in the compound. Leadership in the lineage is in the hands of the older men, who make decisions by discussion and consensus. There are no chiefs or headmen.

The lineage owns houseland, some farmland, and groves of oil and raffia palms. Members support one another in legal disputes, particularly when the interests of the lineage as a whole are involved. A woman usually leaves the custody of her own patrilineage at marriage and comes under the authority of her husband's lineage, though she never becomes a member of it in any sense.

THE PATRILINEAL SUBLINEAGE • The patrilineal sublineage that occupies a section of a compound has some controls over housing and farmland, and occasionally over oil- and raffia-palm groves. Its members participate in ceremonial activities such as title-taking and second funerals, and the group is responsible for the burial of members. Leadership is very informal and is usually vested in the oldest man, although any adult male member may represent the group at meetings of the lineage leaders.

These patrilineal groupings form the basis of political control in the compound and village. Within the compound they are concerned with keeping the peace, particularly among the women, whose ties with the lineage are not so strong as the men's and who are also subject to counterpulls of their own matrilineal affiliations. Social control inside the compound is thought of primarily as a kinship affair, and legal means are usually not employed unless a matter cannot be settled by the sublineage or the lineage.

THE MATRICLAN • A matriclan is defined as a group of persons descended through the female line from a female founder. Because the founder and the depth (that is, number of generations) of the clan are unknown, members are unable to trace their descent to the founder as is possible in the case of the patrilineage. Afikpo matrilineal clans range in membership from a few hundred to several thousand persons. Each is known by a name, often of unknown origin, prefixed by the word ibɛ (side or part).

With their pattern of dispersed residence spreading members through the different villages, matrilineal clans serve as an important unifying factor among the Afikpo. There is a strong sentiment among members, and one will often use the name of the group in greeting another. Traditionally, the clan had the obligation of blood revenge should one of its members be killed by an outsider.

Each clan has a spirit shrine, Nja, concerned with the welfare of its members. Unlike the ma obu of the patrilineage, it is not an ancestral shrine; dealings with matrilineal ancestors are handled directly rather than through an intermediary. Within a clan the relation of the component lineages to the common clan ancestress cannot be traced, in contrast to the precise knowledge of relationships within the patrilineal lineage and sublineages. Thus, the division of a clan into lineages is as much on a residential as on a genealogical basis, the factor of proximity in the same or neighboring villages being more significant than exact genealogical relationships.

Leadership of the clan is almost entirely in the hands of men, for although it is a group based on descent through the female line, women know little of clan affairs. In the fields of policy and group action the clan is supervised by its male elders, whose qualifications are similar to those of leaders in the patrilineage. However, unlike the patrilineal descent groups, the matrilineal clan and lineage do not form the basis of political groupings.

The matrilineal lineage is directly concerned with the affairs of its members and acts as an autonomous group in several areas. It has direct controls over matrilineal farmland;[5] it plays an important role in inheritance and in marriage, burial, funeral, and some title ceremonies; and it supports its members in personal disputes, particularly those concerning a woman's marital relations. Leadership of the lineage is usually vested in the oldest male of the group, who is in charge of allocation of lineage land, gives guidance and assistance to members, and acts as a representative of the lineage to the clan and other groups. There is a similar pattern of leadership among women of the lineage, but pertaining only to women's affairs.

Associations

In addition to having a kinship structure in which descent groups play an important and varied role in the lives of the people, the social organization of Afikpo is marked by well-developed association groupings based on residence, sex, and age in varying combinations. The most important of these are the village men's society, age groupings, and title societies.

Ogo (VILLAGE MEN'S SOCIETY) • The village men's society, *ogo* (village), is found in each of the Afikpo villages. Since all men belong to it, it is a secret society only in that it is closed to females and all uninitiated males, but its rituals and activities have factors in common with secret societies in other parts of Africa. *Ogo* has a number of functions: religious, moral, and recreational. Its patron spirit, *ɛgbɛlɛ*, is concerned with the affairs of the society and with the welfare of the village as a whole, and the society has the authority to make rules of conduct for villagers and to fine offenders. Fear of punishment by *ɛgbɛlɛ* is an important sanction in promoting proper behavior, particularly of women, who are thought to offend the spirit if they imitate men's activities or perform songs or dances associated with the society.

From time to time members of the society produce masked plays of social commentary, *ɔkumkpɔ*, analogous to the revues of Western society, satirizing the behavior of persons who have defied tradition or broken the mores in pointed topical songs and burlesquing their activities in pantomime. Songs composed for these plays become part of the legacy of Afikpo folklore and are sometimes sung many years later by persons who wish to criticize the behavior of others.

A Play of the *Ogo* Society
One of the leaders in an ogo
society play (ɔkumkpɔ) in a
village square, where the play
is presented. Chorus mem-
bers are in the background.
(*Simon Ottenberg*)

During ɔkɔci, the season following the yam harvest when men have little
work to do, much time is given to *ogo* activities. It is then that the initiation
takes place and the ɔkumkpɔ and sometimes other plays are given. During
this time restrictions are placed on nonmembers to prevent them from seeing
or hearing secret activities.

Although the *ogo* society is taken very seriously by both men and
women, who are convinced that its spirit has the power to harm or even
kill persons who offend it, a vein of humor runs through its activities, from
the penetrating satire of its songs to the joking and horseplay of some of its
secret activities. And although women display an attitude of reverence
toward it in the presence of men, they may indulge in the jocular use of
tabooed words or sing forbidden songs in gatherings where no men are
present.

MEN'S AGE GRADES · Afikpo differs from most Ibo groups in having a well-
developed system of men's and women's age sets and grades. Certain of the
men's age grades form the basis of the traditional government of the village
group. An *age set* consists of persons living in one village born within
approximately three years of one another. In contrast to systems common
in East Africa, where boys are initiated into a set in childhood, Afikpo men's
age sets are formed in adulthood. Although the Afikpo were traditionally
warriors, their age sets never formed the basis of regiments. Women's age
sets are composed of the women *married* into a village within a period of
about three years, rather than being formed on the basis of village of birth.
In a village each men's set is paired with a women's set, and each supports
the other in feasting and ceremonial activities.

An *age grade* is a grouping in which several contiguous age sets combine to form a larger body having recognized functions. Although an age

set is an organization lasting from its formation until the death of the last member and identified by a distinguishing name, the members of an age set move in succession through several formal statuses that are age grades. At a given time, an age grade (or "age status") will be occupied by a cluster of age sets.

Within an age set there are strong feelings of loyalty and mutual support among fellow members, or age mates, as they are called. They conduct social meetings from time to time and make money contributions to ceremonies performed by members, being feasted by them in return. If a member dies, his age mates often contribute to the support or schooling of his children. Age sets of younger adults are called upon by the elders of a village to perform civic tasks necessary for the maintenance of the community.

Although age sets are formed on a village basis, age grades are organized on the basis of both the village and the village group, but primarily on the latter, larger territory. On the *village* level there is a young men's age grade, made up of two or three age sets of men usually in their thirties and forties, who form a sort of police force, carrying out rulings laid down by the elders and enforcing law and order in the village. The organization of this grade varies from village to village and is not a part of the age-grade system of the village group.

On the *village-group* level, the men's age grades combine age sets of elders from all the villages. The village-group age grades are a junior grade composed of three age sets of men approximately 55 to 64 years of age, a

AFIKPO MEN'S AGE GRADES

Age Grade	Ibo Name	Approximate Ages of Members	Basis of Organization	Functions
Young men	ukɛ ɛkpɛ ("age group-society")	30–50 years	Village	Village police force
Junior	ɛkpɛ ukɛ ɛtɔ ("age set-three")	55–64 years	Village group	Executive arm of Afikpo government
Middle	ɛkpɛ ukɛ ɛsa ("age set-seven")*	65–83 years	Village group	Legislation and adjudication for village group
Senior	ɔni ɛkara (no English equivalent)	84 years and over	Village group	Retired—limited advisory powers
Residual category	hɔri (no English equivalent)	—	—	—

* Actually there are only six sets in this age grade.

middle grade made up of six sets of men from about 65 to 83 years old, and a senior grade, whose few remaining members are described as "retired." There are at no time more than a dozen or so living members of the senior grade, who are treated with the deference due to age but are usually considered senile and are sometimes referred to as "half dead." There is a residual age category for any who may survive the senior grade. In the 1950s there was one such person in Afikpo.

In the traditional government members of the middle grade compose the chief legislative body for all Afikpo and hold the real power. Members of the junior grade carry out rulings of the middle grade but are considered still on an apprenticeship basis; men younger than they are dismissed simply as "small boys." With the trend toward education and urbanization, leadership positions are gradually passing to younger men, but during the 1950s, the middle grade still maintained an important position in Afikpo affairs and its members were feared and respected by the villagers.

Each of the three village-group men's age grades has a shelter in the central market where members sit on market day, visiting with one another and being greeted by others. Members of the middle grade hold a court at their shelter, where they hear cases dealing with infractions of the laws they have made. Since the functions of the men's age grades are chiefly political and judicial these will be discussed in more detail under the headings of political organization and law.

WOMEN'S AGE GRADES · Women's age sets and grades, although of importance to their members, are less well developed and less highly organized than men's. There is only one women's age grade, $\varepsilon kp\varepsilon$ $uk\varepsilon$ $\varepsilon t\mathfrak{d}$ $nwanyi$ (age set-three-woman), which functions on both the village and village-group levels. Compared with the men's groups, its organization is somewhat nebulous and there appears to be considerable variation in age levels of the members in different villages. Most women questioned knew of the existence of this grade, but few could say what age sets it included, even in their own village. On the village level the women's age grade makes and enforces rulings on the farming and harvesting of women's crops and the women's annual tributes to the Afikpo rain maker. On the village-group level the age grade makes regulations pertaining to all Afikpo women, for example, the number of pots one woman is allowed to sell on one market day. Men's age grades make rulings for both men and women; $\varepsilon kp\varepsilon$ $uk\varepsilon$ $\varepsilon t\mathfrak{d}$ $nwanyi$ has authority only in women's affairs.

TITLE SOCIETIES · A form of association traditionally of great importance is the title society, a group of persons who have taken a title, $Mm\varepsilon m\varepsilon$, by feasting the members and paying a substantial initiation fee. Though virtually defunct by 1960, title-taking was still a going system in the 1950s.

Title-taking Activity The contributions made by kinsmen and friends to an elder who is taking a title are counted. Shillings are placed on the mat in groups of twenty each. An educated man (with cigarette) records the transaction. (*Simon Ottenberg*)

It is based on the idea of personal achievement as expressed in the expenditure of wealth. Since a person taking a title is aided and supported by his kinsmen, age mates, and friends, who share in his honor and prestige, the system has wide social ramifications. Although the main emphasis was traditionally on a person's proving his importance and worth by taking titles, it represented a form of investment also, for the initiation fee of a new member was divided among those who had already taken the title. From the financial standpoint title-taking was a calculated risk: if a man lived long enough he might collect more than he had spent taking the title. However, for most Afikpo this consideration was probably secondary to the prestige and influence involved.

As is true of many other aspects of Afikpo life, title-taking is mostly a men's activity. There is a complicated hierarchy of men's titles, more than twenty in all, whereas there are only two titles women may take. Some men's titles are taken in connection with the *ogo* society and are compulsory for the men of a village.

Traditionally, persons who achieved the highest titles did so after saving for a long time and often at great personal sacrifice. In the 1950s the cost of the highest men's title was about £200, which represented immense wealth in terms of the average per capita earnings. By that time the tide of women's opinion was turning against titles, and no one had taken the higher one since the mid-1940s. Actually, the women appeared to reject the impracticality of an investment for which the only sure return was intangible, while still approving of the basic principle of title-taking. Many seemed to have reinterpreted the term *Mmeme* to mean any socially sanctioned expenditure conferring prestige on the spender. Thus, several women, when asked if they had taken any titles, replied that they had paid for their children's schooling.

A few youths who had been to school criticized their fathers for "wasting their money on titles," but most men did not share the women's attitude. In 1952 a prosperous trader who had built himself a concrete block house with a tin roof and filled it with carpentered furniture and the rare luxury of a gramophone was criticized by his neighbors, who said: "That is nothing. He hasn't taken any titles!" The man laughed off the criticism, but some expressed the thought that once he had rid his system of this eccentricity he would probably start saving his money for titles.

IMPROVEMENT ASSOCIATIONS • A type of association that has come with European contact is the improvement association, sometimes called a union or *mikiri* (a corruption of "meeting"), that is common in Nigerian and other West African societies. Beginning in the 1940s, some young men of Afikpo established so-called village unions, or associations of men of a village who joined together to protect mutual interests. These were usually loan associations in which each member paid monthly dues that were pooled in a fund from which loans were granted to members. These groups included a few educated men, but the majority were unschooled traders, farmers, and fishermen. Although these unions were not set up exclusively as men's organizations, women were not encouraged to become members and did not try to join.[6]

In 1950 a village-group union, the Afikpo Town Welfare Association (ATWA) was formed, with branches in several cities where Afikpo people were employed in any number. ATWA was concerned with civic projects, such as the improvement of roads and markets, the interests of Afikpo traders, the furthering of education, and the general moral tone of Afikpo, as they interpreted the matter. (A controversial issue grew out of their ruling that adolescent girls, whose traditional attire was a string of beads around the hips, must wear clothes when they appeared in public; the ruling elders made strong objection to this, insisting that girls wore clothes only when they had something to hide.) Most ATWA members were men; however, a few educated women also belonged.

Social stratification

Afikpo is a theoretically classless society, with rule by consensus, great emphasis on individual achievement, and traditionally no great differences in economic status, but there are two groups that are historical remnants of social stratification. One is a group of patrilineages in certain villages who are owners of a spirit shrine, ɔtɔsi, that once granted them a privileged position, making them, in effect, an aristocratic class known as *amade*. The first *amade* were people of Aro Chuku who settled in Afikpo in pre-British times, bringing the shrine with them from Aro. They were followed by their descendants and, later, by non-Aro who purchased the shrine at Aro Chuku. Traditional prerogatives of the ɔtɔsi-holders enabled them to exploit nonholders in various ways. At one time only *amade* were allowed to have doors on their houses, and their position was too powerful for non-*amade* to accuse them of theft. Although traditional prerogatives of *amade* were outlawed by British rule, membership in the group continued to carry with it a measure of prestige.

At the opposite end of the social scale was one matrilineal clan, *ibɛ osim* (part [that is, people]-slave). This clan was traditionally not allowed to own land, and its female members were supposed to be available sexually to any man of another clan (the rule of matriclan exogamy held within the slave clan) and had no recourse against them. After they had been "freed" by the British, the position of the *osim* improved somewhat, but they were still discriminated against socially. Although men sometimes married *osim* women they refused to pay brideprice for them for fear that supernatural retribution for marrying a "slave" might cause them to fall ill or die.

MARRIAGE

For Afikpo the chief reason for marriage—and for many the only reason—is to have children. Celibacy is thought not only unnatural but immoral, for it is a person's duty to his descent groups to carry on the line and maintain the strength of the lineage and clan. Though many men are monogamous, the ideal marriage is polygynous. The average number of wives per husband seems to be slightly less than two, and only a few men have more than three wives. Any marriage can be thought of as either polygynous or potentially polygynous, for Afikpo men continue to marry well into old age.

The over-all picture of Afikpo marriage might be called one of "shifting polygyny" for husbands, since they acquire wives—and sometimes lose some—as they grow older, and one of successive marriages for wives. Because the average age of marriage for women is fifteen or sixteen years and for men is close to thirty, elderly men often marry women who are widowed while still young and remarry for the sake of bearing children.

Afikpo think of the relationship between co-wives of the same husband as an essentially hostile one, although this attitude is often not borne out in actuality. Co-wives rarely work together in farm or household tasks, and wives' everyday relations with other women are based primarily on friendship rather than on kinship or marriage.

A marriage is legalized by the husband-to-be's payment of brideprice, *ɛkθ nwanyi* (wealth-woman), to the bride's father, who shares it with his matrilineal kinsmen and the bride's mother. The amount of the brideprice for any Afikpo girl was set at £5 by the ruling elders of the village group in the 1920s. This payment, which is supposed to be made in full before the marriage is consummated, makes the husband the legal father of any children born to the wife thereafter, regardless of who the genitor may be. In contrast to some African societies in which the wife's relatives must return the brideprice if she is childless or does not conduct herself properly, the husband can recover his money only in the event that his wife leaves him and goes to another man, who then compensates the husband in order to validate the second relationship and gain custody of children born to the union. Thus, divorce is formalized only through the wife's remarriage, and a woman who has left her husband but has not remarried is still married in the jural, or legal, sense, though the conjugal relationship has been broken.

In addition to paying brideprice, a husband was traditionally expected to perform bride service *inyo ozi* (working-work), for the girl's parents, though this has largely been replaced by his paying a sum of money, determined by the bride's father, equivalent to the cost of hiring laborers to do the work the bridegroom would ordinarily have done. Although the brideprice has been kept at £5, inflation has crept in, since enterprising fathers have set the amount of the "work money" to conform with their conception of the girl's worth, which in Nigeria is often based on the father's expenditure in rearing the girl. In the early 1950s Afikpo fathers sometimes asked as much as £15 or £20 in addition to the brideprice for a girl who had had a few years' schooling.

Marriage is somewhat unstable in Afikpo, though less so than in many societies. Records obtained in 1952–1953 show that about one marriage in three ended in separation or divorce. Case histories of marriages did not indicate that this instability was a new development. Its explanation seems to lie partly in the divergent pulls on marriage partners inherent in the double descent system as well as in strains caused by social change. With the introduction of schools, Christianity, and the experience of many Afikpo in cities, ideas of the goals and purpose of marriage are changing for some but not for others. Women, particularly, have become concerned with the idea of romantic love and have hoped for its expression in marriage, an expectation that is inconsistent with the going system of polygyny.

LIFE CYCLE

CHILD TRAINING • Socialization and child training in Afikpo are informal and noncoercive. This seems to be associated with the belief that although an infant already has a soul at the time of birth —the reincarnation of one or more persons who have died—the spirit may change its mind about living and decide to "go back," causing the body to die. It is only when the baby has started to walk and talk that it is assumed that the spirit has decided to remain in its present incarnation and the child

Children Helping with a Household Task The children are returning from a stream where they have been washing cassava. They carry, from left to right, a *gari* (cassava meal) grater, a box into which cassava is grated and a bucket, dishes that have been washed, and a child's pot.

is considered fully human. An infant mortality rate of more than 50 percent in the first year of life tends to substantiate this belief. There is a convention of not talking about children, and particularly of never asking questions about them, for combined with the idea of infants' diffidence about life there is the notion that if a person thinks evil of another it may cause him supernatural harm. Children, strongly desired and difficult to rear because of disease and malnutrition (though sickness and death caused by these factors are usually assigned supernatural causes), are a subject of particular sensitivity.

Women traditionally nursed their children for two and a half to three years. During the 1950s a few educated women who had learned to feed their babies canned milk and cereals, and could afford to do so, had shortened this period to a year or a little longer, but most still nursed their children at least two years. It is customary for a woman to abstain from sexual intercourse while she is nursing, for it is thought that should she conceive before the child is weaned it will sicken and be likely to die. In actual practice the offense is not extremely serious if the nursing child has cut its teeth.

Mothers wean children by rubbing their breasts with bitter leaves and offering the child fruits such as bananas and papaya, which are thought of more as food for children than for adults.

No issue is made over toilet training. A child is cleaned up after soiling itself simply and without fuss, usually by an older brother or sister, and when it is thought old enough it is taught to use the compound latrine.

Girls are trained by their mothers, and boys, after early childhood, have much more to do with their fathers than with their mothers. A boy who spends much time at his mother's house is called ɔkpɔ Niɛ (bottom-mother's or mother's tail) because he clings to her. At the age of about five or six years a boy moves from his mother's house to a house, *ulotɛ* (diminutive form of "house"), shared by other boys in that part of the compound, where he sleeps with his friends. A girl continues to live in her mother's house until she marries.

Boys of five or six years may run errands, such as carrying messages for their fathers and other men of the compound, and girls of the same age care for younger children in their mother's absence, but training for adult tasks does not begin until around the age of eight. Then boys are expected to help their fathers with farmwork, and girls begin helping their mothers with housework and farming. By early adolescence a girl is expected to cook and relieve her mother of a considerable part of the housework.

Traditionally, learning has been chiefly by imitation, and, as children round the world mimic their elders, young Afikpo enjoy their own versions of adult institutions. For example, the village men's society (ogo) is imitated by boys, who build small-scale replicas of the men's resthouses in the bush outside the villages, make masks from coconut shells and other materials to represent the men's carved wood masks, and enact as much of the ritual as can be reproduced by noninitiates.

INITIATION · For every Afikpo boy initiation into the ogo society of his village is the beginning of his social adulthood, whether he is two years old or twenty. Membership is compulsory for all males. Although boys were traditionally not initiated until their late teens, it has become fashionable for a father to sponsor his young son in initiation at an early age as a mark of prestige and as a means of giving the son greater privileges as a child than he would ordinarily have.[7] Boys are initiated in groups rather than individually. The initiation involves a test of boys' strength and courage; it does not include circumcision, which is performed in early infancy and does not appear to have any important ritual significance.

Although there is no formal initiation for girls, clitoridectomy, traditionally accompanied by cicatrization and sometimes tattooing of the arms and torso in decorative designs, is the traditional ritual equivalent of boys' initiation into the ogo society, involving the elements of ordeal and preparation for social adulthood. Clitoridectomy is compulsory for all girls and formerly took place shortly before marriage during a period of three months in which the girl was secluded in her future mother-in-law's house and the cicatrization and clitoridectomy were performed. This seclusion, ulo ubu (house-circumcision), is referred to as "the fattening house" by English-speaking Afikpo, though it never involved intensive efforts to fatten its subjects, as has been reported for other Nigerian societies. Now thought "uncivilized" by most Afikpo, cicatrization, tattooing, and ulo ubu have disappeared from the scene, and clitoridectomy is now performed in early childhood.

POLITICAL ORGANIZATION

The Ibo-speaking peoples, with their total of more than two hundred autonomous, self-contained groups, have been described by anthropologists as "ultra-democratic and highly individualistic" (Forde and Jones 1950:24). In Afikpo there are no headmen or true chiefs, though there are influential and powerful individuals. Their control over others is limited, however, because rule is largely by councils of elders, arriving at decisions and taking action as a body. In council meetings the matter to be decided is brought before the group and any member is free to voice his opinion. The matter is discussed by the group until a consensus is reached. If members cannot reach an agreement the decision is postponed, or, if the matter is very serious it may be appealed to a religious authority, such as the oracle *ibini θkpabi* at Aro Chuku.

Although decisions are reached by consensus, some members of the group carry more weight in discussion than others. In Afikpo the criteria for leadership are seniority, the ability "to speak well," and personal achievement, as expressed in activities such as title-taking and the giving of second funerals. For a man to be a respected and persuasive leader he must be an elder (that is, a member of one of the village-group age grades), he must be a good orator, and he must have established his claim to a position of leadership by his achievement; one or two of these qualities are not enough. Hereditary factors are not completely absent here, for if a man's father or grandfather was a respected leader his position is enhanced by this fact, but only if he himself successfully fulfills the qualities of leadership.

THE VILLAGE GROUP • On the village-group level the traditional governing body for the whole of Afikpo is the village-group men's age grades, as mentioned above in the discussion of social organization. Members of the middle age grade have the major responsibility for lawmaking and are also an important judicial authority. Members of the senior age grade, though they do not take an active part in government, act as an advisory body. As has been mentioned, members of the middle grade hold a court in the central Afikpo market, where they try infractions of village-group laws and fine offenders. They act also as an advisory body for all Afikpo. They regulate the annual farm cycle, determining the time for planting and, in conjunction with the village-group yam priest, for the yam harvest; moreover, they set the amount of brideprice and regulate the ceremonial activities connected with marriage.

Members of the village-group junior grade, or executive arm, serve as messengers for the middle and senior age grades, summon offenders to the middle grade for trial, and collect fines for violations of the rulings of the middle grade. They also act as a police force for the central market. They report violations of traditional Afikpo customs to the middle and senior grades, and they may be sent by the former to investigate such matters as charges of adultery. Members of the junior grade may take it upon themselves to fine violators if the outcome of a case seems self-evident, but they do not have the authority to pass laws on the village-group level, for they are considered by their seniors to be lacking in judgment and are sometimes criticized as overeager.

The men's age grades of the village group act jointly in matters such as disputes between Afikpo villages or disasters threatening the welfare of the village group as a whole—excess rain, drought, famine, epidemics, and the like. In the former case they try the disputes, sometimes calling on the neutral elders of nearby Edda village group for assistance if they are unable to settle the matter themselves. In the latter case the elders seek action from the Afikpo rain maker or may consult a diviner or an oracle to find the cause of the trouble and the proper means of ending it. The three village-group age grades traditionally represented Afikpo to the outside world, in precolonial days summoning Afikpo villages to make war on outside groups and making peace settlements afterward. In later years they made decisions concerning disputes between Afikpo and outsiders, for example, rulings forbidding Afikpo people to attend markets of unfriendly groups.

THE VILLAGE • On the village level the three elders' age grades as a group form the ruling body, members of the middle grade being the most influential. Here members of the junior grade are among the lawmakers, gaining experience that will be needed when they move up to the middle grade, and the executive arm of village government is the young men's grade uke ɛkpɛ. There are usually few members of the middle elders' grade in any one village, and the junior grade play a major role in government at that level. Members of the middle grade have controls over village properties and over the younger age grades of the village, and it is they who represent the village to other villages. In most Afikpo villages the elders hold a short meeting on the morning of each market day to deal with village matters, such as proclaiming a law or announcing coming events. This meeting is open to all men and any women who may wish to attend.

In some villages there are powerful elders who may be called eze (chief) and are influential in village and village-group affairs. These are usually wealthy men possessing the qualities necessary for leadership in Afikpo, and they are greatly respected, but they must not override the wishes of their fellow elders lest they lose their support and cooperation.

The interests of the elders' age grades within the village are numerous. They control individuals, for example, forbidding them to travel to some areas outside Afikpo or banishing women who bear twins, traditionally taboo in Afikpo. They regulate the actions of such village groupings as age sets and the village men's society, and they exert controls over village properties, such as farmland, groves, streams, and the yam barn. The village elders perform a limited function as judges in disputes between compounds or patrilineal lineages that the disputants cannot settle themselves, and in trying cases of persons accused of fighting on the farmland, an action that threatens the whole village through possible supernatural retribution. In a manner similar to the elders of the village group, the village elders are responsible for the general welfare of the village, and they are its representatives to the outside world.

THE WARD • Governing activities on the ward level are concerned mostly with disputes between members of different compounds within the ward and with the control of ward properties such as groves, ponds, and streams. The *ukε εkpε* members of the ward intervene in quarrels between persons of different compounds, and they make sure that necessary rituals concerning ward properties are performed. They also carry out certain duties connected with the farm cycle, summoning younger age sets to perform such tasks as maintaining the ward's section of the village yam barn. Since the ward plays a smaller part in the lives of Afikpo than the compound and village, its governing functions are also less important.

THE COMPOUND • Government of the compound is in the hands of the elders of the patrilineage residing in it. In the few compounds inhabited by more than one lineage, the elders of the component lineages function separately in lineage matters but combine in dealing with those concerning the compound as a whole. The elders' authority within the compound is reinforced by the religious sanction of the patrilineal ancestral shrine, *ma obu,* the central symbol of the lineage. This spirit is an intermediary between the living and the ancestors and is concerned with the welfare of the lineage and, by extension, the compound, for the authority of *ma obu* extends not only over lineage members but over their wives as well. The patrilineage elders, one of whom is the shrine priest, are thus guardians of the compound and of the ancestral shrine, dealing with disciplinary matters within the group of kinsmen and their wives and protecting the shrine against offenses to the spirit that would bring harm to the compound.

The elders of the compound settle disputes arising among its members, and they advise members who become involved in serious quarrels with outsiders and testify on their behalf. They have the authority to banish women from the compound and to ostracize men who consistently violate their rulings. In addition, the elders are responsible for the upkeep of spirit shrines owned by the lineage (or the lineages) and for representing the compound to other compounds in the village.

In keeping order in the compound the elders are assisted by the *ukɛ ɛkpɛ*, who have the duty of controlling disputes within the residence group. In the view of Afikpo men an important function of the *ukɛ ɛkpɛ* in the compound is that of keeping the women under control, for, with the tensions of daily domestic life—particularly in conflicts between husbands and wives and between co-wives of the same husband—there are frequent outbursts. As on the village level, the compound *ukɛ ɛkpɛ* acts as the executive arm of the elders, seeing that their orders are carried out and rulings adhered to and performing maintenance tasks concerned with the upkeep of the compound. The members are also responsible for providing materials for sacrifices to compound spirit shrines and, in times of trouble, for summoning and paying a diviner whom the elders consult.

CONCLUSION · In Afikpo government a formal system of checks and balances against the exploitation of power, such as the division of executive, legislative, and judicial powers, or the institution of advisory councils for chiefs is not needed. Individual leaders retain their power only as long as they represent the opinion of the majority, for Afikpo are too self-assertive to allow themselves to be dominated by someone with whom they do not agree. Further, supernatural sanctions act as a curb on individual power. In an essentially democratic religious system, the Afikpo deities allow no such sanction as divine kingship or chieftainship. One person's supernatural resources are potentially the same as another's, and in any case he is judged on his conduct rather than his heritage.

In addition to government by age grades and groupings of elders, some functions of government at the village level are taken over by the *ogo* society. The sanction of its guardian spirit, *ɛgbɛlɛ*, is effective in enforcing restrictions placed on nonmembers, and the biting satire of the society's plays is warning against willful behavior.

Law

Legal procedures are closely connected with legislative functions in Afikpo, since the elders often judge the people's adherence to laws they themselves have made. Seen within the context of the elders' role as the mappers and protectors of the social order, this traditionally operated as an efficient system, accepted and respected by the people.

JUDICIAL JURISDICTION · As has been noted, disputes within the patrilineal lineage are usually handled within the group, as is true also in the case of the matrilineal clan and lineage. In the compound, disputes not settled by the young men's age grade, *ukɛ ɛkpɛ*, are appealed to the elders.

Central Afikpo Market Old women come to a central Afikpo market to sell pots they have made. The village-group middle age grade holds court in this market. (*Simon Ottenberg*)

At the village level the elders hear cases between patrilineages or compounds of the village that the groups cannot settle themselves, and cases arising within a compound in which the litigants have been dissatisfied with the elders' decisions. However, they are not on the whole an active judicial body, since people try to settle disputes at a lower level if possible. Further, there is another group within the village that forms an even higher court than the elders. This is a group within the village men's society who have taken all or most of the *ogo* society titles and are usually elders as well. In addition to being a law-enforcement body within the village, the titled group helps to settle long-standing disputes arising over *ogo* matters. As a rule serious disputes between unilineal descent groups are not settled at the village level but are taken to the village-group elders, the Aro Chuku oracle, or other agencies.

JUDICIAL PROCEDURES · The middle village-group men's age grade, whose members are the chief judiciary body of Afikpo, use two methods of settling disputes. The first is an informal one, used when both parties agree to the need to settle a case. After choosing a meeting place, the parties ask a few elders of the age grade to come and judge the case. Both sides feast them and give them small sums of money. (In theory the elders are not influenced by gifts.) Litigants often ask members of the middle grade who are their kinsmen to judge a case in the hope that the relationship ties will improve their disposition toward the case. In an informal case of this sort the disputants do not have to accept the judges' decision but may take the case to another body, such as the middle grade of the village group as a whole or one of the courts introduced by the British administration.

The second type of judiciary activity of the village-group middle grade is that of the age grade as a body, meeting at their court in the central market. Cases taken to this court are those in which there is doubt as to a person's guilt, property ownership is not clear, or there is a question of violation of traditional custom.[8]

Procedures of the various Afikpo judiciary bodies are initiated as outlined above. In hearings, the judges question the litigants and call on witnesses to testify. As in lawmaking, decision is by discussion and consensus, and cases such as those brought before the middle-grade court in the market may be debated for many meetings before they are settled. In an Afikpo court there is no judge in the sense that there is in European law. There are, however, supernatural authorities to which cases are referred if the judges are unable to come to a decision. The foremost of these is the Aro Chuku oracle, *ibini θkpabi*, through which many cases are settled. Agents of the oracle living in Afikpo escort litigants to Aro Chuku, where the cases are decided. Another means, used particularly in cases in which the judges are unable to determine guilt on the part of a litigant, is to ask him to swear an oath of innocence on one of the several *εrosi* (spirit shrines) used for this purpose in Afikpo. It is believed that if a person swears falsely the spirit will kill him or will make him gravely ill within a year. Refusal to swear is tantamount to admission of guilt.

Most of the cases adjudicated are those concerning property, particularly land, though many involve inheritance, and the settlement of brideprice in cases of wives' remarriage. In precolonial days the greatest crimes were adultery and theft, both of which were punished by the death sentence. In the 1950s the Afikpo still had an abhorrence of theft, and few cases of adultery came before the courts.

RELIGION

In the religion of Afikpo, as in its social and political organization, many forces are at work. Most operate independently of one another, there being no supreme god or hierarchies of deities. In addition to the ground (*ale*) and the spirit of the Aro Chuku oracle (*ibini θkpabi*), there are two major types of spiritual forces: the ancestors and a class of spirits called *εrosi*. All these spiritual forces have an important influence on human behavior, since if a person does not treat them properly they can bring harm not only to him but to others with whom he is associated.

ANCESTORS • The ancestors, *Ndicie Nwe ale* (elders-get [in]-ground), are thought not only to be reincarnated in their descendants but to have power and influence over the living, who must perform prescribed ritual duties toward the ancestors lest they be displeased. Sacrifices are made to them at the time of the New Yam Festival, and rituals are performed for parents after their deaths and in times of special need or misfortune. If a person is remiss in his duties, an ancestor may nudge his memory by making him sick. On the other hand, if he is in trouble, an ancestor may appear to him in a dream and suggest a remedy.

A special class of ancestors are evil ancestral spirits, Ndɛ ma (people-spirit, singular, ma). An evil ancestor does not reincarnate himself, but, without provocation, haunts his descendants in dreams and makes them sick, an action that Afikpo compare with the practice of witchcraft among the living in other Ibo groups, though witchcraft as such does not exist in Afikpo. There is no correlation between the personality of a living person and the behavior of his spirit after death. Although they may be similar, a good man's spirit may unpredictably turn into a ma and start haunting his descendants, or a ma may decide to reform and reincarnate.

If a person is haunted by an evil ancestral spirit he makes a sacrifice to it in the bad bush, an area outside each village where the bodies of dead babies and persons dying of loathsome diseases are thrown and which is the home of the Ndɛ ma. If the spirit haunts him repeatedly after being given the proper sacrifices, he may, on the advice of a diviner, punish it by digging up this ancestor's bones and burning them.

Erosi (IMPERSONAL SPIRITS) • Erosi are a class of impersonal spirits associated with nature and with such interests as fertility, prosperity, and general welfare. Each has a shrine, usually in the form of a small pot or a group of pots, where sacrifices are given it, and some are said to assume various forms, such as an animal, a tree, or a cave. Some ɛrosi are owned by individuals and some by descent and residence groups. Most individual ɛrosi are owned by men or women, but not by both. The ɛrosi belonging to a group is usually served by a priest, a member of the group who acts as intermediary between the people and their spirit. Sacrifices are generally in the form of food, animals, or everyday objects, such as a type of chalk used for body marking.

The ɛrosi are propitiated by sacrifices on ceremonial occasions, when a special favor is requested, or to end some trouble caused by a spirit. Sacrifices to group ɛrosi, such as the spirits looking after the general welfare of a compound or promoting the fertility of its members, are made by the ɛrosi priest. Those to individual ɛrosi, for example, a spirit promoting the fertility of a man's yam crop, or one aiding his wife's success in market trade, are made by the individuals owning the ɛrosi shrine.

From an older kinsman or kinsmen owning its shrine a person acquires an ɛrosi in a ceremony—apata ɛrosi (to take-spirit)—in which the new owner's shrine is made from part of the donor's shrine, usually by transferring some of the contents from a pot forming the old shrine to a new pot. It is only after a person "takes" an ɛrosi that he himself can sacrifice to it; until then any necessary sacrifices to the spirit must be made on his behalf by someone who owns the shrine. Although a person does not usually "take" an εrosi unless instructed to by a diviner as a remedy for a misfortune or illness through which the εrosi is said to be "calling him," by middle age most men and women have acquired one or more εrosi.

Afikpo deal with their εrosi in a straightforward and businesslike fashion. Although the ancestors and the ground are propitiated with respect and even humility, people have a less reverent attitude in approaching an εrosi. A man may bargain with a spirit, offering him a promissory sacrifice when requesting a favor. He may present an egg to the shrine, saying, "If you give my wife a child I will bring you a chicken." A reasonable time having elapsed with no result, he may rebuke the spirit: "I gave you the egg. Why has my wife not conceived?" If the spirit grants the favor and the petitioner does not give it the promised sacrifice, the spirit may retaliate by bringing illness or other trouble to him or one of his family. However, an individual εrosi must in a sense earn its way. If a spirit consistently fails its owner and he feels sufficiently strong-minded about it, he may abandon it by simply leaving its shrine untended or even throwing it away.

Ibini θkpabi • A pervasive force in Afikpo religion is *ibini θkpabi*, the spirit of the Aro Chuku oracle. Shrines of this spirit are owned by both patrilineal and matrilineal groups, and by men who have traveled to Aro to consult the oracle and have obtained the shrines there. Some Afikpo classify the spirit as a very powerful εrosi, but others consider it a god, *ɔbasi na elu* (Efik for "god-in-sky"), who is worshiped through the shrine of *ibini θkpabi*. *Ɔbasi na elu* is said to live in the sky, and some maintain that it is the same as the Christian God, *Chinεkε*.

THE GROUND • Like *ibini θkpabi*, the ground, *ale*, presents problems of classification from the point of view of analysis. *Ale* seems to differ from εrosi in that its principle is not simply one of an automatic supernatural sanction, dealing directly with a wrongdoer if it is offended, but is also one of a jural sanction: a person who breaks the sanction of *ale* is punished by the people of his compound. Offenses against *ale* are the birth of twins, the performance of sexual intercourse on the ground, the impregnation of a girl before her clitoridectomy or by an uninitiated boy, and a baby's cutting its upper teeth before the lower. These are thought to threaten the welfare of an entire compound, inviting retaliation in the form of illness, crop failure, or other misfortune. A person committing such an offense is called *onyε θrθ ale* (person-spoil-ground) and may be punished by banishment, having his parents' houses torn down, and so on, according to the specific offense. Sacrifices are made to *ale* at set times in the farm cycle. Atonement for an offense against *ale* is made by a sacrifice to the guardian εrosi of the compound, ɔma εzi (good-compound), which accepts the sacrifice on the ale's behalf.

Forces of major importance in Afikpo religion are the ground, ibini θkpabi, the ancestors, and impersonal spirits. All these deities are concerned with the survival and welfare of the people. The ancestors must reincarnate for continuity of the social group, aided by εrosi that promote both human and crop fertility. Ale is a sort of guradian of the social order: the ground and its fertility are necessary to food production, and its sanction for proper behavior is carefully observed. Ibini θkpabi is a help in daily life and is called upon as a last resort in cases of special difficulty. The Christian God, Chinεkε—from ci na εkε (god-and-creator), a term apparently introduced by missionaries—is worshiped by a few Christians in Afikpo, and, as mentioned, has become associated with ibini θkpabi—ɔbasi na elu in the minds of some Afikpo.

The impersonal spirits, ibini θkpabi, and the ground have in common the quality that they are by definition good and do not act in an unpredictable or capricious manner: if they are correctly treated they do not cause people harm. Ancestral spirits, on the other hand, sometimes exhibit human failings in the afterlife, and in these cases the living must treat them as well as possible and hope for the best.

MAGIC AND SORCERY · Belief in magic (ekikε) takes several forms in Afikpo: medicines used to influence a person's actions, magic made by using something from the body of a person in order to harm him, and charms used to ward off evil ancestral spirits. Sorcery, or the use of evil magic (also called ekikε), was said in the early 1950s to be a custom recently acquired from other Ibo groups having powerful magic. It was used only by women in the form of medicine obtained from a diviner to "turn the husband's head" from a co-wife to the user. Though magic is used by Afikpo, it is not one of their specialties, and it is less frequently resorted to than appeals to εrosi and ancestral spirits.

A belief analogous to the belief in haunting by evil ancestral spirits is the idea that to think or speak evil of another person may cause his illness, misfortune, or death, and that doing so may bring about supernatural retribution in the form of harm to the offender. Although Afikpo are explicit in comparing haunting by evil ancestral spirits with witchcraft among other peoples, they do not make this observation concerning evil thought and speech, though the underlying principle appears to be the same. Here, however, justice may be automatically meted out in the form of the offender's malice backfiring and striking him down, whereas haunting ancestors must be dealt with by humans.

Another idea widespread in Afikpo is that bad luck is contagious, for instance, that a widow's second husband may "catch the bad luck" of her first husband and die also. This belief seems to apply only to bad luck, good luck usually being attributed to *θwa* (fate).

DIVINATION · A key figure in Afikpo religious belief is the diviner, *dibia*. It is he who diagnoses illness or misfortune by determining what spirit or ancestor may have been offended, or who may have been using magic against a client. With the aid of several *εrosi* that give him the power "to see what has happened," the diviner is able to advise his client concerning the proper means to end the trouble. The diviner also provides his clients with various forms of magic, including those used by women against their co-wives, though this practice is deplored and it is said that a good diviner would not deal in this kind of magic.

CONCLUSION · In Afikpo, religion is not an isolated or compartmentalized part of the people's lives but enters into many spheres. It is a basic essential of farming. It is important in kinship also, for, in addition to a generalized power that the ancestors hold over the living, sanctions such as those of *ma obu* (the patrilineal ancestral spirit shrine) are important in regulating the behavior not only of lineage members but of everyone living in the compound. In addition, each matrilineal clan has a guardian spirit, *Nja*, which looks after the welfare of the group.

Religion plays an important part also in Afikpo government and law. Although religious specialists such as priests and diviners are usually not active politically, and supernatural sanctions for political office are absent, the force of the supernatural is still seen. The men's village society, reinforced by its much-feared guardian *εrosi*, is a major force in maintaining order within the village. Recourse to oracles and to swearing an oath of innocence on an *εrosi* shrine in cases in which legal means fail shows clearly the authority of supernatural forces in the lives of the Afikpo.

Folklore

Afikpo folklore consists of tales, proverbs, riddles, and songs. There is no body of mythology of the type found in some societies explaining the nature of the universe and the creation of man, and there is no poetry.

Tales are referred to by the term *ilu* (story), sometimes followed by the name of the person or animal the tales are about. There are two principal types: historical tales dealing with the origin and development of Afikpo villages, compounds, and lineages, and stories classified by English-speaking Afikpo as "fairy tales" (there is no Ibo word for this category), which have as their characters humans, animals, the sun and moon, rivers, and so on.

Proverbs, *iko aka* (proverb–ancient custom) are cited at any time or on any occasion, mainly by older people. They are frequently used by elders in speeches and legal cases to emphasize a point. They are used as philo-sophical comments on life, to instruct children or warn adults against foolish behavior, and as expressions of group solidarity.

Riddles (*iko ilu*) are used mainly for recreation. Besides those in the form of a tale there are two other common types: one in the form of a simple question and the other in the form of paired proverbs having the same mean-ing. In the latter type the asker states the first proverb, to which the reply is the second. For example, the answer to "Soup in a flat plate cannot be licked," is "White man's work is never done."

Topical songs are composed and sung on many occasions in Afikpo. Usually new words are attached to old tunes that are used time and again in different contexts. The songs most commonly sung are similar to Trinidadian calypso songs in that they are often scathing social commentaries. They are of the call-and-response type, with a soloist carrying the narrative in the verse and others joining in the chorus.

CHANGE

During the first half of the twentieth century Afikpo changed from an isolated group of warring villages to a community where governmental and legal superstructures were erected over the tradi-tional systems by the British administration. The colonial government per-tained to the outward aspects of maintaining order, while matters of "native law and custom" were left largely to the Afikpo to handle in traditional fashion. Along with this came a change in the subsistence level, notably a greatly increased volume of trade and dependence on imported goods. Christianity was accepted by a small number of Afikpo, and a few mission elementary schools were introduced; in 1951, the first secondary school was opened. Western culture left its mark on the people's life and values in the areas of economic and vocational aspirations, marriage, and family life.

Between 1953 and 1960 striking additional changes took place in Afikpo, especially in the economic and political spheres. Two specific developments (in addition to general conditions of prosperity in Nigeria) increased the buying power of the people. The first was the adoption of rice growing and shipping on a large scale; and the second, the demise of men's title-taking and the diversion of money spent for titles into other channels, especially housebuilding and a generally higher consumption level. Thus, markets have become larger and meet more frequently.

Several new schools, both elementary and secondary, had opened in Afikpo by 1960, and most of the boys and a fair number of the girls of elementary school age were attending school. Although only a few years earlier schooling had been thought by the more conservative Afikpo to com-pete with such traditional interests as farming, and girls' education was believed by many not only to be wasteful but to cause women's barrenness, the Afikpo had come to realize the value of education in modern Nigerian life and were willingly sending their children to school.

Christianity had made some further inroads with the building of more mission schools, but the total number of Christians was still small. Although Islam seems to have little appeal to most Ibo peoples and has not been readily accepted by them, most of the people of one of the southern Afikpo villages became Muslims in the late 1950s. Islam seems solidly entrenched there, but there seems little likelihood of its spreading to other villages.

Major political changes occurred in Afikpo in the 1950s as a part of the Africanization of the colonial administration preparatory to Nigerian national independence in 1960. The Afikpo Divisional Council was established in 1952 as a part of a program to introduce self-government at a local level. This body served the whole of Afikpo Division, in which the Afikpo village group was one of fifteen population groups, and it brought the Afikpo into a political contact with their neighbors that they had not experienced before. The council gradually took over the control of major markets, the maintenance and construction of secondary roads, sanitary services, and local taxation. The Divisional Council became the District Council in 1955, and by 1960 it had taken over a number of functions of the traditional Afikpo government. For example, though members of the elders' age grades still sat in their shelters in the main market on market day, the market was under the control of the Market Master, an employee of the District Council, and the power of the middle village-group age grade court was much reduced. The Senior Service officers connected with the government of Afikpo had all been Europeans in 1953; by 1960 they were virtually all Africans. However, these were mostly relatively young, educated men with little interest in traditional life. The rule of the elders that had flourished within set limitations during colonial rule seemed more and more to be a thing of the past.

Notes

(1) Field research was carried out in Afikpo from December 1951, to February 1953, and from September 1959, to September 1960. Work during the earlier period was made possible by the award of an Area Research Fellowship of the Social Science Research Council, New York, and a grant-in-aid from the Program of African Studies, Northwestern University. I wish to thank my husband, Simon Ottenberg, for the use of his field materials and for helpful suggestions on Afikpo government and law. Afikpo culture will be described here as it existed in the early 1950s, a time when a considerable number of Afikpo had had some schooling and had traveled to other parts

of Nigeria and the Cameroons but when traditional values and practices were still followed by the majority.

(2) One such non-Ibo people are the Yakö, described in the works of Daryll Forde. The culture of Afikpo bears similarities both to that of other Ibo peoples and to non-Ibo groups east of the Cross River. A number of other eastern Ibo groups share with them the main features in which they differ from the Ibo as a whole: double descent, compact village organization, and association groupings based on age.

In contrast, the majority of the Ibo-speaking peoples trace descent patrilineally and live in dispersed villages marked by a pattern of paths radiating from a central market. Along a given path live members of a patrilineage, with one patrilineal extended family to each homestead. Traditionally, individuals sometimes held more power than in Afikpo, and there were chiefs in a few Ibo groups. Members of some Ibo groups believe in a supreme spirit *Chuku*—from *ci uku* (spirit-great)—identified with *Chinɛkɛ* (the Christian God) in some areas. In certain Ibo groups a relationship between *Chuku* and other spirits, such as the ground, lightning, and the sky, is postulated that is suggestive of Yoruba pantheons of gods, but less explicit. Finally, there has been considerably more culture change among Ibo of the south and west than among those of the north and east, such as the Afikpo.

(3) Covering an area of 64 square miles, Afikpo village group had a population of 26,305 according to the census of 1953 (Nigeria, The Census Superintendent 1953:25).

(4) The matriclan is exogamous, but the patrilineage is not, with the exception of a few lineages having a tradition of marrying outside the group.

(5) Although the clan is the ultimate owner of farmland used by both its male and female members and of oil- and raffia-palm groves used by its male members, these are controlled by its component lineages. The clan as a whole is concerned only when a dispute arises over their use.

(6) Although women's unions or meetings are common among many Ibo groups, the only one in Afikpo was a short-lived association founded in 1947 by a group of women who considered themselves "a little bit civilized" and wished to set themselves apart from other women.

(7) In some villages there is a special form of initiation for an eldest son, which takes place only every seven years instead of each year and is longer and more elaborate than the regular form.

(8) By the 1950s criminal cases were supposed to go to the colonial government body, the Magistrate's Court, but they were sometimes handled by the middle grade if the matter did not come to the attention of the colonial authorities. At that time the judicial power of this age grade was declining, and serious cases were often handled by the Magistrate's Court or by the Native Authority Court, a body made up of Afikpo but organized and supervised by the British administration.

Bibliography

With a few exceptions the following bibliography emphasizes contemporary work. Starred items (*) include significant bibliographies. Daggered items (†) are cited as references in the text of the chapter.

Achebe, Chinua (1958). *Things Fall Apart*. London: William Heinemann, Ltd.
A novel on the impact of European contact on an Ibo people at the end of the nineteenth century.

Forde, Daryll (1941). *Marriage and the Family among the Yakö in South-eastern Nigeria*. London: London School of Economics Monographs on Social Anthropology, No. 5.
Marriage customs and ceremonials among the Yakö.

———— (1950). "Double Descent among the Yakö," in A. R. Radcliffe-Brown and Daryll Forde (eds.), *African Systems of Kinship and Marriage*. London: Oxford University Press, pp. 285–332.
An analysis of the Yakö system of double unilineal descent.

————, and G. I. Jones (1950*†). *The Ibo and Ibibio-speaking Peoples of South-eastern Nigeria*. London: International African Institute. (Ethnographic Survey of Africa, Western Africa, Part III.)
A survey of the basic cultural features of different groups among the Ibo and the Ibibio, an Efik-speaking people who live southeast of the Ibo.

Green, M. M. (1947). *Ibo Village Affairs*. London: Sidgwick & Jackson.
A study of village organization and law in a southern Ibo group.

Greenberg, Joseph H. (1955†). *Studies in African Linguistic Classification*. New Haven, Conn.: The Compass Publishing Co.

Grove, A. T. (1951). "Soil Erosion and Population Problems in South-east Nigeria," *Geographical Journal*, Vol. 117, Part 3, pp. 291–306.
The relation of soil conditions and economics in a thickly populated western Ibo community.

Horton, W. R. G. (1954). "The Ohu System of Slavery in a Northern Ibo Village-Group," *Africa*, Vol. 24, No. 4, pp. 311–336.
The position of a slave-trading community and the role of domestic slavery in precolonial life.

———— (1956). "God, Man, and the Land in a Northern Ibo Village-Group," *Africa*, Vol. 26, No. 1, pp. 17–28.
Religion and world view of the Nike Ibo.

Jones, G. I. (1949a). "Dual Organization in Ibo Social Structure," *Africa*, Vol. 19, No. 2, pp. 150–156.
An analysis of a common Ibo pattern of division of villages and communities into two complementary sections.

———— (1949b). "Ibo Land Tenure," *Africa*, Vol. 19, No. 4, pp. 309–323.

The relation between farming practices and the development of new communities in a thickly populated area.

Leith-Ross, Sylvia (1939). *African Women*. London: Faber & Faber, Ltd.
A study of the position of women in four Ibo communities having experienced different degrees of European contact.

Meek, C. K. (1957). *Law and Authority in a Nigerian Tribe*. London: Oxford University Press.
Traditional government and social systems of groups among the western, northern, and southern Ibo.

Nigeria, The Census Superintendent of (1953†). *Population Census of the Eastern Region of Nigeria, 1953. Bulletin No. 4, Ogoja Province*. Port Harcourt, Nigeria.

Ottenberg, Phoebe (1958). "Marriage Relationships in the Double Descent System of the Afikpo Ibo of Southeastern Nigeria." Unpublished doctoral thesis, Northwestern University.

—— (1959). "The Changing Economic Position of Women among the Afikpo Ibo," in W. R. Bascom and M. J. Herskovits (eds.), *Continuity and Change in African Cultures*. Chicago: University of Chicago Press, pp. 205–223.
The effect of historic change and economic growth on the respective positions of men and women.

Ottenberg, Simon (1955a). "Improvement Associations among the Afikpo Ibo," *Africa*, Vol. 25, No. 1, pp. 1–25.
The development and functions of improvement associations.

—— (1955b*). "Supplementary Bibliography on the Ibo-speaking People of South-eastern Nigeria," *African Studies*, Vol. 14, No. 2, pp. 63–85.
References to supplement the bibliography in Forde and Jones (1950).

—— (1957). "The System of Authority of the Afikpo Ibo of Southeastern Nigeria." Unpublished doctoral thesis, Northwestern University.
A study of traditional government in Afikpo.

—— (1958). "Ibo Oracles and Intergroup Relations," *Southwestern Journal of Anthropology*, Vol. 14, No. 3, pp. 295–307.
The role of oracles, particularly that of Aro Chuku, in relations between different Ibo groups in the period before intensive European contact.

—— (1959). "Ibo Receptivity to Change," in W. R. Bascom and M. J. Herskovits (eds.), *Continuity and Change in African Cultures*. Chicago: University of Chicago Press, pp. 130–143.
Factors in the culture and geographical setting of the Ibo making them more receptive to change than other Nigerian peoples.

—— (1960). "Double Descent in an Ibo Village-Group," in Anthony F. C. Wallace (ed.), *Selected Papers of the Fifth International Congress of Anthropological and Ethnological Sciences*. Philadelphia: University of Pennsylvania Press, pp. 473–481.
A brief account of the Afikpo double descent system.

———— (1961*). "The Present State of Ibo Studies," *Journal of the Historical Society of Nigeria*, Vol. 2, No. 2, pp. 211–230.
Further Ibo references since 1955.

Ottenberg, Simon and Phoebe (1961). "Afikpo Markets: 1900–1960," in Paul J. Bohannan and George Dalton (eds.), *Markets in Africa*. Evanston, Ill.: Northwestern University Press, pp. 117–169.
An account of the development of Afikpo markets and economic exchange from pre-British times to 1960.

2

THE BANTU TIRIKI
OF WESTERN KENYA

about the chapter

The Tiriki of Kenya are one of the Bantu-speaking cluster of Abaluyia peoples formerly referred to in social science writings on the area as the Bantu of North Kavirondo. Since the societies of the Abaluyia peoples vary from tribe to tribe, they afford the anthropologist a "laboratory" for research by a variation of the comparative method that has been called the method of controlled comparison. The tribes offer examples of closely related cultures, with similar habitats and language, which differ only slightly in major cultural institutions. Thus any given institution in which two Abaluyia tribes differ may be viewed as a variable to be studied to determine the difference the presence or absence of a given form makes in the total cultural configuration.

For example, the Tiriki have a highly developed and formalized system of age groups while age groups among the other Abaluyia peoples are not nearly so elaborated or important. The Africanist wishes to understand this feature of social organization because it is found extensively in East Africa (for example, among the Jie and the Swazi) as well as in other areas of Africa (for example, among the Ibo, the Tiv, and the Yoruba). Sangree's analysis describes all of Tiriki culture, but focuses on age grades as a dominant Tiriki institution. The Tiriki borrowed age grades from the neighboring Terik, a branch of the so-called Nilo-Hamitic (Cushitized Nilotic) Nandi. This alone indicates the functional elasticity of the age grades as a social grouping, for they were borrowed from a herding society by the Tiriki and fitted into their social organization, which rests on sedentary agriculture. Yet Tiriki age grades function effectively as an integrative institution.

Sangree notes that the Tiriki have made a better adjustment to the conflicting pulls of the acculturative situation than have the other Abaluyia peoples. He also observes that Tiriki age grades still function, many "modern" voluntary activities being organized according to age grades. Employing controlled comparison, he concludes that since the other Abaluyia peoples with less complex age groups are less adjusted to acculturation than the Tiriki, structurally elaborated age grades can function to smooth the stresses of acculturation. (Age groups among the Jie show a contrasting pattern; they are almost completely separate from modern activities and reinforce cultural conservatism.) In documenting his conclusion, Sangree uses an analysis that draws implicitly on the "culture and personality" approach as well as on the "structural" approach. He considers age grades both in terms of their functions for social structure and with respect to internalized personality needs and individual role behavior. In this context he describes the way in which the age grade system reacted to the introduction of Christianity.

A last point of significance of the Tiriki age grades is the insight into puberty rites that may be gained through studying them. Like initiation into adulthood in many sub-Saharan societies, Tiriki initiation involves the use of masks and costumes to dramatize the assumption of a new adult identity. As in initiation into the Kpelle Poro, initiation into the first Tiriki age grade means the assumption of manhood, and it involves seclusion and careful instruction. The chapter points out that the initiations are successful partly because the tone and manner of this training involves a discontinuity with previous socialization.

about the author

Walter H. Sangree, Associate Professor of Anthropology at the University of Rochester, received his Ph.D. from the University of Chicago in 1959. From 1954 to 1956 he carried out field research among the Tiriki of Kenya. He has written *Age, Prayer and Politics in Tiriki, Kenya* (to be published by Oxford University Press) and several journal articles on the Tiriki.

WALTER H. SANGREE · *The Bantu Tiriki of Western Kenya*[1]

INTRODUCTION

The Tiriki are one of twenty-two politically discrete, Bantu-speaking tribes living in the North Nyanza and Elgon districts of Nyanza Province, Kenya.[2] These tribes in effect form a linguistic and cultural sub-area where closely related dialects are spoken, common bonds of kinship are recognized, and a large core of common customs and values prevails. In recent years they have become known collectively as the *Abaluyia* or *Luyia*. Their sense of similarity and communality is enhanced by their being surrounded on almost all sides by alien Nilotic and "Nilo-Hamitic" peoples. Today, they are emerging as a distinctive political bloc in Kenyan affairs.

The Abaluyia tribes, probably numbering in all slightly over a half million people (1956), live in an area of approximately 2700 square miles that extends roughly from the equator north for about 90 miles to the southern slopes of Mount Elgon, west to the Uganda border, and east to the Nandi escarpment. The area is hilly, averaging about 5500 feet above sea level in the southern portions, but the altitude drops to about 4200 feet and becomes gently undulating in the northern regions approaching the Mount Elgon massif. The temperature is mild and fairly even the year round, in most places seldom going much above 80° or below 55° F.

LANGUAGE AND PHYSICAL APPEARANCE · Considerable dialect variation is found among the twenty-two Abaluyia tribes. The northern Abaluyia speak dialects rather similar to that of the Gishu (Bagishu) of eastern Uganda, whereas the southern Abaluyia, particularly the Maragoli tribe, speak dialects with close affinities to the language of the Gusii (Abagusii) of South Nyanza, Kenya. The Abaluyia are Negroids, for the most part of medium stature, with heavy-set muscular torsos, but rather slender limbs. The considerable variation in both height and skin color, particularly noticeable among the Tiriki, is quite likely due in part to interbreeding with Nilo-Hamitic and Nilotic peoples to the east and south.

43

GEOGRAPHIC LOCATION AND POPULATION · The Tiriki *badiliji* (people) live in the southeastern portion of North Nyanza District. Tiriki Location, the contemporary homeland of the Tiriki as legally instituted by the Kenya government, is about twenty miles long, and is shaped roughly like a dumb-bell. Of Tiriki Location's total area of just over seventy square miles, almost seventeen square miles in the northeast are uninhabited, government-protected forest preserve. In the remaining fifty-three square miles about 40,000 Tiriki make their homes. This brings the average population density in the inhabited part of the Location close to 750 people per square mile.

The *Pax Britannica*, combined with British success in controlling famine and epidemics, has caused the rather dense pre-contact population level to increase severalfold during the last fifty years. As the population increases so does the absolute dependency on wages from jobs in East African urban centers and on European farms. Because of overpopulation, today probably over half of the Tiriki adult males are *mulugulu* (off-tribe) at any given time, for the most part performing wage labor. Mostly it is the men between the ages of about eighteen and forty who seek wage labor off-tribe; consequently, the tribal population appears to the visitor to consist overwhelmingly of women, children, and old men.

ECONOMY

CLIMATE · The land of Tiriki, although hilly and boulder-strewn, is well watered, and generally very fertile. The rainfall, which averages between 60 and 70 inches a year, usually comes in late afternoon deluges of short duration in the months just following the equinoxes. Lighter showers also ordinarily occur several times a week during the intervening months. The planting is done just before the beginning of the semi-annual rainy seasons in March and September, and the crops are harvested during the dry months following the solstices; thus generally two crops are obtained a year.

CROPS AND DOMESTIC ANIMALS · Yellow maize, successfully introduced by American missionaries shortly after the World War I, has replaced eleusine and sorghum as the principal crop. A fairly informal but nevertheless clear-cut pattern of crop rotation is widely practiced. Every family's landholdings are divided into a number of small plots, and on each plot several plantings of maize or sorghum are generally followed by a planting of beans, and then a fallow period of several years. These crops form the backbone of the present-day subsistence economy of the Tiriki tribe.

This subsistence agricultural activity is today, as traditionally, almost entirely in the hands of the women. The men do nothing to help with these crops except to clear the bush from a fallow area prior to planting, and occasionally to help with the harvesting. Some cassava (manioc) is planted nowadays—also by the women. A banana patch is found a few yards behind most Tiriki homesteads; it is a man's duty to plant these patches, which the men use as places to drink beer in the shade. Except in times of severe shortage, they generally leave all the fruit for the women and children to harvest, eat, or sell.

Animal husbandry—the herding of cattle, sheep, and goats—remains today as traditionally, a fairly significant adjunct to the subsistence economy. Old men and young boys tend the small family-owned herds. The animals are a source of milk as well as meat; in the past they were very important ritually and ceremonially, and today they still figure largely in the bridewealth payments that continue to regularize every marriage. Every homestead has its flock of chickens that serve as household scavengers. Fowl were traditionally sacrificed in many of the rituals connected with the ancestor cult, and then eaten by the menfolk. Live chickens continue to be the usual gifts with which to honor visiting relatives and friendly strangers.

CASH CROPS AND WAGE LABOR • Since 1954 an increasing number of the men not regularly employed outside of Tiriki have been planting coffee bushes in portions of their homestead land holdings in hopes of achieving significant cash returns from the sale of the beans. Also, a few Tiriki eke out a small income cutting trees and making charcoal in the forest areas of the neighboring Nandi tribe.

Today more and more Tiriki are taking up permanent residence on land they have rented from the Nandi. However, the recent practice of renting lands in neighboring Nandi is only a partial and temporary palliative for Tiriki overpopulation. It is improbable that the farming activities of Tiriki women would in themselves be able to support—even at the bare subsistence level—the present-day tribal population.

For some time most Tiriki families have been obliged (except in years following an occasional bumper crop) to buy maize from elsewhere to tide them over the lean weeks that almost always precede harvest time. Cash with which to buy this grain comes in most families from wage earners working off-tribe. The same is true of the cash needed to pay the yearly poll tax (equivalent to about two weeks' pay of a day laborer) levied on every ablebodied man, or to pay for certain foodstuffs such as sugar and tea, and a number of imported or town manufactured articles running the gamut from razor blades to ready-made clothing—all of which are used by every family now and counted as necessities. Also, every man aspires to own a bicycle, and most families now regard it as important to send their children to school for at least a primary education. Schooling at all levels in the mission-run school system entails the payment of school fees. Thus, since opportunities for making money are so limited within the tribal area, economic necessity compels most Tiriki men to seek employment outside the tribal area for several years during their adult lives.

The traditional economic and social system also works, in effect, to encourage the practice of young men seeking employment off-tribe. A principal objective in a young man's seeking such work, Tiriki say, is to obtain money with which to buy cattle, particularly for use as bridewealth. It is the duty of a father to arrange for the acquisition of cattle for his sons' bridewealth payments; but it is equally the duty of every young man to help his father enlarge the family herds.

Traditionally, the young men were warriors. A principal motive for the cattle raids against alien and enemy tribes by the warrior group was to increase the size of the family herds. Both tribal war and cattle raiding were completely quashed by the British in North Nyanza beginning in 1907; even cattle theft has been virtually eliminated. Young men, it is said, used to boast among their peers, particularly in the presence of girls they wished to impress, of their exploits in battle. Today public boasting sessions in which young men tell of their important jobs, influential employers, and exciting exploits off-tribe, are a regular feature of local dances. Thus, it appears that the present day practice of young men seeking employment off-tribe serves as a partial substitute, both economically and prestigiously, for the traditional raiding activities of the warrior age group.

SOCIAL STRUCTURE

The Tiriki indigenous social structure may be likened to a rope of three strands: *lubamba*, plural, *zimbamba* (clans), *lixula*, plural, *maxula* (age groups), and *lusomo*, plural, *zisomo* (territorial units). These three strands, although no longer in themselves sufficient to maintain the social order, combine with the recently developed Christian religious groups and tribal bureaucracy to form the five principal elements of contemporary Tiriki social structure.

Territorial units

THE TRIBE • Traditionally the Tiriki had no tribal chief, or even any regular tribal council. However, circumcision elders of the different subtribes consulted with each other prior to announcing the start of a new initiation period, and it is claimed that ritual elders and war chiefs from different subtribes would gather for consultation and corporate ritual or military action whenever famine, a crushing military defeat, or some other situation arose that seemed to require their combined efforts. Space precludes any outlining of the development of the present tribal chieftaincy. It is sufficient to note simply that the British from, roughly, 1900 on selected a series of young or middle-aged men to serve as tribal chief. They established and initially maintained the chief's authority principally through giving him their own military backing.

Since the 1920s the institution of a tribal chief has been firmly established and generally supported in Tiriki, mainly through the administrative skill and personal attributes of leadership manifested by Chief Amiani. The present chief of Tiriki, Hezron Mushenye, who succeeded Amiani in 1948, has been able to use the authority that the office had by then acquired to re-strengthen the local authority of the judicial elders, and to do much to further primary and secondary education in Tiriki. The net result has been not only to win him the support and backing of the illiterate pagan elders, but also to maintain and increase the stature of the chieftainship in the eyes of the Christians and younger, school-educated Tiriki.

The chief today is aided and advised in his administrative duties by a tribal council consisting of the headmen and two nonsalaried representatives from each subtribe. Prior to 1956, these tribal council representatives were selected by the chief and his headmen from nominations made by the local communities. Since 1956, however, the subtribal representatives have been elected by universal male suffrage from local nominees. In 1956 the headmen and subheadmen were still appointed by the European district officer.

THE SUBTRIBE · In the past, the Tiriki had *zisomo* (subtribes), which contained several constituent communities whose men of the warrior age group were organized into offensive military divisions. Hilltop sacred groves and valley circumcision groves served as the ritual centers of these subtribes. Elders from the member communities would gather there for important ceremonies involving the supplication of past generations. The hilltop groves no longer figure in Tiriki ceremonial life except for their continued use by some pagans in the southern·region of the tribe in a ceremony held for initiates just at the end of their period of seclusion. In fact, traditional subtribal units themselves are now defunct except in connection with the circumcision ceremonies.

Tiriki today (1956) is divided into five subtribal administrative units. These are each somewhat larger in area than the traditional subtribes, and do not follow their boundaries. A government-appointed salaried "headman" is in charge of each of these subtribes. He holds a weekly meeting attended by all the subheadmen of his unit, and by a number of the more important local elders. At these meetings he hears disputes referred to him by the subheadmen, and before handing down his decisions consults with them and attending elders about the nature of the evidence presented and the customary procedure. He also briefs his subheadmen about new policies promulgated by the tribal chief in such matters as road and path maintenance, tax collection, and the like. Although his authority overrides that of his subheadmen in all areas, the headman generally supports and works through them in all community matters. The subheadmen, for their part, are expected to consult with their headmen before taking any matter to the tribal chief.

THE COMMUNITY • The unit that a subheadman represents is the *luhya* (community). Today, it generally consists of about one hundred homesteads, the members of which share a common local meeting ground where the judicial elders gather to arbitrate local disputes.

Traditionally the community was not only the principal judicial unit, but also was the basic military defensive group. The elder warrior age group of each community was organized to mobilize and operate as a unit whenever the defense alarm was sounded by an official known as "the keeper of the war horn." Also, the annual *bwali* (first fruits ceremonies) were carried out on a community basis by the local ritual elders. This aspect of community ritual is now defunct, but one community-based facet of ritual life still remains, namely the care and instruction of initiates while they are in seclusion. (See section on age groups below.)

Contemporary administrative structure: An overview

The contemporary Tiriki administration consists of a neat hierarchy of appointed, salaried tribal officials, each with specific administrative duties within his assigned territorial domain. At the lowest level are the nineteen subheadmen, each in charge of a community. Over them are the five headmen each in charge of a sublocation, and each is aided by his subheadmen. At the apex is the chief, who is responsible to the Kenya district administration for all Location (tribal) affairs. The chief is aided by his five headmen. Finally, outside the salaried administration, are the ten elected members of the tribal advisory council, and the several hundred community elders.

The elders act as the tribal judges. Many regularly serve as judges in the community court sessions held weekly by the subheadmen, and a substantial minority of the more respected and more vigorous elders are urged to attend the weekly courts of their respective headmen. Finally twenty or thirty of the most venerable elders of the tribe who still have the vigor to walk or bicycle to the chief's weekly court at Hamisi are urged to do so by the chief and his headmen.

The Tiriki administration retains to a high degree the informality and flexibility one associates with governmental procedures in a small, intimate face-to-face group in spite of the present size of the tribe and the administration's formal, bureaucratic nature. Crucial in the maintenance of this intimate quality is the presence of the subheadmen and usually several elders from each community at the chief's as well as at the headmen's weekly court and administrative sessions. Thus the formal chain of authority from the chief via the headmen, subheadmen and elders to the people in the communities is supplemented by the personal awareness of both the subheadmen and the community elders of what has taken place at all levels. This intimacy at the local level of intermediate- and top-level administrative affairs serves in Tiriki to foster the smooth acceptance of the administrative activities of the tribal bureaucracy.

The judicial system

The community remains to this day an important judicial unit in Tiriki. The elders say that the contemporary community judicial procedures are for the most part the same as they were in traditional times. It should be noted, however, that certain striking limitations have been placed on their jurisdiction. The judgment of certain serious crimes such as murder and manslaughter was completely removed from both community and tribal jurisdiction by the British. Also today it is possible for a plaintiff to appeal, or take his case directly, to the subtribal or tribal courts, or, if he chooses, to the multi-tribal African Tribunal, whereas in traditional times the community courts usually offered a man his only legal recourse.

The judicial elders who habitually gather at the community center in the mornings may always be prevailed upon by any man in the community to arbitrate a dispute. Boys, girls, and women customarily have their grievances presented by an adult brother or father; a husband, in those cases where he is not the defendant, may represent his wife. The plaintiff pleads his own case or the case of the aggrieved woman or child he represents, and he may bring as many witnesses as he wants to substantiate his story and give supporting evidence. The defendant, or his or her guardian, then presents his own case and names witnesses whom the judicial elders may then summon to give testimony on his behalf. During the entire proceedings all adult men and elderly women present may ask the judicial elders for permission to express their opinions on the case, or add further evidence, and the elders may themselves call on anyone, including women and children, to present testimony. The matter on which the judicial elders finally pass judgment is not necessarily that which the plaintiff first presented. Indeed the original accusation may be judged irrelevant to some other question that arises during the trial and that is deemed of greater importance by the elders. The original defendant may even be acquitted and final judgment made against someone else—even the plaintiff.

There is really no such thing as a simple acquittal of a case, for in any event the plaintiff's good judgment is on trial. If his accusations are disproved or rejected, but otherwise he is judged guiltless, the plaintiff will characteristically be laughed at by the elders for his stupidity (*busilo bwe*) and he will be obliged to pay the elders a chicken or some fee for having heard his

Dispute Settlement An elder is presenting testimony in a land dispute.

case. If the plaintiff is successful in the presentation of his case the defeated party must compensate the elders for having heard the case and then perform whatever else they direct as indemnity to the plaintiff and the community.

In traditional times community courts could administer certain kinds of ordeals to reveal guilt, and also could employ several oath-taking rituals, some Nandi in origin, and some common among the Abaluyia peoples. Tiriki elders say that all ordeals and pagan oaths have been outlawed with the exception of the *xuroza murembe*, an oath that was still occasionally administered under British sanction, but only at the multi-tribal District-administered African courts.

The jurisdiction of the community court is for the most part confined to cases where both the plaintiff and defendant live within the community. Cases heard cover such diverse matters as domestic squabbles, especially between husband and wife, theft, inheritance disputes, delinquency in bride-wealth payment, and assault. Murder and manslaughter, more recently always under the jurisdiction of British magistrates, in traditional times usually involved groups outside the particular community or communities involved; these were clan affairs, whether the killing occurred within one clan or between members of two clans. Elders of most, if not all, of the larger Tiriki clans are found residing in a number of different Tiriki communities. Consequently, final settlement, although usually made at the community of the deceased, generally involved judgment by elders of several different communities, and sometimes of even other subtribes. Accusations of witchcraft and sorcery still occur occasionally in the community courts, but they seldom bring the plaintiff much satisfaction now: today ordeals are never administered, and such accusations are null and void unless material evidence of witchcraft activity can be produced, which is rarely possible.

Kinship and clanship

It would be difficult to discuss questions such as marriage, inheritance, or even religious beliefs among the Tiriki without first sketching out the nature of Tiriki *zimbamba* (clans) and *zinzu* (subclans). Tiriki clans and subclans are primarily of significance in the affiliative, economic, and religious spheres. They supply their members with answers to the questions: "Where did I come from? Who cares whether I live or die? Whom can I depend on for food, land, shelter, and help when I'm sick? Who will remember me after I die?" In short, Tiriki clans and subclans offer their members a sense of social affiliation and continuity, and they give them both continuing economic and supernatural support. The clan, more particularly the subclan, is heavily involved in every funeral, marriage, major disaster, or change of status that may befall homestead members. Sentiments and responsibilities that the Tiriki derive from clan membership circumscribe and regulate people's actions at these times.

There are about a hundred *zimbamba* (agnatic exogamous clans) in Tiriki, each with its own genealogy and history or origin myth. Nearly all these origin stories tell of an agnatic ancestor who came from one or another Abaluyia clan (*luhya* or *oluhya*) accepted Terik age group initiation, was allowed to settle down as a neighbor and fellow warrior of the Terik, and thenceforth was known as a *mudiliji* (Tiriki). The Tiriki today commonly use the same term (*zimbamba*) to refer not only to the hundred or so exogamous clans within Tiriki, but also to refer to the usually larger non-Tiriki clans from which the Tiriki clans claim they originally segmented. Indeed, each Tiriki clan prohibits intermarriage with its parent Abaluyia clan, although today intertribal marriage to members of nonrelated Abaluyia clans is quite common. Tiriki clans vary greatly in size. The two largest clans in Tiriki have about four thousand members each; at the other extreme are a number of clans represented in Tiriki by only one or two families, or even by one or two individuals, but most Tiriki clans have memberships that range in the hundreds. No regular patterns of totemic observances or avoidances are followed by Tiriki clans; thus traditional agnatic genealogies are the sole charters of clan identity.

The largest and oldest Tiriki clans claim genealogies that reach back to a founding ancestor (the first man of their larger Abaluyia clan to reach Tiriki) who lived usually five or six generations prior to present senior living members of the clan. Subclans, in contrast, are groups of agnatic kinsmen who trace descent from an ancestor who lived only two or three generations ago.

In actual operation the subclan is confined to members of such agnatic groups who live close enough and are friendly enough, so that they regularly attend each other's weddings and funerals. Traditionally, the subclan was the group whose eldest male members made an effort to attend important supplications held at each other's homestead ancestral shrines. The sentiments and patterns of mutual responsibility and respect kept alive, however, by the corporate activity of the subclan are regarded by the Tiriki as springing from common clan membership. Indeed a distantly related clansman can and will be treated as a de facto member of the subclan group if he settles nearby and chooses to enter fully their round of activities.

Tiriki clanship manifests itself in four clear-cut ways. First, through their original myths the clans supply their members with a sense of social identity and continuity. Second, clan solidarity is reinforced through clan exogamy. The Tiriki not only prohibit marriage within one's clan, but also marriage within the mother's clan, or marriage into the subclan of the mother's mother or father's mother. Thus clan exogamy, combined with the other marriage prohibitions, prevents not only the development of intraclan friction that might result from clan endogamy, but also works to prevent the establishment of paired or clustered clans, linked by continuous intermarriage. Third, a sense of clan solidarity is further strengthened by patterns of hospitality that may be extended not only to closely related kinfolk and neighbors, but also to all clansmen no matter how genealogically distant. A further corollary of this is that kinship terms are regularly extended to all clansmen. Fourth, in the religious area a man traditionally feels that his welfare is most intimately tied up with his agnatic ancestors. In ritual activity at the homestead ancestral shrines, a person most often supplicated his clan ancestors, particularly those of his subclan. Clanship, per se, has no political significance in Tiriki; in practice, however, where a substantial plurality of the men living in one community belong to the same clan, they tend to control things by virtue of their numbers, and to speak of the area as being their clan region. Matters of property, inheritance, and traditional ancestor cult practices are spoken of as being clan affairs. But in point of fact they are family and, to a lesser extent, subclan affairs.

THE HOMESTEAD • *Mujizi* (homestead), in contemporary Tiriki usage, may denote anything from an establishment consisting of a single round mud-and-wattle thatch-roofed dwelling hut with an accompanying granary and surrounding fields where a man lives with his wife and three children, to a large compound—sometimes hedge-enclosed—containing as many as seven or eight dwelling huts and a number of granaries, where live several dozen people whose age span embraces three or even four generations. All homesteads, although often immediately adjacent to those of nonrelated neighbors,

A Homestead Cluster at
Hamisi, Tiriki

are inevitably backed or partially surrounded by family-owned and -farmed fields.

Ideally, the homestead head, always a male, is elderly, but still vigorous. Often he has two and, in some instances, three or more wives living in separate huts in the compound. In addition, a married son with two wives and offspring, each wife with her own hut, may continue the irregular line or uneven circle of huts in the compound. A second son may have his bride of a few months settled in a newly built hut, while perhaps a younger brother of the homestead head has one of his two wives and her offspring settled in another hut. Finally, a hut belonging to a brother who has gone with his family to live for an indefinite period on a European farm may be serving now as the sleeping place for a half dozen adolescent youths of the community.

In pre-European times two factors no longer operative tended to keep extended families together in large thorn-bush-enclosed compounds. The first was defense against pillage and surprise cattle raids by warriors of enemy tribes; and the second, the rites and rituals of the ancestor cult, organized principally around the homestead ancestral shrine.

Today the large joint-family homestead such as that outlined above is the exception rather than the rule. Polygyny among older men is still rather common; but as often as not the polygynist has inherited his second wife from a deceased clan brother, and she continues to live with her children on the homestead of a former husband, where she is periodically visited by her new husband. In those cases where a man is inclined as well as wealthy enough to procure as a second or additional wife a girl who has never before been married, he often runs into real difficulty today in keeping her in the same homestead with his senior wife. Nearly all women in Tiriki are now practicing Christians, and generally do not take at all kindly to sharing their home with a co-wife. Thus very often the man is obliged to build a hut on land he owns some distance away and settle one of his wives there.

When a young man marries his first wife it is customary for him to live with her in a hut in his father's homestead. Sometimes they move into a new hut built just for them, and in other instances they live in a hut vacated by an elder brother or a paternal uncle who has moved elsewhere to live. The bride, however, is not allowed to do her own cooking. Only after she has borne her husband three children will her mother-in-law and other women of her husband's homestead help her, with requisite ceremony, to set up her own hearth in her hut and permit her thenceforth to cook for her husband and children. A woman is considered to be a member of her husband's homestead from the time she first takes up residence there with him, so far as her own parents and the community at large are concerned. But in terms of her own sentiments, and those of her in-laws, her acceptance there remains highly tentative until she gets her own hearth and starts to cook for her husband and children. Moreover, she never becomes a member of her husband's clan.

After a wife has achieved the right to cook for her husband and children it is quite common for them to leave his parental homestead before many months have passed and establish a new home for themselves either on some land that the husband has been granted by his father, or on land that the husband through his own arrangements has acquired the right to use from a clansman, maternal uncle, or, more rarely, from his wife's kinsman (but never in her paternal homestead), or an unrelated friend. Neolocal residence following initial residence during the first few years of marriage at the husband's (paternal) homestead is today the predominant pattern; and indeed it apparently always has been fairly common for only one or two sons to continue to live in the paternal homestead.

Several months after the death of the head of a homestead, a large meeting of the subclan and neighbors is held to make final distribution of his property. Then all people, related or not, come forth to state whatever claims they may feel they have against the estate of the deceased. At this *lubego* (meeting) the grants of land made to mature sons by the father before his death are reviewed and confirmed or contested and revised. The eldest adult son generally takes over the deceased father's role as the homestead head and becomes responsible for distributing the remaining land to the younger sons as they reach maturity, provided the mothers of these immature sons (that is, the widow or widows of the deceased) are past child-bearing age. Arrangements are made for members of the subclan to inherit the young widows as wives because sons may never inherit their father's young wives. Whoever inherits a widow from a deceased clan brother thereby takes on responsibility for her immature children and the land they will eventually receive from their deceased father's estate. The foster father's reward is being assigned for his own use some of the land of the deceased, as well as gaining an additional wife and becoming the legal father of any children she may bear him. An elderly widow is allowed to remain in the hut her deceased husband built her, and is provided with a garden plot for her own use.

Cattle of the deceased are divided equitably between his sons, with the immature sons later looking either to their elder brother or to their foster father for cattle and help in bridewealth acquisition.

MARRIAGE AND THE SYSTEM OF BRIDEWEALTH · In Tiriki, as in so many African tribes, the payment of *buxwi* (bridewealth) is the crucial element in the legitimization of a marriage. This payment, made by the family of the groom to the family of the bride, grants the husband's clan the right to claim the children of the union. The size of Tiriki bridewealth has fluctuated over the decades, but nowadays at least six cattle are usually involved in the bridewealth given for a previously unmarried girl.

The Tiriki have developed a rather clear-cut folk sociology regarding their custom of bridewealth and the manner in which it affects family relationships. They feel that it in large measure colors and regulates the nature of (1) the father's behavior toward his grown sons; (2) brother-sister relationships; (3) the nature of the father's sister–brother's child relationship; and (4) the mother's brother–sister's child relationship. In addition they say the hyperformality and avoidance behavior characteristic of so many of the in-law relationships arise in part from the strains attendant upon the payment of bridewealth.

I shall now examine these four pairs of relationships, and then mother-child, and grandparent-grandchild relations. It will be seen that each becomes meaningful to the individual at different times, and also that each changes in nature during the course of a person's life.

Once a man's son has been initiated into the tribe (always after the onset of puberty) and is ready for marriage the Tiriki aver he becomes a very mixed blessing to the father, for he has become a rival with his father for bridewealth. "Remembrance" is a dominant theme in Tiriki culture. The Tiriki feel that everyone wants very much to be thought well of and remembered by as large a circle of people as possible, not only while alive but also after death. It is through his own offspring, to a lesser extent through descendants of his clan brothers, and sometimes through *biixwa* (his sister's children) that a person feels his desire to achieve the immortality of remembrance will be primarily gratified. The more wives a man has the greater his chances of having a large number of sons, each of whom may found a lineage that will honor and remember him as the founding ancestor for time immemorial. A son, of course, when he reaches adulthood, begins to harbor similar dreams, and wants to get married. Custom decrees that it is a father's obligation to make arrangements for the collection and payment of the bridewealth of the first wife of each of his sons. Thus the conflict: a father's duty to provide bridewealth for each son's first marriage may oblige him to use for obtaining daughters-in-law the cattle and wealth that he would like to be able to use to procure more wives for himself.

Unmarried adult sons, for their part, are expected to help their fathers economically. Nowadays this means that an unmarried son working away from the tribe is expected to send home a good portion of his wage earnings so that the father may buy cattle, some of which will later be used for that son's bridewealth. The actual planning for the acquisition of the bridewealth remains, however, the father's responsibility. Today, when a son often works hundreds of miles away, the father may take his responsibility rather lightly; and it is not too uncommon for a son to return after several years to find that all the money he has sent home has been spent on cattle used by the father to acquire another wife for himself. A son, however, is not always blameless in his dealings with his father over bridewealth. In fact he often forces his father's hand by running off and eloping with his favorite sweetheart.

Marriage by elopement is today the most common form of marriage, and probably was in traditional times as well. If a boy and a girl are successful in spending a night together uninterrupted by their respective clansfolk at a prearranged rendezvous, the irate father of the girl will generally go to the father of the boy, declare the marriage a *fait accompli* and demand that negotiations be started for bridewealth payments. The father of the boy really has no choice but to provide the couple with a place to live on his homestead just as he would if the pair had been formally married—unless he wants perhaps to estrange his son permanently, which is a serious and rarely taken step. Usually in such a situation the father vents his spleen by driving as hard a bargain as possible about bridewealth payments; often he will not make any payment at all until the birth of the first child; then, however, the community elders will rule that he must pay at least one cow immediately on demand no matter what hardship it may cause him, and a second cow shortly thereafter. An obdurate father can be obliged in like manner to make a minimal payment of two more cows to the girl's family the next two times the girl gives birth. After that—a total payment of six cows—the affair is considered legally closed. Such an arrangement of delayed payments makes a father quite anxious to get his daughter formally married before she can elope, so that he may receive several additional sheep or goats and cash, which are handed over in formal marriage. The practice of elopement also works to help reconcile the father to his son's marriage, since in the long run the father pays less bridewealth, and pays it more slowly, than he would have to pay in a formal marriage.

A father may draw on a number of sources when amassing bridewealth payments for his sons. As mentioned earlier, the son has usually given his father cash from his own earnings, but normally not enough. It is considered fitting that some of the cattle that the father uses should come either from the marriage of a younger sister of the father or from the marriage of one of his own daughters. Next the father may turn first to his brothers and then to other members of the subclan for help. In many instances he may also get help from nonagnatic kinsmen, neighbors and friends who are in one or another way indebted to him.

The Tiriki perceive the custom of bridewealth as working to intensify the brother-sister bond. Before he reaches adolescence a young boy is fully aware that when his sisters marry they bring cattle into the family, which may then be used for his own and his brothers' marriages, and young girls also are fully cognizant of the role they are destined to play in the family fortunes. A boy is especially solicitous toward the sister from whom his father or elder brother has indicated he will receive marriage cattle. Throughout their entire lives brothers and sisters generally feel freer to trust and confide in each other than in their spouses or even their mothers. "After all," Tiriki men point out, "your sister is a member of your own clan—but not your wife, or your mother!"

The bond between brother and sister, reinforced by the custom of bride-wealth, is reflected after marriage in the relationship patterns between a woman and her brother's children on the one hand, and those between a man and his sister's children on the other. A woman (and her husband) and her brother's children call and refer to each other by a special term, *senje*. A *senje* treats her brother's children with great warmth and cordiality; indeed they may choose to live in her homestead for protracted periods of time during childhood, and every visiting brother's child, whether the visit is for an hour or for weeks, can expect, when departing for home, to receive a live chicken from his (or her) paternal aunt. Moreover, children are taught to treat their paternal aunt with great respect for her curse is feared above all curses as a source of sterility. Thus it is this category of kinsmen, one of whom is generally a vital economic link in the marriage of one's parents, to whom the Tiriki attribute the greatest cosmic veto power over the conception of their offspring.

A more openly ambivalent but generally more informal relationship commonly prevails between a *mwihwa* (maternal uncle) and *xoza* (his sister's children). A woman, especially during the first years of marriage returns to her paternal homestead for frequent and sometimes extended visits, bringing her small children along with her. This means that a man frequently sees a good deal of his sister's children even during the first years of her marriage when custom decrees that elders of his homestead must still avoid all social relationships with her husband and his parents; indeed, his family and the family of his sister's husband are frequently in the midst of a legal dispute over the bridewealth settlement. Thus the cards would seem to be stacked against the cordial acceptance of the sister's children who by birth-right are members of the in-law's homestead and clan. Actually, however, a maternal uncle feels a real proprietary interest in his sister's children, an interest that is again attributed by the Tiriki themselves to the working of their bridewealth system. Because a marriage in Tiriki is considered finally consummated and the bridewealth payments truly binding only after the birth of three children, the birth of each sister's child brings greater certainty of tangible lasting material increase to members of her paternal family and works to assure the sister's continued well-being and to improve her status in her husband's homestead.

The formalized aspect of the *xoza-mwihwa* relationships are manifest in certain obligations that the maternal uncle has toward his sister's daughter at the time of her marriage, and in certain rites that a sister's son must be ready to perform following the death of a maternal uncle. Also tradition smiles on a man taking a sister's son as an apprentice to learn a special skill, such as divining or blacksmithing. And a man may ask a sister's son to settle near him if there is land available, or even to become a member of his homestead.

In the informal situation the mother's brother has the right to ask his sister's children to run all sorts of errands for him. Conversely, the maternal uncle is always an "easy touch" for pocket money; and his sister's children can ask for, and receive on more or less indefinite loan, almost anything belonging to him that strikes their fancy.

The *xoza-mwihwa* relationship finds reinforcement in a supernatural correlate in which the sanctions, as almost always in Tiriki, flow from the elder to the younger generation. If you are afflicted with a skin itch or a cloud of flying ants swarming around your head, a maternal uncle's displeasure is often blamed. His curse may bring you barrenness but, it is seldom felt that he, unlike the paternal aunt, has actually taken such a step.

I think it is significant that I never heard the Tiriki try to relate mother-child relationships to the bridewealth system. Tiriki cattle-focused folk sociology does not embrace this area of life perhaps because it is too complex and too important and lacks almost entirely the cut and dried formalized aspects of the previously described relationships. A woman in Tiriki can achieve lasting status and security in her husband's homestead, as an adult, virtually only through bearing a child. Furthermore, the resultant security and respect that remain partial and tentative until she has borne at least three offspring are reinforced and further amplified by her bearing a large number of children of both sexes. To be sure, a few elderly women, more or less regardless of their success at motherhood, gain considerable esteem among the womenfolk for their knowledge of medicinal herbs or, sometimes, for having learned the art of "smelling out" female witches. The crucial point to be observed is that virtually everything in the society is structured to encourage and reinforce a woman's pleasure at becoming a mother.

CHILD TRAINING AND SOCIALIZATION

The care of infants and small children is for most Tiriki women a relatively pleasant and untaxing part of their lives. A woman generally gives birth in her hut in her husband's homestead, attended by women of the homestead and neighborhood. For the first several days after childbirth the mother generally rests, and devotes herself primarily to her infant's wants. After a week or so, the old women of the community gather to shave the baby's head, and help find a name for the infant. The name may not be decided on for several days, the paternal grandparents generally having the principal say in this important matter, but the interest and delight the neighborhood women, especially the elderly women, take in seeing, fondling, and talking about the newborn infant gives a very early introduction to the widespread cuddling and playing with by elders, both related and unrelated, that is every Tiriki baby's lot. The men are conspicuously aloof from this sort of thing during the first year or so of the baby's life, but once the infant begins to be able to walk about unaided they too start to take delight in him.

Usually quite soon after a baby's birth, the mother takes the baby (and the other small children she may have already borne) to her parental homestead for an extended visit, often lasting several weeks or more. After the young mother returns to her husband's homestead, her mother-in-law, elder women of the neighborhood, and preadolescent girls not yet strong enough for regular work in the fields tend the baby while she goes about her regular farmwork. Demand breast feeding is universal, however, which means that the mother never goes so far afield to farm or gather wood that she cannot quickly return if word comes that the baby is crying or seems hungry.

When the baby is about six months old, a small girl, about seven or eight years old, is found to take over the task of looking after the infant when the mother is busy. No infant or small child is ever allowed to scream unattended. Usually the small nurses who tend infants are elder sisters or cousins of the baby, but sometimes a young aunt, or even a nonrelated neighbor child performs this service.

A little boy serves as a nurse only on those rare occasions when no young girls are available. By the time they are five or six most boys are spending much of their day helping neighborhood peers tend sheep and goats. Boys usually graduate to cattle herding when they are about nine or ten. Today probably well over half of the boys between eight and twelve regularly attend primary school; but those not in school, together with some of

A Nurse and Her Infant Charge

the elderly men seem to have little trouble in managing the rather small number of cattle about, which in most instances do not come to more than about one or two cattle per homestead.

As noted earlier, men, with the partial exception of elderly men, remain comparatively distant and aloof from younger children. The Tiriki say that the vomit and drool from a nursing infant will give a man a bad case of skin itch, and offer this as the reason they will have nothing to do with a baby under a year old. It is said that formerly a man would not have sexual relations with his wife after she had given birth until their infant was a year or so old because he was afraid of touching the drool from the infant that might be on his wife's body. If by accident or in an emergency a man did pick up a small infant, or believed he had become contaminated by its drool, he felt obliged to go to a stream and give himself a thorough scouring with water and sand to forestall a case of skin itch. In recent years, however, the notion has developed that a good washing with Lifebuoy soap, widely sold locally, effectively prevents skin itch in all such cases. Men nowadays often start to have sexual relations with their wives after a wait of only two or three months following childbirth, taking a Lifebuoy bath the next morning as a safe and easy decontamination procedure. After a baby is a few months old the mother starts to leave the infant from time to time to spend part of the night with the small children on the other side of the hut; and this is the procedure followed when the husband wants to have sexual relations with her, for husband and wife usually sleep separately.

A Tiriki baby is nursed until the mother's milk fails—usually sometime during her succeeding pregnancy. It is not unusual for a woman to become pregnant today only six months after she has had a child, with the result that her milk supply may fall off and stop before the baby is walking. Children are usually started on gruel and other soft foods when just a few months old; hence in most cases the decreased time nowadays between pregnancies and the resultant shortened nursing period does not create major feeding difficulties. A woman's last child may nurse until three or four years old, and finally stop only because of teasing by peers.

Toilet training is permissive and gradual; in Tiriki huts, which mostly have floors of pounded earth smeared with dung, accidental soiling by a baby does not pose much of a cleanup problem. Babies are not diapered, and the adult or the child nurse is quick to hold the infant away from her body at the first sign of evacuation. Babies astride their nurses' hips are conditioned to going outdoors to a secluded spot, such as the banana patch, to defecate even before they can walk, and after they are walking they soon learn to head for the out-of-doors on their own through being verbally reminded, or, if necessary, picked up and carried to the door. When they are a bit older children learn through the example and admonitions of their elders not only to be modest about excretory functions, but also that it is well to be secretive about these matters as protection against the possible use of their fecal matter to bring them sickness through sorcery.

On reaching the age of five or six, a child is gently nudged and guided by parents and elders to forsake the parental hut at night and start sleeping instead in the hut of a nearby grandparent or elderly relative of the same sex. Even before the child goes to an elderly person's hut to sleep, aged relatives have become the focus of his frequent daytime visits; and after the move, right up until adolescence, grandparents and other old people take a dominant role in the informal instruction of children. A great deal of grandparental interaction with children consists of spinning out anecdotes and reminiscences that punctuate and further illustrate everyday technical skills taught by parents, such as planting, herding, or grinding millet, as well as the social obligations and attitudes toward various categories of relatives and neighbors that are manifest in the actions and brief instructions of the younger adults and older children.

Grandparents and grandchildren exchange a lot of banter; their joking is often sexually toned, and expressions of endearment, such as *ijolwa* (sweetheart), *muxali wanje mudididi* (my little wife), or *musaza wanje* (my husband), are frequently used when addressing a grandchild of the opposite sex. Such informality is in marked contrast to parent-child verbal exchanges that are generally rather restrained and strictly avoid all allusions to sexual matters. Later in life, if a man is having a squabble with his father or guardian, perhaps over bridewealth, he generally turns to a grandfather for support. Also, if a person has been cursed by an elder, or believes he is the victim of sorcery, he may go to a grandfather to beg for his intercession and aid. Complementing the solicitude and warmness of the grandparents for their grandchildren is the expectancy that the grandchildren will readily do chores and run errands for their grandparents and that they will always show them respect and quick obedience whenever these are called for. As a child grows up and comes to realize the ritual, magical, and (in former times) the religious power held by his aging grandparents, disrespect toward them becomes untenable; indeed, sustained rudeness toward grandparents and elders is quite literally viewed as a sure road to *bulalu* (madness). Most grandparents find as they grow older, and their descendants increase in number, a growing fulfillment of their own familial aspirations through care of and concern for their own grandchildren. Grandchildren in their turn come to view grandparents not only as very kind and pleasant people, but also as the storytellers and tutors of worldly wisdom, and, most important, as the people they can depend on to help most in times of real trouble or distress.

RELIGION

RELIGIOUS BELIEFS · Contemporary Tiriki elders, both pagan and Christian, agree that the Tiriki traditionally had no conceptualization of a "high God, Creator of all things," comparable to the mission-taught Biblical God, or to the northern Abaluyia creator, *Wele* (Wagner 1954:20–28). Today Tiriki apparently remember only scattered myths about the origin of the sun, moon and other natural phenomena. These myths, when viewed together and compared one with another, manifest no apparent integrating theme or dominant cosmological focus.

Traditional Tiriki religious beliefs are quite in harmony with the prevailing Abaluyia and general Bantu idea that the spirits of the deceased have a continuing influence over the fortunes of the living. A crucial aspect of the relationship the Tiriki feel exists between the living and the dead is the distinction they make between the *baguga* (fairly recently deceased paternal and maternal agnatic ancestors), and the *misambwa* (the ancestral spirits in general). All the ancestral spirits including recently deceased agnates are believed to live together in a world apart from the living. Tiriki pagan elders are not sure just where they live or what sort of existence they lead, but they agree that the ancestral spirits continue to have access to the world of the living and that they can strongly influence the well-being of the living. It is felt to be of paramount importance, therefore, to secure and maintain the support of the *misambwa*. This support is gained through the rites of supplication, which are most commonly held at the *lusambwa* (homestead ancestral shrine).

Tiriki folk tales give instances of specific phenomena and types of behavior that are good or bad and then offer particularistic explanations as to why; they also support the traditional assumption that the ancestral spirits are the only generalized source of power. If the *misambwa* are indifferent about or angry toward you, you will not receive their strength and consequently will probably soon fall on bad times. The ancestral spirits were never, either in myth or in common pagan judgment, conceived of as themselves a source of evil or misfortune.

Dangers arising from human and other natural and supernatural causes are often illustrated in Tiriki myths, but these dangers are not related in any conscious or formalized way to an overall cosmological tradition. *Manani* (man-eating giants) are probably the superhuman agents of evil in Tiriki myths most frequently alluded to. Wild animals, enemy tribes, those phenomena traditionally considered to bring or be associated with a state of *luswa* (ritual danger), and the action of sorcerers, are other often cited sources of danger. Today, as in pre-European times, *baloji* (witches) are regarded as inherently *damanu* (bad). Witches are believed simply to enjoy using their magical powers to make people barren or to make them sicken or die. They get their evil nature, it is said, either from having a "disposition of blood" present in their family (some subclan segments are reputed to have a predisposition toward witchcraft), or from having been corrupted and trained by a practicing witch.

There are *balyuli, babila* (diviners, sorcerers, and the like) in Tiriki who are not witches; they use their supernatural powers primarily to protect their families and clients from the medicine and spells of witches and enemy sorcerers. Sorcerers are believed occasionally to turn their art against other people principally for two reasons. One reason is *imbodoxa* (jealousy) over other peoples' wealth, health, good luck, and so on. Jealousy, however, is believed to characterize witches, and any known sorcerer who seems by disposition to be especially prone to jealousy may become a witch-suspect; thus everyone, including those tutored in the arts of magic, strives to appear to be free from jealousy. The second reason is *burima* (vengeful anger). A sorcerer may feel this against someone, particularly a younger person, who has treated him disrespectfully; or he may endeavor to harm by sorcery someone whom he suspects of having harmed a member of his family.

No one in Tiriki, either young or old, is felt to become seriously ill or to die simply because he has had bad luck or because his time has come. At every death and serious illness a human agent is suspected unless there is clear-cut evidence before the death or the onset of illness that the person has fallen into a state of ritual impurity (*xugwa luswa*) and has not been properly purified, that he has violated an oath where the sanction is illness and/or death, or that he was being troubled by a *shisyuxu* (ghost) seeking vengeance or company.

It is the role of the elders, particularly the subclan elders, to comfort the immediate family of the deceased and to allay and smooth over any public accusations of sorcery that might be uttered at the graveside. Also it is to his subclan elders that a seriously ill person first turns for counter-medicine against sorcery. If they themselves do not possess the appropriate knowledge for divining the difficulty and counteracting the cause, the elders appeal to nonrelated elders of the community who do. It must be remembered that nearly all magical power—preventive, curative, and destructive—is controlled by old people in Tiriki. A person is not usually taught most of the important magical ritual until he has reached middle age. Furthermore, it is believed that some of the most powerful and dangerous methods of sorcery may make their practitioners permanently sterile. Thus these medicines are almost exclusively the tools of the very old who have passed the age of procreation.

Tiriki readily accept Western medical explanations offered by mission doctors and dispensary nurses about the cause of disease, for example, the role of the mosquito in the transmission of malaria. Their underlying assumptions about the reasons for disease and death, however, still remain unchanged. No one in Tiriki ever denied that the bite of a poisonous snake, for example, was the immediate cause of the victim's death. But Tiriki are not content with this level of explanation. Why did the snake get in the way of and bite *that* man? Why did the malaria-infected mosquito bite *that* baby? Now that they have learned that diseases can be cured relatively easily by Western medicine, they no longer bother to ask who or what was ultimately responsible; they just take the medical cure. For diseases that Western medicine can cure only through extended and extensive treatment, however, or can only alleviate, the services of the diviner and the sorcerer are still widely utilized.

RELIGIOUS PRACTICES · It should be stressed that the Tiriki feel today, as formerly, that among the elders are those who above all others have the power to preserve the well-being of the living—but who also can kill. The death of an elder does not weaken this notion; rather, in the eyes of the Tiriki it reaffirms this idea by suggesting that other elders remain who are as powerful as or more powerful than the one who has just died.

Elders played a crucial role in the supplication of the ancestors that took place at the ancestral shrine found in many Tiriki homesteads. Such a shrine was very simple, consisting of three small stones placed around a stick cut from the *lusiyola* tree (*Markhamia platycalyx*) set up under the eves of the granary opposite the entrance of the hut belonging to the homestead head's senior wife. Care of the homestead ancestral shrine is the responsibility of the homestead head. Only a man who has reached the age of elderhood can keep such a shrine; furthermore, even though he is old enough to have a shrine set up for him in his own homestead by his clan elders, a man is obligated to call in a senior member of his clan to preside at all ceremonies held at his homestead shrine until he himself has reached senior elderhood (that is, he has advanced to the ritual elder age grade; see the chart, page 71). Thus a man who leaves his parental homestead to set up his own independent homestead prior to reaching elderhood is obliged, whenever he wishes to beseech the ancestral spirits about an important matter, to return to the ancestral shrine of his parental homestead, or go to the shrine of a closely related elder clansman, and induce his father or the clan elder to hold the supplication for him.

In times of supplication it is common for the *musaalisi* (presiding ritual elder) first to beseech and praise one or two of his deceased *baguga*, usually mentioning them by name. Then he supplicates the *misambwa* for help and assistance. The ritual elder assumes that the way to get the attention and aid of the *misambwa* is by first remembering and praising deceased forebears whom he remembers from his youth. These forebears, flattered by being remembered and praised, may then feel moved to solicit the aid of the *misambwa* in general on behalf of their living descendants. The Tiriki view a personal connection as being the most helpful in dealing with the supernatural, just as they do in relations with the living.

Tiriki elders also had a strong role in controlling witchcraft in the community. It is believed dangerous to declare someone a witch because that makes the accuser a prime target for the accused's suspected malevolent power. Consequently, most overt antiwitchcraft activity was undertaken by the community elders acting as a group, thereby lessening the danger of individual accusers being picked out for the witches' wrath. Once a year, at the community first fruits ceremonies (which were given up, apparently for good, about a decade ago) it was common for the local elders collectively to curse the witches, no specific names being mentioned, and to ask the ancestral spirits to drive them away. Occasionally a person was openly accused by the community elders of being a witch. If the accused failed to clear his (or her) name through an ordeal (there were several kinds), or some other method, it was not uncommon for him to be severely beaten and warned to desist, or cursed by the elders and driven from the community, or sometimes even clubbed to death. The advent of British justice curtailed beatings and ended ordeals and clubbings for witches; it even made public accusations of witch suspects very rare because the accusations could no longer lead to any definitive decision or public action, and, indeed, might boomerang if the accused instituted a slander suit against one or more of his accusers in the British-instituted African district court.

AGE GROUPS

HISTORICAL ORIGINS AND INITIATIONS • The Tiriki age group organization affects, directly or indirectly, most of the major areas of social activity in Tiriki. The social groupings, rankings, statuses and

roles it institutes are manifest in everything from the largest tribal and subtribal activities to everyday intrafamilial relationships. Yet the Tiriki avow
(and all the evidence I could master supports their opinion) that the age
group organization is not an indigenous part of their Bantu heritage; rather
it is something they received from the culturally and linguistically alien
Terik. The Nilo-Hamitic Terik people are herdsmen, a Nandi offshoot, and
they were the previous inhabitants of the area now inhabited largely by the
Bantu Tiriki. A few Terik have chosen to remain in the region rather than
take refuge in nearby Nandiland, but they are now outnumbered by the
Tiriki probably more than ten to one. Nothing in their present status indicates that the Terik were the people who first permitted straggling remnants
of Abaluyia lineages to settle in the region, or that they insisted that these
newcomers be initiated into Terik age groups. These age groups soon supplied the principal political and ritual basis for Tiriki corporate action.

The Tiriki word *idumi* designates the whole series of ceremonies performed when adolescent boys are circumcised and then initiated into a
lixula (an age group) and achieve adult and full tribal status. *Idumi* is
usually held at four- or five-year intervals. Up until the *idumi* of 1920–1921
the Terik and the Tiriki ceremonies are reported to have been one and the
same, and to have remained substantially unaffected by European contact.
Since then a number of innovations have taken place including the development of separate Christian and pagan Tiriki ceremonies. The pagan Tiriki
ceremony still is essentially the same as the Terik ceremony, and the two
groups of people continue to initiate their youths together in those parts of
Tiriki and Nyangori Locations where they live as neighbors.

Initiation is organized on a territorial basis. As noted earlier, the area
traditionally inhabited by the Terik and Tiriki was divided into about ten
or twelve subtribes, each with a hilltop sacred grove and a circumcision grove
located in a valley. A number of new circumcision groves have been established in recent years by both the pagans and the Christians. No uninitiated
person may enter these groves, and they remain the place where the principal
secret ceremonies of initiation are held. Each circumcision grove is under the
care of a ritual elder who is the chief circumciser and the leader of the entire
initiation procedure in his subtribal area. Generally about a half dozen local
communities share the same circumcision grove.

The infant and childhood socialization procedures of all the Abaluyia
tribes are very similar. The postpuberty circumcision and initiation rites of
the Tiriki, however, differ radically from and are much more involved than
the circumcision and initiation procedures of any of the other Abaluyia
tribes. The Terik-derived Tiriki initiation rites, in the six months of
dramatic and rigorous instruction during seclusion following circumcision,
teach the initiates how to behave as members of the highly formalized graded
age groups that traditionally regulated Tiriki traditional military, political,

Tiriki Initiates Wearing Initiation Garb (*Onni Rauha*)

and ritual activity. A youth can come from another part of North Nyanza, go through the Tiriki initiation, and emerge, in every sense of the word, a full-fledged Tiriki.

A certain directness, candor, and independence of manner characteristically distinguish men initiated in Tiriki from those who have undergone the much simpler and less protracted initiation rites performed in the other Abaluyia tribes. Clearly, however, the rites in themselves do not produce this change in the individual, for an initiated Tiriki, when away from other Tiriki, cannot in most cases be distinguished from other Abaluyia living nearby who speak the same language. But the initiation rites, apparently with marked effectiveness, do give the initiate a sense of belonging to a special tribal brotherhood, and do much to teach him what kinds of social attitudes are appropriate for and expected of members of that brotherhood.

What is the nature of these rites that so drastically alter not only the tribal status but also the social behavior and general demeanor of those who undergo them? I think that very likely the shock the initiates receive because of the contrast the Tiriki initiation cycle presents to all their preceding socialization procedures is probably just as significant to their effectiveness as their actual content. The relentless and dramatic intensity of the initiation is a radical departure from the casual on-again-off-again tutelage and supervision of near peers, women, and old people that guide a youth before his initiation. The principal agents of socialization during initiation (the counselors who supervise every aspect of the initiates' lives during the seclusion) are initiated men still in their physical prime—the very group with whom youths, before initiation, have virtually no contact. Finally, prior to initiation, socialization is generally very permissive in character, whereas throughout the entire six months' initiation period every facet of the initiate's life is characterized by its spartan quality, its strict regimentation, and its focus on group activities to the exclusion of all privacy and all individual undertakings.

The initiation rites themselves fall into five stages, each lasting from four to six weeks. Elaborate ceremonies held in the special circumcision groves, with attendance restricted to the initiates and men already initiated, mark the beginning of each successive stage. The subtribal ritual elders preside at these ceremonies. During the intervening weeks initiates spend their time in or near seclusion huts in a forested area, where their activities are carefully supervised and regulated by the specially appointed counselors belonging to the age group immediately senior to the initiates. The entire initiation cycle subjects the initiate to the following sequence of events:

1. Confession to the elders by each initiate of all taboos he has violated thus far in his life—so as not to bleed to death from the circumcision wound.

2. Initiation in the grove, witnessed only by those already initiated. The operation is regarded as a test of the initiate's fortitude, and he is taunted later in the initiation procedures if he flinches or cries out.

3. A period of ritual impurity and relative inactivity until the wounds heal.

4. Weaving of masks and costumes to be worn by the initiates whenever they appear in public until the end of their seclusion.

5. Protracted instruction and practice in dancing and singing.

6. Periods of intensive drill in the arts of hunting and warfare.

7. A solemn oath taken in front of the elders by each initiate never to divulge any aspect of the initiation rites to the uninitiated on pain of ostracism and death by sorcery.

8. Ritual enactment of the initiate's death and rebirth.

9. Public displays of dancing and singing by the masked initiates.

10. A period of relative license during the last weeks of the initiation period when the masked initiates may wander around freely, begging jewelry and other favors from the girls, food from the women, and beating up any adult male they catch who is not an initiated Tiriki.

11. Final blessing by the elders, emergence unmasked from seclusion, and the triumphal return of each initiate to his parental home, where he is greeted with feasting and ceremony, closely paralleling the welcome given to a bride arriving at the homestead of her groom.

The initiated young man returns to a completely different sort of life from the one he knew prior to initiation. Now he eats with the men and shuns the casual company of women and children; he woos girls, but for a number of years avoids marriage. Today, almost inevitably, he soon seeks employment off-tribe on a European farm or in one of the growing East

African urban centers. Traditionally, he occupied himself with raiding and cattle herding.

The young man returning to his community after initiation has a place among the menfolk whereas before he had none, but he finds himself at the bottom of the male status hierarchy. The endless specific instruction and ritual and illustrative anecdotes he was subjected to during his initiation have prepared him for this by making him very much aware not only that he is a neophyte to the age group occupying the warrior age grade, but also that he is subordinate to the successively senior age groups occupying the elder warrior, judicial elder, and ritual elder age grades.

Prior to initiation a youth has very little contact with initiated men outside his own homestead; his peers are drawn from different clans all over the neighborhood, but his main loyalties are to those in his homestead, clan and kin group. After initiation, however, all these loyalties are in most circumstances subordinated to his age group ties, and to the judicial and ritual authority of the elder age groups. Thus the Tiriki initiation rites quickly orient the initiates to their new status of manhood, indoctrinate them in the intricacies of the graded age group organization, and effectively shift their primary bonds of loyalty and social reference from their extended family to their age group and the graded hierarchy of more senior age groups.

Age group structure

The Tiriki age group organization is directly borrowed from the Nilo-Hamitic Terik who border the Tiriki to the south. There are seven named age groups (Kabalach, Golongolo, Jiminigayi, Nyonje, Mayina, Juma, and Sawe), each embracing approximately a fifteen-year age span. In addition, each age group passes successively through four distinctive age grades. The system is cyclical, as the chart shows, each age group being reinstated with new initiates approximately every 105 years.

Perhaps the easiest way to grasp the difference between age groups and age grades is to review the nature of our college class system. Freshmen entering college in the autumn of 1958, for example, immediately become known as the Class of 1962—the year when they were due to graduate. Thenceforth, for as long as they live, they are known as the Class of 1962. While in college, however, members of the Class of 1962 must pass in successive years through four ranked grades: freshman, sophomore, junior, and senior.

In Tiriki each age group contains those men who were initiated over a fifteen-year age span, not simply during one year. The initiation rites, it will be recalled, traditionally extend over a six months' period, and are held every four years; thus each age group receives recruits from three or four successive initiations. The four traditional Tiriki age grades are *bandu bi lihe, balulu* (the warriors), *balulu basaxulu* (the elder warriors), *basaxulu bi biina, basaxulu bu luhya* (the judicial elders), and *basaxulu basaalisi* (the ritual elders). Before they were prohibited by the British about 1900, handing-over ceremonies were held at about fifteen-year intervals in conjunction with the closing of an age group to more initiates. At this time the age group just closed to initiates became formally instated in the warriors' age grade, the age group that had just been the warriors' moved on to the elder warrior grade, the former elder warriors moved on to the judicial elder grade, and the former judicial elders moved on to the ritual eldership.

The cyclical aspect of Tiriki age groups can also be readily compared with the system of college classes, if one substitutes the Tiriki age group name for "Class of ———," and remembers that each Tiriki age group embraces fifteen years. The Class of '62 at Harvard, for example, has been reinstated every 100 years for several centuries with a new group of college men, and thus can be viewed as part of a cyclical process. In Tiriki each cycle lasts 105 years instead of a century, because the seven age groups, *each* embracing fifteen years, cover a total span of 105 years. The Sawe age group, for example, open for initiates from 1948 to 1963, was previously instated and open to initiates from roughly 1843 to 1858.

Age group functions

Now I shall review briefly the traditional function of the four age grades and then contrast them with their contemporary functions (see chart). The *warriors* were formally given the responsibility of guarding the country. They were said "to hold the land" (*bali na shibala,* and so on). An age group's lasting reputation was principally earned while it was occupying the warrior age grade. Similarly the reputation accompanying a man throughout the remainder of his life and then remembered by his posterity was primarily based on the leadership, courage, and good fortune he exhibited while a warrior.

The duties and prerogatives of the *elder warriors* were neither as glorious nor as well defined as those of the warriors. They had relatively few specialized social tasks, but they gradually assumed an increasing share of administrative type activities in areas that were basically the responsibility of the elder age groups. For example, at public post-funeral gatherings held to settle property claims, usually a man of the elder warrior group was called upon to serve as chairman. His duty was to maintain order, to see that all the claims and counterclaims were heard, to initiate compromises, but always to seek and defer to the judgment of the elders in matters that were equivocal or a departure from tradition. Members of this age grade also served as

	Traditional Age-graded Duties	Age Span	Age Groups
Elders	Elders (deceased or senile)	91-105	KABALACH
Elders	Ritual elders	71-90	GOLONGOLO
Elders	Judicial elders	56-70	JIMINIGAYI
Warriors	Elder warriors	41-55	NYONJE
Warriors	Warriors	26-40	MAYINA
	Initiated / Uninitiated	11-25	JUMA
	Small boys	0-10	SAWE

1954

Age Groups	Age Span	Modern Age-graded Roles	
GOLONGOLO	91-105	Elders (deceased or senile)	Elders
JIMINIGAYI	71-90	Ritual elders	Elders
NYONJE	56-70	Judicial elders	Elders
MAYINA	41-55	Administrators or away at work	Warriors
JUMA	26-40	Away at work	Warriors
SAWE	11-25	In school and away at work	Initiated & uninitiated Small boys
KABALACH	0-10	Babies, baby tenders, cattle herders, and schoolboys	Initiated & uninitiated Small boys

Tiriki Age Groups[3]

couriers and envoys when important news needed to be transmitted between elders of different subtribes.

The age group occupying the *judicial elder* age grade fulfilled most of the tasks connected with the arbitration and settlement of local disputes. This included everything from delinquent or contested bridewealth payments to cases of assault or accidental injury. Any major disturbance or legitimate complaint by the head of a household served as sufficient reason for the community judicial elders to gather at the local meeting ground to hear the plaintiff and defendant, question witnesses, and give a judgment.

The *ritual elders* presided over the priestly functions of the homestead, subclan, community, and subtribe. They presided in homestead ancestral shrine observances, at subclan meetings concerning inheritance and the like, at semiannual community supplications, and at the initiation rites. Also, the ritual elders were accredited with having access to magical powers. They were the group who expelled or killed witches, or at least who were counted on to neutralize their evil powers, and they also were the group who underwrote the death through sorcery of anyone cursed by the community for violating the initiation secrets or for committing some other heinous crime. The advice of the ritual elders was sought in all situations that seemed to hold danger for or entail the general well-being of the community or the tribe. For example, the warriors solicited the auguries of the ritual elders before embarking on a major raid, and postponed the raid if the omens were bad.

Today, over sixty years after the last formal handing-over ceremony, the age group cycle still continues, kept alive by the regular performance of the initiation rites. As the chart shows, the four graded statuses are still manifest in informal social behavior and in current social ideology and action, albeit in relatively informal and altered form. Young men whose age group according to traditional reckoning would now be warriors, are still occasionally called, or referred to as, "warriors," but only in a spirit of friendliness and flattery. Today, instead of fighting, young men of this age grade find a modicum of excitement and adventure through extended employment away from the tribe. A fortunate few are pursuing secondary or advanced studies, teaching school, or holding clerical jobs; but in most cases they, too, are employed or are studying off-tribe. Members of the warrior age grade are no longer held in such esteem as formerly, and no one ever speaks of them as "holding the land." Their active participation, however, in the new and rapidly changing world beyond tribal boundaries still lends the warrior age grade a bit of glamour.

In contrast to that of the warriors, the relative status of those occupying the elder warrior age grade has increased dramatically during the last fifty years. Men of this age grade have assumed nearly all the new administrative and executive roles created by the advent and growth of a centralized tribal administrative bureaucracy. With few exceptions they hold all the salaried offices in the tribal administration. It is quite in keeping with traditional age grade expectations that members of this age grade should occupy the executive and administrative positions, but pre-European conditions provided only a minimal number of such roles.

The judicial elders still serve as the local judiciary body, although it will be recalled that their authority was somewhat altered and curtailed by the British colonial administration.

The ritual elders have suffered a severe diminution of their functions and powers. During the last twenty years, ancestor worship has declined until today the formal aspects of the cult are virtually extinct. They, like the warriors, have been deprived of a major part of their traditional age grade activity; but, unlike the warriors, they have not found any substitute activity. The positions of leadership in the Christian church have been assumed by a small number of men, mostly of the elder warrior age grade. The ritual elders continue, however, to hold the most important positions in the initiation ceremonies, and their power as sorcerers and witchcraft expungers remains almost universally feared and respected.

CHANGE

The age groups, Christianity, and contemporary leadership

The Tiriki have been heavily missionized since 1902 by several Protestant evangelical denominations, and also, more recently, by the Mill Hill Fathers of the Roman Catholic Church. Over the last several decades the missions have fostered the development of a comprehensive network of community churches and primary schools that are now under the charge of African pastors and teachers. Most of the women, and a substantial minority of the men in Tiriki are today at least nominally members of one or another Christian church. At Kaimosi, the largest mission in Tiriki, under more or less direct supervision of American and British Friends missionaries, are a high school, a teachers' training center, a Bible school, and a well-equipped hospital, all of which draw students or patients from a number of Kenyan tribes. The missions have been almost entirely responsible for the establishment and administration of the school system, the value of which is becoming more and more appreciated by the Tiriki as they seek better jobs in Nairobi and other East African centers.

All the missions in Tiriki, with the exception of the small, rather recently established Catholic mission, preach and profess that the consumption of alcoholic beverages is incompatible with leading a Christian life. Missionaries reported to us that the Tiriki have been less receptive to Christianity than have the surrounding Bantu tribes, and that "all but the most intelligent" Tiriki men still reject Christianity because of the appeal of beer. The Tiriki elders themselves, both pagan and Christian, classify all beer drinkers as traditionalists, and all abstainers as Christians. Thus abstinence has come to be a general symbol to both missionary and African of being a Christian.

Systematic questioning of missionaries revealed that few of them had much insight into the motives of so many Tiriki men for staying pagan or for returning to paganism as they grew older. When asked to qualify what he meant by the appeal of beer, a missionary would generally say that all but a few very outstanding Tiriki men simply feel the pull of their tribal ways very strongly and so are not motivated to adopt Christianity.

The Tiriki pagan elders, however, revealed a very realistic working knowledge of the structural factors underlying the reasons for becoming a Christian. They perceived quite correctly that it always had been and continues to be those people outside the tribal *age group organization* who join mission churches and remain members in good standing.

During the first twenty-five years of missionization, very few people except those excluded from the Tiriki age groups were attracted by the

Drinking Beer

alternative affiliation and status offered by mission church membership. In other words, virtually all the converts to Tiriki missions during this period were tribal aliens, outcasts, women who wished to escape from uncongenial husbands, and children attracted by food and clothing or sent by their parents to work on the mission coffee plantation for money, and sometimes also to attend school.

Then in 1927 Chief Amiani was converted to Christianity. Although a member in good standing of his age group when appointed headman in 1911 and then chief in 1924, he tried to continue to maintain an executive type of role as chief even after he had reached the age when his age group had retired to a judicial role. Thus by 1927 he had started to antagonize many of the traditional members of the age groups, and this may have been a factor in his turning to a mission for a new source of support and prestige.

Around 1932 the mission persuaded Chief Amiani to rule that Christian women could not be forced to brew beer for their pagan husbands. Women had customarily brewed the beer for their menfolks' beer parties, which are an integral part of initiated male sociability and also of the initiation feasts. The women, however, were never included in the parties. After this legislative decision, women started joining the churches in increasing numbers, and today hardly a woman can be found who is not a church member. Thus they have escaped the drudgery of brewing beer.

During the last two decades the economic advantages of education of the European type, which can be acquired in Tiriki only through mission schools, have become more and more widely recognized by both Christian and pagan. In consequence, increasing numbers of both Christian and pagan fathers have been sending their sons to school. After having finished school and having returned from initiation, the politically ambitious young man not uncommonly curbs his appetite for tribal beer and sociability and joins a church. Perhaps he may become a preacher, and thence with mission and church group backing may secure a position within the British-instituted tribal governmental bureaucracy. Shortly after getting the government job, he almost invariably starts attending the beer parties of his age group, and consequently he is suspended from his church positions.

Thus today, just as was true twenty-five years ago, men who by Tiriki standards are aliens, witch-suspects, and outcasts form most of the senior African mission church leadership in Tiriki. The rest of the uninitiated—the women and the children—comprise the great mass of the congregation. The Tiriki age group elders are quite contented to see their younger men profit by mission education and church connections without incurring a lasting second loyalty among witches and women—thanks to the missions' stand on beer.

Many women may have been initially attracted to Protestant church membership by a desire to escape the drudgery of beermaking, but in order to understand the ongoing loyalty and active participation in church affairs of most of these women one must recall their traditional position in Tiriki society. The women have no initiation rites and are not incorporated into a social framework comparable to the men's age groups. A woman's social position and the ascription of her social roles were traditionally instituted almost entirely through her clan, her father's family, and later in life also through the family of her husband. It was only through her father or her husband that a woman had any formal connection with the major social and religious rites and institutions of the community. In recent years, with this connection weakened or broken by the prolonged absences of husbands and younger fathers working off-tribe, the mission-spawned local churches, under the direction of young African pastors, have been providing an increasingly important religious and social framework for the women.

The age grades, each grade with its formally ascribed status, role, and social orientation, in effect supply the Tiriki with a set of built-in mutually interdependent social factions that cover the field from "progressive" or "innovative" to "conservative." Also, it is noteworthy that the age group organization functions in such a manner that a modicum of social adaptability and flexibility is demanded of its members; for all men who live out their full three score and ten must succeed and adjust to several formally delineated changes of status, role, and social orientation. In short, the Tiriki have a social system that aligns its male members into several social groupings each of which must adjust to and fulfill throughout the decades sucessive major formally structured social roles.

An analysis of biographical data gathered on recent Tiriki tribal leaders reveals a striking concordance between traditional age-graded social roles and contemporary career patterns. The typical career pattern of the contemporary tribal leader is characterized by a W-shaped zigzagging back and forth between predominantly pagan and predominantly Christian socio-religious affiliations.[4]

The typical successful Tiriki leader has been a church member during the greater part of his life, and through his mission ties he has received great instrumental aid in the sphere of education, employment, and initial leadership opportunities. Whenever a major conflict has occurred, however, between the demands of church and age group affiliations, the age groups have won out. The first break with the missions typically has occurred at initiation, which of course opens the way to manhood and traditional warrior status in Tiriki; the second break coincides roughly with the traditional shift from elder warrior to judicial status.

Clearly one would be forced to regard the correlations between traditional age grading and the career patterns of recent leaders as probably gratuitous and insignificant except for three factors. First, the Tiriki seem to have resolved conflicts presented by the discordant demands of church, modern centralized tribal administration and traditional loyalties considerably more smoothly than have members of the neighboring southern Abaluyia tribes. These tribes have experienced the same sort of "contact situation" as the Tiriki and have cultural traditions very similar to those of the Tiriki except in one area: they have no counterpart to the Tiriki-Terik-Nandi type of age group organization. Instead, their traditional stateless political systems were based on the balancing and interplay of lineage-derived loyalties. Second, the Tiriki continue to organize their social and voluntary type activities primarily according to age grades. Many of these informal associations strongly influence attitudes and decisions in more formalized situations. For example, decisions about most important legal disputes are usually informally reached around the elders' beer pots even before the disputes are presented for adjudication. Third, and perhaps most significant, individual Tiriki frequently rationalize their contemporary periodic changes in status and social activities, in regard to their jobs and their church affiliation, in terms of the traditional age grades.

In summary and conclusion, Tiriki age group system has facilitated the tribe's acceptance of post-contact social and administrative innovations in two ways: it makes rather dramatic changes in social roles and statuses during the course of a lifetime seem not only inevitable but also proper and even desirable; and it supplies a tribe-wide system of stratified interdependent political type of activity, universalistic enough in its patterns of leadership and authority delegation, and specific enough in the demands made of disparate groups, to serve as a fairly adequate bureaucratic prototype. This has facilitated the acceptance and smooth operation of the contemporary, British-instituted tribal bureaucracy.

NOTES

(1) The fieldwork on which this paper was based was carried out by my wife and me during sixteen months' residence in Tiriki between December 1954 and June 1956, under the auspices of the Fulbright Program. Some corroborative data were also gathered during a twelve-day return visit I made to Tiriki in June 1961. This brief return visit was made possible by a travel grant from the Carnegie Foundation-sponsored Non-Western Studies Program of the University of Rochester. Special thanks go to Dr. Alfred Harris for the many helpful suggestions he gave me after reading an earlier, somewhat longer version of this paper. Some of the material here has been drawn and condensed from my forthcoming monograph on the Tiriki, *Age, Prayer and Politics in Tiriki, Kenya,* to be published under the auspices of the East African Institute of Social Research by the Oxford University Press.

(2) Until 1946 North Nyanza and Elgon Nyanza together formed North Kavirondo District, and the Abaluyia were commonly called the Bantu of North Kavirondo.

(3) This diagram is adapted from the diagram of Tiriki age groups that first appeared in *Africa*, vol. 32, 1962, as part of a paper by Walter Sangree and Robert A. LeVine entitled "The Diffusion of Age-group Organization in East Africa: A Controlled Comparison," and that will appear in *Age, Prayer and Politics in Tiriki, Kenya.* It is used here by permission of the International African Institute.

(4) The present leaders generally were born into pagan families and, for the most part, attended mission schools during their boyhood and early adolescence. There they received instruction in the "three R's" and Christianity; they also attended and frequently joined the Christian church. Then they retired, sometimes eagerly and sometimes involuntarily, from school life to traditional circumcision and the subsequent six months of initiation and seclusion. This action, viewed by the Protestant mission authorities as an extremely unfortunate return to paganism, marked the end of school careers of most initiates.

Nearly all the contemporary tribal leaders, however, are recruited from those Tiriki youth who managed, sometimes after a delay of several years, to return to mission schools to complete elementary teacher's training and then to obtain jobs as teachers in the mission schools. Then, as their age group approached the traditional elder warrior age grade, they often took on, in addition to their teaching duties, positions of increasing importance in the local Christian churches. Generally, after several years they became local pastors, and through their pastoral activities, gained recognition both locally and in the eyes of the contemporary tribal leaders as up and coming community leaders.

The next step, coinciding with the approach of the traditional age of elder warrior status, was usually the attainment of a position in the tribal bureaucracy. Finally, as the tribal leaders approach elder status, they typically have taken on the social roles associated with their new age grade. These include regular attendance at community local beer parties for the elders, and polygyny. The former is forbidden by the Protestant missions in Tiriki, and the latter, of course, is forbidden by all Christian missions. Thus, for the second time they fall out of grace with the Christian church, but this time usually permanently. Retirement from salaried tribal administrative posts commonly coincides roughly with the attainment of the judicial elder age grade, and is normally followed by an active judicial and advisory role in community and tribal affairs.

BIBLIOGRAPHY

The Tiriki

LeVine, Robert A., and Walter H. Sangree (1962). "The Diffusion of Age-Group Organization in East Africa: A Controlled Comparison," *Africa*, Vol. 32, No. 2, pp. 97–110.
This article briefly analyzes factors leading to the acceptance of the Nandi type of age groups by the Tiriki, and their nonacceptance by the Gusii of South Nyanza.

Sangree, Walter H. (1962). "The Social Function of Beer Drinking in Bantu Tiriki," in David J. Pittman and Charles R. Snyder (eds.); *Society, Culture and Drinking Patterns*. New York: John Wiley & Sons, Inc., pp. 6–21.

————— (In press). *Age, Prayer & Politics in Tiriki. Kenya*. London: Oxford University Press.

Other Abaluyia Peoples

The following two sources contain early references to Abaluyia peoples.

Dundas, K. (1913). "The Wanga and Other Tribes of the Elgon District," *Journal of the Royal Anthropological Institute*, Vol. 43, pp. 19–75.

Hobley, C. W. (1903). "Anthropological Studies in Kavirondo and Nandi," *Journal of the Royal Anthropological Institute*, Vol. 33, pp. 325–359.

The following sources—monographs, chapters, and articles by Gunter Wagner—are based primarily on his fieldwork among the Maragoli of North Nyanza, and the Vugusu of Elgon Nyanza, which he carried out during the late 1930s. They afford a good overall picture of the Abaluyia culture area.

Wagner, Gunter (1939). "The Changing Family among the Bantu Kavirondo," Supplement of *Africa*, Vol. 12, No. 1.

——— (1940). "The Political Organization of the Bantu of North Kavirondo," *African Political Systems*, M. Fortes and E. E. Evans-Pritchard (eds.). London: Oxford University Press.

——— (1949). *The Bantu of North Kavirondo*. London: Oxford University Press, Vol. I.

——— (1954). "The Abaluyia of Kavirondo (Kenya)," in *African Worlds*, Daryll Forde (ed.). London: Oxford University Press.

——— (1956). *The Bantu of North Kavirondo*. London: Oxford University Press, Vol. II.

Neighboring "Nilo-Hamitic" Peoples

The following sources, two studies of the "Nilo-Hamitic" Nandi and Kipsigis tribes, both of which are closely related to the Terik, give considerable information about the nature of the age-group organization that they share with the Terik and the Tiriki.

Huntingford, G. W. B. (1953). *The Nandi of Kenya*. London: Routledge & Kegan Paul, Ltd.

Peristiany, J. G. (1939). *The Social Institutions of the Kipsigis*. London: Routledge & Kegan Paul, Ltd.

3

THE GANDA OF UGANDA

about the chapter

From journalistic accounts of the modern nation of Uganda the layman knows of the Ganda king, the *kabaka*, and perhaps of the prominent place of banana groves in the Ganda landscape. Southwold notes that these two features of Ganda culture are connected: the Ganda state exists as a strong centralized political structure partly because of the environmental and ecological features, which create a favorable demographic picture.

Unlike many African crops, the banana, the Ganda staple, can be raised on the same plot for decades without exhausting the fertility of the soil. Thus, the laborious bush fallowing and shifting cultivation practiced by groups such as the Kpelle and the Suku are absent in Buganda, where a large proportion of land does not have to be continually reserved for fallow. A dense population results from the intensive utilization of land. Furthermore, without the need for continually clearing brush and breaking ground associated with slash-and-burn agriculture, the role of men in agriculture is reduced. Among the Ganda, women assume proportionately even more of the agricultural burden than they do among the Kpelle or the Suku, where they play an important role. In short, the Ganda support a fairly dense population, which is not typical of the eastern half of the continent, and do so with a minimal demand on male labor. Thus much of the energy of Ganda men has been free for governmental pursuits associated with the kingship.

Generally speaking, large, dense populations live under fairly complex political structures, and the Ganda are no exception. The monarchy centers on the kabaka who, unlike many African kings, is not considered to be "divine" or "sacred" but is royal and has very strong powers. Traditionally, strong centralization was maintained through the granting of offices to a series of lower chiefs or "clients" *directly* by the kabaka, rather than by the linking of some chiefs to the king through an intermediate client. Thus the pattern was similar to, but not identical with, the feudalism of medieval Europe and the clientship in other sub-Saharan societies such as the Hausa, the Kpelle, the Rwanda, and the Yoruba. The Ganda pattern differs from that of the other African monarchies described here also in that the estates and their tenants which went with each office were not transferable if the appointee of the kabaka was transferred or removed from office. This gave the kabaka very great power, but, as in many other African centralized states, there were built-in checks on this power in the form of a queen mother, a prime minister, and a great council, or *Lukiiko*, with certain powers reserved to them. The Ganda are clearly of interest to anyone concerned with comparative political organization.

As noted in Southwold's analysis, the traditional Ganda system is unique in the way it depends on ties of tenancy between individual householders and lesser chiefs or estate holders. A local chief among the Ganda is not a kinsman of some sort to most of his villagers. In contrast to the dominant African pattern, kinship in Buganda is not a major integrative institution. In colonial times the pattern of tenancy became even more complicated through a misunderstanding of indigenous patterns, as explained in the chapter.

Even today the Ganda retain a strong sense of tribal identity centering on their identification with the kabakaship. Their participation in the movement for Ugandan independence and their role in postindependence politics have been contingent upon constitutional recognition of the kabakaship as the core of their society.

about the author

Martin Southwold, Lecturer in Social Anthropology at the University of Manchester, England, received his Ph.D. from the University of Cambridge, where he has also taught. He did field research among the Ganda from 1954 to 1956 and from 1959 to 1960, and has written *Bureaucracy and Chiefship in Buganda* (1961) and "The Inheritance of Land in Buganda" (1956).

MARTIN SOUTHWOLD · *The Ganda of Uganda*[1]

INTRODUCTION

The Kingdom of Buganda[2] is part of the country of Uganda in East Africa, which before independence was a British protectorate. Buganda lies along the northern and western shores of Lake Victoria near the headwaters of the White Nile, and stretches about 200 miles along the lake shore. The country extends inland to an average depth of some 80 miles, with an extension in the northwest reaching the southern shores of Lake Albert. The land area of Buganda is today 17,295 square miles. Most of the country lies at an altitude close to 4000 feet above sea level.

LOCATION · The eastern boundary of Buganda is formed by the Nile River, on the far shore of which live the Soga, a people culturally very similar to the Ganda, and formerly in part subject to them. On the north lies the remnant of the Bunyoro kingdom, Buganda's traditional enemy, and formerly, before she was smashed by the Ganda in alliance with the British, her equal in strength. On the west lie Toro and Ankole, two further kingdoms of the Interlacustrine Bantu. Intersected by the equator, Buganda is near the center of the African continent, which accounts for its long historical isolation from the outside world.

HISTORICAL BACKGROUND AND POPULATION · The first non-Africans to reach Buganda were a few Arab traders who probably got there in the 1830s. The first European visitor was the explorer Speke, who arrived in 1862; and the first Europeans to take up residence were two missionaries of the Church Missionary Society, in 1877. The beginnings of European government can be dated to Lugard's Treaty of Protection in 1890, though it was not until 1894 that the British government formally assumed the protectorate.

Today, Buganda is connected with the outside world by about 800 miles of single-track, narrow-gauge railway leading to Mombasa, Kenya's port on

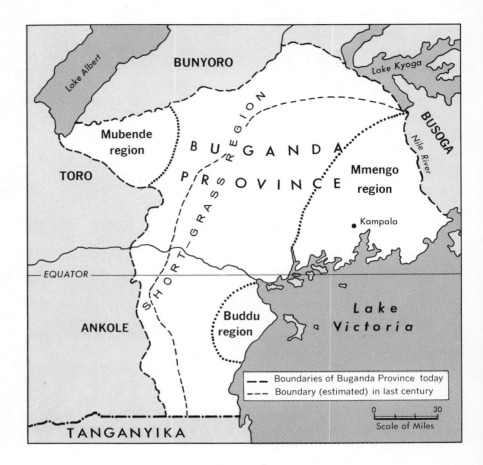

Buganda

the Indian Ocean. Although Buganda's lines of communication are long and thin, their cumulative effect over the past sixty years (the railway reached Lake Victoria in 1901) has been great. A large quantity of imported goods, which are paid for mainly by the export of cash crops, is now in everyday use in Buganda; and the influence of imported ideas and institutions on everyday life is perhaps still greater. Despite the short period of contact with Europe, and despite the fact that the Ganda always retained a good deal of control of their own destinies, the impact of European culture has been profound. The Ganda culture and particularly the Ganda political institutions were already so sophisticated that they were essentially adaptable to European modes. Thus, the history of Buganda over the past hundred years is the history of a people modifying their own institutions, and digesting those of the Europeans, to form an amalgam very different from what existed in the past, but yet organically continuous with it.

At the 1959 census the African population of Buganda was recorded as 1,834,128 persons (there were also some 40,000 Asians and 7000 Europeans). The overall population density is thus 106 persons per square mile, though this conceals a wide variation among different areas. Within the country as a whole there is not yet a shortage of land; but, largely for social reasons, probably as much as three quarters of the population choose to live in areas where the good land is fully (even overfully) occupied.

Earlier in this century the population density was much lower, and, except in the capital itself, people rather than land were scarce. A hundred years ago the population was probably around one million persons, and the area of the kingdom on the order of 10,000 square miles. Allowing for the fact that land was not needed for cash crops, the effective pressure on the land must have been notably less than it is today.

The census of 1959 shows that of the Africans in Buganda only 1,006,101 were Ganda by tribe; indeed, among males, the Ganda form a minority in their own country. The other Africans are mostly immigrants from other tribes who have come to Buganda seeking work. Some of these immigrants work for Asian or European employers, but many are employed as agricultural laborers or herdsmen by Ganda. Some immigrants are essentially "target workers," seeking to save a certain sum as quickly as possible and return home with it. Others, however, settle in the country, and after a few years in employment become tenants in the villages on the same terms as native Ganda.

Obviously, to live in Buganda is not the same thing as to be a Muganda, a member of the tribe. To establish his status as a Muganda a man must demonstrate his descent in one of the recognized clans; though at any one moment this criterion is clear, over time the rules can be manipulated to allow assimilation of people of foreign stock.

PHYSICAL APPEARANCE · Ethnically, the Ganda are clearly Negroid: their skins are dark brown or black, their hair is frizzy, their lips are fleshy, and their noses are squat; the mean stature of men is recorded by Oschinsky (1954) at 65 inches. Some Ganda resemble the "Hamitic" Bahima of Ankole, or the Nilotes now found living to the north and east of Buganda, doubtless as a result of intermarriage at some time with people of those stocks. Such apparent ethnic variations may be aesthetically valued among the Ganda, but they do not correspond to any scale of social evaluation: there are no "castes" in Buganda such as are reported from Ankole or Rwanda.

LANGUAGE · Luganda is a typical Bantu language, placed by the International African Institute in the Interlacustrine Group of the Northern Zone of Bantu languages, and by Greenberg (1955:12) in the Central Branch (subfamily) of the Niger-Congo family of languages. It is closely related to Lusoga, Lunyoro, Kinyaruanda, and so on, and speakers of any one of these languages can easily acquire another.

Culturally, too, the Ganda have much in common with other peoples of the group we refer to as the Interlacustrine Bantu. They are not, however, entirely typical. Cattle play a minor part in the economy, and cattle keeping is not esteemed; as we have seen, there are no "castes" in Buganda. The political organization was more highly centralized and sophisticated than those in the other kingdoms of this group, or indeed than those in most other kingdoms in Africa.

REGIONAL VARIATIONS • The heartland of Buganda is an area in the southeast, extending to a radius of about fifty miles around Kampala, Uganda's capital: I shall refer to this as "the Mmengo region." It lies within the fertile ecological division known as the "elephant-grass zone" (see page 88).

To the north and west the Mmengo region is bounded, fairly sharply, by a drier zone in which the natural vegetation is short grass; this forms a distinct region that is sparsely settled because it is not well suited to the Ganda way of life. Beyond this, two further regions may be distinguished; ecologically they fall within the elephant-grass zone, but culturally they are distinguishable from the Mmengo region. One is in Mubende District, in the northwest of Buganda; this area was taken from Bunyoro at the end of the nineteenth century, and most of its people still regard themselves as Nyoro. The other is Buddu County, to the west of Lake Victoria. Buddu was taken from Bunyoro probably toward the end of the eighteenth century; its people retain some differences of dialect and culture from other Ganda, and their distinctiveness is emphasized today by the fact that they are predominantly Roman Catholics, in contrast to the Anglican predominance in the Mmengo region.

The urban and peri-urban area of Kampala contains perhaps 200,000 people. Not only is it the seat of the central government of Uganda; for the past half century it has been the center and focus of European and Asian commercial, educational, religious, and cultural enterprise. It is, of course, an important center of employment and—today—of African enterprise; its influence is strongly felt throughout the whole of the Mmengo region. But when Ganda speak of "going up to the capital" they have in mind not only the exotic city of Kampala, but also the neighboring township of Mmengo, the seat of the Buganda government and site of the principal palace of the *kabaka* (king).

Because of the influence of Kampala, the Mmengo region is the most fully Europeanized part of Buganda. But at the same time it is the most truly Ganda part, not alone because it contains the royal capital, but also

Landscape near Kampala
The scene shows the spread of houses and gardens.

because it has for longest formed part of the Buganda kingdom. Here the typically Ganda institutions were formed, and here are to be found the places associated with the outstanding events in Buganda's history, as well as the men most steeped in the traditions. I did all my fieldwork in this region, and my account refers to it primarily.

ECOLOGY · The climate of Buganda is broadly of the tropical savanna or modified equatorial type. At Kampala, the principal town, the mean temperature is 69° F.; the highest monthly mean maximum temperature is 83° F., the lowest mean minimum is 62° F. In other words, the temperature is warm and equable, rarely becoming oppressively hot or more than relatively chilly. This is broadly true of the whole country.

Rainfall is heaviest near Lakes Victoria and Albert, falling off rapidly with distance from the shores. In the elephant-grass zone the average annual rainfall exceeds 45 inches, though it falls below 35 inches in parts of the short-grass zone. No less important is the fact that the rainfall is well distributed throughout the year, and is reliable from year to year. The year is divided into four seasons: the heavier rains of *ttoggo* (March–May) and the lighter rains of *ddumbi* (August–December), separated by two drier seasons. Except in the short-grass region, this distinction of seasons is not very sharp; even in the "dry" seasons it is unusual for a week to pass without rain, and even in the rainy seasons more than two hours' rain in a day is uncommon.

Geologically, Buganda is an eroded plateau, and the typical landscape consists of a multitude of small hills, separated by valleys that are commonly filled with papyrus swamp, or sometimes forest. Hilltops are generally about 500 feet above the valleys, and most hills are no more than a mile or so in diameter. Soil types lie in bands along the hillsides: in most places the best soil is a wide band of fertile red clay along the middle of the hillside. The less fertile soils above and below are not cultivated, except where there is great pressure on the land, but provide grass for pasture, and thatching, and so on.

I have distinguished the region where the natural vegetation is short grass of several varieties; the climax vegetation of the rest of the country is of the high grass—low savanna type. It is usual in Uganda now to refer to these areas as forming the "elephant-grass zone," named after its distinctive tall, canelike grass (*Pennisetum purpureum*), and to include within it those small areas where the natural vegetation is equatorial forest. When cleared, land in this zone is excellent for bananas, *robusta* coffee, cotton, and a variety of other crops.

POLITICAL AND TERRITORIAL ORGANIZATION

Buganda was never conquered by the British, but came under British protection through treaties and agreements. As a consequence, the indigenous political system was not destroyed; instead it was reformed to serve new purposes. Moreover, because of this continuity, the indigenous institutions retained their authority, and the Ganda reacted to proposed reforms and changes in terms of their traditional political ideology. For these reasons, the colonial and postcolonial political systems are best seen against the background of the traditional institutions and concepts that underlie them.

Traditional organization

The indigenous political system was notable for its very high degree of centralization, and especially for the very great authority and power attributed to the kabaka. But the central institutions are best described against the background of the machinery of government by which rule was mediated to the people.

CHIEFS · For the purposes of government, the kingdom was divided into *ssaza* (counties). In the early days, when the kingdom was very small, these appear to have been three in number; but with the gradual expansion of the kingdom by conquest, these had increased to ten by the time British over-rule was established. Each county chief had under him a number—usually about half a dozen—of subcounty chiefs, each of whom governed a section of the county. Below these, there were one or more further levels of chiefs, the lowest level being the chief of the *kyalo* (village). Each chief was responsible to the chief immediately above him in level of seniority, just as the area he governed was a segment of the area governed by the more senior chief. A hierarchy of authority was fitted over a segmentary pattern of local governmental units, as it is in most centralized states.

One of the main tasks of chiefs of all levels was the maintenance of law and order. This is described more fully below under "Law." Here we may remark that the ability of a chief to judge cases justly, and his success in maintaining peace and security in his area, largely determined whether he was considered a good or a bad chief by both his superiors and his people. Every chief was responsible for certain kinds of public works: for cutting and keeping open roads, and for building and maintaining the compounds of senior chiefs, of the king, and of some of the gods. The chief also organized his men for carrying out similar tasks within his area, as well as for making and servicing places for drawing water, and for hunting down dangerous wild beasts.

Each chief was also responsible for collecting and leading his men to war when called upon. Usually when the king decided upon a war, he appointed a general, and ordered certain counties to supply troops. The war drum was beaten at the compound of the county chief, and the beat was taken up by junior chiefs down to the village. In each village all able-bodied men assembled under their village chief, who led them to his senior; and so on until the whole contingent had collected at the headquarters of the county chief, ready to march to the rendezvous appointed by the general.

Tax collection was not directly the responsibility of the chiefs, but of tax collectors appointed by the kabaka. But both in assessing and in collecting the tax these collectors were assisted by the local chiefs, who were entitled to a proportion of the tax collected in their areas.

Most of these chiefs were chosen and appointed by the kabaka himself, not by their immediate superiors. This markedly distinguishes the Ganda political system from European feudalism. The kabaka also had the power to dismiss chiefs, or to promote or transfer them as he wished. This tended to make chiefs careful to show loyalty to the kabaka, as well as to make it difficult for them to get too familiar with the people in any one area.

But kabakas never felt sure of the loyalty of the chiefs, and they came to rely instead on another category of officers, the *batongole* (singular, *mutongole*). Originally a *mutongole* was someone who supplied the king with goods or services (for example, a potter or a musician) and who was remunerated with an estate. Because landholding and political authority were inseparable, the *mutongole* governed the people who lived on his estate and thus acted as a minor chief. As a chief, he had to be fitted into the hierarchy of organization in the county; many of the chiefs of lower level were *batongole* and some *batongole* were even found on the level of subcounty chief. But *batongole* were especially "the king's men," and were appointed from among his favorites; the king therefore used them to check and to spy on the other chiefs.

The heads of clans and segments of clans—who were known generically as *bataka*—also held estates, mostly of the size of a single village, attached to their offices; consequently they too had political authority and had to be fitted into the hierarchy of government. Unlike the *batongole*, the *bataka* were not especially loyal to the king; indeed, as the king had only restricted control over their appointment, they were often somewhat resentful of his authority.

THE KABAKA · The kabaka was elected from among the Princes of the Drum, that is, men whose father or father's father had been a kabaka. The choice was made by the *Katikkiro* (prime minister) who survived from the previous reign, in consultation with other senior chiefs. There was no such rule as primogeniture to indicate one prince as heir apparent; and although a king might indicate a preference for one prince to be his heir, this choice was not binding. The electors chose a prince partly on the basis of his personal character, and partly in relation to the strength of support for different candidates among the chiefs. Once a prince had been chosen and proclaimed and had passed through the accession ceremonies, he was kabaka until his death: there was no constitutional means for deposing him.

The kabaka was the supreme authority in the nation, and all other authority was held to derive from him. Chiefs were appointed by him and held office at his pleasure. The rights of the clans were held to derive from grant by some previous kabaka, and succession to every headship of a clan or clan segment had to be confirmed by the kabaka. Even the gods were supposed to derive their position from the fact that the men whose ghosts they were had rendered special services to previous kabakas. The kabaka himself was not regarded as a god, nor was he especially closely associated with the gods: he was not a divine king, nor was he a priest. The authority of the kabaka derived partly from the conquest of Kintu, the first king of the dynasty, from whom he was descended, and partly from the power he held in the nation.

Because the kabaka's authority, the source of all legitimate authority in the kingdom, derives from his power, the Ganda tend to exaggerate the extent of this power; and in the last century they did so also in order to impress the Europeans. Hence the kabaka has often been represented as a despot, but no man can be a despot for long, especially where technology is relatively primitive. It was only in the latter part of the last century, after the introduction of guns, that the kabaka had even a small standing army. The kabaka was always dependent on his chiefs for assistance and even for information. He had a *lukiiko* (council) to advise him, though it had no formal power, and he was not obliged to consult it or follow its opinion. His real power rested on the fact that he appointed all his subordinates, as well as on his position as coordinator of the complicated system of chiefs, *batongole* and *bataka*. But if he angered too many important people at one time, he was liable to be overthrown by rebellion, as many kings were: there were always ambitious princes ready to seize the throne, and dissatisfied chiefs to support them.

OTHER "KABAKAS" · The mother of the king had the title of *Namasole* (queen mother), and the sister with whom he was linked in his succession ceremonies had the titles of *Lubuga* and *Nalinnya* (queen sister). Both ladies were styled kabakas, and had their own palaces and estates and bodies of chiefs. Their power was however much inferior to that of the king, though the queen mother often had considerable influence over her son.

Another officer sometimes styled a kabaka was the *katikkiro*, the most senior of all the commoners. His rank was only slightly inferior to that of the king; because he was in charge of most of the day-to-day business of government, his power was very great. The king could always overrule him or dismiss him, though in practice this sometimes proved difficult. The *katikkiro* could sometimes get rid of the king by encouraging rebellion. Thus the power of the *katikkiro* was not the least of the checks against royal despotism.

The colonial period

The British protectorate was proclaimed in 1894, and relations between the Ganda and the British were formalized under the Uganda Agreement of 1900. This recognized Buganda as one of the four provinces of the protectorate, though in practice its status was always higher than this, and more like that of a semiautonomous, protected state. The kabaka was recognized as native ruler of Buganda, on condition that he obeyed the instructions of the British Governor of the Uganda Protectorate. In most matters concerning Africans in Buganda he had full authority and responsibility, though some matters were reserved to the Protectorate Government. He appointed and dismissed all ministers and chiefs, subject to the governor's approval.

Under the kabaka's surveillance, Buganda was governed by the Buganda government, under three ministers: the *katikkiro*, the chief justice, and the treasurer. They were advised by a council, now formally constituted and known as the *Great Lukiiko*. This consisted mainly of chiefs, and had advisory and legislative powers, subject to approval by the kabaka and the governor.

Under the Buganda government, the country was administered by the chiefs of counties, now twenty in number. Each county was divided into subcounties (singular, *ggombolola*), and these further into parishes (singular, *muluka*), and each unit was headed by a chief. These chiefs were salaried, and, except for most parish chiefs, transferable; they came to resemble a civil service. The pattern was essentially a simplification and rationalization of the traditional system.

THE PARISH · The parish is today the smallest recognized unit of government. It usually contains about three hundred to five hundred taxpayers (adult males), and about eight or ten villages. Over the past half century the boundaries of parishes have been frequently changed, with a general tendency to increase the size of the unit, and it is perhaps as a result of this that people have little sense of identification with, or corporate membership of, the parish.

But, in practical affairs, it is the parish chief who is important in the lives of ordinary people, for he is the person who represents the government to them. Parish chiefs are subordinate to subcounty chiefs, as the latter are to county chiefs, and they have similar duties. They do not have official courts, and therefore cannot try offenses, though they give cases a preliminary hearing, and often successfully arbitrate disputes. The main burden of tax-collecting falls to the parish chief. He also enforces upon his people numerous administrative orders, such as those requiring the destruction of cotton plants after the harvest, or forbidding the possession of "Nubian gin." In most cases, parish chiefs, unlike their seniors, are not transferable (except on promotion to subcounty rank); they are local men, normally landowners, who have usually been promoted from among the petty chiefs, the *batongole*.

The parish is divided into sections, based on the units of landownership, and the people living on each section are under the supervision of a *mutongole*. The *mutongole* is appointed not by the central government but by the landowner (or landowners) for whose tenants he is responsible. His office derives from the traditional axiom that landholding implies political authority and responsibility. Strictly, the parish chief should not communicate officially with any of his people directly, but should act through a man's *mutongole* as intermediary. But because *batongole* receive no government salary, many of them are idle, and most parish chiefs frequently have to bypass this rule. In most parishes I know there are about fifteen *batongole*: the proportion of these who are not incorrigibly idle is sufficient to allow the chief some practical assistance in his work.

As is true of bureaucracies generally, it is the officer of lowest level—

A Parish Chief's House A prosperous *muluka* (parish) chief is seated in front of his house with his three wives, his children, and a kinswoman.

in Buganda, the parish chief, and sometimes the *mutongole*—who has the task of reconciling a remote government with the common people. His task is difficult, for he governs too many people to be friendly with them all, and has too many duties to be able to explain each one patiently. Many parish chiefs side with the government against the people, or the people against the government, but there are also many who successfully establish a bridge between the two and retain the goodwill of both their superiors and their people.

TENANCY AND THE VILLAGE · In the old days, estates were held by chiefs and other prominent persons. Except for estates granted by the kabaka to princes or favorites, it would be more accurate to say that estates were tied to chiefships and other offices, for when a man was transferred he gave up his estate, and when he died it went to his successor in office, not to his personal heirs. This form of tenure is known as "*butongole* tenure."

Although estates varied in size, the basic unit was the *kyalo*, which might be an independent holding or a part of a larger estate. The *kyalo* normally corresponded to a *mutala* (a hillside or sector of a hillside), which was a named unit of settlement. With qualifications we can translate the word as "village."

Each of these villages had a chief, a direct appointee of the kabaka, a man appointed to take charge of this division of the larger estate of a senior chief or officer, or the head of the lineage or clan that owned the estate (see pages 96–97). The village chief was politically responsible for the people living in the village and had political authority over them. He granted to each villager (that is, to each household head) a plot of land on which to build and make his gardens, and could, if he chose, revoke this grant. Equally, the villager was free to desert him and join another chief elsewhere (though his chief, if he learned of the villager's plans, might use force to prevent him from leaving). Although the villager gave produce and services to the chief, these should not be viewed as rent; just as the chief held the estate by virtue of his office as chief, so the villager held his plot by virtue of his status as subject of that chief. The return for the gifts of produce was not the plot of land; it was the chief's hospitality at his compound.

Thus the village or *kyalo* was essentially a group of people linked to the *kyalo* chief by ties of political allegiance. It was not a group of people tied irrevocably to a piece of land by serf-like ties, nor was it basically a localized kin group.

By the Buganda Agreement of 1900, the British altered this system, partly through misunderstanding it. Over 8000 square miles of land were allotted to private individuals, to be held in a form of freehold tenure, known as *mailo* tenure from the fact that allocations were made in square miles.[3] The allottees were supposed to be chiefs and other persons who had held estates under the old system: most of the 3700 who received allotments in fact were in this category, though many of them did not get the same estates they had held before. Each received estates in his private capacity, and ownership was not dependent on continued political office.

The new estates, to which the Ganda gave the name *mailo*, were for the most part based on existing *kyalos* and took the names of those villages. In other ways, too, new *mailo* owners generally acted and were thought of as *kyalo* chiefs. Hence the institution of modern *batongole* chiefs was natural.

As the original grantees died, their estates were divided among their heirs. The Ganda had had no rules for the inheritance of land, for estates, as we saw, were not personal property but were attached to offices; they therefore adapted their rules for the inheritance of moveable property. Where there are several sons, one of them (nearly always the eldest) becomes principal heir and successor (see page 97) and receives rather less than half the estate; the rest is divided among the other sons and daughters. (Where a will is left, small legacies may be given to other relatives.)

Estates can also be given away or sold, in portions or in entirety.[4] Many landowners have sold land in small portions—up to, say, twenty acres—to raise cash. As a result of divisions by inheritance and by gift and sale, there are now between 50,000 and 100,000 owners of *mailo* land.

Titles for the original estates were issued, and the estates themselves were surveyed, by the Protectorate Government's Lands and Surveys Department. All transactions must be registered at one of the land offices, which also attempt to survey the new holdings arising from division of estates. Only recently have the land offices come within sight of bringing their records up to date, and the delays, arising from various causes, that were hitherto customary, have given rise to no little confusion.

When, in World War I, high prices began to be paid for cotton—the cash crop that had spread widely since its introduction in 1904—landowners found opportunities for exploiting their tenants, whom it became increasingly necessary to protect. In 1927 the *Great Lukiiko* was induced to pass the *Busulu* and *Envujjo* Law. Under this law, as subsequently amended and as interpreted by the Buganda courts, once a tenant has been granted a plot of land by a landowner he is guaranteed undisturbed possession of it, and can even pass it to his heir without further negotiation. Normally it reverts to the landowner only if the tenant surrenders it, or abandons it for more than four months at a time; although an eviction order can be obtained for non-payment of rent, the sums due are too small to create difficulties. The same law controls the rent that may be charged, on a sliding scale related to the acreage of cash crops and the number of times beer is brewed. In 1927 the controlled rents were realistic; today the few amendments that have been made have done little to keep pace with inflation, so that rents are quite uneconomic.[5]

In effect, if not in strict legal terms, it is the tenant rather than the landlord who owns the land; and landlords have realistically decided that granting a tenancy is best regarded as a sale. At least Shs. 200/-, and frequently much more, are now charged to intending tenants. An outgoing tenant normally sells his plot to the man who will take it over, but because they are illegal such transactions are troublesome.

CONCLUSION • Thus the village, once a community united by basically political bonds to the *kyalo* chief or *mailo* owner, has now become a collection of independent peasant families each owning its own piece of land. Because of the fragmentation of estates, there are relatively few large landowners now; and very many landowners, large and small, are absentees. The resident landowner who is landlord to a large body of tenants is now a rarity, and the community ties focused on such a figure have disappeared. Because of the peculiar character of Ganda clanship and kinship institutions, which we must now examine, there is little else to bind the village into a social unity.

Clans

According to the traditions, when Kintu, the first kabaka, came to Buganda twenty-four generations ago, he found the people divided into six clans, and living under the rule of their clan heads. Kintu created new clans by granting estates to various of his followers; with subsequent accretions, there are now forty-eight recognized clans in Buganda. Each clan is named from its totem, usually a species of animal or vegetable, which it is taboo for members to eat; and the clans are agnatic (patrilineal), a person deriving membership from his father. Clans are divided into segments, which we may term lineages, though there are specific Luganda terms for each level of segment: a segment of a clan is a *ssiga*, a segment of a ssiga is a *mutuba*, a segment of a mutuba is a *lunyiriri*. (Segments of a *lunyiriri* are not formally recognized.)

Each clan or lineage has a recognized head,[6] who takes the name of the founding ancestor of the group as a title; the position is hereditary, though the choice of successor must be confirmed by the kabaka. The head of a clan or lineage "rules" its members with the aid of a council, or *lukiiko*, consisting of the heads of its subordinate segments (or of leading members in the case of the *lunyiriri*).

Certain princely lineages together make up what is often called the "Princes' clan,"[7] though it has no totem since kabakas have no totem (all princes are associated with their *mothers'* patrilineal clans).

In the old days each clan and each lineage had an estate, usually a single *kyalo*, attached inalienably to it; such an estate was called a *butaka*. Members, or at least important members, of the group were buried at the *butaka* when they died; and it was their ghosts that defended the estate from alienation by the kabaka or anyone else. The kabaka, therefore, forebade the burial of several generations of one descent line in one place, unless he was willing to grant the estate on "*butaka* tenure"—that is, tenure of an estate that was hereditary and inalienable because it was attached to a hereditary office or position. All *butaka* estates are thus regarded as having been originally granted by a kabaka—either to bestow a mark of special favor on an individual, or to allow the natural expansion of a clan.

It was considered good for a person to live at the *butaka* village of his *lunyiriri* or higher segment. Because the *butaka* estates of most clans are widely dispersed over the country (especially in the Mmengo region) a man had a wide choice of places to live if he wished to live at one of his *butaka* villages. However, few Ganda could avail themselves of all the options because many of them do not know where to find the head of their *lunyiriri*, nor can they trace their line of descent back beyond their own grandfathers. Moreover, most Ganda did not want to live at any *butaka*, but preferred to move about between villages held by political chiefs, seeking their own advantage. At a *butaka* of his own clan a man did have a special right to be given a plot, if one was available. Even so, at many, if not most, *butaka* villages a majority of the men were nonclansmen. Thus, to a large extent, the position of a lineage head in his *butaka* village was like that of any other kind of village chief in that many of his subjects were bound to him primarily by political ties—ties of personal allegiance—rather than links of kinship. Clanship, then, gave a man a right to claim land and reside in a certain place, but since this right was often forgone, the clan was not a strongly localized unit.

When *mailo* estates were distributed, most of the *butaka* estates, apart

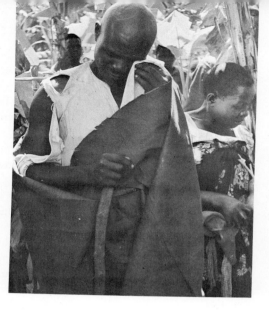

Personal Succession The successor of the deceased is seen at a mortuary ceremony. He has been invested in bark cloth, and his head is shaved in mourning for the deceased, his brother, of whom he was fond.

from those of clan heads and some senior lineage heads, were granted to strangers. This led to vociferous complaints, but probably little real hardship: those few Ganda who actually wish to live at their *butaka* village can generally do so, and heads of lineages were later given a specific right to do so. Even where the land now belongs to a stranger, people still regard the village as the *butaka* of the lineage, and it has as much (or rather, as little) importance to the members as before. In fact, new *butakas* have arisen as men have declared that their *mailo* estates (which are of course inheritable) are *butakas* for their agnates.

In the past, the clans were also responsible for arranging matters of personal succession and the inheritance of movable property (including widows). Every deceased person, unless an infant, had to have a *musika* (personal successor) appointed, who "took the place" of the deceased; always ceremonially, and sometimes in day-to-day affairs, he took the name of the deceased and adopted the kinship terms appropriate to him. He also took the greater part of the dead man's property. The eldest son was ineligible as successor; indeed, it was preferred to pass over sons altogether and choose a more remote agnatic kinsman in order to link groups of relatives somewhat remote by descent, and probably by residence too. (This custom was altered by royal decree in the latter half of the last century—and thereafter sons were preferred.)

Clan membership was also important in the achievement of nonhereditary chieftaincies and in the regulation of exogamy. Thus people had to know their clan membership in order to avoid marrying a spouse of their own or their mother's clan, for clans were exogamous.[8] They had also to know it if they sought appointment to chiefship, since only a true Muganda could be appointed, and a true Muganda was defined as a member of one of the clans. To this day, at the ceremony where chiefship is formally bestowed by the kabaka, an appointee must recite his membership of his clan and its segments; and should the head of his clan disown knowledge of him, his appointment falls through.

Today the clans retain this duty of arranging personal succession and inheritance for their members—and this is important now that land may be involved. But since the dispositions the clan council can make of *mailo* land are limited either by a will or by a precise ordinance issued by the kabaka, and are examined by a special office under the *katikkiro*, the clans have little real power though much prestige.

Traditionally, clans were linked to the kabakaship. Thus each clan had the privilege of performing certain duties for the kabaka, such as supplying bark cloths or herding his cattle, and by this means the clans were linked to the kingship. (The practical economic significance of these duties was probably small, since we know that the kabaka used other means of obtaining bark cloths, herdsmen, and so forth.) Each clan had the opportunity of providing the kabaka's mother,[9] and thus of being especially linked to the kabaka himself; and some rough attempt was made to circulate this privilege through the clans. Each clan also provided boys to serve the kabaka, and the more favored among them might become chiefs, bringing glory and no few advantages to their clans.

On the other hand, the clan was held corporately responsible to the kabaka for the misdeeds of its members; and when a chief gave great offense to the kabaka, he might order his executioners to kill all the offender's clansmen. This is why, my informants said, people are reluctant to reveal their clan membership to strangers. Another consequence was that members of clans under the royal doom pretended to belong to other clans, using their blood brothers to get them accounted members of their clans. Thus many ostensible members of a clan are not truly descendants of its founder; this is one reason why exact knowledge of lines of descent is said to be the affair of the lineage head.

Clansmen held themselves responsible for obtaining justice, through a chief's court, if one of them was killed or injured or wronged. Moreover, a clansman was expected to provide hospitality to a fellow clansman, to provide him with banana shoots to start his gardens when he moved to a new village, and to assist him if he was in difficulty, perhaps through being fined for some offense. As even the smallest lineages were widely dispersed, the incidence of these obligations in practice was haphazard; and, except for royal persecutions, a clansman or group of clansmen was not automatically accountable for a fellow. These obligations—to be hospitable and helpful to a clansman—are still recognized, though people say they are evaded more commonly nowadays. Some people maintain that, as in the old days, a chief may be expected to grant favors to his clansmen; but others assert that it is more valuable to be of the same religion than of the same clan as a chief. Thus, even in traditional times, the Ganda clan was not a strongly localized corporate unit. As we shall see, clans did have important religious functions. They also had mutual aid functions and regulated certain types of inheritance, succession, and exogamy. Finally, through matrilateral ties with the kabaka, clan membership provided potential access to favor and political status, but ties of personal allegiance counted for more than ties of clanship or territoriality.

Although the clans now make little practical contribution to the life of the Ganda, matters of clanship evoke great interest and emotion. One reason may be that membership of his clan, freely and permanently[10] received at birth, gives a person a sense of belonging that softens the hazards of a highly individualistic and competitive way of life. Another reason is precisely because clans were largely ignored in the new dispensation, so that the Ganda, as they sought to throw off British dominance and rediscover their own national identity, found—and are finding—in the clans an embodiment of tradition relatively untainted by foreign influence.

Law

THE TRADITIONAL PERIOD · In the old days each chief had a court, and a man who had a complaint against another would bring a charge before the offender's chief. The accused was then summoned by a messenger of the chief to appear—he might be arrested, though Ganda, who pride themselves on their skill in litigation, are usually quite willing to stand trial—and both parties paid court fees. Each pleaded his case in turn, and if he could, produced witnesses in his support. The chief heard cases in his *lukiiko*; all the people present, including the chief, might closely question the parties and their witnesses and were ingenious in uncovering both inconsistencies and facts about the relationships of the parties that might put the dispute into context. When the issues had been thrashed out, people at the *lukiiko* would state their views of the case, and the chief normally took these into account in giving his decision.

If he were found guilty, the defendant had to pay a fine to the chief, and compensation to the plaintiff. Murder was usually punished by death, as was adultery, though for the latter crime mutilation was sometimes substituted. Thieves caught in the act were killed at once, or if only later brought to justice were punished by fine or mutilation. Another punishment was confinement in heavy wooden fetters.

It was possible to appeal against a decision to the court of a higher chief, though the lower chief was likely to make the appellant suffer for such insolence. Generally the *katikkiro's* was the highest court of appeal, though some cases were appealed to the kabaka himself. It was also possible to appeal to the poison ordeal if one disputed a chief's judgment.

SINCE THE COLONIAL PERIOD · Under British rule murder and certain other defined offenses, as well as cases involving non-Africans, were placed under the jurisdiction of Protectorate Government courts. Ganda courts have tried offenses against uncodified "native law and custom," such as theft, assault, or insolence to a chief, as well as all kinds of civil wrongs not reserved to government courts; and they have also tried offenses defined by laws of the Buganda or national governments, such as adultery, arson, tax default, offenses against agricultural regulations, or drunkenness. Chiefs acting as judges had the assistance of a few subordinate chiefs chosen in rotation, and interventions by the general *lukiiko* have been gradually discouraged. The necessity of producing a written record, however summary, of the cases heard has tended to make the procedure more formal, and such technicalities as the inadmissibility of evidence may be raised. But professional lawyers cannot be employed in Ganda courts, and the chiefs themselves have little or no special judicial training; hence decisions were more usually determined by substantive justice than by legal technicalities. There was right of appeal from the subcounty to the county court, and from there to the principal court at Mmengo; decisions were subject to the revision of the judicial adviser, an officer of the Protectorate Government. Punishment was and is by fine or imprisonment. With the introduction of magistrates (see page 114), who receive some special training, procedures have become still more formal, and there is now only one level of court below that of Mmengo.

Ganda political and territorial organization: An interpretive summary

In order to survive as an independent nation, the Ganda needed a strong political organization, and their institutions of government have much in common with those of the other Interlacustrine tribes who were their enemies. Ecological conditions favored the development of a strong state, since the people were rather densely settled, the labor of men was free for political and military activities, and there was no economic basis for the development of a privileged pastoral caste, such as is found in neighboring kingdoms.

But it was the genius of successive kabakas that ensured the remarkable centralization of power by undermining the strength of localized clans and by keeping the chiefs entirely subordinate and dependent on themselves. In such a system, where royal jealousy curbs the power of subordinate groups in the nation, the individual becomes relatively free. In Buganda the individual valued this freedom, and used it to seek his own advantage by changing his allegiance from village to village and from chief to chief. Such mobility of persons in turn was a further check on the development of autonomous local groups under chiefs or clan leaders.

In modern times, the individualism of Ganda life has perhaps been accentuated by the fact that every man now makes his living in his own gardens, and is not economically dependent on any chief or landlord, let alone his clansmen or kinsmen. The village, once a community focused on a chief, is no longer this, and the groups to which a man belongs, his clan, his church, and perhaps his political party, are themselves national in span. Above all, however, a man recognizes allegiance to the state itself, embodied in the kabakaship. The kabaka is the focus of every Muganda's loyalty and pride, for he is rightly identified with the achievements and glories of the tribe, and with its characteristic institutions and customs. The *namasole*, mother of Kabaka Muteesa I, spoke truly when she said to Speke: "Buganda is personified by Muteesa; and no one can say he has seen Buganda until he has been presented to the king."

KINSHIP ORGANIZATION

KINSHIP · The Ganda have a kinship terminology of the Omaha type.[11] A special feature of the system is the use of specific terms for cross-cousins of the opposite sex, with whom there is an avoidance relationship; but more significant is the fact that many Ganda do not know the correct terms for cross-cousins of either sex. This cannot be attributed to the Europeanization of Ganda life, since Roscoe, writing fifty years ago, recorded several of the terms wrongly. It is due partly to the fact that men prefer to take their wives from villages some distance away, so that the children of a woman and those of her brother generally have little contact; and partly to the fact that kinship terms are used rather sparingly.

Except between parents and children, kinship terms are rarely used in addressing a kinsman; and, even in referring to a kinsman, at least outside one's own elementary family, personal names are used more often than kinship terms. I have even known people to be disturbed because I referred to a kinsman of theirs by the kinship term rather than by name; there is, in fact, a certain tendency to regard kin relationships as an embarrassment.

When a young man marries, he normally, though not invariably, goes to set up a home in a village other than that of his parents or his wife's parents. Some men told me that they had moved to get away from their fathers. Also, it is commonly said that people disperse in this way because brothers inevitably quarrel, especially over the anticipated inheritance (the Ganda maintain, quite unrealistically, that which one of the sons will become successor is unpredictable until after the father has died). Usually, though not always, a man will go to a village where he has a kinsman of some kind who can introduce him to people and help him establish his gardens. Thus Ganda move away from close kinsmen, and toward more remotely related kin; it is kinship in general, rather than more specific ties of blood, that is valued. The Ganda attitude seems to be that kinship is a good thing—but you can have too much of it.

In the old days, people frequently moved from one village to another, whether to escape from a bad chief or from neighbors who were hostile— perhaps making sorcery; or to join another chief from whom they hoped for more advantages, because he was wealthy or powerful, or because he was a clansman or a kinsman, or because he had a reputation for generosity and justice.

Today, village chiefs have given way to landlords, and most people do not take sorcery very seriously; hence these considerations apply less. Indeed, there are now good reasons against moving: houses are more permanent and expensive; coffee gardens, which take four years to come into bearing, represent a major investment; in the Mmengo region at least, it is hard to find unoccupied land; and there are financial difficulties (see page 95) involved in disposing of one plot and acquiring another. Yet, people do still move fairly frequently, so that most people will have had homes in several villages, often widely scattered. One reason for this is, as the proverb says, "A man goes to live where he finds people of his own sort." There is a verb, *kusenguka*, to describe this customary movement, which is regarded with pride as typical of the Ganda—with pride, because they rightly point out that it depends on the ubiquitous power of the kabaka, which means that a man's status as subject of his king counts for more than specific status as kinsman or clansman.

Since people like to be free to move, it is good to have kinsmen scattered over many villages; indeed you rejoice if a kinsman goes away, because, as the proverb says, "The place he has settled adds to the places you can stay." Similarly, people like to take a spouse from, and so make in-laws in, a village some distance away. Some even suggested that it would be slightly incestuous to marry a woman from the same village, since fellow villagers are regarded as kinsmen. Marriages at a distance are also facilitated by the fact noted above that men, and still more women, often go to stay with kinsmen living some distance away. Thus the Ganda system of kinship and marriage is intimately linked with the custom of moving homes from village to village, and its implication that dispersed kinsmen are more useful than a localized group. Perhaps these institutions will change as the increasing scarcity of good land, together with other factors, puts a brake on the free movement of peasants.

In any village, most people have some neighbors they call kinsmen; and this is partly because it is convenient to choose to live in a village where you actually have kinsmen. But, in fact, the most tenuous links—any fellow clansman may be regarded as a kinsman—will be emphasized in order to posit a kin relationship; and it is just as true to say that neighbors are identified as kin as it is that kinsmen are chosen as neighbors. People do not suffer if they have no blood kin in their own village, and kinship connections seem to have little distinctive effect on the patterns of friendship and association within a village. "Friendship is stronger than kinship," the Ganda say—though they add that kinship lasts longer.

An important reason for the lack of a consistent pattern of kin relationships in the village is the fact that Ganda agriculture does not require the cooperation of people outside the single household. Certain less frequent activities, such as housebuilding, do require help from others; but in these days specialists are employed for cash, whereas in the past neighbors were recruited on an *ad hoc* basis. Similarly, if a family desires help in its gardens (as it may, especially with the cash crops), it employs laborers who have immigrated from other tribes. Relationships between members of different households always depended more on goodwill and sociability than on need; now that the cash nexus has replaced the common political relationship to a village chief, there are often only random and tenuous bonds between the residents of a single village.

THE HOMESTEAD AND THE VILLAGE · The domestic unit, however it is constituted, occupies a *maka* (homestead), the term I use to describe the house and huts standing in a yard among the gardens of the plot of the household head. The house in these days is rectangular, about thirty by twenty feet, and is divided into two or more rooms. The walls are built of mud on a framework of canes supported by posts, and the pitched roofs are now more often of corrugated iron or aluminum than of thatch. Most people buy from a local joiner properly carpentered doors to build into the walls at the front and the back of the house, and small windows having wooden shutters that are kept open by day. More prosperous people build larger houses, with such refinements as concrete floors or plastered walls, and some, even in the villages, build in brick.

A separate hut, also of mud on a rectangular plan, serves as a kitchen, and additional sleeping huts must be provided if there are adolescent children, or the household head's mother, living with the family.[12] Other constructions are an unroofed enclosure of canes behind the house in which people bathe in the evening, and sometimes in the morning too; and farther away, the small hut which covers the pit latrine.

The yard that surrounds the house is kept weeded and swept, and often members of the family sit there, especially if they have a shade tree. The front of the yard, some twenty or thirty feet before the house, normally borders a village road or footpath; the other three edges of the yard are marked by the gardens of permanent crops—coffee sometimes, but more often bananas—that soon grow tall and thick enough to form an effective

A Village Main Street There are houses to the right of the man in the *kkanzu* (gown) and behind the cyclist. These and others are concealed by the vegetation.

screen. Because of this, there are not many places in the village from which more than three or four houses are visible.

The Ganda always have their gardens, of permanent as well as annual crops, on the same plot on which they build their houses; and since a plot is generally of five or six acres, homesteads are inevitably dispersed over the band on the hillside where the soil is most fertile. It is impossible to see the houses of the village as a cluster, and as homesteads are on the average thirty to forty yards apart along the road, a visit to the other end of the village involves definite exertion. Just as there is no focus on which house sites are centered, so too there is no social focus of village life. People meet in twos and threes on neighborly visits, and a dozen people will be found most days at a house where beer is being sold; but only at the infrequent marriage feasts or mortuary ceremonies are most of the villagers likely to meet together at one time.

The villages I know usually range in size from thirty to eighty homesteads; but people tend to regard all the homesteads on one *mailo* estate, even if of several square miles, as constituting one village, so that the possible range of size is greater than this.

In the old days, the houses were built of thatched cane, in a beehive shape, twenty or more feet in diameter. Each house was divided into a front and a back room, and many peasants probably had several houses as well as lesser huts in their yards. Chiefs had much larger compounds, with many houses and huts to accommodate wives and children and dependents and slaves, all enclosed in a reed fence. In the village, the chief's compound was certainly a social center, where people spent much of their time sitting around drinking beer and talking. It may also have been to some extent a focus for the pattern of house-sites: at least villages were more compact then, partly because gardens were needed only for food, partly so that people could more easily call for assistance against thieves.

MARRIAGE · One reason given for preferring to take a bride from some distance away is that this makes it more difficult for her to run home to her mother. Marriage is certainly very unstable in Buganda; although it is difficult to collect reliable figures, most people have had several spouses, and have little confidence that the current union will endure. One reason is that it is easy for a woman to travel, and easy for her to support herself; in all villages one meets women who have "retired from marriage," have acquired land as tenants or as owners, and run their own households and gardens. The governments, too, are partly responsible, since they recognize only civil marriage (rarely used by Ganda) and religious marriage (where, except for Muslims, divorce is not recognized). Most marriages in fact follow the customary procedure; since this receives no official recognition, the courts will not enforce the return of brideprice. Brideprice usually amounts to Shs. 200/– and upward, and the groom[13] is likely to spend as much again on the wedding and the reception; hence it is strange that men are prepared to delve repeatedly into their pockets for temporary wives. Some men admit that their spouse is really a *mukwano* (friend) and that there has been no proper marriage with the payment of brideprice; I suspect that this kind of union is more common than people will admit. The Ganda attribute the instability of marriage mainly to the fact that girls in school are taught new ideas of their rights, which jar with the views of men. Traditionally, Ganda husbands were patriarchs, claiming the authority even to prevent their wives from leaving the homestead without permission. Since the father of a child is not defined as the mother's husband, but as the true begetter (genitor), there was reason for such strict supervision (though it is hard to believe that men were able to enforce it). It is impossible to know how much less unstable marriage was in the old days, when the return of brideprice could be demanded and women could not support themselves without a man.

Polygyny is the ideal for most men, except particularly devout Christians; and it is claimed that in the old days, when many women were captured in war, most men had several wives at the same time. But only about one man in twenty now attains this ideal, and these are nearly all men notably wealthier than the average. Poorer men cannot offer sufficient inducement for co-wives to accept the jealousy and quarreling inherent in the situation. If such a man introduces a second wife into the household, it is likely that one or both women will desert. Although *muggya*, the specific term for co-wife, has the same stem as *buggya* (jealousy), co-wives generally do not have different sleeping huts, but only separate bedrooms in the same house; and I was told that in the old days, too, more than one wife might share the same hut. Some polygynists however establish homesteads in different villages for each co-wife.

THE FAMILY · Apart from the compound families of polygynists, the normal residential group is the elementary family; married sons and daughters, even if they live in the same village, invariably have separate homesteads on different plots of land. The actual composition of the domestic group naturally depends on the stage of development of the family. A household may contain a bachelor, or a married couple without children, or a married couple with unmarried children. Because of the instability of marriage, one often finds households containing a man or woman whose marriage has ended, and these sometimes have children living with them. Some households also contain one or more kinsmen of the household head, most often a mother or sister whose marriage, if any, has come to an end. An infrequent but characteristic type is the man who has brought his sister (real or classificatory) to look after him, and perhaps his children, after his wife has left him.

The average size of a household (brought down somewhat by the large number of persons living alone) is about three persons. It is useful to have a woman in the household to take charge of the cooking, the cultivating of food crops, and the fetching of water and firewood, but a man will do these things for himself if he has to. However, women often say that a man is not much use about the homestead.

In the old days men took little part in agriculture, since their only task was the clearing of new land, not frequently required; men built houses, made bark cloths, hunted and in some places fished, but much of their time was spent in attendance on the chief and waiting for the call to go to war, or to labor on public works. Today men are considered responsible for earning cash, usually by cultivating cash crops, so that they can pay taxes, pay for their children's education, and provide their families with clothes, meat, sugar, tea, kerosene, and all the other minor necessities and luxuries of modern life. Men, unless in employment, are perforce cultivators now, at least in the cotton and coffee gardens—though their wives also help with these. Most men put in an average of about four hours' work a day, and spend much of their free time in drinking banana beer, or even brewing it. Women, with their domestic duties as well as their work in the food gardens, have less free time.

CHILD TRAINING AND SOCIALIZATION

Because of the instability of marriage, many children do not grow up under the care of their own mothers.[14] This may be harmful psychologically, but it is nothing new in Ganda life, since there was a custom of sending children away from home to be reared by others. Kinsmen were given children as a favor, to keep the relationship alive; and the mother's brother had a right to half his sister's children, until they reached puberty, unless their father made special payments to keep them. It was considered beneficial to the child to be sent away, since he would receive a stricter upbringing than in the home of his own parents. Where possible, a promising child was sent to the compound of a chief or to the palace of the kabaka, where a boy would learn the arts of government and perhaps later receive preferment, and a girl might make a good marriage. Children sent to relatives were sent very young, usually straight after weaning; those sent to serve chiefs naturally went at an older age.

Similar customs are certainly practiced today, though, since they were condemned by the missions, it is difficult to get accurate information. Infants are often sent to grandparents, or to other kinsmen without children of their own, though such children frequently return at six or seven when school fees have to be found. But, at the same age, other children are sent to live with relatives who live near a good school; if this means living in Kampala, their parents will not only pay their school fees but also make a contribution to their keep.

A few months after birth, the child begins to receive solid food, often much against its will; but it is not finally weaned from the breast until about the age of three. (Some mothers nowadays wean considerably earlier than this.) At two months of age the child starts to be trained to sit up. I do not know when toilet training begins; but before a child can talk it is considered "to have no sense," and is not rebuked or punished for its faults. Once the child can talk, parents take pains to teach it good behavior, especially respect toward adults; toddlers kneel before a visitor and timidly squeak out the formal greetings, and thereafter sit quietly on the floor until dismissed to play or work. As soon as it is able, the child is given tasks to do, taking small pans to fetch water from the spring, or cultivating its own small garden with a miniature hoe. Girls of five or six also help their mothers in the kitchen, and are sometimes able to do most of the work of preparing and cooking a meal. In the old days boys of six or seven began to go out herding the goats.

Nowadays, children start school at about six, or as soon thereafter as their parents can raise the fees; in the areas where I worked, all children—boys and girls—apparently got at least four years of primary education, and the chiefs made trouble for parents who did not send their children to school, although primary education is not yet legally compulsory. Because of attending school, children do not make as large an economic contribution to the household as they used to; however, many children are expected to do an hour's cultivation before setting off for school, and to do some work in the gardens or in the house after school, on weekends, and during the holidays.

Ganda believe in bringing up children strictly, and I was told that they are frequently beaten if they are naughty—though I never witnessed this, partly perhaps because Ganda family life is conducted largely in privacy. Children, though extremely well behaved, do not usually appear to be cowed; and the strictness of discipline is mitigated by the obvious fondness of most parents or guardians for their children. The Ganda are an infertile people—about a quarter of the women never bear children—so people consider themselves fortunate to have children, of their own or others' loins, and cherish them accordingly.

There is no initiation among the Ganda, who express scorn for other tribes who mutilate their bodies. A girl's first menstruation is marked by a family ceremony, but a boy's puberty receives no formal recognition. For boys and for girls it is marriage that really marks the assumption of adulthood. Girls used to marry young, from about thirteen, but nowadays, even among the peasants, girls are not often married before sixteen. Boys used to marry at fifteen or sixteen, but with them, too, marriage is now deferred to the age of eighteen or more.

ECONOMY

SUBSISTENCE CROPS • Most Ganda are peasant cultivators, producing on their plots the bulk of their food requirements as well as cash crops. The staple food is the banana (or plantain), which is cut unripe and eaten steamed and kneaded to form a starchy mass somewhat like our potato. Other varieties of banana are grown for beermaking, and to provide snacks; and parts of the banana plant other than the fruit are used to provide a variety of useful objects. The typical homestead has a banana grove of one or two acres.

Sweet potatoes, grown in small quantities, provide a starchy food alternative to bananas; nowadays each household must cultivate a cassava (manioc) plot primarily as a reserve against famine. Yams are also often grown as another source of starch, though anything but bananas is regarded by Ganda as a second best. Peanuts are grown to make a sauce eaten as relish with starchy food, although they can also be sold for cash; cowpeas and beans are also often grown for the same purpose. Other vegetables, of which the leaves, roots, or fruit may be eaten, are grown in small quantities for relish.

From time immemorial the basis of Ganda economic life has been the banana plant. After land has been cleared of grass and bushes—trees can usually be left—banana suckers, which are given, or nowadays sold, by kinsmen or other neighbors, are planted. Eighteen months later the first bunches of fruit are ready for eating; and though the stem dies, its place is taken by one of the suckers that have developed from its roots. If the first planting and subsequent renewal by suckers are properly planned, the banana grove can provide fruit continuously through the year. Careful farmers mulch the ground between stems with the debris of finished stems, and other waste. When this is done, little weeding is required, and the Ganda maintain that one woman's work can provide food for ten men.[15] With mulching and other care, the soil does not noticeably deteriorate, and if soil and rainfall are suitable, the same grove continues to produce for between ten and seventy years. Thus manpower for clearing new land can virtually be eliminated from the labor budget. One person can be supported from about one third of an acre of bananas, without having to allow further land for rotation; and the necessity to rest land used for cultivating minor food crops can be accommodated within the bounds of a single plot.

Thus, the Ganda were able to support a fairly dense population[16] in which, though individuals often moved, local groups such as villages or chiefdoms were permanent. They supported this population, moreover, with minimal demands on male labor, which made possible the large number of persons involved in government, and the frequent raising of large armies. The Ganda say, "In the old days the work of the men was war"; and if the ordinary peasant spent only a small part of his time on campaigns, and returned with little booty, the effect—with respect to the nation—was profound. Economically, the armies that were sent out each dry season brought in cattle and slaves and wives; demographically, the infertility of the Ganda was counteracted by the influx of captured women and children; politically, the strong organization of the state was a necessity if such powerful kingdoms as Bunyoro were to be successfully raided.

When warfare ceased, with the assumption of the British protectorate, it was not long before the labor of men found another profitable outlet in growing cash crops. Though Buganda's population surely decreased, from a variety of causes, between about 1880 and 1920, since then immigration from other tribes has refilled the country, and has provided a source of labor to replace the slaves of the old days.[17]

LIVESTOCK · Every household keeps a few chickens. The eggs are sometimes eaten, but not by women, for whom they are taboo. Chickens are kept mainly for meat, especially to offer to visitors; *nkoko* (chicken) must if possible be offered to *bako* (in-laws). Most households keep a few goats, or sometimes sheep; but these are not milked. Only a few people keep cattle, although in most villages milk can be bought by those who can afford it. The grasses of the hilltops and lower hillsides provide ample free pasture for those who have cattle, but most Ganda have no interest in cattle raising, and the care of the cattle is delegated to employees, immigrants from tribes to the west. A man who does not provide meat for his family at least once a week will soon lose his wife; the meat is bought, usually on Saturdays, from

A Ganda Woman She is dressed in a *busuti*, and peeling cassava.

local butchers. Some of the cattle to supply this market are brought in from outside Buganda.

CASH CROPS • Cotton was introduced as a cash crop in 1904 and spread rapidly. *Robusta* coffee was indigenous and grown in small quantities by the Ganda, and later as a cash crop especially in the Buddu region; with the rise in world coffee prices it spread widely as a cash crop especially after World War II. Now it is—in financial terms—the leading cash crop. The average household has one to three acres in coffee, cotton, and other minor cash crops; and I would estimate that in 1954 (when coffee prices were at their peak) the annual income of a household in the Mmengo region was commonly between Shs. 700/– and Shs. 1000/–.

HOUSEHOLD BUDGETS AND OCCUPATIONAL SPECIALIZATION • This income of the household head is normally spent for taxes, rent for land, and—in many instances—hired labor, including carpenters who may be called to help with housebuilding. Cash is also used for clothing.

Men like to dress in the *kkanzu*, a long gown like a nightshirt, with shorts underneath; for dress occasions a man likes to wear a jacket over his best *kkanzu*, and often long trousers beneath it. Women generally wear the *busuti*, which consists of a roll of cloth worn as a long skirt, with a bodice sewn to the top, and brassiere and bloomers beneath. Their husbands are wise to buy them several *busutis*. Boys usually wear a shirt and shorts; girls, a dress and bloomers.

Usually cash income is used for meat, for the imported sundries mentioned earlier, and for larger items like the ubiquitous bicycle. Finally, there is beer, which is not often given away, but perhaps a man balances his drinking expenses by his earnings when he himself brews.

A few men are lucky enough to inherit the plot and the house in which they set up their home; others are assisted by their father or perhaps other relatives in paying for the plot and the wife. The impact of all the initial payments may be spread by installment buying, notably for the plot, sometimes for the wife. But, clearly, many young men have to earn a substantial sum of money before they become householders. Hardly ever will a Ganda work as an agricultural laborer, and opportunities for employment as clerks, teachers, shop clerks, craftsmen, or drivers are limited in country areas. Many young men go to work for a period in Kampala. Others earn cash by cultivating their own cash crops on their father's plot; others take a cheap plot on poor soil, sometimes renting it on terms not covered by the *Busulu* and *Envujjo* Law, and by growing cotton for a few years raise the capital to buy a better plot. Loans from an elder brother or other kinsman, a Ganda moneylender (often an old woman), or an Asian trader,[18] often give a young man his start in life.

Some older men also have sources of income other than cash crops, notably by employment in Kampala, but in rural districts these are scarce; there are a few chiefs, clerks, carpenters, bicycle mechanics, butchers, and— near the lake—fishermen. Some men have stalls in the weekly market, of which there are perhaps one to a *muluka* (parish); one man in a village, on the average, may run a small shop, often at a loss.

MATERIAL CULTURE · Most of the items of the traditional material culture have now fallen into disuse. As noted earlier, the house type has changed completely; cloth is universally worn instead of bark cloth and skins; cooking pots have largely given way to aluminum pans; hoe blades are now imported from Birmingham and elsewhere. Most men keep a spear, for self-defense or for the hunt, but shields no longer have a function. Many people have drums, either the tub-shaped type that has cow skins stretched over both ends and tightened by thongs, or the long narrow variety that has a lizard skin at one end tightened by pegs, and the other end open. Professional musicians have one-stringed fiddles or flutes; and, at the palace, the bow-harp, typical of Buganda and otherwise best known from ancient Egypt. But music is more often provided by the phonograph or the radio. Fishermen use dugout canoes, and a larger variety sewn together from rough-hewn planks; they also use fish traps of traditional patterns, but their nets are of nylon or Dacron. Among the typical possessions of the peasants one cannot overlook the bicycle and the fountain pen; and among those more prosperous, the motorcar and the wristwatch. In old Buganda, without writing and without beasts of burden or the wheel, there was nothing even analogous.

RELIGION AND MAGIC

GODS AND CULT GROUPS • The most important
beings in Ganda religion were *balubaale* (singular *lubaale*) or gods. These
are regarded as the ghosts of men who showed remarkable powers during
their lifetimes, at periods after the founding of the kingdom. The fact that
some of them are identical with the gods of neighboring kingdoms suggests
that this account was invented to assert the supremacy of the kingship over
the gods.

The names of more than seventy gods have been preserved, but probably only about a dozen were of more than local importance. The *lubaale,*
Katonda, is supposed to have created the world, but his cult was unimportant. The most important of the gods was *Mukasa,* who controlled the
lake, and also granted health, cured disease, and gave fertility to women.
Kibuuka is also remembered as particularly important: he was the god in
charge of war against Bunyoro, which, as I have remarked, was a major
industry.

Gods were believed to take temporary possession of men and women
and to speak through them; persons who were frequently possessed in this
way served as mediums and were the principal means of communication
with the gods. Leading gods had large temples, each with a staff of mediums
and other servants; the work of the temples was controlled by priests, most
of whom were the heads of lineages or clans. There were also lesser temples;
indeed, each clan and lineage head, and many private persons, had shrines
where the gods could be invited to speak through a medium.

People, the king included, made gifts to the gods to secure favors or
pay for favors received; and prayers might be addressed to a god even when
he was not present in the body of a medium. In general, people appealed
to that god who specialized in what they were seeking, or went to the
temple that happened to be nearest; there were no defined congregations for
at least the major gods, and local or descent groups did not usually have
their own gods peculiar to them.

NATURE SPIRITS • *Misambwa* were the spirits of certain trees, rocks, rivers
or other prominent objects, or of individual wild beasts, such as a leopard or
a snake. In return for gifts they granted favors to people of the locality or
of the lineage associated with the locality. They might also have their
mediums, and indeed seem indistinguishable from the lesser *balubaale.*

ANCESTRAL SPIRITS • Ghosts of the dead were feared, since they might
afflict the living who offended them by neglect or by sin, and they were
therefore placated with offerings. But except for those of important chiefs,

and above all those of former kings, which were housed in permanent shrines and reached through mediums, a ghost was soon forgotten. There was no ancestor cult, unless the remembrance of past kings be described as such.

CHRISTIANITY AND ISLAM • With the initial support of the kabaka, the teaching of the Christian missionaries rapidly took hold on the younger chiefs; after the kabaka had turned against them, the Christian converts, with their Muslim fellows, seized power in 1888 by the traditional means of deposing the king through rebellion and replacing him with a prince of their choice. After a period of civil wars between rival religious factions, Christianity became the established religion, and the temples of the indigenous religion were destroyed. With few exceptions, only Christians, and a few Muslims, were given chiefships; and the common people followed their masters in taking up the new religions. Perhaps 15 percent of the people today are Muslims; the remainder are Christians, mostly either Roman Catholic or Anglican. I met no practitioners of indigenous religion apart from a few who had renounced Christianity for nationalistic reasons; but Christian and Muslim peasants still believe surreptitiously in the traditional gods and spirits and ghosts, and invoke them in spirit-possession ceremonies.

MAGIC AND SORCERY • In the old days, black and white magic were widely used to injure enemies, to detect or harm unknown thieves, to influence chiefs, to ensure human fertility and health, to secure safety and success in war, hunting and fishing, and for many other purposes. There was, however, no agricultural magic (except as prevention against climatic disasters). Medicines and charms are still sold for these purposes, though except for medicines for diseases that do not yield to the Western type of treatment, they are not much in demand. Few people take sorcery very seriously, and many openly scoff at it; litigation and arson are now the favored ways of redressing grievances.

CHANGE

THE CURRENT CONSTITUTION • Under the new (1955) constitution the kabaka became, on paper, a constitutional monarch with a position similar to that of the British queen. The *katikkiro* was to be responsible to the protectorate government for the conduct of the Buganda government. A new *Great Lukiiko* is formed every five years. Sixty members are elected and a smaller number appointed. The *Great Lukiiko* in turn elects a *katikkiro*, who chooses five other ministers to assist him. The ministry is answerable to the *Lukiiko*, which now exercises considerable political power. Political parties of the Western style (such as the

Uganda People's Congress or the Democratic party) play little part in the politics of the *Lukiiko*, partly because of difficulties arising from the indirect method of election, and partly because political parties as such are detested by many Ganda—they have, for instance, been declared "satanic" by many of the clan heads.

Chiefs are now appointed, not by the kabaka, but by an appointments board, and their appointment is not now subject to the governor's approval. But the members of the appointments board itself are appointed by the kabaka—he has made a close kinsman chairman—and hence the kabaka's views are not irrelevant to the choice of chiefs.

The kabaka's views also have a bearing on decisions of policy, since, in general, members of the *Great Lukiiko* are assiduous in loyalty to him. It has been said that the 1955 constitution actually increased the real power of the kabaka, since he was not accountable to the governor for decisions that, in theory, did not emanate from him.

Although not stemming from the 1955 constitution, two other developments of the last decade may be noted. First, chiefs at all levels down to the *muluka* now have formal councils containing some elected members; these councils discuss matters of local interest and pass resolutions on them, and they send resolutions on matters of local or national interest up to the *Great Lukiiko* for consideration. They do not, at least by right, intervene in the chiefs' work; if they pass a resolution concerning the chiefs it is effective only because it is approved by the chiefs; indeed, chiefs use councils to get support expressed for what they intend to do anyway.

Second, Buganda government magistrates have been gradually introduced to take over the judicial side of the work of county and subcounty chiefs; such chiefs now try only minor offenses.

In other respects my account of the situation holds good for the present —except for the changes that accompanied Uganda's attainment of independence in 1962. These will be mentioned in the next section.

POSTINDEPENDENCE DEVELOPMENTS • Uganda attained independence in 1962. It might have come earlier if the Ganda had not refused to cooperate until they were confident that the kabakaship was safe from the jealousies of other tribes and the ambitions of party politicians. This end was achieved partly by giving Buganda federal status within Uganda, and partly by so arranging things that she could participate in elections without yielding power to political parties. Direct elections in Buganda to the *Great Lukiiko* were held in February 1962: these were crushingly won by a neotraditionalistic movement (it rejected the term "party") called *Kabaka Yekka* (The King Alone). While the rest of Uganda held direct elections to elect representatives to the National Assembly in April 1962, the *Great Lukiiko*, dominated by *Kabaka Yekka*, chose Buganda's twenty-one representatives.

These entered a coalition with the party that had won a majority from the rest of Uganda, to form the government that led Uganda to independence. Thus Buganda crushingly defeated the internal challenge of party politicians to the supremacy of the kabaka; and at the same time, by allying herself with non-Ganda politicians, she obtained a decisive voice in the affairs of the central government of Uganda. These achievements, backed by the constitutional safeguards embodied in her federal status, should ensure that the quasi autonomy and other privileges she held under British rule have been guaranteed and even increased.

NOTES

(1) My fieldwork in Buganda was supported by a Bursarship from the East African Institute of Social Research (1954–1956), and a research grant from the International African Institute (1959–1960), two organizations to which I am deeply grateful. I have drawn heavily on the many published works on Buganda, only some of which are mentioned in the bibliography for this chapter. I owe much to colleagues at the East African Institute of Social Research, especially to Drs. L. A. Fallers, A. I. Richards, and C. C. Wrigley. Above all I gratefully acknowledge my debt to many Ganda for their hospitality, help, and information.

(2) *Buganda* is the name of the country. The people who own the country are the *Baganda* (singular, *Muganda*). The language they speak is *Luganda*. Here the Anglicized form without the prefix (Ganda), conventional in scientific works, will be used as a noun to refer to the people, and also as an adjective.

(3) Apart from another 573 square miles which became official land attached to the kabakaship and leading offices and chiefships, the rest of Buganda was allocated to the British Crown. Most of this Crown land became forest reserve or remained unused; although some of it has been occupied by Ganda farmers as tenants, it may be set aside as a considerable factor in the land situation.

(4) Since 1916, alienation to non-Africans, always restricted, has been stopped.

(5) A man with a typical plot of about five or six acres will usually pay between Shs. 20/– and Shs. 30/– a year (20 East African shillings equal £1 sterling, or about $3 U.S.). In the Mmengo region in 1959 the average price for *mailo* land probably approached Shs. 200/– per acre. In 1954, when coffee prices were at a peak, the average return to the grower per acre of coffee in the Mmengo region was almost Shs. 500/–; it was probably about half this figure in 1959.

(6) Some of the members of a clan or lineage are not allocated to subordinate segments, but remain in what is called the "lineage of the roof." It is as-

sumed that, for instance, the founder of the clan appointed most of his sons to be heads of *ssigas*, and that the members of each *ssiga* are the descendants of those sons, whereas the "lineage of the roof" comprises the descendants of that son who was chosen to succeed his father in the headship of the clan. From among them, and normally from among sons and grandsons of former heads, the successor to headship is chosen by the council of the group.

(7) This princely clan was formed as follows. As has been remarked, only sons and grandsons of a previous kabaka, the Princes of the Drum, are eligible to be chosen as kabaka. The children of those not chosen are also called princes (or princesses); but once the line of agnatic descendants of a kabaka is too remote for them to be Princes of the Drum, they are classed as "Peasant Princes," and grouped into formal lineages each descended from a different kabaka or kabaka's son. In style of life Peasant Princes are often indistinguishable from commoner peasants, though their possession of royal blood gives them a higher rank. There was a strict rule that no prince could be appointed to a chiefship; and this is still followed, above the level of the *muluka* (parish).

(8) A few clans, on grounds either of size or of diverse descent of different sections, permit in-marriage to persons of different *ssigas*. The princely clan also does not enforce exogamy.

(9) There were, however, special customs which excluded a few of the clans from this privilege.

(10) There is a procedure for expelling a clansman who has become an intolerable burden or has committed such a sin as incest, but I have not heard of its being used in these times.

(11) The terms are listed by Margaret C. Fallers in her Ethnographic Survey (see the bibliography for this chapter).

(12) It is taboo to have sexual relations when parents and mature children are sleeping under one roof.

(13) A youth's father will at most pay for his son's first marriage, and often not that. If other relatives contribute, it will be from kindness only; for the most part a man is expected to raise the marriage payment as best he can.

(14) Some women who desert their husbands may take their young children and look after them until school age, or even until puberty; in the old days this was never permitted.

(15) On the basis of figures supplied by the Department of Agriculture, I calculate that with four hours' work a day a woman could provide the bananas required by thirty-six persons. Of course such specialization, to the neglect of other crops, would be absurd, except in the areas supplying bananas to the Kampala markets.

(16) Without cash crops, the land around the capital could have supported four or five hundred persons to the square mile, and probably did, although the average density for the whole country was probably not much above one hundred to the square mile.

(17) It has not, however, provided women to the same extent: few single women come in; in any case mutual contempt between Ganda and foreigners makes intermarriage unusual.

(18) Until the organized boycott of 1959, most retail trade was in the hands of Asians, congregated in trading centers, most of which were near county or subcounty headquarters.

BIBLIOGRAPHY

This list covers only the more basic and easily accessible works on Buganda (with three on nearby related peoples); full bibliographies are published in the Ethnographic Survey (M. C. Fallers 1960). Daggered items (†) are cited as references in the text of the chapter.

Apter, David E. (1961). *The Political Kingdom in Uganda*. Princeton, N. J.: Princeton University Press.
A political scientist's account; largely on developments in this century, but has also a valuable account of the indigenous political system.

Beattie, John (1960). *Bunyoro: An African Kingdom*. New York: Holt, Rinehart, and Winston, Inc.
A good, short account of a neighboring kingdom.

Fallers, L. A. (1956). *Bantu Bureaucracy*. Cambridge, England: W. Heffer & Sons, Ltd.
A neighboring tribe, the Soga, whose institutions supply illuminating parallels.

Fallers, M. C. (1960). *The Eastern Lacustrine Bantu*. London: International African Institute. (Ethnographic Survey of Africa; East Central Africa, Part XI.)
A valuable and readable summary, with excellent bibliographies.

Greenberg, Joseph H. (1955†). *Studies in African Linguistic Classification*. New Haven, Conn.: The Compass Publishing Co.

Hailey, Lord Malcolm (1950). *Native Administration in the British African Territories*. London: H. M. Stationery Office, Part I.
Includes a clear, short account of the pattern of administration under the Protectorate Government.

Mair, Lucy P. (1933). "Buganda Land Tenure," *Africa*, Vol. 6. pp. 187–205.

——— (1934). *An African People in the Twentieth Century*. London: Routledge & Kegan Paul, Ltd.
An essential work, describing Buganda society in the early 1930s, and in the last century.

——— (1940). *Native Marriage in Buganda*. London: Oxford University Press. (International African Institute Memorandum No. 19.)

———— (1962). *Primitive Government.* Harmondsworth, England: Penguin Books.
Includes much valuable information on the Ganda and related peoples.

Maquet, J. J. (1961). *The Premise of Inequality in Ruanda.* London: Oxford University Press.
A clear account of another interlacustrine kingdom.

Mukwaya, A. B. (1953). *Land Tenure in Buganda.* Kampala, Uganda: East African Institute of Social Research. (East African Studies, No. 1.)
A clear and detailed account of basic importance.

Oschinsky, L. (1954†). *The Racial Affinities of the Baganda and other Bantu Tribes of British East Africa.* Cambridge, England: W. Heffer & Sons, Ltd.
For physical anthropology.

Richards, A. I. (ed.) (1954). *Economic Development and Tribal Change.* Cambridge, England: W. Heffer & Sons, Ltd.
Mainly about immigrant laborers, but also contains much information about modern Ganda life.

———— (1960). *East African Chiefs.* London: Faber & Faber, Ltd.
The chapter on Buganda gives the best brief account of the political system; see also Chaps. 1, 15, and 16.

Roscoe, J. (1911). *The Baganda.* London: Macmillan & Co., Ltd.
A very rich compilation of fact, essential for the study of pre-European Buganda.

Southall, A. W., and P. C. W. Gutkind (1956). *Townsmen in the Making.* Kampala, Uganda: East African Institute of Social Research. (East African Studies, No. 9.)
The sociology of African life in Kampala.

Southwold, M. (1961). *Bureaucracy and Chiefship in Buganda.* Kampala, Uganda: East African Institute of Social Research. (East African Studies, No. 14.)
A brief account of the growth of the power of the kingship in Buganda.

Speke, J. H. (1863). *Journal of the Discovery of the Source of the Nile.* Edinburgh, London: Blackwood and Sons. Vivid account by the first European to visit Buganda; illuminating and generally sound.

Taylor, J. V. (1958). *The Growth of the Church in Buganda.* London: Student Christian Movement Press.
A brilliant account of its subject, and contains also an excellent portrait of life in a rural *muluka.*

Thomas, H. B., and R. Scott (1935). *Uganda.* London: Oxford University Press.
The best single source for background material.

Wrigley, C. C. (1959). *Crops and Wealth in Uganda.* Kampala, Uganda: East African Institute of Social Research. (East African Studies, No. 12.)
An excellent agrarian history, shrewdly set in the sociological context.

4

THE HAUSA
OF NORTHERN NIGERIA

about the chapter

The Hausa are influential in northern Nigeria and in some of the adjoining regions as well, not only because of their large population, which numbers over five million, but because their language is a lingua franca in the area as a result of their activities as itinerant merchants.

Like the Yoruba to the south, the Hausa developed large pre-European cities, which are the focus of their extensive trading activities and formidable governmental centers. Studying this society sheds light on the nature and history of urbanism. Again like the Yoruba, the Hausa developed large, elaborate markets and guildlike groups of occupational specialists, but among them these institutions are more highly organized than among the Yoruba. Thus, the very large number of occupational specialists among the Hausa reminds one of traditional India. As in India, the occupational groups are ranked, but the stratification so characteristic of the Hausa has not been elaborated into the caste principle because it is countered by other principles and softened by a formal etiquette based on superficial egalitarianism.

Smith points out that the principle of stratification operates also in the political context, and that "ruling" is seen by the Hausa as the most prestigious occupation. The political organization of the Hausa (which has changed little since the achievement of Nigerian independence) offers an intriguing model for the political scientist because it combines principles of kinship, clientship, and office (and, in the

119

past, slavery) in centralized kingdoms known as emirates. Clientship appears as a principle in several of the societies described in this volume, including the Rwanda and the Kpelle. In addition to the structural principles mentioned above, the Hausa emirate combines the traits of feudalism, despotism, and bureaucracy. Centralized states with which this state may usefully be compared include that of the Ganda, the Rwanda, the Suku, the Swazi, and the Yoruba.

The ethnic mixture of Fulani conquerors and Hausa—ruler and ruled—is a further subject of interest in the Hausa state. Comparison of the "Hausacized" Fulani elite, described in this chapter, with the pastoral Fulani (Chapter 9) provides an illustration of how the pastoral overlords of a conquest state became absorbed by their agricultural subjects. Some earlier Africanists mistakenly hypothesized that this never occurred.

A strong overlay of Islamic religious and social forms is characteristic of Hausa society. A long, proud tradition of literacy in Arabic and the availability of written records in Arabic and Arabic script make this society one of the few African societies for which it is possible to trace developments over several hundred years. For students of Islam or culture change, the Hausa (as well as the Fulani and the Somali) offer an excellent opportunity for observation of the transformation of Islam in an African setting.

about the author

M. G. Smith, Professor of Anthropolgy at the University of California, Los Angeles, has been the recipient of several honors and prizes awarded by the Royal Anthropological Institute of Great Britain and Ireland: The Wellcome Bronze Medal for Anthropological Research in 1953, the Curle Bequest Prize in 1955, and the Amaury Talbot Book Prize in 1960. He received his Ph.D. from the University of London in 1951. He has taught at the University College of the West Indies, Jamaica, and been a Research Fellow of the Institute of Social and Economic Research of that institution and of the Nigerian Institute of Social and Economic Research. Dr. Smith has carried out field research among several Hausa groups in Nigeria and Niger (1949–1950 and 1958–1959) and in the West Indies at Grenada (1952–1953) and Jamaica (1955, 1960). His published works include *The Economy of Hausa Communities of Zaria Province* (1955), *Government of Zazzau 1800–1950* (1960), *West Indian Family Structure* (1962), and *Kinship and Community in Carriacou* (1962).

M. G. SMITH · *The Hausa of Northern Nigeria*

INTRODUCTION

LOCATION · The Hausa are a numerous West Sudanic people settled in northwestern Nigeria and adjoining regions of Niger. Most Hausa are Muslims, and most Muslim Hausa live in Nigeria, their homeland lying between latitudes 10½° and 13½° north, longitudes 4° and 10° east. It is these Muslim Hausa of northern Nigeria whose culture and society I shall try to describe; but first, it is important to see how they differ from their pagan cousins.

BACKGROUND: MUSLIM VS. PAGAN HAUSA · The pagan Hausa-speaking peoples of this region go under various names, such as Arna or Azna, Bunjawa, Maguzawa, all conferred on them by the Muslims. These pagan Hausa live in small villages of exogamous patrilineal kin, worshiping nature spirits known as *bori* or *iskoki*, and deriving their subsistence almost entirely from farming and gathering. Wherever they are in close contact with the Muslim Hausa, they are subordinate.

Muslim Hausa are organized in a number of large centralized chiefdoms, some of considerable antiquity, and all having their government and economic centers in a large fortified city. The technology and economy of these Muslim Hausa are highly developed. They involve agriculture for subsistence and exchange; a wide range of craft specialization; an extensive network of trading relations and institutions, including markets, currencies, long-distance caravan traffic along protected routes, and customs duties; and judicial systems enforcing Islamic law. In place of exogamous patrilineages, among these Muslim Hausa we find an elaborate stratification based on hereditary occupational classes, the various strata being integrated by ties of clientship, allegiance, political interest, Islam, and historical tradition. Thus the differences between pagan and Muslim Hausa reveal influences of commerce, technological development, and urban growth, as well as conquest and Islam. In history and culture, the Muslim Hausa may perhaps be taken as representative of the more developed Islamic societies of the Western

Portrait of a Hausa Man

Sudan. Along with the Dahomeans, Ganda, Ashanti, and Yoruba, the Muslim Hausa belong at the upper limit of the developmental range to be found in indigenous African societies. To the student of African history, the Hausa have a special interest since we can trace the outlines of their development through written records. Political scientists may also find that knowledge of Hausa government illuminates feudalism, bureaucracy, and despotism, as well as the political institutions of Islam.

In the Nigerian census of 1952, Hausa were estimated as 5.5 million, most of whom lived in the area delimited above. However, apart from scattered pagan communities, this area also includes another large ethnic group, the Fulani, who numbered about 3 million at that date. Some Fulani are pastoral nomads, moving with their cattle within and beyond the limits of Hausaland. Others, perhaps one half the total, are settled among Hausa as their rulers, and have adopted Hausa language and culture as their own—with certain differences that express their greater emphasis on Islam and their pastoral cultural antecedents. In this account, I include the settled Fulani ruling class within the general term "Hausa," except where clarity requires differentiation.

PHYSICAL APPEARANCE • In consequence of their heterogeneity, the population varies greatly in physical type. Pure Fulani are likely to be tall, lean, and with markedly aquiline features; but even in this category, some are black and others are of light copper color. The "pure," non-Fulani, Hausa type is rather shorter and stockier and has more heavily Negroid features; but these are ideal contrasts rather than average types. Generations of interbreeding has produced an extremely variable physical type.

LANGUAGE • Thus Hausa are a heterogeneous group, whose most obvious common features are a common language and habitat. The Hausa language, from which these people take their name, is classified as belonging to the

Chad subfamily of Afro-Asiatic (Greenberg 1955:103), along with Kotoko, Yedina, Mubi, and Musgu, found in the Chad Basin farther east. However, perhaps a fourth of the Hausa vocabulary is of Arabic derivation and many terms for basic institutions and skills are of Kanuri origin, the Kanuri of Bornu, west of Chad, having dominated the Hausa, politically and culturally, from the fifteenth to the eighteenth century. Since 1900, the Hausa have acquired yet another layer of loanwords from English, and so their language reflects their cultural history.

ECONOMY

Ecology

Hausaland is open, rolling savanna, at a general elevation between one and two thousand feet, broken only by numerous rocky outcrops and thickly wooded watercourses. Aptly described as orchard-bush, this vegetation, like the rainfall, thins out to the north. At latitude 12°, rainfall averages between 40 and 45 inches per annum.

The Hausa year divides sharply into a long dry season, followed by a period of rains from May to early October. Brilliant electrical storms in late April and May herald the coming of the rains. During *damina* (the wet season) the country is clothed in green, and the people grow the bulk of their food for the following year. In August there is a brief break in the rains, when bulrush millet and maize are harvested; the first peanuts are picked in late September. *Kaka* (the main harvest) begins in November with wet rice, cowpeas, late millet and Guinea corn and continues until February when the sweet potatoes, cotton, sugarcane, and tobacco have all been reaped. The *kaka* season is followed by *rani*, when days are cool and clear and the nights chilly. *Rani* ends when the harmattan blows from the desert, bringing clouds of dust and a dry burning heat with noon temperatures of about 100°. *Bazara*, this season of the harmattan and meningitis epidemics, ends with the rains, to everyone's relief.

Throughout Hausaland temperature varies greatly by season and day, from a diurnal range of about 12° and an average of about 80° in the rains to a mean of about 100° in *bazara* with a greater diurnal range. To keep track of seasonal movements, Hausa employ an Eastern calendar that divides the year into 27 periods of 13 days each, and a last, *Jabaha*, of 14, each division taking its name from a constellation that rises at the time.

Grain is the staple diet, Guinea corn, millet, maize, and, to a lesser extent, rice being the principal varieties. Supplies permitting, the Hausa eat grain twice daily, for their main meal in the evening as *tuwo* (a heavy porridge) seasoned with *miya* (a peppery stew), and for a midday snack as *fura* (a dough ball) taken with milk or tamarind. The diet is short of protein but has a fair variety of sweetmeats, bean cakes, and snacks, that women prepare. Honey and sugarcane are available, and stimulants, particularly kola nuts, are in constant use.

Agriculture and animal husbandry

Besides the crops already mentioned, Hausa cultivate a number of roots, such as *rizga* (Kaffir potatoes), *gurjiya* (*Voandzeia subterranea*, the Bambara groundnut), cassava, and where conditions permit, yam and cocoyam, as well as onions, chili and other peppers, okras, *rama* (Indian hemp), pigeon peas, and indigo. They distinguish different soil types, and distribute their crops accordingly, marshland with its capacity for dry-season cultivation being highly prized, and intercropping the general practice elsewhere. Green manure, cattle manure, and periodic fallowing are employed, Hausa cultivation being based on a rotation of fields, except that home plots, heavily manured with household refuse, receive little rest.

In addition to what they grow, Hausa gather wood and grass from the open parkland for fuel, building, thatch, basketry, and mats. They use the tamarind, locust-bean, baobab, deleb palm, horseradish tree, and date palm as sources of food; the silk cotton for kapok, shea tree for oil from its nuts, raffia for building, and gutta-percha for export. Hunting and fishing yield very little, though monitor lizards and guinea hens add variety to the diet.

For meat, milk, and butter, the Hausa depend on the pastoral Fulani, who graze their herds near village markets where they purchase the foodstuffs and services they need, sometimes undertaking to quarter their cattle on a villager's farm for an agreed time, in return for money and grain. Apart from a very few cattle employed in farming, livestock raised by Hausa consist of horses, donkeys, goats, sheep, turkeys and other poultry. Of these, goats and poultry are in women's hands; sheep, rather less so. Horses are a man's pride but donkeys are the main means of local transport.

Occupations and crafts

Most Hausa men farm and also practice some other occupation. Only aristocrats, officials, wealthy merchants, and leading *mallamai* (clerics) do not cultivate their fields themselves. Even in the rains men practice nonagricultural specialties as much as they can. In contrast, few women take part in farming, although they are called on to harvest peanuts, cotton, *gurjiya*, and certain other crops. Women therefore have considerable freedom to pursue various female craft and trade activities throughout the year.

A simple list of the more important traditional male occupations will indicate the level of economic and technological complexity in Hausa society. Hausa classify men as hunters, fishers, builders, thatchers, butchers,

A Woman Weaving on the Women's Loom

tanners, leatherworkers, saddlers, weavers, dyers, woodworkers, blacksmiths, brass and silversmiths, calabash-workers, potmakers, drummers, musicians of various types, praise-singers, barber-surgeons, tailors, embroiderers, washermen, porters, commission agents, traders of various kinds, including *fatauci* (specialists in long-distance overland trade), makers of sweetmeats, makers of baskets or mats, tobacco grinders, specialists in herbal medicines, clerics rulers, officials, and their agents [*fadawa* (courtiers) or *jekadu* (intermediaries)]. Though incomplete, and excluding all recently developed specializations, this catalogue indicates high levels of technological self-sufficiency within a chiefdom and of economic integration among its various communities.

Moreover, Hausa women also have occupational specialties. They process sweetmeats and foods for local sale; thread, for local weaving, and make both the standard Hausa *gwado* (cotton blanket) and pots; raise goats and poultry for sale; trade in medicines, vegetable oils, cigarettes, and other small items; maintain the cult of spirit-possession (*bori*), and also are its main devotees and exponents. An unmarried woman may act as a praise-singer or *jakadiya* (female messenger), or as a prostitute, in which case she either enters the local guild or works independently.

Material culture

Given this range of occupational specialization, only the salient outlines of Hausa material culture can be treated here. Iron has been mined, smelted, and worked for as far back as Hausa traditions extend, the main woodworking tool being an adze, although small axes are used to hew trees. Local metallurgy provided Hausa with their tools for farming, sewing, leatherwork,

, warfare, and so on, as well as decorative ornaments, such as the lver *mundaye* that women wore on their wrists and ankles.

fighting, cavalry formed the main striking force, organized in several divisions. Horsemen wore armor of chain mail or quilted cotton, the latter also covering the flanks of their mounts. Swords of local manufacture broke easily; hence tempered blades were imported from Morocco and the Near East. Shields of hide, bows, and arrows (some poisoned, others shot aflame into besieged settlements), muskets, daggers, lances, and *kagai* (light battle-axes) were the weapons mainly used. Towns were fortified for defense, their walls surrounded with a deep ditch, their gates closed with heavy iron sheets, and the entrances recessed to hamper attackers. Captives were chained together by their ankles for the homeward march.

Hausa leather reached Renaissance Europe through Morocco and bore that name. The best leather comes from Katsina goatskins, tanning with acacia and local potash being a special art. Leather was used for loincloths, shoes, horse trappings, saddles, sheaths, quivers, and satchels for the Koran, as well as for buckets, snuffboxes, cushions, and other domestic articles.

Clothworking is a traditional Hausa industry. Women spin the locally grown cotton for weaving by both sexes, the lighter men's weave being sewn into clothing for men and women, and also serving as a traditional currency in certain areas. Women's cotton blankets are traded far afield. Embroidery with locally processed silk is a male craft; it is frequently combined with Koranic study by sedentary Fulani.

The local script, known as *Ajemic*, employs Arabic characters but differs from standard Arabic. For centuries, chiefs and wealthy traders in Hausaland have used this script in government and commerce. A special branch of clerical activity is devoted to copying Arabic manuscripts, both local and foreign, as well as preparing amulets and charms, many being worn on the person in leather cases. *Mallamai* also teach the Koran in their homes to young children. For this they receive token gifts from the children's parents, and more substantial shares of the *zakka* (the grain tithe at harvest ordained by Islam). In these schools, children learn the first sixty suras of the Koran by heart with little explanation. On graduation, they acquire the honorific title of *Mallam*, and are encouraged to study further the essentials of Arabic, Muslim law, Koranic exegesis, and rhetoric. Keen students travel long distances to study under a scholar of high repute in special fields and, on returning home, transmit their knowledge to others.

Dyeing with locally grown and processed indigo is a skilled occupation. Dye pits are sunk eight to ten feet in the earth, being narrow at the mouth and lined on the inside with traditional cement made from old indigo dye, cow dung, ashes, and horsehair. The locally grown dye is vigorously stirred in this cylinder by hired men using long poles. It gives a dark blue color, and is also beaten dry onto the cloth. When not in use, dye pits are covered with

conical thatch to reduce evaporation. As permanent capital, these pits are inherited through males.

Exchange and markets

Most Hausa men practice their craft or trade on a part-time basis, after farming, or on market days. Only where there is an assured market for craft
products can craftsmen become full-time specialists. In the cities and on the
borders of large pagan groups, some crafts, such as weaving, tailoring, leatherwork, or metalwork may support full-time specialists.

Traders are more likely to devote full time to commerce than craftsmen
to their crafts. General trade in local staples as well as foreign goods, large-
scale kola-nut trade, and cattle shipment to Southern Nigeria, clearly require
constant attention. In city markets, *dillalai* (brokers) also find it profitable to
specialize, as do courtiers, praise-singers, and a few others. Butchers rank
low in Hausa society, but they are important and often wealthy, since they
control market supplies of meat, hides, and skins. To dispose of meat rapidly,
they pay drummers to announce the coming kill, and also help one another
to sell it. Without an announced supply of beef, markets are poorly attended.

EXCHANGE · For the most part, Hausa combine production for subsistence
and exchange, subsistence being derived primarily from farming and gathering, while cash income comes from cotton, peanuts, and other cash crops,
livestock, forest products, craft products, services, and trade. Rural expendi-
tures focus on those traditional needs which households are unable to produce themselves. Survey data show that during 1950 in rural Zaria, roughly
one half of the consumption of ninety households was self-produced, the
remainder being acquired through exchange. There is great variation in the
extent to which individual households participate in the exchange sector.
This depends partly on their capacity to do without local commodities and
services.

The Hausa system of exchange has three distinct levels. There is a
complex pattern of gift exchange at kinship ceremonials such as naming,
weddings or funerals, at the main Muslim festivals, *Id-el-Kabir* and *Id-el-Fitr*,
and at harvest when *zakka* (tithe) is distributed. Gift exchanges confined to
males tend to be uneven in value. Commercial exchanges proceed at two
levels, within and beyond the community. Intracommunity exchanges consist
mainly of craft products and services, whereas intercommunity exchanges for
the most part involve cash crops, meat, and imported goods. Trade within a
Hausa community never ceases; children hawk cooked foods around the
village from dawn till dusk; petty traders keep tables laden with kola nuts,
cigarettes, matches, soap, kerosene at their entrance hut, while carrying on

some craft or conversation. However, the great bulk of exchanges takes place at the regular market meeting.

MARKETS • Hausa settlements may be classified as urban or rural, according to the frequency and size of their markets. Cities like Kano, Zaria, and Katsina have several markets that meet daily, as well as regular night markets. Important rural market towns also have a daily market, several full-time specialists, and some European trading posts staffed by Southern Nigerians. Smaller towns and villages have a regular market once or twice weekly. In eastern Hausa, village markets seem to meet more frequently than in Sokoto Province. The market days of nearby communities are arranged to form a cycle so that the market meets at a different village every day. Adjacent market cycles tend to overlap partially, but attract the same group of outside traders, who move easily among them since their price structure is much the same.

City markets are centrally located near the merchants' quarter. Village markets often stand on the village perimeter, in an open site with rows of sheds to accommodate traders. In rural areas the market assembles about ten in the morning, reaching its peak around two in the afternoon and breaking up at dusk. Fulani pastoralists, whose women attend in order to sell milk and butter, settle themselves in a group to one side and take little part in the trading. Hausa girls in their best clothes also attend in bevies, some hawking foodstuffs and snacks, kola nuts or cotton thread, while others wait for the young people's dance when market is over. In and around the sheds vendors group themselves by commodities, the 'yan koli—who deal in antimony, mirrors, needles, European thread, ginger, caps, cloves, black pepper, beads, natron—sitting in one place; potters, in another. Other specialists have their separate places. Commission agents or brokers, and young folks hawking snacks or kola nuts, keep moving throughout the crowd. If tax is overdue, the village chief or his representative may attend to remind late payers.

Underlying the noise and movement is a clearly defined organization. Each market has a headman (the Sarkin Kasuwa or Magajin Kasuwa) responsible to the village or town chief. He in turn has a number of assistants, the Sarkin Awo (Chief of the Grain Sellers, often a woman), the Sarkin Pawa (Chief Butcher), the Sarkin Dillalai (Chief Broker), and so on. Each craft official knows the group he represents, and is regarded by its members as their market leader. Accordingly, craft headmen remain with their various groups to settle minor disputes about payment or quality of goods, price, and the like, before these become serious, or to bring them to the market chief, who can refer them to higher authority. Perhaps for this reason quarreling and blows are very rare at these markets. One senses that for many who attend it, the market is a major social event, while others derive pure pleasure from trading, irrespective of profit or turnover, and still others attend of

Procession in Kano The emir's bodyguard is shown in a procession in Kano. (*British Information Service*)

necessity to earn the money with which to buy articles they urgently need. Markets provide the largest regular assembly of Hausa, and are scarcely visited by the ruling Fulani, who nonetheless, through the market organization, ensure that these assemblies meet and disperse peacefully, insulated from political agitation.

TERRITORIAL ORGANIZATION

THE CITY · The pattern of Hausa settlement is compact, and the people classify their settlements as cities, towns, or hamlets. Residence in cities carries most prestige, in hamlets least. Each state has one pre-eminent city, the *birni* (capital) where the ruler and senior officials live, the main administrative and economic institutions of the state are located, and learning, crafts, and communications are most advanced. Such capitals have long had separate wards, some reserved for visiting immigrant groups, including Tuareg, Arabs, Nupe, Kanuri, Fulani, and others. Nowadays large settlements of Southern Nigerians have grown up around these old cities, and most also contain a European suburb, occupied mainly by commercial and administrative personnel. These Hausa state capitals vary as much in size and population as the states themselves. Kano City now contains over 150,000 people, while Hadeija, Daura, and other small emirates have capitals with populations of less than 10,000. The centers of large emirates, such as Katsina, Sokoto, and Zaria, each held over 50,000 in 1952. Despite these large urban centers, the great majority of the Hausa are rural folk, living in villages and hamlets.

Most Hausa cities contain large structures more than a century old,

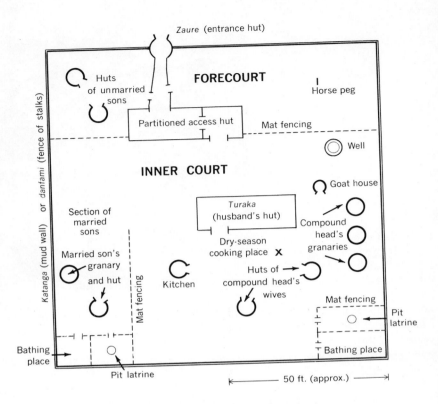

A Hausa Compound (Gida)[1]

such as the ruler's palace, mosque, and main official compounds. Such structures have high mud walls and mud-roofed rooms built around interior courtyards. There are two main ways in which the heavy mud roofs are supported. In Sokoto, vertical pillars within the room bear the weight; in Kano, Katsina, and eastern Hausa, ant-proof wooden beams are cantilevered to produce a vault, which is then plastered over with mud, whitewashed on the inside, and coated above with the traditional Hausa cement. With periodic repair, at these latitudes, such roofing may remain waterproof indefinitely.

The compounds of noblemen and wealthy merchants often include two-storied structures, with windows, interior stairs and metal gutters. Exterior decorations include whitewashing and plaster arabesques. Such prominent units as these may serve as the *kofa* or *zaure* (entrance) to the compound forecourt where horses are tethered and slaves formerly dwelt. Fenced off from this entrance may be one or more interior courtyards, which are entered through rectangular buildings having mud or thatch roofs and one or more rooms, the doorways being arranged so as to limit vision inward. At the rear of the compound, through another fence, one enters the *cikin gida* (women's

Women's Quarters (*Cikin Gida*) in a Prosperous Compound

quarters). Each holds as many huts as wives, and in addition the householder may have a *turaka* (separate hut) of his own. Hut types vary from the round windowless ones with thatched roofs and mat-covered doorways to rectangular huts with one or more rooms and an enclosed porch. An intermediate type is the *adadu,* in which an outer room with curving walls leads into the round hut. Small granaries made of mud or cornstalks stand around the *cikin gida.* There may be a light, thatched structure for wet-season cooking in addition to open hearths. Households that can afford them have their own wells, or —nowadays in the cities—a piped water supply. In one corner by the rear wall, behind a cornstalk fence, are the pit latrine and the bathing place.

In the design of its women's quarters the ordinary home does not differ greatly from this pattern but it lacks elaborate forecourts and mud-roofed rooms. Poor compounds may even lack a *zaure* (entrance hut), having instead a recessed entrance known as a *kofa.* Rural compounds are typically fenced with Guinea-corn stalks which require annual repair. Most compounds have a small round hut in the forecourt where young boys and visitors sleep. The *zaure* is the place in which the men of the compound sit, plying their crafts and talking with their neighbors and friends. Noblemen and merchants conduct their private interviews in one or another of the interior rooms.

A *gida* (compound) with only one entrance is regarded by the Hausa authorities as a single social unit, having one head, the *maigida.* Such a unit may, in fact, contain two or more domestic groups, each with separate granaries and food stores. Such domestic divisions may be expressed by partitions in the women's quarters up to the forecourt fence. However, until new entrances are cut in the compound wall, it is officially treated as one unit under its senior male.

THE VILLAGE • The Hausa word *gari* denotes a rural town or village. Hausa do not distinguish rural units with daily markets from others with less frequent markets. To them, differences between old and "new" settlements are more enlightening. Thriving new townships are mainly found on motor roads near ferry points, or on railroads laid down by the British, but many settlements on these routes have a long history. Most older villages or rural towns were walled and fortified against raiders. Parts of these walls still stand, although they have not been repaired for the past sixty years. Such walled villages are the typical capitals of village areas and contain the local market, the mosque and the official priest, the village chief and his residence, and the great majority of the population in the area under his charge. The principal *mallamai*, traders, and craftsmen of the local community will also be found at its capital. These villages vary in size between one and four thousand people, but in Katsina and Kano, several contain 8000 or more.

The great majority of rural people identify themselves as *talakawa* (commoners), in distinction from their *sarakuna* (rulers or chiefs) or *masu-sarauta* (administrators or office-holders). These distinctions are relative to the context of discussion. Village chiefs and officials may rank as subjects at the level of emirate organization, but as "rulers" in their local communities. The folk distinction is useful mainly in directing attention to the divergent interests of rulers and subjects, and to their relations.

A village area is a clearly demarcated territory that traditionally formed a fief, and under British rule, this served as the smallest unit of local administration. Besides the village capital it normally contains a few hamlets, scattered within the area. Each hamlet forms a separate administrative ward under a resident ward-head, who is either the founder or some member of the putative founder's family. The village capital is likewise divided into wards, each under a resident head, some wards being inhabited by families of the same occupational group, for example, dyers or blacksmiths.

POLITICAL ORGANIZATION

The institutions of office, kinship, slavery, and clients have provided the main principles of Hausa government from the sixteenth century until recently.

The concept of office

Traditional and modern government proceeds through a system of titled offices (*sarautu*, singular, *sarauta*), each of which is in theory a unique indissoluble legal corporation having definite rights, powers and duties, special relations to the throne and to certain other offices, special lands, farms, compounds, horses, praise songs, clients, and, formerly, slaves. Until the British occupation of 1900–1903, the principal offices of any Hausa state were distributed among the dynasty, noble lineages (most of which were Fulani), certain clerical groups, the ruler's clients, eunuchs, and throne slaves. An order of occupational officials, which was mainly reserved for commoners, had little direct political importance, though of value administratively.

The interplay of kinship and office is seen in the position of noble lineages. These are units that have maintained prominent political positions over the generations. Some clerical lineages with hereditary interests in judicial and priestly offices form a distinct section of this nobility. In most states, though not in Zaria, the major offices are traditionally distributed among these descent groups, so that each office tends to be filled from one or two lineages that lack claims to other offices of the system. Under these conditions, rank and lineage intertwine closely. A noble lineage contains a number of competing descent lines, with historic rivalry among them, and with differing ties of alliance and clientship. The relative rank of these descent lines depends on their political successes, and genealogical segments that have failed to maintain political prominence often fail to maintain lineage status.

DYNASTIC OFFICE · Divisions arising on the basis of competition for office within such noble lineages are naturally most acute and important in the ruling dynasty. Some states, such as Zaria and Katsina, have two or more dynasties, each divided internally in various degrees. Others, such as Kano or Sokoto, which have only one ruling line, display the same essential structure, the single dynasty being quite as effectively subdivided into competing segments or "houses," as is Zaria with its three or four royal lineages.

Under both the Sultan of Sokoto and the British, candidates for a vacant throne were customarily subject to the evaluation of an electoral council composed mainly of official clerics from that state. This council's selection was subject to veto or approval in the last century by the sultan; in this, by the British. No members of a royal line could sit on these councils, which generally recommended the rotation of kingship among the local dynasties or rival segments of a single dynasty in order to reduce the chances of conflict. In deciding among otherwise eligible candidates for their nomination, the council paid special attention to the support that rivals could muster among their kin, but even more so through their clients and slaves. Nowadays, even at the village level, appointments still depend on these estimates of popular support, as shown by the number and character of kin and clients.

On appointment, a new ruler or official sought to put his close kin, clients, and slaves into strategic administrative positions, appropriate to their status. The greater the proportion of senior offices vested in particular descent lines, the fewer remained for the ruler to dispose of freely. Largely as an effect of their political histories, states differed significantly in these features.

Traditional offices differed in function, powers, and rewards. Territorial offices allocated to the dynasty, noble lineages, and the emir's senior clients, entailed both military and civil duties. Such officials administered dispersed fiefs that were permanently attached to their title, they attended the ruler at court, and took part in state councils and on campaigns. From their fiefs as required, they levied taxes, supplies, labor, and military forces. To communicate with the fiefs, each appointed a subordinate staff of titled assistants, these being drawn mainly from the officeholder's clients, close kin, and slaves. These titled staff members were each separately responsible for the administration of a particular fief, and as their reward, subtracted an appropriate portion of the tax and supplies they collected before passing on the remainder to the lord, who then removed his portion, and turned the rest over to the ruler. On campaigns, a lord's titled staff members acted as captains of the troops drawn from their several villages.

Each state had two official priests, who presided over the Friday mosque and the two annual Sallahs (Id-el-Fitr and Id-el-Kabir), respectively, and generally sat on the electoral council. Other offices reserved for clerics included palace priesthoods, judgeships, legal assessorships, official scribes, and the Sarkin Mallamai (Chief Mallam).

Throne eunuchs and slaves had responsibility for the treasury, the harem, the ruler's farms and granary, the royal stables, insignia, drums, the town gates, and also served as warders, policemen, and executioners. Senior eunuchs and slaves were the main channels of communication between the emir and important officials. In war, throne slaves attended the ruler, and formed part of the fighting force.

Besides clerical offices, certain special functions were allotted to free officials of high rank, for example, supervision of major public buildings, such as new towns, control of caravan routes and collection of tolls, control and maintenance of waterways, and the like. The ruler's bodyguard and senior palace officials were also freemen, directly dependent on him for their maintenance.

Clientship

Until men become heads of their own compounds, they remain political minors, though technically responsible for their actions at law. As compound-heads they may enter into clientship independently, although sons generally maintain the relations established by their fathers. Destitute men seek protection, food and shelter from prominent men as yaran gida, barori (menial clients or house servants), the master providing their clothes, tax, food, accommodation gayauna (personal farm plot), and, in due course, bride-wealth for marriage. Clients of independent means retain their mutumci (manhood or self-respect) by restricting their relations to jural and political issues. The economically independent client visits his lord to seek advice

and political assistance in his affairs, to keep the lord informed of developments that affect him, to offer advice and greetings, and, at the lord's request, to discharge some duty compatible with the client's status.

In all cases, clientship links individuals of unequal status, fortune, and
political position or prospect. *Mallamai* and wealthy merchants render *chapka*
(allegiance) to those who rule them, but maintain *barantaka* (clientship)
with some nobleman holding high office or prospects. These clients themselves have others who treat them as patrons and whom they regard as their
clients. Clientship of proven strength and value provides a basis for generous
economic aid, political appointments, and intermarriage, the patron often
giving his loyal client a kinswoman as wife. Traditionally, lords also gave
their clients horses, along with saddles, swords and other fighting equipment,
the clients in return being obliged to attend the lord on campaigns or as
otherwise required. Abolition of war has not eliminated this feature of clientship entirely, but horses are reserved by the lord nowadays for his *fadawa*
(courtiers), *jekadu* (agents), and immediate entourage.

It is a rule that the clients may have only one lord whereas the lord
has many clients whose individual attachment to his interest is shown by
their actions on his behalf. Those clients more closely identified with the
patron's interest are most likely to receive political appointments from him.
However, in all cases, although in differing degrees, clientship entails mutually beneficial relations and solidarity of interest of client and lord, even
where the relations of clientship lie direct to an office, rather than to its
holder.

Political structure under the British

Under the British, fief-holders were reduced in number and transformed into
resident district heads. The number of Muslim courts and judicial assessorships increased until almost every district had a court under a qualified
Muslim judge. Except for ward-heads, all officials have been placed on
salaries. The emir's office now handles the bulk of his official correspondence,
and the state treasury has been separated from the ruler's privy purse and
greatly developed to handle budget preparation, and the administration of
emirate funds. New departments of the emirate administration administer
public works, schools, prisons, police, sanitation and native dispensaries,
agriculture, veterinary work, forestry, and the like. The emir selects and appoints these departmental heads, as well as the judges, district heads, and
other senior officials on traditional principles. Some old titles have accordingly changed their function while retaining the same *sarauta* (ruling) form.

Nowadays the capital contains the ruler's court, the departmental head
offices, the treasury, the state prison, the court of appeal, and the agencies of
the Northern Regional government. With recent liberalization, the powers

formerly vested in the emir are now shared with a council, the members of which are the senior departmental heads living in the capital and selected by the emir. A popular element represented by an "outer council" meets periodically to receive reports from the emir's councilors on the progress of local schemes. However, the emir still retains decisive power.

THE DISTRICT HEAD • The rural areas are organized in districts, each containing between ten and thirty village units, under its district head, whose capital contains the district court, and representatives from the main emirate departments. Through his staff of messengers and state police, the district head enforces emirate regulations, court orders, and generally supports the district departmental officials. A district council on which the villages are represented meets periodically to discuss local development plans. Within the district, its head retains decisive control. Traditional relations between the district head and both the village chiefs and the villagers persist substantially.

THE VILLAGE CHIEF • Under the British the district head replaced the fief-holder, resident in the capital, in whose jurisdiction the village traditionally lay. This man customarily selected the village chief, although the latter was formally appointed by the emir at court with turban and gown. The village chief's duties included maintenance of public property, especially the mosque, the village walls, the market, and the official compounds reserved for the fief-holder and the chief, and cultivation of the fief-holder's farm, all done by corvée labor of the villagers. Village chiefs also used corvée labor to cultivate their own fields. As instructed by the fief-holder's agent or representative (the *jekada*), the chief also organized collection and dispatch of stated amounts of tax, formerly paid in cowries and cloth, supplies, especially grain or craft products, or men for work at the capital or for campaigns. Villagers transported these items as required. When summoned for a military expedition, the village chief assembled all his local horsemen, together with as many foot and bowmen as required. In recompense for these duties, the village chief exercised ill-defined powers to make levies on the local market, to employ forced labor in working his farm; he also received some of the tax collected in his area. During the last century he exercised a customary jurisdiction over minor issues such as divorce, *fada* (quarrels, fighting) that arose in his village, together with inheritance, where the estates were not large enough to interest the fief-holder. The village chief had to keep the fief-holder informed of all noteworthy local developments, such as the arrival of strangers, the withdrawal of villagers, the movements of pastoral Fulani through the fief, news of raids or caravan movements, harvest failures, epidemics, the deaths or disloyalty of officials, popular disaffection, and the like. Ward-heads were thus subject to dismissal by the fief-holder or his representative on recommendation of the village chief.

Today, the village chief controls unoccupied land in his village area, but generally delegates to their resident heads power over land which borders bush hamlets. He may likewise authorize heads of village wards to administer unoccupied plots and house sites in their wards, but usually retains these powers himself. A stranger wishing to live and farm in the village area approaches the head of a ward in which his friends or kin are settled, seeking an empty compound or house site and lands for farming. The ward-head informs the village chief, who might allocate some unused fallow land or compound to the immigrant and may also give him some grain. When the stranger has thus received fallow sufficient for his home farm, he selects a tract of uncleared bush for the main field and inquires of the ward-head if it had ever been farmed. Fallow belongs to its last occupant, unless he has died without heirs or moved away permanently, in which case control reverts to the village chief or to the head of the hamlet. Usufructuary rights in land vest in the man who cleared it, provided he resides in the territory of its village chief. Land rights are thus contingent on community membership, expressed as allegiance to the community chief, whose office includes trusteeship for the community over its unoccupied land.

THE WARD-HEAD • As noted above, a village area is a clearly demarcated territory that traditionally formed a fief, and, in addition to the village capital, normally contains a few hamlets. Each hamlet forms a separate administrative ward under a resident ward-head. It was noted that the village capital is likewise divided into wards, each also under a resident head.

Ward-heads bear traditional village titles and are often drawn from particular families living in the ward that have traditional claims to these offices. Besides residence and descent, a good reputation, good health, a fair body of supporters, and the attainment of middle or senior age are important considerations for appointment. Equally important is personal loyalty to the village chief, expressed as *chapka* (allegiance) or clientship.

When a ward-headship falls vacant, through death or dismissal, the village chief may call on ward elders to select a suitable successor from the ward, or he may simply appoint a *mukaddas* (interim deputy) and await the approaches of candidates. Having selected someone for the post, he organizes support among the ward elders, and then informs his immediate superior, the district head, that a successor has been found. After a formal check to discover the elders' reactions, the district head summons the village chief and his nominee to the district headquarters, and formally invests the latter with turban and robe, after some instruction in his duties and obligations. The district head appoints the candidate only as head of the particular ward. The new ward-head receives his village title from the village chief to whom he is directly responsible.

Village titles generally repeat the more ancient and important titles of their emirate, such as *Madaki* (war leader), *Galadima* (chief civil administrator), *Ma'aji* (treasurer), *Sarkin Fada* (head of the ruler's palace staff), *Limam* (imam or priest), *Ciroma* or *Magaji* (heir), and the like. In stable communities, each of these titles is traditionally linked with headship of a particular ward, and often with particular families in them. As new wards emerge through population growth, immigration, or the founding of hamlets, new titles may be taken from the emirate list or, in the case of hamlets, the new offices may be left with its bare designation of *mai-anguwa* (ward-head).

OCCUPATIONAL TITLES · Titles allocated to occupational groups in villages were also replicas of traditional offices held in the emirate capital. At both levels each *sana'a* (major craft or trade) formed a unit under the charge of an official head drawn from its practitioners. Thus, blacksmiths, butchers, brokers, and others all had an officially appointed head, responsible for collecting occupational taxes, for organizing work required by the rulers, for informally supervising the market, and for consulting with other craft heads or the chief as necessary. Most of these craft titles at the emirate and lower levels were filled by non-Fulani Hausa.

To discharge their duties and especially to collect the occupational tax craft officials appointed by an emir appointed assistants to subordinate titles, also drawn from the emirate's main series of titles. Thus, *Sarkin Makeran Kano* (the Chief of the Blacksmiths of Kano City) was appointed by *Sarkin Kano* (the Emir of Kano), and was responsible for blacksmiths throughout the emirate. He appointed as assistants a *Galadiman Makeran Kano*, a *Madaki*, and others, giving each responsibility for dealing with the blacksmiths in certain districts. Usually the titled assistants of a senior official were drawn from his close kin, clients, and slaves. These titled assistants in turn recruited their helpers from similar categories.

At the village level, craft heads were selected and appointed by the village chief from resident families engaged in these specialties, and they would also appoint titled assistants with responsibility for their craftsmen in particular wards. The local craft head called on these assistants as required in his dealings with the village chief or with the representative of the head of his craft in the emirate. Occasionally a local craft head, such as the *Sarkin Pawa* (Chief Butcher) would also serve as a ward-head; but with the exception of butchers, who experience some residential segregation, and dyers, whose homes surround the block of dye pits where they work, this coincidence was unusual. Ward-headship is a territorial office, whereas craft titles combine duties and responsibilities for a given occupational group, the members of which are generally dispersed. These occupational offices persist despite loss of their major manifest functions.

POLITICAL ORGANIZATION: AN ANALYTICAL SUMMARY • Hausa
society as an association of rulers and ruled, nobles and commone
ethnic terms, Fulani and Hausa. These dichotomies are useful l
quate. There is a complex continuous stratification that does not exactly cu.
respond to ethnic or political distinctions. Most rulers are Fulani, but most
Fulani and most rulers themselves are subject to others.

The most appropriate model of Hausa stratification is that based on occupational class. This model applies mainly to males, since females are jural
minors, have differing occupations and modes of ranking themselves, and,
marrying several times, do not take their husband's status. Among men, occupation tends to be hereditary, sons learning their father's craft or trade during youth. Thus a system of occupational ranking ensures high social stability
while accommodating individual movement and some shifts in the relative
status of the differing occupational groups. Even so, there are numerous exceptional cases, linked with differences of age, wealth, birth status, residence
and types and number of occupations that an individual combines; but the
occupational model still serves Hausa as a useful preliminary guide to their
social order. In this scheme, *sarauta* (ruling) is an occupation and outranks
all others. *Mallanci* (Koranic learning) and *kasuwanci* (successful trading),
which have universalistic emphases, rank next. Below these comes the great
majority of the traditional Hausa occupations; ranking lowest of all are
butchers, praise-singers, drummers, blacksmiths, house servants, and
hunters.

This scheme corresponds very roughly with Hausa distinctions between
the rich and powerful—those who are economically independent and observe
Islam—and the economically unstable strata whose observance of Islam is
questionable. Bonds of clientship that presuppose status difference link individuals of different strata into local and wider political factions. Through
these ties, which extend laterally to kinsfolk, the different strata are effectively linked into a system of contraposed segments whose leaders all declare
allegiance to the same institutions of government and Islam. The ceremonious
etiquette of social relations minimizes the very real status differences in male
society and emphasizes mutual respect.

Ethos

The Hausa ethos stresses patient fortitude in the face of adversity, self-control, industry, thrift, pride in workmanship, and enjoyment of social relations. Hausa need these qualities in the face of annual epidemics, vagaries
of weather, marital instability, a high infant mortality, and personal misfortune in their dealings with superiors. The commoners are habituated to
obedience and tolerance, their rulers to political control. *Kunya* (shame) is a

major sanction compelling individual conformity to custom. Its strength is shown in the rejection and lifelong avoidance of the first-born by all Hausa parents.

KINSHIP ORGANIZATION

The domestic group

Two or more men, their wives and families, who work a common farm, live in the same compound, and share common food supplies, form a *gandu* (joint family *or* family farm). Such a group is regarded by the ward-head and village chief as a unit under the authority of a single man, normally its senior member. Officials therefore address their communications to junior members of the *gandu* through its head, who is also responsible in their eyes for the conduct of all his dependents, for the payment of any fines they incur, for the unit's total tax, and for such labor or supplies as may legitimately be required from the group.

In addition, the *gandu*-head, who is also the *maigida* (compound-head) must provide for certain group needs from the proceeds of the *gandu*. He oversees the provision of the unit's food throughout the year, seed for planting, farm tools, huts for members, and bridewealth for the marriages of young males. At *Sallah*, that is, *Id-el-Fitr* and *Id-el-Kabir*, he bears the cost of meat, kolas, and other delicacies consumed by the group, and he also provides the ceremonial gifts of boiled chicken and grain sent by the group to kin, neighbors, and friends at their weddings and naming ceremonies. The group is subsumed in those relations of clientage that he, as its head, maintains. To balance these obligations, the *gandu*-head controls the unit's male labor force within traditional limits. At his direction all work daily on the *gandu* until the *Azahar* prayer at 2:30 P.M., except on Fridays, the Muslim Sabbath. Dependent males are free at other times to pursue their special interests.

A householder farms with the aid of his sons, to whom he allocates small plots known as *gayauna*, which thereafter become theirs, together with the produce. As sons mature, their father increases their *gayauna* portions from the old farm, while clearing more bush with their aid for new family fields. In late adolescence, when marriage is near, boys become liable for the tax, and are enrolled on the village population register compiled annually by the village chief and the ward-heads as the basis for tax assessment within the village. It is at this stage that village authorities begin to describe the unit formed by the householder and his sons as a *gandu*. Thereafter, the tax due for each youth increases slightly each year until he marries and has his first children.

Normally, young men remain in their father's compound for some time after their marriage, continuing to work with their father on the family farm, while devoting their leisure to crafts or trade, as well as to their *gayauna*. If there are several sons, as they marry, living space in the family compound increasingly fails to accommodate all in comfort. The eldest son, being the first to marry, is usually the first to have several children and to seek a second wife of his own instead of his parents' choice. By this time, the younger sons should also have married, and the eldest may ask his father's permission to move out and establish his own compound nearby. Some men prefer to make this suggestion themselves, without waiting for their son's request.

When the new house site has been approved by the ward-head, the group sets about building, usually with help from neighbors, affines, and friends. When the compound is ready for occupation, the father gives a final portion of the family plots to his departing son. If the family owns valuable trees, such as baobab or locust bean, one or more of these may be transferred. Thereafter the new compound forms a separate unit for farming and domestic economy, as well as for payment of tax. Nonetheless, the young compound-head continues to defer to his father and communicates with officials through him.

Ganduna (singular, *gandu*) vary in their composition, the two most common forms being units that consist of a man and his sons, their wives and dependents, and those that represent a later phase of development, based on two or more brothers, their wives, and issue. Rarely do brothers continue to operate a *gandu* for very long after their father's death; and only exceptionally do we find the children of two brothers as the senior members of a common *gandu*.

Despite its great prestige among the Hausa, we rarely find that more than a quarter of the households in rural areas at any given time have the *gandu* form. In part, the low incidence of this ideal reflects the influence of economic differentiation on family structure, but even more clearly it exhibits the structural instabilities of this family organization itself. High divorce rates, coupled with polygyny and affectionate attachments to one's matrikin, operate to disperse paternal half brothers, especially those of similar age, who are subject to economic demands from their wives and have divisive polygynous aspirations. In these circumstances, brothers generally seek an amicable division of their father's estate and then either subdivide the compound formally by cutting a new entrance or separate, the younger generally moving out. Even when they merely partition the interior of the compound, but retain a common *zaure*, each takes charge of his own household as a separate economic unit, although the elder continues to be regarded as the compound-head.

A Housewife at Her Cooking Place

Marriage

MATRIMONIAL RELATIONS · Relations between husband and wives are governed by a mixture of *al'ada* (Hausa custom) and *shari'a* (Muslim law). The traditional division of labor among Muslim Hausa involves a pervasive separation of the sexes and emphasizes their divergent interests, even within the framework of marriage. Men are solely responsible for providing the traditional household needs: shelter, food, water, firewood, and an annual outfit of clothes for their wives. Some husbands, when short of grain, may not provide for a midday snack, leaving their wives to supply this themselves from their craft earnings. Men often become indebted to their wives for sums used to purchase foodstuffs or to pay the tax. Women have ample leisure, especially in polygynous households, and derive a useful regular cash income from their craft and petty trade.

Women's domestic obligations, on the other hand, involve no regular cash outlay, but consist simply of cooking, tending infants, and sweeping their quarters. Since sewing and laundry are male activities, husbands either undertake these tasks for their wives themselves or arrange for their performance by others. Farming; repairing buildings and houses; gathering firewood, grass, and forest products; marketing and transporting household supplies—all these are male responsibilities in which wives take no part. Even their own children do not necessarily bring husband and wife together, since fathers especially, and mothers to a lesser degree, are obliged to display marked restraint toward their own issue, although free to fondle or tease the children of unrelated persons or of kinsfolk of the next descending generation. Thus co-wives address one another's offspring with greater ease than they do their own; and both sexes are obliged to maintain a lifelong avoidance of their first-born, which includes reciprocal teknonymy. This avoidance often extends to the second and third child, though with diminishing intensity; and these early children are the ones most likely to be adopted by their grandparents, or by close collaterals, such as the mother's brother or the father's sister. Such adoptions are especially likely if the parents divorce, as often occurs.

A wife may not utter her husband's name or the names of his parents and elder siblings. The husband is expected to observe similar restrictions with regard to his wife and her senior kin. Correct behavior when approaching her husband requires that the wife express deference, for example, by kneeling, remaining to one side out of the direct line of vision, talking quietly, addressing him as *"Mallam,"* and always by her actions emphasizing his precedence and authority. The husband exhibits such behavior in relation to his wife's senior kin. The facts that a woman is a legal and political minor, and that after her marriage authority over her is divided between her brother as guardian and her husband, do not entirely account for this highly brittle and formal relationship. Many polygynists value warm relations with women. Traditionally, concubines, recruited from the slaves, provided these, the master distributing his concubines between his wives equally, or *daki-daki* ("hut by hut") as Hausa say, each co-wife, her children, and concubine forming a *daki* (separate segment) of the compound family, socially and at law. Now that concubinage is rare, prosperous men in large towns seek more equal heterosexual relations with leading prostitutes, the mistresses of local salons, whose wit and charm they admire.

Poorer men, after a brief experience with polygyny, may elect to maintain one wife only, although aware that this increases their dependence on her. They also face the difficulty of bridging the traditional gulf between wife and husband by establishing common interests and bonds. This may be more easily done if the two inhabit a separate compound of their own, where they may talk freely and without formality or strain, but few women enjoy such isolation. To maintain domestic peace polygynists are obliged to display identical behavior toward all their wives. This condition places a premium on formality and on the maintenance of social distance, on co-wives as well as on the husband; hence many men seek warmth elsewhere, and women often regard divorce as their only escape.

A man's first wife is known as *uwargida* (mother of the household). Co-wives rank in seniority in order of their marriage to the common husband. Such ranking may have little significance outside the household; but within it, the *amarya* (young bride) is definitely subordinate to her seniors. Since divorce is easy and general, junior co-wives are apt to seek relief from their senior rivals by behavior designed to promote the latter's divorce, and failing this, themselves to withdraw from the unit. The Hausa term for co-wife is *kishiya* ("the jealous one"). Under these conditions, only wealthy and powerful men with three or four wives may enjoy security against divorce. Data from Zaria suggest that, on the average, women marry three or four times each.

Under Islam, a man may not have more than four wives simultaneously, but as many concubines as he wishes. After the Hausa came under British rule, concubinage almost disappeared. By Muslim law, a concubine who bore her master a child was freed on the master's death, and her child had a share in the estate equal to that of other issue of the same sex. Although several emirs in the last century were sons of concubines, in most cases a man's children by concubines did not seem to inherit equally with those borne by wives. By custom, each wife undertakes to cook for the household two days in turn, sleeping with the common husband on those nights. Concubines attached to a wife's hut would discharge her chores for her, but receive only a half share of the husband's attention.

Hausa marriage is virilocal, and often, as we have seen, initially patrilocal also. Parents arrange their children's first marriages, when girls are thirteen or fourteen, and boys about twenty. The society has no legitimate role for unmarried adults. Women believe that in order to qualify for *Lahira* (Paradise), they must die in wedlock. The same term—*bazawara*—denotes widow and divorcee. All unmarried adults are equally *karuwai* (prostitutes, profligates); even married pimps and praise-singers do not receive this term. Yet the social stigma attached to those adults who remain single after widowhood or divorce is small compared with that directed at those, especially girls, who delay their first marriage beyond the customary age. The condition of such maidens is doubly abnormal. Being past childhood, they cannot rank as children, but being unmarried they lack adult status also. Even the status of prostitute is not open to them, since a previous marriage is its essential condition. Under these circumstances, young girls are not likely to resist indefinitely their parents' plans for their first marriage, since they cannot wed without their parents' active interest.

Parents prefer their children to marry close kin, especially first cousins. Fulani, following Islam, give the father's brother's children first preference. Native Hausa custom prefers marriage between cross-cousins, and with the mother's brother or the father's sister's daughter almost equally. Occasionally, we find the children of two sisters married to one another. Marriage between second cousins (either cross- or patrilateral), like that between first cousins, is frequent. Marriages between kin of different generations are exceedingly rare. Hausa rationalize their preference for cousin-marriage by claiming a greater stability for these unions than statistics may warrant.

PLAY ASSOCIATIONS · Despite much emphasis on seniority by age in the allocation of status and roles, Hausa society lacks a firm age grading. Children form play associations under titled leaders of their own choice, and by imitative play learn the rudiments of political behavior and etiquette. Even today, in certain areas, youths hold dry-season meetings known as *kallankuwa* in little "townships" of Guinea-corn stalks to which recently circumcised youngsters are brought for enrollment, where appointments are settled and titles distributed, and the group's dry-season schedule is discussed, or assignments given by the village elders are organized. Girls, who have a separate association under a leader of their own, are invited to this site for dances, courtship, and *tsaranci* (petting). Indiscipline in either group is countered by formal trials under the group head, the *mama* (head girl) or *Sarkin Samari* (Chief of the Youths) and by punishment consisting of special chores, money fines, or mild whippings. Without significant tasks, official sanction, or ritual functions and support, these associations also lack effective organization and continuity. On marriage, their senior members withdraw into adult roles, girls abruptly, young men somewhat less so. Rarely do girls marry their *tsaranci* partners, nor may a betrothed couple practice *tsaranci* together. Circumcision takes place at about seven years for boys, clitoridectomy occurs at naming for girls, and neither serves to ritualize any significant change of personal status; nor is there any initiation rite in the young people's play associations. The central *rite de passage* for both sexes takes place at their first marriage; hence the peculiarly anomalous condition of those who do not marry at the appropriate time.

BETROTHAL AND MARRIAGE CEREMONIAL · Marriage preambles are negotiated by the couple's parents, and include a number of minor transfers once betrothal is agreed, these sums being handed by the groom's family to the bride's parents for distribution among all the latter's kin to inform them of the coming event. An agreed amount of bridewealth must then be handed over to the girl's father, after which the wedding date is set. The boy, meanwhile, should give his future bride small presents, including money, especially at the main Muslim festivals.

Islamic marriage ceremony does not require the couple's presence. Before a small assembly of neighbors, the couple's fathers, and close kinsmen, a *mallam* recites the relevant Koranic prayers and passages, and the *sadaki*, a small sum of about ten shillings essential to the marriage in Muslim law, is handed by the groom's father to one of the bride's kin chosen as her *waliyi* (legal guardian) to be given to the bride. This simple ceremony completes the legal marriage. The customary *rite de passage* to which both groom and bride are subject on first marriage concludes that day, with the removal of the bride, veiled and on horseback, to her new home. It is this customary ceremony that translates young people into adulthood by marriage. Although the Muslim ceremony undergoes no change in subsequent marriages, the ritual seclusion, struggles to escape, washing, and staining with henna that mark the seven days' ceremony in first marriages are never repeated for the same persons, and usually the bridewealth transferred on behalf of a woman is also less in a second marriage. Such a marriage is celebrated with little ritual.

DIVORCE • Data collected during 1950 in Zaria show that about 8 percent of the men over twenty years of age in rural areas are likely to be wifeless at any moment, while 37 percent of the remainder have two or more wives. Under these conditions nearly 60 percent of the married women in these communities live in polygynous establishments. Despite the unusually high divorce rate characteristic of Hausa, the cultural rejection of spinsterhood means that divorce merely transfers women from one household to another.

Under Muslim law, a man may divorce his wife by word of mouth, and if he dismisses her thrice, divorce is final and no bridewealth may be reclaimed. The woman simply reports to the district court that her husband has dismissed her. He is summoned and questioned, and if the court finds the woman's report is true, she is instructed to return to her parents' compound for the three months' period of continence known as *iddah*, which Muslim law requires before she may remarry. However, if a woman appeals to the court for divorce and rejects reconciliation, the judge takes the amount of bridewealth into account, and decides how much should be returned according to the length of the marriage, its fertility, and other factors.

TYPES OF MARRIAGE • Hausa classify marriages according to the degree of wife seclusion involved, their mode of arrangement, and as first or later marriages. *Auren kulle* (purdah or complete wife seclusion) is mainly practiced by wealthy merchants, aristocrats, and clerics. *Auren tsare* (partial seclusion), under which the wife may obtain her husband's permission to leave the compound rather more easily, is very widespread. No wife seclusion, *auren jahilai* ("the marriage of the ignorant") is typical of butchers and other low-ranking strata.

Unions distinguished according to their differing bases include *auren zumunta*, "the marriage of kin or close friends"; *auren sadaka*, in which a maiden is given to some suitable *mallam* as representative of the Prophet without his prior knowledge and without request for bridewealth; *auren daukisandanka*, in which the woman remains in her own home and receives visits from her husband, this form being favored by young widows whose reputation requires their remarriage, but who desire to remain in their late husband's compound to protect their children's inheritance rights; and, finally, *auren mutsaya*, or marriage by exchange, traditionally used by owners to arrange marriages for their slaves and now extremely rare. These and other categories are of social rather than legal significance; at law, the obligations of husband and wife are constant in unions of each type. In this social classification of marriages, perhaps the most important dichotomy is that between *auren zumunta* and *auren so* (marriage of desire) or *auren bare* (marriage of nonkin). My data from Zaria communities in 1950 indicated that about one fourth of the unions current at any one time in the rural areas were based on kinship between spouses. Given current divorce rates, this implies a much higher incidence of kinship between spouses at their first marriage.

Other kinship features

Kinship terminology reflects historical factors, and is not properly classifiable as Eskimo, Hawaiian, or other. There are important alternatives, and, indeed, two quite different modes of reference, one very general and inclusive, the other equally specific and exact. In areas long subject to Fulani influence, the Fulani terms *goggo* and *kawu* (father's sister and mother's brother) have been adopted by Hausa. In Daura, Maradi, and other independent Hausa communities, father's sister is *baba*, a difference of tone distinguishing this clearly from the term for father which has the same spelling. A man's siblings and his parallel or cross-cousins of any degree are equally *'yanuwa* ("children of [my] mother"; singular, *danuwa*). But cross-cousins of either type are also addressed and described as *abokan wasa* ("joking relations"), whereas special terms distinguishing elder and younger brother and sister are generally restricted to real siblings, although often applied to cousins of either sort. These terms that distinguish siblings by birth order combine easily with terms for parents and children to provide an exact system of kinship denotation that Hausa employ whenever they wish. Thus a categorical statement about Hausa kinship presumes the selection of some kinship usages and the rejection of others. It seems sounder to relate these differing alternatives and their use to the general conditions of Hausa history and social structure.

Besides his cross-cousins and preferred spouses, a man jokes with his father's and mother's parents, real or classificatory, his grandchildren in similar range, and the younger siblings of his wife or wives. He has specially warm relations with his mother's brother, and father's sister, and his full or uterine sisters' children. He also enjoys affectionate relations with his last-born, who is known as *auta*, and approximates a grandchild; but his closest ties are to his mother. Respect and obedience are due his father and father's brothers, and his elder brothers and ortho-cousins. He may be married to his father's brother's daughter, or may be adopted by the father's brother, whose wife is addressed as *inna, uwa* (mother). He avoids his first-born, his wife's parents and elder siblings, his younger siblings' spouses, and, in the presence of others, his wife also. Teknonymy marks these avoidance relations.

Despite the agnatic basis of domestic groups, as illustrated by the *gandu*, and despite the unilineal features in this nomenclature, Hausa kinship is prevailingly bilateral, except among the political aristocracy and urban Muslim intelligentsia. A man's *zuri'a* or issue include those tracing descent from him through females as well as males. His paternal and maternal kin are verbally balanced as *dangin jini* (kin by blood) and *dangin nono* (kin by milk), or, more commonly, *dangin wajen uba* (kin on the father's side) and *dangin wajen uwa* (maternal kin). Cross-cousin marriage extends equally in either direction as does adoption, which is an important institution of Hausa kinship. The distribution of differentiated relationships between the paternal and the maternal kin is almost identical, given that agnation is the basis of joint and extended family groups.

Although the group identified as maternal kin have an agnatic core, Hausa commoners nonetheless lack a unilineal organization. Their agnatic descent groups are shallow, residential units that fade as sons move out, or brothers separate after their father's death. Islamic emphasis on the sub-divisions of estates among heirs, males of the same degree of kinship receiving twice the portion of females, except for shares fixed by law, coupled with Hausa custom by which a man distributes his land to his sons as they marry and establish their households, eliminates corporate property interests among agnates at this social level. In consequence, it is rare to find commoners who can trace kinship beyond their great-grandfather, and outside the range of siblingship, such ties involve no clearly defined interaction, common interests, or obligation. Men are free to stress bonds of kinship with such agnates as they wish, or with their maternal kin; and they may also rely more deeply on relations of clientship or bond-friendship.

Unlike commoners, aristocrats and clerical families having common interests in property and offices emphasize descent correspondingly. The competition of several lineages for political office reinforces their corporate status and interests simultaneously. Facial markings indicate an aristocrat's lineage permanently. Such marks may also serve as certificates of ethnic and social status. Lineages whose former members held large estates or founded slave villages retain common interests insofar as these property units persist undivided. An old compound in the capital also unites the group if it continues as corporate property in which the senior member lives and the family heirlooms and library of Arabic texts are preserved. Even so, rivalry between segments of a noble lineage especially over political appointments is handed down the generations and is a fertile source of fission.

CHILD TRAINING AND SOCIALIZATION

As male and female interests and roles are sharply distinguished, so are the typical male and female life cycles. Domestic rituals are a prime female interest, whereas extradomestic activity engages men. Pregnancies are only slightly marked by ritual actions, and most women give birth in their husband's compounds. Young mothers have to be then ritually compelled by their kinswomen to touch their first-born and suckle it. After delivery, the new mother engages in daily ritual ablutions of her pudenda in very hot water for a period of five months, her husband having devoted the last months of her pregnancy to assembling the necessary firewood. On first delivery, and less regularly thereafter, the mother returns to her parents' compound with the infant for this ritual washing on a visit known as *bangwalle*. Before she departs on the seventh day, a ram is sacrificed at the Muslim naming ceremony for the child. These repetitive childbirth rituals mark a woman's advancing maturity and achievements as a mother.

Children are breast-fed for about two years, during which time the mother should avoid sexual relations. Weaning occurs when the toddler is removed to a kinswoman's compound for *tallafi* (adoption), or, failing that, the mother anoints her breast with bitter foods. The child, already accustomed to the softer Hausa foods, then shifts to the standard diet of grain porridge and stew. Toilet training is gentle, children learning from those immediately older than themselves. Typically, an elder sister nurses the infant, and carries it about on her back when the mother is busy. The special attachment for their elder sisters that adult men retain has this childhood basis. At night in the women's huts, children listen to folktales, fables, and garbled history, but have little to do with their father and his brothers.

Circumcision, which young boys undergo at seven, perhaps with one or two others, is almost entirely devoid of ritual. Young girls at this time learn the arts of self-decoration, dress, and flirtatious talk. Their informal socialization continues within the compound, in the young people's play associations, at the markets, and often at Koranic school, and the regular round of farming, trading, *Sallah*, and Ramadan also helps to impress cultural patterns firmly upon them. (See "Play Associations," pages 144–145.)

Friendship

In later childhood, special friendships develop between children of the same sex and age who are not kin. Such bond-friends share their activities, resources, and secrets, hunt, trade, and visit together, and continually exchange gifts. At the rites of first marriage, an individual's bond-friends help to reduce the personal strain. In adult life, each man gradually singles out one of his former bond-friends as his *babban aboki* (special friend) with whom gifts, secrets, advice, and labor are freely shared. Besides kinsmen, only the *babban aboki* may freely enter a man's compound. These relations, which emphasize equal status, common interests, and mutual trust, are inherently exclusive and difficult to replace, once broken by emigration, betrayal, or death.

On their part, women, whose marriages involve movements between compounds and often between villages, seek to establish new bond-friendships wherever they live. A woman may therefore maintain such relations with several others of similar age, only a few of whom may be near neighbors. Given their seclusion in compounds and dispersal by marriage, women formalize their bond-friendships much more than do men. Although the gifts or labor that men exchange vary with their situations and abilities, women maintain a *biki* (formal exchange) in which gifts double at each transfer until their value forces a new beginning for the series. Women exchange these *biki* gifts whenever their partners have kinship ceremonials requiring some special outlay, such as a wedding, a childbirth, or a naming. The gifts themselves consist mainly of cash, derived from craft production and petty trade. By this institutionalized exchange, women are able to mobilize at short notice the amounts they need for these periodic outlays without getting into debt as their menfolk do. Thus despite their marginal position in the cash sector of the economy, women provide the main outlay on kinship ceremonies and consequently control them.

Among women of different families, ages or generations, formal relationships emphasizing status differences may be established on the model of male clientship. The senior woman, who is always patron, is consulted by the junior, who may also undertake certain tasks for the patron, receiving advice, instructions, and gifts in return. Like bond-friendships, these female client relations are individually exclusive, although a female patron may have several clients as do males. Ceremonial exchanges at the main Muslim festivals are a feature of all formal friendships.

RELIGION

For Hausa, Islam is a way of life as well as a set of beliefs in Allah and his Prophet. The five daily prayers, attendance at mosque on Fridays, the three main annual festivals, the yearly grain tithe, the annual Fast of Ramadan, and the recurrent fact of pilgrimage together represent local Islam most forcefully. In addition, the courts administer Muslim law modified by Hausa custom and the traditional schools teach Muslim texts. Much of Hausa folklore is Islamic, together with urban house types, dress, script and other cultural forms; and the standard Islamic injunctions and taboos are regularly observed in the country towns as well as in the cities. Within the Malikite framework, Hausa also align themselves either with the Tijjaniya or Kadiriya *tariqa* (schools), even when they do not enroll personally. The same sanctions of shame and ostracism which compel observance of Hausa custom apply also to Islam as Hausa know it, and they would find it very difficult to discriminate all their own indigenous institutions from the Islamic overlay. Even in rural areas, men of middle status eagerly attend visiting *mallamai* to learn Islamic lore and tradition more

Sallah (Festival) at Zaria
The scene is in front of the
emir's compound.

deeply; expeditions for this purpose are a standard dry-season activity of
their juniors. Thus whatever Hausa Islam might seem to the learned outsider, it is the dominant theme of life to the Hausa themselves. Actual com-
prehension of Islam may be inadequate, especially among the rural peasants;
but if questioned, any Hausa would point to their history as evidence of
Islamic affiliation.

Islam reached Hausa from the West in the mid-fourteenth century. As
caravans came to Kano and Katsina, the number of its adherents increased.
Elsewhere, paganism persisted even under the domination of Muslim Bornu.
In 1804–1810, the Fulani under Othman dan Fodio as *Sarkin Musulmi*
(Chief of the Muslims) came into conflict with the Hausa chief of Gobir,
and launched a *jihad* (holy war) for the purification of Islam in the seven
Hausa states by conquest. The *jihad* was successful, partly because of assistance from Muslim Hausa and Fulani settled in these areas. Dan Fodio's
lieutenants administered as his emirs the chiefdoms they had conquered. His
successors, as sultans of Sokoto, maintained this empire until the British under Lord Lugard established their Protectorate of Northern Nigeria in 1900–
1903. Throughout this century and the last, the ruling Fulani have justified
their dominion over the Hausa in terms of maintaining, extending, and
strengthening Islam, the same motives that underlay the Shehu's *jihad* of
1804–1810.

Today, overt deviance from Islam is limited to the spirit-possession cult,
which draws support mainly from women, butchers, hunters, blacksmiths,
praise-singers, and prostitutes, the latter providing the continuous organization on which cult activities and survival depend. As Greenberg has shown,
Muslim Hausa *bori* (spirits) have pagan Hausa antecedents, but also include
certain Arabic elements derived from the *jinn*, together with the practice of

spirit-possession. By appealing to spirits, women particularly seek benefits or personal relief as well as entertainment. The women's exposure to Islam having been restricted severely by those conditions that subordinate them to men while segregating them from men, women's greater interest in the traditional cult is easy to understand.

CHANGE

Like other African peoples, the Hausa have been subject to change during the past sixty years; but, perhaps as an effect of Lord Lugard's policy of indirect rule, their adjustment to changing conditions has been relatively smooth. With the introduction of railroads, automobiles and adequate roads, telegraphs, airplanes, and radio, the urban Hausa populations have acquired a modern communications system that has influenced the direction and the nature of trade. For example, cotton and groundnuts, shea nuts, hides and skins, and kapok are sent south on freight cars for export, as are Fulani cattle, locust beans, some grain, and other Northern products. In return, Hausa purchase palm oil, kolas, ginger, and Yoruba cloth from Southern Nigeria, and import an increasing number of manufactures from abroad. By air they go to Mecca in increasing numbers; the wealthier Hausa have their own motor vehicles, including some for commercial purposes. These innovations have encouraged the spread of mechanical skills, particularly in the large cities, but the countryman still knows only the old technology. Literacy, likewise, though low everywhere, is mainly found in the towns. A Roman script introduced by the British is now in official use. Christianity has made little headway in this population, Lugard having guaranteed the preservation of Islam; but Christian missionaries have helped to spread Western attitudes toward health, child care, and education. Currently the Hausa rulers are greatly concerned to increase elementary education and adult literacy.

In 1952 the principle of electoral representation was introduced by the British. The Hausa supported a regional political party, the Northern People's Congress, along with the Muslims of Bornu, and this party has since dominated Northern politics. Within the emirates, popularly elected councils have been created at both district and emirate levels. Although these changes are not very noticeable in the rural areas they have important implications.

Notes

(1) This diagram first appeared in *Baba of Karo* (London: Faber and Faber, Ltd., 1954) by Mary F. Smith and was reprinted in *The Economy of Hausa Communities of Zaria Province, Northern Nigeria.* (London: Her Majesty's

Stationery Office, 1955) by the present author. It is reproduced here by permission of Faber and Faber Ltd., Mary F. Smith, and the Controller of Her
Britannic Majesty's Stationery Office.

Bibliography

The following bibliography emphasizes both recent and historical works.
Daggered items (†) are cited as references in the text of the chapter.

Arnett, E. J. (1922). *The Rise of the Sokoto Fulani.* Kano, Nigeria: Emirate
Printing Co.
Part translation and part paraphrase of Sultan Mohammed Bello's *Infak'ul
Maisur,* this is a detailed account of the context and development of the
Fulani Jihad of 1804–1810, with concise historic précis and dating by Arnett.

Barth, H. (1961). *Travels in Nigeria, 1850–1855* (selected and edited and with
an introduction by A. H. M. Kirke-Greene). London: Oxford University
Press. Passages from the detailed journals in which Barth describes the Muslim
Hausa, Fulani, and Kanuri peoples as he found them in the mid-nineteenth
century. With a scholarly appraisal of Barth and his work.

Cole, C. W. (1949). *Report on Land Tenure in Zaria Province.* Kaduna,
Nigeria: Government Printer.
Useful especially for its summary of the legal context of claims to land based
on the Jihad of 1804–1810 and for concise statements of prevailing Hausa
forms of land tenure.

Denham, D., and others (1826). *Narrative of Travels and Discoveries in North-
ern and Central Africa in the Years 1822, 1823, and 1824.* 2d ed. London:
John Murray.
Journal of the first successful European exploration of Northern Nigeria,
describing conditions in Bornu and the Fulani empire at the time of Sultan
Bello.

Greenberg, J. (1946†). *The Influence of Islam on a Sudanese Religion.* Monograph of the American Ethnological Society, No. 10. New York: J. J.
Augustin.
Ethnography of the pagan Hausa (Maguzawa) of Kano tied into careful
documentary and field studies of the Muslim Hausa cult of spirit-possession
to shed light on pre-Islamic religious practices among Hausa, and certain
conditions of Islamic conversion.

——— (1947). "Islam and Clan Organization among the Hausa," *Southwestern Journal of Anthropology,* Vol. 3, pp. 193–211.
Brilliant sociological analysis of conflicting Muslim and pagan Hausa rules
of kinship and marriage, again with decisive implications for Hausa ethnology.

——— (1955†). *Studies in African Linguistic Classification.* New Haven,
Conn.: The Compass Publishing Co.

Heath, F. (1952). *A Chronicle of Abuja*. Ibadan, Nigeria: Ibadan University Press.
Translation of two volumes by Mallams Hassan and Shu'aibu, members of the royal house of Abuja, describing the ethnography and history of this Habe successor-state of Zaria (Zazzau).

Hogben, S. J. (1930). *The Muhammadan Emirates of Northern Nigeria*. London: Oxford University Press.
Terse histories of Muslim emirates and empires of northern Nigeria drawn from provincial gazetteers and placed in the wider context of the history of the western Sudan.

Meek, C. K. (1925). *The Northern Tribes of Nigeria*. London: Oxford University Press, 2 vols.
Excellent ethnographic account of this region, its peoples, and their cultures at a time when European influence was still weak. Especially useful for comparative and ethnological studies.

Palmer, H. R. (1908). "The Kano Chronicle," *Journal of the Royal Anthropological Institute,* Vol. 38, pp. 58–98.
English version of the Arabic text giving best single account of the history and development of a representative Hausa state from earliest times.

———— (1926). *Sudanese Memoirs*. Lagos, Nigeria: Government Printer, Vol. III.
Potpourri of translated Arabic texts relevant to the histories of Bornu, Kano, Katsina, Daura, and Azben (Air), with learned commentaries and disquisitions by one of northern Nigeria's most distinguished administrators and scholars. Full of useful suggestions and ethnological hypotheses.

Perham, M. (1937). *Native Administration in Nigeria*. London: Oxford University Press.
Lucid and well-documented study of local administration under Indirect Rule throughout Nigeria twenty-five years ago, with special emphasis on the northern area, by Lord Lugard's biographer.

Rattray, R. S. (1913). *Hausa Folklore, Customs and Proverbs*. London: Oxford University Press.
Useful introductory ensemble by the future ethnographer of Ashanti.

Robinson, C. H. (1899). *Hausaland, or Fifteen Hundred Miles through the Central Sudan*. London: Sampson, Low.
Vivid account of Hausa and other areas of northern Nigeria by the last of the pioneers before Lugard imposed the *Pax Britannica*. Robinson, who trekked north to Kano, spoke fluent Hausa.

Rowling, C. W. (1949). *Land Tenure in Kano Province*. Kaduna, Nigeria: Government Printer. Tight and informative analysis of land tenure, and the changes that accompany modern population movements, increase, and registration.

Smith, Mary F. (1954). *Baba of Karo: A Woman of the Moslem Hausa*. London: Faber & Faber, Ltd.; New York: Praeger (1964).

This old Hausa woman's life story, spanning the last decades of the last century and the first half of this, gives valuable data on feminine roles and attitudes, especially in kinship, ritual, socialization, and marriage.

Smith, M. G. (1955). *The Economy of Hausa Communities of Zaria*. London: H. M. Stationery Office.
A report on a social and economic survey of Zaria Hausa that seeks to place the economy in its social and historical context.

———— (1959). "The Hausa System of Social Status," *Africa*, Vol. 29, pp. 239–252.
Summary description of stratification in Hausa societies.

———— (1960). *Government in Zazzau, 1800–1950*. London: Oxford University Press.
An attempt to combine structural analysis with a detailed history of one of the larger Hausa states—Zaria—drawing on data supplied by the *Chronicle of Abuja*, translated by F. Heath, above.

Tremearne, A. J. N. (1913). *Hausa Superstition and Customs*. London: John Bale.
Useful collection of ethnographic data describing non-Islamic as well as Islamic practices observed among Hausa by an early British administrator with anthropological interests.

———— (1914). *The Ban of the Bori*. London: Heath, Cranton, Ltd.
Used by Greenberg in his study of pagan and Muslim Hausa spirit-cults, this study describes the beliefs and practices of spirit-possession found among the Muslim Hausa early in this century.

Trimingham, H. S. (1959). *Islam in West Africa*. London: Oxford University Press.
A classic study of tremendous range and depth of the variety of patterns found among west African Muslims, including Fulani and Hausa.

———— (1962). *A History of Islam in West Africa*. London: Oxford University Press.
Easily the best and most penetrating introduction to this topic in English, a permanently valuable contribution to history, to Islamic, and to African studies. Perfectly places the Islamic penetration and the Fulani conquest of Hausa in context.

5

THE JIE OF UGANDA

about the chapter

The Jie of Uganda are one of the Nilotic cattle-herding peoples of East Africa whose life centers about their livestock, especially their cattle. In many ways they typify the cultural type of East African cattle herders prominent in the theories of early Africanists. Although agriculture provides most of their staple food, livestock products such as blood, meat, and milk are important in the Jie diet, as other animal products are in the economy. Transhumance, as one pattern of animal husbandry, shows an adjustment to the features of habitat, as it does among the pastoral Fulani and the Somali.

In his structural analysis Gulliver points out that the herds are important as stores of social as well as economic value, and that the transfer of livestock is important in establishing and maintaining social relationships. As among the Somali, prestige devolves from large herds, but even more from the ways in which the beasts are used. The transfer of livestock establishes marriage and hence ensures the continuity of the family. In this respect there is a strong resemblance to the pastoral Fulani. Gulliver describes how animals are distributed among household groups and wider kin groups in a way that recognizes both the corporateness of the group and its ties with other groups. In addition to kinship ties, ties of friendship with trading partners and other "stock-associates" are established and maintained by the transfer of animals. Cattle are indispensable too for settling disputes and for the proper carrying out of ritual, but they have no special spiritual value for the Jie as they do for some other Nilotic groups.

The Jie religion and age group system are fused into one integrated institution. Traditionally, the Jie had no chiefs, and their society

157

was, and largely still is, organized not in terms of political functionaries or of a centralized political structure, but in terms of communal rituals carried out at territorial levels. The requirement that all men—men from different kin groups and different settlements—unite for the carrying out of crucial ritual means that age group membership, like tribal fraternity membership among the Kpelle, cuts across the narrow bonds of genealogy and residence to provide a network of wider ties. Furthermore, age group membership gives each man a position of relative seniority in relationships with other men and a designated role in the communal ritual. Junior men are supposed to obey the orders of senior men on pain of supernatural punishment and ritual impurity. This gives weight to the elders' enunciation of norms on ritual occasions, and even to their intervention in instances of open violence. Thus Gulliver's analysis demonstrates that the age group organization, although primarily ritualistic in focus, takes on marginal judicial and political functions and serves as an integrative institution. This fusion of religious and political institutions is characteristic of many sub-Saharan societies including the Bantu Tiriki, the Kpelle, and the Tiv.

An understanding of the Jie is important to anyone interested in cultural change in Africa today, for they, like many Nilotic herders, show a strong resistance to acculturation, including Westernization. Jie habitat is one with limitations that restrict the utility of Western technology and ideas and hence possibilities of change. Their resistance is based also in part on their adherence to pastoral values, which focus on individualism and the social and economic worth of livestock.

about the author

P. H. Gulliver, Reader and Lecturer in African Anthropology at the School of Oriental and African Studies, University of London, received the Wellcome Bronze Medal for Anthropological Research of the Royal Anthropological Institute of Great Britain and Ireland in 1957. He received his Ph.D. from the University of London in 1952, and has taught at that institution in the London School of Economics, as a visiting professor at Harvard University, and in the African Studies Program at Boston University. From 1952 to 1958 he was Research Sociologist for the government of Tanganyika, where he did extensive field research. Dr. Gulliver has also conducted field research in Kenya (1948–1950), in Southern Rhodesia (1961), and in Uganda (1950–1951). He is author of *Preliminary Survey of the Turkana* (1951), *The Central Nilo-Hamites* (with Pamela Gulliver, 1953), *The Family Herds* (1955), and *Social Control in an African Society* (1963) and editor of and contributor to *The Family Estate in Africa* (with Robert Gray, 1964).

P. H. GULLIVER · *The Jie of Uganda*[1]

INTRODUCTION

LOCATION · The Jie[2] are a small tribe, numbering 18,200 people in 1948, living in the north-central part of Karamoja District in northeastern Uganda. Culturally and linguistically they are part of the Teso Cluster, an eastern Nilotic group, which comprises a number of related peoples in contiguous territory in eastern Uganda, northwestern Kenya and the southern Sudan.

LANGUAGE · The dialects of this cluster of people are mutually intelligible, though clearly distinctive. They have conventionally been classified in the Nilo-Hamitic language group (Tucker and Bryan 1948); alternatively the group is identified as the Great Lakes subdivision of the Nilotic branch of the Eastern Sudanic subfamily of African languages (Greenberg 1955:62).

PHYSICAL APPEARANCE · The Jie have no outstanding physical characteristics to distinguish them from surrounding East African peoples. They are of average height and have a fairly uniform dark brown skin: only a few individuals have lighter or reddish skins. Hair and facial features are of the Negroid type. As a result perhaps of their well-balanced and generally adequate diet, the people have a good physique. Their children, who are always given priority in the distribution of milk, appear to be healthier than those in many African societies.

ETHOS · The life of the Jie is based on a mixed economy; but although agriculture provides the bulk of the staple food—sorghum for porridge—the Jie themselves give major importance to the care and value of their livestock, particularly cattle. From these animals they obtain additional food staples, and hides and skins. Unlike agriculture, livestock have a significance beyond food production. They have a notable aesthetic value, and they are essential to the rich complex of rituals that would be thought ineffective without the slaughter of oxen. Above all, livestock are the agents in all important social relations and transactions. For the Jie, every major bond of kinship or formal friendship creates a channel along which livestock may pass in either direction so that the two people may assist one another. For these reasons the herds are stores of value, economic and social capital, and the only capital the Jie have. Some prestige accrues to the owners of a large herd, but greater prestige accumulates from the proper use and disposal of animals in ongoing social life. Unlike some African pastoralists, the Jie ascribe little spiritual significance to their animals. Critically important though they are, cattle are not thought to have or to symbolize mystical qualities.[3]

In all social transactions (including rituals) involving domestic animals, the "small stock" (goats and sheep) are used as the lesser units but for essentially the same purposes as cattle. In addition, most families have one or two donkeys for pack purposes—to carry water in the dry season, to carry loads on barter trips, to transport thatching grass, and so on. Little or no aesthetic value is attached to small stock or to donkeys.

ECONOMY

Pastoralism

The Jie are comparatively wealthy in livestock, with an average of three to four cattle, and four small stock, per human being. Their cattle are the humped Zebu type, and they provide milk and blood, meat, and hides. Children are given preference for milk when it is in short supply toward the end of the dry season, but it is a favorite food of both adults and children. Blood, taken from the necks of living animals, is consumed fresh or mixed with other foods. The principal occasions on which meat is eaten occur when an animal is slaughtered for ritual purposes; beasts are rarely killed simply to provide meat. Jie do not normally milk she-goats and ewes, regarding their milk as much inferior, but children are permitted to take it if they wish.

HABITAT AND CLIMATE · Because the Jie environment is harsh and tropical, it closely affects their subsistence economy. Jieland lies in the semiarid savannas of upland East Africa, at an altitude of about 4000 feet, with almost no higher land except on the extreme borders (see map). There are two major divisions in the year: the rainy season, lasting from about late March to early August, with a dry spell of at least two or three weeks in about June; and the dry season, during which virtually no rain falls and when torrid conditions are exacerbated by hot, dust-laden winds from the semidesert lands to the east. Although Jieland is small—roughly sixty-five miles from east to west, and twenty-five miles from north to south—there are two fairly distinct ecological regions. In the eastern region, about one third of the country, rainfall is not more than about twenty-five inches in the

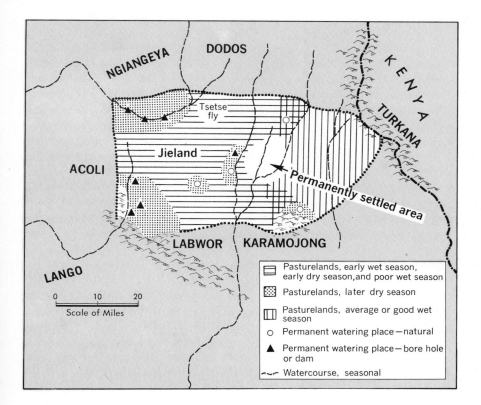

Sketch Map of Jieland[1]

season; here there is open, treeless savanna thinly covered with seasonal short grasses, and without water soon after the rains cease. In the western region rainfall is probably up to thirty-five inches, it is more reliable in both quantity and distribution, and the season tends to be more prolonged. Here are moderately dense bush and small trees with a thick cover of long perennial grasses; water is more plentiful, and there are a number of permanent watering places. The Jie attempt to make best use of their meager natural resources by pastoral transhumance between east and west regions, which they use for their herds in the rainy and dry seasons, respectively.

SETTLEMENT PATTERN · Permanent settlement is limited to a small area in the middle of the country, in the borderland between the two regions. Here in fixed homesteads arranged in stable communities live some four fifths of the population—women, children, and most of the men—at a local density of about 130 persons per square mile; here, too, are all the arable lands. The bulk of the herds are kept in separate mobile camps in the pasture lands and are tended by youths and young men subsisting directly off the livestock. Only small dairy herds and a few small stock are kept at the homesteads, and even these are sent to the camps toward the end of the dry season when local pastures and water are exhausted. A camp is an easily built affair—a ring of brushwood often suffices to keep the animals enclosed at night. It may be divided into the kraals of the separate owners, but not always. In the dry season herders usually sleep in the open under cattle hides; in the rainy season rough shelters are put up. A few essential utensils for milking, making butter, and storing blood and fat are all that are needed. Each herder has his own spears, necessary to protect the animals against hyenas, leopards, and lions. A camp can be abandoned and another made with ease. The pasture lands are dotted with deserted camps, for the Jie always build a fresh camp in a new location after a move.

PASTORAL CYCLE • The pastoral cycle is briefly as follows: by about the middle of the rainy season the stock camps are all located in the eastern region, where, by that time, new grass has grown sufficiently and surface water collects in pools and stream beds. Camps are scattered throughout the region. Dairy herds are at their largest in the homesteads, and milk supply is at its peak. As the dry season sets in, both grass and water quickly become exhausted and camps must shift westward. There is an irregular migration of the camps, for it is entirely the responsibility of each herd owner to determine the timing and direction of movement as he assesses the situation. At first in the western region water supplies are sufficient to allow a widespread scatter of camps, but as the time of the last rains recedes, surface water dries up and camps are compelled to converge on one or another of the half-dozen permanent watering places for the remainder of the season. The choice of watering place is a matter for each herd owner to decide, although usually he tends to put his camp near the same one each year. Nevertheless, some readjustment of locations does occur each dry season when some places tend to become overcrowded or when men decide to shift for personal reasons. With the onset of the next rainy season it again becomes possible for camps to scatter through the western region as fresh grass and water are available. Then there is a shift back to the east, where the rains come a little later.

In this pastoral cycle each camp shifts at least four or five times a year. No individual Jie, nor any group, can lay claim to any particular part of the pasture lands, which are entirely communal. Environmental conditions are the only controlling force, with a single exception: intense public disapproval effectively prevents a camp from remaining in the western region throughout the rainy season (though this is physically possible). It is recognized that western pastures should be rested and allowed to reseed naturally, and it is also considered logical to leave those pastures for later use while taking advantage of the purely temporary pastures in the east. In addition, camps in the east are rather nearer the homesteads, and men like to have their herds as near as possible during the latter part of the rainy season, when animals are frequently required during that time of intense social and ritual activity. Also the young men at the camps are then able easily to visit and to participate in such activities.

Although the camps are the domain principally of youths and young men, older men visit their herds frequently, staying a week or two, in order to supervise arrangements and perhaps to make a decision on the spot regarding a move. Women make briefer visits, bringing some cereal foods for their sons and taking back milk and butter. The young men make visits to the homesteads, perhaps alternating with their brothers and cousins so that each can spend some time at home. As cows come into milk, some of them are transferred to the homestead; cows that go dry are sent to the camp; and some animals have to be fetched to the homestead for various purposes.

If the herds are large enough and if enough herders are available, small stock are put in a camp separate from the cattle. But usually only the wealthiest owners maintain camps of their own: generally the herds of two or three owners are kept in a single camp and herded together in the pastures, with duties shared by the younger brothers and sons of the owners. The commonest cooperators in this way are close agnates, but a man may choose to share a camp with friendly clansmen, maternal kin, or affines.

Agriculture

Animal husbandry is pre-eminently the concern and dominating interest of the men in Jieland; female concern is mainly in domestic activities and agriculture. Although men often assist in milking, women and girls normally act as the dairymaids in the homesteads. But women cannot own livestock nor do they share in their management. There is a common saying that "sorghum is the cattle of women." As men acquire names based on their outstanding oxen, so women gain names from agricultural contexts. As Jie see it, only men can properly protect the herds from predatory animals (and formerly from raiders). Animals are closely associated with the solidarity and continuity of the family, with marriage and affinal relations, with ritual, and with law—and formerly with war making. All these are primarily men's concern, and therefore it is logical and appropriate that men should take the responsibility for the practical side of stock management.

Women own both the arable lands and the produce from them. Each married woman makes her own fields by clearing a patch of bush conveniently near the homestead. A field can be cultivated for three to six consecutive seasons before being allowed to lie fallow; there is no use of manure or other fertilizer. A woman aims to hold several sets of fields, one of which is in cultivation while the rest lie fallow. Rights over resting land are well established and a woman cannot use another's fallow without express permission. On her death, or in the infirmity of old age, a woman's land is taken over by her daughters if, after marriage, they live nearby; but most of it is taken by sons' wives as they come to live at the homestead. Small informal parties of co-wives and neighbors cooperate in the work of digging up each other's fields immediately after the onset of the rains. Then each woman plants, tends the growing crop, and harvests it on her own land. Over nine tenths of the crop is sorghum, which is best suited to the erratic rainy season and low rainfall. The remainder is finger millet (for beer) and tiny "luxury" crops of tobacco, peanuts, and gourds planted around the homestead. Each wife stores the produce of her own fields in large granary baskets in her own courtyard, and uses it as she herself sees fit—mainly, of course, to feed herself, her children, and her husband. Some of it, at her discretion, she may give to kinswomen in need, or she may use it in barter for small items she requires. She also makes beer occasionally and, nowadays, she profits from any cash sale of this.

The sorghum yield under simple hoe cultivation is low even in good years, for this is marginal country for cereal production. Occasionally there is an almost complete failure, but even in moderately good years sorghum supplies frequently do not last until the following harvest without stringent rationing. And yet scarcely a day passes when cereal porridge is not a main food in the homesteads, although it is variably augmented by milk, blood, some meat, and (in the rainy season) wild vegetables and fruits gathered in the bush.

Trade

The additional grain needed is regularly obtained from neighboring agricultural peoples to the west: especially the Labwor, the southwestern neighbors, but also the Acoli, Lango, and Ngiangeya (see map). It is acquired by barter: hides and skins, milk, butter, meat, small stock, and sometimes male calves. Men are chiefly responsible for this trade, which occurs mainly toward the end of the dry season and in the early wet season when Jie provisions and milk supplies are at their lowest. Each Jie man has one or more bond-friends among those peoples with whom he maintains a trading relationship. He obtains grain directly from his bond-friend, or uses him as an intermediary with fellow members of the tribe who have produce available. About one third of the men are likely to be away from the homesteads on barter expeditions at any time after the middle of the dry season.

The Jie also trade with the Labwor to obtain ironware (spears, knives, hoe blades, ornaments, bells), pots, and gourds. Still mainly by barter, this trade is conducted directly with the Labwor specialists in their own centers, or as they occasionally make trading journeys. These specialists are also often suppliers of cloth and beads (the remaining external needs of the Jie), although nowadays these articles are available in one or two local stores (alien-owned) in Jieland. Thus the Labwor barter trade is doubly important to the Jie because of the inadequacy of their agriculture and the poverty of their material culture, which contains no ironmaking and almost no potmaking.

Material culture

On the other hand, Jie are able to provide themselves with a sufficient range of utensils for domestic and dairying purposes by the use of wood and leather —wooden troughs and bowls, leather and wood bottles, cups and jars, leather bags. Cowhide is used for thongs and thread, sandals, mats, and covers. Women continue to dress the skins of goats, sheep, and calves for their skirts and cloaks, although almost all the men have taken to calico cloth cloaks when they wear clothing at all. There are no drums or musical instruments. The main aesthetic expression occurs in the beaded decorations on women's clothing, in personal adornment with beads, wire, and fine wire-work, and the fashioning of the horns of their oxen.

Traditionally, Jie men have gone naked, older men wearing a leather cover on the back. Nowadays most men wear a cloth cloak, but commonly this is thrown back over the shoulders, for the covering of nudity is still regarded with some suspicion. Few young or middle-aged men go far from home without their pair of long spears; invariably a man carriers a stout stick and his wooden stool-headrest. Uninitiated men allow their hair to grow uncut, and they fashion it into a large bun that sticks out at the back of the head. Sisal string, dyed red, is wound around this to give the appearance of a fez. After initiation a man wears a rather smaller bun covered with gray clay, which falls on the nape of the neck. (See the central figures in photograph on page 188). The hair above the forehead is covered with a mudded plate stretching from ear to ear, and decorated in six or eight different colored ochres. In both the mudded bun and the head plate small holes are made into which ostrich feathers can be set on festive occasions. Older men wear an intricate metal waistband; younger men wear bead necklets, earrings, and armlets; ivory armbands and lip plugs are common.

Unlike western Nilotic peoples women and girls never go naked. Girls wear a rather shapeless back-skirt and a short apron suspended from the waist. A wife's skirt is more elaborate: the hair is left on the animal skin and the skirt is flared and gored all around. A leather cloak is worn over the shoulders unless the woman is busily working. The hair is fashioned into a mass of ringlets, though the head is shaved above the ears, and some bead necklets and sometimes a metal or an ivory lip plug completes the ensemble. (See photograph on page 176.)

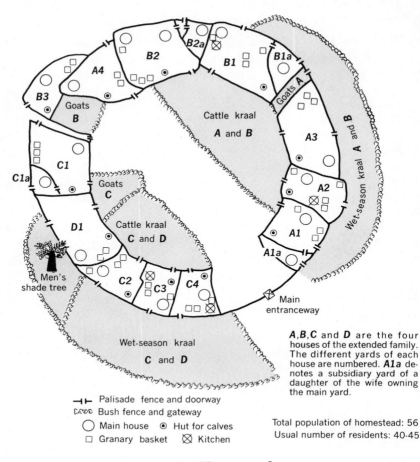

A Jie Homestead

Legend:

⊣⊢ Palisade fence and doorway
〰 Bush fence and gateway
◯ Main house　◉ Hut for calves
□ Granary basket　⊗ Kitchen

A,B,C and *D* are the four houses of the extended family. The different yards of each house are numbered. *A1a* denotes a subsidiary yard of a daughter of the wife owning the main yard.

Total population of homestead: 56
Usual number of residents: 40-45

KINSHIP ORGANIZATION

THE HOMESTEAD · In its physical construction, as the diagram shows, a Jie homestead is a series of contiguous enclosed yards roughly in the shape of a horseshoe, with the width of the open end—the entrance—varying according to the number of the yards. In the middle of the homestead is an open space for one or more cattle and goat kraals. Although there may be some irregularity in the time and standard of construction and of the consequent abutment of yards, in general there is the appearance of a continuous, curving fence, whether viewed from outside or within the central kraal area. The fences are made of stout, tightly packed palisades six to eight feet high, with tiny doorways about three feet square leading into each yard from either side. This solid construction used to be

A Jie Homestead

necessary, say Jie, to safeguard the homestead against enemy raiders, but it serves a persisting purpose in making decisively clear the exclusive identity of the group of people within the fence.

Typically the homestead is the residence of an extended family. Ideally this comprises a group of men who are the descendants of one grandfather, together with their wives, sons, sons' wives and children, and unmarried sisters and daughters. On the average a homestead contains six to eight adult men, and about the same number of yards—thirty to forty people. There still exist some of the larger homesteads of traditional type that contain several extended families, all the members of one clan, the residents of which may number up to one hundred or more in fifteen or twenty yards. On the other hand, some extended families have now become divided residentially so that only some portion, two or three yards, occupies a single homestead.

Each yard is the household and home of a wife and her children. An unmarried mother, or a married daughter who has not yet gone to live with her husband, has her own small yard made by cutting off a corner of her mother's yard. On coming to her husband's homestead a wife has the right to her own yard (initially prepared for her by his womenfolk) and is responsible for maintaining its fences and keeping the bare earth floor clean and hard. In each yard is a small beehive-shaped house whose grass thatch scarcely rises above the fence and reaches more or less to the ground. It is used only for sleeping and for shelter during a storm—a simple, dark room with no window and a tiny doorway entered only on hands and knees. Another small hut, with rather higher walls and larger doorway, shelters the calves at night and often serves as a temporary kitchen in wet weather, though some women build an extra, open-sided hut for that purpose. Generally, cooking is done on an open fire at one side of the yard, and nearby, often hung on the fence, are cooking pots, bowls, gourds, and other domestic utensils. Each wife has several granary baskets of woven saplings (men's work) and shaped like gigantic pots about six feet tall, mudded, and mounted on low platforms.

THE HOUSE · The word *ekal* is used by Jie for both the physical yard and the group consisting of a wife and her children whose home it is. The yard in its social sense is, however, but a dependent unit within a larger, autonomous group. This is the "house"—again using the word in its social meaning —that is founded by a set of full brothers. Like a yard, a house focuses on a single mother, and Jie see the origin of a house in an earlier yard. The house contains all the yards established by the brothers' wives. Usually, though not invariably, all the yards of a house occupy a single segment of the family homestead, and often each house has its own kraals for its livestock. The house is vitally important in Jie society because it is the stock-owning and controlling unit, and it consistently acts as an integrated whole in its relations with the rest of the extended family and the outside world.

It is perhaps easiest to indicate the particular nature of the Jie house by saying that there is no domestic or nuclear family within it. Although a man may eat and sleep in his wife's yard he is not a member of it, for that is a subunit founded by her with her children. Structurally speaking, a child is the offspring of a house, rather than of a particular father, but he is marked off from his half brothers and cousins by maternal origin. He recognizes a group of fathers—his physiological father and the latter's full brothers—and ultimate authority comes from the eldest of these. The real father's death does not affect a son's status and social role so long as his father's full brother remains alive. A son commonly prefers his real father before the others, and a man takes a greater interest in his sons than in the sons of his brothers. He may well support his sons against his nephews, but he is limited in this because of his obligations to his brothers and the overriding unity of the house.

The Jie themselves think of a house primarily as the group of full brothers under the acknowledged leadership of the eldest, and they attach greater importance to the unity (in residence, cooperation, mutuality, and amity) of full brothers than to any other relationship. It represents the fundamental moral premise to these people and is directly connected with the control of a herd of livestock. A man does not possess a herd independently, but only in concert with his brothers. The leadership of the senior brother is chiefly exercised in relation to the administration and use of this herd that the house inherited as a group. Animals may not be used for any purpose whatever without at least the tacit approval of the senior brother, and it is he who formally accepts or disburses gifts of animals on behalf of the house. Younger brothers, even when old men, leave it to their senior to conduct transactions, although they do not refrain from influencing him in such matters. Ideally, and commonly in practice, the head of a house should manage the herd in the best interests of his juniors and the whole group; but so pronounced is the emphasis laid on his status that he can sometimes take advantage of it to act in his own interests and the possible detriment of the rest.

The pre-eminent unity of the house is generally reinforced by considerable affection among the brothers, which often goes to the extent of self-denial in the others' interests. These men spend a good deal of their time in each other's company. Even the more autocratic senior brothers continually consult with their juniors and are much influenced by their opinions and personal interests. Even where, nowadays, some extended families have become residentially divided, and where tensions and quarrels are common, it is exceedingly unusual when full brothers do not live together in a single homestead. It requires a catastrophe to cause this and even then is universally condemned by Jie. In other cases where fraternal conflict is troublesome, the authority of the senior brother is sufficient to override potential dissension. This authority is buttressed by certain ritual prerogatives he exercises on behalf of the group, and by the belief that supernatural retribution follows deliberate flouting of his decisions. But despite this, the fundamental integrity of a house lies in its moral value, the values of cooperation, and the joint inheritance and use of the common herd.

Because of this joint ownership some conflict may occur over the divergent aspirations of the brothers and—when they become adult—their sons. Clearly one brother cannot plan to use many of the cattle for his son's marriage while another hopes to do the same for his son and a third is anxious to acknowledge and improve his relations with outside kinsmen by making a number of gifts of animals. There is an established regulation of the various claims and needs of different members, and here the control of the senior brother is paramount. There are two major allocations of the house's herds: for domestic economic purposes (as described below) and for bridewealth. Since a house must find about twenty cattle for each bridewealth (see page 177) this is a great strain on resources: not only can a house not tolerate the marriages of two members at the same time; other claims against the herd must be tempered by marriage needs and the necessity to leave enough animals to retain the nucleus of a herd and to ensure some milk. Allocation of animals for bridewealth, and therefore permission to marry, is made in strict order of seniority: first, by order of age among the full brothers; second, by a set order among their sons. In this matter the wives (and thus their yards) of the full brothers are ranked by the order of their marriages. Sons of a single mother are ranked in order of birth. Then, as between sons of different mothers, where the difference in age is not large (less than about five years) the son of the senior yard has seniority over his half brother or cousin irrespective of age; where the difference in age is larger (more than five years or so) the older son is given seniority irre-

Bridewealth Cattle in Transit
Bridewealth cattle are driven to the bride's homestead. They are led by her father's junior wife and driven by his agnatic kinsmen.

spective of yard ranking. Within a generation, men should marry in order of seniority; and a man should not marry a second time until all his juniors have married once, although this is sometimes ignored when no unmarried peer is of an age to marry. Sometimes, too, the senior full brother may take advantage of his position to marry again before a younger one—even though he is old enough to marry—takes a first wife.

LIVESTOCK DISTRIBUTION IN THE HOUSE • As far as outsiders are concerned, the group of full brothers controls its own single herd of animals. Within the house, although ultimate control remains with the brothers, many of the animals are allocated to particular wives and their children (that is, to yards) for domestic purposes. When a wife comes to live at her husband's homestead, to establish her new yard she is allocated a number of cows from the main herd, usually an ox or two, some small stock, and perhaps a donkey. The brothers retain a reserve of animals that are not allocated to any wife.

Domestic allocation to yards does not affect the legal and pastoral unity of the herd and transfers only limited rights and responsibilities to a wife and her yard. Adult animals, after allocation, remain in the central kraal and are herded and watered with the rest. Each wife has both the responsibility and the right to milk the animals attached to her yard (to obtain food for herself and her children) and to care for them (for example, to remove ticks). When animals are received by the house, as in bridewealth, each yard should receive a share. When the house makes a payment, animals are taken from each yard as determined by the full brothers, although the yard of a son who marries surrenders a few more than do the others. A wife herself cannot dispose of animals allocated to her yard.

On the other hand, there is a gradual, intensifying differentiation within a house as the founding full brothers grow older, and especially as their sons reach adulthood. As sons grow up they come increasingly to think of the yard's allocation as "our animals," in contrast to those of half brothers and cousins. Adult sons, therefore, begin to chafe when stock are taken for the benefit of men of another yard. There is an emotional aspect to this, for at least some of the animals have been tended as calves in the yard and cared for as they mature. The animals are bound up with the strong attachment to the mother by Jie sons who, even as young men, spend much of their leisure time in her yard.

Above all, there is their developing awareness that, sooner or later, when their fathers all die, they, the sons of one yard, will become the founders of a new house, separate from their peers' houses. From early adulthood, sons' aspirations are strongly conditioned by the promise of ultimate autonomy. Other centrifugal forces are the separate matrilateral ties and, in due course, the separate affinal kin of each yard. Rivalry among yards is common, though it may be reduced by interpersonal affections that cut across yard lines, and by their fathers' attempts to preserve unity. Yet it is inevitable that sets of full brothers should diverge because of the practical and moral emphasis which the Jie sedulously give to the special unity of such men.

THE HOUSE LINE • It is only when the last of the fathers—the founding full brothers—dies that their house dies. Until then, even though sons are mature, married adults, they remain subject to their seniors. After that each yard becomes a new, autonomous house. Strictly speaking, it is the set of full brothers who, with their wives and children, make a new house, but both the mother and their unmarried full sisters belong temporarily. At the death of the last surviving father, the single herd is divided and inherited by each successor house. Each new house takes the animals that were formerly only allocated to it—this is straightforward and rarely causes dispute. Any unallocated reserve of the old herd is then divided by the rule that the more junior houses should get a larger share, the more senior a smaller share. Jie justify this on the grounds that the more senior a yard is (and therefore usually the older the men in it), the more chance they will already have had to use animals for bridewealth.

The group of houses that together are the successors to a former single house may be called a house line. Jie themselves see this as the male patrilineal descendants (and their wives) of a common grandmother, and they use the same word—*ekal*—as for a yard and a house.

With the completion of inheritance and the simultaneous recognition of the full autonomy of the successor houses, the former rights and obligations between half brothers and cousins also come to an end. Each new house becomes principally concerned with husbanding its own herd for the benefit of its own members. But a house cannot normally afford to exist quite independently: few houses have the resources to make up a full bridewealth; hence, although other kinsmen are asked for help, it is to near agnates in other houses that men look first. In the early days after the dissolution of the old house, its former members still feel closer to one another than to other members of the extended family. Their past association and their division of the former single herd continue to be powerful factors. Thus, although the seniority order of marriage is no longer enforceable, it still guides men's actions. It is still thought that men *should* marry in that order, and any attempt to avoid it is likely to be disapproved in a practical manner: other houses may refuse to contribute cattle for the bridewealth of one who seeks to ignore precedence. There is a vital idea, too, that every man has the firm right to marry once, and to gain assistance to do so. But when some men begin to prepare to take a second wife conflict sets in, for men of other houses may desire to use their herds for their own additional marriages (and other purposes also, of course) rather than assist the ambitions of others.

The autonomy of a house and the tendency of houses to conflict is here explained in terms of marriage and bridewealth payments, because that is how the Jie themselves perceive it. Marriage and the procreation of children are the main way of developing a house and account for the major non-domestic use of animals. The problems of gathering bridewealth are raised early each wet season—the time for negotiating marriages—and each successive year tends to show a growth of rivalry among houses, and increasing unwillingness on the part of each to give as generously as before to the others. Half brothers and cousins cannot refuse outright to assist a man and his house by denying the agnatic obligations to contribute to his bridewealth: such a refusal would be morally indefensible, and would invite isolation from the rest of the extended family. It is explicitly recognized that agnates should assist one another, both as a duty and in return for similar assistance, past or future. There is no authority whatsoever to compel these obligations, but the practical values of reciprocal assistance are self-evident to Jie. These obligations do not only concern bridewealth, for a house needs assistance and support at other times, both in livestock and otherwise.

Over a period of years, and by trial and error, relations among houses in the new house line come to find a rough balance at a level both tolerable and yet valuable to each house and every one separately. This level is not necessarily quite the same for each pair of houses in the house line, though Jie say that a "proper" bridewealth contribution is three to four cattle. Considerations of friendliness and trust, or alternatively of hostility and rivalry, clearly affect the situation. Houses with larger herds or fewer demands on them may be able to give more generously and therefore to make heavier demands in return. In any event, the Jie are specific that the principal factor is reciprocity—the idea of helping another house as much as that house helps yours. Jie are quite prepared to concede that at a particular time the state of a house's herds and the other legitimate claims of all kinds against the herds may prevent the men from giving as many animals as they had received

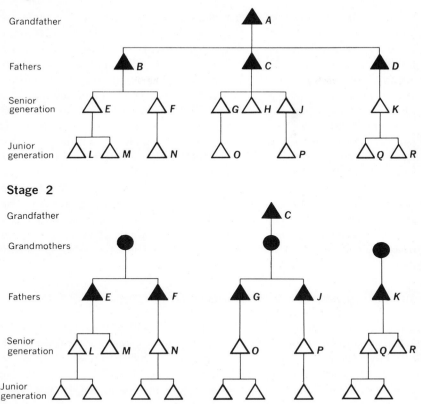

Stage 1

Grandfather

Fathers

Senior generation

Junior generation

Stage 2

Grandfather

Grandmothers

Fathers

Senior generation

Junior generation

The Development of an Extended Family

earlier. But Jie stress not only the number of animals but the spirit of generosity that impels the gift. On the other hand, a house that is chronically unable to match the gifts it receives begins to find that assistance to it diminishes after a time.

THE EXTENDED FAMILY · A number of house lines make up the extended family. The *ideology* is that each line originates with a grandmother, and that all these grandmothers were the wives of the common grandfather who founded the family. This conception is associated with the notion that, although now separate stockowners, each of the constituent houses has acquired a part of the grandfather's original herd as that has been passed on by his sons to his grandsons and their children. Thus genealogical identity is reinforced by the exclusiveness of the family's herds. What is of practical importance, however, is the pattern of continuous cooperation, common residence in the homestead, relatively heavy commitment to mutual assistance in livestock, and the everyday contacts and interests that exist between the various houses of the extended family. There is usually a good deal of pastoral cooperation, for relatively few houses have both enough animals and enough youths and young men to tend them so that they can be entirely independent in day-to-day management. If the men of a house are unwilling to cooperate with other houses, they may be able to share a camp with, for example, a matrilaterally linked house; but Jie prefer if possible to restrict cooperation in these matters to their agnates who, they feel, are likely to be more trustworthy and also more easily kept under surveillance.

Conflict among houses is not uncommon, but it tends to be most marked among men of fairly new houses—that is, before a modus vivendi is reached between them. Among more mature houses, whose senior members are, of course, older men, the major emphasis is on collaboration for recognized mutual benefit, for such men have no longer to insist on their autonomy, which has come to be taken for granted.[4]

The kinship network and stock-associates

Each Jie man stands at the center of a particular network of formal, personal relations with certain other men. Some of these relations are established by birth (patrilateral and matrilateral kin), some by marriage—his own and those of his sisters and daughters (affinal kin), and some by deliberate pledge (bond-friends). A man looks to these people for friendship, sympathy, advice, and affection. He often visits them and he gives hospitality and assistance to them. More than this, they are the people with whom he maintains reciprocal rights to claim gifts of animals in times of need. While never neglecting the initial basis of the relationship—kinship—Jie always lay greatest stress on the exchanges of livestock at such times as marriage, shortage of milking animals, the desire for a particular kind of ox or goat, or the need to pay a judicial fine or to provide a specified animal for ritual purposes. For that reason I refer to these men as "stock-associates." A Jie refers to them collectively as "my people," but they do not form a corporate group since they act with respect to a particular individual, and seldom at all together. Every man is a stock-associate, in differing ways of course, to a number of men. Apart from his agnatic kin within the extended family, no two men's associates are quite the same—not even those of two full brothers who share the same matrilateral kin but have different affinal kin and bond-friends.

Jie recognize two kinds of stock-associates: those with whom reciprocal rights involve cattle, and those involving only small stock. In the first category come all agnatic kin, mother's full brothers and their sons, close affines (fathers and brothers of wives and sons' wives, sisters' and daughters' husbands and their brothers), and bond-friends. In the second category are more distant maternal and affinal kin and clansmen. The distinction is not precise and depends on the particular conventions established, but usual practice works out like that. The nature of reciprocal rights has already been discussed in connection with interhouse relations in the extended family, and the same general principles apply in the case of other kin. In emphasizing the rights and obligations over animals, I am following Jie conceptions. I do not wish to ignore the many other kinds of assistance or affections, but, like the Jie, I stress the most vital aspects of the relationships.

Jie explain the potentialities of stock-association by saying that where animals have once passed a path is made along which other animals can travel in either direction. The initial path between agnates is created by inheritance; the passage of animals in bridewealth establish future rights on each side between affinal kin and, in the subsequent generation, between a man and his matrilateral kin. With his mother's full brothers in particular a man feels especially warm affection and strong links. Friendly equality typifies relations between brothers-in-law, but a wife's father has a more distant and superior status.

Bond-friends are not kinsmen, though relations with them have a pseudo kinship quality, setting those men off from unrelated persons. Essentially bond-friendship rests on an informal contract in which the element of reciprocity is paramount. Beginning usually in ordinary friendship, the two men agree to accept claims by each against the other for gifts of livestock. No formal pact is made—no witnessed agreement nor ritual act. A man is able by this means to extend the range of his stock-associates deliberately. Many of these bonds persist through a lifetime, and some are even inherited by the originators' sons; others founder as one of the men defaults, voluntarily or not, in his obligations against rights received. Most men continue to seek new bond-friendships—a wealthier man finds it easier, a poor one more difficult. Older men have at least one or two bond-friends outside their country, not only to gain rights there, but also in order to ensure a center of security and hospitality if travel is necessary. And every Jie man has a bond-friend in Labwor, and often other trading areas too, with whom he maintains the valuable barter relations previously described (page 164).

Marriage and bridewealth

The significance of Jie marriage is twofold. First, there is union between a man and woman, leading to the procreation of children and their upbringing in a new unit (the yard) founded by their mother in the father's house; and second, vital affinal links are created between the husband and his wife's fathers and brothers, and between the close agnates of both parties. These conscious aims are accomplished over a period of not less than five years dur-

Jie Women Dancing at a Wedding

ing which time the woman gradually advances from betrothed girl, to bride wife, to full wife; and affinal ties are progressively strengthened as the men change from relative strangers to close associates. In one way this period is measured by the rule that a wife does not shift to her husband's homestead and become a full wife and a member of his extended family until she has reared two children to the walking stage. Until then she remains at her father's homestead. In a different but related way, the period covers a number of chronological, ritual stages creating and strengthening the marriage, the fertility of the woman and the affinal link, and these culminate in her formal incorporation into her husband's family.

Wives become full members of their husbands' family, and they automatically lose membership in their natal group. They are little involved in the cooperative pastoral arrangements of their men, but, living in the same homestead, women cooperate in their own activities: expeditions to collect firewood or thatching grass, to gather wild fruits in the bush, to fetch water from a distant watering place in the dry season. Co-wives commonly form the nucleus of hoeing parties at cultivation time, and they accompany one another to the fields when going to work. There is a good deal of sharing and borrowing of food and utensils, and joining in leisure activities.

Marriage rules are straightforward: a man cannot marry a girl of his own clan (see below), nor of the clans of his mother, mother's mother, or father's mother. No man would receive help in building up a bridewealth or performing rituals were he to attempt to ignore these rules. But equally important in Jie eyes is the common-sense prohibition on marriage into a house that is already affinally linked to one's own. To do this would only confuse the reciprocal stock rights existing between the two houses, and it would also foolishly waste the opportunity to extend the range of kinship and stock-association. But most Jie prefer not to marry into any extended family with which there are even remote affinal links already. Other than this, there are neither prohibitions nor preferences in the choice of a wife: a man seeks the girl of his choice, subject to the approval of his father and hers.

Marriage is legalized by the transfer of bridewealth from the groom to the bride's kinsmen. An average bridewealth consists of about fifty cattle and one hundred small stock, and most of these are handed over on the day of the wedding, the remainder following very soon after. The house of the groom provides about twenty of the cattle; the rest are contributed by his various stock-associates, to each of whom he goes to gain approval of the marriage and to seek a gift of animals. Perhaps fifty people or more contribute in this way. On the receiving side, the animals are distributed among the stock-associates of the bride's father, his house retaining about twenty cattle. Other than the rare compensation payments for homicide or adultery, the transfer of bridewealth (a common event each rainy season) is the most important occasion for the exercise of stock rights.

The size of bridewealth is a matter for negotiation between a man and his prospective father-in-law. The only prescription is that a man should give according to his ability—that is, the size of his house's herd and the number of his associates. This a Jie always attempts to do, both as a matter of prestige and in order to create the most favorable conditions for the new affinal bonds. Hard bargaining over the animals is quite antipathetic to Jie notions, for it seems to them irreconcilable with subsequent relations.

The transfer of bridewealth gives the husband marital rights over his wife, but these are not wholly acquired in practice until she comes to live with him permanently as a full wife. All children she bears belong to his house and agnatic line, and they automatically gain rights in the herd and claims to support. But, say Jie, bridewealth alone cannot make a marriage: the subsequent ritual stages are essential for that. The whole marriage is completed when the wife and her first two children are ritually led through the main entranceway (the cattle entrance) into her husband's homestead.

There is no other form of marriage among the Jie. Divorce is so rare that I was unable to obtain full information on a genuine case. A widow does not remarry, but remains the wife of the dead husband. She may accept another man, preferably from her husband's house or at least an agnate, as pro-husband, but any children she bears by him are reckoned as members of their mother's yard within her husband's house.

Child training and socialization

A Jie mother and father, and their adult kinsfolk, show unreserved affection toward babies and small children. Adults are markedly permissive toward them and rarely (ideally, never) are children chastised physically or verbally for their behavior. Jie say that small children have little sense and that they mean no wrong in what they do; therefore it would be wrong to punish them. Thus, if a small boy chases a calf round the kraal, causing commotion among the animals and perhaps upsetting utensils, and so on, he is the object only of tolerant amusement, to be picked up and put out of harm's way.

There is, however, a radical change as a boy grows older. By the age of about seven he is expected to begin helping with the herding of young animals around the homestead; and soon after he accompanies an elder brother or cousin with the dairy herd, which is absent all day from the homestead. Mothers now have little to do with the training of their sons, and fathers become sharply disciplinarian toward them. The boy-herder who loses a goat is likely to be beaten rather severely; he who is clumsy in dealing with the animals is verbally castigated. When they get a little older (say, about eleven years) most boys spend much of their time in camps, away from the homestead and continuous parental control. Then they learn mainly from their peers and immediate seniors on terms of friendly equality. The particular timing of these stages for a boy depends on the need for herding labor and the supply of herdboys available in his house. Mothers are usually warmly affectionate toward their sons, but are separated from them in activities and interests (and often in residence) for long periods.

There is no corresponding change in the upbringing of girls. They remain continuously with their mothers until several years after marriage, as noted above, and gradually learn and share more and more of a woman's conventional work at home and in the field. A daughter might be beaten by an exasperated mother, but not often and not heavily. Fathers have little to do with their daughters' training. By puberty a girl should be capable of doing all of a woman's tasks and she is probably already cultivating her own arable plots more or less independently of her mother.

TERRITORIAL ORGANIZATION

As described already, the main part of Jieland consists of communal pastures where there is no permanent settlement. The settled area, about ninety square miles, is roughly in the center of the country. This area is divided into seven named districts, each containing a number of settlements that themselves comprise a number of clan-hamlets. The boundaries between these residential groups are not visible on the ground, and often there is a more or less continuous stretch of homesteads. The Jie cannot indicate specific boundary lines, but they are perfectly aware to which group any homestead belongs since determination of this is sociologically well established. These units at whatever level are groups of people kept together by important moral, economic, ritual, and general cooperative ties. Nevertheless, each unit is in effect a discrete territorial entity, and there is no geographical intermingling of the homesteads of two or more.

THE CLAN-HAMLET • The clan-hamlet contains all the members of a single clan: that is, the males born into it patrilineally, their unmarried sisters and daughters, and their wives and mothers who have been ritually incorporated into it on becoming full wives. Each clan, of course, is made up of a number of extended families, but in no case can the people trace any kind of genealogical link between these families. There is usually a dogmatic assertion of forgotten patrilineal links, but Jie see no particular importance in this and are content to affirm common clanship.

The clan is exogamous, and therefore there are no affinal links between members. To each clan are ascribed certain specific procedures that its members must follow in their ritual activities. The general pattern of Jie rituals (concerning marriage, death, illness, and so on) is common to all the people, but it is modified in its detailed observation by these clan prescriptions. Concomitant with this is the necessity for all (or at least as many as conveniently possible) of the clan members to participate in the clan-determined rituals of any of its families. In fact, differences in the ritual prescriptions of different clans are usually quite small, and they never affect the more significant acts; but for the Jie the minutiae of ritual observance are quite essential for efficacious results, and they perceive these distinctions between clans as crucial.

THE SETTLEMENT • Although because of the closeness of the homesteads to one another, there is much cooperation, gossip, and joint leisure activity among members of the hamlet, nevertheless this kind of day-to-day and face-to-face contact is extended to all members of the same settlement. The hamlets of a settlement are located close together—perhaps strung along a low ridge—so that everyday contacts are easy and frequent. One or two settlements contain a single clan (clan-hamlet), but most comprise two or three hamlets, and some have four or five. There is no explanation why the constituent clans should be united in one settlement, though changes seem not to occur: there is no notion of putative kinship, nor is any clan considered to be superior to the rest. Exogamy does not extend beyond the clan, and therefore a network of affinal and matrilateral links reinforces the useful relations of neighborliness between families of different clans.

The men of a settlement associate together in all their informal activities, as well as in formal matters such as ritual. There are usually two or three popular shade trees where men collect to gossip and carry on their handicrafts, and where they can discuss their problems with friendly confidence. These men, and their wives also, know each other's lives intimately. The women only rarely gather together, but there is much visiting between homesteads as well as informal cooperation, such as collecting firewood or carrying water. Most of the arable land of the women lies in and around the settlement. There are no set boundaries within which women of a settlement must find their fields, and it is not unusual that the arable lands of adjacent settlements intermingle. But the Jie are able roughly to indicate the general cultivated area of each settlement, and often that area is identified by the use of the settlement name. When the dairy herds are at the homesteads, all or some of the men arrange a cooperative herding schedule, and they arrange to meet and help each other at watering time.

The sense of unity of a settlement is demonstrated by its possession of a rainy-season pond and a ritual grove. The pond is located in some dip in the land where water naturally collects and often a small dam wall is maintained to prevent runoff. The pond is cleaned when it has dried out, usually just before the rainy season, by the joint labor of all the men. It is used both for domestic supplies and for watering animals, and groups of youths and men gather there to bathe. Apart from pools left after a storm, there are no natural water supplies in the center of Jieland, and the maintenance of these ponds makes it unnecessary for people to go to one of the few streams that flow in the rainy season. Each settlement is therefore self-sufficient but responsible for its seasonal water supply. Members of one settlement do not take their livestock to the pond of another settlement when their own dries up, but must go to the only permanent watering place that lies beyond the western limits of the settled area.

The ritual grove of a settlement is a small clump of trees and bush adjacent to the homesteads. It is considered a sacrilege to cut these trees, which often are almost the only ones standing in the bare land created by agricultural clearing and heavy grazing. At the grove all rituals are performed that affect the settlement as a whole (rainmaking, warding off disease and misfortune, and so on), and also those public rituals of resident families that contain a regard for the welfare of the settlement even though chiefly concerning the particular family. The settlement is the primary *ritual* unit for the Jie, for even family rituals (whose specific form is determined by clan membership) are performed by members of the whole settlement under the leadership of the most senior male. Neighbors are therefore not only dependent on one another for their general welfare, but also for the efficacy of the rituals that personally affect them in life's crises. Since the Jie have a rich body of rituals, this means that the settlement is frequently assembling as a corporate group for purposive activity. It includes not only the ritual performance itself, but involves also the commensal feast from the slaughtered animal. This provides the main source of meat, for Jie do not approve of the slaughter of beasts merely for eating.

THE DISTRICT · A district is made up of several contiguous settlements; unlike the settlement, it is not a unit of everyday and general cooperation and contact, nor do members of different settlements have so close a knowledge of and concern for each other. Today the district is principally a ritual group; formerly it was important also as a military unit in that each had its own war leader and contributed its own contingent under that leader to the Jie offensive army. This no longer applies, although the memory of it persists and serves to activate a district (rather than the tribe or the individual settlements) in its relations with the central government.

The district is mainly concerned now with the rainmaking rituals, which are described later. But as an entity it also has responsibility at certain stages of the marriage process. Occasionally the district assembles in a ritual attempt to combat the more severe threats to social life—human and animal epidemics, locusts, and so on. Each district has its own ritual grove, separate from those of its settlements. In view of the ritual importance of the age group system, it is logical that the district is the major unit for its organization, as explained below.

THE TRIBE • The whole tribe, comprising the seven districts, is also significantly a ritual group, and there are at least three tribal groves at one or other of which tribal assemblies are held twice a year. In addition to this crucial activity, the Jie are markedly conscious of their tribal identity in a number of ways. The tribe was the largest unit of internal peace, except for the *Pax Britannica*, under the British protectorate. It is therefore a grave offense —and one believed to affect rainfall and fertility adversely—for one Jie to kill another, whether by intent or not. Homicide must be dealt with by compensation payment of livestock and by ritual purification; lesser offenses also have their limits at the tribal boundaries and should similarly be treated by regular judicial procedures. To kill a non-Jie, to take his cattle, or to seduce his daughter is not, by Jie evaluations, a crime or a sin; in fact, it is thought rather admirable. But Jie accept these as offenses nowadays insofar as the central government can compel them to do so. Finally, the tribe is recognized by its communal possession of the pasture lands, from which non-Jie are excluded.

Beyond the tribe and tribal land the Jie world reaches little more than thirty or forty miles. Beyond that there are few or no contacts and little interest in or knowledge about even the countries of their immediate neighbors. Peoples living farther off, even though culturally related (for example, the Teso of central Uganda), are but vaguely recognized. The local center of the government is some sixty miles from central Jieland (at Moroto in Karamajong country), and Jie are lightly administered. They have a poor understanding of this alien power except as it impinges directly on them at home through irregular visits of officials and through decisions of the local, appointed chief.

The age group system

Among most Nilotic (or Nilo-Hamitic) peoples an age group system is of primary social importance, though there are many crucial differences between the various systems. That of the Jie is somewhat exceptional because it has only marginal significance in the political, judicial, or economic life of the people. Almost exclusively it provides the organizational basis for the performance of their communal rituals in two principal ways: first, it establishes the ritual efficacy of adult males through formal initiation in and membership of an age group; and second, by the order of seniority inherent in the system, it provides an established ranking and obligation of leadership at all levels of ritual activity, from the whole tribe down to the extended family. The system is concerned only with males; girls undergo a mild form of initiation but do not form groups, nor are they able to participate in rituals outside the extended family.

AGE GROUP STRUCTURE • All Jie males are ordered into fixed generations so that members of one generation are all the sons of the members of the immediately preceding one, irrespective of age. Usually there are two established generations in existence at any one time: the senior generation, all of whose members are initiated; and the junior generation, some of whose members are still too young to be initiated. Although male babies are considered to be born into a generation, the group of males is not inaugurated, named, and given formal recognition until all the members of the preceding generation have been initiated.

A new generation is publicly established at about twenty-five-year intervals by a ceremony held at a special tribal grove. This event should be administered by surviving members of the generation of grandfathers of the new group[5] because it is necessary that the spiritual power of ritual efficacy be passed on by the old men to their grandsons. This is done by ritual anointing and blessing of the seniormost member of the new generation (the senior grandson of the seniormost member of the grandfathers' generation), who in turn passes the power to the senior man in each district. Later each district's senior man formally gives ritual power to the seniormost man in each new age group in each settlement. This power is therefore passed from the grandfathers and dispersed through the whole of their grandsons' generation; in due course the latter pass it on to their grandsons.

The intervening generations of the fathers of the new generation and, later, that of their sons play no part in this, for generations are linked alternately only. This grandfather-grandson link appears in a number of contexts among the Jie—for example, the whole complex of the extended family is ideologically based on the grandfather, and boys are personally named after a grandfather and obtain an ox-color from him. According to the Jie, the names of age groups are all taken from the grandfathers' generation and in the same order as they occurred there; this is not true in practice, although some of the earlier names are repeated.

The final inclusion of a man into his generation comes with his initiation into an age group. This occurs by the ritual spearing of an ox or he-goat, after which the initiate is anointed with the undigested stomach contents of the animal by the senior member of his settlement. His new ritual status is acknowledged by his participation, together with the other initiated men of his settlement, in a commensal feast of the meat.

When a new generation is permitted to begin initiations, a large number of men, some of whom are at least middle-aged, have had to await the end of initiations in the preceding generation. Thus, a single large group, which necessarily contains a wide age span, is quickly made up in the first year.[6] Thereafter, age group membership gains a more truly coeval basis as males come forward periodically at about the age of eighteen to twenty. Initiations are held only in good rainy seasons—that is, about once in three years. Usually a new group is begun in each initiation year, though this is not essential.

The name of a new group is chosen by the seniormost men of the district, though there is consultation between districts so that most names have a tribe-wide application. As more groups come into being they become gradually arranged into three sets, which are named after the senior age group in each. This is a fairly loose arrangement that recognizes the principal age differences within the total age span of some fifty or more years within the single generation. Men invariably sit in their groups at all rituals, and groups of the same set cluster together. Later, in the senior generation, men tend to think in terms of the set rather than in terms of the age group. The generation itself takes the name of its most senior group, that name having been acquired at the inauguration of the generation at the tribal grove. The pattern of generations, sets, and groups is illustrated on page 184 by the actual conditions in the Kotido District in 1951.

THE OPERATION OF THE AGE GROUP SYSTEM • In this system relative seniority can easily be calculated between any two Jie men. First, men of one group are all senior to men of a chronologically junior group. Within a group, a man is senior to all his fellow members whose fathers were junior to his father in the preceding generation. Seniority is not, then, a matter of physical age.

In communal rituals the age principle determines the patterns of seating and participation. Emphasis is always laid on the primacy of the most senior man of the unit involved. In some settlements, of course, he may perhaps not be a member of the most senior age groups; in others, or in a district, he is likely to be a very old man, often too infirm to do more than make a symbolic appearance, leaving the actual duties to his more active juniors. Senior men arrange rituals, determining the times, the donors of animals, and so on; at the rituals they supervise the proceedings and lead supplications to the High God. Junior men clear the ritual site, prepare branches

JIE AGE GROUPS

Age Set	Age Group	Number of Men Alive in Each Group in 1951
Deceased Generation—Giraffes		all dead
Senior Generation—Buffaloes		
Buffaloes	Buffaloes	all dead
	Lions	all dead
	Elephants	all dead
Jackals	Jackals	1
	Kongoni	3
	Tortoises	5
	Grasshoppers	2
Snakes	Snakes	13
	Plovers	12
	Stones	19
Junior Generation—Topi		
Topi	Topi	31
Leopards	Leopards	32
	Red-poll cattle	31
	Giraffes	32
	Gazelles	11

All names are in English translation.

The total number of men in each group was as follows:

Senior generation	55
Junior generation	137
Uninitiated men over twenty years	54
TOTAL	246

Most uninitiated men were of the junior generation, but some were sons of senior members of that generation (that is, the Topi set) and therefore were of a subsequent but as yet immature generation. Many younger males also belonged to the junior generation: over half of the members of that generation were by then initiated, but at least another ten years remained before initiation would be completed. The Topi set began in about 1935.

and leaves for their seniors to sit on, bring firewood, tend the fires, and cook the meat. Men of middle seniority have a more passive role, no longer servants but not yet senior enough to take responsibility—except in their settlement where a smaller number of men are involved.

On ritual occasions, after the completion of the supplications, the meat is ordered to be cooked, and when ready it is distributed by the seniormost man to the age groups seated in order. Within each group, the meat is then distributed by the seniormost member to his juniors in strict order.

Senior Age Sets Members of the seniormost age sets are shown during marriage rituals in a homestead.

At the settlement level, in the small group of everyday cooperation, organizational responsibilities of ritual leadership are not heavy; rituals are arranged and carried out as part of the continuum of neighborhood life. At the district level, responsibilities are greater, for they require the cooperation of men of different settlements who are not in daily contact. It is necessary for the seniormost men of each settlement to meet in order to make arrangements for an assembly, and to ensure that men know what is expected of them. This is the duty of the district's seniormost man or, if he is too old, his immediate juniors. Because the districts are not large, the difficulties are not great; but the locus of responsibility is clearly determined. At the tribal level the problem is more serious, for then it is required to assemble all or most of initiated Jie men at the tribal grove on a certain day. Each district must have adequate warning so that its members may arrange to obtain an ox that they drive to the grove as their offering for ritual slaughter and subsequent feast. That this is successfully accomplished at least twice a year stands as a measure of the leadership pattern provided by the age group system in this noncentralized society, in which politically and economically the small kin and neighborhood groups are autonomous and without direct intercommunication. Because of its central location in the settled area, senior men of the Kotido District tend to act as a clearinghouse for information and arrangements on a tribal basis, irrespective of their particular seniority vis-à-vis the seniormost men of the other districts. This tendency has probably strengthened in recent times with the establishment of the chief's headquarters and the main store center in Jieland in that district, for people visit these from all other districts.

As is true of all men who achieve responsibility and influence in this society, those who by their seniority status begin to exercise ritual leadership begin simultaneously to acquire mystic power from the High God, whose agents they have become. Thus, the propitious grove, the right day, the color of the ritual animal, the name of the new age group are all dictated by the High God to one or more of these men in dreams. Such divine recognition is believed to give the old men sanctity and power. In ritual matters, more junior men should in any case obey their orders on pain of punishment and ritual impurity; but to disobey, say Jie, is also sacrilege against the High God, and it is met by supernatural punishment. A highly senior man should never be offered violence, physically or verbally, and because of this it is claimed that fights and quarrels can be stopped by the physical intervention of these men. Were this generally true, it would give an added political function to the age group system; in fact, a senior man seldom concerns himself with mundane affairs that do not already affect him in his ordinary role as a kinsman. He may, by virtue of his ritual status, enunciate the accepted moral values of the people on some occasion when they have obviously been contravened. But, even then, he is content to point up the situation and does not himself initiate procedures to redress the matter. When a senior man uses his prestige to stop open violence, he is moved to act in this way primarily because the shedding of blood, or even the threat of it, is thought to prevent rain and spoil ritual efficacy until the pollution is removed.

Although the age group and seniority system is only marginally concerned with the nonritual aspects of Jie public life, it is the only large-scale organization they have. Settlements are united into functioning districts, and these again into the whole tribe, principally by ritual requirements and through the mechanism of the age group system. And although the age group is only a weak corporate group (as compared with some of the Nilotic peoples), nevertheless bonds of friendly equality between members of a group cut across the parochialism of clan and settlement to provide a wider network of personal links than kinship and neighborhood afford. Both district and tribe are significantly defined in ritual terms, but the unity obtained in this way spreads over into nonritual matters to give a general cohesion to the society (Gulliver 1953c:158–168).

RELIGION AND RITUAL

In such a region of meager and unreliable rainfall, each year's precipitation is of the utmost importance both for crops and for pastures. Jie know well how capricious the rains can be and the disastrous effects of a bad year—perhaps one in five years. Without rain, hunger is a stark reality: the land remains bare and unfruitful; human beings are made miserable and their children suffer; animals get in poor condition and their young are ill-nourished and susceptible to disease. In a moderate or good year, food is plentiful, grass is lush, and animals are in good condition. Rain has therefore come to be directly associated not only with a sufficiency of food, but with the welfare and fertility of the people and their livestock. Rainmaking rituals are consequently of the first importance, aiming not only at plentiful rain itself but also at general welfare and the absence of maleficent influences. The Jie explicitly recognize the necessity for cooperative and coordinated ritual efforts to these supreme ends.

Thus the first of the three main categories of Jie rituals is the annual cycle concerning rainmaking, fertility, and general welfare. In early March, before the rains begin, there is a tribal assembly of initiated men to ensure the coming of the new season and its fruitfulness. This is immediately followed by secondary assemblies in each district separately, both to bring the rain and to keep it when it arrives. If the rains are late or poor, further rituals are held in each settlement. In about June, during the normal dry spell between the May and July rainfall peaks, a second tribal ceremony occurs to bring back the rains and to seek good harvests; and this again is followed up by district rituals. In July, approximately, all initiated men and all livestock of each district assemble at their district's grove, where they are blessed and strengthened as the turn of the year is marked when all herds are finally in eastern pastures. Toward harvest time, rituals are performed in each settlement either to give thanks to the High God for good rains and abundant crops, or as a last-minute attempt to gain amelioration of a poor year. During the following dry season each district holds one or two assemblies to maintain contact with the High God, and to prepare the way for the next rainy season. On any of these occasions, should particular troubles have arisen (for example, a cattle epidemic), special attention is given to them in the ritual.

Second, a number of ad hoc rituals are aimed at promoting of some particular public interest, or at preventing or mitigating impending misfortune. The opening of a new generation, the kindling of new fire when general misfortunes accumulate, or the prevention of an epidemic—all call for rituals at tribal and distinct levels—often followed up by lesser assemblies as each settlement attempts to safeguard its own special interests. At that level, too, there are occasional rituals to deal with local misfortune or threats to welfare—damage by fire or by the dust devil, violence in the settlement, witchcraft, and so on.

Third, there is the series of rituals connected with the marriage process (see pages 176–177). Although these are mainly of a private nature, all are performed by the initiated men of the settlement of husband or wife. One or two of them also require the attendance of initiated men of the district, although occurring in the homestead or at the settlement grove.

There are specified acts and observances in all these kinds of ritual, especially marked in those concerning marriage, but their main feature consists of appeals and requests to the High God, *Akuj*,[7] who lives in the sky, where he has a vast homestead and huge herds. He is wholly a power for good, but chronically careless of human beings unless constantly exhorted; above all, he controls the rain. Although not thought of as the source of morals, he may punish wrongdoers, particularly if their disapproved conduct is brought to his notice by responsible or senior Jie.

Marriage Ritual Members of the extended family are being ritually anointed by its seniormost man.

At a ritual assembly, supplications are made by a leader, supported by the chorus of the other men present. The seniormost man present, holding a ritual wand, stands in the open space inside the cluster of seated men; he addresses *Akuj* directly, explaining the reason for the assembly and seeking benevolent assistance. Interspersed in the monologue are communal supplications led by the standing man, in which his specific pleas (for example, for rain, or for the fertility of a new wife) are echoed by the others' chorus. After the seniormost man, other seniors in turn take up the leadership. When a man begins to assume this role with the approval of his more senior associates he has achieved notable seniority.

The reinforcement of the role of a ritual leader by his recognition by the High God has been noted (see page 185); the same reinforcement occurs in respect to the head of a family or of a house and, formerly, a war leader. Modern chiefs and headmen are not thought to have this supernatural support. In particular the High God gives power to diviners, one or two of whom live in each district. A diviner is visited by the High God in his dreams and given instructions on how to act and what agents to use to accomplish beneficent ends. Diviners are also skilled in the reading of entrails of ritually slaughtered animals in order to foretell the future and diagnose the past. They have some knowledge of herbs, but they tend to lay most emphasis on magical and ritual acts to effect cures and stimulate good fortune. They are able to detect witches and provide protection against them. Occasionally a diviner announces, by divine revelation, that a certain settlement or district must perform specified rituals in order to combat threatened misfortune. A diviner himself does not conduct rituals, nor does he lead communal supplications; often he does not attend ritual assemblies.

Apart from their beliefs in the High God and their actions relating to him, Jie have only vague ideas about the supernatural. Even he is so remote that he does not impinge on everyday life. There are thought to be witches, and they seem invariably to live in a settlement other than that of the victim. Jie are inclined to attribute death, disease, misfortune, and so on, to failure to reach *Akuj* properly, or to natural causes, rather than to the machinations of their fellowmen; on the other hand, they are inclined to think of non-Jie as powerful witches.

It is in keeping with this generally mundane attitude that Jie have no mystical practices in connection with economic or judicial affairs. Homesteads, camps, and kraals are not ritually established or maintained; cattle in themselves have no spiritual characteristics; agriculture is entirely a practical matter. The people seek to obtain the benevolence of *Akuj* to give favorable conditions (rain, fertility) in which they may apply their technology and their notions of human relations.

JUDICIAL AND POLITICAL AFFAIRS

The Jie have no centralized political system. The limits of kinship are relatively narrow, and beyond the settlement they are more or less peculiar to each individual. Other than in ritual affairs, there are no acknowledged leaders of territorial groups, nor is coercive authority or decision-making responsibility ascribed to specialized roles and particular persons. In modern times, by fiat of the colonial government of Uganda, there was established a chief, with subchiefs and headmen under him; the chief also heads the court of first instance. The authority of these officials is limited largely to the administration of government business—collection of the tax, enforcement of orders and edicts. They have little concern with the public or private affairs of the Jie, nor do the people look to them for responsibility. Although now constrained to accept court jurisdiction in certain major crimes (for example, homicide), Jie remain unwilling to use the courts in regard to their own affairs.

Where an injury is committed against the person, property, or interests of a Jie, it is entirely his own personal responsibility (or that of the head of his house) to initiate steps to obtain restitution, compensation, or other settlement. There are generally accepted norms that describe right behavior and that prescribe legitimate compensation in the case of their contravention. For example, it is commonly said that forty to fifty cattle are payable for homicide, and proportionately less for bodily injury; theft of animals should be compensated by the return of two animals for each one stolen; adultery calls for a fine equal to bridewealth. But these are only generalized norms and there is no one to enforce them in a particular instance.

An injured person often makes a direct contact with the offender and may be able to achieve some redress by moral argument and informal pressure. If the injury is serious, he does not work alone but seeks the support of his stock-associates—those individuals with whom he is personally linked, and who are bound to give him both material and moral assistance. If a man has to pay compensation, he looks to them for contributions of animals. Thus, the two parties to a dispute assemble as many of their associates as possible, and negotiations are held between the two groups. A man who belongs logically to both groups is often able to act as go-between by virtue of his joint acceptability—though the precise value of this service depends on the relative closeness of his bond to either party.

There are various courses open to an accused offender. He, with his associates, may admit to the offense and accept the demand for compensation. This seldom happens. Usually he may admit to the offense, but dispute the size of the compensation demanded. He may, however, deny the offense and thus any claim for compensation. Finally, he may ignore all demands and messages and refuse to recognize the dispute. If offense is admitted, then the two parties can concentrate on negotiating the compensation; this is done at a joint meeting, probably in the offender's settlement, where the whole matter is discussed and assessed and, with good fortune, an agreement reached. Except in the most blatant offenses, it is unusual for the eventual agreement to settle upon as large a compensation as the ideal norm allows, for the injured party must generally be prepared to temper his demands lest he risk further delay or get nothing at all.

Whether the offense is admitted or not, if compensation is denied, the injured party can accept the *fait accompli*, feeling unable or unwilling to do anything else because the difficulties are not commensurate with the gravity of the offense. On the other hand, he may threaten to use force by attacking the offender's homestead and seizing animals or by committing acts of vengeful violence against his person. This kind of threat is intrinsic to the situation; whether or not it is made with real intent depends on estimates of the relative strengths of the two parties and their chances of success. Jie clearly feel that an injured person has the moral right to resort to force if that is the only way open to him to gain a settlement. More peaceful pressures are also exerted: for example, by using a go-between, by appealing to the need to restore amity in the neighborhood, or by arousing public opinion in favor of the injured. Where the offense is fairly clear, some of the offender's associates may be unwilling to support him in his refusal to negotiate, and others may become lukewarm in assistance. Conversely, the injured person's associates may be reinforced by righteous indignation and the expectation of success. On the whole, in so small a society where little happens that is not well known and widely discussed, it is usually impossible for genuine offenses to be persistently denied. An offender has to continue to live in his community, and his associates in theirs, and this is made difficult where there is flagrant contravention of others' interests.

When the two disputants are entirely unrelated and live at a distance from each other, such public opinion may be ineffective. The process of dispute settlement is not altogether efficient, and some offenders are able to deny or ignore the consequences of their acts. This is not common, for relations between any two men are likely to have some effect on a large number of other people. It is more probable that an offender, by his calculated recalcitrance, is able to avoid the full consequences of his act. The injured man must assess the degree of support both he and the offender can muster, the gravity of the offense, the difficulties of exerting persistent pressure on the offender, previous relations between the two men, and so on. Usually a balance can be struck somewhere so that some compensation is obtained—enough to satisfy the injured without completely alienating the offender.

It is only occasionally that some matter arises that affects the welfare of a number of people of different families, and in which it is inappropriate for particular individuals to initiate action. Most usually someone feels sufficiently threatened to act on his own behalf, with little or no thought for more general interests. For example, in one district a number of cases of alleged witchcraft occurred together. At first, persons who thought themselves involved took individual action against the accused woman; but as further misfortunes accumulated, and the rainy season turned out poorly, people began to see her as a general threat to the whole district. Eventually, with little formal organization, and led by some of those who felt themselves particularly injured, people of the district assembled at the woman's homestead. There she was compelled to admit to her misdeeds, and to declare that she would not use witchcraft again; and her husband provided an ox for slaughter to accompany ritual supplications to the High God.

The district is the usual level at which relations with the outside world are ordered: offensive warfare formerly, and nowadays dealings with the central government. There is little or nothing of communal deliberations and decision making at the tribal level.

To sum up this aspect of Jie life: there is no continuously operating system of public administration outside the ritual sphere. Law and order are maintained by the common acceptance of the norms of conduct (that is, the unitary culture of the people), and these are declared and as nearly as possible enforced by any individual who is injured by their contravention. In this he is assisted by his stock-associates. The norms are also reiterated by ritual leaders on what are primarily sacred occasions, in order to bring generalized moral pressures to bear and to prevent the spoiling of ritual. Decision making is largely a matter for the individual, influenced more or less by his associates; but if enough people are seriously affected, public decisions *can* be reached at settlement or district levels. Finally, insofar as the ritual and age organization places persistent emphasis on the essential unity and interdependence of all Jie, on internal peace and the norms of right behavior, it powerfully reinforces mundane unity and cooperation and serves as the major integrative factor in the society.

CHANGE

There have been few changes in Jie society during the twentieth century,[8] and Jie have remarkably little knowledge of or interest in preceding times. Colonial intervention began in the first decade of the century, primarily as a military operation to end ivory poaching by foreigners and to prevent intertribal warfare on the eastern borders of the then new Protectorate of Uganda. For the latter purpose, an important limitation was imposed on the Jie: not only were they compelled to abjure warfare[9] but, to reduce the possibilities of conflict, the majority of the people were made to live permanently in the settled area in central Jieland. Previously, as the dry season advanced and milk and water supplies failed at the homesteads, the whole population had shifted into the stock camps, leaving the settled area deserted until the rainy season began. This compulsory change brought hardship, especially because of acute water shortage until bored wells were introduced in the 1940s. It also exacerbated overgrazing and erosion in the settled area, as cattle have been retained there rather longer each dry season than hitherto. On the other hand, it is probable that the operative unity of both settlements and districts has been intensified now that most members of those groups no longer scatter for several months each year. Conversely, the district lost part of its *raison d'être* since it had been the unit of military activity.

The colonial government appointed a chief and headmen over the Jie; their potential roles have not been understood by the people, who have passively accepted them as alien impositions. The first small mission and school opened in 1949; it has expanded since, but there are still few even partly educated Jie, and few who know or care about the outside world. On the whole, the colonial government remained remote, primarily keeping the peace, and interfering little in everyday life. Compulsory cattle sales began in the 1940s to reduce stock numbers, to supply meat to the more populous areas of Uganda, and to introduce cash into the Jie economy. Without compulsion it is doubtful that the Jie would have sold many animals, and they converted much of the money into goats and sheep purchased from their eastern neighbors. The one or two foreign-owned stores opened in the settled area have provided a source of foodstuffs alternative to the traditional barter trade, which, however, is still the more important. Ox plows, first introduced in 1951, have been enthusiastically welcomed; as a result cultivation is now primarily men's work, but in their wives' fields. There is no cash crop.

The population of Jieland has probably doubled during the twentieth century, increasing the dangerous pressure on meager natural resources. It seems possible, but not yet certainly demonstrated, that the increase in the numerical size of extended families has diminished their unity. This has been encouraged by the prevailing peace that has allowed the breakup of the old large homesteads, formerly thought necessary as a vital defense measure. Agnatic conflict can now be expressed and avoided by residential separation, and the overriding need to maintain unity is less evident.

The Jie are an example of the many peoples of the semiarid East African savannas for whom pastoralism and the economic and social values of livestock are all-important. Like so many of these peoples, and especially the Nilotes, they have thus far been relatively little affected by the impact of the outside world. In part their culture, and especially the strong individualism it fosters, is intrinsically unreceptive to change; more important, they inhabit country whose environmental limitations restrict the usefulness of Western ideas and techniques and the possibilities of change. The Jie sociopolitical system, typical in principle of the eastern Nilotes, is of a kind still relatively poorly studied. It has neither the centralized unity of traditional chiefdoms nor the particular integrity of the segmentary unilineal societies that have been so thoroughly examined by anthropologists in Africa.

NOTES

(1) The sketch map of Jieland and certain ethnographic material in this chapter appeared previously in *The Family Herds* (London: Routledge & Kegan Paul, Ltd., 1955) by P. H. Gulliver. The map and ethnographic material are used here by permission of Routledge & Kegan Paul.

(2) The tribal name has two syllables, and is written as it is pronounced (Ji-e). The people call themselves *Ngijie*, masculine plural, singular *Ejiot*; there are comparable feminine and diminutive forms. Their country is *Ajie*.

(3) For a good example of the mystical importance of cattle among a pastoral people of East Africa, see Evans-Pritchard (1956).

(4) A detailed analysis of the process of family development is given in Gulliver (1955: Chap. 4).

(5) Sometimes no one of these is alive when the time comes, and senior fathers have to act instead.

(6) Initiations occur only at the end of the rainy season, after the main harvest.

(7) The name is associated with *kuju* (up, above). There is some anthropomorphic concept of Akuj, but notions about his nature are vague.

(8) The ethnographic present of this essay is about 1950. A first visit was made to Jieland in 1949, and the main fieldwork was carried out between November 1950 and June 1951.

(9) In any case, Jie had been largely on the defensive in the preceding decades, mainly against the stronger Karamojong and Dodos.

Bibliography

With a few exceptions the following bibliography emphasizes contemporary work. Starred items (*) include significant bibliographies. Daggered items (†) are cited as references in the text of the chapter.

Colson, Elizabeth (1962). "The Role of Cattle among the Plateau Tonga of Mazabuka District," in *The Plateau Tonga of Northern Rhodesia*. New York: Humanities Press, pp. 121–171.
An excellent account of pastoralism in a Bantu society.

Dyson-Hudson, N. (1958). "The Karamojong and the Suk," *Uganda Journal*, Vol. 12, No. 2, pp. 173–180.
A brief account of the southern neighbors of the Jie.

Evans-Pritchard, E. E. (1939). *The Nuer*. London: Oxford University Press.

——— (1951). *Kinship and Marriage among the Nuer*. London: Oxford University Press.

——— (1956†). *Nuer Religion*. London: Oxford University Press.
This trilogy contains the best available account of an African pastoral people. The Nuer are a western Nilotic group, with an ecology and economy similar to those of the Jie.

Fosbrooke, H. A. (1948). "An Administrative Survey of the Masai Social System," *Tanganyika Notes and Records*, Vol. 26, pp. 1–50.
The best single account of the Masai, a seminomadic group of eastern Nilotes.

Girling, F. K. (1960). *The Acholi of Uganda*. London: H. M. Stationery Office (Colonial Research Studies No. 30).
Deals with the western neighbors of the Jie. The Acholi are western Nilotes.

Greenberg, Joseph (1955†). *Studies in African Linguistic Classification*. New Haven, Conn.: Compass Publishing Co.

Gulliver, Pamela, and P. H. Gulliver (1953*). *The Central Nilo-Hamites*. London: International African Institute. (Ethnographic Survey of Africa, East-Central Africa, vii.)
A general survey of the peoples of the Teso Cluster, including the Jie.

Gulliver, P. H. (1951*). *A Preliminary Survey of the Turkana*, Cape Town University (Communications from the School of African Studies No. 26).

A general survey of the eastern neighbors of the Jie and the people most closely related to them.

———— (1952a). "The Karamajong Cluster," *Africa,* Vol. 22, No. 1 pp. 1–21.
A historical and ethnographic survey of the Jie and their most closely related neighbors.

———— (1952b). "Bell-oxen and Ox-names among the Jie," *Uganda Journal,* Vol. 16, pp. 72–75.

———— (1953a). "Jie Marriage," *African Affairs,* Vol. 52, pp. 149–155.

———— (1953b). "The Population of Karamoja," *Uganda Journal,* Vol. 17, pp. 178–185.
Deals mainly with Jie demography in the twentieth century.

———— (1953c†). "The Age Organisation of the Jie Tribe," *Journal of the Royal Anthropological Society,* Vol. 83, Part 2, pp. 147–168.
A full account of the Jie age group system.

———— (1954). "Jie Agriculture," *Uganda Journal,* Vol. 18, pp. 65–70.

———— (1955†). *The Family Herds: A Study of Two Pastoral Peoples in East Africa, the Jie and Turkana.* London: Routledge & Kegan Paul, Ltd.
A full account of family and kinship, stock-association and property rights, bridewealth, and the economy of the Jie and the Turkana.

———— (1958). "The Turkana Age Organisation," *American Anthropologist,* Vol. 60. No. 5, pp. 900–922.

———— (1963). *Social Control in an African Society: The Arusha, Agricultural Masai of Northern Tanganyika.* Boston: Boston University Press.
The social system of a Masai-speaking people.

Huntingford, G. W. B. (1950). *Nandi Work and Culture.* London: H. M. Stationery Office
This and the following source contain a general account of one of the main Eastern Nilotic peoples, with a similar economy to that of the Jie.

———— (1953a). *The Nandi of Kenya.* London: Routledge & Kegan Paul.

———— (1953b*). *The Northern Nilo-Hamites.* London: International African Institute. (Ethnographic Survey of Africa, East-Central Africa, xi.)
This and the following source are general surveys of the Eastern Nilotic group other than the Teso Cluster.

———— 1953c*). *The Southern Nilo-Hamites.* London: International African Institute. (Ethnographic Survey of Africa, East-Central Africa, viii.)

Lienhardt, G. (1961). "The Western Dinka," in *Tribes without Rulers,* J. Middleton and D. Tait (eds.). New York: Humanities Press.
The ecology and political system of a large Western Nilotic group in the southern Sudan.

Peristiany, J. C. (1951).   "The Age-Set System of the Pastoral Pokot," *Africa*,
    Vol. 21, pp. 188–206.
        A system similar to that of the Jie, among another eastern Nilotic people.

Tucker, A. N., and M. Bryan (1948†).   *Distribution of the Nilotic and Nilo-
    Hamitic Languages of Africa*. London: Oxford University Press for the
    International African Institute.

6

THE KPELLE OF LIBERIA

about the chapter

The Kpelle live in a part of tropical Africa where rainfall is sufficient for the growing of rice without paddies, as is done in many regions of Asia; upland, or dry, rice is their major crop. The laborious steps in their slash-and-burn agriculture are common in many sub-Saharan societies as dissimilar as the Yoruba, the Rwanda, the Suku, and the Swazi. Other features of Kpelle society include a strong agricultural role for women and the correlation of the farming cycle with a cycle of social and ritual activity. Since these patterns are typical of sedentary agricultural societies of equatorial Africa, they are of interest to the geographer as well as to the anthropologist.

Central to the cultural configuration of the Kpelle, as in many other societies of Liberia, Sierra Leone, Guinea, the Ivory Coast, and their peripheries, are secret societies, especially tribal fraternities such as the Poro, and a parallel association for women—the Sande. Political, correctional, religious, educational, and integrative functions are all partially vested in these tribal societies. Fulfillment of these functions is enhanced by the secrecy, mystery, and ritualism that surround the societies, and which are expressed in the dramatic appearances and nocturnal sounds of masked figures and in forest initiation "schools."

These exotic features drew the attention first of explorers and, more recently, of social scientists. Kpelle chiefs capitalize on them and, above all, on the ritual authority of masked society figures and other society officials. In fact, Kpelle chiefs are themselves highly placed in the Poro. Thus, there is a fusion of ritual or supernatural power which is somewhat analogous to the situation among the Tiv and among the Suku. Moreover, the Kpelle societies combine the secrecy and ritual sanctions with universal membership—a feature of age groups which, as in age-graded cultures such as the Jie, the Swazi, and the Tiv, is strongly integrative. Accordingly, the secret societies enforce a strong degree of adherence to the norms and values of traditional Kpelle society. The fusion of ritual and secular powers in Kpelle political organization results in a unique and compelling centralized structure, "the polycephalous associational state," which is of special interest to both the political scientist and the anthropologist.

The chapter combines the "structural" approach with a focus on ethos, which marks the "configurational" approach. The control and regulation of the tribal societies is directed partly against the stress on individualism and achievement in the Kpelle ethos, which is reflected in various aspects of social organization. Some of the forms that express the achievement motif are common to other sub-Saharan societies; clientship, for example, is found also among the Hausa and the Rwanda. But alongside these are more unusual institutions that give expression to the same theme, such as some of the forms of marriage and a minimal development of unilineal kin groups.

The Kpelle, like the Suku and the Tiv, offer a unique cultural configuration, yet they typify sub-Saharan Africa and thereby give us an indication of the range of diversity characteristic of Africa.

about the author

James L. Gibbs, Jr., is associate Professor of Anthropology at the University of Minnesota, where he received the Distinguished Teacher Award of the College of Science, Literature, and the Arts in 1961. He received his Ph.D. from Harvard University in 1961, and has taught as a visiting professor at Cornell University. In 1957 and 1958 Dr. Gibbs carried out field work among the Kpelle of Liberia as a Ford Foundation Fellow. He is editor of the present volume and has written several articles on the Kpelle as well as "Compensatory Blood-Brotherhood: A Comparative Analysis of Institutionalized Friendship in Two African Societies" (1962) and "Social Organization" in *Horizons of Anthropology* (1964).

JAMES L. GIBBS, JR. · *The Kpelle of Liberia*[1]

INTRODUCTION

Stretching from Portuguese Guinea to the western Ivory Coast and as far north as Mali is an area of Africa in which powerful, well-organized secret societies are one of the major cultural institutions. The functions and activities of universal membership secret societies for men and women reach into many areas of tribal life, creating a fascinating and complex type of social organization. The Kpelle are one of the tribal groups possessing this mystery-dominated cultural configuration unique to that part of Africa.

LOCATION · The Kpelle of Liberia are found primarily in Central Province and also in Western Province.[2] They occupy a great wedge that almost bisects the country. In addition to the 86,000 (Porter 1956) Kpelle who live in Liberia, there is another group at least as large,[3] sometimes referred to as the Guerzé, who live in the bordering country of Guinea. The description here is of the Kpelle of Liberia, with details applying particularly to those of Panta Chiefdom.

LANGUAGE · The Kpelle speak one of the tonal Mande-Fu languages of the Mande subfamily that is part of the large Niger-Congo family (Greenberg 1955). There are significant dialectical differences within the Kpelle that mirror the presence of four recognized subgroups differing slightly in culture: the Kpelle of Guinea, those of Liberia's Western Province, and, in the Central Province, a southwestern and a northeastern group.

PHYSICAL APPEARANCE · In physical appearance the Kpelle are not as tall as the Malinke and other Mande-speakers of the north. They range in color from a pale, coppery brown to almost black. Their noses are not as broad nor their lips as everted as those of the more typically Negroid people farther west on the Guinea Coast.

199

HABITAT[4] · The Kpelle area falls entirely within the tropical forest zone of the Guinea Coast, although the vegetation is largely secondary bush. Virgin forest is uncommon, especially in Central Province.

Actually, the geographical habitat of the Kpelle is reasonably uniform. Most of the Central Province is an area of low plateau that varies in elevation from 600 to 1500 feet. The elevation increases gradually as one moves from southwest to northeast, the plateau being punctuated with occasional hills. The Bong Mountains and the Reputa Escarpment are the most prominent of these. The second distinctive feature of this part of Liberia is the presence of numerous swamps that wrap themselves around the areas of hills and high ground. On the trail one gets the impression of a series of gentle, forested hills and ridges with a swampy area in the valley that separates each.

Liberia's climate has two distinct seasons, a rainy season and a dry season whose intensity lessens as one moves northward. Rainfall in the Kpelle area varies from 175 inches a year at the southwest fringe to 50 inches a year in the extreme northeast. The rainy season is from May to October; the dry, from November to April. The average monthly temperature varies little with the seasons, lying in the 77–79° range. However, the daily range varies 6–10° from the dry season to the wet season.

ECONOMY

CROPS · The Kpelle are—first and foremost—rice farmers, growing upland rice as their subsistence crop and main cash crop. A term used as a synonym for farm (*gbalaŋ*)[5] is *tii* or "work." Thus, when a man says *a tii ka ti*, he means either "That is my farm" or "That is my work." The use of the same term for both meanings is significant, for meaningful work to the Kpelle is rice farming. The second most important subsistence crop is cassava (manioc). Women also grow garden vegetables: yams, eddoes (taro or cocoyam), okra, tomatoes, pumpkins, eggplant, onions, —and to season all the others—red peppers. Some fruits are also grown: bananas, plantains, papayas, pineapples, soursops, oranges, grapefruit, and limes.

Peanuts are a cash crop grown by women, who also save palm kernels for sale to traders. Both men and women raise sugarcane, which, as a cash crop, is used to produce a simple type of distilled rum. Men, particularly, are the gatherers of kola nuts for which there is a steady market in the drier regions to the north. Cotton is grown, not as a cash crop, but for producing homespun cloth.

LAND TENURE · Formally, land is said to be "owned" by the paramount chief, who divides it into portions for each town in the chiefdom, using for boundaries cottonwood and kola trees, creeks and hills. Each town chief divides the land for his town into segments for each quarter, using similar boundaries. These portions, in turn, are further split by the *kwili namu* (quarter elder, literally "quarter owner") into parcels for each of the "families" or unnamed lineages (*kala* or *suu*) of shallow depth that form the significant subgroups within the quarter.

Because each man in the lineage is entitled to the use of a portion of the land, the lineage head cannot refuse to allot a piece of it to each household head in the lineage. Once land is parceled out, it stays within the lineage and reverts to the quarter elder or other original "owner" only when a lineage dies out or some other unusual event occurs. Thus, although a town chief, a quarter elder, or a lineage head is, like the paramount chief, called "owner of the land," each is really a steward, holding the land for the group he represents.

Actually, in everyday situations, the head of a household to whom lineage land has been allocated is spoken of as the owner of the land. He decides which bit of "his" land he will work during a given year and which portions he will allow to lie fallow. Most farms are individually owned by the heads of the households and are worked with the help of the farmer's household group and cooperative work groups. A man's farm will usually be near that of his patrilineal kinsmen or others who live in his quarter; occasionally brothers or a father and grown sons will plant a joint farm. Women, in addition to working their husbands' plots, often have individual gardens of upland rice or swamp rice, the latter being customarily thought of as a woman's crop. Women have complete control over the income from these individual plots.

If the land that a man has access to through his agnates is inadequate for his needs, he may be allowed to use land that belongs to his mother's brother or his wife's family. Or, if he wishes, he may ask for the use of land that belongs to a total stranger. In return for the use of such land, at harvest time he will pay a small amount of rice to the owner. In Panta Chiefdom there is enough land available so that the use of borrowed land is freely arranged, and people do not feel land pressure, as evidenced by the fact that disputes about land are very rare.[6]

The agricultural cycle

Because there is very little virgin forest left in the Kpelle area, most of the farms are made in what is secondary bush, an area that has been cut for farming and has been allowed to lie fallow for an indefinite period. It is readily distinguishable from virgin forest, but is formidable in appearance, being a dense, tangled mass. A Kpelle farm hardly seems that to the unaccustomed American or European eye. It is a large clearing in the midst of bush, in which the trunks of felled trees are left for the maturing rice to "lean on," giving the field a rather untidy appearance. Yet the clear green color of the growing rice, which becomes a soft tan on maturity, contrasts markedly with the surrounding bush, an indication of man's transformation of the rain forest.

The agricultural season begins in January with the clearing of undergrowth, a task carried out by men and women. The vines and large bushes that have grown up during the fallow period are cut and piled to dry. In late March and April, the men cut down the trees but leave cottonwood trees and economically useful oil palm, kola, and citrus trees standing. Tree branches are lopped off and piled with the underbrush to dry. Just before the rains come, all this dried material is burned. The rains beat the ashes into the soil, where they act as fertilizer. The plot is then cleared of unburned brush and branches, leaving only felled trunks. In July, after the rains begin, the women begin *mɔlɔŋ si* (scratching rice), planting the seed rice. For two weeks, almost the entire population of a village will sleep on the farms in order to be on hand to drive away the weaver birds who come to eat the germinating seeds. Weeding of the rice, another operation carried out mainly by women, takes about a month.

After this comes the mid-season lull in farming activity. For about six weeks during this period in August and September the town is full of people during the day. This respite is short-lived, however. Soon the rice heads are maturing, the weaver birds are back in force, and everyone returns to the fields to "drive birds." In a short time the crop is ready and "cutting rice" begins. This harvesting, which takes place anywhere from October to December, may, on a very large farm, take several weeks. To prevent spoilage due to dampness, the rice, which is cut stalk by stalk, is allowed to dry in the sun for a few weeks before being taken to the granaries, which are built by the men. The filling of the rice loft marks the end of the farming season and a period of celebration that, even in remote, non-Christian villages, centers on Christmas Day.

This type of slash-and-burn agriculture is demanding of all who farm. Farms are as much as two hours' walk from town, the workday is from dawn to dusk, and the slack months are few. *Tii* is an all-consuming activity. Even more significant is the dominant role played by women: among the Panta Kpelle they participate in all steps except felling trees and burning off and building granaries.[7] As we shall see, this has implications for the operation of the stratification system and the incidence of divorce.

From the ripening of the rice in September until the cutting of the new bush in February, there is a period of intensified economic and social activity. Farmers sell any rice left over after meeting the previous year's subsistence needs. After the lean period preceding the harvest, those without such a surplus are happy to sell a little of the newly harvested crop. The money is

A Kpelle Farm A cooperative work group (*kuu*) eats
its midday meal after a morning spent "burning-off" the
farm.

used for buying new clothes or other consumer goods, such as hunting
lamps. It is also the inevitable period for repaying to Malinke[8] traders any
loans made since the previous harvest season. Looms are set up, men weave,
women make pots and fish nets, and everyone participates in house building
and repairing. This is also a time for tending to social and political matters:
the chiefs devote time to whittling away a backlog of untried disputes and
wives may make extended visits to their families. In short, the trading and
social cycles parallel the agricultural cycle.

ANIMAL HUSBANDRY, HUNTING, AND GATHERING · Farming being as important as it is in Kpelle eyes, animal husbandry does not make a significant
contribution to the economy. After chickens, goats and sheep are the most
commonly kept livestock. Guinea fowl, ducks, and pigs are found occasionally. Rarest of all are cattle, which, in a tsetse-resistant breed, are kept only
by men of great wealth, primarily for prestige purposes. They will be
slaughtered for occasional feasts or visits of important government officials.
Hunting, fishing, and gathering also play a relatively minor role among the
Kpelle. The forest of Central Province has been largely hunted out, so that
men, who do the hunting, do not find game a dependable source of meat.
Fishing, in the hands of women, adds a small, steady contribution of animal
protein to the diet; other supplements are certain wild leaves, roots, and
honey. As noted earlier, kola nuts are gathered for trade purposes.

OCCUPATIONAL SPECIALIZATIONS AND TRADE · Occupational specializations
are also secondary to farming, and specialists always work at their specialties
on a part-time basis while farming for their basic subsistence. For men the
traditional part-time specializations are acting as a *zo* (medicine man, plural,

Packing Kola Nuts Kola nuts are packed for sale to Malinke traders.

zoŋa) and blacksmithing. Newer occupations are sawing timber, tailoring, operating a shop or café, and sandal making and repairing.

It is significant that many of those who follow the newer trades are people of other tribes who live among the Kpelle or are Kpelle who have had long contact with other tribal groups: the commercial spirit is poorly developed among the Liberian Kpelle, as is also evidenced by the lack of large, periodic markets. However, simply by displaying them in front of her home, a woman may gain some income by petty trade of garden produce or prepared items like palm oil, fried bread, or pots. Or she may serve as a midwife and medical practitioner. Serious trade is mainly in the hands of Lebanese or "Mandingoes." The latter, whose proper tribal name is Malinke, are an Islamized group from Guinea who live scattered among the Kpelle as semi-itinerant traders. They buy rice and kola nuts and sell hand-crafted items from the north such as homespun robes, bedclothes, raffia bags, as well as "medicines" and charms, or such imported wares as cooking pots.

MATERIAL CULTURE • The blacksmith has high status in any Kpelle community and his craft is considered very important. In the not distant past, iron was smelted from ore; but nowadays implements are usually forged from scrap iron, such as discarded automobile springs. Tools made include machetes, hoes, and knives, although factory-made imported machetes are now extremely common. The blacksmith also makes his own anvil, hammers, and tongs. It is a virtual certainty that the smith makes whatever implements are used in Poro ceremonies (see section on the tribal societies below), such as the knives that cut the initiates' cicatrices. The maker of these implements must know how they are used. Therefore, the high status of the blacksmith is partly explained by the fact that he produces agricultural tools; but another reason for it is that he is necessarily party to privileged information regarding the tribal societies.

In addition to iron, the habitat yields wood, which is made into mortars, rice spoons, stools, chairs, and occasional figurines and masks. In some cases the smith is also the carver. Clay is used for pots. Piassava (a bamboolike reed) is used for winnowing trays and chair seats; raffia is used for making twine, hammocks, and skirts for some types of dancing. Many of these items are produced by individuals for their own use; part-time artisans specialized in the manufacture of each item do not exist. The same is true of fish nets, which women make from the twine they produce from the fronds of the oil palm, and of the baskets they make with various grasses.

Musical implements include drums of several types, harps, rattles, resonators, and side-blown horns.

In the past the Kpelle produced many items that are now seldom seen: wooden *malaŋ* (*wari*) game boards, elaborate "chief's chairs," brass anklets and bracelets, and iron spears and arrow points.[9] Many items of tribal manufacture, such as sleeping mats, bed covers, and chiefs' gowns are commonly imported from Guinea. Kpelle there have maintained more of the old craft tradition and items are fabricated with more artisanship. The presence of larger, periodic markets has probably favored this trend. The Kpelle are very pragmatic and, when compared with examples of many African craft traditions, such as that of the Dan of Liberia and the Ivory Coast, their craft products seem poorly finished and crudely executed. The focus is on utility more than on craftsmanship or aesthetic refinement.

Kpelle grow cotton, which is made into yarn by women and woven by men on looms that produce a strip of coarse, durable cloth about six inches wide known in Liberia as "country cloth" (Kpelle, *siɣe*). The strips may be all white or striped with white and either blues, blacks, tans, or combinations of white, blues, and either of the other colors. They are sewn into larger pieces of cloth, which are used as bed covers or made up into garments. In Guinea white and black strips are made into bed covers with a striking checkerboard pattern. These are widely traded in the Liberian Kpelle area.

Kpelle women wear a two-yard piece of cloth called a *lapa*, which is wrapped around the body under the arms and fastened by tucking one end into the other. This is very rarely made of homespun nowadays; brightly printed trade cloth is much more common. More acculturated women replace the *lapa* with a fitted, sewn bodice and a *lapa*like cloth worn from the hips as a skirt. A smaller piece of cloth tied around the waist is used to carry a child in the small of the back. Virtually all women wear a bright tradecloth head tie or kerchief tied around the head. Occasionally one sees a very old woman wearing the traditional toque of homespun. Old women also sometimes fashion false braids out of the combings of their younger and

The Town Chief of Gwinyee with Part of His Family His robe is of homespun cloth. The house in the background is typical in form and construction.

black-haired friends and co-wives, which they wear fastened under their head ties to frame their faces.

For important occasions chiefs and other men of standing wear homespun gowns with voluminous draped sleeves and underneath modified Turkish or European trousers. A few older men wear shifts of homespun cloth for everyday, but more common are garments of similar cut made of trade cloth, which is far cheaper, if less durable. Younger men wear a European style of shirts and shorts of trade cloth. Most Kpelle go barefoot, although a very large proportion of people wear sandals fashioned out of discarded tires and strips of inner tubing, and those who can afford to do so wear leather sandals or shoes. A man who considers himself to be no longer tribal will almost always wear long trousers and shoes to symbolize this.

The Kpelle house, built of wattle and daub with thatched roof, is described in a section below, "The Household." Other Kpelle architectural types of similar construction include larger buildings used as courthouses by paramount chiefs, farm shelters, granaries, and occasional chicken coops. Open-sided thatch-roofed pavilions called "palaver houses" are used by town chiefs as courthouses, and open-roofed bathing enclosures are built of saplings and vines.

THE COMMUNITY AND TERRITORIAL ORGANIZATION

THE TOWN AND THE QUARTER • As noted earlier, a Kpelle town is divided into wards or quarters (singular, *kwili* or *kwei*), which are social as well as territorial entities. Those who live in one quarter are *kwili ɓela tɔnɔ* (literally, the portion of people who live in one quarter), or *kwili ɓela* (the quarter people). The core of the quarter consists of several groups of patrilineally related males heading their own households, a man, his brothers, and his grown sons all living near each other. These groups are not named, nor do they have many corporate functions.

The ties between the most senior members of these groups, the elders of the quarter, are difficult to trace and sometimes are fictive. Actually, the overall composition of the quarter often deviates markedly from the ideal that says that all household heads should be patrilineally related to the *kwili namu* (quarter elder). Some men live there because of matrilineal ties; others have ties of clientship or perhaps lapsed bonds of pawning or slavery that no one will articulate. A few are "strangers" who have come because of an affinal link; in the larger villages, one finds people who "sit down" only by permission of the *kwili namu*—that is, they are Kpelle who lack even affinal ties—and members of other tribes.

In spite of these variable links, the *kwili ɓela* think of themselves as the quarter elder's people, a kinship unit. But the quarter is not rigidly exogamous. This is true even though the Kpelle have patrilineally inherited food taboos, and the people of one quarter are sometimes characterized by those of other quarters as "the people who can't eat such-and-such." People with the same food taboo may marry if they cannot trace actual common genealogical ties.[10] The *kwili ɓela* are, all in all, more neighbors than kinsmen.

The quarter, as noted earlier, is technically a landholding unit; but most of the corporate functions center on the duties to the government rather than the private needs of the *kwili ɓela*. The quarter is the unit in which taxes are collected and laborers are recruited for "government work."[11] One of the few tasks in which the people of the quarter work together is tidying up the quarter or brushing near the village paths. People of the quarter may also express their unity in subtle ways: by forming cooperative work groups for farming, or by exerting pressure on a blacksmith to give members of his own quarter first preference during the busy season of toolmaking. The quarter has few corporate functions; large-scale kinship groups are not very significant in Kpelle social organization.

THE HOUSEHOLD • The most significant kinship unit among the Kpelle is the household. In composition, three quarters of the households are of the polygynous, nuclear family type: a man, his wives, and their children. The most frequent deviation from this pattern is the household consisting of a man and one or two of his grown brothers and possibly their wives. Another variation is the addition of a spouse's parent (usually the husband's mother) to the polygynous family. Although the Kpelle are patrilocal, the extended family is relatively rare, for an adult Kpelle male who is married prefers to live in his own house, even though it is usually close to that of his father.

This residence pattern is evidence of patrilineality as are the patrilineal food taboos and the pattern of inheritance, which runs from a man to a brother or a grown son.

The most important corporate activity of the household is farming. Although each person may plant and tend an individual farm or garden, all the members of the household cooperate in working the fields of the household head, which are, in reality, the family farm.

Kpelle say the household head should manage the income from the rice so as to pay the hut tax, provide his wives and children with items for which cash is needed, such as clothing and medicines, and supply his sons with brideprice when they marry. The wife is, as everywhere, cook, house-keeper, and child-tender. One of her significant roles is regulating the flow of rice from the granary. Keeping the key, she guards the reserve of seed rice and also determines how much rice is to be used for subsistence and how much her husband may sell. Although a woman's formal status in the home is low, her tasks there are as crucial as those in the fields.

Children are expected to help with as many farm and household tasks as they are able until they marry and establish their own households. (See the section "Child Training and Socialization" below.)

The house itself is of wattle-and-daub construction, with a vertical framework of saplings lashed together horizontally with vines. Over this is applied wet earth mixed with mud from a termite hill and finished, where available, with a waterproofing layer of cow dung and a final coat of white clay. The roof has a similar framework thatched with leaves of the oil palm or piassava. Men build and keep in repair the framework and roof; women, the walls. The traditional round, windowless house has in most towns been largely replaced by a rectangular structure divided into quarters to form three rooms and a porch. In polygynous households each wife and her children have a separate room; it is very rare for each of several co-wives to be established in a separate dwelling.

LIFE CYCLE

Child training and socialization[12]

Kpelle babies are not born at home, but in the bush or in a special house built for that purpose. The mothers are attended by a *zo* or a *fia lee zo* (female medical specialist) because men are not normally allowed to be present at birth. The mother returns to her house after three days if the infant is a girl; after four, if a boy. An expressed ideal is that a first-born child should be raised by its maternal grandmother from the time it walks, but this is apparently infrequent in practice. Children are nursed at least until they walk and usually until age two or three, during most of which time the mother observes a postpartum taboo on sexual intercourse with her husband. Children are weaned between the ages of two and four unless the mother becomes pregnant again. In that case, the baby is usually weaned immediately. The most common method of weaning is for the mother to smear her breasts with a bitter substance. Other methods are to send the child on a visit to a grandmother or to offer the child sweets. The weaning is never sudden, for the child is given rice water from the first few days of life. This is often force-fed as the mother blocks the nostrils and grips the child with her legs so as to restrain movement. Soft foods, such as mashed banana, and then solid foods are introduced, and the child is expected to be able to eat regular foods with the family by the time he is walking. At this point, because their children are no longer largely dependent on the breast, Kpelle mothers consider the children "weaned" and that they themselves are no longer bound by the postpartum sex taboo.

Kpelle parents do not give their children much help in walking. However, if the child does not walk by a certain time, there is anxiety that is expressed by applying "medicine" to his feet. With talking, in contrast, there is conscious concern from the beginning. The child is prompted and corrected, for the Kpelle feel that a person should use language well.

Mothers often fondle their small sons' penises, especially while nursing them, and boys are not punished for autoeroticism. A child is expected to be able to control his urination by the time he is walking well and to have completed toilet training by the time he is three. With toilet training and with walking there is an apparently *laissez-faire* attitude that masks underlying concern with achievement and mastery. Permissiveness with regard to genital manipulation seems more thorough.

Mastery becomes important in role training and the assumption of household tasks: A girl is given her first tasks around the home at six, when she can heat water and sweep the floor. By eight, she can hull and winnow rice, haul water from the creek, care for younger siblings, and help her mother on the farm. Two years later she knows how to cook most dishes. A boy's responsibilities begin a bit later, with a stress on agricultural activities. By mid-adolescence he could farm on his own if he wished to. Two values that are expected to be internalized by both boys and girls are working diligently and showing respect for older persons.

Genital operations are usual for both young men and women: either circumcision or a clitoridectomy (see page 222). Both postpubescent girls and boys commonly engage in teasing as mild sex play and exchange gifts and personal services—such as a girl washing a boy's clothes for him. Assignations culminating in sexual intercourse are not uncommon, although parents seem to remain overtly unaware of them. Betrothal and marriage do not usually occur before a woman is sixteen or eighteen and a man somewhat older.

Marriage

BETROTHAL • In the past, the Kpelle practiced infant betrothal and childhood betrothal, but neither of these forms is any longer followed, and they have been outlawed by the Liberian government. A man who wishes to marry will present his sweetheart with a *wɛli sɛŋ* (love token), such as twenty-five or forty cents in coin[13] or a bracelet, saying, for example, "I love you, I want you to be my wife." She will then present this to her parents, asking their permission to marry the suitor. If they assent, the man will follow this up by presenting them with a small sum of money, the *iyeei ŋa sɛŋ* ("something from your hand") which affirms the honorableness of his intentions.

In choosing a spouse, a Kpelle man or woman has virtually free rein, for preferential marriage is not institutionalized. Kpelle say that it is good to marry a matrilineal cross-cousin or a wife's sister, but genealogies show that this is rarely done.

MARRIAGE CEREMONIAL • On the day set for the wedding itself, the two families meet at the bride's house, and each family will have a person designated as a spokesman. The ceremony itself involves an exchange of prestations. Among the Kpelle, bridewealth is paid in installments throughout the life of the marriage, and the initial payment is made at the time of the marriage ceremony. It is often made in cash, but it may also take the form of livestock, such as a sheep or a goat, or goods, such as bracelets or enamel basins. Marriage payments are very low.[14] In the vivid idiom of hinterland English, "It can be two cents itself!" When the parents are particularly fond of the prospective son-in-law, they may not require a marriage payment at that time. The parents show their consent by presenting the woman to her husband along with a token that binds the husband to care for her (*neni dei sɛŋ*, "woman giving thing," or *ŋei ke ma,* literally, "put your eyes upon her").

It is the giving of this token that effects the marriage. As long as the woman has been turned over "on something" the marriage is legal, even though there has been no marriage payment. A Kpelle wedding, in contrast to a Kpelle funeral, is not marked by much in the way of public display or festivity. In fact, there is often an almost clandestine air about it as a few people gather casually in the room or the house.[15]

FORMS OF MARRIAGE • The Kpelle differ from some African groups in having several forms of union loosely referred to in casual conversation as "marriage." These forms differ in terms of the effecting ceremonial and the rights transferred to the husband.

The first form, *endowed marriage,* is the ideal form described above where the woman is turned over to her husband with a token and an initial marriage payment is made. In this form of marriage the husband obtains complete personal rights (rights *in personam*) over her: he can take her to his home to live, he has control over her sexual activities, children born to the union belong to his lineage, and he can command her economic services. In the second type of marriage, *token transfer marriage,* a woman is turned over to her husband with a token, but no marriage payment is made. This form of marriage also transfers all full rights *in personam* over the woman, but it is a less prestigious form of union.

In *bride service marriage* the groom elects to work for his wife's parents in lieu of paying brideprice. In the ceremony, *he* is turned over to *them* with a token, agreeing to work for a variable period of time. Living in his wife's house, he cannot determine her residence nor command her labor. Children born to the couple before the completion of the period of bride service belong to the wife's family. The only right *in personam* he can claim is control of her sexual activities, and thus, the ability to claim adultery damages.[16] *Male concubinage,* rooted in clientship, is another form of union in which the husband's rights over the woman are severely limited. A young man who does not have the means of obtaining a marriage payment will go to a chief or other wealthy man and ask to be given one of the wealthier man's wives as a consort. The woman remains legally the wife of the tɔ nuu (patron), but the tii kɛ nuu (client) cohabits with her in a house provided by the patron-husband. Although the patron gives up sexual access to his wife, he retains the right to collect any adultery damages that may be incurred by her actions, and children born to her and the client legally belong to the patron. In addition to working their own farm, both the woman and the client work on the farm of the patron, who gains labor and political support from this arrangement. In a formal sense, the client gains little more than sexual access to a woman.

Two forms of union that give no legal rights *in personam* at all are *trial marriage* and *cohabitation.* In each case, for one reason or another, the man and woman simply live together without going through a ceremony. The difference between the two forms is that in trial marriage the couple intends to become formally married, but the woman goes to live in the man's house "to look around to see if she likes his ways," for the Kpelle feel that a marriage can be successful only if the partners know each other well and like what they see of each other.

The relationship between a man and his wife is not characterized by an open show of affection but more by reserve, formally rendered respect, and a calculable exchange of stipulated gifts and services. For example,

Co-wives Hulling Rice Domestic animals, such as the goats and chickens seen here, are not usually fed, but allowed to forage.

Kpelle spouses address each other by the "respect form" of the personal name, a form that is otherwise used in addressing older people and certain affines. In addition a man and his wife spend much of their time in separate activities.

POLYGYNY · Among the Kpelle, polygyny is the cultural ideal, and most men wish to acquire secondary wives, for this is the way to acquire prestige and, hence, wealth and political power. A man's first wife will have considerable interest in her husband's wish for additional wives because it gives her the status of head wife and less work. She will help her husband to save money for bridewealth and may even say, "I have seen so-and-so, who looks like she works well. Here is some money to pay brideprice for her as *our* wife" (emphasis mine).

Although the second wife may be welcomed by the first one, her advent often alters a head wife's relationship with her husband, for the second wife being young—and new—is often favored by the husband to some extent. Such disparity in the treatment of co-wives has effects on the relations of the wives with each other. Their feeling of companionship and sharing of work and activity is frequently almost obliterated by the undercurrent of jealousy and envy that often takes the form of witchcraft accusations that are lodged between co-wives more than between other people.

A second way of acquiring secondary wives is through inheritance, for when a man dies, his eldest son inherits all his wives (except his own mother, of course). In most cases where a man has more than two wives, most of the secondary wives are inherited in this pattern I term the "filial levirate."

This practice may create tension between the elder brother and his younger brothers, who have no legal claim on their deceased father's wives.

Such tensions are aggravated by Kpelle incest regulations, which allow a man to have sexual access to the wives of his father, his son, and his brothers (real and classificatory). However, a father does not usually exercise his option of sleeping with his son's wives, although the reverse is much more often true. Similarly, a thoughtful man does not sleep with his brother's wives without obtaining consent, for to do so—while permissible—creates tension in the family.

Such liaisons within the family do not count as "adultery" but when formed with a nonfamily member, they do, and entitle the cuckolded husband to collect "adultery damages," which are fixed by law at ten dollars. Taking lovers, both by men and by women, is not unusual in Kpelle society and informants express pleasure in the air of excitement and zest added by the demands of discretion, the pleasure of new sexual experience, and the flow of gifts involved in an extramarital affair. Such affairs are a frequent element in divorce in Kpelle society.

DIVORCE • An outsider first attending court sessions among the Kpelle is struck by the lack of variety of cases. Nothing occurs with the regularity of *kule meni* ("women palaver"), which includes both adultery and divorce. Adultery is more likely to be settled out of court, so that most courtroom cases of *kule meni* are divorce cases.

Divorce is customarily instituted by the woman, and, because fault is held to lie with the person who institutes suit, a man who wishes a divorce will usually mistreat his wife until she initiates proceedings. Such an action consists of two parts often held in one hearing. First there is *da taa* (literally, "they scattered"), the determination of fault. If a judge decides that a divorce is in order (and he usually does), he then goes on to the the the *seŋ kau kula lee meni* ("digging-out-the-money-left-behind-palaver," or, more prosaically, refund of brideprice action).

A divorced woman held at fault loses her rights in the rice harvest, the major common property. In such cases, full brideprice is returned, even where children have been born of the union. This is quite unusual in African societies. Children of the marriage are held to "belong to the man," which means mainly that a father can collect his daughter's brideprice when she comes of age. Young children usually stay with their mother, however, for it is felt that it is better to have a stepfather than a stepmother. The ceremony of divorce is the reverse of that for marriage, the chief, serving as judge, places the woman's hand in that of her father with a token provided by the husband.

The divorce rate is moderately high, and Kpelle men claim that their wives are quick to divorce them. Moreover, divorce is a frequent topic of discussion among the Kpelle; people consider it something of a social problem. This marital instability is deeply rooted in some features of Kpelle society previously described. For example, the several forms of union mean that a man can have genuine doubt as to whether or not a woman is really married and therefore legitimately open to his attentions. Similarly, a man can achieve valued goals, such as access to women and acquiring children of his own, without marrying. Because these goals are not even scarce outside marriage, they cannot serve as rewards for those who marry and manage to stay married. The crucial role women play in farming and in regulating the household economy means that they are a source of wealth and much sought after (see "Stratification" below). Knowing this, they are quick to leave a husband who displeases them, for they are always welcome elsewhere. Finally, the weak role of the kin group means that it cannot effectively buttress faltering unions by applying such sanctions as withdrawing access to farm labor. The conclusion suggested by this line of analysis is that Kpelle marriage is unstable because its norms are uncertain, conformity to them is not strongly rewarded, nor is deviance from them punished.[17]

STRATIFICATION

The Kpelle have an incipient class system that distinguishes three classes: tɔ nuwai (rich men), lɔi loŋni (sons of the soil), and tii kɛ nuwai (workmen or clients)—an upper class, middle class, and lower class, respectively. This is termed an "incipient" class system because the range of attributes on which the classes differ is small, the ratio of intraclass interaction to interclass interaction is small, and the number of people in both the upper and lower groups is small.

This class system has historical origins because it stems from the domestic slavery once practiced by the Kpelle, although slavery has, of course, been abolished by the Liberian government. In earlier times there were three classes: freemen, slaves, and pawns.

The upper class among the Kpelle are referred to as tɔ nuwai (singular, tɔ nuu), which literally is "upstanding or upright person," but is also used to mean rich men or prominent men as well as chiefs. To be a tɔ nuu is to be in a position of power and respect. The tɔ nuwai are those men who are looked up to by their fellows, the bearers of prestige and the molders of opinion. Most important, it is from among such men that paramount chiefs and other chiefs are chosen. A tɔ nuu is a person who helps others when they are in distress. If a man is pressed to raise the money to pay his hut tax or to pay a court fine a tɔ nuu will help him out with a loan or a gift. He would be reluctant to see a man go to the funeral of an affine with empty hands or to see someone die for the lack of the wherewithal to consult a zo. Thus it is not the possession of wealth alone that marks a tɔ nuu, but the way in which it is used.

An earmark of the tɔ nuu noted explicitly by the Kpelle is the fact that he has many wives. They are the major source of his wealth. A polygynist's wives form the main continuing source of labor for his rice farm, both by working themselves and by bringing to the farm the various cooperative work groups to which they belong. In addition, each woman may have her own individual rice farm, whose crop helps to support her and her children. Moreover, a prominent *tɔ nuu* will often have more wives than he can satisfy sexually. He may acquiesce if his wives form adulterous liaisons because he can then collect adultery damages from each named adulterer— and double damages if he is a chief. A man with dozens of wives may achieve an income of moderate proportions from this source. The control of the sexual functions of many women provides a third source of income. As noted earlier, a *tɔ nuu* may allow some of his wives to become the consorts of poor men from the lower class who become his *tii kɛ nuwai*. These clients are another source of labor to work the patron's farms and perform such tasks as cutting palm nuts. But if the patron is a chief or a would-be chief, they constitute a ready-made claque, for they are sure to "praise the man's name."

Although a *tɔ nuu* is not immediately identifiable among other people in Kpelleland, there are subtle differences. He lives in a house that is distinguishable from that of his neighbors by its size and its embellishment: it may have a tar-paper or a galvanized roof and it may be finished with cement and commercial whitewash instead of clay and cow dung. Ordinarily, he will dress much like everyone else, wearing shirt and trousers of trade cloth. However, they are tailored in the native fashion, and he rarely affects completely European dress. On special occasions, fine homespun robes and, perhaps, shoes set him apart. Such a man is marked by his wealth in livestock as much as by his wealth in women. To own a cow or a steer is a sure indicator of status, as is the possession of more than one or two goats, sheep, or pigs. Livestock, like women, are used to enhance a *tɔ nuu's* reputation. Since they can be sold quickly, they are easily convertible assets, adding to the ability to raise money to aid a neighbor in distress. Livestock also means meat in the cooking pot for entertaining chiefs, a district commissioner, or potential political supporters.

It is significant that this stratification system makes class distinctions on the basis not only of wealth and material goods, but of the possession of women and children. A *tɔ nuu* has several wives and many children sired not only by himself but by the consorts of his surplus wives. A *lɔi lɔŋ* is a man with one wife (or not more than three wives) and his own children. The *tii kɛ nuu* has a consort and children that are not, in the last analysis, his. From one point of view this is a tripartite class system composed of wife-lenders, wife-keepers, and wife-borrowers: a system based on the locus of rights *in uxorem* (right of sexual access) as well as on differences in wealth.

The stratification system is connected with political organization because to become a chief, one must first become a tɔ nuu. It is the Kpelle man's goal to enlarge his household by plural marriage and with the wealth produced by his wives (as laborers and as producers of adultery damages) to begin to attract the following of people that makes political success possible.

POLITICAL ORGANIZATION

Most tɔ nuwai aspire to becoming one of the several types of chiefs. However, there is no single king or chief who serves as the head of state for all the Kpelle or even the Liberian Kpelle. Instead, there is a series of paramount chiefs, all of equal authority. Serving under them are district chiefs, town chiefs, and quarter officials, whose political control is reinforced by the activities of an associational group, the Poro Society. Thus Kpelle political organization can be termed the "polycephalous associational state."

THE PARAMOUNT CHIEF • A paramount chief's domain is his "chiefdom," the largest tribal administrative unit into which each of the interior districts that compose the provinces of Liberia is divided (see note 2). The unity of the chiefdom is traditional, deriving from dialectal differences, hazy tales of common origin or migration, former common enemies, and allegiance to common chiefs who were historical figures.

Although he is the highest ranking tribal chief, a paramount chief (kaloŋ, "chief") is also a salaried official of the Liberian government and, as such, mediates between his people and the government. Much of the respect that attaches to his office stems from the fact that he carries out the traditional tasks of hearing disputes, preserving order, keeping up paths, and —seldom mentioned nowadays—maintaining "medicines." As a government official, he carries out orders of the district commissioner, collects taxes, and recruits laborers. It is the performance of these latter duties, viewed more ambivalently by the tribesmen, that imposes the greatest demands and requires most judiciousness and tact. Missteps are somewhat minimized by the fact that deliberations and responsibility can be shared: paramount chiefs and subordinate chiefs down to the level of the town chief administer with the aid of a council of elders. District chiefs, town chiefs, and quarter elders of the headquarters town customarily comprise the paramount chief's council. As is true of many parts of Africa, a chief who adheres closely to government regulations is likely to find his constituents somewhat dissatisfied with him and, conversely, if his administration is highly popular with his tribesmen, it is likely that the central government views it as less than ideal.

The difficulties of a paramount chief's position are outweighed by the tangible and intangible rewards he receives as a politically successful tɔ nuu.

A Paramount Chief Settling a Dispute The defendant's mother "begs" for her son in a case heard out of court on the porch of the chief's home.

Besides his government salary, he receives a commission on hut taxes collected in his chiefdom, a commission from Firestone Plantations for laborers recruited for employment, a portion of court fees collected, a stipulated amount of rice from each household in place of the traditional labor requirement,[18] and—usually—a stipend for serving as a party chairman for the True Whig party. Gifts of one sort or another are brought by people who have come to request favors and intercessions, for one cannot "beg the chief with an empty hand." Certain portions of large game are also presented to the chief, but the scarcity of game has deprived this privilege of its economic value. The intangible rewards are to be surrounded by trappings of power—uniformed messengers, a literate clerk, and symbols of wealth—many wives, embroidered gowns, and freedom from manual work in the rice fields.[19]

THE DISTRICT CHIEF · Each chiefdom is divided into two or more districts, which in Liberia are called "clans" although they are not primarily kinship groups or even compromise kin groups but territorial units.[20] Each district is administered by a district chief who, like the paramount chief, is "elected" after having been named by elders.[21] He is not simply the paramount chief's lieutenant, but a liaison between his people and the paramount chief. He represents them in the deliberations of the chiefdom council, transmitting their grievances as well as informing them of the administrative decisions of the paramount chief. In most districts the district chief has a close relationship with his people, and a paramount chief who wishes to remain successful in office must work closely with his district chiefs. Neither the role strains nor the compensations of a district chief are as extensive as those of the paramount chief, but they are broadly parallel.

THE TOWN CHIEF · In his town the town chief is *the tɔ nuu*, the "big man." More than the comparatively remote paramount chief, he is in many

ways the ideal of every growing Kpelle boy: receiving visitors bearing bowls
of hulled rice, chickens, or government letters; relinquishing the machete
in favor of hours spent swinging in a hammock of his palaver house settling
disputes or discussing the pressing affair of the moment; and distributing
his largesse as a host. His townsmen feel freer to carry their complaints
and dissatisfactions to him than to his superiors. He, on his part, is more
sensitive to and reflective of their consensus than to what is known in Kpelle
as *game pawa* (government power). This paternal and intercessionary role
is one that enhances his eminence as *to nuu*. In official duties, the town
chief is to the district chief as the district chief is to the paramount chief.
As a member of both the district chief's and the paramount chief's councils,
he participates in the decision-making aspects of tribal administrative and
legislative processes.

QUARTER OFFICIALS · As noted above, a Kpelle town of any size at all is
divided into two or more quarters headed by a *kwili namu* (quarter elder).
He hears petty palavers, oversees tax collection, and—if he is tradition-
minded—cares for the quarter medicines.

Nowadays a parallel functionary is the *kwili kalon* (quarter chief)
or *koti* (not translatable). He is a younger man who is responsible for the
quarter affairs pertaining to the central government, primarily the recruitment of laborers. It will be he who locates porters to carry the load of a
passing chief or government official, or designates who will fill the quarter's
monthly quota for labor. He often collects taxes for the *kwili namu*. The
post of *kwili kalon* is significant because it is the first rung of the ladder
to high political office. It is for this reason viewed as a desirable position
even though the duties are generally considered to be onerous. A quarter
chief is in a position to be publicly observed, to demonstrate his abilities, to
begin to act in the manner of the *to nuu*.

THE *loi namu* · In the past each area that corresponds to a chiefdom
had an official known as the *loi namu* (owner of the land). His office was
a hereditary one, vested in the lineage said to be the first one to settle in
the area. The office of *loi namu* was complementary to that of *kalon* (chief),
the former having ritual power and the latter secular power. The *loi namu*
had important ritual functions, such as making sacrifices in the time of
war or other emergency. He also had an important role in settling disputes
pertaining to the Poro Society or to ritual offenses. Kpelle informants are
reluctant to discuss the role of *loi namu* because it is so bound up with Poro
activities, but it is clear that the office still exists in some chiefdoms as well
as in some towns. However, the role and the power attached to it vary
from area to area, having waned where adherence to traditional practice
has fallen off.

THE TRIBAL SOCIETIES

The authority that chiefs and elders wield as political figures in Kpelle society is supplemented by the ritual authority they hold as highly placed members in the Poro,[22] a tribal fraternity. Presence of the Poro; the Sande,[23] a tribal sorority; and other tribal secret societies is often noted as a cultural feature characteristic of the culture area surrounding Liberia. Much has been written about these societies—a great deal of it in an exotic or adventuresome vein. There is no reliable study based on detailed observation of the activities of the Poro and Sande but the general features and functions are known.[24]

The Poro society

Secrecy is a part of both societies, and it has received much attention in published reports, partly because it is the one feature of which the outsider will be made aware! Each of the societies meets in a secret, sacred grove in the bush, and its affairs and meetings are not a matter of public knowledge.

The Poro, the more important of the two universal membership societies, will be the one discussed here. The corporate identity of the Poro is personified by the Great Masked Figure or Grand Master. In Kpelle he is called ŋamu (for which no translation is available) or lɔɔ seŋ (forest thing). In some Kpelle chiefdoms, he may make occasional public appearances; in others, he can be seen only by the initiated. When he appears in public, he is always masked, wears a costume that reveals nothing of the body, and speaks in a special disguising falsetto. The mask, regalia, and accompanying attendants mark his public manifestation. In some Kpelle areas other masked, costumed figures perform publicly as dancers or stilt walkers and are known as mala-ŋamu and gbada ŋamu, respectively. They should not be confused with ŋamu, the Grand Master (cf. Welmers 1949:231). When ŋamu visits towns at night to call meetings of the Poro members, his only manifestation is his voice, a distinctive type of music, that warns women and non-initiates to withdraw and to shutter themselves tightly in their houses. The voice inspires as much dread and respect as the mask. An uninitiated boy who would happen to see ŋamu would be immediately initiated; a woman would probably be poisoned. The special music is attributed to ŋamu as one being, but it is made by several musicians (Welmers 1949:233–234). The Grand Master is a person selected by his peers who are high officials of the Poro, and on these visits when he appears only before initiates, he probably appears undisguised.

SOCIAL CONTROL FUNCTIONS • The masquerade is no mere frivolity: it generates the deference and fear that must surround ŋamu if the Poro is

Masked Poro Figure A Poro figure (*mala* ŋamu) appears publicly in honor of Liberian Independence Day, July 26.

to carry out its social control functions that link it to political institutions. Breach of the rule of secrecy or of other Poro regulations is dealt with by Poro authorities in the Poro grove. Moreover, the Poro also enforces compliance with certain society-wide norms, such as the violations of incest regulations or—in the past—the commission of arson. Judicial procedures of this sort can be thought of as a type of canon law that parallels secular law. Even the uninitiated know that the Poro contains a series of graded inner orders and ranks or "degrees," such as Masonry has. Thus the Poro court that hears accusations consists of men who have taken "higher degrees" and who are therefore not only significant political figures but zoŋa (medicine men or authorities on the supernatural). Most of them are undoubtedly lɔi *namus* as well (see page 218). These Poro offices thus involve a fusion of secular and ritual roles. There is evidence that some of these positions are filled by hereditary selection. Traditionally, the authority of these Poro officials was supreme: they could even depose a chief who was not their equal in Poro. It is said that their council was the court of highest appeal, even higher than that of a political chief.[25]

In such cases ŋamu sits as the judge, apparently in his masked manifestation. The mask itself is called *sale* (medicine) and is said to possess great power. As is true of the neighboring Mano tribe, the mask is probably viewed as a repository of spirits—ancestral, animal, or totemic and natural, and the wearer's person is believed to merge with the spirit when he dons the mask (Harley 1950:3, 6, 41, 43). The tribunal's decision is issued by ŋamu, in effect, in the name of the mask: "Obtain[ing] a decree (and even the act of execution) from the spirit world itself" (Harley 1950:x). It is not the act of a fallible man but of the Poro masks functioning as "agents of social control" (cf. Harley 1950). Punishment often takes the form of ritual medicines that must be administered by the medicine men (Welmers 1949:

234). Here we see the significance of one of the most crucial attributes of Poro officials: their dual sacred-secular role mentioned earlier. They are both chiefs and priests, and control material and nonmaterial affairs. The canon courts enable them to penalize deviance while deflecting resentment away from themselves to the supernatural.

Several bits of field data confirm the view that political power and Poro power tend to be lodged in the hands of the same individuals, and it is not unlikely that chiefs utilize Poro mechanisms to underscore their political decisions. By "putting the country under Poro oath" all of the men of a given area can, under penalty of Poro sanctions, be required to carry out a specific action or abstain from one—for example, working in a particular man's fields.

OTHER SUPERNATURAL ACTIVITY · Speaking of the supernatural principle that underlies such mechanisms, one writer (Harley 1941:4) has said: "Not only are the men supposed to meet the ancestral spirits in the sacred grove, but they conduct rites and sacrifices of the type suggesting the worship of higher gods."[26] In fact, in Panta chiefdom today, the tribal secret societies seem to be the main focus of ritual activity (see pages 228–229). Because the secrecy surrounding the societies is strong, ritual activity that takes place in this context is protected from ridicule and direct acculturative contact and pressures.

SOCIALIZATION FUNCTIONS · The fear and respect for authority and the awe of and deference to the great societies as an institution are inculcated during the initiation, one of their most striking features. Initiation involves attendance at a "bush school" or initiation school in which the initiates receive instruction during a period of rigid seclusion in a special area.[27] Among the Kpelle, the number four is associated with maleness; three, with femaleness. Accordingly, male initiates were traditionally secluded in the initiation school for four years; girls, for three. In present circumstances the period of instruction has, in most places, been substantially reduced. Ideally, Poro and Sande initiation schools are operated alternately in a given area every fourteen years, although actual practice varies somewhat from this ideal. During the four-year period of Poro initiation and for the four years following, men have ritual supremacy in a chiefdom. Then the ritual authority is transferred to the women in a striking ceremony, and they have supremacy for the three years of the Sande initiation and the three years following (cf. Welmers 1949:237). The handing-over ceremony involves a mock argument and fight in which the women drive a ŋamu into the forest. Women thus have the right to alternate with men in the rule of the forest (Welmers 1949:247).

While a boy is in the Poro bush, he is instructed in tribal lore: farming, house building, crafts, the use of medicines, dancing, warfare, history, the treatment of women, and deportment before chiefs and elders.[28] Physical ordeals, hazing, and the meting out of harsh punishment not only ensure that he learns well but that he acquires a deeply ingrained willingness to submit to authority because it is authority.

When a Poro initiate enters the bush it is said that he is "eaten" by ŋamu. By the time he comes out, he has acquired a lɔi laa or "bush name," by which he is known thereafter. The uninitiated person has died, and a new person has been born in his place. His new status and rebirth are also evident in the cicatrices on his back and chest, said to be the teeth marks of the Great Masked Figure imprinted in the process of disgorging the initiate at his rebirth. Circumcision is usually arranged individually before the boy becomes an initiate.

The initiation school for the Sande involves parallel instruction in domestic arts and sexual knowledge. A clitoridectomy is part of the initiation for women. The effect of the separate initiation schools is to intensify the links between the members of the same sex. It also results in the lessening of the strong mother-son tie that is a result of Kpelle child training practices.

In spite of the vitality of the Poro and Sande as institutions, non-membership seems to carry no great disadvantage. An uninitiated man can hold land and property and marry, which, it is said, would not have been possible in the past. The long interval between Sande initiations meant that in Panta chiefdom in 1958 there were many women who were married and had children although they were not members of the Sande. Although membership may not have tangible advantages, it is an important part of being a Kpelle and accounts for much of the pride that Kpelle have in their culture. It has been correctly pointed out that the attachment most Kpelle feel to the tribal societies and their secrets is similar to European and American conceptions of patriotism (Welmers 1949:236).

INTEGRATIVE FUNCTION • Membership in different lodges or units of the Poro or Sande is an important integrating factor, for the unifying bonds of society membership crosscut the divisive links of kinship and territorial affiliations.[29] They even link members of different tribes: a Kpelle Poro member can participate in the activities at lodges in adjoining tribes after the proper passwords and signals have been given. The society bonds are particularly strong among those who have shared the long seclusion of the initiation school and, in Panta chiefdom, this results in the formation of named initiation sets. However, the secrecy of the Poro and other restrictions make it difficult to know anything of their functions in the formation of other groups, in the selection of persons to fill secular political offices, and the execution of the chief's decisions.

In sum, the Poro and Sande are secret, universal membership societies. Each has assumed multiple functions: social control, socialization, social integration, and the maintenance of basic Kpelle values and of constituted authority.[30]

Other sodalities

THE COOPERATIVE WORK GROUP · Many of the operations in the farm cycle are not carried out by the farmer and his family alone but by a cooperative work group known as a *kuu* (plural *kuu ŋai*). Such a group is made up of from six to forty people, and goes in rotation to the farms of each of the members, performing whatever work is in season. *Kuu ŋai* are organized on an individual basis. A person who has leadership and organizing ability will announce that he is going to be a *kuu laa nuu* (a *kuu* leader, literally, "a person whose name is attached to the *kuu*"). Usually the core of the *kuu* will be made up of people who live in the same quarter as the *kuu laa nuu* and people who are related to him in various ways. However, many people in the group will have no link with the leader other than friendship. A person will join a *kuu* with his best friend so that he can be with that person much of the time. Co-wives will join different *kuu ŋai* for the opposite reason. The more different *kuu ŋai* a household has membership in, the more groups will come to work on its farm, and the more the work is lightened. The most important thing about the basis of recruitment of the *kuu* is that everyone is free to join whichever one he or she likes.

A day at a farm with a good *kuu* is a day of hard work. But it is a day of pleasure as well, for the farmer-member who is host for the day provides a rich meal for the long break at noon. (In fact, *kuu* also means "feast" in Kpelle.) Sometimes a musical group provides continuous rhythmic accompaniment, and a *kuu* with marked *esprit de corps* may even outfit itself with costumes for the bits of dancing that go with cutting bush or sowing rice. Because of this, a person's ties with fellow *kuu* members may become very strong, for he spends much of his time with them. One could make a case for the *kuu* as being the most time-consuming, if not the most important, corporate group in Kpelle life. Its strong development helps in part to explain the relative lack of importance of the lineage and other wider kin groups in Kpelle social organization.

OTHER VOLUNTARY ASSOCIATIONS · The Kpelle have several other societies that are all bound up with *sale* (medicines), but they cannot be described here because of lack of space. They are the *kali sale* or *kwenuŋ* (Snake Society), the *mala* (Witch Driving Society; see page 228), *moliŋ sale* (the Spirit Society), and *gbɔ* (the Thunder Society) (cf. Welmers, 1949).

LAW

Dispute settlement among the Kepelle involves the intervention of a third party, and this principle is expressed in many areas of Kpelle life: lovers will ask a go-between to help in arranging a rendezvous; schoolboys sleeping in the same room wishing to ask each other about an outstanding loan may write a note to be carried by a third person; a person may be asked by a kinsman to intervene in a marital dispute; and someone of status in a community, such as a teacher or a chiefdom clerk, may be asked to mediate a dispute informally.

COURTS • Serious disputes are taken to court, and the system of courts is, of course, built upon this principle of third-party intervention. Paramount chiefs and district chiefs have official government courts where they may try civil cases involving two Kpelle individuals who are "tribesmen" (persons not officially literate)[31] where the amount of money or property involved does not exceed a fixed amount. Certain actions, such as murder, assault, and rape, are considered by the government to be serious criminal offenses that must be tried by an official of the central government and not by a chief. Each paramount chief or district chief has a clerk whose job it is to assist with the issuance of writs and summonses, the transcriptions of cases, and—in practice—the interpretation of government regulations.

A case begins with a pretrial hearing when the plaintiff brings his grievance to the chief or his clerk. If a legitimate grievance is felt to exist, a date is set for a trial and a summons is sent. In a Kpelle trial in a paramount chief's court, the court consists of a paramount chief and a council of subordinate chiefs. Order is maintained and litigants and witnesses are summoned by government messengers, known to the Kpelle as *soja* (soldier) because their uniforms closely resemble those of the Liberian Frontier Force. The trial itself follows a simple four-step procedure common to many legal systems. First, the plaintiff makes his complaint, and the defendant is then given a chance to reply. As a third step, witnesses will be called if they exist and are needed. Finally, a decision is reached and announced.

Such a bare outline of procedural steps omits many of the overtones that distinguish a Kpelle courtroom hearing. Any of the attending chiefs may question either party; moreover, any spectator may question either of the litigants. Indeed, the litigants may even question each other. Even with this high degree of participation, the courtroom is usually quite orderly. In examination of witnesses, the court sometimes resorts to the use of the conditional oath, when there is some reason to doubt the testimony of a witness, or when the testimony of witnesses is in conflict. In such a case, a messenger is ordered to administer a spoonful of *kafu* (or *gberɔ*) to the witness(es).

Kafu is a colorless liquid kept in a stoppered whiskey or wine bottle and is believed to have supernatural potency. In taking it, the witness swears that, "if I bear false witness . . . then the *sale* should kill me." It is believed that a person who breaks such an oath will be "caught" by the *kafu*. His stomach will swell and he will die, or some other sickness will eventually strike. In the tropics, such a misfortune often occurs fairly soon, thereby supporting the belief in the efficacy of the liquid. Questioned about the nature of the liquid, Kpelle chiefs professed to know nothing about it except that it was brought in by Malinke, a group with a general reputation for skill in preparing charms and "medicines," and that it worked.[32]

The decision is handed down by the presiding chief, often with little or no consultation with his council. A chief will frequently use proverbs as a way of bringing home the meaning of his decision, and he will not ordinarily cite precedents, since there is no written body of Kpelle law. Informal reprimands and admonitions are often directed at the losing party. Sanctions usually take the form of the request for damages and often, in addition, the payment of a fine; confinement in jail for short periods of time is another punishment.

As noted earlier, most of the cases that come before a Kpelle court involve disputes over women. Other types of cases heard include simple assault, theft, breach of contract, possession of illegal charms, and damage to crops by livestock. Among the southwestern Kpelle, where land pressure is great, disputes over land also occur. Town chiefs also have courts, but they are not official government courts; hence procedure there is less formal but is basically similar to those before higher chiefs. Quarter elders settle disputes very informally within a quarter.

The Kpelle courtroom hearing is formal and is somewhat coercive in its basic tone. A detailed analysis of courtroom-hearing transcripts shows that this is the result of several procedural features, such as the public nature of the hearing and the presence in the courtroom of tangible symbols (such as the khaki-uniformed messengers) of the physical force that backs the judiciary actions of the chief. A second source of the coercive and arbitrary tone is the influence of Poro values that, as noted earlier, condition submission to authority.[33]

THE MOOT · Besides the court, the Kpelle have an informal dispute settlement forum known as a *berei mu meni saa* (a "house palaver" or moot). This is an ad hoc council of kinsmen and neighbors of two complainants who come together to help them settle disputes involving marital matters or other domestic problems that are seldom initially taken to court.

The moot is not held in a courthouse but in someone's home. Several features of the moot give it a more informal and consensual flavor than the court hearing: the participants are dressed in everyday clothes; at the beginning and end of the moot the group participates in pronouncing blessings and appealing for group harmony and consensus. Perhaps most important is the open and full participation of all those attending. Being among friends and neighbors, the parties feel free to air all their grievances and to cross-examine each other vigorously. At the close of deliberations, if one person is found to be at fault, a formal apology is made. The wronged person is presented with apology tokens and other small gifts by the losing party, who openly and ceremonially begs his or her pardon. At the end of the moot all the participants drink together, symbolizing the re-establishment of group consensus, and blessings are again pronounced.

With such a focus on harmony and conciliation, it is not surprising that in dealing with marital disputes the moot is more likely than the court to bring about a reconciliation between spouses. The court, by its formal nature, tends to drive the husband and wife farther apart. But the moot's procedures have many of the features of group psychotherapy, such as catharsis, and commonly result in a consensual solution that is agreed to by the couple, who can start off on a new footing with the insights gained in the group session.[34] The moot is a specialized dispute settlement process that is not a substitute for the courts but a complement to them that is especially effective in resolving a type of dispute common in African societies, one involving parties who are linked by some ongoing relationship—kinsmen, spouses, neighbors.

RELIGION[35]

The Kpelle are pragmatic in their world view, and their religious beliefs and practices are not highly elaborated. There is a supreme god ɣala to whom people direct prayers and in whose name blessings are invoked. Occasional sala (sacrifices) are made to him, especially in the time of calamity or prolonged disaster, such as a smallpox epidemic. The only time when a sacrifice must be made is when human blood is shed in a fight or altercation. Then a sheep should be sacrificed because human blood contains a principle of life, and to shed it is apparently ritually dangerous. However, theological beliefs about ɣala are not well articulated, and some Kpelle claim that such sacrifices are really directed to the ancestors, who most Kpelle feel are somehow intermediaries between the living and ɣala.

The ancestors are known as ŋamua or ŋamoa and, formerly, were important in Kpelle religious life. It is felt that ancestors can influence events in the lives of their living descendants, but there was common agreement among several informants that they intercede only to bring good things and are never responsible for misfortune. Evil deeds are done apparently by evil spirits of the recently dead (mɔliŋ or gɔfɛ), spirits that have not yet had

A Funeral In the ceremony that starts the deceased on the path to ancestorhood, a family elder receives condolence gifts brought by relatives and friends.

time to become ŋamua and, hence, harmless. The ŋamua would be fed periodically at certain shrines that were evidently open to anyone. They were customarily large cottonwood trees, sometimes banana groves, and occasionally other trees, or even objects, such as a pot. The ancestors would be left bits of rice, rice meal, palm oil, yams as an offering (*sala*), or even livestock as a sacrifice (also *sala*). Sacrifices were not routine, but were offered especially when things were not going well. Nowadays such offerings are very seldom made, and sacrifices are almost rare.[36]

In addition to the spirits of the dead, the Kpelle recognize several other types of spirits, although they do not agree on the names applied to them. The individual spirit of life or personality that each individual possesses is called *nyina* or *ŋina*. ɣai Ɓela (water people) are like human beings, but they are white in appearance and live under the water, conducting their affairs much as people do. Certain individuals, especially the successful, are felt to have the backing of an individual water spirit who gives them power and supernatural support. Some people are believed to have close spiritual ties with animals, being able to displace their spirits into wild animals or favorite livestock, such as steer.

A witch spirit is called *wulu-nuu* (sometimes *mɔliŋ* or *gɔfɛ*), the belief in witchcraft being one of the strongest elements of Kpelle supernatural belief. It is thought that witches sustain themselves through eating the spirits of kinsmen (even their own children) and neighbors, thereby causing their death. This is done nocturnally, while the witch gives the appearance of deep, deathlike sleep. His witch-nature goes to consume a portion of someone's spirit, perhaps bringing it back to share it with other witches in a feast. Nonwitches are invited to participate, and, like the partaking witches, incur a debt that must eventually be repaid by providing the meal for a future gathering. Witches are also believed to cause illness and deformities.

The sign that one is probably engaging in witchcraft activity is to dream of eating meat, probably a common occurrence among the protein-poor Kpelle. If several people have a similar dream about eating meat on the same night, it means that they are participating in witchcraft together. Most Kpelle feel that witchcraft activity is unconscious and that the potential for witchcraft may be inherited through either parent, or that a person is drawn into the activity through the malevolent supernatural actions of others. Women are said to be witches more often than men, and, as noted earlier, witchcraft accusations are most commonly made between co-wives.

A person who feels that he or someone in his family is being bewitched may go to a *teli kpε nuu* (diviner), in order to discover whether or not witchcraft is present and—if so—who the witch is. The diviner may "cut the sand" or even resort to a *zolo* (ordeal) if there are several strong suspects. The victim or his representative may also "set a medicine," that is, ask people to swear a conditional oath. *Sale* (medicine) is used in many senses by the Kpelle. It can be a substance with pharmaceutical or supernatural curing power; a substance with supernatural prophylactic power, such as a charm or a fetish; a poison or a bit of magic; and any substance, action, or organization with unusual powers (cf. Welmers 1949). In one form of setting a medicine for witchcraft suspects, one prepares the *sale* by catching water that has been used to wash a blacksmith's hammer, an object having great supernatural power. The suspects, often all the members of a household, will be asked to eat kola nuts dipped in the charmed liquid and to swear an oath of innocence. The principle is the same as the one that underlies the operation of *kafu* in the courtroom. In time, it is believed, the guilty party will become ill. But if the witch confesses his or her witchcraft in time, he may recover before the illness becomes fatal. Each Kpelle town is also said to have a lodge of the Witch Driving Society, whose function is to control the evil influence of witches (Welmers 1949).

This principle of oaths and confessions is important in one other area of Kpelle life. At the beginning of the farming season, it is customary for a man to ask his wives to touch the sharpening stone and confess the names of any lovers they have had during the previous year. If an adulterous wife does not do so, it is felt that the rice crop will fail. It is this practice that makes possible the assessment of adultery damages and their collection, a cornerstone of the *tɔ nuu* complex in social stratification.

Magic and sorcery are also a part of Kpelle supernatural practice. Charms or medicines are used by individuals for such diverse purposes as warding off contagious diseases or attracting wives. An individual's excreta may be used to cause him harm through sorcery, and the use of poisons is a well-understood art. In the past, chiefdoms and some towns had "medicines" (fetishes or charms). There is some evidence that this is still true, although the medicines are not openly renewed.

In the day-to-day talk in the byways of a Kpelle village there are plentiful references to "medicines," to witches, and to water people. However, the concern is not with the manipulations of ancestors or other spirits and, through them, the regulation of human affairs; nor are offerings and sacrifices very much a part of daily life. Rather, the focus is on the supernatural manipulation of other people or supernaturally fending off their manipulation of oneself. In their daily religious expression the Kpelle are people-oriented, although they are not "sorcery ridden."

Offerings and sacrifices were more common in the past. The decline is not due to inroads by the great faiths, since the percentage of Kpelle who have adopted Islam or Christianity is still quite small. This is suggestive if one assumes that collective ritual action dealing with the representation of and interaction with the supernatural or symbolization of social values and groups is part of every culture. As hypothesized earlier, such ritual activity of this type as exists among the Kpelle is probably concentrated in the protective confines of the society groves (see page 221 and note 36).

ETHOS

Kpelle culture has two conflicting dominant themes. The first is a stress on personal autonomy and the individual achievement of status. Eligibility for high rank such as chieftaincy is not ascribed primarily on the basis of birth as a member of a particular lineage or clan as it is in many middle-range African societies. Rather, it is achieved on the basis of individual effort. A Kpelle may climb ahead of his fellows through the possession of certain obtainable skills. Most important is the ability to work hard, that is, to farm well, and to manage his economic resources skillfully. This will enable him to attract wives, themselves the major source of wealth, for Kpelle women claim to be drawn to a man mainly by his industriousness. The possession of interpersonal skills enables a man to hold his wives and the clients whom they may attract. He will then become known as a man who knows how to "hold people good," and, if he has a gift for oratory and settling palavers, he will be selected for political office. Some of this know-how he may acquire by starting adult life as the client of a prominent man or by working in bride service for the daughter of such a man. The variability of marriage forms and residence patterns in Kpelle society exists because men make marriages less to give expression to a particular kinship principle than to enhance their status by taking a step in the process of acquiring power over people.

The basic quest is for the individual acquisition of wealth through hard work and shrewd investment of this wealth in persons. At advantageous times one collects the social debts thus created. Throughout there is not too subtle a stress on the instrumental manipulation of others to one's own advantage. What is significant is that this is an individual enterprise, not one of a corporate group. However, if a man is prudent, he will not neglect his supernatural resources. He will protect and enhance his gains by investing in medicines and charms to hold his wives and protect his crops; perhaps he will use sorcery to slow the progress of his rivals. But he will approach the creator god or the ancestors only when in dire straits.

In a society where the achievement principle is widely followed, it is clear that competitive rivalries and shifting allegiances can be a source of considerable friction. This is especially true where, as in Kpelle society, kinship groups are weak and exercise few restraints on the individual. Those in constituted authority are constantly faced with the unsettling possibility of being replaced by the newly powerful.

The counterweight to the theme of individual advancement is the stress on conformity and regulation as exemplified in the tribal societies.[37] Through the initiation schools they assure the continuity of basic Kpelle values and by the application of combined ritual and secular sanctions, they ensure adherence to those values. This means that individual Kpelle are guided by the same expectations in the competition for power. They play by the same rules and for the same stakes, which means that no one goes too far in the means he uses to acquire position. If he does, the sanctions are forceful and effective. Through its officials, the Poro regulates the speed with which a man with a following may acquire formal political or Poro office.

Using game board maneuvers as an analogy, one would say that no one can advance along the game board too fast. Thus only those men who have demonstrated respect for proper authority and traditional values win the game, whereas others are not allowed to proceed too far. In short, those with ritual and secular power who form the top echelon of the Poro and society as a whole take care to allow themselves to be replaced only by those who share their outlook. This is especially significant if, as noted above, these Poro gatekeepers are themselves selected by the inherently conservative ascriptive hereditary principle. Thus, the Poro minimizes the disruptive effects of the achievement principle and competition for individual status, and serves as a stabilizing and conserving force in society.

Other themes of the Kpelle ethos are the instrumentality noted above, a practical orientation, and a belief in the formal superiority of men over women.

In the major features of culture and social organization, the Kpelle are strikingly similar to most of the neighboring tribes whose cultural configuration centers about the tribal societies: the Vai, Gola, Mano, Dan, Gio, Loma (Toma), Mende, Kissi, and others. For example, the rice-centered agriculture, the polycephalous associational state as a political form, and the central role of the Poro and the Sande are closely parallel. Variations occur in details of society organization, in the type and number of smaller secret societies, in the elaboration of religious beliefs and cosmology, and especially in the strength of unilineal descent groups.

CHANGE

Liberia was colonized by freed American slaves in 1822, and the Westernization of the Kpelle followed as the American *émigrés* began to pacify the interior. One of the first changes was the introduction of money, which also filtered in from Sierra Leone and what was then French Guinea. Both French and British currency have been used in the Kpelle area, and American currency, which is the official currency in Liberia, is still counted in shillings by the Kpelle. (For example, a dollar is five shillings.) Along with this came traders and a rapidly increasing desire for imported objects such as lanterns, brass buckets, and guns. In order to get the money to pay for them—and for taxes that were inevitably introduced —the Kpelle began to grow surplus rice for sale on the coast and to plant cash crops. After the 1920s and the establishment of the Firestone plantations, Kpelle could work at wage labor as rubber tappers.

The settlers also brought Christianity and encouraged missions in the hinterland. However, the southwestern Kpelle are more Christian than those in the northeast, since they have had longer contacts with the coast. The Lutheran Church has had the most effective missions in the Kpelle area of Liberia.

The 1940s marked the completion of an all-weather road that runs from Monrovia to Saniquellie, near the border with Guinea, transecting the Kpelle area. The building of that road and those that followed has intensified the changes that began with colonization. However, the Kpelle are less acculturated than the coastal tribes of Liberia, such as the Bassa, Kru, Vai, or Gola. Although many Kpelle work as rubber tappers or for the iron mines that have recently opened in or near the Kpelle area, comparatively few of them work on the coast as domestic labor, in semiskilled trades such as truck driving, or in the lower grades of the Liberian civil service. Rather than do this, an ambitious Kpelle man will save enough money to buy a sewing machine and set himself up in business as a tailor in his own village. The Kpelle hinterland dweller talks about events in Dukor (the Kpelle name for Monrovia); he may even visit there. But considering the fact that his is the largest of the Liberian tribes, he lives there in small numbers. He seems to wish to get the best of both worlds by keeping his culture but augmenting it selectively with particular borrowings from the West.

Evidence of change of this sort is found everywhere in Kpelle villages: the "country buses" (pickup trucks) that provide public transport on the main roads, the open-fronted shops of the Lebanese traders with their wide variety of imported goods, the government and mission schools and dispensaries, and, in some of the larger towns, the small mosques and chapels. Such changes reach into homes where tar paper and aluminum sheets may replace palm thatch as roofing. Moreover, each hut is sprayed yearly with DDT by an agency of the World Health Organization and the Liberian government.

The greatest direct changes in tribal institutions came with the instituting of a form of indirect rule by the Liberian government that fixed chiefdom boundaries, making it impossible for towns to follow the old pattern of shifting allegiance from one chief to another when one became too autocratic or too weak. The government has also outlawed capital punishment by tribal authorities and removed the trial of serious offenses from the chiefs. These changes would seem to weaken the authority of the chiefs. In actuality, they have narrowed the area in which the Poro acts judicially, have made the chiefs less susceptible to Poro regulation, and, hence, have concentrated their power by lessening some of the indigenous checks on their authority. These checks have been replaced by new ones, for each chief is subject to the authority of the district commissioner and the Department of Interior.[38]

A modern chief must satisfy his people and his government. Like most Liberian peoples, the Kpelle as a group are overwhelmingly supporters of the True Whig party, the party of President William V. S. Tubman and of his National Unification Policy, which was designed to accelerate the integration of tribal peoples into Liberian national life. In the interior regions, however, this does not take the form of organized political units and activities except at election time.

The pace of change among the Kpelle is slow and steady. Nativistic movements and other strong forms of reaction are absent. By and large, the Kpelle are still the people of the machete, oriented to their traditional culture and the cycle of activity bound to the rice—as the Kpelle say "our rice is what we know."

Notes

(1) This chapter is based on data collected during a period of seventeen months of field research carried out among the Kpelle of central Liberia in 1957 and 1958 while I was holding a Ford Foundation Foreign Area Training Fellowship. The Ford Foundation, of course, bears no responsibility for what appears here. Much of the analysis was completed while I was the holder of a predoctoral fellowship from the National Science Foundation. Here is an appropriate place to acknowledge with gratitude the support of both foundations, of the Kpelle people, the Liberian government, and the many other

individuals who helped to make the study possible. Lack of space prevents repeating the additional acknowledgments found in Gibbs (1960).

(2) At the time of this writing the Liberian government has announced a change in the makeup of the internal administrative divisions of the country. The three provinces are to be replaced by counties: Western Province by Loffa County; Central Province by Bong and Nimba counties; and Eastern Province by Grand Gedeh county. The four counties will be administered by super-intendents directly answerable to the president. This position replaces that of provincial Commissioner. An official government source indicates that the office of district commissioner is likely to be retained, with the commissioners serving under the superintendents instead of under provincial commissioners.

(3) Picot (1958:273) gives the population for the Kpelle of N'zérékoré Circle as 130,000. The Kpelle of Guinea are heavily concentrated in this circle, with much smaller numbers in Macenta and Beyla Circles.

(4) Much of the material on habitat is drawn from Porter (1956).

(5) The orthography for Kpelle terms used here is drawn from Welmers (1948). Although Kpelle is tonal, like many African languages, it is written for native speakers of the language without tone marks. In the interest of sim-plicity, that convention has been followed here.

(6) In the areas closer to the coast, land has been surveyed and alienated, having been sold to individuals or granted to concessions. In such areas land pressure is greater and disputes about land are more common.

(7) Kpelle men in the southwest participate in more of the steps of the agricul-tural cycle; nevertheless, the role of women is the dominant one.

(8) For a brief desciption of the Malinke and their role see page 204.

(9) Descriptions and photographs of the material culture of the wider culture area in which Liberia is included are found in Gunn (n.d.). Excellent photographs of the full range of the material culture of the Liberian tribal groups, including the Kpelle, are found in the appendix of Schwab (1947).

(10) Westermann (1921) felt that these patrilineally inherited food taboos that are not totemic are evidence of factual common descent. My data, which indicate marriage between people with the same food taboo, belie this.

(11) In Liberia all male tribal citizens who are not regularly employed for wages work a certain number of days per year on public works duties (such as repairing roads or acting as porters for government officials) in lieu of taxes. See Government of the Republic of Liberia (1952).

(12) The field data upon which this section is based were collected by my wife, Jewelle Taylor Gibbs.

(13) American currency is used as official currency in Liberia, although a few Liberian coins are used, including a two-cent piece.

(14) According to Liberian law, brideprice must be a minimum of forty dollars, but this is observed more in the breach—notably when a court determines the amount of brideprice to be returned at divorce—than in the practice.

(15) The ceremonial is so slight that some observers have declared that the Kpelle have no wedding ceremony. Picot, writing of the Kpelle of Guinea, notes, "No formality is necessary for the celebration of the marriage. The marriage is formed from the moment the woman goes to live with the husband" (1958:278, my translation). Similarly, Mengrelis (1946b:26) states that in Guinea there is no ceremony to "ratify" a Kpelle marriage although he describes a prestation of first bridewealth whose acceptance establishes the marriage.

(16) Among the Gola, another Poro-centered tribe, bride service marriage is associated with upward mobility. A group contracts such a marriage to marry into a lineage with higher status (d'Azevedo, 1962b).

(17) This line of analysis is presented in detail in Gibbs, 1963b.

(18) This was a requirement of working personally for the chief, usually on his rice farms. Today, gifts of rice substitute for this, and, as noted earlier, labor is now required for the tribal administration or for the government rather than for the chief as a separate person.

(19) Chiefs often go to their farms but usually to supervise rather than to participate actively in the labor.

(20) Similarly, chiefs of these units are designated in Liberia as "clan chiefs." I use the term "district chief" because it is less confusing to persons with a knowledge of anthropological terminology.

(21) Paramount chiefs are now elected. They were formerly selected by a loose hereditary principle.

(22) In Kpelle, the name for the Society is *pɔlɔŋ*. In the literature, this is usually written in an Anglicized form of the Mende term, *pɔrɔ*. Because it has such wide currency, it will be used here.

(23) The Kpelle term is *Saneŋ*.

(24) Some attributes of the Kpelle Poro are described in Welmers (1949); Westermann (1921); Mengrelis and Sibley and Westermann (1928). The most detailed treatment of the Poro in Liberia appears in the writings of Harley (1941, 1950), who describes the institution as it existed among the Mano people. Relevant and insightful material on the Poro among the Gola appears in d'Azevedo (1962) and, among the Mende, in Little (1949). All these materials on the Poro must be interpreted with some caution because all are based on informant reports that, because of the secret nature of the society, cannot be verified by observation.

The tribal pride in the great societies and their centrality as an institution has been given explicit recognition by the Liberian government, which has taken steps to protect the societies from the incursions of nonmembers, including those of researchers and scholars. This action undoubtedly does much to preserve the fabric of tribal social structure and should therefore be commended. Too rigidly applied, however, it could prevent the recording of core customs before that inevitable day when the societies lose their present position. Because of this policy, I made no direct inquiries about Poro or Sande activities in Panta chiefdom. However, a few inferences could be drawn from material collected on other tribal institutions. These have been interwoven with the descriptive material from published sources in order to indicate the broad outlines of how the societies function.

(25) Because of the Liberian government's policy with regard to inquiry into Poro activities, I can say nothing as to the extent to which Poro tribunals still operate as a complement to secular courts.

(26) Welmers (1949:250, 241) contradicts this, saying that the Poro "has no concern with sacrifice or religion except by indirect implication." This runs contrary to all that we know of the Poro from other published reports and to Welmers's own statement as to the role of the "nonmaterial" in the affairs of the society. Yet he is probably correct when he states that "the primary character of the initiation seems to be concerned with attitude rather than information."

(27) A general statement about these schools is Watkins (1943). Details appear in those works on the Poro in Liberia cited in note 24.

(28) Welmers (1949:230) states explicitly that the initiation does not consist of instruction in tribal customs "or anything else that would correspond to teaching as we know it." This differs from all other published reports on the Poro.

(29) The precise territorial limits of lodge membership for the Kpelle are not known, but it is definite that some units include more than one town.

(30) D'Azevedo (1962a) treats the Poro historically, suggesting that it arose during a period of social disruptions as a device for increasing social stability and order.

(31) In Liberian usage it is customary to refer to the "Americo-Liberian" portion of the population as "civilized" and the tribal people as "natives" or "the native people." Here I have followed the more neutral terminology used by McCall (1956) and I have referred to the tribal people as "tribesmen." McCall refers to the Americo-Liberians as "citizens." In actuality, both groups are, of course, citizens of the Republic of Liberia. In a personal interview District Commissioner Charles Williams of Gbarnga noted that a tribesman who has been educated as far as the fourth grade is counted as literate and hence a "citizen" and therefore no longer subject to the judicial authority of a tribal chief. If he wishes, he has the right to have any litigation in which he is involved heard by a district commissioner or higher government official.

(32) A description of the preparation of *kafu* in the Vai and Gola areas of Liberia is instructive. There witnesses took an oath of their own choosing and Malinke elected to take *kafu*. "A sura from the Koran was written out on a wooden slat and the writing was washed off with water which was ceremoniously prepared with some rice flour and put into [a] bottle. When a witness took oath to the kafu some of it was poured into a spoon given him to take internally" (Government of the Republic of Liberia 1955:11).

(33) A detailed ethnolegal analysis of Kpelle courtroom procedures appears in Gibbs (1962).

(34) An analysis of the moot as a therapeutic device for the informal settlement appears in Gibbs (1963a).

(35) Kpelle religious beliefs are not highly systematized, and informants' reports are often inconsistent and contradictory, especially in terminology. The most complete and integrated report on Kpelle religion appears in Welmers (1949), which I have draw on heavily in this section for variations in Kpelle terminology. In other details my own field data support his statements.

(36) In seventeen months in the field I saw no offerings and could verify the making of only one sacrifice. Other observers have made the same report. Rev. P. Lassort and M. H. Lelong, in an article comparing the Kpelle of Liberia with those of Guinea with whom they were more familiar, write: "We have seen neither sacrifice, nor other religious acts, because we were only passing through. But we have seen many enclosures for the male initiations. We have also seen initiates coming out of the entrances [to the initiation groves] the same day that we arrived in their villages" (Lassort and Lelong, 1947:19, my translation).

(37) Contention between these two principles is also characteristic of the Gola. D'Azevedo (1962b) has traced the process there in detail, noting with more precision than is possible for the Kpelle the relationship between Poro structures and the variation in kinship structures.

(38) See note 2.

Bibliography

Starred items (*) include significant bibliographies. Daggered items (†) are cited as references in the text of the chapter.

The Kpelle

Gibbs, James L., Jr. (1960†). "The Judicial Implications of Marital Instability among the Kpelle." Unpublished doctoral dissertation, Harvard University.

—————— (1962†). "Poro Values and Courtroom Procedures in a Kpelle Chiefdom," *Southwestern Journal of Anthropology*, Vol. 18, No. 4, pp. 341–350. A description and analysis of dispute settlement procedures in the paramount chief's court of Panta chiefdom.

—————— (1963a†). "The Kpelle Moot: A Therapeutic Model for the Informal Settlement of Disputes," *Africa*, Vol. 33, No. 1, pp. 1–11. A description and analysis of procedures in the Kpelle moot.

—————— (1963b†). "Marital Instability among the Kpelle: Towards a Theory of Epainogamy," *American Anthropologist*, Vol. 65, No. 3, pp. 552–573.

A description and analysis of Kpelle marriage showing how its instability is rooted in many features of Kpelle social organization.

Lassort, P., and M. H. Lelong (1947†). "Chez les Kpèllè du Libéria et les Guerzés de la Guinée française," *Études Guinéennes* (no volume), No. 2, pp. 9–20.

Mengrelis, Thanos (1963). "Esquisse sur l'habitat guerzé," *Africa,* Vol. 23, No. 1, pp. 45–53.
A description of Guinean Kpelle agricultural techniques, settlement patterns, and house building. Contains a short section on funerary customs at the death of a chief. Mengrelis also has a series of other papers briefly treating aspects of Kpelle life including the Poro. They are in French and appear in *Africa* (vol. 22, 1952) and in *Notes Africaines de l'Institut Français de l'Afrique Noir* (vol. 29, 1946).

Picot, J. (1958†). "N'zérékoré." (Monographies d'Afrique Noire) in *Annales Africaines.* Paris: Imprimerie Guillemot et Lamothe; publiées dans les auspices de la Faculté de Droit et des Sciences Économiques de Dakar, Université de Dakar, pp. 273–286.

Sibley, James L., and Diedrich H. Westermann (1928). *Liberia, Old and New: A Study of Its Social and Economic Background with Possibilities of Development.* New York: Doubleday & Company.
Chapters 5–9, containing a general account of Kpelle culture prepared by Westermann, are essentially an English translation of large portions of his *Die Kpelle.* (See below.)

Welmers, William E. (1948†). "Spoken Kpelle." Sanoyea, Liberia. (Mimeographed for private distribution by the Lutheran Mission in Liberia: Monrovia, Liberia, and in 1955 by the United Lutheran Church in America.)

———— (1949†). "Secret Medicines, Magic and Rites of the Kpelle Tribe in Liberia," *Southwestern Journal of Anthropology,* Vol. 5, No. 3, pp. 208–243. By far the best treatment of Kpelle supernatural beliefs and practices.

———— (1962). "The Phonology of Kpelle," *Journal of African Languages,* Vol. 1, pp. 69–93.

———— (1964). "The Syntax of Emphasis in Kpelle," *Journal of West African Languages,* Vol. 1, pp. 13–26.

Westermann, Diedrich H. (1921†). *Die Kpelle: Ein Negerstamm in Liberia.* Göttingen, Germany: Vandenhoeck und Ruprecht.
This is a general monograph on the Liberian Kpelle based on four months' field research carried out by Westermann in 1914. The brief fieldwork was based on Dobli Island in the St. Paul River, an area into which the Kpelle have moved in comparatively recent times. Many of the patterns reported show the strong influence of the neighboring Gola. These facts, plus the brevity of Westermann's field period, probably explain the discrepancies between his results and mine. (cf. Sibley and Westermann, 1928 above.)

Other Liberian Tribal Groups

Recent studies by professional anthropologists, with virtually no exceptions, have not focused on tribal groups located entirely in Liberia, but on peoples who reside in Liberia and either Guinea or Sierra Leone.

d'Azevedo, Warren L. (1962b†). "Common principles of Variant Kinship Structures among the Gola of Western Liberia," *American Anthropologist,* Vol. 64, No. 3, pp. 504–520.
An insightful treatment that shows that a common principle underlies the apparent variation in Gola domestic groups and descent groups and that this principle is given expression in, and regulated by, the Poro.

Goverment of the Republic of Liberia (1952†). "Revised Laws and Administrative Regulations for Governing the Hinterland, 1949." A mimeographed edition of "The Revised Interior Administrative Regulations passed by Legislative Enactment and approved December 22, 1949." Issued by the Department of Interior, Monrovia, Liberia.

———— (1955†). "The Tribes of the Western Province and the Denwain People." Monrovia, Liberia: Bureau of Folkways, Mores, and Customary Laws of the Department of Interior (mimeographed).

Harley, George W. (1941*†). *Notes on the Poro in Liberia.* Cambridge, Mass.: Papers of the Peabody Museum of American Archaeology and Ethnology, Vol. 19, No. 2.
Deals with the Poro among the Mano. (See note on next reference.) A usefully long segment of this work is reprinted in "The Mano of Liberia," pp. 344–379, in *A Reader in General Anthropology,* Carleton S. Coon (ed.). New York: Holt, Rinehart and Winston, Inc., 1948.

———— (1950†). *Masks as Agents of Social Control.* Cambridge, Mass.: Papers of the Peabody Museum of American Archaeology and Ethnology, Vol. 22, No. 2.
Describes and analyzes the activities of the Poro among the Mano. Although based on informants' reports, rather than on direct observation, this volume offers the most complete available treatment of the Poro in Liberia.

Holas, B. (1952*). *Mission dans l'est liberien: Resultats demographiques ethnologiques et anthropometriques.* Memoires de l'Institut Français de l'Afrique Noir, No. 14, Dakar: IFAN.
Contains material on some of the tribes of eastern Liberia: the Grebo, Dru, Kra (Krahn), Gio, Dan, and Ge. Especially good for the lengthy bibliography on Liberia.

Little, Kenneth (1949). "The Role of the Secret Society in Cultural Specialization," *American Anthropolist,* Vol. 51, No. 2, pp. 199–212. This paper is reprinted in *Cultures and Societies of Africa,* Simon and Phoebe Ottenberg (eds.). New York: Random House, 1960, pp. 199–213.

———— (1951). *The Mende of Sierra Leone: A West African People in Transition.* London: Routledge & Kegan Paul, Ltd.

———— (1954). "The Mende in Sierra Leone," in Daryll Forde (ed.) *African Worlds: Studies in the Cosmological Ideas and Social Values of African Peoples*. London: Oxford University Press, pp. 11–37.

McCullock, Merran (1950*). *Peoples of the Sierra Leone Protectorate*. London: International African Institute. (Ethnographic Survey of Africa, West Africa, Part 2.)

Paulme, Denise (1954). *Les Gens du riz: Kissi de Haute-Guinée française*. Paris: Librairie Plon.

Schwab, George (1947†). *Tribes of the Liberian Hinterland* (edited with additional material by George W. Harley). Cambridge, Mass.: Papers of the Peabody Museum of American Archaeology and Ethnology, Vol. 31.
A general overview of the tribes of Liberia that contains relatively little specifically on the Kpelle. However, the photographs in the appendix give a very complete inventory of the culture of the Liberian tribes, much of which is uniform for the entire country. Much specifically Kpelle photographic material is included in this appendix.

The Modern Liberian Nation

These works are included for the reader who wishes to understand the nation of which the Liberian Kpelle are a part. They will also provide useful background for understanding the acculturation of Liberian tribal peoples—a pattern of acculturation that is unique in that there has been no European colonial power as in other west African countries.

Fraenkel, Merran (1964). *Tribe and Class in Monrovia*. London: Oxford University Press.
A well-documented study of social stratification in Monrovia, Liberia, with a special focus on the acculturation and absorption of tribesmen.

Liebenow, J. Gus (1962*). "Liberia," in *African One Party States*, Gwendolen M. Carter (ed.). Ithaca, N. Y.: Cornell University Press, pp. 325–394.
This is the best overall treatment of the modern nation of Liberia, avoiding the two extremes of many past treatments: overromanticism or ridicule and burlesque.

McCall, Daniel F. (1956†). "Liberia: An Appraisal," *Annals of the American Academy of Political and Social Science*, Vol. 306, pp. 88–97.

Porter, Philip (1956†). "Population Distribution and Land Use in Liberia." Unpublished doctoral dissertation in geography. London School of Economics and Political Science.
Contains a good description of the Liberian habitat along with detailed land-use maps and a population estimate based on a count of huts made from aerial photographs of almost the entire country.

Solomon, Marvin D., and Warren L. d'Azevedo (1962). *A General Bibliography of the Republic of Liberia.* Evanston, Ill.: Northwestern University Press (Working Papers in Social Science, I).

Related Topics

d'Azevedo, Warren L. (1962a*†). "Some Historical Problems in the Delineation of a Central West Atlantic Region," *Annals of the New York Academy of Sciences,* Vol. 96, pp. 512–538.
Discusses the cultural features and history of the culture area dominated by the Poro and related societies.

Greenberg, Joseph (1955†). *Studies in African Linguistic Classification.* New Haven, Conn.: The Compass Publishing Co.

Gunn, Harold D. (n.d.†). *A Handbook of the African Collections of the Commercial Museum-Philadelphia.* Philadelphia: The Commercial Museum.
Has a brief introduction to African art and crafts. Especially useful for photographs of African craft products grouped according to material or product and according to culture area.

Livingstone, Frank B. (1958). "Anthropological Implications of Sickle Cell Gene Distribution in West Africa," *American Anthropologist,* Vol. 60, pp. 533–562.
An insightful attempt to relate sickle-cell gene distribution to the distribution of linguistic, botanical, and culture evidence in order to reconstruct some of the history of the area that includes the Kpelle.

Watkins, Mark Hanna (1943†). "The West Africa 'Bush' School," *American Journal of Sociology,* Vol. 48, pp. 666–675.
A general description of initiation schools such as that of the Poro.

7

THE !KUNG BUSHMEN
OF THE KALAHARI DESERT

about the chapter

For the anthropologist, the Bushmen are one of the world's most intriguing peoples, as they are virtually unique physically, linguistically, and culturally. The physical anthropologist cannot place the Bushmen in any one of the recognized major racial groupings: Caucasoid, Mongoloid, or Negroid. Similarly, linguists have placed their language in a category, Khoisan, apart from other African language families. The velar "clicks" that characterize Khoisan languages are apparently found nowhere in the world outside of Africa.

The culture of the Bushmen shows the imprint of their harsh and barren desert habitat, and, as Marshall points out, the ethos of their culture is dominated by the quest for survival. Many Bushman cultural institutions are molded by certain ecological constants: water, the location of water holes, water-storing plants, and other edible wild plants, the movements of game. The size of the band, the daily cycle of labor, the low incidence of polygyny, are all aspects of culture marked in this way. Certain other Bushman institutions, however, are not simply cultural creations passively molded by habitat; rather, they give the Bushmen better than even odds to defy the limitations which their habitat imposes. Such culture patterns are their skillful hunting techniques, their institutionalized patterns of sharing, and their strong striving for cooperation and harmony. Few cultures give the observer such a rich opportunity to study the two-way interaction between habitat and culture.

Marshall shows how specific customs reflect the dominant quest for water, and she portrays the feeling of Bushman culture as well as providing an ethnologist's construct. In this configurational model focusing on ethos, she indicates how derived themes or postulates, such as the stress on cooperation, relate to the most basic theme. Comparison of the !Kung Bushmen with the Mbuti Pygmies, the other foraging group represented in this book, reveals that even though these groups occupy very different habitats some features of their cultures are similar. These include not only elements of technology, for example, the use of poisoned arrows, but themes such as the stress on cooperation and the minimizing of intragroup conflicts, features that are a functional requisite for the close, face-to-face relationships in a foraging band. Thus a study of the Bushmen offers insight into what may be minimal and hence universal features of the foraging band as a culture type.

Bushman culture is also of interest to those concerned with African culture history, for archaeological remains of societies with a similar material culture have been discovered scattered over a much wider region of the eastern part of the continent than the Bushmen now occupy. Many anthropologists feel that the bearers of these early cultures were Bushmen, or Bushmanlike in racial type. An understanding of Bushman culture gives us insight into the cultural and behavioral setting to which the mute artifacts may have belonged.

about the author

Lorna Marshall lives in Cambridge, Massachusetts, and, with members of her family, has conducted several expeditions to the Bushmen of the Nyae Nyae region of South West Africa (1951, 1952–1953, 1955, 1959, 1961), of Bechuanaland Protectorate (1955, 1961), and of southeast Angola (1959). She received her M.A. from Radcliffe College in 1928. Her writings include "The Kin Terminology System of the !Kung Bushmen" (1957), "N!ow" (1957), "Marriage among the !Kung Bushmen" (1959), "!Kung Bushman Bands" (1960), "Sharing, Talking and Giving: Relief of Social Tensions among !Kung Bushmen" (1961), and "!Kung Bushman Religious Beliefs" (1962).

LORNA MARSHALL · *The !Kung Bushmen of the Kalahari Desert*[1]

INTRODUCTION

LOCATION · The Bushmen live in those parts of the Kalahari Desert in southern Africa that lie in the British Bechuanaland Protectorate, in South West Africa, and in southeastern Angola. A few additional remnants of Bushman groups still exist in Northern Rhodesia and at Lake Chrissie in South Africa. In the past Bushmen had a much wider distribution.[2]

Many Bushmen live among, and some work for, the Bantu-speaking tribes in settlements where sufficient water resources have been developed to support cattle, and some Bushmen work for white farmers in the Ghanzi area of the Bechuanaland Protectorate and in South West Africa. However, many still live in small, independent, nomadic groups, widely dispersed in the vast areas of the desert.

It is very difficult to arrive at a precise population count of the Bushmen, but a recent estimate gathered from various contemporary sources (Tobias 1956) indicates that in 1955 there were 55,531 Bushmen.[3] These figures are higher than any previously propounded (cf. Schapera 1939) and come as a surprise to many.

The Bushmen are linked with the Hottentots, a southern African people who resemble them physically and with whom they have linguistic affiliations, but who are a pastoral people with a more complex social structure. Bushmen and Hottentots together are called the *Khoisan* peoples, a coined term combining the Hottentots' term for themselves (*Khoi*) and their name for the Bushmen (*San*). The Khoisan peoples have been referred to as a distinct race (Murdock 1959: 8) or, as Howells puts it, "a major racial variety of man" (1959:306). The obscurity of their origins and racial affinities are in themselves subjects in which research continues and interesting postulations engage the attention of scientists in various fields.[4]

PHYSICAL FEATURES · The physical features of the Bushmen have drawn much attention from anthropologists. Bushmen are of small stature (adult

243

A Headman 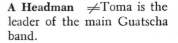Toma is the leader of the main Guatscha band.

males average approximately five feet, two inches) with yellowish brown skin that becomes heavily wrinkled in old age. They have very little facial and body hair, and their short, black, head hair is so curly it spirals into peppercorn tufts. The Bushman face is flat and triangular; the brown eyes are set rather wide apart. A variety of eye folds narrow the apertures of the eyes. The nose is extremely broad with a very low bridge, the lips are everted but not protruding or only slightly so, and the ear is somewhat square in shape with a deeply rolled rim (helix). The Bushman body and limbs are slender; the frame is delicate. A notable feature is the inward curve of the small of the back. The penis is semierect. In women there is what is called the "Hottentot apron" (elongation of the *labia minora*). Steatopygia (fat on the buttocks) is invariably mentioned in the literature as one of the important physical characteristics of Bushman and Hottentot women and recorded as being very prominently developed in some. By comparison with the extreme examples that are seen among some Hottentot women and in illustrations, the northern and central Bushman women whom we observed did not have marked steatopygia, although some had buttocks that could be called plump.

LANGUAGE • Bushman languages and those of the Hottentots are classified as a language family known as Click or Khoisan (Greenberg 1955:80). Clicks are so unusual as to be almost unique to Bushman and Hottentot (they occur also in two East African languages—Sandawe and Hatsa—according to Greenberg) and are so distinguishing a feature of these languages that much attention is given them.

The Khoisan clicks, striking implosive sounds, are velaric suction stops (Heffner 1960:119; cf. Beach 1938:73 ff.). The northern and central Bushman languages have four, made with the tongue, as follows: the dental (/), lateral (//), alveolar (!), and palatal (≠). The southern Bushman languages, some now virtually extinct, were characterized by a fifth click made with the lips, called the kiss click (⊙). In addition to clicks, the Bushman languages have tones: high, middle, low, rising, and falling. Oswin Köhler has given special attention to tone as well as to other features in his study of Bushman languages, especially Barakwenga (Köhler 1962).

Each of the large divisions of the Bushman languages—the northern, central, and southern divisions (see Bleek 1956)—differs markedly from the others. Within each group are several languages, sometimes resembling each other enough to be considered merely dialects of the same language, but more often differing so widely as to be distinct, mutually quite unintelligible languages. The !Kung described in this chapter (Köhler's and Westphal's !Xū) belong to the northern group.

HABITAT · The Kalahari Desert, some 1200 miles long, with a mean high altitude of about 3000 feet, forms part of the great plateau of southern Africa. It is a basin in form, covered with wind-blown sands, sometimes red, sometimes white, to a depth of 300 to 400 feet. The underlying rock crops out rarely in ridges and a few low hills.

Stamp (1953:78) classifies the Kalahari as a semidesert. Its conditions are not the most extreme. Our expeditions recorded daytime air temperatures in the shade up to 115° F. and sand temperatures in the sun up to 140° F. In winter the temperature at night falls below freezing but for most of the year the nights are temperate. Although they seem acclimated to the heat, the Bushmen appear to find the colder temperatures very uncomfortable and shiver violently if they are away from their fires when the cold south winds blow.[5]

The rainfall, which comes in summer thunderstorms—6 to 10 inches, increasing in the better-watered parts toward the north, according to Wellington (1955:61)—though slight, is sufficient to sustain a varied drought-resistant vegetation, and the country is covered with grass, brush, and scant small trees. In the northern and northwestern parts, the trees are more numerous and taller and include shivi groves and nut-bearing mangetti—important sources of food to the Bushmen. And in all the areas of the desert that Bushmen inhabit are found edible plants, in scant, far-apart patches perhaps, but existing. The vegetation, furthermore, provides material for fires, shelter, weapons, implements, tanning, poison for arrows, and juices (for example tsama melons, on which these people can live when there is no water). In short, this desert provides the things that make life possible; otherwise the Bushmen would be dead or somewhere else.

The desert is a forceful shaper of the outlines of Bushman culture, and both the possibilities it permits and the limitations it imposes have been meaningfully summarized by Robert Story in a personal communication:

A lack of permanent water is probably the most trying of the difficulties which beset the Bushmen of the present day in the country which shelters them. However, it is this very disadvantage which has ensured their survival, for while they have been dispossessed of their country and exterminated in the less arid parts, in the "Great Thirst Land of the Kalahari" they have been comparatively safe from their European and Bantu enemies. The austerity and hardships of the Kalahari are offset to some extent by its deep level mantle of sand, which prevents run-off of the rainwater and makes it readily available for plant growth. "Clay, for example, is as dry as dust to the plant when it contains 18% of water, while most sands are very nearly saturated with 18% of water" (Schantz 1911). This means not only that the sandy soil can support more luxuriant plants in greater variety, but also that storage organs are common among them, for drainage in sand is so rapid and thorough that shallow-rooted plants at least are in a stronger position if they are able to collect and store the water before it sinks into the deeper layers.

Although some of the storage organs are poisonous, the Bushmen still have numerous edible bulbs, tubers and roots at their disposal. Thanks again to the sand, they can harvest these quickly and easily with wooden digging-sticks which would be inadequate in a heavy or stony soil. Other storage organs which they do not eat because of bitterness or high tannin or fibre content are nevertheless important indirectly through being eaten by the various antelopes that are the Bushmen's meat supply.

Hunting is easier as well, for as there could be few better tracking surfaces than the Kalahari sand and, as a wounded animal can thus be followed with very little risk of loss, hard-hitting weapons and careful aim are not necessary. Instead, the Bushmen use small poisoned arrows which have the advantage of being effective on any part of the body and of bringing death as certainly to big game as to small.

LINGUISTIC AND BAND GROUPINGS · The major groupings among the Bushmen cannot correctly be called tribes; they are, rather, linguistic groupings and the names by which they have been traditionally known by Europeans refer to language: for example, !Kung-speaking Bushmen, Naron-speaking Bushmen. The Bushmen themselves and their Bantu neighbors use a multitude of names by which they refer to various combinations of local groupings. Our own tentative and incomplete comparisons lead us to say that the language groups differ from one another markedly in some customs while they are much the same in others.

The language groups have no political unity among or within themselves. The only social unit larger than the family is the autonomous band composed of several families and headed by a headman (see "Political Organization," p. 267). Each of the major groupings has many bands within it.

The Bushmen whose social structure I describe in this chapter are a group of !Kung-speakers who call themselves *ju /õassi* and who live in the Nyae Nyae region of South West Africa. It is a region of about 10,000 square miles, centered approximately at Gautscha (about 19°48'30" S, 20°34'36" E). The region lies for the most part in South West Africa, but extends into the Bechuanaland Protectorate to a number of Tswana and Herero settlements along the border. We arbitrarily call this particular stretch of country a region because it is a region in the minds of the Bushmen. In it are some 27 bands living independently in their own traditional way and 9 groups employed by the Tswana and Herero—a !Kung population of about 1000. These !Kung intermarry. They have not formally structured the region as an endogamous unit, but they remain within it by custom and preference. They know there are other !Kung-speakers living to the north and northwest of them, but consider them strangers, as they do the Auen-speaking and Naron-speaking Bushmen to the south.

ECONOMY

It is vividly apparent that among the !Kung Bushmen, ethos, or "the spirit which actuates manners and customs," is survival. Their time and energies are almost wholly given to this task, for life in their environment requires that they spend their days mainly in procuring food. The band organization is important to their survival, and, to secure the mutual support and companionship that it affords, they seek to regulate their social actions to reduce tension and potential hostility among the individuals within the band. They also strive to avoid the possibility of conflict between bands. Similarly, in their religious concepts and practices, the emphasis is on survival in this life on earth, not a looking forward to the eternal life in the sky after death.

WILD PLANT FOODS (*veldkos*) · The !Kung of the Nyae Nyae region have no agriculture. They subsist mainly on wild plant foods, which we refer to by the convenient Afrikaans word *veldkos*. The game the hunters of a band manage to kill is an important part of their diet and much desired, but it is by no means the daily sustenance. In this region the !Kung know more than a hundred different kinds of veldkos (cf. Story 1958). Several species of berries exist, dry and hard for the most part. A few fruits ripen suddenly in a short season. Leaves, resembling spinach, make a spring salad for a short time. Morsels of gums from certain trees are cherished like sweets. Tsama melons and wild cucumbers grow here but do not abound in this region as they do in some other parts of the Kalahari where some Bushman groups can live on them for certain seasons without having access to any water. Most important to the daily sustenance of the Nyae Nyae !Kung are the edible underground roots, tubers, and storage organs of certain drought-resistant plants. We observed the gathering of 23 different kinds of these; doubtless there are more. In addition to the roots and tubers, there are sev-

Gathering Mangetti Nuts

eral large groves of mangetti trees (*Ricinodendron rautanenii* Schinz) in the region, all on great waterless white sand dunes, and one extensive area in which *tsī* grows. *Tsī* (*Bauhinia esculenta* Burch) is the seed of the vine that runs along on the surface of the ground. Both mangetti nuts and *tsī* are excellent foods, rich in oils and proteins, and so important to the !Kung that they organize their lives to a considerable extent around them.

Each band, according to !Kung social structure, owns and lives within what we call a territory. The band, through its headman (in a way to be explained later), owns the veldkos and water resources within its territory. The territories are varied in size and shape and sometimes consist of portions that are not even contiguous. The boundaries are vague, for the need to draw fine boundary lines is not great. In the interior of the region, where water is so scant, in roughly 8000 square miles live only 17 bands, comprising 447 persons. The other bands and employed groups live on what we call the periphery of the region. The !Kung say that one cannot eat the ground itself so it does not matter to whom it belongs. It is the patches of veldkos that are clearly and jealously owned, and the territories are shaped in a general way around these patches. The !Kung of the interior have settled themselves in such a way that every band has access to areas of edible roots and to either a mangetti grove or a *tsī* patch. A few bands have both.

The strong concepts of ownership of veldkos by the band operate almost like a taboo. No external force is established to prevent one band from encroaching on another's veldkos or to prevent individuals from raiding veldkos patches to which they have no right. This is just not done. Fear of fighting is one of the deterrents. The poisoned arrows of the Bushmen are as deadly to man as to game and they are always at hand. A mere nick and a speck of poison in the bloodstream can be fatal. There are no known antidotes.

As skilled trackers of game, Bushmen develop their powers of visual observation and train their visual memories to such a high degree that they know everyone's footprint as well as his face. This is another deterrent, for no one could steal veldkos without leaving his marks and having his identity detected. Theoretically, in !Kung society the thief may rightfully be killed by the person or the band from whom he has stolen, but he may fight back, and relatives could also become involved and the fighting would spread. In the opinion of the !Kung, situations likely to engender hostility are assiduously to be avoided, to say nothing of actual fighting. Breaches of this intention are very rare.

Life throughout the seasons is planned around the veldkos gathering. The people know at what seasons the various veldkos will ripen and about how much each patch will yield if the rains have been good or if they have been poor. The !Kung are not, according to our way of thinking, exactly conservation-minded, but they do plan to consume their veldkos in advantageous order. They eat the perishable short-seasoned leaves and the few fruits as soon as they ripen. They leave until the dry season is advanced certain beds of roots and tubers that are edible the year around if they remain in the ground.

The headman of the band has the authority and the duty, according to !Kung social regulations, to plan the band's movements, to say to which veldkos area they will go and when, and, if the band separates temporarily into segments, to know where each segment is going and, in general, what veldkos it will consume. It is a matter of life and death to plan and control as best they can and not to travel for days, counting on food and finding that one segment of the band has eaten it all, unbeknown to the others.

Each type of veldkos and each area presents its problems of logistics, water being the determining factor in the plans, for usually water and veldkos are not in the same place. During the big rains and for several weeks after, the pans and vleys become shallow ponds and small, temporary water holes are filled. It is the time of relative plenty. The people find sufficient water to enable them to move about with comparative freedom in their country, wherever there is something to gather. When the dry season sets in, the problem is to carry enough water from the water hole to the veldkos area in ostrich egg shell containers and to carry enough veldkos back to the water hole. It is a ceaseless labor.

The distances the !Kung travel between water and fertile areas in these gathering trips vary from a few miles to twenty or thirty. The people do not manage greater distances except in the rainy season, when they go as far as seventy-five miles to a mangetti forest.

When the people go to gather mangettis or *tsi*, the men always ac-

On the Move A Bushman hangs his possessions on a carrying stick and thrusts his assegai under the stick in back to distribute the weight onto both shoulders.

company the women and help to gather and to carry the heavy loads—as much as they possibly can—back to the water hole.

Though the men help, especially with *tsi* and mangettis, gathering and digging are the work of women and the work that takes up the greater portion of their energy and time throughout their lives. Their digging implement is a sharpened, unweighted stick about three feet long. When we were living with the Gautscha bands at the Gautscha water hole in the dry season, the women went to gather every day or every second or third day, depending on the distance and on how much food they could carry back. They would plan which patch or fertile area to go to and start out in small groups, some to one place, some to another. They would walk five or ten or fifteen miles to their destination and then pick berries or dig roots, which may lie two feet or more under the ground, until the mid-afternoon, and then start back to the werf (campsite) at the water hole. They carry their infants tied to them, small children on their shoulders, and the loads of veldkos in the bulges of their karosses (skin capes). When they near the werf, they pick up two or three logs for the night fires.

The veldkos that each woman gathers belongs to her and with it she feeds her own family, sharing with whatever relative or friend she wishes. Custom does not require her to share it in a systematic way with others as meat must be shared. She cooks her veldkos in the coals and hot ashes, pounds fibrous roots and hard berries in her mortar, and serves the food to her family as a family meal, usually in the evening. During the day, however, people may cook and eat little snacks at odd times.

Although there are numerous kinds of veldkos, we must not give the impression that there is a great abundance. In fact, the opposite is true. Food is scarce all over the arid Kalahari, where drought is the scourge on all—the cattle raisers, the dry farmers, and the gatherers of the wild foods.

There has been much intermarriage in the Nyae Nyae region. Families therefore may have close relatives—with whom they have the right to live—

in several different bands, and they may choose among them. A band that owned comparatively good resources would tend to attract more members than a band with scant veldkos. This flexibility of residence pattern is one of the reasons that one finds the bands of the interior of the Nyae Nyae region relatively in balance with their resources, and varying in size.

WATER • Two or more bands may share the ownership of a water hole. Water holes keep their own rough population balance because, if water is very scarce, people will go to live elsewhere when they have the possibility of doing so.

In the interior of this region, in roughly 8000 square miles, there are three water holes that can be called really permanent. In the driest years these do not fail. Four others dry up only in years of severe drought. Six more are semipermanent: in a very good year they may yield a little water right through, but in a dry year they are sure to dry up. When the semipermanent water holes go dry, the bands who own them may break up temporarily and the families may go to live with relatives who are at permanent water holes, or they may go as whole bands to another water hole where they have relatives.

Water is not owned as exclusively or as jealously as veldkos. Water seems to belong more to mankind, as the animals do, and the ownership of water holes emphasizes more the managing than the withholding of the water. The headman controls the water. His permission should be asked by travelers or visitors before taking water, "because he knows what he has and what can be done," we were told. We saw small temporary water holes marked with bundles of grass thrust into forked sticks. This was to tell visitors or travelers that the owners of the water hole were in residence, as it were, and were counting on the water. We believe that in these circumstances water would not be taken without permission. Occasions are not likely to arise where permission need be refused. The !Kung know where the others are, or are likely to be, at a given time and know how much water is available. They plan better than to get themselves into desperate situations.

One source of water appears to be owned by individuals. It is the rainwater that collects in hollow mangetti trees. The water in trees is not stolen by others who go to gather in the same mangetti forest. Water, incidentally, is the only beverage of the !Kung in the interior of the region. They have no alcoholic drinks and use no infusions of herbs.

HUNTING AND MEAT SHARING • !Kung hunting regulations do not confine the hunters to territories. The game animals belong to no one until they are shot, and the hunters may follow them anywhere the spoor leads and may cross the territorial boundaries of any band. If hunters have made a kill in the territory of a neighboring band, they would not fail to give a present of meat to the owners of the territory should they happen to encounter them, but this is a gift, not an obligatory tribute. The vastness and emptiness of the country allow this freedom in hunting rights and the wandering nature of the game requires that the hunters, if they are to succeed at all, be free to look for game wherever they can find it.

The !Kung eagerly pick up tortoises, certain kinds of lizards, snakes, ostrich eggs, and grasshoppers, and they relish termites when these insects swarm out in nuptial flight. These items provide incidental delicacies and gathering them is like the gathering of veldkos. The person who gathers them may keep them for himself and his own family. Men gladly shoot small animals and birds if they happen upon them—wart hogs, duikers, other small antelope, porcupines, badgers, pythons, spring hares, ostriches, paouws, guinea fowl, red-winged partridges, occasional migrating geese, and other birds. They may keep them for their own families. They do not, however, devote their hunting time to the smaller animal creatures if they find fresh spoor of the larger ones. Hunting the big game animals that feed a whole band is the work of a man's prime and is incumbent on him.

Hunting parties usually consist of from two to four or five men. A man cannot hunt effectively alone in this country. Several parties hunting in different directions are more advantageous than one larger party. Any man may organize a hunting party, with relatives and friends from his own band or from neighboring bands—men he likes to hunt with. No one is formally a leader; the men talk and plan together and are likely to fall in with the suggestions of the one whom they consider the best hunter. Participation in any given hunting party is voluntary. What !Kung society urges is that the hunters hunt; it does not restrict the ways and means. The force of public opinion upon men not to sit in the werf, not to be lazy but to do their share, is tremendous.

The game the !Kung hunt deliberately and purposefully are the several big antelopes found in the region: eland, kudu, gemsbok, wildebeest, hartebeest, springbok. They also hunt the more rarely seen buffalo and occasionally manage to shoot a giraffe. Although there is this considerable variety of kind, there is not a great abundance of game. The herds are small and the hunts long and hard.[6] The antelope, because they can go for long periods without drinking, move and drift about anywhere in the vast monotonous veld and are very difficult to find. Hunters often search for days, covering scores of miles, before finding spoor fresh enough to follow, and they may follow it for days before catching up with the animal. Their little arrows kill by poison rather than by piercing deeply, and, when an animal is shot, if it is big, it may wander for three or four more days until it dies of the poison. Smaller animals succumb in a shorter time. The hunters must track the animal and find it before the lions, leopards, hyenas, jackals, or vultures devour it. Thus, according to our observations, a !Kung band gets on an average only about fifteen to eighteen large animals in a usual year.

The meat of the large game animals does not belong to the hunters to do with as they choose. However, they always have the prerogative of eating the liver at the site of the kill and, if their hunger is not satisfied, they may eat more. The bulk of the meat is then carried to the band, where it is distributed among the members according to a system. The meat belongs to the owner of the first arrow that penetrates the animal so that it stays in. He has the responsibility of making the first distribution.

Anyone in the band may be the owner of the arrow. A hunter carries arrows he acquires in three different ways. Each man has his own that he makes himself, shaping the points with some little distinction so that he will know them from the arrows of other men. In addition he carries arrows that have been given or lent to him. When an arrow is given to him, he is the owner as much as if he had made it himself, but if he uses that arrow he must make a special gift of meat to the donor. When he uses an arrow that is loaned to him, he merely shoots for the person who lent it and who remains the owner of the arrow. !Kung society makes a great deal of giving and lending arrows. Women and old men, as well as men in their hunting prime, receive arrows as gifts and may give them or lend them to a hunter, asking him to shoot for them. A hunter cannot refuse an arrow— as a person cannot refuse any gift—without offending the giver. He accepts the arrow and with it an obligation, but he gives or lends arrows in return and involves others in obligation to him. Hunters choose to use one or another of their arrows, with the result that the responsibility of distributing the meat, with its advantages and obligations, is shared by members of the band as is the meat itself.

In the first distribution the whole animal is divided among a few persons, who receive whole sections on the bone, unless the animal is so large that the meat has to be cut off in strips to be carried. The first of these persons are the hunters, each of whom gets a fore- or hindquarter or the equivalent. The giver of the arrow (if the arrow was not made by the owner himself) receives a generous portion. The owner of the arrow, who may be one of the hunters, or anybody, keeps the rest.

In the second distribution, the several persons who got meat in the first distribution cut up their shares and distribute them further. The amounts depend on the number of persons involved, but should be as much as the giver can manage. In the second distribution, close kinship is the factor that sets the pattern of giving. A man's first obligation at this point is to his wife's parents. He must give to them the best he has in as generous portions as he can while still fulfilling other primary obligations, which are to his own parents, his spouse, and offspring. He keeps a portion for himself at this time and from it would give to his siblings, to his wife's siblings, if they are present, and to other kin, affines, and friends who are there, possibly only in small quantities by then.

Everyone who receives meat gives again, in another wave of sharing, to his or her parents, parents-in-law, spouses, offspring, siblings, and others. This meat may be cooked and the quantities small. Visitors receive small amounts of cooked meat from their hosts. It ends in everybody getting some meat.

In the later waves of sharing, when the primary distribution and primary kinship obligations have been fulfilled, the giving of meat from one's own portion has the quality of gift giving. !Kung society requires at this point only that a person should give with reasonable generosity in proportion to what he has received and not keep more than an equitable amount for himself, and that the person who receives a gift of meat must give a reciprocal gift of meat at some time in the future. People give to whom they please, this time to some, next time to others, more generously or less generously according to their own (to us often unfathomable) reasons. We are certain, however, that the motives are the same as in gift giving in general: the person gives to measure up to what is expected of him, to make friendly gestures, to win favor, to repay past favors and obligations, and to enmesh others in future obligation.

Aside from the practical advantage of using up meat while it is still fresh, the !Kung custom of meat sharing has enormous social value. It does a great deal to mitigate tensions. The fear of hunger is lessened. People are sustained by a web of mutual obligation. Moreover, they are fully conscious of these values, and the custom is so strongly established and so faithfully followed that the idea of not sharing is virtually unthinkable to the !Kung.

Meat is not habitually cooked and eaten as a family meal among the !Kung. When an individual receives a portion he owns it outright. He may give and share it further, as he wishes, but it never becomes family or group property. The men, women, and children may cook their pieces when and as they wish, often roasting bits in the coals and hot ashes and eating them alone at odd times. Or someone may start a big pot boiling and several people will bring their pieces to put into it at the same time, each taking his own piece out when it is cooked.

The sense of possessing one's own piece personally is, I believe, very important to the !Kung. It gives one the responsibility of choosing when to eat one's meat and struggling with hunger as best one can when it is finished, without occasion or excuse for blaming others for eating more than their share.

It has often been reported that, when Bushmen kill an animal, they gorge themselves until they can hardly walk. We have seen the Nyae Nyae !Kung eat hearty meals of meat when plenty appeared and they had been long without, but nothing more than we considered a normal amount.

They hang meat in the bushes to dry and can keep it for some time. It is not uncommon for them to eat quite sparingly and save bits for a coming journey or against a future day of hunger, as they eat sparingly of mangetti nuts and *tsi* when they must make a supply they have carried from a great distance last as long as possible.

The !Kung are well accustomed to restraining themselves in regard to food. Thus when a visitor comes to a fire where people are preparing food or eating, he should sit at a discreet distance, not to seem importunate, and wait to be asked to share.

Although the hunters supply only about a fifth of the people's food and the women four fifths, the women play a dependent role in !Kung society. Nevertheless, the men do not ill-treat the women and require no extreme form of obedience or subservience of them.

The primary factor in the dominance of the men is undoubtedly strength. !Kung men are small and slender, but they are wiry and vigorous and, with their strength, they carry and protect the very life of their people.

Another factor that brings men clearly forward is the character of hunting and its reward. Women bring the daily food, but there is nothing splendid about returning with vegetables and wood. Many of the vegetable foods, furthermore, are rather tasteless and harsh and are not very satisfying. The return of the hunters is vastly different. The intense craving for meat, the anxiety that goes with the hunt, the deep excitement of the kill, finally the eating and the satisfaction reach to the very core of the people, engaging powerful emotions. Once a young man, /Qui, who was said to be the best hunter in the region, had been charged by a magnificent cock ostrich on a big open pan where there was no refuge. He knelt, facing the creature, until it was within close range and shot an arrow straight into its heart. Back in the werf, while the meat was being cut up and distributed by /Qui's wife's brothers, he slept exhausted on the mound of black and white plumes and the women—some of the plumes in their hair—danced a dance of praise around him. This is the role of !Kung hunters.

MATERIAL CULTURE

HOUSE TYPE AND SETTLEMENT PATTERN • The building of the scherm—the Bushman reed-and-grass dwelling—is women's work, associated with vegetation and gathering. Each woman builds for her own family. However, unless no better shade can be found or unless it is raining, the women often do not bother to build these shelters. Especially after the long days of walking, it is easier just to settle in the bushes.

In the Nyae Nyae region, wood and grass are everywhere, and a woman can gather her material and build her scherm in less than an hour. She breaks up flexible branches about six feet long, digs holes with her

A Bridal Scherm The groom, to the right, and the bride, to the left, are with companions. This scherm is a particularly well-built specimen of the Bushman house.

digging stick in a crescent curve, and tamps the branches into them. She weaves the branches together at the top and perhaps ties a few with fiber cord. This makes a frame half a hemisphere in shape, four to five feet wide on its open side, three to four feet deep, and perhaps five feet high at the peak. The woman then lays armloads of grass against the branches.

The fire, not the scherm, is the visible symbol of home for a !Kung family. Summer and winter, each nuclear family has its own fire. The families cover their coals with ash during the day and fan them up for cooking. Toward evening, men and women go to the veld to gather wood and bring back whole dead trees, enough to keep their fires burning brightly all night.

The werf is the group of fires of all the families in the band. A !Kung werf has no fixed pattern of orientation except to cluster closely together. With all space around them, the band with whom we lived—Band I of Gautscha, consisting of thirty-two persons with eight family fires—usually huddled into a place roughly forty to fifty feet by about twenty. The light and warmth of their fires together wall them in from infinity and darkness and protect them from predators.

The !Kung never return to a werf they have once abandoned. They come season after season all during their lives to the same water holes and veldkos areas, but always choose a fresh spot to make a new settlement.

ARTIFACTS · The artifacts of the !Kung are simple and few but well made and well cared for. These people use stone only for sharpening metal blades, for stretching carrying nets, and for pounding things. Informants said they had never seen or heard of stone arrow points or blades. They still use bone and wood points occasionally but have for the most part changed over to metal for knives, axes, assegai blades, and drills, as well as for arrow points.

From wood the men make bows and quivers as well as sticks for making fire, digging, carrying, and stirring; handles for knives, axes, and assegais; bowls, spoons, mortars, and pestles; and musical instruments—the five-stringed //guashi and a one-stringed violin. Reed and bone are available in plenty for arrow shafts. There are abundant fiber and sinew for the excellent cordage that men and women make. Little tortoise shells are dippers and cosmetic boxes. Hides, although not abundant, are sufficient—in the Nyae Nyae region at least—for everyone to have a kaross, for the men to have breechclouts, and for the women to have modesty aprons and skins to wear around the buttocks. All have sewn skin bags. These objects of hide are made by men because they are products of the hunt. Frequently there are surplus hides for trade.

Ostrich egg shells are used for water containers, and women make ostrich egg shell beads. This is the one important craft of the women and the one for which Bushmen are noted among the surrounding peoples. Good ostrich egg shell bead ornaments are the most prized possessions of the !Kung. The women also make ornaments of European beads and of grass and thongs and tsī nuts. They very much enjoy ornamenting themselves.

The !Kung decorate their artifacts occasionally with rather meager scratched designs but have not developed graphic, pictorial, or sculptural arts to any appreciable extent.

The !Kung trade with their Tswana and Herero neighbors, offering well-tanned hides, ostrich egg shell beads, and a red powder they make from the dead heartwood of a certain tree. Usually what they want most of all in exchange is tobacco—for they are passionately addicted smokers— and malleable metal from which they shape their arrow points and assegai blades. They also want knives, axes, European beads, and either the round-bottomed Ovambo pots or European iron pots. Once in a while they get an old chisel or file, a basin or cup, or a few miserable scraps of cloth garments. The little Bushmen find the bigger, more aggressive Bantu hard bargainers and are rather at their mercy.

The significant thing about !Kung artifacts from a social point of view is that they are not accumulated as wealth and their possession does not symbolize high status or bestow prestige. It is not advantageous to multiply and accumulate in this society. Any man can make what he needs when he wants to. Most of the materials he uses are abundant and free for anyone to take. Furthermore, in their nomadic lives, without beasts of burden, the fact that the people themselves must carry everything puts a sharp limit on the quantity of objects they want to possess. They do not even want one each of the common tools of their lives. They borrow from each other, and there is less to carry.

Instead of acquiring prestige by accumulating possessions, the !Kung seek it in the opposite way. They practice a custom of gift giving to such an extent that their belongings all move in a slow flowing current among them and no one keeps anything of particular value very long. !Kung society requires that gifts be made in return, and the custom serves as a means to mitigate jealousy, to express friendly intent, and to weave people together in mutual obligation.

SOCIAL ORGANIZATION

THE FAMILY AND THE DOMESTIC GROUP • The family is the primary and the most cohesive social unit of the !Kung. By far the strongest bonds they feel are those of the nuclear family—the bonds between parent and offspring, between siblings, between spouses. These relationships are the basis of residence; by that I mean that people live together and have membership in their bands and rights to its food and water resources because they are linked to the band by one of these relationships. I believe that, in addition to the structured aspects, there is great emotional cohesiveness in !Kung families and that this is observable in the way families within the band build their fires near each other, come and go together, or, if there should be a quarrel, literally stand by each other, drawing close together.

The !Kung family passes through four phases. In its simplest nuclear form it consists of a man, his wife, and such children as are born to them. First marriages are always with just one wife. A later nuclear phase may be polygynous. When the daughters of a !Kung couple marry, and the daughters' husbands come to live with their brides' parents to give them bride service, the unit becomes an extended family. In a second extended phase, the married sons may have returned from bride service with their wives and offspring. In this phase, the married daughters with their husbands and offspring may stay or they may go to live with their husbands' people.

The headship of a family is strongly associated with males. A widowed mother is regarded as a dependent, not as a family head. When the old father of an extended family dies, that particular family ceases to be an extended family. Families of siblings may live together in the same band, but no one of them has authority over another unless one of the siblings happens to be headman of the band. If they are no longer involved in bride service themselves, and their offspring are not yet married, these families become independent nuclear families again, to become new, extended families when the offspring marry.

Both the father and mother expect and receive respect and obedience from their children. Although the mother's influence is always felt, I believe that the father's authority is greater. It is not formalized or expressed in a harsh or domineering way. As long as the father lives, he is the head of the family, symbolically. Even when too old to hunt, if he is still a forceful person, he remains the one in authority, the leader of the sons-in-law and his daughters, of his sons and their wives. Gradually, however, when he becomes very old, the younger men make their own plans without necessarily consulting him.

!Kung families are responsible for dependents. Thus, old, dependent parents are unfailingly supported by their offspring and may choose with which one of their offspring they will live. Orphaned children are taken by their grandparents or by a sibling of their parents. It happens occasionally that a person has no living parent, offspring, or sibling. In that case, other relatives assume the responsibility.

THE NAME RELATIONSHIP · Although !Kung society has developed no formal political structure under which the bands are united, and there are no organizations outside the bands, these people have a means of extending the concept of kinship beyond close consanguineous relatives and affines and of recognizing, in what we call the name relationship, the web of remote interrelationship that long intermarriage within the region has established.

Invariably the first son and the first daughter are named by their father for their paternal grandparents. Other children are usually named for their mother's parents, the siblings of their parents, and the spouses of those siblings, and may occasionally be named for other relatives. Thus, a few names are used over and over through the generations. We recorded only forty-six men's names and forty-one women's names in the region. The !Kung assume that persons who have the same name are related, though the exact nature of the relationship is forgotten. They believe, also, that people with the same name somehow have a common entity. They bestow upon each other kin terms that are appropriate to the name, according to a system. The !Kung have intermarried within the Nyae Nyae region to such an extent that everyone has a kin term he associates with each one of the names. This means that the people of the whole region are what we call name relatives, all applying kin terms to each other.

From the !Kung point of view the custom has two values. It regulates the incest taboo in its furthermost extension, especially the joking relationship that symbolizes the taboo. (For example, a man should not marry or make sexual jokes with a woman who has the same name as his mother.) The !Kung feel secure in righteousness when they know they are behaving properly in these matters, and the kin term they apply guides their behavior with everyone they meet.

The other value is obvious. The !Kung of the whole Nyae Nyae region, in their thirty-six separate bands or groups, are drawn together by a feeling of belonging to an in-group. The familiar names and the use of the kin terms make them expect from each other behavior suitable to kinsmen— sharing food, gift giving, restraint from expressing jealousy or other hostili- ties, conforming to group opinion, all the things they do that are conducive to peaceful living together. This sense of belonging gives security and com- fort to these people in whose language the word *dole,* which means "strange," means also "harmful" and "bad." They call themselves *ju /ōassi. Ju* means "people"; */ōassi* connotes something like "true" or "pure" and can be para- phrased as "just ourselves."[7]

INHERITANCE PATTERN · The !Kung have no named, structured patriline- ages, but they have a patrilineal emphasis. Inheritance passes from father to eldest son, as does the succession in headmanship.

There is not much property to inherit. Land and the resources of food and water are owned by the band, not privately by individuals. A consider- able amount of an individual's personal property is destroyed at the time of his death. This is not done to provide implements for the spirits in the after-life. The !Kung believe that the spirits of the dead have their own heavenly objects and need nothing from earth. It is done because no member of the family wants to use the common objects of the dead, which too vividly remind them of their loss. Only the more rare and important pos- sessions are kept, such as assegais and fine ornaments. These are inherited by the eldest son. Failing a son, the spouse or a daughter or sibling or, failing these, some other close relative who was present would take the things. Whoever took them would be expected to give some of them to other relatives.

MARRIAGE · As I mentioned, the Nyae Nyae !Kung rarely marry outside the region, although !Kung women not infrequently marry Tswana or Herero men in the border settlements.

First marriages are arranged by parents while the children are still young. Either the parents of the boy or those of the girl may first ask for the betrothal. Parents of boys have their eyes on every girl baby and may say to parents of an unborn infant, "If it is a girl, let us have her for our son."

No property settlements enter into the marriage choices or marriage arrangements among the !Kung. Rather, they say about the basis of their choice that they seek an upstanding family for their child to marry into, people who are not lazy and not "far-hearted" but who are dependable and generous and behave with propriety, obeying the social rules and the various taboos. They wait for the children to grow up, hoping that they will be like their families in these qualities.

The marriage takes place when the parents agree, but it must be after the boy has killed a game animal and is scarified. The age at which young people marry varies greatly. We know girls who were married for five or six years before they menstruated; others were somewhat older at marriage.

!Kung society rigorously, and without exception, requires that all men, in first and subsequent marriages, go to live with the parents of their brides, and give them bride service. This service is essentially hunting. "Our daughter's husband must give us meat." "We shall soon be old; we need a young man to hunt for us." These are the refrains of the people.

The duration of bride service is indefinite. The !Kung say it should be long enough for three children to be born. Since the girls are so young, it may mean that eight or ten years elapse before three children have been born. Divorce may terminate bride service. After his obligations are fulfilled, a man has the right to return to his own people with his wife and dependents or he may choose to stay with his wife's people.

The young couple is expected not to have sexual intercourse until the girl is ready. No social rule patterns the time, which is a matter of individual adjustment, but the boy must not force the girl. If she complained to her parents, they might disapprove of the boy, dissolve the marriage, and send him away. His parents would have to try to find another bride for him and he would have to wait for years again for her to grow up.

The !Kung are polygynous. First marriages are ordinarily arranged by their parents between children who have not been previously married. Only occasionally is a young girl betrothed for her first marriage to a man who had been married before, perhaps a young man who had lost his wife by death or divorce, or possibly, but rarely, to her sister's husband or some other man as his second wife. Usually second marriages are contracted later in life when a woman becomes available for remarriage through widowhood or divorce. In such marriages, the man and woman concerned make their own arrangements. The number of wives a man may have is determined not by social rule but by the man's ability to obtain and support them. This limits him usually to one. There is no great excess of women, and prestige and wealth do not concentrate in !Kung society to give certain categories of men, such as headmen or medicine men, more power or right than others to acquire wives. A sampling of eighty-eight marriages showed that only nine of the men had two wives. None had more than two.

Although the first wife is considered to have a somewhat more esteemed and dominant position, no property or other material advantage is given to her and no important social advantage accrues.

!Kung co-wives live very closely together. They share one scherm and one family fire. They care for and nurse each other's children. Even when they are jealous of each other, as they so often are, !Kung society demands of them that they preserve a decent semblance of harmony and, by self-control and silence, avoid disturbing other people with jealous wrangling.

The band itself, as a structured unit, is not a factor in regulating marriage. Persons may marry either within their bands or outside them if relationships and marriage regulations permit. Neither the sororate nor the levirate is obligatory, but marriage with a brother's wife or a sister's husband is considered to be good and suitable, particularly as a second marriage, should death or divorce make it possible for these affines to marry again. These relationships are not especially preferred in first marriages.

Marriages are forbidden in !Kung society only on the basis of the incest taboo, which is very strongly felt. It rigorously prohibits the !Kung from marriage with members of the nuclear family. It also extends to step-parents, stepbrothers and stepsisters, stepchildren, and to three additional categories of persons: certain kin, certain affines, and certain name relatives, whose relationships are considered to resemble those of the nuclear family.[8]

The !Kung conform strictly to the marriage regulations where they feel the internal sanction strongly, as they do with close kin and affines. But with the more remote relatives, third cousins, and even second cousins, and with name relatives, they deviate without any apparent sense of guilt and without incurring the grave disapproval of society.

Widowers may marry again without restriction. A widow is supposed to wait until one rainy season has passed so that "the rain may wash the death away," but often she does not.

A couple may divorce without formality. This may be by mutual consent, or one spouse may simply leave the other. No religious or legal dispensation is involved and parental consent is not a requirement. No property entanglements present difficulties for there is no dowry or bride-price to be resolved. Divorce does not change people's status in the community in any way, and they are free to remarry without restrictions. Although the !Kung do not consider divorce reprehensible, they deplore it because it is untoward and can cause trouble. Divorces are not uncommon among young people of about the age at which young people in our society would be getting married, but, once a compatible mate is found, there is a notable stability in the marriages.

!Kung society forbids any sexual relations outside marriage, with one exception, called /kamheri. /Kamheri means that two men may agree to exchange wives temporarily, provided the wives consent. When deviations from the sexual regulations do occur, the usual form is adultery, since almost all Bushman women are in the married state from early youth. But adultery meets with deterrents in this society. The strongly felt incest taboo prevents extramarital sexual relations as well as marriage with close relatives. Ease of divorce enables persons who really wish to change mates to do so. Lack of privacy makes it almost impossible to keep an affair secret, and violent jealousy and anger can be aroused. Fearing any disruptive force, the !Kung disapprove.

LIFE CYCLE

CHILD TRAINING · !Kung parents are gentle, protective, and permissive with all their children and express their affection especially with babies. It is a most common sight to see fathers fondly kissing them with pursed lips and smacks. The mother, wherever she goes, carries her infant tied to her left side, skin to skin, in a little leather sling where it can reach her breast. When she sits, she takes the infant out of its sling, holds it, lets it nurse the other breast.

The !Kung believe that long nursing is essential to the survival and development of their children and encourage them to continue until they are three or four or older. These people practice infanticide and, in explaining it, say that they must space their babies so that each will be able to nurse long enough to ensure his having strong legs. An infant cannot thrive on their harsh foods, they say, even though they chew the food and put it into the infants' mouths, and the mother cannot support two entirely with her milk, excellent though !Kung lactation appears to be. They supplement the milk with adult food as soon as the child can eat it, so that a child is accustomed to it and ready to be weaned at three or four when the next baby comes. But, even so, the mother weans gradually, letting the older child have a drink of milk occasionally through the day. If the mother does not have or keep another baby but still has milk, she will allow or encourage her child to continue nursing. Other children tend to make fun of a child who nurses until he is six or so, and, in response to their teasing, a child may wean himself quite abruptly.

Babies are naked and, since there are no floors but the desert sand, not much is made of their urinating wherever they are. When they defecate, they are wiped with grass and the fecal matter is cleaned up at once by some older child or adult and carried off. As soon as children can walk fairly well they are led by the hand and encouraged to go out of the werf for their toilet needs, at first for the sake of cleanliness and, as they grow older, for the sake of modesty as well. (!Kung adults are exceedingly modest about uncovering their genitalia. Their incest taboo influences this behavior, I think, very strongly.)

Infants sleep in their mothers' arms. Young children sleep wrapped in karosses beside their parents' fire. Boys from the age of about eleven or twelve sleep at a boys' fire, not far from the family of one of them. Girls at that age go to sleep with a grandmother or some widow, or several of them together may sleep near the parents of one of them, but not exactly at the parents' fire.

Within the frame of protectiveness the parents are very permissive and make few, if any, demands on their children. With no houses and few utensils, there are not many household tasks to assign. Children are not sent off alone to do any of the daily work of fetching water or wood or gathering veldkos. Although lions, leopards, and hyenas tend to mind their own business, they are present in the country and share the water holes with the Bushmen. Poisonous snakes are a very real danger. Furthermore, as the hunters say, it takes a lifetime to learn the country well enough not to be easily lost in the featureless grass and brush. The adults do not let their children out of their sight. In their parents' presence the children imitate adult activities in vital, active play, very engaging to watch, and participate in actual work as they are able. The adults pause to show them how to hold a digging stick, or a toy bow or drill, so that play and learning merge.

The !Kung have a rich variety of lively group games, with pantomime, singing, dancing, and other rhythmic movements, that children and adults together enjoy playing in the werf when the heat of the day is over. In most of their games boys and girls play separately, but they dance and sing together.

!Kung children are never harshly punished. One father said that if he had a boy who was quarrelsome or who disobeyed the rules—for instance, the absolute rule of the !Kung against stealing food or possessions—what he would do about it would be to keep the boy right with him until he learned sense. The children on their part do not often do things that call forth punishment. They usually fall in with group life and do what is expected of them without apparent uncertainty, frustration, or fear; and expressions of resistance or hostility toward their parents, the group, or each other are very much the exception.

PUBERTY • When the fathers of the present old men were young men, the Nyae Nyae !Kung adopted the ceremony of the *Choma*, which they said was taught to them by a !Kung man who had married into another language group in the south. The *Choma* resembles some Bantu initiation ceremonies at certain points. The men who have had the ceremony and are therefore *Choma* owners take the boys to a place far enough from the werf to be out of hearing of the women, who, the !Kung claim, would die if they heard some of the *Choma* sounds. The men and boys dance all night for several nights to special *Choma* songs with special rhythms that differ from those of the other dances. A secret bull-roarer plays a part in the ceremony. At the end the boys are scarified with a vertical line down the middle of their foreheads and are given a special *Choma* haircut. Circumcision or other genital operations are not practiced by the !Kung. The *Choma* is not compulsory; most boys take part but a few refuse. *Choma* owners do not form a corporate sodality. !Kung society has no such units except kinship groups.

Another ceremony for boys, which is presumably ancient and traditionally Bushman, must be performed before a boy can marry. This ceremony is performed twice for each boy, individually, on the occasion of his first killing a large game animal, once for the first male, once for the first female. The meat is cooked at a special fire, which women must avoid, and is eaten ceremonially by the men. The boy is scarified, by his father or another male relative, on his right side for the first male animal, on his left side for the first female. Little vertical cuts are made in his skin in lines on his arms, chest, back, and forehead, and a paste of charred meat and fat is rubbed into them. This is to ensure his seeing well, shooting well, and having a heart that will say to him, "Why am I sitting here in the werf? Why am I not out hunting?"

The passage from childhood to adulthood is marked for a !Kung girl by a ceremony at her first menstruation. The girl is isolated in a special scherm for the duration of the flow only. She must be covered by a kaross because the sun must not shine upon her, and her feet must not touch the ground. When she must go out to urinate or defecate, she is carried on the back of the old woman (not her mother) who attends her. It is not the menstrual blood but the girl herself who must be kept from touching the ground. She would get thin if she disregarded this taboo. Men and boys must not look at the girl and she must not look at them lest the men become highly visible to animals and unable to get near enough to them to shoot.

Every day that the girl is in the menstruation scherm, the women who are present and one or two old men dance a special dance called the Eland Dance and sing a special cycle of First Menstruation music. The Eland Dance is full of sex symbolism. The two old men should be free from even the most attenuated, symbolic extension of the incest taboo with respect to the girl, and it follows that they should have what is called the joking relationship with her. The usual strict modesty of the women is set aside. They take off their karosses (leaving their aprons on, however) and hang strings of beads from their waists down over their bare buttocks. The old men, with forked sticks tied to their heads to represent eland horns, imitate the gait and carriage of elands, and dance among the women with subtly erotic gestures. The other men and boys of the werf must stay at a distance.

When the girl stops menstruating she is washed, rubbed with *tsi̅* and fat, and her face is painted with red lines. She then may go among the people again, but the first time she takes water from the water hole and the first time she cooks and eats veldkos, the water and veldkos must be

The *Choa* Ceremony The
mother takes the girl's hands
to scrape the *tsí* out of the
ashes.

choa-ed. The old woman who attends her performs this part of the ceremony
(or her mother may do so). She scrapes a root called *sha sha* into the water
hole. To *choa* the veldkos, the old woman takes the girl's hands in hers and
together they place the veldkos in the fire. When it is cooked, they scrape
it out together and the old woman puts *sha sha* in her mouth, chews it,
and blows on the girl's hands and on the veldkos. This protects the girl
from having an upset stomach. Each veldkos must be *choa*-ed the first time
the girl eats it after the First Menstruation ceremony.

No ceremonials mark subsequent menstruation periods, and the women do
not seclude themselves during the flow or avoid gathering veldkos or dipping
water from the water hole. They continue only to practice certain avoidances
that in general have to do with men's hunting. The menstruating woman
must not touch hunting gear; it would be very bad, for the arrows would
be useless. She must not have sexual intercourse with her husband; it would
make him tired and thin. Men in the years of their hunting prime should
not talk or listen to talk about menstruation, for to do so might make them
lazy in hunting.

The girls who are married before their first menstruation have the
same menstruation ceremony when the time comes as do the unmarried girls.

There is no genital mutilation practiced among the girls and women
of the !Kung. Girls are scarified, but not at the time of the menstruation ceremony. The scarification is begun when the girl is about seven or eight and
is continued little by little over several years. Stripes are made on the legs,

thighs, up the buttocks to the waist, and on the cheeks and forehead. The !Kung say the stripes are made only for beauty[9] and are in imitation of gemsbok—big, stately gray antelopes with spectacular black markings.

POLITICAL ORGANIZATION

The only social grouping above the family in !Kung society is the autonomous band. A band is a group of families who live together, linked to one another and to the headman by kinship bonds, in a manner that will be illustrated presently. Nuclear families do not live alone among the !Kung. An extended family might do so, if it were a strong unit with enough young hunters and gatherers to sustain it; it would then be a band. Most of the Nyae Nyae bands were composed of several families and ranged in size from twenty or twenty-five to fifty or sixty members.

Each band belongs to its own territory, or, we can say, owns its territory and the resources within it. Two or more bands may belong to the same territory. The focus of the band's ownership of the territory is the headman, who is called *kxau* (owner). He does not own the resources as private, individual property is owned, to withhold or give as he pleases. Members born to the band have a kind of inalienable right of their own to the resources. The headman personifies those rights and gives them organization and continuity. The continuity is expressed by the attachment of the headmanship to the territory. If a headman leaves the territory to live else-where—except temporarily for bride service—he ceases to be headman and the headmanship falls on someone else who remains in the territory.

!Kung society accords to the headman the authority to coordinate the movements of his own people in relation to their consumption of resources, and his chief duty is to plan when and where the band will move. He should protect the resources from encroachment from outsiders.

When the band moves, the headman's position is at the head of the line. He chooses the site for the new werf and has the first choice of a spot for his own fire and scherm. He has no other rewards or prerogatives. He carries his own load and is as thin as the rest.

It is not a headman's duty, as headman, to instigate or organize hunting parties, trading trips, the making of artifacts, or gift giving, nor does he make marriage arrangements. Individuals instigate their own activities. A headman is not in any formalized way a judge of his people, nor must he punish a wrongdoer. He may have great influence, if he is an effective leader, but wrongdoing is judged and controlled by public opinion, usually expressed in talk. Occasionally a person who is wronged seeks to avenge himself by fighting, which is greatly deplored.

If a headman is too young or too old, or lacks personal qualities of leadership, the people may turn quite informally to some other man for leadership in their daily life—ask him for help and advice, fall in with his plans. Such a leader has no authority and receives no honors or rewards.

Headmanship is inherited by the eldest son from the father. If that son dies or leaves the band, the headmanship passes to the next eldest son.

No strictly formulated rules, insofar as we know, provide for further succession. We have no observations of our own of situations in which a headman had no son.[10]

The rule of succession does not provide for a headmanship to pass collaterally to a headman's younger brother. However, a younger brother may set up a band of his own in the same territory if he does not prefer to live under the headmanship of his older brother or if he does not continue to live with his wife's people. The younger brother has his own rights to the veldkos and water that derive from his father and he can share them with his family and band. Nevertheless, as long as a son of the headman in rightful succession is living in the territory, he has higher authority and is responsible for the overall planning. Should the principal headman's band die out or realign itself, the collateral band led by the younger brother would become the principal one.

The bonds that bring the !Kung into membership in bands are the same consanguineous and affinal bonds on which a nuclear family is formed: the bonds of parent-offspring, siblings, and spouses. Everyone who lives in a !Kung band is linked by one of these bonds with the headman, sometimes directly or sometimes in a chainlike manner through one or two other persons. A description of a typical band will illustrate this point. Band II of Gautscha has forty-one members. The headman, Gao Beard, has two wives and four young children. With Gao Beard live his younger brother, one of his younger sisters, each with spouse and children, and his elderly, dependent and widowed mother. Gao asked his first wife's father, Old ≠Toma, whom he likes very much, to join his band. Old ≠Toma brought with him into the band his wife, a married son with wife and child, two younger sons, his wife's sister, and her son by a now divorced husband. He also brought sixteen other persons—Gau and his people. Gau belongs to another band but was at the time living in Band II because he had married, as a second wife, Old ≠Toma's wife's sister and, middle-aged though they are, he was in bride service to her people. After a time Gau can choose whether to stay on in Band II or to go back to the band in which he originated. He said that he thought he would decide to stay with Old ≠Toma and Gao Beard because he likes Old ≠Toma and because Gao Beard has a mangetti grove.

People retain throughout their lives their membership in the band in which they were born and their rights to its veldkos and water resources.

If they leave the band they may return. Affines and the families of affines have equal rights to the resources while they are present but do not retain them if they leave.

RELIGION

RELIGIOUS BELIEFS • In the many strange old tales of the !Kung appears a protagonist named ≠Gao!na–Old ≠Gao. He had supernatural powers, but he looked like a man and lived on earth. Like mankind, he was subject to passion, hunger, wrongdoing, failure, frustration, and humiliation, but men imagine his feelings in larger scale and as more grotesque than their own. Themes of incest, hunger, and cannibalism run through the tales. The !Kung claim that this old protagonist and the great god of their present belief are one and the same: they have the same names, but if the present great god is the old ≠Gao!na, he is mightily changed.

The !Kung now believe that there are two gods. The great god lives in the eastern sky where the sun rises; the lesser, in the western sky where the sun sets. The great god is the creator of all things. He created himself and named himself. He then created the lesser god and a wife for each of them. The wives bore them children. The great god gave names to all these beings. Then he created the earth and the water holes, the sky and the rain, the sun and the wind, the things that grow on the earth, and the animals with their stripes and colors, and he gave them names. He created a woman and then a man. He commanded the man and the woman and the animals to breathe, for without breathing they would not live. From the beginning he created men and women to be mortal. When mortals die he takes their spirits to the place where he lives in the eastern sky, where there is a certain tree that has no name. He hangs the spirits in the tree, makes a medicine smoke in a pot beneath them, and transmutes them into the //gauwasi, the spirits of the dead, who live in the sky with him and are his servants. He has a medicine with which he renews himself, the //gauwasi, and the other heavenly beings and thus keeps them immortal.

The great god gave men bows and arrows and poison and digging sticks and taught them how to shoot animals and dig for food. Everything men know he taught them. Having created all things, the great god is the owner and the master of all things and commands their movements.

To "praise" himself, the !Kung believe, the great god gave himself seven divine names and one human name. The divine names are *Hishe, Huwe, Kxo, !Gara, Gani ga, ≠Gaishi ≠gai* and *//Gauwa.* The human name is *≠Gao!na,* the one he shares with the old protagonist.

Although there is not an absolute taboo upon saying the names of the gods, the !Kung fear to do so because it displeases the gods and draws their attention and they say, "Who is calling my name?"

The lesser god who lives in the western sky is the namesake of the great god, who, as the belief goes, gave the lesser god all seven of his own divine names, but not his human name. Although they insist in this belief, the !Kung never used any name but //Gauwa, one of the seven divine names, when they referred to the lesser god and we never heard them actually use this name for the great god. It would seem, then, that the lesser god is the old evil spirit, //Gauwa, who appears in the beliefs of the Hottentots and other Bushman language groups as the destroyer and the black chief, the one who sends death, disease, and misfortune. This evil spirit was an entity distinct from the good spirit who was variously named by Bushman groups Hishe, Huwe, and so on.

In present !Kung belief, however, neither the great god nor the lesser god is all evil or all good. Both are capable of being pleased or displeased with man and of sending favors or misfortunes. The lesser god is subservient to the great god and is supposed to do his bidding. The lesser god, however, has his own entity and does instigate his own actions, sometimes even disobeying the great god. Often they disagree between themselves.

The great god looks like a man, like a Bushman, but he is "the tallest of the Bushmen" and has long black hair that is not twisted and knotted like Bushman hair. He rides a horse across the sky—you can hear him—and he has a gun as well as bows and arrows. Some say he never comes to earth but always sends //Gauwa, or the spirits of the dead, the //gauwasi, to bring the good or evil that he sends to men. Only the greatest of medicine men have ever seen him.

//Gauwa, however, is commonly seen by the medicine men. They describe him as small. One said he was about two feet tall; another, that he was as small as a guinea fowl; a third, that he was as small as a mouse. Several agreed that he was covered with yellow hairs. One, however, a humble man, said that while in trance he had seen //Gauwa and that he was like a gray mist.

RELIGIOUS PRACTICES • The !Kung say that they pray spontaneously to the gods. Whenever the thought comes to them they put their prayers into words and say or think them to themselves without any formality. When they speak in prayer to the great god they address him by the respectful term !Nau, used for any old man, or use a title Gaoxa (chief), or call him "father." Sometimes they use one of his names. The prayers, a mingling of mild imprecation and pleading, reveal the major concerns of the !Kung: hunger, sickness, and death.[11]

The great god, responsible for sending sickness and death to men, also created and gives to men a mystical curing power that is called gaoxa (the same word as the title of respect). The !Kung say it is strong medicine: /num. The !Kung take for granted his giving to man both sickness and the power to cure it, and account for the power's sometimes failing to cure by saying that the all-powerful god allows it to work, or not, according to his pleasure.

He gives the curing power to medicine men (called num kxao, medicine owners), appearing to them (usually in dreams, sometimes in what seem to be waking hallucinations) and putting the power into them. He has also put a curing power in the medicine songs that the people sing at the dances, songs named Rain, Sun, Giraffe, Eland, Honey, Buffalo, Mamba, and Spider —all powerful things. The great god gives the power freely. It is rare to find a man among the !Kung who is not a medicine man. The function of the medicine men is only to cure. They are not sorcerers or witch doctors. (The !Kung are not a witch-ridden people.) !Kung medicine men receive no rewards or special prerogatives. They work together apparently without rivalry. The medicine men may cure at any time but their strongest curing occurs at the dance.

Whether or not anyone is sick, the people dance two or three times a month, sometimes more often. Anyone who wants a dance may start one simply by asking people to come and begin. The !Kung like to dance for many reasons. There is the inherent physical pleasure in moving to rhythm. Music and dancing are their arts, from which their aesthetic pleasure comes. The dances are also social gatherings in which all participate, men, women, children, visitors—everybody. A dance draws them together as nothing else does. Even more important is the fact that the dance is one concerted religious act of the !Kung and brings people into such unison that they become like an organic being.

At the dances not only may the sick be cured, but pending evil and misfortune averted. The !Kung believe that the great god may send //Gauwa or the //gauwasi at any time with ill for someone and that these beings may be lurking, awaiting their chance to inflict it. The medicine men in the dances combat them, drive them away, and protect the people.

Usually there are several medicine men performing at the same time. To cure they go into trance, which varies in depth as the ceremony proceeds. The curing cannot be described in words; it must be heard. When a man begins, he leaves the line of dancing men and, still singing, leans over the person he is going to cure, going eventually to every person present, even the infants. He places one hand on the person's chest, one on his or her back, and flutters his hands. The !Kung believe that in this way he draws the sickness, real or potential, out of the person through his own arms into himself. To demonstrate that this is in fact going on and is hard to do, he grunts with shuddering grunts that intensify in tempo and pitch into shrieks and reach a high piercing, quavering yell. Finally, the medicine man throws up his arms

The Ceremonial Curing Dance A medicine man is going into a trance.

to cast the sickness out, hurling it into the darkness back to //*Gauwa* or the //*gauwasi*, who are there beyond the firelight, with a sharp, yelping cry of "*kai kai kai.*"

The medicine men are usually only in shallow trance at this point, but, when the curing has been going on for some time, they begin to reach a state of patterned frenzy. They no longer go around to the people, their spasms of grunting and shrieking become more frequent and violent, their stomachs heave, they stagger and sway. They rush to the fire, trample it, pick up the coals, set fire to their hair. They believe that fire activates the medicine in them. People hold them to keep them from falling and beat out the flames. The medicine men rush out into the darkness, where //*Gauwa* and the //*gauwasi* are lurking. They hurl burning sticks and swear at them. "Filthy face!" they screech. "Take away the sickness you have brought. You are bad. You want to kill us. Go away. . . . *Hishe*, you are a liar. This man will not die." At this point the medicine man may fall down in deep trance and appear to be unconscious or semiconscious, with eyes closed, stiff as a board, unable to walk. This stage of trance may last only a brief time or may continue for hours—even into the next day. Gradually it is resolved and the medicine man takes up his normal activities.

The !Kung believe that at the time of deep trance the medicine man's spirit leaves his body and goes out to meet //*Gauwa* and the //*gauwasi*. They call this "half death." It is a dangerous time. The women must continue to sing the medicine music. The man's body must be watched over, rubbed, and kept warm by other medicine men who are in less deep trance.

The violence and excitement of the ceremony have the effect, as in a drama, of releasing the emotions of the people and purging them, in the Aristotelian sense. Fear and hostility find an outlet and the people have acted together to protect themselves. In this there are support and solace and hope.

CHANGE

Today (1962) the pattern of life for the Nyae Nyae !Kung has begun to change radically. Many Bushmen of other language groups have had prolonged contact with the Bantu peoples among whom they live, and some have worked on Europeans' farms. Systematic studies of their social changes are lacking. The Nyae Nyae !Kung, as described here, had contact with Herero and Tswana neighbors in trade, but this contact did not appear to change the social structure of the independent !Kung. They are only now beginning to feel the impact of European contact. They were remote; they are no longer so. When, in 1951, we first worked our way to their area from the outposts of the farm lands, we were eight arduous days en route, in trackless, waterless country of bush and heavy sand, our four trucks heavy with water and petrol, equipment and supplies. Today a well-cleared track gives access in a day. Farmers began to come into the area to get the Bushmen to work for them and have their eyes upon the land.

The government of South West Africa, realizing the problem of the Bushmen, has appointed one of their most competent administrators of native affairs to be Bushman Affairs Commissioner, and is supplying him with funds and equipment. He and his wife are in the Nyae Nyae area and are working with several families of !Kung. He is leading one group of them into agriculture and this year they harvested a crop of corn. Others of the men are employed in road building and are being paid a cash wage, currently a shilling a day. It is too early to say what will happen to their social forms in so radical a change, which ones they will lose entirely, which they will retain and adapt to new conditions. All we know is that the !Kung who are taking part in the experiment have expressed themselves as willing and anxious to try to develop a new way of life.

NOTES

(1) Some of the ethnographic material used here has been previously published in my articles in *Africa* which are cited in the bibliography appended to this chapter. The ethnographic material is used with the permission of the International African Institute and the editor of *Africa*.

(2) Skeletal remains of Bushmen are found associated with late stone age implements in South Africa, but not with early or middle stone age (Schapera

1951:26). In East Africa are sites indicating that people of common origin with Bushmen inhabited those regions, and this suggests that Bushmen in past ages migrated from the northeast (Schapera 1951:27) into South Africa, where they distributed themselves from the Zambesi River to the Cape of Good Hope. Hottentots also came into southern Africa—from East Africa in all probability—bringing with them herds of cattle. Bantu-speaking Negro tribes migrated into southern Africa, it is believed during the fourteenth and fifteenth centuries. White settlers began in 1652 to establish themselves at the Cape of Good Hope. Negroes, Hottentots, and whites encroached upon Bushmen, who were expelled from the better-watered lands or assimilated or exterminated. With the exception of a few individuals, the surviving Bushmen are found now only in the Kalahari Desert.

(3) The numbers of Bushmen found in various political divisions in 1955 as listed by Tobias (1956) are as follows:

Bechuanaland Protectorate	31,000
South West Africa	20,311
Angola	4,000
Northern Rhodesia	200
Union of South Africa	20

(4) Hooton classified Bushmen and Hottentots as a composite race, predominantly Negroid (1946:628) "whose racial ambiguity will probably continue to haunt us" (p. 633). [Cf. Schapera (1951:27), who says that it is generally regarded that Pygmies and Bushmen probably both diverged from a small variety of Negro; and Tobias (1961:19) who points out that no fossil remains have yet been found to provide definite evidence of this.] The resemblance of some of the physical characteristics of Bushmen to those of Mongolians is generally thought to be fortuitous (cf. Tobias 1957:4 ff.). Coon (1962:193) places the Bushmen among "tag-ends of ancient humanity, culturally as well as physically archaic," hard for classifiers to "fit into categories, let alone explain." The reader is referred to Schapera (1951) and Howells (1959) for judicious presentations of what is and is not known about these peoples.

(5) Studies on the adaptation of the Bushmen to heat and cold have been published by Wyndham and Morrison (1956).

(6) The nature of the Bushman hunt is graphically and empathetically portrayed in a most effective and widely acclaimed film, "The Hunters," made by Mrs. Marshall's son, John Marshall, while following !Kung hunters. Information about purchase or rental of the 70-minute film may be obtained from The Film Study Center, Peabody Museum of Archaeology and Ethnology, Harvard University, Cambridge 38, Mass.—ED.

(7) I think that in the name relationship of the !Kung we can see the potential beginnings of a kin group. It would seem that it could be a *deme* if it existed. A deme is a name Murdock proposed for a bilateral endogamous local group, in the absence of unilinear descent, "comparable to the sib both in size and in the traditional rather than demonstrable bonds of kinship which unite

the members" (Murdock 1949:62 ff.). This definition very nearly fits the
!Kung name relationship, but we are convinced that the !Kung do not think
of the region as having a consciously structured grouping to which authority
is attributed, such as, for example, a rule of endogamy.

(8) Among consanguineous kin, ego is forbidden to marry siblings of parents,
cousins (first, strictly; second, less strictly; and third, only theoretically), and
nephews and nieces. Ego's marriage with great-grandparents, grandparents,
grandchildren and great-grandchildren is also forbidden, but is not a concern.
Discrepancy in age and the realization of close consanguinity combine to make
the idea ridiculous and almost unthinkable. The affines whom ego must not
marry are numerous, including spouses of offspring and parents of the spouse,
also spouses of uncles and aunts.

Ego must not marry his sister's husband's father or brother's wife's
mother, because, as marriages with the sister's husband and brother's wife are
preferred, it seems improper to marry parents of one of these affines. Similarly,
marriage with the husband's brother and wife's sister are preferred, so it seems
logical to the !Kung to forbid marriage with the husband's brother's son or
the wife's sister's daughter. Marriage with the parent of a son's wife or a
daughter's husband is forbidden, for if ego married these affines that would
make the son and son's wife or the daughter and daughter's husband step-
brother and stepsister, which would be most awkward. Marriage with the
wife's brother's wife or the husband's sister's husband is also forbidden; the
reason for this lies in a complexity of the joking relationship.

Lastly, marriage is prohibited with certain name relatives whose names
associate them with kinsmen to whom the incest taboo is extended. Ego is
supposed not to marry anyone with the same name as his parent or offspring
or anyone with the same name as his spouse's parent or offspring's spouse.
He should not marry the parent or offspring or sibling of anyone with the
same name as himself.

(9) When the people go to the mangetti forests after the rains have begun, the
young girls draw on the soft, smooth, gray bark of female mangetti trees.
They make diagrammatic representations of their genital aprons, of the bead
ornaments that they wear in their hair and that are male and female symbols
(the long rectangular ones are male, the triangular ones are female), and of
the stripes of their leg scarifications. This suggests that the scarifications were
associated directly with fertility, although now the women claim they are
made only for beauty.

Incidentally, the Nyae Nyae !Kung know nothing of the cave paintings
or rock engravings that abound in other parts of southern Africa. We found
none in the country around them. There were drawings, however, on baobab
trees, abstract-looking forms different from the girls' drawings on the mangetti trees.

(10) We believe that one of several possible adjustments might be made. Strictly
speaking, a daughter does not become headman (though we heard people

refer to one woman as a "headman"), nor does her husband. A headman's daughter, as it were, holds the place until her son is born to fill it. Primogeniture would be in force: the eldest daughter's son would take precedence over a younger daughter's son. If a daughter's husband is an effective person by nature, he could lead the band and perform the functions of headman indefinitely. The band, on the other hand, might find it more advantageous not to wait for a son to be born to the headman's daughter but to realign itself under another headman. Within the proper frame of kinship this is a voluntary matter.

(11) I paraphrase some of the prayers as follows:

"You have created me and given me power to walk about and hunt. Why do you lead me in the wrong way so that I find no animals?"

"Give rain, !Nau, wet the earth. Let there be veldkos. We are starving because we have to stay by the water hole where there is no more veldkos. You have favored some people with rain. Will you not favor us?"

BIBLIOGRAPHY

With a few exceptions the following bibliography emphasizes contemporary work. Starred items (*) include significant bibliographies. Daggered items (†) are cited as references in the text of the chapter.

Beach, D. M. (1938†). *The Phonetics of the Hottentot Language.* Cambridge, England: W. Heffer & Sons, Ltd.

Bleek, Dorothea F. (1927). "The Distribution of Bushman Languages in South Africa," *Festschrift Meinhof,* pp. 55–64.

———— (1928a). "Bushmen of Central Angola," *Bantu Studies,* Vol. 3, No. 2, pp. 105–125.

———— (1928b). *The Naron: A Bushman Tribe of the Central Kalahari.* Cambridge, England: Cambridge University Press.

———— (1929). *Comparative Vocabularies of Bushman Languages.* Cambridge, England: Cambridge University Press.

———— (1956†). *A Bushman Dictionary.* New Haven, Conn.: American Oriental Society.

Cole, Desmond T. (1960). "African Linguistic Studies, 1943–1960," *African Studies,* Vol. 19, No. 4, pp. 219–229.

Coon, Carleton S. (1962†). *The Story of Man.* Rev. ed. New York: Alfred A. Knopf, Inc.

England, Nicholas M. (n.d.). "Music in the Societies of Certain Bushman Groups in Southern Africa." Doctoral dissertation, Harvard University (in preparation).

Greenberg, Joseph (1955†). *Studies in African Linguistic Classification*. New Haven, Conn.: The Compass Publishing Co.

Gusinde, Martin (1953). "Anthropological Investigations of the Bushmen of South Africa," *Anthropological Quarterly*, Vol. 26 (n.s. 1), No. 1, pp. 20–28.

Heffner, R.-M. S. (1960†). *General Phonetics*. Madison: The University of Wisconsin Press.

Hooton, Earnest Albert (1946†). *Up from the Ape*. Rev. ed. New York: The Macmillan Company.

Howells, William (1959†). *Mankind in the Making*. New York: Doubleday & Company, Inc.

Jones, J. D. Rheinallt, and C. M. Doke (eds.) (1937). "Bushmen of the Southern Kalahari," *Bantu Studies*, Vol. 10, No. 4; Vol. 11, No. 3. Reprinted by University of Witwatersrand Press, Johannesburg, Union of South Africa. (Contributors: Bleek, Breyer-Brandwijk, Dart, Doke, Drennan, Kirby, Mac-Crone, J. F. Maingard, and L. F. Maingard.)

Köhler, O. (1960). "Critical Linguistic Aspects of the Theory of the Hamitic Origin of the Hottentots" ("Sprachkritische Aspekte zur Hamitentheorie über die Herkunft der Hottentooten"), *Sociologus*, n.s., Vol. 10, No. 1, pp. 69–77.

——— (1962). "Studien zum Genussystem und Verbalbau der zentralen Khoisan-Sprachen," *Anthropos*, Vol. 57, No. 3–6, pp. 529–546.

Lanham, L. W., and D. P. Hallowes (1956). "An Outline of the Structure of Eastern Bushman," *African Studies*, Vol. 15, No. 3, pp. 97–118.

Maingard, L. F. (1957). "Three Bushmen Languages" (dʒu/ʔõã:si and //ganakwe), *African Studies*, Vol. 16, No. 1, pp. 37–71. Also, "Three Bushman Languages. Part II: The Third Bushman Language" (!Kõ).

Marshall, John (1958). "Man as a Hunter" (the !Kung Bushmen), *Natural History*, Vol. 67, No. 6, pp. 291–309; No. 7, pp. 376–395.

Marshall, Lorna (1957a). "The Kin Terminology System of the !Kung Bushmen," *Africa*, Vol. 27, No. 1, pp. 1–25.

——— (1957b). "N!ow," *Africa*, Vol. 27, No. 3, pp. 232–240.

——— (1959). "Marriage among !Kung Bushmen," *Africa*, Vol. 29, No. 4, pp. 335–365.

——— (1960). "!Kung Bushman Bands," *Africa*, Vol. 30, No. 4, pp. 325–355.

——— (1961). "Sharing, Talking, and Giving: Relief of Social Tensions among !Kung Bushmen," *Africa*, Vol. 31, No. 3, pp. 231–249.

——— (1962). "!Kung Bushman Religious Beliefs," *Africa*, Vol. 32, No. 3, pp. 221–252.

Murdock, George Peter (1949†). *Social Structure*. New York: The Macmillan Company.

———— (1959†). *Africa: Its Peoples and Their Culture History.* New York: McGraw-Hill Book Company, Inc.

Schantz, H. L. (1911†). "Natural Vegetation as an Indicator of the Capabilities of Land for Crop Production in the Great Plains Area," *U.S. Department of Agriculture Bureau Plant Industry Bulletin* 201.

Schapera, I. (1939†). "A Survey of the Bushman Question," *Race Relations,* Vol. 6, Part 2, pp. 68–83.

———— (1951*†). *The Khoisan Peoples of South Africa: Bushmen and Hotten-tots.* New York: The Humanities Press.
This work provides an important treatment of the work on the Bushmen and related peoples.

Silberbauer, George B. (1961). "Aspects of the Kinship System of the G/wi Bushmen of the Central Kalahari," *South African Journal of Science,* Vol. 57, No. 12, pp. 353–359.

Stamp, L. Dudley (1953†). *Africa: A Study in Tropical Development.* New York: John Wiley & Sons, Inc.

Story, R. (1958†). "Some Plants Used by the Bushmen in Obtaining Food and Water," *Botanical Survey of South Africa,* Memoir No. 30.

Thomas, Elizabeth Marshall (1959). *The Harmless People.* New York: Alfred A. Knopf, Inc.

Tobias, Phillip V. (1955*). "Les Bochimans auen et naron de Ghanzi: Con-tribution à l'étude des 'anciens jaunes' sud Africains," *L'Anthropologie,* Vol. 59, pp. 235–289.

———— (1956†). "On the Survival of the Bushmen," *Africa,* Vol. 26, No. 2, pp. 174–186.

———— (1957†). "Bushmen of the Kalahari," *Man,* Vol. 36, pp. 1–8.
This work discusses questions of physical characteristics and origins.

———— (1961†). "Physique of a Desert Folk," *Natural History,* Vol. 70, No. 2, pp. 16–24.

Wellington, John H. (1955†). *Southern Africa: A Geographical Study.* Cam-bridge, England: Cambridge University Press.

Westphal, Ernst (1962a). "A Re-classification of Southern African non-Bantu Languages," *Journal of African Languages,* Vol. 1, No. 1.

———— (1962b). "The Classification of the non-Bantu Languages of Southern Africa," *African Language Studies,* No. 3.

Wyndham, C. H., and J. F. Morrison (1956). "Heat Regulation of MaSarwa (Bushmen)," *Nature,* Vol. 178, pp. 869–870.

8

THE MBUTI PYGMIES
OF THE CONGO

about the chapter

The Pygmy populations of the world are known to school child and specialist alike because of their unique physical features which, Turnbull suggests, are a somatic adaptation to their forest environment. For the physical anthropologist, they pose the problem of determining the degree of closeness of their relationship to the full-statured Negroids of Africa. The African Pygmies vary among themselves in hunting and gathering techniques even more than do the !Kung Bushmen, so they offer an opportunity for fruitful use of the comparative method to understand the consequences of variations in subsistence techniques for cultural configurations in foraging societies.

The Mbuti Pygmies of the Ituri Forest of the Congo are hunters and gatherers with a primary stress on hunting. Some bands are archers and others hunt with large nets. The form of hunting that is dominant affects the size and composition of the band, the division of labor, and the nature of relationships with surrounding Negro villagers. Net-hunting, especially, requires a large measure of cooperation, which is ensured by the informal social controls, including the institutionalization of the role of the clown. Here there are obvious parallels with the !Kung Bushmen.

Turnbull traces the dominant leitmotif of Mbuti ethos: the feeling of identification with the forest as the benevolent provider of life and all good things and the protector from the malevolence of nonforest people. Rituals associated with birth, puberty, sickness, and death all give expression to this value and usually involve physical and symbolic contact with forest substances to symbolize the Pygmy-forest identification.

The Pygmy attitude toward the forest contrasts with that of their agricultural neighbors, who despise and fear it, and this is the key to much of the Mbuti relationship with their neighbors. Turnbull's field work shows that the traditional view of the Pygmy as being dependent on his Negro agricultural "overlords" is false. The Mbuti appears to be subservient while in the villages, but he ridicules the villagers when he is back in the forest. Moreover, the Pygmy keeps many of the patterns of his culture secret from his neighbors.

Like the pastoral Fulani and the Bantu Tiriki, the Mbuti face problems of maintaining their identity and autonomy while surrounded by peoples with a different mode of subsistence and social organization. Physical flight or retreat is used by both the pastoral Fulani and the Pygmies. In other published studies Turnbull has noted that the Mbuti, like the Bantu Tiriki, follow the custom of holding common initiations with adjoining tribes, accepting partial assimilation in order to preserve ultimate autonomy. He indicates that several other Mbuti cultural institutions also serve this end. Subtle or direct, they exist, he concludes, because "as the Pygmies are physically ill-adapted to village life, so are they sociologically ill-adapted."

about the author

Colin M. Turnbull, Assistant Curator at the American Museum of Natural History in New York, holds the D.Phil. degree from Oxford University, and has taught at Columbia University. In addition to three periods of field research among the Mbuti (1951, 1954–1955, and 1957–1958) he has done field work in India (1949–1951). He is author of *The Forest People* (1961), *The Lonely African* (1962), *The Peoples of Africa* (1962), and numerous papers on the Mbuti Pygmies.

COLIN M. TURNBULL · *The Mbuti Pygmies of the Congo*

INTRODUCTION

LOCATION · Considering that the Mbuti[1] are one of the few people left who still live a nomadic hunting and gathering existence, with no knowledge of how to make fire, it is remarkable that there has been so little scientific work carried out among them. Our knowledge in general of the various Pygmy and Pygmoid groups in Africa is parlous, and I am confining myself here to the one specific area that has been studied in the most conscientious manner, the Ituri Forest, bordering on Uganda to the east and the Sudan to the north.

This is not intended to imply that this is the only area of Pygmy occupation, but it does, from every account, seem to be far and away their major stronghold. Pygmoid groups, called Twide by Dr. Martin Gusinde, or Batwa and Batswa by other authorities, are scattered widely throughout the equatorial forest belt, from the edge of Rwanda and Burundi to within a hundred miles or so of the Atlantic coast, in the Gabon.[2]

The Mbuti of the Ituri Forest have not been subject to census, but the distribution of the numerous hunting bands is reasonably well known, and most estimates agree that the total Pygmy population in the area is around 40,000. Far more important than the population size, from our point of view, is its relative isolation, and the resultant purity of the Mbuti as a sociological and biological entity. There has been considerable dispute over the extent of acculturation with neighboring tribes of Negro cultivators, and this will form one of the major points in the present study.

PHYSICAL APPEARANCE · The physical appearance of the Mbuti varies in most features except that of stature, which, for males, averages slightly below four feet six inches, with four feet as a rare adult minimum, and four feet six inches as a rather more frequent maximum. Women tend to be an inch shorter, on the average, than men. The skin color varies from a light yellowish-brown to a fairly deep chocolate red, underarm tests revealing a yellow-brown shade distinctly lighter than and different from that of the Negro.

A Mbuti Man

Observation shows that the Pygmies tan rapidly when exposed to direct sunlight, as they are during their visits to village plantations. Body hair, of the peppercorn variety, is much more prevalent than among the neighboring Negro tribes, sometimes thickly covering the entire body of an adult male, though generally it is downy, and not very noticeable. Further distinguishing the Mbuti are wide-set eyes and an extremely broad nose, sometimes as wide as the mouth. But perhaps the most evident physiological difference, even more evident than the stature, is the proportionate length of the trunk and arms over the rather short, sturdy legs. The physique of both male and female is powerful and their health is generally excellent, deteriorating most rapidly when they are exposed to sunlight and to other conditions specific to the villages, which they sometimes visit for a week or more, ostensibly to barter.

Not enough work has been done with blood groupings for accurate evaluation, but it seems that again there is a significant difference between Pygmies and Negroes. The origin of the difference remains obscure, some authorities claiming that they are separate races, others regarding the Pygmies as a subrace of the Negro.

Here I might only mention two indisputable facts relevant to any sociological discussion, one being that the color and stature and general physique of the Pygmies lend themselves admirably to life in a forest environment. The Pygmies are naturally camouflaged to the point of being virtually invisible at a few yards, they are able to move quickly and silently in the undergrowth, and to climb trees with ease, often without the aid of vines, using only lateral pressure on hands and feet. The other point is that, conversely, they are ill-adapted to village life, being prone to sunstroke (rarely seeing direct sunlight in the forest) and to various diseases against which the villagers have some immunity.

A point that will arise in the following discussion is that just as the Pygmies are physically ill-adapted to village life, so are they sociologically ill-adapted. This has bearing both on their present relationship with the various neighboring tribes of village cultivators, and on their future existence, as hunting and gathering become increasingly unproductive because of commercial exploitation of the forest. Only the fact that the extent of the forest area approaches a quarter of a million square miles has made it possible for the Pygmies to retain their integrity thus far.

SYMBIOSIS: PYGMY AND VILLAGER

Historical genesis

Perhaps three or four hundred years ago, or less, the Mbuti found their forest preserve invaded by a number of Bantu and Sudanic tribes, forced in largely from the north, east, and southeast by more powerful tribes. The invaders were grassland cultivators and pastoralists who found the forest a harsh environment for adaptation. It was totally alien to them, and they made use of the Pygmies they found there as guides, and even as mercenaries—particularly as spies and scouts—in their intertribal warfare. The Pygmies, finding themselves in a situation that rendered their free nomadic existence as hunters and gatherers somewhat precarious, allied themselves to whichever group of invaders happened to be nearest to them. The major tribes concerned were the Bira to the south, the Lese in the east, the Mangbetu and Azande to the northwest; and the Mamvu-Mangutu to the north. The Bira themselves split in two, one branch keeping to the eastern plains and retaining some pastoralism, the other group penetrating deep into the southern part of the forest with their kindred tribes, the Ndaka and Mbo.

In this way bands of Mbuti that may well have been interrelated through marriage found themselves affiliated with opposed groups, especially as both the Lese and the Bira fragmented into a series of more or less independent clan groups without any effective centralized chieftainship. Each Negro village was in danger of conflict from the next.

The isolated Mbuti bands quickly picked up the language of their patrons, and as quickly, it seems, lost their own. There is no certainty concerning the original language of the Mbuti, though remnants are clear in some contexts, and there is current thought that one or other of the languages now spoken by the village invaders is perhaps basically that of the earlier Mbuti. One linguistic feature of the original language clearly remains, however, in the tonal pattern of speech. Regardless of which of the diverse Bantu or Sudanic languages they are speaking, all Mbuti of the Ituri Forest speak with an almost identical intonation. So much so, that at a distance, where the individual words cannot be clearly heard, even Mbuti themselves cannot be sure which language is being spoken. Yet, these same languages, spoken by the villagers to whom they properly belong, could never be confused.

The early relationship of the Pygmies to the invading Negro tribes seems fairly clear, and the many legends and historical tales told by both groups confirm that the villagers acted as patrons to their Pygmy clients. Unable to hunt with success or safety, the Pygmies sold their service to the invaders in return for food and protection. The invaders had to cut down great clearings from the forest for their plantations, and no doubt they were also helped in the maintenance of these plantations by the Mbuti. But as the situation changed, the invaders becoming more securely established and settled, so did the relationship change.

Previous scholarly interpretations

Written records on the Pygmies, including both descriptive and interpretive materials, appeared as early as the Sixth Dynasty in Egypt. Although much of what has been written in the elapsed span of time is grossly misleading, this is especially true of material pertaining to the Pygmy-village relationship.

The record from Egypt's Sixth Dynasty appears in a tomb and tells of the discovery of Pygmies in an area apparently corresponding to the present Ituri Forest (Pharaoh Pepi II; a letter to Herkhouf). Although little detail is given, it does appear that nearly five thousand years ago the Mbuti were living much as they are today, and the account reveals evidence of a highly developed ritual expressed in dance and song.

Herodotus (c.440 B.C.; ii. 32) and Homer (c.800 B.C.; *Iliad* iii. 3, 7) also introduce an element of myth, and by the Middle Ages Pygmies were represented as speechless troglodytes or anthropophagous Blemmyes, "whose heads do grow beneath their shoulders" (Moir and Letts 1955). The Portuguese explorations of Africa began in the sixteenth century and the divers explorers who succeeded them still treated the Pygmies as a legend. The seventeenth-century anatomist Edward Tyson "proved" that Pygmies were chimpanzees. Even the tales of the early twentieth-century travelers in Africa were in the same vein although, in the latter half of the nineteenth century, Miani, Schweinfurth, and Stanley had all produced incontrovertible evidence not only as to the existence of Pygmies but as to their humanity.

The first and only person to make an overall survey of the Pygmies was a follower of the anthropological school of Wilhelm Schmidt in Vienna, Father Paul Schebesta. A second follower of the school, Father Schumacher, studied the Batwa pygmoids; and a third, Father Gusinde, worked in the same general area as a physical anthropologist. Schebesta, having made his initial survey, returned several times to make more detailed studies of the Mbuti in the Ituri Forest, for he considered them the most "pure" culturally and physically. His work resulted in numerous publications, both popular and technical. His *Die Bambuti Pygmäen vom Ituri* formed, together with Gusinde's account, the only substantial scientific study until my own field-work, which was much narrower in scope.

Misconceptions about Pygmies and Pygmoids have a historical tradition of their own, and they have persisted into the mid-twentieth century. The myth has grown up that the Pygmies are now completely dependent on the villagers, not only for food and metal, but also for culture itself. Some claim that the Pygmies have lost all their culture and have adopted that of their former patrons, who are now rather in the position of masters. They cite language as an example, and the apparent adoption by the Mbuti of certain sacred and secular institutions peculiar to the villagers.

Schebesta's account does not go quite this far. Yet, even he, with his considerable insight about and partiality for the Pygmies, claims a much greater degree of dependence than exists. This highly significant misunderstanding was due to limitations in the field that were inescapable at the time he carried out his field research. The major obstacle was the inaccessibility of the Pygmies themselves. Schebesta used villagers as intermediaries and porters in reaching the Pygmies and thus depended on villager goodwill. Because the villagers have illicit plantations in the forest, their cooperation was limited. Moreover, it is my own experience that the presence of just one villager in a forest hunting camp changes the entire context from forest to village, affecting every activity and even the structure of the band. Thus even when he was in the forest Schebesta was, for the most part, observing Pygmies in a village context.

To understand the differences between the interpretations of previous writers on the Pygmies and that which my own data yield, one must be aware of the fact that my own initial contact quite fortuitously circumvented the otherwise inevitable village headman. In 1951 I was the guest of Mr. and Mrs. Patrick Putnam. Putnam was an anthropologist of long residence who had the trust and confidence of both the Pygmies and the villagers of the region. Because of our friendship and close physical resemblance it was generally accepted that we were near relatives. This meant, first, that I was able to go into the forest with the Pygmies without village assistance. It meant also that, although the villagers did not exactly like this, at least they were not so concerned about my coming across their illegal plantations, and I was able, if I wished, to go about unaccompanied by anyone but Pygmies.

Because of this chance, however, my own initial picture was just as one-sided as Schebesta's. If he saw things mainly in the village context, I saw things mainly in the forest context, for even when we were in a village I was treated by the Pygmies, with whom I also lived even in their village camps, as belonging to the forest, rather than to the village. For example, Schebesta (1933) states that the Pygmies have no song, only drumming and dancing. Similarly, as in his major works (1938, 1941, 1948, 1950) he gives very short shrift to music, dismissing song as being of little interest, and dance as being largely erotic. My own findings in 1951 were directly to the contrary. I found virtually no drumming, but a great deal of song of the greatest complexity and of deep ritual significance. What Schebesta did not see, far from being negative, proves to be of utmost positive value. It is essential to put both our points of view together to get a complete picture, not only of the relationship between the Pygmies and the villages, but even of the nomadic hunting and gathering life of the Mbuti in the forest. It is important to keep this in mind when reading narrative accounts of the situation, because it is almost impossible to present both sides at once.

A new interpretation: Asymmetrical symbiosis

PYGMY DEPENDENCE · The question of economic dependence is something that has to be settled before either the village or the forest context can be fully understood, and certainly before the exact nature of the relationship between the two peoples can be appreciated. It is claimed, for instance, that the Mbuti are economically dependent on the villagers for food and for metal. It is said that the forest foods are insufficient, and that the Pygmies rely on plantation foods such as bananas, cassava (manioc), beans, rice, and corn. I can only state that in many hunting camps I have seen the Mbuti thrive on forest products alone and at all times of the year. The honey season, in the middle of our calendar year, is perhaps the time of greatest plenty, but at no time is there any shortage that could lead to serious hunger, let alone starvation. The Mbuti, among whom laziness in the hunt is a serious offense, have a saying that the only hungry Pygmy is a lazy Pygmy.[3] There are innumerable varieties of edible mushrooms, nuts, berries, roots, and fruits. When one goes out of season, another comes into season, so there is a year-round supply. Moreover, there is never a shortage of game, though the migration of game, around which the nomadism of the Mbuti is partly based, may be affected by the plantation activities of villagers and cause temporary difficulty in the hunt.

Generally, each small hunting band, of anything from three to thirty families, may have several hundred square miles of forest territory, and if the game is not in one part of that territory it is in another. The same boundaries that limit the movement of game limit the movement of hunting bands, especially rivers and streams, and also ravines and rock escarpments. After about a month, as a rule, the fruits of the forest have been gathered from all around the vicinity of the camp, and the game has been scared away to a greater distance than is comfortable for daily hunting. As the economy relies on day-to-day quest, the simplest thing is for the camp to move to a totally new one, perhaps ten or twenty miles away, perhaps farther. The moves are always unpredictable, depending on the two factors of the immediate whereabouts of game and forest food.

All my own experience has shown that there is always an area within their own territory to which the Pygmies can go and where there is food in plenty. Their independence of plantation products was amply demonstrated during my last field trip, in 1957–1958. The fact that they have come, over the years, to acquire a taste for plantation foods does to some extent influence their nomadism, but only to the extent that a hunting band may be tempted to remain within a day's march of the village even when hunting in that vicinity is poor. But from the Pygmy point of view, the village is merely another source of food—acquired by another form of hunting as often as not. For if the villagers do not give of their free will, then the Pygmies are not above raiding the plantations and stealing what they want.

The source of metal forms a rather more cogent argument for asserting some degree of dependence of the Pygmies on the villagers, though it is still an inconclusive one. Of the various metal artifacts supplied by the villagers, few are anything like essential. Metal cooking vessels are needed only for village foods that have to be boiled, such as rice; all forest foods can be cooked either by roasting or baking in leaf containers. To the extent that village foods are not essential, neither are their cooking vessels. Metal arrow tips and spear blades are equally far from indispensable. Generally, the Mbuti prefer to use poisoned arrows, which have fire-hardened points only, no metal. The reason is that they frequently have to shoot at a sound or at a movement of leaves rather than at a visible target, and so have no way of aiming at a vital spot. Also, as they themselves say, their small bows are far from accurate at any distance, and with poison all they have to do is to graze the animal and it will die, whereas with a metal tip, which cannot be poisoned, they have to strike in exactly the right place.

Spears are generally a weapon for defense rather than offense, except in the northwestern part of the Ituri. In either case, however, fire-hardened points are considered as effective as metal except against buffalo or elephants. Old Pygmies assert that even large game such as this can be successfully hunted with fire-hardened spears. Spears are still made in this way for and by children, although they are seldom now used by adults.

Slit bamboo and slit reeds provide sharp cutting surfaces, though they dull quickly and are now infrequently used, metal knife blades having taken their place, but there would be no difficulty except possibly in skinning game if the metal blades were unavailable. Thorny vines make admirable scrapers for roots and vegetables. Far more essential are the machete blades, and the blades for axes used in cutting down saplings for hut frames and in chopping honey out of holes in trees. When asked what they would do without these

Smoking a Banana-stem Pipe

implements many older Pygmies say, "We would use stone," but it seems they say this without any remaining knowledge of how to make stone tools. Their statement is possibly prompted more by the occasional discovery in the forest of old stone axes rather than by any continued knowledge of their manufacture or use. Even so, it can be seen that the dependence of the Mbuti on the villagers for food or metal is minimal, and is expressed better in terms of convenience than of necessity.

VILLAGE DEPENDENCE • In reverse, the villagers stand in a more real need of the Pygmies, though here also it is still largely a matter of convenience. The forest, which the villagers till by slash-and-burn technique, is thought of by them as hostile for its refusal to support their modest crops while it nourishes the luxuriant vegetation of the forest and its immense, towering trees. The hostility is thought of as a conscious act on the part of the forest itself, and of the spirits that inhabit it, and here we have one of the keys to the true nature of the relationship between the Mbuti hunters and Negro villagers, for it is a relationship between a forest people and a nonforest people. The Pygmies regard the forest as the source of all good—of the plenty, safety, and good health that is, for them, the norm; consequently, they have no concept of evil spirits and no fear of the forest. The nearest they can get to a notion of conscious malevolence is in their attitude toward acts of destruction against the forest. The villagers are constantly performing such acts by cutting it down, which creates a hostility that may be superficially concealed for the sake of mutual convenience but is always present and always reciprocal.

With their fear of the forest, the villagers do not hunt. They dig pits and set traps around the fringes of the plantation, but the game quickly learns to avoid them. To bolster their otherwise vegetarian diet (goats and chickens play only a small part as food in village economy) the villagers rely on the Pygmies to bring them meat, in return for which the hunters are provided with cassava, rice, or plantains. But the villagers also have other needs. They need saplings to build their houses and leaves to cover their roofs. Since the immediate vicinity is soon cleared of all such saplings and leaves, the villagers, unwilling to move or venture deep into the forest in search of fresh supplies, have to rely on the Pygmies to provide them.

But perhaps the most genuine dependence in the relationship was caused by the Belgian insistence that villagers plant cotton and produce a surplus of certain foods above their own needs. This meant that there was more work than they could handle, particularly since many of the able-bodied men were taken to work in road gangs. More than ever, the villagers came to rely on the Pygmies as a vital and necessary source of labor. Instead of regarding them as parasites, stealing from their plantations and giving little or nothing in return (Pygmies are notoriously reluctant to part with meat and, as stated by villagers themselves, excessively lazy when in villages), the villagers began to regard their forest neighbors as an essential part of their economy. The problem was how to effect some kind of control. One of the most interesting features of the relationship is how the villagers, on the one hand, try to assert control, and how the Pygmies, on the other, devise means of evading it, retaining for themselves the ultimate whip hand of refuge in their forest home. This affects every aspect of the life of the Mbuti. That is why this general discussion of the relationship between the forest and the village is necessary prior to an examination of that life.

PYGMY SOCIAL AND ECONOMIC ORGANIZATION

INTRODUCTION: ARCHERS VS. NET-HUNTERS • In essentials the hunting and gathering nomadism of the Mbuti can have changed little over the past few thousand years, for until the advent of the villagers there have been no changes that we know of in their circumstances. However, the discussion here relates primarily to those Pygmies who are net-hunters, rather than to those in the southeastern section of the forest who are archers. Schebesta concentrated on the latter, whom he calls "Efe," and who are connected more with the Lese than with the Bira.[4]

The structure of Pygmy bands differs according to the economy. The Efe archers are, for one thing, more bounded by roads and foreign settlements—administrative, mission, and medical—than are the net-hunters. Consequently, the game supply is less adequate, and in such circumstances their hunting technique is not as productive as that of the net-hunt. It is natural, then, that they should make much more use of the villagers and that their relationships with the villagers should vary accordingly, at least on the surface. But the variance is only superficial, as far as I can judge from my own experience among the Efe, and what has to be said of the net-hunters can be taken as a guide for what to expect from the archers. The major difference is that a net-hunting band is generally larger than an archer band and demands more cooperation. But both kinds of band are characterized by the same process of constant fission and fusion.

THE NET-HUNTERS

We shall now look at the four aspects of social life among the net-hunters: domestic, economic, political, and ritual, and see what the nature of the structure is and how it allows for the necessary establishment of relations with the villagers. In this way we shall see the present hunting and gathering community as it really is, not as it ideologically was. It is constantly shifting and changing, with one unbreakable thread running throughout—the sanctity of the forest, giving it shape and consistency and constancy.

Marriage, the family, and kinship

MARRIAGE · In considering the domestic life of the net-hunting Mbuti, the keynotes are simplicity and egalitarianism. The family is the basic unit of any hunting camp, net-hunting or archer, and the family is generally a monogamous union of man and wife, and their children. There are exceptions, however. Adoption is not infrequent, particularly where one family has a large number of children and another has few or none, or where there is separation by divorce or death. Similarly, a man may sometimes have two or even three wives, though this is the exception and usually comes about by accident.

Such an accident may happen when a couple becomes betrothed and lives together. The betrothal is marked by no ceremony other than an exchange of gifts. The boy will give his in-laws some game he has killed, as proof of his ability to hunt and support their daughter, and he may also give his father-in-law a bow and some arrows. Bands are generally exogamous by preference, regardless of their kinship composition, and the entire adult population of each band will have separately discussed the betrothal of their children and each band will have reached a united decision. A union is not considered final, however, until a child is born and shows, by surviving the first few days, that it has come to stay. A couple may cohabit without producing children, and after a year or so the two will then separate without formality and each will look for another spouse. It happens sometimes that a man will take another wife almost immediately, this being economically desirable, and may then learn that his first wife has, after all, become pregnant by him. He will then take her back, and keep her as well as his second wife. Or his first wife may decide that she loves her first husband too much, child or no, and simply return. This is also likely to happen if she left him, which she may do in a fit of temper, *after* giving birth to a child.

In such circumstances a man may acquire two wives. In very rare cases, in a brave effort to outdo the villagers, a boastful Pygmy may deliberately flaunt custom and take three wives.[5] But such bravado, though tolerated, is not favored, and is likely to cause disputes.

Structurally, however, such variations from the norm of elementary biological monogamous families have little effect. The only inheritable wealth is the hunting net, bow and arrows, spear, ax, machete, and bark-cloth hammer on the male side; and on the female side the gathering basket, paring knife, and perhaps a mortar and pestle and cooking vessel stolen from the villagers. Both types of wealth are inherited along sex lines; sons from fathers, girls from mothers. In the case of a parent dying before the children have reached adulthood, the father's brother or the mother's sister may hold the inheritance in trust, inheriting at the same time the status of their deceased sibling. It is not necessarily the oldest brother that takes charge of the children, but the brother deemed most fit by the band as a whole.

KINSHIP · With the family being the basic unit, economic as well as domestic and, as we shall see, political, with no effective unit above it except the hunting band of which it forms a part, and in the absence of much inheritable wealth, there is no call for an elaborate kinship system. In fact, it would be a disadvantage, as the composition of any band is constantly changing, and the classic lineage system would fragment it into opposed sections that would have no structural validity.

It is common for a whole family to pack up and go to visit relatives in a distant camp. This may be done to give the children an opportunity for meeting marriageable age mates, or it may be to avoid any tension that may be building up around that family through some minor dispute or jealousy. It is rare indeed to find a hunting band, particularly among the net-hunters, that does not include at least one family unit that normally hunts with another band. With a traditional lineage system such a family would find itself uncomfortably in a minority, and without adequate privileges of sharing in the produce of the hunt in general should its own hunting be unproductive. The system of sharing will be made clear when we deal further with economic life, but here we may state that, although the entire group cooperates in the hunt, each family has its own net and has first claim to game that falls into that net. It happens often enough that in several days there may be nets that by chance trap no game. There is, therefore, a rather loosely defined system that obliges every net owner to share his catch with

Mbuti Women Preparing Food

others; certain parts of the animal being his, others being the due of his parents, others of siblings, and lesser parts being the right of his children. The kinship terminology of the Mbuti in this area of the Ituri (and, I believe, elsewhere), however, is such that every member of the band has some claim as a relative to the catch of every net, though the claim is exerted only if he or she is genuinely without food.

Kinship terminology is generational, sex differentiation being made only at parental level and between spouses. Thus you have, as terms of address and reference, Grandparent, Father, Mother, Sibling, Child, and In-law. For husband and wife the terms of reference are "man" and "woman," personal names being used more often for address.[6] The system is broadened still further by the fact that the term for sibling is also used to mean "Friend," which means that friends of one's father are thus classified as "Father," and so on. Further still, removing the system yet another step from the more classical systems, is the custom of upgrading an elder brother to the status of father if he is sufficiently older to be in a senior age group. The terminology used, then, appears to be concerned more with age and economic status than with other kinship relationships.

This is borne out in the daily life of the band, in which almost every activity is organized on an age basis rather than according to kinship ties. Women of the same age help each other with the building of their huts, in gathering, and in cooking food (see photo). A mother will frequently give her children over to some other possibly unrelated woman to look after, even to suckle, if she is called elsewhere. The children call all their mother's female age mates "Mother," and they expect the same privileges from them all and acknowledge the same responsibilities toward them. So also with fathers. Men discipline children, play with them, teach them, make miniature bows and spears for them, almost without regard for the degree of relationship. However, the elementary family does acknowledge itself as such and feels these bonds more closely than any others.

Although a band states its preference for "marrying far," that is, into distant hunting bands, the presence of stranger families makes endogamy possible without violating the rather vague laws of incest (first-cousin marriage is unknown). Also, patrilocality is a stated norm, but exceptions often occur, such as when a man belongs to a large hunting band and his wife to a small one. Thus, the band cannot be called a patrilineal, patrilocal unit although this is what it tends to be. A band cannot be considered as a kin group except in the most general terms and will nearly always include some families related only by the most distant affinal ties.

External relations: Pygmy-villager links

At the domestic level, then, although the individual family can be called the basic unit, it has little significance beyond its function in rearing children and as a participating unit in communal activities, such as camp building, hunting, gathering, singing, and dancing. This is of no small significance in considering the relationship of the Pygmies with their village neighbors.

The villagers try to assert control over the Pygmies by arranging their marriages for them, and by claiming hereditary rights over the offspring on a patrilineal/patrilocal basis modeled after their own kinship system. Pygmies sometimes undergo these village marriage rites, allowing their "masters" to make elaborate preparations, including a feast and the exchange of bride-wealth between the "master" of the groom and the "master" of the bride. As far as the Mbuti are concerned, it is a good occasion for a three-day holiday with free board and lodging, with the possibility of making off—after it is all over—with some of the wealth. Occasionally such marriages correspond to the wishes of the individuals themselves, in which case the Pygmies consider it as they consider their own betrothal system: if a child is not born or does not prove that it has come to stay, the betrothal is not considered binding, and the couple may separate. Alternatively, the Pygmies may go through with a village-sponsored marriage simply for the sake of the feast. In either case the villagers are in difficulty, for the failure of the two Pygmies to stay together and produce children means that bridewealth has to be returned, and tribunal records are full of disputes between villages over such situations.

But perhaps more important, even if the marriage succeeds and children are born, the "master" of the groom is likely to be upset if he discovers that his Pygmy, instead of marrying patrilocally has married matrilocally and is living with his bride's band. This means that the bride's "master" not only has the bridewealth, but the bride, the groom, and the children.

The village and forest systems are incompatible, and one suspects that this is the way the Pygmies intend it. Although a villager will claim hereditary patrilineal rights over specific Pygmies, he will only be able to tell where a small proportion of them are at any one time, and he will only have the services of an even smaller proportion, and then on the very erratic and unpredictable basis of Pygmy whim.

The Pygmies feel nothing of the alleged hereditary allegiance, although it is convenient for a band to have more or less stable relations with one or more villages on the fringes of its hunting area. But they will go wherever they get the best bargain, and they will play one village against another. Where a happy relationship is established and persists for any length of time, then the Pygmies, when in the village, fall in with the accepted village pattern and refer to their hereditary "masters" as such—BaKpara. But back in the forest they laugh at the idea, and talk freely of all the various villagers, each one of whom thinks he is their master.

The very fluidity of the composition of any hunting band renders the band as such incompatible with a hereditary relationship with any one village in its territory; the band's mobility and knowledge of the forest give the villagers no chance of keeping track of its location or of pursuing it, and the bilaterality of the kinship system and the generational system of terminology mean that external individual relationships are effectively as meaningless as the group relationships. In short, the domestic life of the Mbuti is in no way controlled by the villagers, and the only adaptation that it makes is by adopting the necessary manners and customs when in a village context.

The villagers, although never abandoning their theoretical hereditary ownership of specific Mbuti patrilineages, acknowledge the facts of life and make what use they can of whatever Pygmies happen to be hunting in their vicinity. The neighboring villages will all be doing the same, and there is a dispute among the BaKpara only if there is a particularly valuable kill, such as elephant or okapi, by a Pygmy while outside the territory of his alleged hereditary master. In point of fact, then, a hunting band deals with the most convenient and congenial village, and the hereditary system works out in practice only by the accident, as it were, of the hereditary masters being convenient and congenial.

Within each village individual Pygmies will attach themselves to individual villagers, though their dealings with these villagers are by no means exclusive of others. The extent to which exchange between Pygmies and villagers is carried on depends on a number of factors, not the least being the whim that seizes Pygmies, every now and again, to have a holiday from hunting and to live a life of leisure in the village. In this mood they will come to the village bringing whatever meat they have left over, and other small gifts from the forest.[7]

In the village there is a constant battle between the villagers, who make every attempt to put the visiting Pygmies to work, and the Pygmies, who use all their guile to *avoid* being put to work. When their welcome is outstayed,

A Forest Camp

and the villagers refuse to give any more handouts, the Pygmies simply return to the forest.

Subsistence

THE CAMP • A major activity is the building of a camp, and this is largely communal, although each individual family attends primarily to its own needs. Men usually gather the saplings while women search for the *mongongo* roofing leaves, and the total produce of all who took part will be divided according to individual needs. A man with a large family will need —and will be given—more than a childless couple. But in the actual collecting, with his brothers and friends, nobody will have expected him to collect more than the others.

Generally it takes three days for a camp to acquire its full form, but throughout its duration of a month or so it is constantly changing in subtle ways. The little beehive-shaped huts, built by the women, have narrow entrances, and are built in small clusters. Again these clusters represent friendships and hunting partners rather than kinship ties. Brothers may be at opposite ends of the camp, but they tend to be together. The reason is that the norm is for patrilocal marriage: brothers grow up learning how to hunt together and often find each other ideal hunting partners. But brothers who may have been separated in childhood, as often occurs in an excessively large family where one child may be given into the care of a relative, may feel no such bonds. Friendships and hostilities are accurately reflected in the clustering of huts. In a series of diagrams of camp plans made among one band over a period of twelve months it was impossible to detect any consistency on grounds of kinship, but, throughout the duration of any one camp, internal relationships were clearly manifest in the way the entrances to the huts were constantly adjusted to point them in the direction of friends and away from enemies or rivals.

DIVISION OF LABOR • The few domestic activities in which kinship relationships are more strictly observable, apart from cohabitation, are so insignificant as to be negligible. They are limited to the making of a few personal possessions, but even these may be exchanged freely with friends.

Recreation also goes beyond the bounds of the individual family and involves a much larger proportion of the band, if not the band in its entirety. Dances are necessarily communal, being mimetic and involving a number of actors. Similarly, bopi (special playgrounds) are cleared near the camp, and all the children play there together. The only individual song is the lullaby, which is considered the personal possession of the mother or father who sings it. All other songs, by their technique (which involves canon and hoquet)[8] demand the cooperation of a number of people.

Nor in domestic life can any clear division of labor be seen even on the basis of sex. Certain activities are generally performed by one sex or the other, but not exclusively so. This applies also to economic, political, and ritual life, where roles may overlap or even be interchangeable.

THE HUNT • For a band of net-hunters the day starts at dawn. After bathing, the women cook a meal while the men inspect their nets and ready themselves for the hunt. Men may eat at the household hearth just outside their hut, or in a group by themselves, the women placing food in the center of the group for everyone to share.

After the meal the hunt sets out in a long straggling line of men, youths, women, and children. A few of the older Pygmies will be left in the camp to look after the children that stay behind. Thus, the elementary family is at once broken up, and even adult brothers, each with his own net, may not necessarily hunt side by side but may choose other "Sibling-Friends" in preference. The youths may either stay with their fathers or scatter to the extremities of the semicircle of nets in the hope of catching game that escapes around the edges.

The net-hunting technique calls for each family to set up its net and fasten it to the net on each side (every elementary family owns one net, up to three hundred feet in length). As the men and youths are silently forming this semicircle, the women and girls form an opposite one, and at a given signal from the men, close in, beating the undergrowth with branches and making a distinctive whooping cry.

Any animal falling into the nets is immediately killed with a spear, and the owner of the net into which it fell will give it to his wife to put in her basket. If the animal is too large for this, it is cut up and divided on the spot; otherwise the division takes place back in camp. The ultimate sharing

Setting Up a Net

follows no clear-cut kinship lines, though the owner of the net and the owner of the spear that killed the animal have first priority. Momentary individual needs seem to be given much more consideration, and portions will be given to those who were unable to come on the hunt or whose nets trapped no game.

This technique is, in all its essentials except the net, similar to the *begbe* hunt of the archers. In the *begbe*, armed with spears and bows and arrows the men and youths form a much more compact and smaller semicircle; the women, acting again as beaters, make for themselves leaf petards with which to beat the ground.

All decisions concerning the hunt are made by joint discussion, in which women take part. Gathering is combined with net-hunting, so it is important that the hunt should go in a direction in which there is vegetable food as well as game. Younger married men and women, being the most active hunters and gatherers, tend to have more say in such discussions, but there is no tendency whatsoever to individual leadership even on charismatic grounds.

It is normal for enough food to have been acquired by early afternoon to satisfy the band's needs for one or perhaps two days. Whether or not any surplus is sent to the village depends largely on how far away the village may be, and that in turn depends on where the hunting is best. Even with the hunt at its worst the net-hunters are never dependent on the villagers, their terrain being such that good hunting is never more than a day's march away. Although there is no individual leadership, there is sometimes an individual who is referred to by the villagers as headman of the band, and who accepts for a while the responsibility for seeing that at least token respect is paid by the band to its exchange obligations. Such an individual is generally more addicted to village luxuries than others and so is more willing to spend time there. Even so, the band as a whole never acts in concert with regard to the village, but individual Pygmy families deal directly with individual villagers.

One of the major differences between forest life and village life among the net-hunters is that in a village context the band is composed of individual families, whereas in the forest context it is an egalitarian unit, acting by unanimous accord. It seems that the net-hunters deliberately avoid this unanimity when dealing with the village, recognizing that it would make it easier for the village to deal with them.

At the time of the honey season, a change takes place in the composition of the hunting band. For the net-hunters this is a time for fission. Being a time of abundance, the band breaks up into sections that can still exist easily with complete independence of village supplies. The sections tend to be formed along patrilineal lines, but by no means necessarily. Above all this is a time when the tensions built up over ten months of communal hunting may be released. It is perfectly possible for two brothers to break at this time, each forming his own section, without incurring any undue or lasting stigma.

For the two months of the honey season there is very little interchange of any kind among the various sections until toward the end, when the sections gradually combine. First they will combine to form two or three minimal net-hunting bands of seven or eight families each; then they will converge on a common campsite and once again form a single unit. But in the process of fission and fusion there will have been changes that are perpetuated in the new composition of the total hunting band, which is never the same year after year.[9]

It is also a time when a large band (up to thirty families) has an option of splitting up and forming two separate hunting bands within the same area, or of splitting less evenly, the major segment remaining in undisputed possession of the territory, the smaller segment joining a neighboring band that has perhaps dwindled to somewhere near the minimum number of seven families. With the beaters, seven nets may form a circle of only one thousand feet in circumference, and little more than a hundred yards in diameter. In the forming of any circle less than this the game would be alarmed into escaping before surrounded. On the other hand, any circle formed by thirty nets may be up to nearly a mile in diameter, and so become both difficult and dangerous to control effectively.

All these considerations determining the composition of the hunting band are totally independent of the village. The net-hunters, with their efficient technique and their generally favorable situation, consider the village and its economic needs only so far as it suits their own convenience. They regard the products of the plantations as theirs to take when they wish, and their claim is even acknowledged by some villagers who offer the Pygmies first fruits of any new plantation as recognition that the land really belongs to them.

There is, however, no evidence at all that "silent trade"[10] was ever carried out. Exchange is not necessarily simultaneous, but there is no indication that there was ever any consistent avoidance during exchange.

A Pygmy bringing in meat from the forest may be anxious to return quickly without being questioned as to the whereabouts of his band and without being pressed to stay to help his *MuKpara*. In such a case, or if he happens to come at a time when his exchange family is at work on the plantation, he leaves the meat on a high platform that keeps it out of the reach of dogs, or places it inside the house and then leaves. Villagers, on the other hand, never leave food out in return, as they never know when their Mbuti are likely to appear next—and they also know that they will, in any case, take what they want.

THE ARCHERS

The bow and arrow is less productive than the net, and the game supply of the archers is further reduced by the fact that most of them live in areas that have been open to mission and administrative settlement; to economic exploitation by mining, commercial plantations, and tourist centers such as Beni and Mount Hoyo; and, finally, to consequent road building. In particular the southeast corner of the forest, the area most intensively worked by Father Schebesta, has been subject to such disturbances, all of which affect both the movement of game and the movement of the hunters. Hunting bands in parts of this area are still able to subsist on the forest, but only with great difficulty. Among the archer bands the village is regarded as an important if not absolutely essential source of food, and consequently there is need for a more stable relationship than that between the net-hunters and the villagers.[11]

This need reflects itself in the structure of the hunting bands in a curious way. An archer band has much less call for cooperation than a band of net-hunters, and as few as three elementary families can survive satisfactorily. During a large part of the year the archers are fragmented into such small groups, all of which, however, feel themselves as belonging to a larger unit that corresponds in size to the normal unit of the net-hunters—between ten and thirty families. When the band is fragmented, there is need for some kind of organization to ensure that the village patrons receive sufficient attention. Consequently, there is an embryonic form of centralized authority in the form of an individual referred to by the villagers as headman of the band. But the Pygmies call this headman by his title (*capita* or *sultani*) only when he discusses village food exchange or labor supply. In any forest context, he is referred to either by his personal name or by the appropriate generational term. In an archer band, this headman is generally, but not necessarily, heeded when he reports the demands of the villagers and translates them into more practical terms. He not only suggests a suitable compromise, but also suggests how the villagers' needs can be fulfilled. Thus, he may allocate hunting to one section of the band and the gathering of leaves and saplings to another, and he may tell a third to supply labor. If there is dissent, he has no means of enforcing his orders. He is held responsible by the villagers, and his only reward is their favor, expressed in terms of food, clothing, and tobacco. It is by no means a coveted position, and there are instances where there has been dispute as to who should fill an empty post of headman.

If, from the villagers' viewpoint, the archer band presents a picture of unity, from the inside it presents, for most of the year, an equally misleading picture of internal disunity. The band is split up into a number of small autonomous sections, often consisting of three or four brothers and their families, but equally often it is formed merely on grounds of hunting compatibility. There is no leadership, though men or women may gain special respect in certain fields because of personal charisma. Each section is independent of the others, and cooperates only when called on to do so by the headman for some purpose related to the village. Even then, if a section is enjoying particularly good hunting, it may refuse to cooperate. In a common hunting technique several adult males set off early in the morning and find where the game is. They will then climb trees in strategic positions around the game trails, and either wait for the animals to pass by, or call them by imitating their cries. Dogs are also used to put up game. Any game caught is carried back to the camp, where it is divided, cooked, and eaten. If members of another section of the band are known to be having bad luck in the hunt, meat may be sent to them or they may come and demand it, but contact between the sections is more often for a social purpose than for economic exchange. The women are not needed on the hunt, and spend their time gathering vegetable foods, attending to repairs on the huts, or doing other camp chores.

But once a year the band reasserts itself as a whole, ostensibly for the purpose of a *begbe* hunt. This hunt is like the net-hunt in technique, only without the nets, and it similarly demands the cooperation of men, women, and children in much larger numbers than could be supplied by any one section of the band. All sections, therefore, gather together at this time and build a single camp. The area surrounded by the *begbe* is smaller than the area in the net-hunt, and more animals escape, but the technique is otherwise the same.

The *begbe* seems to coincide with the honey season, and is referred to as marking the beginning of a new year. For the net-hunters the honey season itself is the mark of the new year, and is also accompanied by a structural change in the composition of the band, though a very different one. For the archers the *begbe* not only reaffirms the unity of the band as a whole, it also provides an opportunity for discussion of matters of general interest, such as betrothals, or the election of a new headman to deal with the villagers. It is a time for general socializing, for song and dance (much of which is of ritual significance), and ultimately for the realignment of the smaller sections, whose composition is never the same year after year. Petty hostilities and jealousies are removed during this festive season, which lasts about two months; old friendships are renewed and new friendships are formed.

For most of the year each archer band maintains almost daily contact with the villagers, and the archers' daily diet includes plantains and cassava. Only during the *begbe*, which is a time of plenty, may these Mbuti rely entirely on the forest. But there is still no set exchange rate, nor are forest products and village products necessarily exchanged at the same time. Almost every day the headman will send someone in from the forest to collect more plantains or cassava, and perhaps only once a week will he send in any meat. Individual sections of the band may independently carry on exchange with individual villagers, but this is independent of the headman's dealings with the village chief. When staying near the village, or when working on the plantations, the Pygmies tend to act as individuals under the general supervision of their headman, but if they have any cause for dispute with a villager either they will merely go back to the forest and leave the headman to argue it out, or they will call on their headman to take up the dispute with the village chief. The only recourse of the villagers on the failure of the Pygmies to fulfill their side of the exchange bargain is to penalize the headman by depriving him of gifts of food, but they are reluctant to do this, for the headman may quit, leaving them with the difficult task of negotiating with a new representative.

Generally, the economic balance is maintained by mutual desire and convenience, each side claiming that it is being cheated but not making any great attempt to do anything about it. The archers find plantation food a more important supplement to their diet than do the net-hunters, however, and they make a more consistent effort to keep the villagers satisfied.

Pygmy-village dependency: A conclusion

Far from giving the villagers any measure of control over the Pygmies, economic dependence, which has so often been stated to be the necessary core to the relationship between the Pygmies and their village neighbors, actually places the villagers in a position of some insecurity. Indeed, they themselves frequently complain that they are being "eaten" by the Pygmies. The exchange "system" is so loose and so dependent on mutual convenience and goodwill that it can barely be called a system. It certainly seldom works

Mbuti Dancing in a Negro
Village

out, in practice, along the theoretical lines of hereditary ownership claimed by the villagers. This latter theory exists, it seems, for the purpose of ensuring that no one village or villager can secure a monopoly at the expense of other villages by providing theoretical grounds for settling an exchange dispute. In practice, both the direction and the extent of the exchange are in the hands of the hunters.

Merely by being placed in such an unfavorable position, the villagers redouble their efforts to maintain some kind of control over the "parasites" that otherwise would, they believe, devour them. But just as they have little opportunity for influencing the Pygmies in their domestic or economic life, so they have little opportunity for effecting any kind of political control. It seems likely that the Mbuti hunting bands always were egalitarian communities, much as they are now, but the present excessive fluidity of band composition may well be a response to the attempt by villagers to assert political authority over them. The villagers consequently attempt to assert supernatural control by accepting Mbuti boys into the village *nkumbi* initiation ceremony, but this too is largely ineffective (Turnbull 1957, 1960d).[12]

AUTHORITY AND SOCIAL CONTROL

Leadership of the sections into which bands are divided cannot be said to be founded on the principle of lineal seniority, though older people always receive respect as such. Even more when the bands are united, be they archer or net-hunting bands, their composite nature proscribes centralized leadership on lineal grounds, just as the necessity for cooperation proscribes or at least renders unnecessary any form of individual leadership.

Among both groups of hunters, whether acting as bands or as segments, leadership of a sort exists, but it is divided into a number of different fields, in each of which several adults will jointly be recognized as deserving more of a hearing than others. Nearly every adult is accorded this respect in one or more fields, and every adult has the right to express himself in any field.

These areas over which some kind of cooperative authority exists broadly include hunting and gathering (a joint area for the net-hunters, separate for the archers), womanhood, manhood, betrothal and marriage, conjugal harmony, individual crisis and dispute, group crisis and dispute, and relationship with the villagers. Thus the younger married men, who are the most active and acute, have the most say in the daily discussion as to the direction in which the hunt is to go. They also tend to settle minor squabbles over the allocation of the spoils. The younger married women, again being the most active, settle matters concerning gathering. Among the net-hunters, the daily discussion concerns both men and women, so they air views jointly. In such discussions older men and women may add words of advice, or may complain about the hunt going too far afield for them to follow; younger unmarried men and women have little to say that will be heard, unless any of them have come across indications of abundance in any particular region.

There is virtually no ritual celebrating puberty or marriage, except for the *elima* festival (described below), but any questions that have to be settled are generally settled by the older married men and women. The younger married couples have little to say about this, but the unmarried people are listened to and heeded. It is the older married couples who enter into any disputes of a conjugal nature, and it is they, together with the elders, who may be widows or widowers, who step into the midst of any other serious disputes that arise.

If a dispute becomes so serious that it threatens to split the camp, thus disrupting the cooperative economy, it is generally either a widowed elder or else a stranger member of the band (one with few or even no direct kinship relationship with the several lineages of which the band may be composed) who assumes authority. Even then, however, as in other disputes, formal judgment is never given because there is no formal law. But it is a stated fact that a noisy camp is a hungry camp, and therefore anyone who "makes a noise" is acting to the detriment of the common good, and the mediator will simply tell both parties to the dispute that they are committing this crime. This direct appeal to the stomach is nearly always effective. The dispute will be shelved, perhaps continued behind the scenes by the two individuals, or simply forgotten. If the elder fails to reconcile the disputants, then the entire band takes part, and it may ultimately split into two, one section continuing to hunt while the other goes to a village, or both continuing to hunt in different areas, or one section going to visit in-laws in another territory.

Finally, there are two kinds of individual fitted for special responsibilities. There is, in almost every band, a clown. He is often an unmarried man, of whom there are few above the age of twenty, who is at the same time a great hunter and therefore entitled to respect. Yet, having no family responsibilities he is, rather like the stranger, in a good position to mediate. But he does so not by speaking with a voice of wisdom, for he is too young, but by lampooning one or both parties. Alternatively, he may be singled out as the cause of the dispute and take it all on himself, laughing it off and making light of it by his antics in song and dance. Ridicule, a powerful deterrent in Pygmy society, is consciously used to prevent or put an end to disputes if reason fails. The other type of individual fitted for special responsibility is the person who, perhaps like the clown (and sometimes they are one and the same), has a knack of dealing with tricky situations without getting seriously involved himself. But he must also have a taste for village life, a liking for tobacco and palm wine and hemp, and for village foods. He is the one generally found to act as headman in relationship with the village. He is a past master at the art of trickery and is willing to be subservient in front of villagers because he can laugh it off in the forest.

Authority, then, is divided among the entire population of any hunting band, and even my attempt to describe the nature of authority perhaps suggests too much systematization, for there is so much overlapping.

Perhaps in the reaction to crisis we can best see the way in which authority is divided throughout the band, where its source lies, and what is the basis of the unity that persists in the midst of the flux that is so characteristic of Mbuti society.

One such crisis occurs when sorcery is practiced by villagers against Pygmies, generally as a final attempt to exact what they consider their due in terms of economic exchange. The Pygmies do not practice sorcery or witchcraft themselves and therefore do not have the same means of recourse that is available to the villagers. The Pygmy attitude is ambivalent: they do not believe in supernatural powers of this order; yet they have seen enough of the efficacy of village sorcery (poison is sometimes used) to be wary of it. But their reaction is not one of fear, even when their fellows die, as I have seen. Nor is it colored by any desire for revenge, nor even by anger or hatred. It is expressed best by themselves when they say that the village has become a dirty place, full of the trickery that may be expected from animals but not from human beings. Their reaction is one of concern that they might become contaminated with that dirt, and their remedy is to return immediately to the forest. What is particularly significant is that they consider that sorcery cannot reach them in the forest because the forest, they say, is their protector. It not only protects them physically, for the villagers cannot pursue the Pygmies there, but it also protects them spiritually, and against such foreign supernatural powers as might seem to exist.

The decision to return to the forest, however, is not made by the victims of the sorcery, nor by their immediate families, but by united agreement arrived at during a discussion in which the entire band takes part, or at least that part of it that happens to be in the village at the time. It is just about the only kind of occasion on which the band does unite while in the village.

LIFE CYCLE AND RITUAL ORGANIZATION

The crises occasioned by the normal course of the life cycle do not call for any protective ritual comment by the Mbuti, for their understanding of life is that one is born, grows to maturity, marries and rears a family, and then dies. It is when one does *not* do any of these things that the Pygmies think it strange. Nonetheless, the traditional *rites de passage* that anthropologists have come to expect, if not demand, are evident in elementary form.

Infancy and childhood

When a child is born it is not named for a number of days, until it has proved that it is going to stay. It is bathed in water mixed with the juice of a forest vine, it is clothed with a vine circlet around the waist, decorated with one or two small pieces of pierced wood, with similar circlets around the wrists, and it is an object of pride and interest and concern to every member of the band. The vine circlets, the juice, and the wooden ornaments are not only for decoration, but to place the child in this way always in physical contact with the physical forest, which as well as being the protector is the life-giver. There is no formal ritual, no invocation of supernatural aid other than this insistence on physical contact.

CHILD TRAINING AND SOCIALIZATION · Children are breast-fed for at least eighteen months, often for three years. If the mother's milk does not prove sufficient, the child is given to another woman, usually but not necessarily related to the mother. It is only in this connection that the Mbuti express any feeling about twins, for they would make this preferred long period of breast feeding difficult. There is no stated practice of killing one twin, but so far there have been no reports of both twins surviving.

Upon weaning, a child may demand and expect food from any family in the band, but may equally expect to be disciplined by any adult. From the moment it can crawl it is encouraged to imitate adult activities, and as soon as it can walk it is expected to make its own way beyond the edge of the camp to relieve itself, and down to a nearby stream to wash. By the age of four, children are playing games, sometimes with adults, in imitation of hunting and gathering activities. They are taught, again by any youth or adult, how to make miniature bows and arrows, carrying baskets, and bark-cloth hammers, and how to build houses and cook. At six years old both boys and girls will already be contributing in a small way to the general economy, helping with camp chores and setting off on hunting and gathering forays on their own in the vicinity of the camp. Any food they get in this way they will cook and eat themselves, often at one of their playhouses.

At about the age of nine they accompany their parents on the hunt and are increasingly given adult responsibilities. At this age they also begin to look after smaller children, girls carrying their infant brothers or sisters while their mothers are gathering or hunting. Up to this age any misdemeanors are punished by a sound slapping, but from now on the more usual return for any failure on the part of the child is ridicule.

Girls continue to sleep in the huts of their parents until betrothal, but at twelve or thirteen boys may occupy a deserted hut together. Only a bachelor of marriageable age may build a hut for himself, but if he does this then he is likely to be joined by many other youths. Girls are never officially invited into such bachelor huts, flirtations generally taking place during the daytime and off in the forest.

The whole process of child training is characterized by informality and by an emphasis on the child's responsibilities to the band as a whole.

Puberty rites: The *elima* festival

So also with maturation, there is no formal initiation such as the *nkumbi* of the villagers, but only the *elima*, which is occasioned by the first menstrual period of a girl, and which celebrates, at the same time, not only her maturity but that of the boys who also take part. This has been described in some detail elsewhere (Turnbull 1960a) but the essentials are simple. Whereas the village people think of menstruation as unclean, and of a girl's first menstrual flow as being particularly dangerous, even as being indicative of illicit intercourse, to the Mbuti it is an occasion for great public rejoicing because it is a sign that the girl is now a potential mother. This means that she can now become betrothed.

One function of the *elima* is to provide an opportunity for teaching the girl (and her friends, who may join her for a month or so in the special *elima* hut) the art and responsibility of motherhood and womanhood. Another function is to give public recognition to boys who are considered old enough to flirt, if not to become betrothed. Betrothals and successful marriages may well arise from associations formed during the course of the *elima*, providing an opportunity as it does for boys and girls to get to know each other intimately, though I never found even any recollection of a pregnancy arising from the intercourse that takes place with no more sanction than mutual agreement of the two partners and the permission of the mothers, who always stand by to guard the hut against unwanted suitors. The women are perfectly capable of keeping any boy at bay because he is considered too young, or undesirable for any other reason.

The *elima* involves more physical contact with vines and leaves of the forest, used for decoration and clothing and bedding, but it also places the girl in a special ritual relationship to the forest. Together with her friends she is taken during the daytime on secret sorties far away from the camp. Sometimes these sorties are to introduce them to other bands where there may be eligible bachelors, but often they are for other purposes one of which, I strongly suspect, is to teach them certain ritual dances connected with the forest and with fire.

As far as boys are concerned, the mere fact that the women have allowed them to participate is tacit admission of their entry into adulthood. However, there being no obvious clear-cut physiological indication of adulthood for boys as there is for girls, the boys have to prove themselves and this is the time to do it. Proof of courage is given by the boy's success in fighting his way through the women, armed with sticks and stones, who may give him a very hard time before they finally allow him through. He still has to face the girls, who may all set upon him and beat him, and there is no doubt that considerable physical endurance is called for, though older Pygmies say that the *elima* is less rough than in former days.

The boy also has to prove his adulthood by showing that he can provide for a family, and this he has to do by killing one of the larger antelopes, or perhaps even a buffalo. When he has done this he will, if he wishes to marry, present the game to the girl's parents. He may also be accorded recognition, though there is no formal ceremony, by having his forehead tattooed with tiny triple vertical marks. The skin is slit with an arrow, the flesh beneath is gouged out, and a paste made from ashes of forest woods and herbs is rubbed in and remains as a visible physical evidence of the presence of the forest in the body of the man. (Tattoos are made on arms or wrists in connection with hunting also, and again the Mbuti think of their importance as representing physical contact with the forest.) The *elima* peters out as unostentatiously and informally as it began, and the participants from then on gradually assume adult responsibilities. These are not thrust upon them by any sudden formal status transition, but are conferred according to general opinion as to the ability of the individual.

Marriage follows the same pattern, but is perhaps best considered as a natural sequel to the *elima*, requiring no further formality beyond the proofs of manhood on the one side and the ability to bear a child on the other. There are no visible marks by which married people are distinguished from unmarried, though for a man to bear the forehead tattoos is an indication that he is a hunter, and therefore should be married.

Personal disaster and death: The *molimo* festival

Before we consider the ultimate crisis of death, we should consider two rather rare crises—sickness and bad hunting. The reaction of the Mbuti to such crises strongly marks a fundamental magico-religious opposition between them and their village neighbors. It is more than the fact that the villagers practice magic, witchcraft, and sorcery whereas the Mbuti do not, though this in itself is a startling contrast between two peoples living so close to each other and with so much contact. In almost every conceivable crisis the villagers, be they Bantu or Sudanic, either invoke magical aid, make accusations of witchcraft, or practice sorcery. These are remedies known to them. In their world every misfortune is due to some malevolence, human or supernatural, and they counterattack in kind.

As pointed out earlier, to the villagers the forest is harsh and hostile, whereas to the Mbuti it is beneficent. Thus in a crisis such as sickness or poor hunting, when they have taken every practical remedy they know and to no avail, rather than thinking of the situation as being due to malevolence, the Mbuti think of it as being due to a lack of normal benevolence. This is clearly seen in the steps they take when all practical medicines (of which they have an abundance) and all hunting endeavors fail. There is no evil spirit to counter, the only requirement is to attract the benevolence that has been, for some reason, withdrawn. They do not need to be specific in their requests, and one does not hear invocations asking for sickness to be cured or for the hunting to be made better, though of course such hopes are freely expressed in ordinary conversation. But as the norm, in their world, is for everything to be right and good, and as this is due to the presence, they believe, of a benevolent forest deity, all they have to do is to attract his attention. He will then see their plight, and because he *is* benevolent everything will come right. This is done in a festival known as the *molimo*.[13]

In this context the *molimo* involves a nightly gathering of all adult men, who begin to sing the *molimo* songs once the women and children have shut themselves up in the hut. A few stray women may still be wandering about at the early stages of the singing, but later on they are expected to remain hidden and silent. There are no song leaders, but the men with better voices, young and old, are largely in effective control. The words of the songs are simple, mainly expressing devotion to and trust in the forest: "The Forest is kind," "The Forest is good" are examples. The stated object of the singing is to "rejoice" the forest, and/or to "awaken" it, so that it will see the plight of its people. The *molimo* generally lasts a month, and during that time, in the natural course of events, bad hunting becomes good again. I have never known of poor hunting to last for more than two weeks in any one place that had not recently been hunted out. So, one way or another, it seems to the Mbuti that the forest awakens and restores the norm of good hunting.

When a *molimo* is held for a sick person, during its month's duration it is likely that either that person will become better, in which case again the Mbuti attribute it to their having successfully attracted the attention of the forest, or else that person will die. In the case of death, once again the *molimo* comes into operation, but with significant differences. For instance, there are certain songs that are only sung on occasions of death, one of which is more wordy and likens death to darkness. It states the Mbuti rationalization and acceptance of death in the following terms: "Darkness is all around us . . . but if Darkness *is* [if the forest allows it], then Darkness is good." Having awakened and rejoiced the forest, then anything that happens, say the Pygmies, must be at the will of the forest, and therefore good, though they may not understand it. When someone dies there is great expression of personal grief at a personal loss, but there is no formal mourning, no feeling of injury, no suspicion of sorcery or witchcraft, and the immediate task is to set about restoring normality to the lives of the survivors. The death cannot be ignored, though the burial consists simply of pulling down the hut of the deceased over the body and abandoning the camp. The memory of the dead person must be honored and then expunged, and although the *molimo* festival for death is basically similar to that for bad hunting or sickness, there are vital ritual differences.

For the present account, reverting to the observation on the intimate nature of the relationship between the Mbuti and their forest environment, the *molimo* death festivals are of particular significance. For all other misfortunes the Mbuti believe that the norm of good fortune will ultimately prevail and that they themselves can bring it about through song. Through song they also believe that they can even improve on the norm, in hunting results, for instance. But song is not used in the way that the neighboring villagers use magic, in the belief that it is necessarily and practically effective in itself if properly performed. This is seen clearly when song is used in the *molimo* festivals that follow death. On these occasions there is no thought of bringing the dead person back to life, or even of protecting the survivors against further deaths.

The object of the *molimo* on such occasions is rather to accept and recognize the new situation, to emphasize that nothing abnormal has happened, and to stress the continuity of the hunting band as a whole. This is one difference between the death *molimo* and the hunting *molimo*. It is achieved, it would seem, by ritual acts that are performed so informally as hardly to appear to be such. These acts reinforce the absolute necessity for cooperation among all members of the band. Stress is also laid on the undesirability of individual leadership, even in religious matters, and on the importance of the band as a whole. But perhaps even more important than this, and certainly much more prominent, are the constant reminders of the dependency of the band as a whole on the forest for all the necessities of life. And finally, the opposition between the forest world and the world of the nonforest is formally acknowledged.

A vital ritual difference between hunting and death *molimo* festivals is that in the latter a wooden trumpet, also known as *molimo,* is used. It is traditionally made from a special wood, but with typical informality the Mbuti make use of whatever material is at hand. The important thing, they say, is the sound it makes. It is expected to imitate the leopard and the elephant in particular, both animals that the Pygmies respect. The purpose of making these sounds is not clear to anyone, except that these are the "great animals of the forest." But far more important than making animal sounds on the fringes of the camp, and sometimes in its midst, the *molimo* trumpet sings. A young man, noted for the excellence of his voice, echoes into it the songs the men sing around the fire. He may be far off in the forest, and the stated objective is that the song should be passed on as far as possible so that the sleeping forest is sure to hear its *bamiki nde ndura* (children of the forest) and awaken. When not in use, the trumpet is concealed from women and children by hiding it—in water during the month-long festival and high up in a tree at other times.

The *molimo* trumpet is brought into direct ritual contact with the four elements into which early man elsewhere divided the material universe— water, fire, earth, and air. For example, whenever the trumpet is carried over a stream, it is lowered into it and water is made to flow through it. The *molimo* "drinks." Glowing coals are placed in its mouth so that it "breathes fire"; ashes and earth are rubbed into it. But of all the elements, fire seems to be of the most significance. The Mbuti have no knowledge of how to make fire, and it is carried with them wherever they go. They say that without fire they would die. The most startling part of the death *molimo* is the appearance of an old woman, sometimes assisted by a younger married woman and some theoretical virgins, who invade the sanctity of the *kumamolimo* (*molimo* hearth) and not only assert their power over man by literally tying all the men together with the twine used for making hunting nets, but who also attempt to stamp out the sacred fire. The efforts of the old woman, during an elaborate dance, are countered by the men, who gather up the scattered embers and rebuild the fire, fanning it into life with a wild erotic dance that imitates the act of copulation.

The symbolism is too rich for an analysis even to be attempted here, but it all points to the basic recognition among the Mbuti of the physical world around them, and of their dependence on it. The intervention of women in the otherwise strictly male *molimo* festival is an acknowledgment of the mutual interdependence of men and women, stressed also in legend (according to one legend women had fire before men). The sacredness of the forest and the profanity of the village are expressed by a seemingly informal ritual closing of any path that might lead off to the village; the festival is never carried out in the presence of even a single villager.[14] Further, toward the climax of the festival, there is greater insistence on divorce from village contact. Forest foods are preferred, anyone wearing an article of village clothing is scorned, and the songs of devotion to the forest are sung with increasing passion. The attention of the singers is focused either on the fire or on the forest around and above them—never on each other. They adorn themselves with vines, feathers, leaves, or flowers of the forest, and when the *molimo* trumpet is brought into the camp in the early hours of the morning it is concealed from any curious women who might be awake by a band of youths, all carrying leaves and branches that hide them as well as the instrument. This is a time when troublemakers are singled out, but when huts of miscreants are attacked by the youths, they are beaten with branches and not with fists. It is the *molimo*, not man, who judges.

The final act of the festival, after a month or more of singing every night from dusk to dawn, is the dramatic extinction of the *molimo* fire itself. It is slowly trampled out by the youths, holding the trumpet on their shoulders, and by the older men still desperately singing the *molimo* songs while stamping out the fire of life with their feet. When every last glowing spark has been extinguished, the trumpet is borne away by the youths with a triumphal song, carried far off into the forest and hidden up in a tree until it is called for again.

Ownership of the trumpet is unclear. Apparently almost everyone can have one, if he wants to go to the trouble of making it and is willing to accept the responsibility that goes with it—for the owner is expected to see that food and wood are provided for a *molimo*. In effect, every family usually has at least one close male relative who possesses a trumpet, but if this is not so and a family member dies, they can and do borrow a trumpet from anyone. For an important death of an old person or a great hunter, more than one trumpet may be used. But one thing is clear, and that is that these instruments do not fulfill the function ascribed to them by the villagers, who have a counterpart that imitates the voice of the clan totem (animal or bird), but never sings. For the villagers the voice of their totem protects them from the evil spirits that congregate at the scene of death, and this is their understanding of the *molimo* trumpet of the Mbuti, which they have heard but not seen.

Not so visible in the ritual acts associated with the *molimo*, but plainly visible in the organization of the festival, is the function that this institution plays in separating the two worlds, the forest and the nonforest. It has already been shown briefly how it emphasizes forest values, and in this way incidentally makes clear the division between forest and village, but there is evidence that the institution is now fulfilling an additional function beyond the establishment of the new status quo following a death. It appears that originally the *molimo* was the individual concern of each hunting band. With the stated ideal that each family should have its own trumpet, it might seem that the bands were originally more patrilineal/patrilocal than they now are. The fact that the bands have become cognatic, or are now cognatic, correlates with the fact that the *molimo* now is also cognatic, and that *all* adult men within the territory of a band that has suffered death, regardless of their relationship or lack of it, are expected to participate. During a *molimo* one of the major topics for discussion is the goodness of the forest as against the badness of the village, and it is undoubtedly a time, now, when Mbuti from a number of different bands have an opportunity to gather together and combine in their common opposition to the nonforest world.

In the light of the increasing contact between the two peoples in recent years, it is significant that the *molimo* should, during that time, have become more a matter of common concern among neighboring hunting bands. Even though there is still not yet the slightest evidence of any development of centralized authority either within the hunting bands or among them, it is undeniable that the *molimo* is now functioning as a political as well as a religious institution, giving the Mbuti a wider sense of political unity, if only vis-à-vis the villagers. There is as yet no need for any stronger internal political sense, for each band is still virtually autonomous, and all are, if they wish, independent of the villages.

This aspect of the *molimo* further illustrates how superficial has been the acculturation that many see among the Pygmies, and how erroneous is the notion that they are dominated, physically and culturally, by their village neighbors. The essence of the relationship of Pygmies to villages, marked as it is by outward acceptance of the village way of life when in the village, is the unalterable and increasing opposition to the nonforest world expressed implicitly and explicitly in the forest ritual. That the opposition is conscious as well as unconscious can be clearly seen in the creed often and concisely expressed by the Mbuti themselves: "The Forest is Mother and Father, because it gives us all the things we need . . . food, clothing, shelter, warmth . . . and affection. We are the children of the forest. When it dies, we die."

CHANGE

The Belgian government, prior to independence, made several attempts to "liberate" the Mbuti from their alleged dependence on the villagers by teaching them how to cultivate. This met with as little success as did the few sporadic attempts made to entice Pygmy children into schools, or to make use of them for wage labor. Belgian thought in the matter was that if the Pygmies could be taught to cultivate successfully this would free village labor for other uses, at the same time solving the problem of the unproductivity (from the administrative point of view) of this large segment of the local population.

On the few "model" plantations where the Pygmies were heavily bribed to remain (mostly around the administrative posts of Mambasa and Beni, where hunting is at its very worst), the Mbuti showed themselves perfectly capable of learning how to cultivate, but they degenerated socially and physically at an alarming rate, losing all sense of individual or family responsibility and dying from sunstroke and stomach disorders. Any form of settled cultivation, where the plantation requires constant attention, is likely to meet with equal failure, the only possibility being one where the crops planted can be left largely untended for considerable periods, allowing the Mbuti bands to continue their hunting and gathering activities. Even this, however, will demand radical changes in the social organization of the band.

One of the greatest obstacles to any form of social change is that of the lack of incentive. For one thing, it is clear that the Mbuti do not need "liberation," and they themselves ask why they should work on plantations and grow their own crops when it is much easier to steal from village plantations. Throughout the forest the Mbuti are aware of the threat to their hunting and gathering way of life through outside economic exploitation of the forest, and they were equally aware of the administrative attempts to encourage them to cultivate. But they clearly see and state that once they abandon their nomadic forest existence they will cease to be Mbuti, and it is significant that both young and old talk more of what they regard as the resultant moral degeneration than of the physical degeneration that would come with change.

Their values are so centered on the forest that the mere suggestion of change is, to them, not only without any immediate economic necessity, but in itself a hostile act, and therefore on both grounds to be rejected. Even those who have had contact with Europeans and with schools and hospitals are no more than temporarily amused by "civilization." They make intelligent and pertinent comparisons in terms of their total experience, but still cannot see that civilization has anything to offer that will in any way improve upon what they already have.

Reports from villagers during the years following independence indicate that in face of the lack of such real incentives, such as trade tobacco, Mbuti visits to the villages are increasingly infrequent, and this situation is likely to continue until outside economic exploitation of the forest is resumed.

Notes

(1) The prefix is dropped from BaMbuti and from the Bantu tribal names in line with recent usage in African studies.

(2) Of these the best studied have been the BaTwa Pygmoids of the Kivu District discussed at length by Father Schumacher (1949–1950). But they, and

nearly all the others, show considerable signs of acculturation, physical as well as social, and are no longer true Pygmy hunters and gatherers. Perhaps the Binga on the western bank of the Ubangi River retain more of their early characteristics than the others, but most accounts from this and other areas are in the nature of travelogues rather than serious scientific discussions. The total number of all Pygmy and Pygmoid groups is probably in the neighborhood of 150,000, but in the absence of anything approaching a reliable census, this is only a guess.

(3) The opinion of the villagers, and of most Europeans who have had any dealings with Pygmies, is, of course, that they are the most lazy and unreliable of all people.

(4) Unfortunately, Schebesta does not always distinguish exactly to which kind of group he is referring, and so his account is a generalization for both kinds of economic band.

(5) One of his wives will generally in turn go away to visit relatives, or a boy friend, leaving her husband with a more manageable two. Each wife will build her own hut, and the husband is expected to divide his attentions equally, both with regard to cohabitation and food sharing and eating. But it is obvious enough to the Pygmies that monogamy is a much more trouble-free arrangement, and far less likely to cause difficulty. It also demands less of a husband as a hunter, and it is significant that one Pygmy who had three wives not only compared himself with the wealthy villagers who had several wives, but boasted that his hunting ability was so superior that he could support them all.

(6) In fact, personal names are frequently used in all cases for both address and reference. The few generational terms are the only ones ever used in the forest, even though the village system, using the same language, is much more complex, and is well known to the Mbuti.

(7) If they intend to stay more than a few days they may first, for a few weeks, preserve meat by smoking it, specifically for the purpose of bringing it to the village: for themselves they never smoke meat, having no need for preservation with the readily available supply of fresh meat all around them.

(8) The Mbuti create harmony, among other ways, by repeating the same melodic phrase at successive intervals, so that up to sixteen parts may be sung simultaneously. They add complication to this, especially in hunting songs, by dividing the melodic phrase among the singers so that each singer has one note and the phrase can only be completed by each singing his note in turn and at the correct moment.

(9) In-laws who come to visit may decide to stay; brothers who have separated may decide to remain separated, one of them joining his wife's band.

(10) The Pygmies and their Negro neighbors have been reported to have engaged in "silent trade" or dumb barter, "an exchange of goods between hostile people without face-to-face contact and without the aid of middlemen."—E. Adamson

Hoebel, *Man in the Primitive World* (2d ed.; New York: McGraw-Hill Book Company, Inc., 1958, p. 644).

(11) It is significant that in the northern section of the archer territory, where there is less foreign settlement and greater distance between roads (over a hundred miles), such stability is much less noticeable.

(12) *Nkumbi* is an initiation rite of adjacent Negro villagers in which Mbuti boys are initiated side by side with village initiates. Although Mbuti voluntarily participate to establish and formalize their relationship with the villagers, they reject most of the significance ascribed to the *nkumbi* by the Negroes and, when in the forest, ridicule much of what takes place in the *nkumbi*. Going through *nkumbi* does not in Mbuti eyes make a boy a man; it has little more significance for them than a villager-arranged marriage may have. A description and analysis of the ceremony is found in Turnbull 1957 which is reprinted in *Cultures and Societies of Africa* edited by Simon and Phoebe Ottenberg (New York: Random House, 1960), pp. 421–442.

(13) All significant elements of Mbuti religion are contained in the two religious institutions, *elima* and *molimo*, which are primarily the concern of women and men respectively.

(14) I was permitted to observe what I did (and there may still be more that I did not see) only after three years among the Mbuti, during which time it had become well established that I was much inclined in favor of both the forest and its people.

BIBLIOGRAPHY

With a few exceptions the following bibliography emphasizes contemporary work. Starred items (*) include significant bibliographies. Daggered items (†) are cited as references in the text of the chapter.

Ballif, Noël (1955). *Dancers of God*. London: Sidgwick & Jackson, Ltd.

Gusinde, Martin (1956*). *Die Twiden: Pygmäen und Pygmoide im Tropischen Afrika*. Vienna: Wilhelm Braumüller.

Herodotus (c.440 B.C.). *The Histories*.

Homer (c.800 B.C.). *The Iliad*.

Joset, P. E. (1948†). "Buda Efeba: Contes et légendes Pygmées," *Zaïre*, Vol. 2, pp. 25–56, 137–157.

Letts, Malcolm (1955†). "The Pictures in the Hereford Mappa Mundi," in *The World Map in Hereford Cathedral*. Hereford, England: The Cathedral Press.

Moir, A. L. (1955†). *The World Map in Hereford Cathedral*. Hereford, England: The Cathedral Press.

Putnam, Patrick (1948). "The Pygmies of the Ituri Forest," in *A Reader in*

General Anthropology, Carlton S. Coon (ed.). New York: Holt, Rinehart and Winston, Inc., pp. 322–342.

Schebesta, Paul (1933†). *Among Congo Pygmies.* London: Hutchinson & Co., Ltd.

———— (1936†). *My Pygmy and Negro Hosts.* London: Hutchinson & Co., Ltd.

———— (1937†). *Revisiting My Pygmy Hosts.* London: Hutchinson & Co., Ltd.

———— (1938†). *Die Bambuti-Pygmäen vom Ituri: Geschichte, Geographie, Umwelt, Demographie und Anthropologie.* Mémoires, Institut Royal Colonial Belge, Collection 4, Vol. 1.

———— (1941†). *Die Bambuti-Pygmäen vom Ituri: Ethnographie der Ituri-Bambuti, Die Wirtschaft der Ituri-Bambuti.* Mémoires, Institut Royal Colonial Belge, Collection 4, Vol. 2, Part 1.

———— (1948†). *Die Bambuti-Pygmäen vom Ituri: Ethnographie der Ituri-Bambuti, Das Soziale Leben.* Mémoires, Institut Royal Colonial Belge, Collection 4, Vol. 2, Part 2.

———— (1950†). *Die Bambuti-Pygmäen vom Ituri: Ethnographie der Ituri-Bambuti, Die Religion.* Mémoires, Institut Royal Colonial Belge, Collection 4, Vol. 2, Part 3.

———— (1952*†). *Les Pygmées du Congo belge.* Mémoires, Institut Royal Colonial Belge, Collection 8, Vol. 26.

Schumacher, Peter (1949†). *Expedition zu den Zentralafrikanischen Kivu-Pygmäen, I: Kivu-Pygmäen (Twiden).* Mémoires, Institut Royal Colonial Belge, Collection 4, Vol. 3.

———— (1950†). *Expedition zu den Zentralafrikanischen Kivu-Pygmäen, II: Die Kivu-Pygmäen (Twiden).* Mémoires, Institut Royal Colonial Belge, Collection 4, Vol. 5.

Trilles, P. (1932). *Les Pygmées de la forêt équatoriale,* in Bibliothèque Anthropos Ethnologique, Vol. 3, Fasc. 4.

Turnbull, Colin M. (1957†). "Initiation among the Bambuti Pygmies of the Central Ituri," *Journal of the Royal Anthropological Institute,* Vol. 87, pp. 191–216.

———— (1959†). "Legends of the Bambuti," *Journal of the Royal Anthropological Institute,* Vol. 89, pp. 45–50.

———— (1960a†). "The Elima: A Premarital Festival among the Bambuti Pygmies," *Zaïre,* Vol. 14, Nos. 2–3, pp. 175–192.

———— (1960b†). "The *Molimo:* A Men's Religious Association among the Ituri Bambuti," *Zaïre,* Vol. 14, No. 4, pp. 307–340.

———— (1960c). "Field Work among the Bambuti Pygmies, Belgian Congo: A Preliminary Report," *Man,* Vol. 60, pp. 36–40.

———— (1960d). "Some Recent Developments in the Sociology of the Bambuti Pygmies," *Transactions of the New York Academy of Sciences,* Series 2, Vol. 22, No. 4, pp. 267–274.

—————— (1961†).   *The Forest People*. New York: Simon & Schuster, Inc.

—————— (1963).   "The Lesson of the Pygmies," in *Scientific American (Reprint Series)*. San Francisco: W. H. Freeman and Company.

—————— (n.d.).   *The Mbuti Pygmies: An Ethnological Survey* (In press: Anthropological Papers of the American Museum of Natural History).

Tyson, E. (1699).   *The Anatomy of a Pygmie Compared with that of a Monkey, an Ape, and a Man*. 2d ed. London: T. Osborne.

Van Bulck, G. (1948).   "Où en est le problème des Pygmées de l'Ituri?" *Zaïre*, Vol. 2, pp. 423–436.

—————— (1953).   "Les Pygmées asiatiques et les Pygmées africains, constituent-ils une race unique?" *Zaïre*, Vol. 2, pp. 845–850.

9

THE NORTHERN PASTORAL SOMALI
OF THE HORN

about the chapter

The pattern of pastoralism of present-day Cushites such as the Somali of the East African Horn may provide anthropologists with some clues as to the nature of early pastoralism in East Africa, for some of the earliest pastoralists of Africa appear to have lived in this area. A series of modern studies, in conjunction with archaeological and other direct historical research, should eventually enable Africanists to assess the extent to which Cushitic ("Hamitic") influence encouraged the development of pastoralism among other East African pastoralists such as the so-called Nilo-Hamites (Cushitized Nilotes)—for example, the Jie—and among Bantu-speaking, cattle-keeping agriculturalists—such as the Bantu Tiriki and the Swazi.

The Somali are strongly patrilineal and fiercely militaristic, and these qualities, often referred to as "pastoral values," support their herding subsistence mode and shape the form of their political organization. Unlike many East African pastoralists, such as the Jie (and the neighboring Cushitic Galla), the Somali have no age groups. Political organization, like that of the Tiv, is based on the principle of balanced opposition among strong segmentary lineages. Formalized political offices are few, and the social order itself depends on maintenance of the strength of the lineages: the size of lineage herds, lineage military strength, the payment of compensation, and the good offices of religious leaders.

Interlineage relations are not viewed completely in terms of the

319

genealogical idiom, for lineages commonly relate to each other through the making—and modifying—of formal contracts. This is a striking deviation from the usual operation of the principle of segmentary opposition in sub-Saharan societies. In fact, violation of such contracts is sometimes a cause for feuding or warfare—Somaliland is one of the few places in Africa where resort to arms is still a normal part of the traditional political process. In his analysis Lewis shows how this tendency to resort to force is kept in check through being balanced by other values.

Like the Hausa and the pastoral Fulani, the Somali are Islamic, but the Islam of the Somali has been modified by contact with sub-Saharan Africa, so that traditional Muslim forms exist side by side with such forms as the cult of saints, which reflects the ancestral cult widespread in Africa. And Islamic custom has blended with African custom in other institutions, such as marriage and law, as in other sub-Saharan Islamic societies. Undoubtedly one reason for Somali acceptance of Islam is the strong parallel between the dominant values of their culture and those of the Muslim pastoralists of Arabia. The syncretistic fusion of two cultural configurations makes the Somali of interest to both Africanists and students of Islam.

In their subsistence and in their relationship to their herds the Somali reveal many of the patterns observed among the Jie and the pastoral Fulani, with whom a careful comparison is helpful. Lewis shows how subsistence centers about the stock complex; the composition of households and of smaller economic units, as well as their nomadic movements, shows an adjustment to the features of habitat and the needs of the livestock. However, the herds are significant not merely as the source of subsistence, but because of their connection with significant Somali social institutions such as marriage and clanship.

about the author

I. M. Lewis, Lecturer in Anthropology at University College, University of London, received the D.Phil. from Oxford University in 1957. In addition to teaching at the University College of the Rhodesias and Nyasaland and at the University of Glasgow he has served as a research assistant in the preparation of the second edition of *An African Survey*, edited by Lord Hailey. His field work among the Somali was carried out from 1955 to 1957 as a Colonial Social Science Research Council Fellow, in 1962, and in 1964. In 1959 and 1960 he did field work among the Kaonde of Northern Rhodesia. He is author of *Peoples of the Horn of Africa* (1955) and *A Pastoral Democracy* (1961), and co-author (with B. Andrzejewski) of *Somali Poetry* (1964).

I. M. LEWIS · *The Northern Pastoral Somali of the Horn*[1]

INTRODUCTION

LOCATION · The union in 1960 of the British Somaliland Protectorate with the United Nations Trust Territory of Somalia to form the independent Somali Republic represents a partial political realization of ethnic frontiers in the "Horn" of Africa. Despite their marked ethnic and cultural unity, however, the Somali, who dominate this arid region of northeast Africa from French Somaliland around the periphery of Ethiopia and along the Gulf of Aden and Red Sea coasts to northern Kenya, are still partly divided by colonial frontiers. They make up about half the population of the *Côte des Somalis* (French Somaliland) (about 37,000 in 84,000), which remains an overseas territory of France; in Ethiopia (mainly in Harar Province) they number probably about 750,000; in the Somali Republic itself their strength is some 2,250,000,[2] and in the new North-Eastern Region of Kenya, whose population consists almost solely of Somali, they number over 240,000. Other Somali are settled mainly as traders and entrepreneurs in other towns and ports in East Africa, in Aden and the Gulf of Arabia, and in some European and American ports where Somali seamen have established small immigrant communities. Although there is no complete census, it seems likely that the Somali have a total strength exceeding 3 million.

Ethnically and culturally, the Somali are generally classified with the southeastern Cushites (or "Hamites")—the Afar (Danakil), Saho, Galla, and Beja. The Afar, with whom they share French Somaliland and with whom their relations are traditionally unfriendly, are their northern neighbors. To the west, in Ethiopia, they are bounded by the Galla peoples of that region, and in the south by the Boran Galla of Kenya.

PHYSICAL APPEARANCE · Physically, the Somali are generally tall, taller than most of the other southeastern Cushites; their heads are long and narrow; their hair is frizzy; and in skin color they range from light brown with a reddish or coppery tinge to extreme dark brown. They also exhibit traces of Arabian blood,[3] and, in the south of the Somali Republic, among the

321

A Young Warrior This warrior is of the Gadabuursi clan in the northwest.

Digil and Rahanwiin groups, physical evidence of their contact with the "pre-Hamitic" Negroid peoples whom they and the Galla met when they entered this region several centuries ago.

Although Somali do not see themselves as Arabs, they take great pride in their Arabian ancestry in keeping with their centuries' long attachment to Islam. Ultimately, Somali genealogies go back to Arabian origins, indeed to the Prophet's lineage. And however unfounded historically, these traditions have great importance in validating the whole Muslim basis of Somali society. They also reflect the long-standing trade between Somaliland and Arabia, which, over the centuries, has brought Arab families and individuals to the country and with them Islam and various elements of Islamic culture.

LANGUAGE • Thus in their language there are a number of Arabic loanwords. Yet Somali retains its distinctiveness and is classified as a single unit (Tucker and Bryan: Part III, 1956) in which there are a number of dialectal variations. The main division is that between the speech of the northern Somali, who are the subject of this essay, and the southern Somali to whom only passing reference will be made. Greenberg (1955) classes the Somali language as belonging to the Eastern branch of the Cushitic subfamily of the Afro-Asiatic family.

Intracultural divisions

This primary division in the Somali nation is based on culture, economy, and history as well as geographical location. The northern Somali are those

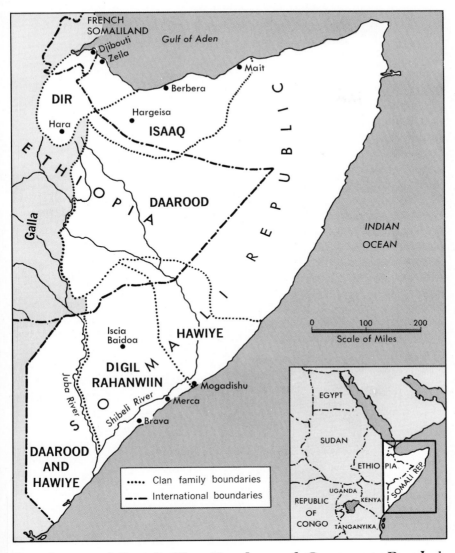

Distribution of Somali Clan Families and Contiguous Peoples[1]

clans and lineages who are dedicated to a mainly nomadic existence and who extend northward from the Shibeli River in the south to French Somaliland in the north (see map). They also occur again south of the Juba River in the Somali Republic, and reach into Kenya, where they form the dominant Somali element. The southern Somali form an enclave between the Juba and Shibeli rivers.

This distribution, which has brought northern Somali to the most

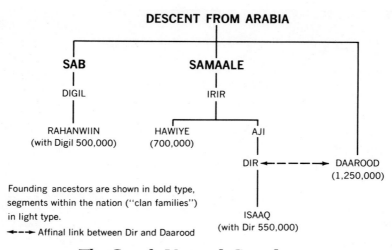

DESCENT FROM ARABIA

SAB
│
DIGIL

SAMAALE
│
IRIR

RAHANWIIN
(with Digil 500,000)

HAWIYE
(700,000)

AJI

DIR ◀ ─ ─ ─ ─ ▶ DAAROOD
(1,250,000)

ISAAQ
(with Dir 550,000)

Founding ancestors are shown in bold type,
segments within the nation ("clan families")
in light type.

◀─ ─▶ Affinal link between Dir and Daarood

The Somali National Genealogy

southerly boundaries of the nation, is the result of a concerted series of migratory movements from the north over the last ten centuries. In the course of these, earlier Negroid and Galla groups (the latter predominating) were displaced or absorbed by conquering Somali. Those Somali who settled in the arable regions between the Shibeli and Juba rivers—the only permanent watercourses in the entire area—turned to cultivation and intermingled with a number of small Galla groups. This has led to the formation of the agricultural southern Somali as a distinctive group with its own habits, culture, and dialect—and with a more hierarchical political system, founded on territorial ties, than that of the northern Somali described in this essay. The further movement of northern pastoral Somali into Kenya, largely at the expense of the Boran Galla and the Warday (Bararetta Galla), took place mainly in the late nineteenth and early twentieth centuries, and was only effectively arrested by the establishment of administrative posts about 1912.[4] No sociological study of these southerly representatives of the northern pastoralists has yet been made, but with a few exceptions, they appear to have the same culture and social structure as described here.

As a whole the Somali are divided into groups on a lineage basis, patrilineal descent being the fundamental principle of social and political division. By reference to his ancestors a man's relations with others are defined and his position in society is established. Somali themselves say that what a person's address is in Europe, his genealogy is in Somaliland. And here, of course, far more is implied than a person's address actually signifies in Western society today. For by virtue of his genealogy of birth, each individual is provided with a wide range of agnatic kin with whom he cooperates at different levels of grouping as occasion demands. The whole Somali nation is encompassed in the single national genealogy shown in the diagram. This is a simplified version, and the population figures given on the diagram are only approximate estimates for which no great accuracy can be claimed. [For fuller details see I. M. Lewis, *A Pastoral Democracy* (1961; 7–15)].

The primary division in the genealogy is between the descendants of Sab—the Digil and Rahanwiin—and those descended from Samaale—the Dir, Isaaq, Daarood (connected by marriage to the Dir), and Hawiye. The former are the southern Somali,[5] the latter are the northern pastoralists.

TYPES OF AGNATIC GROUPS • The six agnatic groups (the Dir, Isaaq, Daarood, and Hawiye, and in addition the Digil and Rahanwiin) shown in the genealogy represent generally the upper limit of agnatic affiliation within the Somali nation and are conveniently referred to as "clan families." Each clan family is a large, highly segmented lineage, with a genealogical span to the founding ancestor of sometimes as many as thirty named generations. These vast lineage units are widely dispersed and are too unwieldy and too widely scattered to act as corporate political entities, although clan-family affiliation has a political value, especially in modern party politics. Their largest component lineages, which for convenience I refer to as "clan," do, however, frequently act corporately in politics.

Clans range in size from groups of 10,000 to groups ten times that strength and have a genealogical span of up to twenty named generations to the clan founder. They are vaguely localized in the sense that the pastoral movements of the members of a particular clan tend to follow a similar pattern over the years. But no pastoral clan has a rigidly defined territory. In keeping with this tendency toward some degree of territorial exclusiveness, many clans have clan heads, generally styled "Sultan," an office that will be discussed in detail later.

Within the clan the next significant lineage grouping that can be usefully distinguished is that of the "primary lineage." This has a named generation span of approximately six to ten generations, and is usually an exogamous group. There is no office of leadership at this level of grouping nor a tendency toward localization.

Finally, within the primary lineage and at the base of this system of lineage political divisions stands the "dia-paying group." This is the fundamental political and legal unit in northern pastoral Somali society. It is a corporate group of a few small lineages tracing descent through from four to eight generations, and having a strength of between a few hundred and a few thousand men. The title "dia-paying group" applied to this order of lineage division by the administration refers to the unity of the group in payment and receipt of blood compensation (Arabic, *diya*; Somali, *mag*). This will be examined in detail in a later section. In the northern regions

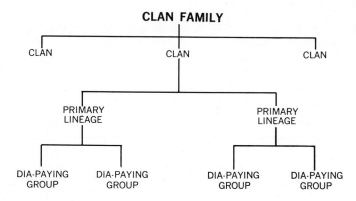

Types of Somali Agnatic Groups

of the republic, with an estimated population of some 650,000 individuals, there are some 360 such dia-paying groups. Dia-paying groups are led by their elders, and have traditionally no single office of leadership. But their distinctiveness is such that it has long been administrative practice to appoint dia-paying group headmen.

These four orders of lineage division are all that need be distinguished here. But although corporate action most commonly occurs at these levels of segmentation in the lineage system, it should be appreciated that the possible range of social and political action is not solely confined to them. In principle every ancestor in the genealogies represents a point of potential unity or division. And the fact that the diffuse agnatic loyalties of the individual are most commonly limited by contract at the level of the dia-paying group does not prevent the mobilization of extended agnatic loyalties by wider contracts. Finally, for an understanding of Somali culture it is only necessary to emphasize that patrilineal descent and contract are together the fundamental principles that order social, political, and legal behavior, and, indeed, pervade all aspects of Somali life.

Ethos

The northern Somali are highly egalitarian and do not have a hierarchical system of political offices. Policy is made by ad hoc councils at which all adult men speak; and in their harsh environment the pastoralists excel in guile and strategy. At the same time, although no firm political units existed beyond the clan[6] prior to colonization in the nineteenth century, Somali have nevertheless an extreme sense of national pride and superiority. They are also warlike, and competition over access to water and pasture readily engenders disputes and bloody feuds that smolder for generations. Even under modern administration, unsettled disputes are left to the test of military strength; and the assumption that might is right still has over-whelming authority. Apparently in keeping with the ease with which force is resorted to, magic, witchcraft, and sorcery do not feature prominently, and in general occur only in contexts where fighting is inappropriate or impossible. The northern pastoralists, indeed, are markedly pragmatic in their assumptions, with, however, a deep trust in the power of God and in the authority of his Prophet.

Not all men are warriors. A minority of men among the pastoralists hold the role of *wadaad* (man of religion), as opposed to that of *waranleh* (warrior, literally, spear bearer). However else he may gain his livelihood, he who practices as a religious expert is a *wadaad*; and all others are *waranleh*. By definition if not always in practice, men of religion are excluded from direct participation in fighting, and the role that ideally they are expected to sustain is that of mediation between man and man and man and God. The extent to which this ideal divorcement from secular affairs is realized in practice will be seen later.

Finally, it must be emphasized that despite some seventy-five years of alien government and a great extension of contact with the outside world, as well as many modern developments in trade, education, social services, and party politics, the traditional northern pastoral system continues in full vigor.

ECONOMY

ECOLOGY · The country occupied by the So-mali as a whole is not an enviable environment, and the conditions with which the northern pastoralists have to contend are particularly harsh. Much of the land over which they move is semidesert, the rainfall in most places is scanty, and the prevailing vegetation is coarse grass and scrub bush. Following the salient ecological and climatic characteristics, Somali distinguish three main topographical zones. From the coast inland these are known as *Guban, Ogo,* and *Haud.* The Guban (from *gub,* to burn) is the scorched coastal plain that extends from French Somaliland in the west to Cape Guardafui in the east and includes the barren northern escarpment of the maritime foothills. Over most of this dry zone the annual rainfall rarely exceeds four inches, occurring mainly in the comparatively cool months from October to March. Despite the general desiccation, however, water is relatively easily available immediately below the sandy topsoil.

The next zone, the Ogo highlands, rises behind the Guban and extends as a declining plateau toward the south, its extension in this direction being roughly defined by the most southerly permanent watering places of the northern regions. From a height of some 6000 feet at the edge of the northern escarpment, the Ogo drops to 3000 feet in the south. Rainfall

A Stretch of the Northern Coast

varies roughly with altitude from four to twenty inches in the northwest, where to some extent pastoralism gives place to the cultivation of sorghum.[7]

This zone is again fairly well watered, but wells—often in dry river beds, for there is no permanently flowing water—have to be sunk to a greater depth than in the Guban. Two main types are distinguished, a shallower "mud well" and another type that is deeper. Because of the considerable labor expended in their excavation, maintenance, and use, the deep wells are regarded as the property of specific clans and lineages. Exclusive rights to use the shallower mud wells are similarly claimed by smaller lineages and groups of agnatic kin. But in those areas of the Ogo where water is especially abundant in all seasons, exclusive rights are usually not asserted and men and stock of different and even rival lineages frequent the same wells. The water resources of the Ogo are particularly important for they provide the "home wells" of those lineages and clans that in the dry seasons inhabit this zone and contain the places where their grazing camels are watered.

To the south, the Ogo descends into the third topographical zone, the Haud, which is a vast area of rolling plains and often red soil with—after the rains—a rich covering of tall grass interrupted in places by belts of thick scrub. This zone has no permanent water, but its rich grasses provide excellent pasture, especially for camels. And in many places in the Haud are natural basins that flood after the rains to form ephemeral lakes. Here tall Acacias grow, and these seasonally flooded basins are the sites of small, semipermanent trading settlements. For the pastoralists these pools provide water for human consumption, and for the needs of the less hardy stock: sheep, goats, cattle, donkeys, and horses; their water is too precious to be given to the grazing camels. When the pools dry out, as they usually do quickly unless the rains are exceptionally abundant, resort is had to the shallow wells usually found in close proximity to them. These are generally the property of individuals or of groups of close kin (for example, brothers or cousins). They, too, dry up periodically and often yield only a little water after much expenditure of effort in their excavation. Like the ponds with which they are often associated, they are used to satisfy the needs of man, of the weaker stock, and of an occasional milch camel.

In some parts of the Haud, to alleviate its deficiencies in water, artificial basins have been excavated, often with government help. Some are lined with cement and hold thousands of gallons of water, which is distributed by vehicles owned by enterprising individuals. This provides a lucrative income in the dry seasons, and extends considerably the grazing movements of sheep and goats.

Throughout these three zones there are four main seasons, two wet and two dry, as well as a host of subsidiary seasons that cannot be discussed here.[8] In the Ogo and Haud generally the *gu* (main rains) fall in the spring, beginning about April in the south and west, and May in the north and east, and generally coinciding with the advent of the southwest monsoon. In good years, *gu* is the season of plenty, when fresh green grass abounds and milk is plentiful. The breeding of most stock is regulated so that most of the young are born after the spring rains; this is also the time of marriage and a general expansion of social activities.

About June or July, as the southwest monsoon winds are at their height, blowing dust everywhere, the *hagaa* (dry season) begins. The vegetation and pastures dry up more or less rapidly according to the abundance of the *gu* rains, and the dry season pattern of watering starts. A short hot period at the end of *hagaa* heralds the arrival of the *dayr* (autumn) rains, which, falling about September or October, provide another, briefer breeding season. The southwest monsoon drops and veers to the northeast. The *dayr* rains fall most heavily on the Guban coastal areas and last sporadically until December or January, when the *jiilaal* (main dry season) commences. This normally is the severest season of the year when stock are likely to die of thirst and debilitation, and man's life also may be endangered. At best people manage to survive at a mere subsistence level, but the line between survival and disaster is precariously narrow.

Pastoralism

Northern Somali pastoralism is based on the husbandry of sheep (the black-headed, fat-tailed "Persian" variety) and goats, camels (single-humped dromedaries); cattle (Zebu), donkeys, and horses.[9] Sheep and goats supply milk and, in the dry seasons, especially, when these animals are often killed for meat, their skins are bartered or sold to traders, who export them in large quantities. Camels also supply milk and the means by which the nomad's collapsible hut or tent is carried from place to place in his pastoral movements. However, they are not usually ridden. On festive occasions their meat is eaten, their skins are used to make sandals and other articles and are also exported. Cattle, which are not very common among the nomads of the north, are bred for export as beef stock, and also for milk for domestic consumption. Donkeys are raised purely as beasts of burden and are common in the towns and in some of the more arid areas of the northwest. Finally, horses, which, though in short supply today, retain their value as the prestige possession par excellence, are ridden on ceremonial occasions, sometimes in battle, but more generally as the traditional means of rapid transport.

DIET • The milk of sheep, goats, camels, or cattle forms the staple of the pastoralist's diet. It is drunk fresh or curdled but is also made into a clarified butter used as a cooking oil for grain or rice and meat. Meat is mainly from domestic stock, little use being made of game. Tea is widely drunk and is prepared as a milky, heavily sweetened, and most sustaining beverage.

SEASONAL PASTORAL MOVEMENTS • The cycle of the year is the rotation of the four seasons and the annual system of movement conforms to it. Through their livestock the Somali pastoralists are acutely conscious of their heavy dependence on their scant natural resources. They are also well aware of the extent to which their lives conform to the rhythm of the seasons and of the delicate balance between adequate food supplies and famine: as one proverbial expression puts it, "Abundance and scarcity are never far apart; the rich and poor frequent the same houses." Indeed, there is an overall complex of movement of people and livestock between Guban, Ogo, and Haud in response to the seasonal distribution of pasture and water.[10]

In general outline the pattern is that, in the spring, about April or May, when the Guban coast becomes unbearably hot and dry, groups pasturing there move up toward the cooler highlands. These in turn have been largely deserted by those other groups whose home wells are in the Ogo and who have moved away southward into the Haud in search of new pasture there. This distribution, with some return to the Ogo home wells, more or less persists until the *dayr* rains of September or October. Then the northernmost lineages return to the coast, which at this time of year offers fresh grazing. And as *dayr* rapidly gives place to the drought of *jiilaal*, the groups that are

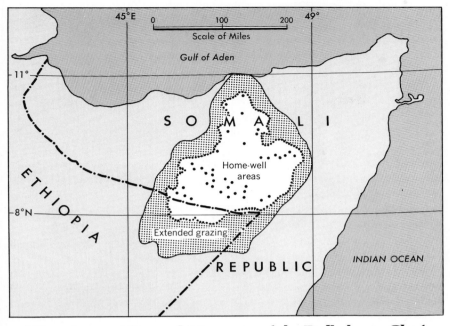

Main Areas of Pastoral Movement of the Dulbahante Clan[1]

in the Haud withdraw toward their home wells in the Ogo highlands.

Thus the pastoral cycle of movement is primarily dictated by the occurrence and distribution of water and pasturage. Other subsidiary factors affecting movement are the prevalence of disease (for example, seasonal malaria), the availability of salt grazing for the stock, and a number of social factors. The most significant of these is the state of the relations among lineages competing for access to the same pastures. Hostility tends to force groups apart and, if conditions permit, leads them to adjust their movements so that contact is minimized. Equally, administrative direction, often imposed to reduce conflict or to safeguard grazing, may affect the pattern of movement.

In general, it must be emphasized that, despite these fairly well-defined four seasons, the annual rainfall varies considerably in both amount and distribution. The seasons are thus by no means constant and, with the small margin that exists between subsistence and famine, necessitate an exceedingly tight adjustment of the pastoral life to its environment. Thus there is no strict localization of pastoral groups in northern Somaliland. Pasture is regarded as a gift from God to Somali in general and not as something to be parceled out among specific groups. Men of different lineages and clans move with their stock where grazing and water are available. Ultimately the only limitation on the movements of the individual is the necessity to

Framework of a Somali House

be within call of his kin should their help be required. Hence lineages are widely deployed in the pastures, intermingling with those of the same and other clans wherever water and grazing are plentiful.

Yet at the level of the clan there is some tendency, based largely on regular usage, toward an association with particular areas of grazing, subject always to the ability to defend these against hostile intrusion. In the nomadic flux, the main points of localization are the home wells where particular lineages water their grazing camels in the dry seasons, and the small trading settlements found close to watering places all over Somaliland. These are not immutable, however. Titles to wells are spread widely, no group relying on home wells in one place only—and wells periodically dry up. Trading settlements, also, are abandoned from time to time in favor of new sites in response to changing patterns of pastoral movement. The prevailing picture is therefore a fluid arrangement of men and livestock on the ground. Permanent ties to locality consequently are not a significant feature of northern Somali pastoralism.

Grazing units

In response to their ecological resources, the pastoralists have developed two separate grazing units: the nomadic hamlet, which is essentially a sheep- and goat-herding unit; and the camel camp, which contains only grazing camels. This division reflects the superior endurance of camels and their less-demanding watering needs in comparison with those of sheep and goats. In the dry seasons, sheep and goats require regular watering every few days and must move in close proximity to water. Camels, on the other

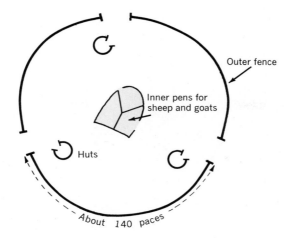

Outer fence

Inner pens for
sheep and goats

Huts

About 140 paces

The Somali Nomadic Hamlet

hand, can go without water for fourteen days or longer on dry grazing, and have a correspondingly wider range of movement.

THE NOMADIC HAMLET · Physically, the hamlet consists of a cluster of nomadic huts, each of which is made of skins and mats draped round a hemispherical frame of curved wooden supports and held together by bark rope lashings and tethering ropes. On the move, the main house supports are packed upside down on the backs of the pack camels, with the mat and skin coverings and all the other furnishings and accouterments. Each married woman, or widow, has her own hut, the huts of the hamlet being arranged within a roughly circular fence of thorn bushes for protection against wild animals and other marauders. As will be seen from the diagram, similar thorn-fence pens are erected within the enclosure to house the sheep and the goats at night. Usually each married woman has a separate pen for her flock, and the husbandry of the sheep and goats is essentially the province of women and unmarried girls. From an early age, the latter plait bark ropes in the shade of a bush as they shepherd their flocks, often at a considerable distance from their hamlet.

Socially the *guri* or *reer*[11] (nomadic hamlet) consists of a group of nuclear families whose heads are principally closely related agnatic kin, with their flocks, pack camels to transport their *aqal* (tents) and effects, and occasionally a few milch camels or cattle. The hamlet may be no more than the domestic group of a man and wife, or wives, and their young children, with the livestock necessary for their support. Often, however, it consists of several nuclear or polygynous families of brothers, or of other closely related agnates with their dependents. Affines and other nonagnatic

On the Move A Somali family is on the move. Note the supporting poles and covering mats for houses lashed on the pack camels.

male kin are also frequently included, for the hamlet does not have an exclusively agnatic composition.[12]

Some conception of the composition of a typical nomadic hamlet may be gained from that led by Ahmad Faarah of the Dulbahante clan, *reer Farrah Hagar*, as it was camped in an area of poor grazing in the *jiilaal* of 1956. Besides Ahmad and his wife and four young children, there were the families of two other men of Ahmad's dia-paying group. Each family had its own hut, and a separate pen for its sheep and goats, few of which were in milk at the time. Ahmad's wife had a flock of some ninety head, and the wives of the other two men, seventy and eighty, respectively. There were five pack camels used jointly by the three families in their movements.

Thus constituted as essentially a domestic group of a man with his wife or wives, with his father and brothers and their families—or more frequently of close agnates of the same dia-paying group with their dependents—the hamlet itself is an unstable unit. Through the seasons, and from year to year, a given hamlet fluctuates considerably in composition. This is not merely the effect of changes due to different stages in the formation, growth, and dispersal of families. All men do not leave their father's hamlet when they marry, nor do brothers always separate on their father's death. Many of the fluctuations in hamlet composition are quite independent of such processes. At one time a man's several wives may live together in the same hamlet; at other times they move as widely dispersed units among whom their husband shares his time and affection. Men, moreover, move about considerably among their kin and relatives, attaching their families now to one group of kin, and now to another. Thus in the grazing movements of a single season, the same individual families often assume quite different patterns of grouping, although these are mainly within the field of agnatic connection.

On the average, nomadic hamlets contain three nuclear families. Sometimes, however, they swell to include five or six families, but rarely more except in time of war, when larger aggregations afford better security. Whatever its composition, the hamlet is generally led by the eldest man of the lineage whose members are numerically dominant in it.

THE CAMEL CAMP • The husbandry of the flocks is essentially women's work and women load and unload the pack camels. Although men assist the women with the watering of the flocks, their attentions are mostly taken up with the management of the grazing camels. As soon as they reach the age of about seven or eight years, boys are sent out to the camel camps to learn the stern art of camel husbandry. The camel camps are the initiation schools to the nomadic life. There is, however, no formal system of initiation, for the northern Somali have neither age grades nor age-set organization. Thus, although boys are circumcised shortly after birth, or more generally at about the age of puberty, to make them *halaal* (clean) in a religious sense and fit for marriage, this is not an occasion for formal instruction, esoteric or otherwise. The act, which is not a great ritual occasion, is usually performed individually and never on a whole group of boys at a time.

In the camel camps, the youths and boys—sons, younger brothers, nephews, and occasionally hired servants of the camel owners—live mainly on the milk of the camels in their care. Often they have no means of cooking, and so sleep in the open, in a huddle, in the center of the camp among the camels. In the dry seasons especially, when milk and water are scarce, their lot is exceedingly hard. In addition to the physical rigors of their existence, the regular movements from pasture to pasture, and the long treks to the wells, they must also be constantly alert for raids or attacks. Yet after the rains, when fresh green pasture and milk are abundant, and the young camel herders have less to do and can move from hamlet to hamlet in search of unmarried girls, their privations are forgotten.

Physically, the camel camp is a much more rudimentary affair than the nomadic hamlet. It consists merely of a rough thorn fence cut out of the bush and generally thicker than that surrounding the hamlets. Within this protecting fence are separate herds of camels, and at the center is the small clearing where the herders sleep. Camps rarely have more than four or five herds, each containing upwards of a hundred camels. And these are almost exclusively those of close agnatic kin, within the same range of patrilineal affiliation as is found in the composition of the nomadic hamlet.

In contrast to the hamlets, however, camel camps very rarely include the stock of nonagnates. This markedly agnatic character of camel-herding units relates to the role of camels in Somali society. Although individuals have primary rights over them, camels are also regarded as part of the joint stock-wealth of a lineage. And unlike sheep and goats, which carry the brands of their individual owners, camels bear a common lineage brand, usually that of the dia-paying group. Camels, indeed, in a sense represent agnation, and apart from their use as a source of milk and as beasts of burden, are also the primary currency in marriage and blood-compensation: it is in terms of them that the value of a man's life is expressed.

Sheep and goats, on the other hand, are used primarily to fulfill subsistence needs. Consequently, whereas the nomadic hamlets are essentially domestic groups, the camel camps contain the capital resources of lineages. At the same time, the division between the two herding units coincides also, as has been seen, with the division of labor between the sexes. For although women are responsible for the loading and unloading of the hamlet's pack camels, camel husbandry is essentially the province of men. Moreover, while women may inherit sheep and goats and other property—though generally their rights in inheritance are much weaker than those of male heirs—it is extremely rare for them to possess full rights in camels.

The grazing settlement

Because of their different watering and grazing requirements, the hamlets with the sheep and goats and the camel camps move separately for most of the year and to some extent quite independently of each other. They tend to be closest in the wet seasons, when stock feeding on fresh green pasture need little or no watering, and the herds have greater freedom of movement. In the dry seasons, when the grazing movements of the hamlets are most restricted, the camel camps are often far distant. And like the hamlet, the camel camp does not have a constant composition. Men move their herds from one camp to another frequently but always seek to place them in a camp where there are herds belonging to other agnatic kin.

Where pasturage is sufficient, groups of hamlets or camel camps congregate to form temporary grazing settlements called *degmo* (from *deg,* to pitch camp or settle). These vary in size and density of population according to the extent of the grazing available, the local political situation, and other factors. Often about thirty or so hamlets settled temporarily in one place occupy about twenty square miles with a density of population of over twenty persons per square mile (the overall population density in the northern regions is probably about ten persons per square mile). The distance between individual hamlets varies between a few hundred yards and a mile or more.

These encampments are not stable local units. They have no formal leader; as the grazing deteriorates and in response to reports of better pasture elsewhere, they split up at random, each hamlet or camel camp moving separately, or with a few others closely related, to a new area of grazing. Here a new grazing settlement results that is often entirely different in composition. Nevertheless, despite this shifting picture, where people settle temporarily in such transitory clusters they tend to distribute themselves on the ground according to their lineage affiliation. Thus in the temporary encampments of both hamlets and camel camps residential patterns by lineage grouping are evident. This tendency of men, when they settle, to congregate according to their kinship connection is most marked in time of war, when kinsmen cluster together for support and safety. At other times, all the members of a lineage, unless their number is very small, are rarely found together in the same place.

Material culture

In dress the pastoralists of the interior still largely favor the traditional *maro*, which resembles the Roman toga and is worn by both men and women. For men the *maro* consists of two widths of trade cloth about three yards long stitched together. Great variety exists today in the way in which this traditional man's robe is worn: with or without a shirt, trousers, or jacket, or used, like a kilt, to cover the lower part of the body. On women, the flowing robe is fastened on one shoulder only, and wrapped tightly round the upper part of the body. Beneath its folds, those who can afford to, sport voluminous petticoats; brightly colored cotton bodices and dresses are also fashionable.

Men, especially the elderly or sheikhs and men of religion, usually have their heads closely shaven and covered by a small cloth cap around which a cloth turban is wound. Many, however, in the interior also go bareheaded. In some parts of the northern regions, men still often favor the older Somali style in which the hair is worn in a long and luxuriant mop without any covering; this is particularly common among young men in the interior. Venerable elders cultivate dignified, pointed beards, sometimes stained bright red with henna dye.

To a greater degree than with men, the manner in which women wear their hair reflects their social age. At the age of about four or five years, girls are shaved completely except for a little crop usually in the center of the head. Later as the hair grows again it is worked into long, full braids that signify eligibility for marriage. After her marriage, and especially after the birth of her first child, a woman gathers her hair into two buns, one behind each ear, and held in place by a net covered with a brightly colored scarf. The pastoralists regard the wearing of the Muslim veil as incompatible with the exigencies of the nomadic life, and usually it is only wives of some well-to-do traders and officials living in the towns who have their faces shielded from the public gaze.

In keeping with this nomadic existence in which the less a man has to carry the more rapidly he can move with his stock, the northern pastoralists have few possessions and their material culture is sparse.[13] Wood, fiber, and skins are the chief raw materials of their crafts. Various cooking utensils and spoons are made of wood as well as *diil* (milk and water vessels), which are carved from a single piece of wood. Similar in construction is the *wayso* (wooden bottle) used for carrying drinking water and water for ablutions before prayers. Today many of these traditional utensils have been replaced by imported metalware, but the great woven bark-fiber *haan* (water-storage vessels), which are strapped to pack camels, are still seen everywhere. Bark and aloe fiber are also indispensable as the raw material for the many ropes that the nomad uses in the construction of his house and for other purposes (drawing water, tethering camels, and so on). Many of the mats that form the walls and roof of the nomadic hut are also made from bark and grass or from palm fiber. These woven products are made by women.

Somali poetry

However limited the achievements of the pastoralists in material technology, their accomplishments in oral literature, especially in poetry, are outstanding. All aspects of Somali life are represented in an extremely wide range of types and styles of song and poetry. These range from the melodious work-songs chanted at the wells and the light-hearted ditties sung by trade-truck drivers and other young men, to the long, serious, and intricately constructed *gabays* (heroic poems) that deal with the fundamental issues of life in a way that invites comparison with Arabian poetry and the Norse sagas.[14]

This classical poetry plays an extremely important role in Somali society, for poetry is used as a means of public communication to influence opinion. Some poems are designed to incite kinsmen to avenge past wrongs; others, to forget them. Praise and blame are most effectively spread about the country through this medium. It is hardly surprising, therefore, that modern Somali political parties should make extensive use of poetry in their propaganda.

SOCIAL ORGANIZATION

Castelike groups

Leather- and metalworking are left mainly to three specialist class groups known as *Midgaans, Tumaals,* and *Yibirs*.[15] These people were traditionally bondsmen attached to Somali families and lineages, although today many have achieved at least a partial enfranchisement.[16] They number in all only a few thousand in northern Somaliland. Traditionally they are excluded from marriage with other Somali and have their own separate social organization modeled on and attached in subservience to that of their patrons. Only recently have they begun to form independent dia-paying groups with the same status as those of other Somali. The *Midgaans,* who are the most numerous of the three groups, and the *Yibirs,* who are the least numerous and who enjoy a considerable reputation as sorcerers, both make leather goods: prayer mats, saddles, bridles, whips, shields (now rather obsolete), sandals, and amulets, and so on. The *Midgaans* also practice a lucrative trade as barbers in the main towns. The *Tumaals*, on the other hand, are primarily metalworkers and are skilled in making spear points, a variety of types of knife, and ax heads, and so on. They do much of the metal repair work on automobiles. Today they also repair and maintain rifles, which to a considerable extent have replaced spears as weapons.

Child training and socialization

Traditionally children were not weaned until their second or third year, but today are often weaned earlier. In their early years children are brought up permissively, little emphasis being paid to toilet training. The sexual difference between boys and girls is stressed, however, from an early age, girls always wearing clothes that conceal their genital organs. From the age of about seven or eight, while girls remain with their mother to learn the woman's work connected with the husbandry of sheep and goats, boys are sent out to the camel camps.

Marriage and kinship

Girls marry for the first time usually between the ages of fifteen and twenty, and men between the ages of eighteen and twenty-five. The choice of a bride is not a matter for the individual alone. Parents and other senior agnates still exercise considerable control over matchmaking, for marriage not only unites the bridal couple but also establishes a new and important relationship between their respective lineages.

BETROTHAL · The favorite time for seeking a marriageable girl is the *gu* (spring). At this season the camel camps are often close to the hamlets, and in the evening the young camel herders go around adjacent hamlets serenading girls and inviting them to join them in dancing. Sometimes youths and girls dance together; more generally, perhaps, the sexes dance separately and songs are exchanged in which would-be suitors boast of their riches in livestock and the strength of their lineages. The girls reply obliquely and often in a teasing vein. Such occasions are, however, highly restrained, for the pastoralists are puritanical to a degree and set a high value on virginity at marriage. A girl's virginity prior to her wedding night is safeguarded by infibulation, which usually takes place about the age of ten to twelve years, but is sometimes performed earlier.[17]

Yet, however decorous, such fleeting contacts often enable a young man to select a girl whom he would like to marry. Here, of course, the immediate appeal is physical, but the ultimate criteria are the wealth and standing of the girl's family and lineage, her own disposition and physical strength, and the desirability of the union in the context of the current political situation.

The formal approach to the girl's family is made by some elder kinsman of the suitor. If the proposal is pleasing to both sides, the first matters that have to be arranged are the marriage payments. The first of these is a *gabbaati* (betrothal gift) paid in livestock or cash, and rarely more than some thirty dollars in value, which establishes the engagement. After receiving this gift, the bride's kin are liable to pay damages should they accept any other offers for their daughter. The fiancé, on the other hand, may forfeit his payment if he breaks off the engagement or is unreasonably slow in completing the remaining and more substantial marriage payments.

MARRIAGE • This bridewealth payment is known as *yarad*, and in all satisfactory unions its receipt evokes a corresponding dowry called *dibaad*. Thus the marriage payments involve an exchange of wealth between the families and lineages concerned, the amount varying with the wealth of the parties and the desirability of the union.

Unless the young man is independently employed, the bulk of his first bridewealth comes from his father's stock. This may be augmented from the groom's own "navel-knot" stock—the small herd that has developed from the beast or two he received at birth as the nucleus of his rights in livestock. Other contributions are likely to come from elder agnates within the dia-paying group, and from maternal uncles. On the girl's side, the bridewealth received is added to her father's herds and flocks, smaller portions being distributed more widely within the same range of kin as have contributed to the outgoing bridewealth payments.

As indicated, the principal medium in which the marriage payments are made is livestock. Money, however, is also widely employed for this purpose, so that the total bridewealth is often paid in a mixture of stock (principally camels), money, and other goods. Although the return dowry gift often includes milch camels, it consists essentially of pack camels laden with mats and skins, and all the parts of the nomadic hut and its furnishings. There will also be a flock of sheep and goats. The aim of this gift is to provide the couple with their house and accessories and enough sheep, goats, and camels to set them up as an independent stock unit. Thus the bridal house—the nomadic hut that the wife will use during her marriage—is a gift from the woman's kin to her husband. It is erected at the bride's own home, where the wedding normally takes place and where the bride may stay a few months— or until her first child is born—before moving off with her new house and flocks to assume the normal pattern of virilocal residence. The wedding festivities last seven days and are usually concluded by a party in which the *mawliid* (Prophet Mohammed's birthday service) is read. During the wedding period the couple are entertained at the expense of the bride's family.

Camels Are a Major Form of Bridewealth These camels are watering in a dry river bed.

The essential purpose of the bridewealth and dowry transactions is to establish an effective affinal relationship between the lineages of bride and groom (Lewis 1962). The definitive marriage transaction is not these, but the Islamic *mahar* (personal dower), a separate gift given by the husband to his bride and normally of much less value than the bridewealth. The dower is agreed to in the presence of witnesses before the sheikh or man of religion who solemnizes the union of the couple. It is this brief Muslim ceremony, including the husband's undertaking to give his wife a stipulated dower, that creates the marriage union. It is performed *before* the couple enters the bridal house as man and wife and *before* the marriage is consummated. In practice, however, this personal dower is rarely actually given to the bride at the time it is promised. Usually it is held over as something the wife may claim on divorce, although even then many women do not claim it.

Nevertheless, it is this dower agreement and not the exchange of bridewealth and dowry that joins a man and woman in legal marriage and gives the husband full rights over all the children born of his wife during their union. This is seen very clearly in elopements where bridewealth and dowry are dispensed with, at least initially, but never the *mahar* dower ceremony.

The exchange of bridewealth and dowry, on the other hand, serves to establish an affinal link and, in the next generation, a matrilateral tie between the lineages concerned. The content of the relationship so set up is seen in the customs of widow inheritance and the sororate. Once bridewealth and dowry have been exchanged, a man has a pre-emptive right to marry the widow of a deceased brother or other close kinsman, and similarly a right to a replacement for his wife in the event of her death. Both types of union give rise to new families, and in the case of widow inheritance children are born to the name, estate, and lineage segment of the new husband. Full bridewealth and dowry are not normally exchanged in such marriages, but in each case the contraction of a new personal dower is essential.

There are no preferential unions in northern Somaliland. But the primary lineage is normally, and the dia-paying group always, exogamous. In genealogical terms this means that people must be separated by at least six or more generations before they can marry. These proscriptions are not enforced by ritual sanctions, nor notions of incest, which are evoked only in relation to sexual intercourse between very close kin. They are, however, enshrined in customary law and supported by fines and other penal sanctions. They are explained in terms of preventing any weakening in the solidarity of strongly united groups. The converse of this is that marriage is encouraged between distantly connected groups, or between groups who have no direct agnatic relationship, for here marriage is regarded as a means of providing social links where few or none exist.

DIVORCE • Despite the distinct corporate aspects of marriage and in many cases its quasi-political significance, divorce is common. Thus in a group of 77 marriages, 16 were broken by death, and 19 by divorce, giving a divorce ratio of 32 percent (Lewis 1962). This fairly high rate of divorce in this strongly patrilineal society appears to be correlated with the fact that although marriage gives a man full rights over his wife's procreative powers during their union, it does not result in the legal identification of a wife with her husband's group. Thus the burden of responsibility for a married woman's blood-debts, should she incur any, lies with her own kin and not with her husband's kin.

There are many possible causes of marital discord that, unless overridden by other considerations, may lead to divorce. These include friction among *dangalo* (co-wives, literally, "those whose interests cross"), barrenness, and infidelity on the part of the wife.

When divorce occurs, the children of the union are at the disposal of the husband. The husband holds inalienable rights over all his wife's children born during their marriage,[18] and these rights are further safeguarded by the Islamic proviso whereby a divorced woman (or a widow) may not remarry until three menstrual periods have passed, showing that she is not pregnant. In practice most husbands allow a divorced wife to take her young children with her, to be returned when they are older. And when the husband is in the right (and this includes barrenness of his wife) he is entitled to the bridal house and to a partial return of bridewealth, according to the circumstances. Quite frequently, too, a woman anxious to escape from a partner who has become intolerable gladly gives up her rights to her stipulated dower.

FAMILIAL AND EXTENDED KINSHIP TIES • Since polygyny is practiced within the limits of Islamic law, marriage gives rise to both *raas* (the nuclear family) and to *raasas* (the polygynous family). Each nuclear family grouped about the mother and her hut is allotted its own flock of sheep and goats by

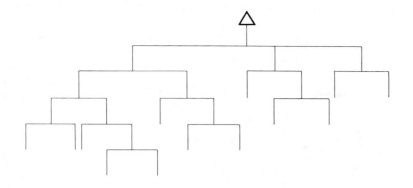

Form of Lineage Segmentation

the head of the family and forms a separate uterine estate.[19] And the children borne by a man's wives either in concurrent or successive unions[20] are regarded as siblings on the father's side but of different mothers (*walaallo is ku aabbe, waanaa kala hooyo*). This division according to maternal or uterine origin within agnatic descent is important not only in relation to property rights and inheritance within the polygynous family but also in lineage relations generally.

Although a number of words in Somali denote lineage, the commonest being the term *reer*, they do not refer to specific levels of lineage division. Specific groups are spoken of by reference to their founding ancestors as recorded in the *altirsiinyo* (genealogies, literally, reckoning of ancestors). And in seeking to establish the character of social relations that should obtain between groups or individuals, what is significant is the "number of generations counted apart" before a common ancestor is reached, or, as the pastoralists put it, before their genealogies "come together."[21]

To determine a person's agnatic group and his corresponding social and political obligations—in other words, to place him—one asks "What is your lineage?" This question is then repeated and descent traced either up or down the genealogy of the person questioned until a group socially significant to that of the questioner is named.

LINEAGE SEGMENTATION AND POLITICAL STATUS · As families develop over the generations and as lineages expand, not all their segments grow at the same rate. Some families and groups multiply more rapidly than others, and some lose many of their members through war, disease, and famine. This process of uneven development over time is reflected in the genealogies, which do not present an array of equally balanced segments at every generation, but have, on the contrary, the form shown in the diagram.

This uneven segmentation has great political significance in a society where, in the last analysis, force is paramount and fighting strength is at a premium; thus the larger or "long branch" lineages have superior political status to their "short branch" rivals.[22] In this situation, small, weak groups are often driven to ally with stronger collateral lineages. Such alliances may be based on real or putative uterine ties, for within the extended lineage system as much as within the polygynous family these provide points of unity and cleavage. Or, again, *gaashaaanbuur* (simple alliances, literally, pile of shields) may be struck without the benefit of uterine connection.

Alliances such as these are normally ad hoc measures rather than permanent unions and are not generally accompanied by the incorporation of the smaller group in the genealogy of their stronger allies. The genealogies of the northern Somali are not adjusted to validate the coalitions and alliances that the weak are obliged to join because of the uneven historical developments of lineages. Genealogical manipulation, so common a feature of other segmentary lineage systems, is not characteristic of the northern Somali organization. This is consistent with the fact that, although *tol* (agnation) is the basic structural principle of society, it does not unaided bind individuals and groups in political and legal unity. This binding is achieved by the equally pervasive *heer* (the principle of contract), which acts throughout the field of agnatic descent and occasionally outside it. It is contract that galvanizes and gives explicit content to the implicit bonds of allegiance that agnatic connection establishes.

POLITICAL ORGANIZATION

Political structure and leadership

The northern Somali pastoralists are, as has been said, highly egalitarian, and in accordance with the shifting character of their lineage divisions possess no formal hierarchy of firm political offices. At every level of lineage grouping, political leadership lies with the elders of all the constituent lineage segments concerned, and only at the level of the clan is there sometimes in addition a special political office—that of clan head. At every level of segmentation, all adult men are classed as *oday* (elders) with the right to speak in the *shir* (ad hoc councils), which deliberate matters of common concern and decide policy. Traditionally only the attached bondsmen (*Midgaans, Tumaals,* and *Yibirs*) are excluded from full participation in lineage affairs, but today this exclusion is being relaxed.

The position of men of religion and *wadaad* (sheikhs) as distinct from that of *waranleh* (warriors) requires some comment, however. Although men of religion participate in the councils of the warrior lineages to which they belong, their role is ideally a rather passive one. They are expected to bless and guide the council proceedings rather than to formulate policy, particularly in regard to war. Yet the division between the two classes of men is not absolute and sometimes those who act as men of religion in other contexts speak in council as warriors.

Subject to these qualifications, all adult men have in principle an equal say in the formulation of lineage policy. Naturally, however, the words of different men carry different weights, for respect is given to such factors as wealth, inherited prestige, skill in oratory and poetry, political acumen, wisdom, and age. Some or all of these factors, other things being equal, tend to allow one man's counsels to prevail over those of his peers. Where large groups are involved, delegations are chosen to represent the constituent lineages concerned and here, in addition to the above criteria, the strength of an elder's lineage becomes highly significant. Such council meetings are called by groups as the need arises; there are no set times or places of assembly nor offices connected with them. Usually the participants sit in the shade of a convenient tree, in the central clearing of a hamlet, or they may meet in a tea shop (universally known as a coffee shop, although tea, not coffee, is served) in a trade village or town. Decisions reached follow the consensus.

THE *Akil* OR LOCAL AUTHORITY • Despite the absence of any formal political office in the dia-paying group, it has long been customary for these groups to select an elder to represent them in their dealings with the administrations.[23] Such men, styled *Akils* or (in the former British protectorate) Local Authorities, normally receive a stipend that, though only moderate, is sufficient to attract competition for the position. An informal office of dia-paying–group headmen has thus been established, but does not carry great authority. *Akils* are regarded by their peers merely as convenient go-betweens for themselves and other groups and the government.

Although they thus fulfill a useful function, the *Akils* are frequently caught between two fires. The administration expects them to act in accordance with governmental interests and with those of the country at large, while they are expected by their own dia-paying–group kinsmen to stand by them, whatever the circumstances. Consequently, where there is a clash of interest between one dia-paying group and other dia-paying groups and the government, the *Akil* is placed in an unenviable position that takes great skill to handle. Not surprisingly, *Akils* are frequently dismissed for what the administration regards as inefficiency. Nevertheless, the position is now so well established that groups compete to have recognized *Akils* and Local Authorities and the possession of at least one of these offices seems more and more to be one of the criteria for the recognition of a lineage as an autonomous dia-paying group.

THE SULTAN OR CLAN HEAD • The position of clan head or *suldaan* (sultan),[24] that many but not all clans possess is also generally recognized by the

administration and is usually accorded a higher status and salary than that of
Akil. This position is again invested with very little real authority, for the
clan head is merely a first among peers—the other elders of his clan. The
sultan has no political or legal court, and no formal administrative or executive machinery at his disposal. Nor does he live more lavishly than does
many another prominent elder. Essentially his role is to mediate in internal
clan affairs, and to act as a representative of his clan in dealings with other
clans, although in this he would never act alone unsupported by other clan
elders. These pacificatory functions are, of course, encouraged by the administration, but only a sultan of outstanding ability and character is able to
perform them with vigor.

The office itself is not always rigidly tied to a specific lineage within the
clan, and it is possible for a wealthy and ambitious elder who has no royal
connections to run as a candidate for office. Even where the office is tied to
a particular lineage or group of lineages, the appointment is inevitably subject to popular approval. Frequently, clan conflict turns on the recognition
of candidates for office. The installation ceremony, which is one of the greatest social occasions of Somali life, involving the assembling and feasting of
great numbers of clansmen in one place, includes as its essential act the
public acclamation of the approved candidate when fresh green leaves and
flowers are showered on his head. Other aspects of the ceremony bring out
the ritual aspects of the office, for the clan head is thought of to a certain
extent as mediating between his clansmen and the clan's founding ancestor.
He is also regarded as symbolizing peace and prosperity in general and most
clans thus expect rain to fall during the installation ceremony.

Political functions

THE CONTRACTUAL PRINCIPLE · Contract for the Somali is not simply a
legal principle; it is also a political one, for many of the relations that bind
lineages of different levels are stated contractual ties. Moreover, much of
their "political" activity involves the enforcement of these contractual obligations and hence has a strongly legal character.

The Somali term *heer,* which has usually been translated as "custom" or
"customary law," means rather "contract," "compact," or "treaty." Two or
more men or groups are said to be of the same contract (*waa is ku heer*)
when their relations are regulated by a common agreement either entered
into by them directly, or inherited from their fathers and accepted as defining their relations. Although binding on all those concerned while in force,
these treaties can be contracted into by others, or contracted out of, subject
always to bilateral agreement. By extension, *heer* means customary procedure,
or even common habits and customs.

Heer, then, denotes a body of explicitly formulated obligations, rights,

Livestock Offered as Compensation Clan elders examine livestock offered as compensation in the settling of a feud. (*C. J. Martin*)

and duties. It binds people of the same treaty together in the regulation of internal affairs and delicts and also defines their collective responsibility in external relations. The most important delicts recognized by all Somali are *dil* (homicide), *qoon* (wounding), and *daliil* (insult or loss of honor). The last embraces a very wide range of infringements of rights, from adultery to defamation. For these three main categories of offense the corresponding indemnities are full *mag*[25] (blood-wealth), *qoomaal* (wound-compensation), and *haal* (damages for loss of face or honor). The amount of compensation payable for physical injury and homicide is assessed by sheikhs and *kadis* (government-appointed Muslim judges), according to the standard legal manuals of the Shafi'i School of Islamic Law, which Somali follow. These Muslim rates apply generally, although with some local variations, and form the basis for the specific compensation rates embodied in the dia-paying treaties of lineages.

Between lineages at all levels of grouping, settlement can be reached by the payment of compensation. The sanctions that control the payment of damages and compensation, however, differ according to whether the individuals or the groups concerned are or are not parties to a common treaty. *Between* dia-paying groups, and at other higher levels of lineage division where the disputants are *not* bound together by a common contractual agreement, unsettled disputes are placed before arbitrating panels. Here settlement ultimately depends on the willingness of the parties to compose their differences, which, of course, is in turn related to the current political situation and pressure of circumstances. A settlement does not have to be made. *Within* dia-paying groups (that is, within the confines of contract) on the other hand, the solidarity and common treaty obligations of the parties oblige them to reach a settlement. If necessary, this will be enforced by the elders of the dia-paying group as a whole, young men being sent to bind the recalcitrant party to a tree before which some of his livestock will be slaughtered until he agrees to obey his contractural obligations. It is this direct enforcement of sanctions within the dia-paying group that marks it off as a distinct political and legal entity.

ARBITRATION PANELS · Disputes between dia-paying groups can be taken either to a government court, or to a neutral panel of arbitrators. If the latter fail to settle an issue, it will inevitably come to the notice of the government and be tried by a government court. *Guddi* (arbitrating panels) are ad hoc bodies summoned for the occasion and consist of elders chosen for their probity, knowledge of Somali custom, and skill in mediation. Frequently a panel consists of only four or five such elders sitting in the shade of a convenient bush.

The procedure is briefly as follows. Either directly or through a representative especially skilled in the art of oratory, the plaintiff presents his case in the form of pleadings. After the plaintiff has presented his version, the defendant is summoned to speak. After hearing both sides and collecting their fee, the arbitrators deliberate in private, discussing the essence of the matter at dispute. No cross-questioning occurs: the success or failure of the plaintiff's case depends in the first place on the support of his witnesses. Three witnesses are normally required, and their joint corroboration of the plaintiff's statements decides the case in his favor. If only two witnesses support him, however, he is required to establish his case by swearing a triple oath. Where the plaintiff has the support of only one witness, those of the defendant are summoned and the same procedure is repeated on his side. The testimony of three witnesses or of two and the defendant's own triple oath are sufficient to refute the plaintiff's charges. Once the case is decided, either party may appeal and a new set of arbitrators will be appointed. Usually three hearings are the maximum allowed by custom before a dispute is judged insoluble by arbitration and more drastic means of redress are sought.[26]

Not all disputes, of course, are first taken to arbitration or to an administrative court. Frequently a wrong sustained calls immediately for revenge and there is no thought of peaceful settlement. Small incidents, such as the seizure of a few camels, or a quarrel over precedence at a well, readily lead to bitter feuds involving an ever-widening circle of clansmen on each side as incident follows incident. Here ecological competition plays an important part, for although it is not always competition over access to pasture or watering that sparks off a feud, these aggravating factors reduce the possibilities of the speedy settlement of a quarrel. Moreover, in such circumstances there are almost always old scores that, though patched up and dormant for years, are readily recalled when the struggle for survival reaches a climax in the dry seasons. At the same time, it has to be remembered that the Somali pastoralists admire military prowess and universally aspire to strength of arms. For, in the last analysis, even under modern administration, as in international power politics, it is force that decides who will prevail. Thus, even where under administrative pressure quarrels and feuds are settled by the payment of compensation and not by further fighting, the weak pay up with greater alacrity than the strong. And only men of religion to a certain extent stand aloof from this intensely competitive struggle for power.

ADMINISTRATION COURTS • Cases of serious assault or homicide that come to the notice of the administration lead to prosecutions which, if successful, culminate in sentences ranging from a few years' imprisonment to execution. If the culprit is sentenced to ten or more years of imprisonment, no blood-wealth is awarded to the injured group. But if a smaller sentence is given, or, as often happens, if the case for the prosecution fails through lack of evidence, the wronged group lodges a claim for compensation. Such claims proceed initially at least through subordinate courts that have limited juris-diction mainly within the field of customary law. In cases of injury the com-plainant appears before a *kadi* with a medical certificate defining the extent of his injuries. Compensation is then assessed according to Islamic law and a claim for this is lodged in a subordinate court. Here the court assessors may reduce the amount of the *kadi's* assessment if the injury is judged to be of a technical rather than substantial nature. These courts, established under foreign rule, are now part and parcel of the nomadic social system and ac-cepted as such.

Dia-paying codes are submitted in the form of petitions to district offices, where they are filed for future reference. And since the collective re-sponsibility defined in dia-paying contracts is that recognized by the adminis-tration, it is thus that *ḥeer* becomes a source of law. It will be appreciated that these agreements are not static; on the contrary, they are constantly being revised in the light of new conditions. Revisions to existing treaties are similarly brought to the notice of the administration. Government, in fact, has become a third force in the system of relations among rival groups. Within this system contractual agreements for defense and offense remain basic principles in the organization of social and political life. Their action is typified in the structure of the dia-paying groups and in their internal ac-tivities.

BLOOD-WEALTH AND THE DIA-PAYING GROUP • Dia-paying group treaties that the courts may be called upon to enforce show some variation in details, but in essential features conform to a common pattern. *Mag* (full blood-

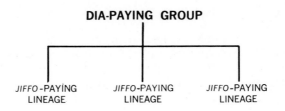

DIA-PAYING GROUP

JIFFO-PAYING
LINEAGE

JIFFO-PAYING
LINEAGE

JIFFO-PAYING
LINEAGE

Structure of a Dia-paying Group

wealth) is divided into two portions. *Mag deer* (the larger) is paid and received by all the male members of the group as a whole. *Jiffo*[27] (the smaller) rated frequently at thirty-three and a third camels (the third being paid in other currency) is paid and received by the immediate kin of the party directly involved. This twofold division of responsibility corresponds to the internal segmentation of the dia-paying group into subsidiary "jiffo-groups." Each constituent jiffo-group meets all liabilities up to the amount of the *jiffo* independently of its collaterals, calling for their support only when damages greater than this amount have to be paid.

Within the dia-paying group, homicide is regarded as being particularly dishonorable, since it defies the common solidarity of the group, and although no ritual expiation is required, the rates of compensation imposed reflect its damaging character. In most dia-paying groups the amount of compensation exacted is the *jiffo*. Since this is paid by the culprit and his immediate kin, and not by the dia-paying group as a whole, it is in practice a heavier punishment than that incurred in homicide outside the group when, although the amount of compensation due is higher, it is paid collectively by the whole dia-paying group, the murderer's contribution often being very small.

Among those clans and lineages that are rich in livestock, the contribution and distribution of compensation is assessed according to the male strength of the jiffo-groups. Male children are reckoned as well as adults, each jiffo-group paying more or less according to its numbers on the assumption that liability is measured by male strength. But in areas where livestock are less plentiful, payment is assessed on the basis of the actual wealth in stock of each family or jiffo-group. The former procedure is known as "penis-reckoning."

In an individual case of payment of compensation, whether for assault or homicide, the amounts actually contributed or received by the members of a dia-paying group tend to vary with the size of the group. In general, the larger a group is the less its individual members have to pay. This means that where a murderer belongs to a large dia-paying group his direct personal liability may be minimal. Hence, although payment of bloodwealth may reduce immediate hostility, it is generally not a sufficient deterrent to prevent further outbreaks of violence in the future.

RELIGION

The northern Somali are passionately attached to Islam, and as Sunnis adhere to the orthodox tradition of the Prophet and the "Community." In doctrine and law they follow the teachings of the Muslim jurist Shafi'i. They are devout believers and take their religious duties seriously: the daily prayers (observed more strictly by the old than the young), almsgiving to the poor, the fast of Ramadan, pilgrimage to Mecca (when possible), and the regular confession of the faith: "There is no God but Allah, and Mohammed is His Prophet." These words, indeed, spring readily to their lips in all circumstances.

Somali, however, do not follow in detail all the regulations of the Shafi'ite code of Islamic law. Where there is a serious conflict between Islamic rulings and the demands of customary practice the latter often prevail. Thus, in inheritance, Somali accentuate the rights of men and of agnatic kin at the expense of women and maternal kin to a greater degree than is consistent with the Shafi'ite provisions of Islamic law. Equally, although the Shafi'ite code stipulates that a man guilty of deliberate homicide should pay the bloodwealth due unaided and without any support from his kin, bloodwealth is paid in concert by the culprit's dia-paying group.

The pastoralists adhere firmly to the belief that God is the ultimate source of causation, conceiving of Him as a largely impersonal power before whom man is impotent and helpless. Sickness and health, good and ill fortune —all exist with His consent and are in His power to withhold or bestow. And although magico-religious procedures based mainly on the mystical power of the Koran are applied in the treatment of disease, illness is very rarely ascribed to magical causes. Nor is it necessarily regarded as a direct reflection of God's wrath. For awards and punishments do not automatically fall due in this life, but may be received after death. Man, in any case, is held to be by nature wayward and sinful; hence God's displeasure is seen as a constant condition rather than viewed as an immediate punishment for transgression.

Although the pastoralists pray to God frequently through the Prophet, they feel far removed from Him, and rely heavily on Muslim saints to intercede on their behalf. The cult of saints (Sufism, the mystical side of Islam) is strongly developed in its external rather than its esoteric aspects. To a considerable extent this is consistent with the lineage structure of society (Lewis 1956), for important lineage ancestors are venerated as Muslim saints (whatever they may have been in life) and are thus in effect canonized. Yet not all the saints venerated in the regularly performed services, in sacrifices, and in pilgrimages to their tombs are lineage ancestors. Of equal ritual authority to that of ancestors, such as Daarood and Isaaq, founders of the corresponding clan families, are the founders of the religious orders that Somali follow.[28]

Almost all Somali belong to one or another of these orders (or their subsidiary branches), and although few Somali are full initiates, adherence to them is practically synonymous with the profession of the faith. The orders have a vaguely hierarchical organization that cuts across sectional divisions in the lineage system. But all Somali, whether warriors or men of religion (the latter often holding positions of authority in the orders), are ultimately subject to the demands of their lineage loyalties. This is even the case in the few sedentary religious communities that have been established as teaching centers of the orders.

Thus, although ideally the division between men of religion and warriors relieves the former from participation in fighting and feuding, men of religion cannot afford to ignore their lineage and contractual ties: in the final analysis it is these that provide for the security of their persons and property. Yet men of religion are loath to engage directly in hostilities and seek to avoid overt participation in lineage rivalry. Their role is to conduct the religious life of the group with which they live. They solemnize marriages, officiate at funerals, lead the weekly Friday prayers and all religious ceremonies. They also teach Arabic and the elements of Islam and they make prophylactic potions and charms; in lineage politics, ideally they figure as negotiators and peacemakers. For all these functions they are rewarded by gifts; in fact, some men of religion are almost entirely dependent on charity.

In keeping with this ideal if only partly fulfilled role of neutrality, they are regarded as being mystically protected against wanton attack. It is not only shameful but also dangerous to molest the person or property of a "poor"[29] man of religion. Thus, men of religion are in a sense complementary to warriors: ideally they stand for the transcendental values of Islam that unite Somali over and above their sectional lineage divisions. In contrast to the position in some other Muslim societies, in Somaliland men of religion are not secular political leaders. Yet, on occasion, and especially when an issue touches on the common solidarity of Somali as Muslims, they can assume temporary positions of politico-religious authority. The outstanding example is Sheikh Mahammad 'Abdille Hassan (the so-called Mad Mullah), who so effectively defied the British, Ethiopian, and Italian authorities in the holy war that he led against them between 1900 and 1920 (see Jardine 1923).

SOMALI SOCIETY:
AN INTERPRETIVE SUMMARY

Despite their often similar environment, and their linguistic, cultural, and historical affinities with their Afar neighbors to the north, and their Galla and Boran Galla neighbors to the west and south, the northern Somali pastoralists have developed a mode of life and social structure that differ considerably from those of these other southeastern Cushites. Thus, although they are not quite what the French in North Africa call "grandes nomades," the northern Somali are nomadic pastoralists on a grander scale than the Afar or those Galla groups who do not cultivate. Moreover, unlike the Galla, they have no age-grade system, and their egalitarian segmentary lineage political organization has no parallel among these Galla who have so far been described (Huntingford 1955). The Afar, on the other hand, do appear to have some form of lineage structure, but it seems to differ considerably from that of the northern Somali; and the Somali are certainly more egalitarian than the Afar.[30] Paradoxically too, though the Somali are perhaps more firmly attached to Islam than the Afar, the political and social institutions of the latter suggest closer parallels with the Bedouin Arabs of North Africa and Arabia. However, a full assessment of the uniqueness of northern Somali institutions within their culture area will have to await the publication of more material on the Afar and Galla.

In a wider view, a number of characteristic features of northern Somali society are of special interest. There is first the particular ecological adjustment that the pastoralists have made with their wide-ranging and shifting patterns of grazing movement and the associated lack of firm territorial ties. This absence of effective ties to locality seems to give clanship in northern Somaliland greater priority as an organizational principle than is the case with other and otherwise comparable segmentary lineage societies. Certainly descent is utilized over a much wider range of genealogical connection as a basis for corporate political action, however transitory, than in the majority of other similarly structured systems.

On these criteria, the social system of the northern pastoralists might be held to represent a particularly well-developed example of segmentary lineage organization. Yet this is not entirely the case, for the Somali system differs in several important respects from the conventional segmentary lineage structure. Descent is not the sole basis for political and social solidarity; it is the complementary principle of contract that is of overriding importance and that binds agnates in temporary political union at different genealogical levels. And the inconsistencies that arise between the genealogical positions of groups and their real political status are resolved by contract, and generally without the genealogical rearrangements so prominent a feature of other segmentary lineage societies.

Both because of the explicit way in which the pastoralists evaluate political power, and because of the continuing prevalence of feud and war in their intensely competitive environment, these questions appear in Somaliland with unusual clarity. Moreover, the strength with which these institutions are invested is seen in the continuing vitality of the pastoral way of life and assumptions. These readily accept new items of culture, institutions, and procedures, modifying them in the process and appropriating them as new fields for the interplay of traditional sectional interests. Certainly, today, the endemic competition among lineages is deflected increasingly into a wider struggle not merely for legislative control, but also for the maximum possible share in new economic developments, in social services, in education, and in progress in general.

CHANGE

The advent of colonial rule toward the end of the nineteenth century intensified Somaliland's external contacts, which, until that time, had been primarily with Ethiopia, Arabia, and the East. Colonization, however, did not lead to any considerable influx of European settlers nor to the development of industries on a sufficient scale to make a revolutionary impact on the traditional economic and social structure. Habits of European dress were adopted in varying degrees; knowledge of European languages and culture (English, French, and Italian) spread both from the schools and from the employment that the administrations brought; many new imported goods replaced traditional articles; and although money currency was not unknown, its use spread extensively. The main new factor was the presence of a neutral, overriding authority capable of mediating between rival lineages which, in the past, were subject to no such control.

The traditional pattern of life has shown marked resilience and tenacity in the ability to adopt new values and items of culture without producing fundamental changes and to syncretize many new features. Yet towns and trading centers have played an important role in spreading foreign influence, which has given rise to aspirations that do represent a fundamental challenge to the old order. In keeping with the greater personal and social security provided in towns, townsmen generally, and especially traders, civil servants, and men of religion, feel less need of the support of their dia-paying kinsmen in the pastures. They find it increasingly irksome, too, to continue to participate in blood-dues for actions in which they have no direct part. A new conception of society exists among these new classes produced by the towns, who have a vested interest in change. Their notions have been strongly reinforced by the aspirations of the steadily growing elite of "new men" and by the policies of the administrations, which since 1950 conceived their main task to be that of preparing the Somali for independence.

While adopting its present form in response to these stimuli and to the example of African nationalism elsewhere, modern Somali nationalism draws much of its strength from the traditional cultural unity of Somali—despite their lineage divisions—and from the unifying appeal of Islam. National political organizations have grown up that are largely consortiums of rival lineage-group interests representing the common denominators of these often widely opposed interests. The strongest of these is the Somali Youth League, which began as the Somali Youth Club in Somalia in 1943. An important opposition group is the Independent Constitutional party (formerly known as the Digil Mirifle party), an organization that represents the bulk of the southern cultivating Digil and Rahanwiin clan families. The existence of this party shows the significance of the primary division in the Somali nation as a whole between the "Samaale" predominantly pastoral clans, and the "Sab" cultivators. Other parties formed in British Somaliland were the Somali National League and the United Somali party. After Somalia and British Somaliland had gained autonomy, they merged to form the Somali Republic, a state with a unitary constitution. The two existing governments (S.Y.L. and S.N.L.–U.S.P.) also merged to form a joint provisional government confirmed in power by a national referendum held in June 1961, although there was some opposition from the northern regions (the former British Protectorate).

The realization of the Pan-Somali ideal of merger of the Somali Republic with French Somaliland, the Somali area of Ethiopia, and the new North-Eastern Region of Kenya remains a burning issue, although it is the last area that at the time of writing commands particular attention. There is also a growing national awareness in a modern sense, which—by extending education and curtailing nomadism—the government of the Somali Republic hopes to promote as a corrective to the particularistic interests that divide the country and threaten its unity. Other modernist trends are evident in the tendency among political leaders to discount their proud traditions of Arabian origin and their sense of "Hamitic" particularity, and to see themselves as Africans in the new society of African nations.[31]

Notes

(1) This essay is based primarily on field research carried out between 1955 and 1957 mainly in what was then British Somaliland and was financed by the Colonial Social Science Research Council, London.

The map "Distribution of Somali Clan-Families and Contiguous Peoples," page 323, appeared in I. M. Lewis, *Pastoral Democracy* (London: Oxford University Press for the International African Institute, 1961) and is reproduced here by permission of the International African Institute and Oxford University Press.

The map "Main Area of Pastoral Movement of the Dulbahante Clan," page 331, is adapted from J. A. Hunt's *A General Survey of the Somaliland Protectorate 1944–1950* (London: Crown Agents for Overseas Governments and Administrations, 1951).

(2) The results of the recent political referendum held in the republic, however,

would imply a population of between 4 and 5 million in that territory alone. An accurate assessment of the size of the total Somali population will have to await more accurate census data.

(3) For serological data see Goldsmith (1959).

(4) On these movements of expansion and the general history of the area see Cerulli (1957), Lewis (1960a), and Lewis (n.d.).

(5) As will be seen from the genealogy, the Rahanwiin and Digil are not genealogically Somali because they do not trace descent directly from the eponymous ancestor "Samaal," who is generally taken to be the source of the name "Somali." It appears that the ethnic name "Somali" has been extended to include the Sab (Digil and Rahanwiin) in much the same way as the term "English" has come to denote all the inhabitants of the British Isles.

(6) It should be added, however, that from as early as the tenth century a number of coastal sultanates existed precariously on the fringes of Somali nomadism. Sporadically these united larger groups of Somali, particularly in the sixteenth century wars against Christian Ethiopia. See Lewis (1960a) and (n.d.).

(7) There is not space in this essay to deal with this small area of northern Somaliland. For an account of its conditions and such social changes as accompany the adoption of cultivation (they are not yet great) see Lewis (1961b:90–127).

(8) For an excellent general account of climatic and ecological conditions, see Hunt (1951:54–119).

(9) For fuller information on animal husbandry see especially Mares (1954) and Lewis (1955a:67–71, and 1961b, chaps. 2 and 3).

(10) For a full discussion of northern pastoral movements and the ecology of the area generally, see Lewis (1961b:31–56).

(11) The term *reer* also denotes a lineage, or a group of people in general.

(12) For further details see Lewis (1961b:59–72).

(13) For general accounts of Somali material culture, see Puccioni (1936: *passim*), Drake-Brockman (1912:114–122); and Lewis (1955a:82–87).

(14) For recent introductions to Somali oral literature, see Laurence (1954), and Andrzejewski and Lewis (1964).

(15) Although Somali traditions postulate an indigenous pre-Somali origin for these despised classes, they appear to have much the same physical characteristics as Somali. Nor, apart from their specialist occupations, are they culturally different from other Somali. See Goldsmith and Lewis (1958).

(16) In an effort to abolish discrimination against these groups, the National Assembly of the Somali Republic has recently passed legislation forbidding the use of these and other derogatory class names.

(17) The vulva is scarified and then drawn together and held until its sides have knit together but for a small orifice. A portion of the clitoris is also excised

to make the girl clean in a religious sense, this being the female counterpart of circumcision. The operation is usually performed individually, often by a *Midgaan* woman, and without much ceremonial. It is designed to prepare a girl for marriage and to protect her virginity until that time.

(18) During the union all children borne by the wife are the husband's, even if some may be the issue of other men with whom the woman has successfully conducted clandestine love affairs.

(19) The size of the flocks at the disposal of families varies greatly. A wife and young family of four or five children, however, will require at least fifty to sixty head if they are to survive.

(20) It is unusual for a middle-aged man of from forty to sixty years not to have married at least twice either in concurrent or successive unions. And the incidence of polygyny (concurrent unions) is fairly high (Lewis 1962: chap. 2).

(21) All agnatic kin who can trace descent from a common ancestor by a number of generations that differs only by one call themselves reciprocally *adeer*, a term which in its minimum extension is that used reciprocally between a man or woman and his or her father's brother. This term is quite distinct from that used for father (*aabbe*), father's brothers being classed not as "fathers" but as "uncles." The children of brothers call themselves reciprocally *ina'adeer* (literally, son of *adeer*) and this term is applied to all agnatic kin other than *walaal* (siblings) who trace descent through the same number of generations to a common ancestor. Strictly, if two persons differ in genealogical connection by two or more generations they should refer to each other as *awow*, the restricted meaning of which is grandfather/grandson. But in practice, young people tend to call their elders *adeer*, and their equals *ina'adeer*; indeed, the latter term is used as a polite way of addressing people in general (even when they are not agnatic kin) and has the sense of "clansman."

(22) For a fuller discussion of genealogical growth and lineage development and for other topics dealt with in this section, see Lewis (1961a and 1961b: chap. 5).

(23) This practice was applied by the Egyptians during their brief rule on the coast (1874–1885) but may have a longer history.

(24) In addition to this Arabic loanword, the purer Somali expressions *Ugaas*, *Boqor,* and *Garaad* are also widely used.

(25) In Arabic *diya*, whence "dia-paying group."

(26) For a further account of the operation of these arbitrating panels, see Lewis (1961b:228–233).

(27) *Jiffo* is literally the metal ferrule at the base of the shaft of a spear and has the sense of pinpointing the responsibility for homicide.

(28) The main orders are the Qaadiriya and Ahmadiya, both widespread in the Islamic world, generally, and highly orthodox. The former is the oldest order

in Islam with its historical center at Baghdad; the latter is a reformist movement founded in the nineteenth century at Mecca in Arabia.

(29) To Somali this word connotes physical weakness as much as if not more than poverty in worldly goods. And the pastoralists, seeking power in everything, believe that where it is not found in physical force it exists in supernatural resources. See Lewis (1963b).

(30) See Cahiers de l'Afrique et l'Asie (1959:45–163); and Lewis (1955a: 155–173).

(31) For fuller information see Lewis (1960b, 1961b:266–295, and 1963a).

BIBLIOGRAPHY

With a few exceptions the following bibliography emphasizes contemporary work. Daggered items (†) are cited as references in the text of the chapter.

Andrzejewski, B. W., and I. M. Lewis (1963†). *Somali Poetry*. London: Oxford University Press.

Cahiers de l'Afrique et l'Asie (1959†). *Mer Rouge—Afrique orientale*. Paris: J. Peyronnet & Co.
A symposium containing articles on the Somali and the Afar.

Castagno, A. (1959). "Somalia," *International Conciliation*, No. 522, New York: Carnegie Endowment for International Peace, pp. 339–404.
An excellent short account of social and political developments in Somalia up to 1958.

Cerulli, E. (1957†). *Somalia: scritti vari editi ed inediti*, I. Rome: Amministrazione Fiduciana Italiana.
A most valuable collection of Cerulli's articles on Somali history and Islam in Somalia.

——— (1959). *Somalia II*. Rome: Amministrazione Fiduciana Italiana.
A collection of articles on Somali ethnography and linguistics including previously unpublished material on the Hawiye.

Drake-Brockman, R. E. (1912†). *British Somaliland*. London: Hurst.
Contains a good deal of material on ethnography, animal husbandry, and so on.

Goldsmith, K. L. G. (1959†). *The Bloodgroups of Somali Tribes with Special Reference to Anthropology* (unpublished Medical thesis). London: London University, Westminster Medical School.
An excellent work on Somali blood groups.

———, and I. M. Lewis (1958†). "A preliminary investigation of the Bloodgroups of the 'Sab' bondsmen of Northern Somaliland," *Man*, Vol. 58, pp. 188–190.

Greenberg, Joseph (1955†) *Studies in African Linguistic Classification.* New Haven, Conn.: The Compass Publishing Co.

Hunt, J. A. (1951†). *A General Survey of the Somaliland Protectorate, 1944–1950.* London: Crown Agents for the Colonies.
A mine of information on climatic and ecological data including also genealogies of the main Northern Somali clans.

Huntingford, G. W. B. (1955†). *The Galla of Ethiopia.* London: International African Institute.

Jardine, D. (1923†). *The Mad Mullah of Somaliland.* London: N. Jenkins, Ltd.
A firsthand account by an official intimately involved in the campaigns against Sheikh Mahammad.

Laurence, M. (1954†). *A Tree for Poverty.* Nairobi, Kenya: Eagle Press for Somaliland Protectorate.
A lyrical and generally fairly accurate evocation of Somali poetry and prose.

Lewis, I. M. (1955a†). *Peoples of the Horn of Africa.* London: International African Institute.
A general account of the Somali, the Afar, and the Saho, based on a survey of the literature up to 1954.

———— (1955b†/56†). "Sufism in Somaliland: A Study in Tribal Islam," *Bulletin of the School of Oriental and African Studies,* Vol. 27, pp. 581–602; Vol. 28, pp. 146–160.

———— (1958). "Modern Political Movements in Somaliland," *Africa,* Vol. 28, pp. 244–261, 344–364. (Reprinted as International African Institute Memorandum No. 30.)

———— (1959). "Clanship and Contract in Northern Somaliland," *Africa,* Vol. 29, pp. 274–293.

———— (1960a†). "The Somali Conquest of the Horn of Africa," *Journal of African History,* Vol. 1, pp. 213–229.

———— (1960b†). "Modern Leadership and Loyalties in Somalia and Somaliland," *Civilizations,* Vol. 10, pp. 49–62.

———— (1961a†). "Force and Fission in Northern Somali Lineage Structure," *American Anthropologist,* Vol. 63, pp. 94–112.

———— (1961b†). *A Pastoral Democracy: A Study of Pastoralism and Politics among the Northern Somali of the Horn of Africa.* London: Oxford University Press.
Discusses in detail the lineage structure of the Northern Somali in relation to ecology and pastoralism and shows how traditional clan and contractual loyalties affect modern developments.

———— (1962†). *Marriage and the Family in Northern Somaliland.* Kampala, Uganda: East African Institute for Social and Economic Research.

Deals with family structure, marriage, and divorce, and discusses the stability of marriage in patrilineal societies.

———— (1963a†). "Progress in the Somali Republic," *The World Today,* Vol. 19, No. 3, pp. 167–173.

———— (1963b) "Dualism in Somali Notions of Power," *Journal of the Royal Anthropological Institute,* Vol. 93, Part I, pp. 109–116.

———— (n.d.)   *The Modern History of Somaliland: From Nation to State.* (In press) London: Weidenfeld and Nicolson.
Offers a comprehensive history of the Somali area as a whole. Deals in detail with the colonial period, the rise of modern Somali nationalism, and recent political and international developments in the area.

Mares, R. G. (1954†).   "Animal Husbandry. Animal Industry, and Animal Disease in the Somaliland Protectorate," *British Veterinary Journal,* Vol. 110, Nos. 10–11, pp. 411–423, 470–481.

Puccioni, N. (1936).   *Antropologia e etnografie delle Genti della Somalia.* Bologna: Niccola Zanichelli, Vol. III.

Tucker, A. N., and M. Bryan (1956†).   *The Non-Bantu Languages of North-Eastern Africa.* (Handbook of African Languages, Part III.) London: Oxford University Press for the International African Institute.

10

THE PASTORAL FULANI
OF NORTHERN NIGERIA

about the chapter

Many theories about the Fulani of the western Sudan by earlier
Africanists have described several striking facts about them: their
distinctive physical appearance, their pastoral mode of subsistence, their
language, and their migrations. In the light of recent linguistic analysis
these theories which posited "Hamitic" origins for the Fulani now seem
farfetched, but the "wandering Fulani" remain the center of romantic
admiration, and are now a focus of systematic research.

In their subsistence modes and in their beliefs about their livestock, the pastoral Fulani show many close parallels with the Jie (see
introduction to Chapter 5) and the Somali. The role of dairy foods
and animal products in the diet is almost the same, although the
Fulani, unlike many East African pastoralists, do not consume the
blood of their cattle. With them, too, hides and other animal products
are significant in the economy. As Stenning notes, the needs of cattle
and the identification of people with cattle influence many Fulani institutions, ranging from the formation of the family and the domestic
cycle to personal taboos and extragroup political relations. These
parallels among different peoples suggest the obvious conclusion that
certain features are basic to African herding cultures in whatever part
of the continent they are found.

Pastoralism is much more characteristic of East Africa than of
West Africa, but the Fulani are probably the most thoroughly pastoral
of the societies of sub-Saharan West Africa, which is so predominantly
agricultural. For this reason the Fulani, like the Bantu Tiriki and the

361

Mbuti, have had to develop methods of accommodating to neighboring groups more than have many of the East African herders. Tracing such extragroup relations, which are one of the most striking things about Fulani culture, is an important contribution of Stenning's research. As he notes, they are rooted in Fulani husbandry practices, their patterns of transhumance and migration, and their ethnic self-conception.

In some cases the accommodation has been so complete that herding or "cattle Fulani" have become the semisedentary or even wholly sedentary "town Fulani" who rule over agricultural populations, such as the Hausa. In Hausaland many town Fulani have given up their language and have intermarried with the Hausa. Two facts make this dominant political role of the town Fulani almost paradoxical: (1) the Fulani hold their culture and physical features to be superior to the customs and the appearance of their neighbors, so it is surprising that Fulani would ever accept cultural or genetic mixing. (2) The pastoral Fulani themselves, unlike the Hausa, have both an egalitarian and rather informal political organization. Although, unlike many African pastoralists, the Fulani are adept urban dwellers, the *pastoral* Fulani have the greatest prestige among other Fulani, and are thought of as being "most Fulani." Thus, study of the Fulani gives us insight into the processes of cultural assimilation and the way in which pastoralists may become sedentary agriculturalists.

The Fulani are Muslims and their migrations for the sake of their herds have been supplemented by their movements as an aspect of Islamic holy wars. As transhumants and especially as alien rulers, they have been a strong force in the spread of Islam in West Africa. Islam molds many of the least typically African Fulani customs, such as parallel cousin marriage and other intralineage marriages. Nevertheless, the form of Islam that the pastoral Fulani practice is modified by their concern with their cattle. The pastoral Fulani, along with the Somali and the Hausa, illustrate the modification of Islam when it is introduced into African societies.

about the author

Derrick J. Stenning was, at the time of his death in 1964, Chairman of the East African Institute of Social Research, Makerere College, Kampala, Uganda. He received his Ph.D. at the University of Cambridge and had been Research Secretary of the Applied Research Unit of EAISR. He taught at the University of Cambridge and at University College, University of London. From 1951 to 1953 he carried out field research in northern Nigeria and from 1956 to 1958 in western Uganda. His writings include *Savannah Nomads* (1959).

DERRICK J. STENNING · *The Pastoral Fulani of Northern Nigeria*[1]

INTRODUCTION

LOCATION · This chapter concerns the Wodaabe pastoral Fulani of Bornu in northeastern Nigeria. The Wodaabe are only a small part of the Fulani, a numerous, widespread, and diverse African people about which a great deal has been written.

These Fulani populations are scattered over the western Sudan, in the savanna belt, from Senegambia in the west to parts of the Central African Republic in the east. It is likely that populations describing themselves as Fulani or speaking the Fulani language number well over six million, distributed roughly as follows:

Nigeria	3,630,000
Mali	850,000
Guinea	720,000
Cameroun	305,000
Niger	269,000
Gambia	58,700
Dahomey	54,000
Ivory Coast and Upper Volta	52,000
Portuguese Guinea	36,000
Mauritania	12,000
Ghana	5,500
Union of Central African Republics	no estimate

The most important concentrations of Fulani are found in Senegambia, the Guinea Highlands (Fouta Jalon), on the upper and middle Niger, in the Northern Region of Nigeria (Sokoto, Katsina, Kano, Bornu, Bauchi, and Jos Plateau) and in the Adamawa Highlands (Adamawa, Bamenda, and Ngaundere).

These populations are known by various names in various areas. The Wolof term "Peul(s)" is widely used in French publications. In Gambia they are known by the Bambara term "Fula." The peoples of the Chad Basin call them "Felaata." In German works they are called "Fulbe."[2] This, with its singular "Pullo," is their term for themselves. Following northern Nigerian usage, they will be called "Fulani" in both singular and plural in this chapter.

PHYSICAL APPEARANCE · The zone in which Fulani are found has for many centuries been the meeting places of Caucasian (Mediterranean) and Negro peoples, and the Fulani are a classic example of racial mixture. They themselves attach great importance to a number of non-Negroid features: light, copper-colored skin, straight hair, narrow nose, thin lips, and slight bone structure, which, they say, make them different from their neighbors. But Fulani communities, as well as individuals within them, display a remarkable range of combinations of Negroid and non-Negroid physical traits.

LANGUAGE · The classification of the Fulani language, generally known as "Fulfulde," has long been a matter of controversy. This has been partly due to several of its distinctive features, such as noun classes and initial consonant alternation, that were not present in most other languages of the western Sudan. Confusion also arose through attempts to correlate the distinctive features of Fulfulde with Fulani non-Negroid physical traits and with hypotheses concerning the way they had spread over the western Sudan. Fulfulde is now classified, however, with the West Atlantic group of Sudanic languages included in the Niger-Congo family (Greenberg 1955).

It is clear that such a widespread people must speak a number of dialects. Much work has yet to be done in determining these, but there appear to be significant dialect differences in these areas: Senegal, Fouta Jalon, upper and middle Niger, Upper Volta and northwestern Nigeria, northern Nigeria, Adamawa Highlands, and Bagimiri.

There are some structural differences between these dialects, but the major dialectal differences lie in the vocabulary, which is adapted freely from the dominant or autochthonous languages of the area concerned. In addition to their own tongue, Fulani usually speak the lingua franca where this is not Fulfulde, and often master an additional minority language. Moreover, the mobility of the Fulani population must have always placed speakers of different Fulfulde variants in the same community as it does today. Continuous and often rapid linguistic changes occur. Numerous writers have commented on the comparative richness, refinement, and flexibility of Fulfulde, which must be due to these circumstances.

TERRITORIAL ORGANIZATION

Fulani communities

This chapter is about the pastoral Fulani, but in addition to these there are other Fulani populations that differ in their modes of life and social organiza-

Fulani Cattle in Katsina Province (*British Information Service*)

tion. These must be described if pastoral Fulani social organization is to be understood.

THE PASTORAL FULANI · Pastoral Fulani are known by several terms they do not use to describe themselves—Burure, Bororo, and Abore. They retain non-Negroid physical features to the greatest extent, speak the purest Fulfulde, and have in general been least amenable to conversion to Islam. Pastoral Fulani populations are found in those areas of the savanna belt where the population density is lowest, and also in well-favored highland areas. Their subsistence and wealth derive solely from their herds of cattle, although they also own sheep and goats. But pastoral Fulani do not live exclusively on dairy produce; they exchange surpluses for cereal foods in the markets. They also invariably practice a form of transhumance described below. The simple or compound family is an important domestic and economic unit in pastoral Fulani life, but agnatic lineage groups are a further strong feature of their social organization. Attention to cattle keeps the pastoral Fulani aloof from the life of village and town, but even this involves special relations with sedentary populations for rights of access to water and pasture. Historically, this has brought them into the orbit of the Muslim states of the western Sudan, in whose politics and wars they became involved principally to maintain or extend their pastoral opportunities.

SEMISEDENTARY COMMUNITIES · Semisedentary Fulani communities not only raise cattle but also have farms. The result is not mixed farming, but a dual mode of subsistence in which farming and stock raising at once complement and circumscribe each other. Farms are made according to local practices of shifting cultivation, but are likely to be smaller and to concentrate on food rather than on cash crops. Herds are also likely to be small and moved in a restricted cycle of transhumance. The farm is regarded as "home," and often lies at a convenient point for transferring labor from pastoral to agricultural work, especially for farm clearing and harvesting. The domestic unit of the simple or compound family is likely to be split annually to carry out these tasks.

Semisedentary Fulani communities arise mainly through loss of cattle. Many a pastoral Fulani genealogy is studded with such cases, which come about mainly when widespread cattle disease makes the customs of loan or gift of stock impossible. Although semisedentary Fulani often return to the fully pastoral mode of life, these communities may also be regarded as a transition to a completely sedentary, agricultural one. The pressures of maintaining a dual mode of subsistence often hasten this process. Also, in highland areas, semisedentary communities have arisen that depend on wealth in cattle and the availability of non-Fulani labor to work on farms and help tend the large herds.

SEDENTARY COMMUNITIES · Sedentary Fulani communities merge into the major ethnic groupings in which they are found and, while having strong communal and kinship links with them, also recognize traditional bonds with pastoral Fulani groups. Sometimes they simply exemplify a further stage in the process of becoming sedentary sketched above. In fact, some are communities of ex-slaves established by Fulani pastoralists in the nineteenth century, whose masters may have moved on to new pastures, or who, in the twentieth century, have relaxed control of them as a result of legislation. Also, there are communities of Fulani who, on their pilgrimage to Mecca, are forced by circumstances to halt for a period. These are found mainly in Sudan, rather than in the countries mentioned earlier. Sedentary Fulani (and semisedentary ones as well) are sometimes referred to in the literature as "town Fulani" to distinguish them from pastoral or "cattle Fulani."

STATES · The communities described briefly above are distinguished mainly by their mode of subsistence. In them, or in contact with them are specialists, the Fulani Muslim holy men. They live on fees for performing religious offices, but some also have farms or are craftsmen or traders. They may work alone, or may form hamlets with kinsmen or friends from which they travel in pursuit of their calling; some have attained considerable importance and have attracted large followings. The geographical zone in which Fulani are found has also been the scene of the rise and fall of state organizations for many centuries, and Fulani, especially holy men, have played their part in these events.

The rise of a number of empires in the nineteenth century was due to the efforts of the Fulani under outstanding leaders. These were all devout, not to say fanatical, Muslim holy men who were moved by the laxity of the Muslim states in which they lived. The general pattern of events was for the Fulani reformer to preach until he had mustered a considerable body of sympathizers and had called down the displeasure of the ruler. He then fled, like the Prophet Mohammed, and went to a poorly administered part of the country, where he collected a force and raised the flag of the Holy War. Most of these revolts were successful, and resulted in the establishment of a new dynasty (or set of dynasties). They also resulted in the establishment of a new administration in which taxation and levies of all kinds were usually considerably expanded. They resulted in a new polity in which attacks were mounted on neighboring states in the name of religion, and, in the same cause, on pagan enclaves for the purposes of obtaining slaves. It was in this way that the nineteenth-century Fulani Muslim empires of Fouta Jalon, Fouta Toro, Macina, and—eminently—Sokoto were founded.

Evolution and differentiation of Fulani communities

The different types of Fulani community or organization described above are related factually and historically over very wide areas of the western Sudan, by the process of migration. The general mass movement of Fulani appears to have started about the eleventh century in Senegal, and to have taken place eastward. By the beginning of the nineteenth century there was a sufficiently wide distribution of Fulani to make them a common factor in similar politico-religious developments in areas as far apart as Guinea and northeastern Nigeria. Since that time, and as a result of the pacification of hitherto inaccessible areas by colonial administrations, Fulani have penetrated still further, as far as parts of the Central African Republic and into Sudan. This west-east distribution of Fulani, totaling some three thousand miles, has been achieved in about eight hundred years.

The main impetus of this movement has been provided by the pastoral Fulani. Their transhumance systems have probably always been conservative, involving the knowledge of the grazing potentiality of relatively limited tracts of country. In this, small social units have been crucial, and the formation of extended groups having well-defined grazing and water rights in specific tracts to be defended by force has not occurred. Thus, herds have been maintained *not* by cattle raiding, feud, and war, but by continuous adjustment of transhumance to subtle ecological changes.

The resultant movements may be described as "migratory drift."[3] Living in their close-knit, small groups, pastoral Fulani have always formed minorities in wider societies. When state policy was adverse to them, they reacted by the more dramatic movement known as "migration." Moreover, the growth of a state's territory opened up new pastoral possibilities that Fulani skillfully seized, also by migration. In this movement they have left behind them those who might be called the casualties of pastoralism: the semisedentary and sedentary communities, and also those who represent the peak of their influence in a given area—the slave community.

For the pastoralists the savanna of the western Sudan was a vast potential grazing ground. For the Fulani holy men it was simultaneously a field of missionary endeavor among both non-Fulani and Fulani populations. It is thought that the Fulani were converted to Islam before the eleventh century in Senegal, and that Fulani holy men were themselves moving eastward. Their efforts resulted in the formation of widely dispersed religious brotherhoods in which Fulani ethnic feeling and language had a strong place. This ethnic feeling and wide dissemination of Fulani communities supported the development of the Fulani Muslim states.

THE WODAABE PASTORAL FULANI · This background is essential to an understanding of the way of life of the Wodaabe pastoral Fulani of Bornu in northeastern Nigeria, whose culture is described in this chapter. Their material equipment is rudimentary, their social groupings are small and isolated, their interests are circumscribed by the demands of their herds. But none of the features described above are alien to them. They have been, and are still, part of the great migration. Epidemics of cattle disease and political misfortunes have made some of them capitulate to the sedentary life. They trade and barter continuously with non-Fulani communities, and most of them use two languages other than their own. Some of them have visited the capitals of Muslim states where they lived, not as homeless migrants, ill-adjusted to the life of the city, but in centuries-old ethnic wards. The Wodaabe have been converted to Islam by holy men. They worship, however imperfectly, the God of millions of coreligionists. They help the pilgrim on his way to Mecca, and one or two of them have made the pilgrimage. Their legends are those of Muslim kings, and the religious wars that have swept the country. Their tribal heroes are men who profited by the wars, who acquired slaves and horses for services rendered to kings. The Wodaabe, like other Fulani communities, are historically and culturally part of the Islamic world of the western Sudan.

But they do all this on one condition—that the welfare of the herds on which they depend, and the maintenance of the family system to which cattle are so closely bound, shall not be disrupted unduly. This gives their whole social life a certain opportunistic flavor, combined curiously with certain firmly held moral notions that we shall now explore.

ETHOS

The "Fulani Way"

Despite their involvement in so many ways with the general current of western Sudanese culture, the pastoral Fulani know very well what the vital core of their society is: the maintenance of families and herds in a proper relation. For a Wodaabe man right conduct is still mainly the exercise of familial virtues. Fulfillment of duties toward elders, wives, and coevals ensures the smooth working of the family and the lineage group as economic and cooperative units. Fecundity means herdsmen and milkmaids. Good husbandry ensures that the next generation is provided for. Proper arrangement of children's marriages secures them in a social system in which they can count on the same satisfactions their fathers had. These general rules which they believe to be distinctively Fulani, are collectively called *laawol pulaaku* (the "Fulani Way").

However concrete these virtues are in practice, pastoral Fulani have made abstractions of them linguistically. The prime factor in *pulaaku* is the Fulani language. Fulfulde means not only the language spoken by Fulani, but the whole range of rights and duties peculiar to a Fulani. To say that a man "hears Fulfulde" implies an acquaintance with the language. To say that he *"has* Fulfulde" implies not only this, but that he is acquainted with Fulani social usage.

There are three other components of *pulaaku*. These are *seemteende* (modesty and reserve), *munyal* (patience and fortitude), and *hakkiilo* (care and forethought). Like the English words that seem to translate it best, *munyal* is a somewhat negative quality. A man must have *munyal*, for example, in bereavement, in polygynous marriage, at the height of the dry season, and in epidemics of bovine disease. *Hakkiilo* is mainly a technical virtue. For example, a man with *hakkiilo* never fails to inspect his cattle in the morning and never fails to obey the water spirit who first gave the cattle to the Fulani: lighting the corral fire before the herd comes back at dusk and putting it out as they leave the corral for the morning grazing. *Hakkiilo* is nowadays also used to describe the qualities of a man who is punctilious toward constituted authority. *Seemteende* is the virtue of correct conduct in personal relations in a given situation within the Fulani group to which a man belongs.

Prime among the institutions that ensure right conduct is the system of first marriage by betrothal, through which families and herds, the basic units of society, are established. These marriages are usually made between close kin, and by this means an agnatic lineage group is believed to conserve its moral purity and, indeed, to prevent its own dissolution.

This type of marriage maintains and fortifies moral virtues, and is also believed to conserve the physical type of the descent group. Members of some Wodaabe groups in which there has been a high degree of endogamy take pride in what is often their distinctive facial likeness. A Wodaabe proverb runs: "See the nose, understand the character." But, in general, Fulani can no longer correlate these desirable physical traits with lines of descent. Then the association becomes curiously reversed, so that a man or woman possessing these features is regarded as being more likely to possess the moral virtues of a Fulani. By definition, non-Fulani cannot possess these qualities because they do not follow the Fulani Way. This attitude is consistently expressed, not only in myth, but in everyday linguistic usage! Non-Fulani behave in ways that are abhorrent to Wodaabe. They eat in public and with women and children; they work unclothed; their elders dance; moreover, they are black and their noses are wide. Intercourse with a non-Fulani is in theory incompatible with membership of a Wodaabe community. On the other hand, the nose is, for the Wodaabe and the pastoral Fulani in general, one of the chief criteria of beauty, as well as the sign of moral probity.

The Guardian

These notions can be seen at work in the family. But in the past there was a still wider field of ceremonial to demonstrate these basic ideas. In the wet season, when agnatic lineage groups concentrated, they came under the control of a figure who not only was a model of conduct but who affirmed the corporateness of descent groups, and who was armed with sanctions against offenders. This was the *maudo laawol pulaaku* (Guardian of the Fulani Way). He succeeded to this office patrilineally and by primogeniture, ensuring that he was the descendant of first sons of marriage by betrothal. He was the epitome of virtue by descent.

He provided milk for the communal meal of all lineage heads that inaugurated the ceremonial cycle. He officiated at cattle fertility rites in which new stock bulls were introduced formally to their herds, and in which old stock bulls were killed and eaten ceremonially by their owners. The Guardian was responsible for initiating youths and maidens and he officiated at weddings. In short, he was the focus of a short but intense annual period of ceremonial life.

The Guardian was also a judge. He had the power of banishing one who had infringed the Fulani Way. A man who flouted the Fulani Way was regarded by the Wodaabe as mad, since he denied himself the material and moral benefits of living with his clansmen. He was also regarded in a sense as physically ill, for the moral qualities of the Fulani are associated with certain organs of the body.

It is in this context that the relation between the qualities of the Fulani Way and the basic facts of clan life—possession of a herd, wives, and children, and the cooperation of kinsmen—is best illustrated. Fulani feel that without forethought a man is likely to lose his cattle. Under certain circumstances this might be phrased the reverse way. Cattle are lost through lack of forethought, but when cattle are lost, seemingly without reference to the qualities of their owners, then the latter lose these qualities. When widespread annihilation of herds accompanied the 1897 rinderpest epidemic, Fulani cattle owners left their families and wandered unclothed in the bush, their heads unshaved, eating dust, looking for their dead livestock and, we may infer, their sanity.

ECONOMY

Ecology

West Africa may be divided into a number of lateral ecological zones. The zone of West Africa in which the economic strains of zebu cattle may be kept is generally stated to be the savanna zone, a belt of more or less open woodland or orchard bush, interspersed with grassland. The savanna zone itself is divisible into two. The southernmost of these divisions, the Guinea Savanna, has a heavier type of woodland, with many varieties of tree that are not fire-resistant. It coincides strikingly with the mean annual rainfall belt of 45–60 inches. The more northerly division, the Sudan Savanna, is a zone of lighter woodland, with a greater proportion of fire-resistant trees. It coincides with the 30–45-inch rainfall belt.

Much of the savanna is infested with certain varieties of tsetse fly, the carriers of human sleeping sickness and bovine trypanosomiasis. For convenience these will be called simply bush tsetse and riverain tsetse. The activities of tsetse, insofar as they affect cattle, are associated with seasonal changes in temperature, humidity, and vegetation cover. These changes also affect the availability of pasture and water to cattle.

Seasonal changes in northern Nigeria are brought about by the alternate action of the dry northeast monsoon from the Sahara, the harmattan, which brings the dry season; and the moist southwest monsoon from the Gulf of Guinea, which brings the wet season. The dry season starts earliest in the north of the savanna zone, in September or October, and lasts longest there, till April or May. The wet season comes to the southern part of the savanna zone in March or April, and lasts longest there, till September or October. With the onset of the dry season in the northern part of the savanna zone, standing water is evaporated and herbage is dried by the sun. As dry season conditions extend southward, they begin to affect the zone in which tsetse are prevalent. Riverain tsetse are greatly affected by this desiccation, and retreat along watercourses, or are isolated in patches of standing water. Bush tsetse retreat to thickets in underpopulated stretches of bush, where game is likely to be found. As the wet season in its turn moves progressively northward, vegetation again recovers, pools of standing water again appear, and water flows along the river and stream beds. Both bush and riverain tsetse again attain their maximum distribution. In Nigeria, this accounts for all but a small northern portion of the savanna zone.

TRANSHUMANCE MOVEMENTS · These seasonal changes also have their effects on the zebu cattle of the pastoral Fulani. At the height of the wet season, the bulk of the cattle in Nigeria are concentrated in the fly-free zone, which extends across the northern parts of the northern region.

When the dry season begins, it is the northernmost herds, in Niger and Sudan, that first experience shortage of pasture. Although cattle are watered from wells, there is a southward movement of herds in search of pasture. These conditions progressively affect areas farther south, from which tsetse has itself retreated, and the cattle population spreads into pasture lands from which a major hazard has been removed. Sometimes in a long dry season, herds may impinge for fodder on areas to which bush tsetse has retreated, or may be forced to water at streams or at water holes in stream beds where riverain tsetse is prevalent. Pastoral Fulani are well aware, so far as their own practical purposes go, of the relation between tsetse fly infestation and trypanosomiasis.

This regular seasonal movement of cattle, southward in the dry season in response to shortages of pasture and water, northward in the wet season to avoid tsetse, is a consistent pattern of transhumance among the pastoral Fulani of the savanna zone. The speed and length of these seasonal movements vary from area to area and from year to year, and may be correlated with a number of local conditions.[4] Among these the principal factors are the duration of wet and dry seasons, the size of herds, the presence of other herds, the density of the sedentary population, and extent of farmland under crops, and last, but not least, the availability of suitable markets where dairy products may be sold or exchanged for cereal and root foods.

Pastoralism and the family

In seeking their subsistence on herds of cattle in this habitat the Wodaabe rely primarily on small, independent, and highly mobile groups. It is the household based on the simple or compound family that deploys the herd of cattle it owns.

HERDING HUSBANDRY • A Wodaabe herd is a distinct group of cattle consisting of at least one stock bull and a complement of cows, heifers, calves, and pack oxen. It is distinct since it normally inbreeds, spends the daytime grazing apart from other similar herds, is watered separately, and spends the night in a corral reserved or constructed for it and marked by its special smudge fire. The corral is part of the homestead of the male herd owner, who is responsible for its day-to-day management.

In the homestead of the male herd owner live the members of his household: normally a simple family composed of himself, one wife, and her children, or a compound family composed of himself, his several wives, and their children. In circumstances in which cattle are the sole basis of subsistence for such a household, meat does not form a regular or staple diet and animals are not often sold. Killings are confined to male beasts or, where possible, sick or maimed animals; such killings occur only on ceremonial occasions. Sales take place only when there is an overriding need for cash, for example, to buy corn in a bad dry season or to raise tax money. In these circumstances the family lives on milk, for, unlike some East African pastoralists, Fulani do not drink cattle blood or make blood foods. Either milk or milk products must be drunk or eaten continually or milk must be sold or exchanged for other foods.

If the milk output falls temporarily below a certain minimum, cattle will have to be sold to pay for food, thus potentially reducing still further the fecundity of the herd. Humans share milk with calves; if they make too great a demand on the milk of the herd, the well-being or even the lives of the calves, and therefore the future fecundity of the herd, is prejudiced.

Good husbandry for a Fulani herd owner thus involves maintaining a milk yield sufficient to support his dependents at all seasons. Lactation must not only be adequate, but continuous. Since lactation is dependent on the birth of calves, the main interest of the herd owner is a steady yearly increase in his herd.

All pastoral Fulani find themselves in a situation of seasonal shortages of water and pasture and severe endemic diseases, in harsh tropical conditions in which maintenance of the herd in the state required merely for continual subsistence may be achieved only by constant seasonal movements and periodic migration. Cattle have to be capable of long miles of trek to, from, and between pastures, and able to undergo seasonal irregularities in both the amount and type of fodder and water. The herd owner therefore maintains his milk yield, not by a dairy technique directed to realizing the milking potentialities of individual animals, but by one in which other qualities are important. Thus, culling, when practiced at all, is based on a standard of excellence referring to color and conformation rather than to milk production, and breeding is done with an eye to maintaining aesthetic standards as well as avoiding disease.

We have here been considering the herd as supporting the human family dependent on it; we have taken the family as "given" and examined the general properties of the herd associated with it. But the human family also supports the herd. Fulani cattle are not natural groups of wild animals followed and exploited intermittently by human beings. Fulani herds are domesticated in a particular way, and this entails special organization in the families dependent upon them. For example, desirable pastures have to be sought and cattle led to them, and water supplies have to be arranged and cattle watered regularly. Diseases and accidents of many kinds have to be avoided, or their results treated, and the birth of calves has to be assisted, for the pastoral Fulani believe that a calf born in the bush brings ill luck on the herd, and should be sold on weaning.

Among the Wodaabe the division of these and related tasks between the sexes is clear cut. Men have to do with cattle, their seasonal movements, daily pasturing and watering, and veterinary care. Women have to do with milk and its marketing in addition to their domestic tasks of food preparation and the care of the homestead both at rest and on the move. Adult men are herd owners and managers, male children and adolescents are herdsmen. Adult women are dairywomen and purveyors of milk, female children and adolescents are dairymaids. The Wodaabe family is a herd-owning and milk-selling enterprise.

Given a strict division of labor and a herd of a certain size, a herd owner's family must attain a size commensurate with its responsibilities toward its herd. It must also maintain a balance of the sexes, so that these responsibilities may be efficiently carried out by appropriate members of the family. A herd owner must have at least one wife. Man and wife must reproduce at a certain minimum rate and in a certain proportion of potential milkmaids and herdsmen. When the size and increase of the herd and the family are adequate for the control of the former and the subsistence of the latter, then family and herd may be said to be in equilibrium. In the life history of a family, expressed as the lifetime of the male household head, such a state of equilibrium is never permanent. One party to the disequilibrium—the cattle —can do nothing to adjust the state of their affairs, though the Wodaabe quite reasonably believe they may approve or disapprove of certain acts of their owners. The other party—the human beings—can and do take action on both the herd and themselves to readjust the relationship of family and herd.

The herd and the family are brought into existence by first marriage by betrothal, the procedure and symbolism of which demonstrate the interdependence of family and herd. The maintenance and increase of herds are effected largely by seasonal movements and by cooperation between herd owners. The adjustment of family size and composition is carried out by subsequent monogamous marriages, polygynous marriages, and the divorces these may entail.

Material culture

The material culture of the Wodaabe is simple, and they practice a few crafts.

HOUSEHOLD AND PERSONAL EQUIPMENT · Household utensils consist mainly of receptacles for milk, for which calabashes of many different shapes and sizes are bought in the market and then decorated by the women. In addition there is usually an earthenware pot for cooking cereal food, sometimes with its iron tripod. All adult women have a decorated headring for carrying calabashes. Most own a bradawl for decorating calabashes, in hairdressing, and as a surgical tool.

The care of cattle demands many kinds of ropes—tethers, hobbles, halters, and lashings. Men make these, mainly from baobab bark, and rope-making is their constant preoccupation. One or two important ropes—the main calf rope, and certain fittings for a wife s store of calabashes—are made of leather and have a ceremonial as well as utilitarian importance. All adult men carry a herding staff with magical properties.

Cowhide is used very rarely today for clothing, being confined to garments worn by youths on ceremonial occasions, and to the workaday sandals worn by all except small children. Women wear a single piece of cloth fastened above the bosom, but carry with them another similar piece to be used as a cowl, or a covering at night, or simply to be folded decoratively on the head. Men wear pantaloons of an Arabic type, a sleeveless shift, and a decorated Islamic cap. A man might have a long, full-sleeved white gown, and perhaps another pair of gowns in a colored or patterned material. He might own another cap for ceremonial occasions, and perhaps a large straw sun hat. He will possibly have a pair of red or yellow leather shoes of Arabic design. All these items are bought in the market, usually when a beast has been sold to pay the tax and there is cash to spare.

The important remaining items of personal equipment are tools, weapons, and saddlery. Most Fulani men own an ax, but few own a hoe, for which there is little use. Most have a small knife, which is used as a razor, and many an arm dagger. Some have swords, but only a few possess spears, which were never used in combat but for hunting giraffe. Shields and bows and arrows, which are said to have been important weapons, are never seen nowadays.

About one adult man in five owns a horse, and consequently a saddle. These are of Arabic design, with runners and a high pommel and cantle. They are set on numnahs or saddle pads, the topmost of which is often highly decorated. A very few Fulani possess some item of quilted horse armor, or even chain mail, which they display only on the most important ceremonial occasions. Bits are mostly of traditional design, although English bits are finding favor. Stirrups are of the shovel type, the sharp corners acting as spurs. Harness is made of traditionally worked leather, which, because it is inadequately dressed and receives much hard use, is continually breaking. All these items—particularly the horse, which is their raison d'être—demonstrate high status but are luxuries for which a man ought not to sell cattle. Perhaps in weapons and saddlery the conflict between material and pastoral values is most clearly seen. Men like to own horses and saddlery and weapons, but cannot afford to maintain them; on close inspection they appear old or shoddy or unreliable—and Fulani men are well aware of this. A well-turned-out "cavalier" is nowadays an anomaly worthy of suspicion.

THE HOMESTEAD • The homesteads and camps of the Wodaabe seem haphazard and rudimentary. In the wet season even a large camp blends with the bush, and in the dry season it is possible to pass within a few yards of a homestead without realizing it is there. Household equipment is limited to the amount that may be carried on the head or on pack oxen, and shelters must be made of whatever tree foliage the district has to offer.

The pastoralist has no sense of attachment to a specific plot of land he calls home. Rather, he is at home in any of the favorite pastures where he or his father have tended their herds, in any of the markets where his womenfolk sell milk, and on the cattle tracks and footpaths that join them.

Nevertheless, the homestead, though impermanent and simple, exhibits important elements of formality and uniformity.

Wodaabe homesteads and camps always face west. In the context of the homestead, west is synonymous with "front," and east with "back." In Fulfulde, north and south are used for the left and right sides of the homestead, respectively, as seen by an observer facing the homestead looking east. In all but overnight camps a curved fence of branches cut from nearby trees is put up at the back to ensure privacy, to keep out hyenas, and to deflect the course of stampeding cattle frightened by hyenas' nightly visits in the wet season. Other details of the homestead arrangement are described in the following section.

SOCIAL ORGANIZATION

Family and kinship

THE FAMILY • Although the range of equipment and the nature of the dwelling of the Wodaabe may be simple, they are nevertheless closely related to the structure and activities of the basic domestic unit—the simple or compound family. (See page 372.)

The whole homestead takes the name of the male head. But it is divided into two parts by the "calf rope," a long, two-stranded leather rope to which the calves of the household are tethered when the herd is in its corral. The part of the homestead to the east of the calf rope is the female section. The bed shelters are the dwellings and property of the wives who arrange them in a line of order of seniority from the north. Other shelters here are also for women—for a daughter in her first pregnancy or for a widowed mother of the household head. The only males who sleep here (east of the calf rope) are the household head (whose wives take turns to feed him and sleep with him), and his infant sons. No male who has to do with cattle goes into this part of the homestead except to help set it up or in an emergency. It is the province of the wives and daughters of the household head, who do all the chores there.

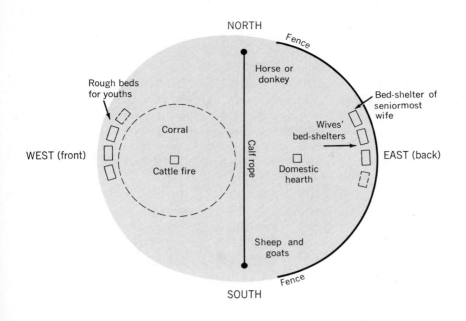

NORTH

Fence

Horse or
donkey

Rough beds
for youths

Bed-shelter of
seniormost
wife

Corral

Wives'
bed-shelters

WEST (front)

Calf rope

Cattle fire

Domestic
hearth

EAST (back)

Sheep and
goats

Fence

SOUTH

Plan of a Wodaabe Homestead

West of the calf rope is the male part of the household, where the cattle are kept. It is sanctified by the cattle fire, which burns there from dusk to early morning. While the cattle are away grazing nobody goes into the corral. In the early morning the householder and his sons sit there and discuss and inspect the cattle. Wives come into the corral only to milk, and the special cooperative task of men and women is for the former to release calves from the rope, which then go to their dams to initiate milking by the wives. Menfolk eat to the west of the cattle corral and some sleep around it to guard the herd by night. Menfolk spend a day in camp under a tree to the west of the corral.

When returning to, or visiting, a homestead a man approaches from the west and a woman from the east. Males are buried on the west side of the cattle corral, females to the east of the back fence. When a whole household moves to new pastures it does so in the order dictated by these arrangements. The household head sets off initially to the west, followed by the herd flanked by his sons. Behind the herd come the wives, their shelters and domestic equipment lashed to pack bulls. With them are the children of the household and its small stock.

Immediately in front of the back fence are set the beds of the household. Four stout forked stakes are driven into the ground to form the corners of a rectangle three by eight feet. Poles of about four inches in diameter, which are part of the domestic equipment, are placed on the stakes to form the two long sides of the rectangle. Thirty or forty special sticks, an inch or so in diameter, are laid crosswise on them; these may be adjusted to fit the curvature of the body in repose. One or two basketry mats serve as mattresses, bark-fiber mats are used as blankets, and bark-fiber chafing pads from a pack bull's harness as pillows. The shelter for this bed is a structure similar to it but on longer uprights, forming a platform on which are placed the household utensils. In the wet season the small cross poles of this structure are extended as a framework for additional basketry and bark-fiber mats, which provide some shelter from the rain.

Alongside or in front of these bed-shelters there may be other shelters put up for specific purposes and the domestic hearths.

Also near these shelters and in front of them are kept the household's stock other than its herd of cattle—a horse or a donkey hobbled and tethered to a forked stake, and a small flock of sheep or goats sheltered in a fold of stout branches.

In front of this group of shelters the calf rope is staked down. In front again of the calf rope is the cattle corral, often merely a patch of earth trampled by the beasts' hooves. A corral fence is not often made. Around the corral under convenient bushes or trees there may be rough beds. In the center of the cattle corral is a smudge fire around which the cattle gather in the early morning and in the evening when they return from the pasture. The fire is always lit, even in the rain, on the return of the cattle and extinguished after they have gone out to pasture the next morning. The corral fire maintains or increases the herd by magical means, and its importance for the well-being of the herd is attested by a number of myths.

THE LINEAGE · The Wodaabe family is a close-knit economic unit, devoted to the welfare of its herd. But even if families have a high degree of economic independence, they are linked by various forms of cooperation. At the founding of a new family its cattle come from another family's herd, and the first and subsequent wives of a family head come from other families. If a family finds itself unable to cope with its economic tasks, or if its herd is too small to support it, it has to rely on the help of other families or use the resources of their herds. On a family head's death his wives' unmarried children and his cattle are allocated to other families. A number of families join together to perform these essential functions and choose a leader from among the family heads.

The principle of this association of families is primarily the agnatic relationship of male family heads—their descent through male links from a common male ancestor. We now turn to a consideration of the small corporate groupings based on it, which we shall call agnatic lineage groups or, more briefly, lineage groups.

Lineage Activity Members of a Fulani clan attend market at Katsina market. (*British Information Service*)

First, a lineage group has a name that usually refers to its component household heads as the agnatic descendants of a common ancestor generally not more than three ascending generations removed.

The second characteristic of lineage groups is that their households are coresidential, their homesteads being grouped together to form camps. When a man's sons marry they set up their homesteads to the north of his homestead and in line with it. The differential development of families and the continued presence of members of previous generations produce different arrangements in camps of this size, which are, however, consistent with age, generation, and the genealogical principles outlined above.

Besides this coresidence, a third characteristic of a lineage is that its herd owners also cooperate to ensure that each household has sufficient stock and an adequate labor supply. There is a system whereby, if some herds are deficient in certain types of stock—such as pack oxen, pack bulls, stock bulls, or milch cows—these may be borrowed. Each member of the lineage group who is himself a herd owner is expected to provide stock when formally asked by a member whose stock is deficient. In addition, if a man's herd has been depleted by bovine disease or theft, he might recoup his losses by means of gifts from the other herd owners of his lineage group.

A fourth characteristic of the lineage group is its control of the marriages of both its male and female members, particularly the first marriages by which families and herds are set up. A distinctive principle of Wodaabe marriage, and, indeed, of pastoral Fulani in general, is endogamy. Thus spouses are found for members of a lineage group primarily within that group or from others related agnatically. The types of preferential marriage based on this principle will now be summarized. (The shading in the diagrams that follow designates the marriage partners referred to in the text description.

1. A most important form of preferential marriage is that between the son and daughter of two brothers or half brothers. In this type of marriage, the partners trace descent to a common grandfather through male links.

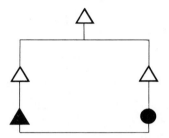

The fathers of the marriage partners are full brothers or half brothers. The marriage partners are patrilateral parallel cousins or "children of uncles."

2. The marriage partners may trace their descent through male links to a common great-grandfather. The fathers of the marriage partners are actual patrilateral cousins, while the marriage partners themselves are classificatory patrilateral parallel cousins.

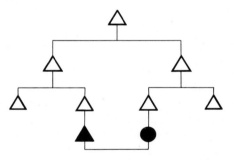

3. In a third type of preferential marriage the partners have a common male ancestor more than three generations removed.

These three types of preferential marriage are based on an insistence on the strict agnatic descent of the partners, endogamous for lineage groups of a depth of three ascending generations from the marriage partners. In each of the three types, the fathers of the marriage partners are brothers, or at least "lineage brothers." A man looks to another man of his lineage group to supply a spouse for his son or daughter.

4. In a fourth type of marriage the man marries the "child of a paternal aunt," whereas the woman marries the "child of a maternal uncle." The

marriage partners trace descent to a common grandfather, but the female partner does so through her mother. The marriage partners are actual patrilateral cross-cousins.

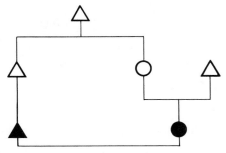

5. In another type of marriage the marriage partners are classificatory patrilateral cross-cousins. But now their common descent is traced to a great-grandfather, that of the wife through her mother.

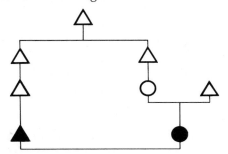

6. In the third of this class of preferential marriages, depending on clan brother and sister, descent is traced to a common male ancestor at more than three ascending generations, the female marriage partner tracing it either through her mother or through the mother of her father or grandfather.

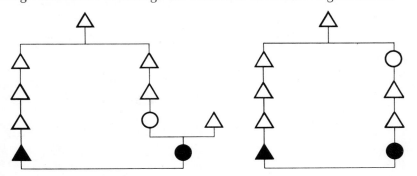

In a further set of three types of preferential marriages the operative relationship is not that of two clan brothers, or of clan brother and sister, but that of man and wife. A man looks to his wife's agnatic relatives for a marriage partner for his son. This means that in tracing the common descent of the marriage partners, it is the male partner who does so by a female link.

7. Here the partners trace descent to a common grandfather, the male marriage partner doing so through his mother. A man marries his mother's brother's daughter, whereas a woman marries her father's sister's son.

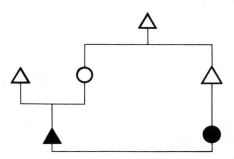

8. Here the partners trace descent to a common great-grandfather, the husband through his mother.

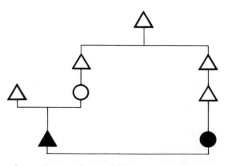

9. Here again the relationship of the partners is to a common male ancestor more than three generations removed, the male partner tracing his descent through his own mother or through his father or grandfather.

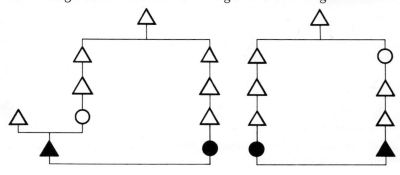

Marriage types 4–9, which utilize a female connection or link, are not at first glance endogamous for lineage groups. They tend to unite two different lineage groups by using the sisters of the wives of the men of that descent group as links. But where these women have themselves married endogamously, a marriage of this kind in the next generation is automatically endogamous for the lineage group.

The types of preferential marriage presented here show that the lineage group aims, primarily, at keeping the young woman in order to betroth her to one of its own young men (marriage types 1 and 2). Second, it passes her on to a lineage group that is believed to be related agnatically (marriage type 3). Third, it uses the connections established by the marriages of its own women, and takes spouses to the lineage groups from which its wives have been drawn (marriage types 7–9).

There is a further type (10) in which neither the marriage partners nor their fathers can trace common descent, but are aware that the lineage groups to which they belong do intermarry, that is to say, belong to the same clan. The marriage partners and, for that matter, their fathers, are known as "people of one body."

Wodaabe regard *kooggal* (the endogamous system of "betrothal marriages") as a cornerstone of their traditional morality, and as a practice that marks them off, physically and culturally, from non-Fulani populations. Their system is closely connected with the structure of the agnatic group and its existence as a corporate body under a special set of ecological conditions.

The fifth characteristic of lineage groups is the control exercised over the inheritance of the cattle of a deceased herd owner. The aim of an elder is to pass on more cattle to more sons than his father was able to do. But inheritance of cattle is not primarily a system of legacies in the sense that a herd is shared among a man's sons on his death. A man's sons, during the lifetime of their father, acquired progressively more rights, both to possess and to dispose of cattle, in proportion to their steadily increasing duties and responsibilities toward the herd. There is a clear distinction in Fulfulde between the cattle to which sons acquire rights during the lifetime of their father and those cattle received as a legacy on the father's death. A son does not properly own cattle until a separate homestead is made for him, and his betrothed wife and first child have taken up residence there. He then has a valid voice in the camp conferences concerning future moves, and in periods of stress or danger, as in epidemics and famine, his decision to move away independently will be respected.

A father's rights in his herd grow less in relation to those of his sons as more sons are born to him, take up their herding duties, and marry. But a father retains a general supervisory control over his own and his sons' herds until his last son has married. When this point is reached all his cattle have passed into the hands of his sons. When a man dies leaving unmarried children, or no children at all, there is a residual herd to be shared among his heirs. The administration of an estate is the duty of the dead man's lineage group.

The estate is subject to prior changes, for it is by no means freely distributable in its entirety by the administrators. First they have to decide how many pack animals are heritable. This is determined by the inheritance of the widow of the dead man by one of his agnatic kinsmen. Next the administrators have to decide what proportion of the estate is held under the various agreements for loans of stock between cattle owners. Although in the administration of an estate these various arrangements made by the dead man have to be recognized, they do not lapse automatically on his death but are carried on by his senior heir.

Pastoral Fulani inheritance is firmly, although not exclusively, patrilineal. The formal order of inheritance, counting the original estate holder as (I) is as follows (see diagram):

    II. The estate holder's son
   III. His full and half brothers
   IV. His brother's sons
    V. His father's brothers
   VI. His patrilateral parallel cousins.[5]

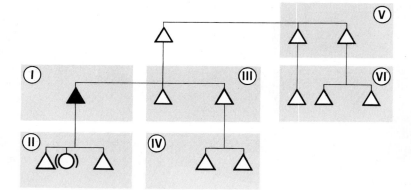

No women inherit in this system, but nowadays provision is often made for sisters of the heirs to inherit half shares, as is customary in Islamic law.

Although the cattle that are heritable in this way represent those not as yet used for the dead man's unmarried sons, the only competent direct heirs are those males who have homesteads of their own. Those who, by the marriage of all their children, have relinquished the right to a homestead are not competent heirs. The portions of those who have as yet no homestead pass into the hands of guardians who become the trustees of their inheritances and have the obligation of initiating or continuing their betrothal arrangements.

Within each category, each heir's portion is similar. Also, the sons of the dead man inherit, not from the total heritable stock, but from that proportion of it in which their own mother has milking rights. Among the Wodaabe a first wife is allowed more cattle to milk than her co-wives, but in practice the number of cattle milked by a wife depends also on the size of the matricentral segment of the family for whose feeding she is responsible.

Although the portions claimed by or allotted to each heir are similar numerically, priority of choice is given to older over younger siblings. Where the estate is a large one, some care is taken to ensure that the portions form at least the nuclei of balanced herds. The authority of the senior heir or the guardian might be maintained, at least temporarily, by placing in his portion the serving bulls of the estate.

The lineage group is interested not only in the disposal of cattle, but also in the disposal of women and children particularly on the death of one of its members; this is the sixth of its characteristics. The administrators of a dead man's estate have the duty of finding a husband for his widow from among the younger brothers or junior agnatic kinsmen of the same generation as the dead man. A younger brother is bound to take over the wife or wives of his dead elder brother, even if only for a short token period.

The final characteristic of the lineage group is that it has a leader. This office will be discussed later.

THE CLAN · There are wider groupings in Wodaabe society. These are clans, composed of clusters of lineage groups joined by the principle of agnation. This is not the known descent of household heads from the common ancestor of the group, but the putative agnatic relationship of several of these ancestors with each other; they are believed to have been brothers, patrilateral parallel cousins, and so on. Not only were these groups related by the putative agnatic kinship of their ancestors; they were also groups within which betrothal arrangements might be made because these were assumed to have been carried out in the past. Clans were called by a term that means "people of one body." A clan had a name, but this was not usually derived from a founding ancestor but was a nickname or referred to a locality with which the group had been associated in the past.

The lineage groups in a clan were not of equal status. The factors conferring high status on a lineage group of a clan were similar to those making a household prominent in a lineage group. The groups that had most effectively preserved their agnatic character through the generations by maintaining families and the herds associated with them at optimum size and composition had the highest status. As well as making possible numerous endogamous unions, their large herds attracted wives from other groups, so that a higher rate of polygyny contributed further to their cohesion and prosperity. By contrast, groups with low status were those whose past had been checkered with misfortune or lack of skill in pastoral affairs, thus forcing them to associate with stronger groups and so destroying the continuity of their agnatic lines.

These characteristics of clans have been phrased in the past tense, not because they do not exist today, but because other features of clan life that make them meaningful have either disappeared or become attenuated. In particular the coresidential properties of clans are less in evidence, and so are the many ceremonies that demonstrated these features in the wet season gatherings. Also, new political factors have supervened, making the clan relationships of lineage groups less important for their corporate welfare. These factors have been touched on earlier and will be mentioned again below.

Marriage

BETROTHAL MARRIAGE · The first stage of the formation of the family and herd is by *kooggal* (betrothal marriage). Childhood betrothal is common; in any case the girl should not be older than the boy, and there is a general preference for an age disparity of about three years. Betrothal marriages include preliminaries, bride removal and "sleeping out," first pregnancy of the bride, name giving to the child, and establishment of the homestead.

The sibling group of the boy's father seeks to betroth him at any time after his circumcision. Now the boy is beginning to work with the herd, and his father furthers his interests in it by adding to the cattle already set aside for the boy at his naming ceremony. He is also formally introduced into the cattle corral. Next the future services of a wife are considered. "There is the herd; the milkmaid must follow." The boy's father's representative goes with a witness to the father of a suitable girl. The successful completion of these preliminaries is marked by a feast at the camp of the girl's representatives for which a feast bull is provided by the boy's father.

The next stage is the betrothal ceremony proper, which nowadays usually includes a conventional Islamic wedding ceremony. This takes place at her father's homestead when the girl has begun to menstruate. The boy's father provides two bulls to be slaughtered, the various fees to the scribe, and the kola nuts that are an important element. *No bridewealth changes hands at this or any other stage in a betrothal marriage.*

Next follows the bride removal. This takes place in two stages. In the first stage the boy's father provides a feast bull and a gift of gowns for the bride. After this the boy is no longer represented by his father's siblings but by his own siblings, who take the gifts to the girl's father's home. The girl's mother provides her with a ceremonial but miniature set of calabashes. The bride removal is accompanied by jollity. Milk is blown over her by her future husband's age mates. She may be struck with branches of the Fulani blessing-tree. One of the bridegroom's sisters may threaten to belabor her with a grain pestle. She is taken to her mother-in-law's home, where she stays for two days and nights during which no men are allowed near. She then goes back to her own father's homestead for a week.

The bride is then brought back for a second time, and is now expected to sleep with her husband. But she is not given a married woman's shelter; her husband's bed at the edge of the cattle corral is made more comfortable with the addition of a rudimentary roof. This first period of residence of the young couple is unobtrusive. The husband behaves like any herding youth. The young wife spends all her time with her mother-in-law, helping her as a daughter would in domestic chores, with the exception of milking. This period of first residence comes to an end when the bride is discovered to be pregnant and goes back to her father's homestead, where she is under many ceremonial prohibitions, for the birth of her child.

After the birth of her child the young mother stays in her father's homestead for about two and a half years, after which she returns to her husband at his father's homestead. On this ceremonial occasion the parties to the betrothal marriage join in providing the partners with the symbols of full marital status. The husband is now said to "know his cattle." The wife is elevated to the status of wife and mother and acquires the right to milk in her husband's herd. The husband's brothers clear a homestead space to the north of his father's or elder brother's. His father makes the calf rope and its stakes, and his mother sets it in place. The husband's father provides a pack-bull with its lashings, and his wives make its chafing pads. He also buys gowns for his daughter-in-law. All these are taken to the bride's father's home. She is arrayed in the gowns; her mother gives her the materials for her bed, and also a ceremonial set of calabashes. Her child is provided for by its maternal grandmother with a decorated halter, the halter of a young calf, which she places on its neck. The bride's party sets off for the bridegroom's camp, where a feast in which the couple have no part takes place. After the feast the bride attaches to her calf rope the calves belonging to her husband's cattle, which now return to them after grazing rather than to the calf rope of his father. The new family and its herd are now in existence.

Marriage by betrothal is an institution closely linked to the inheritance of cattle, the establishment of herds, and the status of both men and women as married adults. It is binding on men because of its connection with the dominant forms of property in Wodaabe society. Women, as we shall see, are nowadays free to refuse or avoid its provisions.

CICISBEAN MARRIAGE · There is no rule of monogamy in Wodaabe society. Polygynous marriages are of several kinds—cicisbean marriage, contract marriage, widow inheritance, gift marriage, and concubinage.

Cicisbean marriage results mainly from the breakdown of arrangements for betrothal marriage and is a union in which the previous marriage of the wife has not been properly dissolved by tribal or Islamic authority.

A woman leaves her husband without divorce, and goes to a man with whom she may have been friendly for some time. The couple are usually of different or strange clans. The man has a bull slaughtered in his own home, and it is eaten by his kinsmen, who witness his declaration of marriage to the girl. The latter's family are not represented, and there is no officiating scribe. There are none of the presentations associated with other types of Wodaabe marriage. These marriages frequently prove to be childless or of short duration, the wife returning to her previous husband to whom, usually, she has been betrothed.

The status of a runaway wife is generally no more favorable than if she had stayed with her father or husband. She usually has the status of daughter of the household without the support of her own family, as she has in betrothal marriage. She may be a substitute for her lover's betrothed wife, who is away in her first pregnancy. Usually if the runaway returns home she will lose the status of betrothed wife she holds there, especially if she runs away before taking up first residence with her husband.

The father of such a runaway usually makes a strong attempt to get the girl back, since he is interested in carrying through her betrothal marriage, but there is rarely a common political tie between himself and his daughter's new husband. The help of a Muslim scribe is of little use in this case. The girl's father often has no choice but to offer back to his opposite party in betrothal the cattle provided to date for the betrothal arrangements.

Cicisbean marriage is a recent institution. It has increased in proportion to the decline of the Guardian with his control of betrothal marriage. The opening up of markets and communications has resulted in increased personal mobility; the admixture of immigrant Fulani groups in Bornu is also a contributory factor. Some Wodaabe chiefs have made a specific attack on cicisbean unions by attempting to protect the rights of the girl's party in betrothal. In general the spread of formal Islamic marriage is tending to limit the cicisbean type of union.

CONTRACT MARRIAGE · The term "contract marriage" is a translation of the general Fulfulde term "to marry." It may be used to describe the stage of betrothal marriage, widow inheritance, and gift marriage that includes Muslim ceremony. Applied to marriage between pastoral Fulani, contract marriage is an Islamic marriage a man makes for himself after he has been married to someone else by betrothal. Contract marriage often takes place between clansfolk but between more distantly related partners than in betrothal marriage, and the transfer of bridewealth is a part of such marriages.

WIDOW INHERITANCE · At her husband's death a widow undergoes the period of continence and mourning (edda) prescribed by Islamic canon law.

If she has adult sons she stays with them; if not, she goes to her father or guardian. We have seen that the dead man's lineage has the right to his wife and the duty of taking care of his children. His younger brother often takes over his wife for a short period, but other eligible kinsmen may make the widow an offer of marriage during her mourning. The widow is remarried at an Islamic ceremony, and the bride changes residence without a feast. The woman might marry a man of her own choice, but in this case her husband's heir may claim the equivalent of the cattle slaughtered for the woman's betrothal, if she is childless, or he may claim the children of a woman's marriage.

A widow's choice in the matter of remarriage depends on her age and her children. If she is old she is unlikely to remarry but will stay with her sons. If she is young, and her husband dies in her children's infancy, she will expect to be inherited so as to guarantee support in her old age. If she marries away, either she will lose her children or they will be at a disadvantage in inheriting their stepfather's cattle.

Pressure may also be brought on a widow, for if she was a close kinsman of her dead husband, the administrators of his estate might also exercise parental or quasi-parental control over her.

GIFT MARRIAGE · Gift marriage arises from a man's desire to make a gift with an Islamic motive. The gift is his daughter, who is married without bridewealth to a man in his own, rather than in his daughter's, generation. The Wodaabe cases of this form of marriage involved girls who might make difficult matches—for example, a deaf and dumb girl. Also, a newcomer to a chiefdom might give his daughter to a chief or a chief's relative as a form of tribute.

CONCUBINAGE · In Wodaabe society, concubinage is defined as a union between a Fulani man and a non-Fulani woman. The woman is not wedded in Fulani or Islamic ceremonies, and her family plays no part in the arrangements. She has a defined domestic position, however, although it is inferior to wives of other categories. She has her own cattle to milk, although only in exceptional circumstances are these inherited by her sons. Although concubinage is regarded as a possible union by Wodaabe, no instance of it was found in field inquiries; however, it is still practiced in other Fulani communities in northern Nigeria.

DIVORCE · In Wodaabe society, as in pastoral Fulani society in general, the dissolution of marriage by divorce is permitted, easy, and frequent. It is allowed to both partners in a marriage, but it is probably easier, and therefore more frequent, for a man to divorce his wife than for a wife to divorce her husband.

De jure or legal divorce is preceded by a period of conjugal separation, the wife returning to her father or guardian. After this her husband may divorce her in Islamic fashion by making a declaration of repudiation before his chief and witnesses. In doing so, he forfeits all and any payments he may have made in respect of the marriage and also forfeits his claims to any infants in the wife's care at the time of the separation. When the wife divorces the husband, he does not forfeit these things. The repudiation is followed by a divorcée's *edda* of three months in order to insure that the newly divorced woman is not pregnant. *De facto* (informal) divorce often occurs when a woman makes a cicisbean marriage in a "stranger clan."

When an endogamous betrothal marriage ends in divorce, it is not feasible for the husband to demand the return of the slaughtered bulls consumed at the *kooggal* feast from the wife's family who are, after all, his clansfolk. The greater stability of these marriages rests not on the economics of bridewealth but on the moral norms of *pulaaku*. There is, among the pastoral Fulani, a correlation between the degree of adherence to Islam and the *decline* of both cicisbean marriage and *de facto* divorce—and with the *rise* of *de jure* divorce and the observance of *edda*.

CHILD TRAINING AND SOCIALIZATION

It is convenient in this section to consider socialization in relation to age categories. Age is not the basis of any corporate group in Wodaabe society, but status in such groups is heavily influenced by age, and most behavior is divided and characterized along age lines.

Wodaabe recognize five stages of life—childhood, youth, young adulthood, senior adulthood, and senility. Within these there are subdivisions of conventional duration.

CHILDHOOD • A child is "one" in its first week, before it is named. Until then it is not considered a person; no distinction is made between a child dying in its first week and a stillbirth; a baby under a week is called by an impersonal pronoun.

The naming ceremony is the Wodaabe version of the feast prescribed by Islamic canon law, which recommends that at the ceremony a child should be named, its head shaved, an animal sacrificed, the meat eaten within the family circle, and the greater part of it given away in alms. The blood of the sacrifice should not be smeared on the head of the newborn, nor should the child be circumcised on this occasion. The Wodaabe carry out this ceremony strictly, and with some additional rigid injunctions of their own. A child is named with an Arabic name appropriate to the day on which it was born.

Children later acquire other names—grandparents' names, nicknames, and adopted names.

When a child is born it is given undiluted cow's milk for a day or two. A period of exclusive breast feeding then follows, lasting until the ninth month. The infant's diet from then until the age of two years is a gradual replacement of mother's milk by cow's milk and solids. Final weaning may occur when the child is placed in the care of one of its grandmothers, usually when the mother becomes pregnant again. It is said that a suckling gives up the breast to its younger sibling after two years. Before this it is carried slung on its mother's back in a cloth. There is no term for a child who has newly learned to walk. A child is taught to speak by its mother, who playfully chants elementary words, the child repeating them as best it can; the mother passes over difficult terms, coming back to them later.

The terms for children who are no longer in the care of their mother, but do not leave the homestead, are sexually differentiated. When older lads are in camp, little boys sit with them and are given a share of their tasks, but when left alone the youngsters play freely with little girls of their own age. A girl of this age "follows" her mother and helps her in small ways, but she also goes off to play with her age mates. This regime of domestic tasks and interests, and the way in which even the youngest are gradually inducted into it, is shown in the leisure activities of young boys and girls. They make figurines of clay, the boys fashioning horses and long-horned cattle, the girls making female busts, the heads stylized with no attempt at facial representation, the breasts large and carefully pricked to represent tattooing. In the homestead itself, these boys and girls are happy to imitate the tasks of their elders.

YOUTH · The stage of youth is divided for both males and females into pre- and postpubertal phases. A boy leaves childhood behind when he is circumcised, although this is not a prominent event and has no group ceremonial. At the age of about ten a boy is fit to herd cattle, and his father introduces him to the corral, and earmarks cattle for him that will form the nucleus of his own herd. He gives the boy a staff with magic properties and a set of Koranic charms to prosper his herding. His mother gives him a small calabash bottle for his day's water. Now the boy moves his bed from the women's side of the homestead to the edge of the cattle corral; he eats with the men, and may take part in the moving-day conference.

This phase merges into that of the onset of puberty. A boy now takes a fuller part in the activities of the youths. He flirts in the market, he becomes interested in fashion and ornament, and learns love magic. He goes to the young people's evening meetings in the wet season and learns dance steps and love songs. Later he enters the *gerewol*. In this dance performed before

Fulani Herdboy Tending Cattle on the Jos Plateau, Northern Nigeria (*British Information Service*)

elders the youths, dressed in their finery, dance unaccompanied by drums while praising in song the charms of the maidens. In this way the girls are graded in order of beauty. Meanwhile the maidens, dancing in a circle nearby, choose the most handsome and the best-dressed youth. In this way two or three of the "best" youths and maidens have been paired. These couples now spend the night together, the rest of the dancers pairing off as they may. The *gerewol* is connected with courtship, but it does not regulate betrothal or first marriage, which are determined in an entirely different way. It arranges the youths and maidens in a status order, which is unimportant after a short time, when they become married. It seems likely that the *gerewol* was formerly part of the instruction of youths and maidens in adult sexual practices.

During this period of youth an interim stage is reached when a young man's betrothed wife takes up residence. This does not mean that a young man now gives up *gerewol* but that he has a more supervisory role in the ceremonies.

The girl's period of youth is similarly divided. There is no event in the girl's life corresponding to circumcision and the assumption of herding duties, but she takes up household responsibilities in an analogous way. She now goes to evening meetings and *gerewol*. But as soon as a girl begins to menstruate the father of her future husband may claim her, her hair style and her place in the dance showing him that she is ready for first residence with her husband.

YOUNG ADULTHOOD • The establishment of a homestead and a herd marks the beginning of young adulthood for both sexes. A young man gives up his youthful finery and has his head shaved. He may now grow the beard of an elder. A young woman now enters two fields where she may demonstrate her status: the camp and the market place. But although adult, both men and women are junior adults, who have to prove their skill, fecundity, or probity.

SENIOR ADULTHOOD • A man in the stage of senior adulthood is an elder. He is a herd owner and has a wife or wives and has begotten children. His homestead is placed in such a way as to demonstrate his seniority in a camp. He has a full place in the deliberation of the elders, but this is conditioned by the size of his family and his herd. In the corresponding period a woman is expected to have borne at least two children. There is no term to indicate how many children a woman has borne but this was formerly indicated by the number of heavy brass earrings worn.

SENILITY • The state of senility is defined for women when they have ceased to bear children and for men when their sons have all married. When the latter event takes place a husband and wife no longer live in a homestead. The wife's calabashes and the husband's cattle have all been passed on to their children. An old man lives in a rudimentary hut to the west of the cattle corral. An old woman lives in a small shelter near the back fence of her eldest son's homestead. It will be remembered that these are the places where men and women are buried. The old couple are separated, and sleep, one might say, over their own graves, for they are already socially dead.

POLITICAL ORGANIZATION

The basic political unit of the Wodaabe of West Bornu consists of the males of the small agnatic descent group and their families, comprising perhaps twenty families or about a hundred persons, and about five hundred cattle. This group associates with other like groups in the wet season but separates from them as the dry season progresses, itself often dividing into individual families or pairs of families. Formerly the large wet-season groups were clans but now they have a more varied composition. In the past it was the Guardian who exercised jural control over the clan, but his duties, as we have seen, were concerned with the internal affairs of the group, which had no corporate external relations. (See page 370.)

Nowadays the wet-season groups have a political head, and the leaders of their constituent groups are arranged in a hierarchy by titles; but this hierarchy hardly conceals the essential fluidity of the basic pastoral groupings. All the offices and groupings above the agnatic descent group level are the product of specific events in the history of the Wodaabe in Bornu, which cannot be dealt with fully here. The main trend of these events was that Wodaabe, themselves a fluid, segmentary society, had to guarantee their own economic welfare by maintaining links not only with alien groups of similar order whom they encountered in their pastoral life, but also by rendering allegiance to states in whose territory they pastured. Now follows a sketch of the principle political offices and the groups with which they are concerned.

THE *ardo* (LEADER) • The *ardo* (leader) is the most "traditional" of the political offices, for it is concerned with the basic political group in Fulani society, the agnatic descent group.

Several criteria govern the selection of an *ardo*. He must have established a herd and household in the usual way and must have wives and children. It is preferred that he be a prosperous man and have a reputation for being not only fortunate in his pastoral affairs but skilled in conducting them. It is an advantage for him to be the son or younger brother of his predecessor, but he must be related agnatically to his forerunner. The most important factor, however, is that he commands the support of his entire group. Indeed, there is no room for dissension over leadership in these pastoral groups, which split rather than harbor divided counsel on the important matters affecting them.

The *ardo* is charged with general responsibility for his group's social, political, and economic affairs; formerly he organized the members for defense and attack. He is the spokesman of his group in dealings with like groups within Wodaabe society and with all those outside Wodaabe society who will treat with him. Non-Fulani are usually very clear about the duties of an *ardo* and will deal with him in a wide range of matters concerning the men and women of his group. Thus, when the protectorate system of taxation was set up among the Wodaabe in 1915, it was conceded that an *ardo* might hold one tax receipt for his group, and this is the practice today.

But an *ardo* does not command, he advises, as is best seen in the conferences preceding pastoral moves. The *ardo*'s duty is to elicit all forms of evidence from the youngest herdsboy to the oldest herder, and to sum up the feeling of the group. Thereafter any householder can go where he will without restraint and with no ill feeling.

THE *laamiido* (CHIEF) • In Fulani society at large the term *laamiido* is a very flexible one considered in terms of the powers wielded and the groups involved. It may connote an emir of a large kingdom with provincial status; or it may be applied to a minor chief with a few hundred persons in his charge. But whereas the term *ardo* generally conveys the ideal of leadership of Fulani in a pastoral context, the term *laamiido* connotes rulership, not only of Fulani but of others, and in a wider context than the life of the pastoral camps. It also suggests that a greater range of sanctions is available for the control of the political unit involved.

Among the Wodaabe it is very likely that rulership was unknown before the Holy War. It grew during the latter half of the nineteenth century and was adopted by both the British and the Wodaabe to suit the circumstances of the protectorate.

The British found three Wodaabe chiefdoms when they began to administer West Bornu effectively in 1913. Their first main administrative aim was to ensure the collection of the tax—in this case the cattle tax. To do this they had to break the dual allegiances of the Wodaabe, and the first method they adopted was to offer them a District of Bornu, for which the Wodaabe would supply the district head. This the Wodaabe rejected. Next, in 1915, the British persuaded the chiefs to establish permanent settlements in the neighborhoods to which their followers would return in the wet season. The chiefs would be responsible for collecting the cattle tax, and the leaders would be responsible for their own pastoral groups, registering themselves with the *laamiido*. This the Wodaabe supported since it removed some of the abuses of a more direct system of collection that had operated earlier. The chiefs later became the salaried employees of the Bornu government and their duties were widened to include responsibility for the sedentary population.

Let us turn to the working of a chiefdom today, considering it solely from the point of view of the pastoral Wodaabe, from whose nineteenth-century organization it was adapted.

The chief resides in his village, which is located in an area proved to be desirable for wet-season grazing by the Wodaabe. But all these areas are not equally endowed, and their suitability varies from year to year. Thus, despite strong social links to their chief, his followers may be forced to spend the wet season elsewhere than in his village area, and he is not free to move in their company. This results, at the least, in difficulties in collecting the tax and in holding wet-season ceremonies, and, at the most, in a change of allegiance of pastoral groups from one chief to another. Moreover, the chief, in general, finds it difficult to exercise leadership of the kind congenial to Wodaabe pastoral groups. He himself is not a practicing pastoralist; indeed, many chiefs no longer own significant numbers of cattle. A few chiefs manage to maintain effective personal communication with their followings at most seasons of the year. Others rely on a body of messengers to keep in touch with the affairs of the camps, which often lie sixty to eighty miles away at the height of the dry season. But all find that government and village matters interfere with these activities, and a chief's performance is not assessed primarily by his control over pastoralists—except during the short tax season.

The social bonds between a chief and his following are by no means uniform. His following may consist of up to ten pastoral groups, each under its leader. The groups are informally ranked in terms of affiliation, length of allegiance, degree of intermarriage, and wealth in cattle. The leader of each of these groups has to weigh his social obligations to the chief against the demands of his cattle. The chief, for his part, has the administrative duty of collecting the tax upon which his livelihood depends. In practice the tax cannot be related directly to the actual numbers of cattle possessed, for it is assessed somewhat arbitrarily by the administration. The chief has therefore to pamper those groups who are lowest in the hierarchy. In a good tax year he is able to relieve those with whom he has the closest social bonds.

Ceremonial, too, plays a variable part in the cohesion of a chief's follow-ing. There are two sets of ceremonial, the familial and the political. Those familial ceremonies that were under the Guardian's control are fading in im-portance (see below), but may still be valuable cohesive factors when com-bined with political ceremonies. Whereas for the groups highest in each chief-dom hierarchy the two coincide, and indeed blend in a very vivid way, the lower-order groups find themselves divided in their ceremonial commitments. The main wet-season ceremony that will bring these groups into closer touch with others in the chiefdom is marriage and, partly for ceremonial and partly for political reasons, a chief will foster marriages between the higher and lower groups in his chiefdom's hierarchy.

A Wodaabe chiefdom is a fluid organization. This derives partly from pastoral demands made upon its constituent groups, but also from their in-compatible social commitments.

RELIGION AND LAW

Islam

It will have been apparent that the Wodaabe regard themselves as Muslims. All the important life crises of an individual are accompanied by ceremonies that, while having many important indigenous elements, are unmistakably Islamic. A baby becomes a person, grows up, is married, and dies to the ac-companiment of Islamic prayers, and every one of his days is divided in a similar way. A man feasts and fasts (the latter not always with good grace) according to the dictates of the Islamic calendar. Quite outside the system of tribal cooperation, the poor are assisted with alms as the Koran commands. If he cannot go on the pilgrimage himself, a man speaks of the pilgrim with awe and helps him when he can. The details of the lives of local saints are known, and the Muslim scribe is honored. If a man achieves worldly success in the form of a title or a chieftainship, his accession is marked with an Islamic ritual.

Cattle

But somehow all this organized religious activity—and it is considerable—seems to touch only a part of the Wodaabe life, and to affect the people, as it were, casually. This is because nothing in their experience of the Islamic faith touches that other vital part of their being, the cattle. The traditional religion of the pastoral Fulani has been described as "cowmania without cowdolatry." Indeed, when we look closely at its elements it seems as though Wodaabe dealings with cattle, when not hardheaded manipulation of a vital resource, are an apparatus of magic. But in addition, or rather joined with these acts, runs the firm belief that cattle pass judgment on human beings, and that therefore Wodaabe must rule their lives in ways of which the cattle can approve. This is the basis of the wide range of ritual prohibitions on personal acts that have as their reference not simply the welfare of the cattle but the latter's active sanction. Indeed, the Wodaabe are called by a name that indicates their preoccupation with this relationship with cattle.

The vital element lacking in Wodaabe traditional religion today is a firsthand knowledge of the full cycle of the Guardian's wet-season ceremonies, which raised these personal and often negative acts into a coherent system made vivid by corporate ceremonies. In the past the *maudo laawol pulaaku* was the focus of communal activities of the clan in the wet season. These included livestock contests in which the prize beasts of the clan's herds were paraded and judged. The Guardian also presided over herd owners' feasts in which a man whose stock bull had served ten seasons presented it to his clansmen at a meat feast. The cattle contests and feasts were probably fertility rites, although informants do not describe them in this way. Even today the *maudo laawol pulaaku* will convene periodic wet-season assemblies at which he will exhort the elders to prevent their young people from adopting practices or fashions conceived to be out of tune with the traditional Fulani way of life, but many of the West Bornu elders leave their families and their cattle behind when they attend.

The Wodaabe religious beliefs have an important relationship to law, to which we now turn.

Law

The only courts of law at the disposal of the Wodaabe are those of the government of Bornu, presided over by Muslim judges, or at a lower level by district heads. In civil affairs Wodaabe hardly avail themselves of these courts, partly because they are few and the pastoralists are continually moving, partly because their civil disputes can be settled otherwise. The only frequent Wodaabe case before the *alcaali*'s (Muslim judge's) court is divorce where a woman is the plaintiff. Otherwise these courts serve as courts of criminal jurisdiction as far as Wodaabe are concerned. However, by virtue of their mobility and inadequate law enforcement, the Wodaabe are able to a large extent to avoid criminal judgment.

By virtue of his government office as a subordinate of the district head, a Wodaabe chief is expected to exercise the police functions of inquiry and apprehension. This he does when the culprits are likely not to be Wodaabe, or when he has little choice in the matter. But usually the Wodaabe chiefs are at pains to keep these functions dormant as far as Wodaabe are concerned, particularly those of their own followings, who are likely to drift away from a chief who is too zealous. The chiefs have no constituted judicial functions in the government hierarchy.

It will be seen that outside his own lineage groups, and to a lesser extent outside his clan, a man is in an alien legal system. In both criminal and civil cases his case will be tried by the rules of evidence and procedure of an Islamic court, not in his natal language (although this is a frequent provision in such courts), and with no assessor (an assistant to the judge) who knows his tribal customs intimately.

Customary legal procedures are therefore carried out in and between descent groups, and the key figure is the leader. We must remember that these groups cannot harbor long-standing disputes, and that their pastoral dispersal automatically affords a way of minimizing tension, and may act as a sanction on a wrongdoer. Also, Wodaabe religious beliefs concerning the many and intimate sanctions wielded by cattle exercise a strong control over an individual's actions.

It might seem from this that no wrongs or disputes ever occur in Wodaabe pastoral groups. This, of course, is not so. But what does happen is that the group itself, in the form of its elders, is continually in session, sitting in judgment on the actions of its members. They are also continually taking the most valuable form of evidence, the state of the cattle. This takes place in the morning meetings in the cattle corral, but more particularly in the meetings of elders in the afternoons, either under the shade tree in the camp or in the market. Disputes therefore rarely take these pastoral tribunals by surprise, and a disputant is coached in advance on the reactions of his immediate social group, which may in fact move him to modify his intended course of action. In this way, disputes between male elders are rare, since a man is either extracting his full rights from his group and rendering it his full duty, or he has no identity of interests and pastures his cattle elsewhere. But frequent adjustments of relations are made, and in this the leader, voicing the consensus of the elders' group, plays an important part.

CHANGE

It is not possible to say for how long the Wodaabe have been part of the Islamic world of the western Sudan, but it is safe to assume that they could not have entirely escaped the early days of the Holy War of 1804, by which the Empire of Sokoto was founded. During the later stages of the empire in northeastern Nigeria, we know that they participated actively from about 1820 on. They did so opportunistically, now seizing a chance to join an emir's army, now holding back. We also know that, for about a century, Wodaabe have been prepared to involve themselves in state politics and state wars, although less so in the twentieth than in the nineteenth century. During all this time, it is equally clear that their overriding motive has been the welfare of their herds. Wars have been joined and tribute has been given in order to enhance Wodaabe pastoral opportunities. Slaves, horses, and titles were simply the by-products of this involvement.

The values derived from this activity are the antithesis of those attached to the family system that Wodaabe hold to be so important. These values are public, status-conscious, and martial, as opposed to familial, egalitarian, and peaceful values. The latter set of values, although still coherent and expressed to a large degree in present-day institutions, have undergone considerable erosion. As we have seen, chiefs with wider fields of competence have arisen at the expense of the Guardians. Moreover, the norms and practices of Islamic religion have been disseminated and Islamic legal provisions have become more effective. The result is a dualism in Wodaabe values that is demonstrated in many of their ceremonies and rituals and in other dimensions of life.

There is evidence that before the protectorate these changes accumulated slowly. Since protectorate times, when the British took specific measures to draw the Wodaabe into the protectorate's fiscal and legal system, they have proceeded apace. This process will surely be accelerated in the future. Even by 1951 involvement with the government was beginning to be viewed as a dubious advantage.

In the developments of the past century and a half there has been one feature of Wodaabe life that, involving themselves with the state or withdrawing from it, they have been able to use effectively. This feature—their physical mobility in unfrequented tracts of country—has guided their reaction to attempts to introduce them to ranching as an alternate form of cattle raising. It will, perhaps, also guide their response to much future change.

Notes

(1) This chapter includes an abridged version of *Savannah Nomads* (London: Oxford University Press for the International Africa Institute, 1959). It appears here by permission of the International African Institute and Oxford University Press.

(2) This term is properly written FulƁe. The Anglicized form will be used here. Similarly, Wodaabe, Fulfulde, Laamiido, and Ardo should be written as WoɖaaƁe, Fulfulɖe, Laamiiɖo, and Arɖo, respectively.

(3) The various Fulani transhumant patterns are described and analyzed in Stenning 1957.

(4) See Stenning 1957 for a more detailed analysis.

(5) No category might inherit while representatives of a prior category were eligible. Each category inherited to the exclusion of subsequent categories. Thus an estate could not be divided among a son, a brother, a nephew, an uncle, and a patrilateral parallel cousin of the dead man even if representatives of all these categories were available.

Bibliography

With a few exceptions the following bibliography emphasizes contemporary work. Starred items (*) include significant bibliographies.

General

Stenning, Derrick J. (1959*).   *Savannah Nomads.* London: Oxford University Press for International African Institute.
All the material in this chapter is treated more extensively in this work.

Dupire, Marguerite (1962b).   *Peuls nomades: étude descriptive des Woɖaabe du Sahel Nigérien.* Paris: Institut d'Ethnologie (Travaux et Mémoires 64).

Subsistence

Dupire, M. (1961).   "The Place of Commerce and Markets in the Economy of the Bororo (Fulbe)," in Paul J. Bohannan and George Dalton, *Markets in Africa.* Evanston, Ill.: Northwestern University Press.

——— (1962a).   *Les facteurs humains de l'economie pastorale.* Paris: Secretariat Institut Français de l'Afrique Noir Niger.
Includes material on the Fulani.

Stenning, Derrick J. (1957).   "Transhumance, Migratory Drift, Migration; Patterns of Pastoral Fulani Nomadism," *Journal of the Royal Anthropological*

Institute, Vol. 87, Part 2. Reprinted in Simon and Phoebe Ottenberg (eds.), *Cultures and Societies of Africa.* New York: Random House, 1960.
An analysis of the main modes of pastoral Fulani movements.

Social Organization

Hopen, C. E. (1958). *The Pastoral Fulbe Family in Gwandu.* London: Oxford University Press for International African Institute.
A general account of the Fulani family in a semisedentary population.

Stenning, Derrick J. (1958). "Household Viability among the Pastoral Fulani," in J. R. Goody (ed.), *The Developmental Cycle in Domestic Groups,* Cambridge Papers in Social Anthropology No. 1.
Discusses the limits of herd and family association.

Political Organization

Bâ, A. Hampaté, and G. Dieterlen (1961). *Koumen; texte initiatique des pasteurs peul.* Cahiers de l'Homme, n.s., No. 1. Paris: Ecole Practique des Hautes Etudes.
The most complete account of the Fulani pastoral religion.

Froehlich, Jean C. (1954). "Le Commandement et l'organisation sociale chez les Foulbe de l'Adamasua," *Études Camerounaises,* Nos. 45–46.

Smith, M. G. (1960). *Government in Zazzau.* London: Oxford University Press for International African Institute.
Parts 1 and 5, especially, discuss the nature of Fulani state organization.

Other

Dupire, Marguerite (1963). "The Position of Women in a Pastoral Society [Wodaabe] in *Women of Tropical Africa* edited by Denise Paulme. Berkeley and Los Angeles, California: University of California Press, pp. 47–92.

Greenberg, Joseph H. (1955†). *Studies in African Linguistic Classification.* New Haven, Conn.: The Compass Publishing Co.

Hopen, C. Edward (1964). "A Note on *Alkali Fulfulde:* A Reformation Movement among the Nomadic Fulbe (Fulani) of Sokoto Province," *Africa,* Vol. 34, 1964, pp. 21–27.

11

THE RWANDA OF RWANDA

about the chapter

The romantic appeal of the Tutsi (Watutsi), with their tall, gracile Nilotic physical type, has made them one of the few African groups widely known outside of Africa. But, more important, Rwanda, the wider society of which they are a part, is of special interest to the Africa specialist, especially the anthropologist and the political scientist. D'Hertefelt's analysis demonstrates that orderly principles underlie the complexity of the Rwanda nation. The kingdom is composed of three separate hereditary groups—the Tutsi, the Hutu, and the Twa —which differ in occupation and physical appearance but speak a common language. Since they speak a common language, Kinyarwanda, the Rwanda are considered to be one people—in older terminology, one tribe. However, the culture of Rwanda shows intracultural variations and, less recognized by anthropologists, regional variations as well. An important conclusion of the chapter is that even in nonurban nations principles that integrate a society may not operate identically in every corner of its territory.

Traditionally, the institution of divine kingship served to hold the diverse Rwanda castes together in one society. Rwanda, like Hausaland and Swaziland, was a "conquest state," and, more than any other African kingdom, it was organized on a caste principle. For the Africanist, a comparison of the operation of the stratification principle in Rwanda and in Hausa is useful. For other social scientists, Rwanda provides the basis for comparing caste phenomena in Africa with caste in other areas, and a study of the nature of an African variety of bureaucracy and "feudalism."

Closely connected with the kingship was the institution of client-

ship, which appears in various forms in many African societies, such
as Hausa, Yoruba, and Kpelle societies. From among his kinsmen
and direct clients (largely Tutsi), the king (also Tutsi) appointed his
councilors and heads of territorial units into which the state was
divided for administrative purposes. As in most sub-Saharan kingdoms, there were checks on duplicity and some concentration of
power in hands other than the king's. Crucial to understanding political
organization and social stratification in Rwanda is the fact that
although these features operated to give the Hutu majority some institutionalized protection from arbitrary misuse of power by their Tutsi
overlords, they at the same time operated to preserve and even increase
Tutsi power and to continue the inferior position of the Hutu and
the Twa.

In the recent successful movement for the independence of
Rwanda—described by d'Hertefelt—the numerically dominant Hutu
wrested power from the Tutsi and, rejecting the basic premise of Rwanda
society, overthrew the monarchy and replaced it with a republic. The
situation offers valuable case material illustrating how a modern political party created a sense of self-awareness and unity among a segment of society formerly lacking cohesion. It also shows how a hereditary elite, whose attachment to its own myths and symbols of power
was rigidly institutionalized, could not move with the current of history. Rwanda is one of the few African countries which is linguistically
homogeneous, but its unity mainly rested on the symbols and the
idiom of the deposed kingship. D'Hertefelt's analysis provokes the
question: Will the long-term substitute that is found for the kingship
—whatever it may be—employ the same symbols, albeit negatively.

about the author

Marcel d'Hertefelt, social anthropologist of the Institut pour la
Recherche Scientifique en Afrique Centrale, Butare, Rwanda, teaches
at the National University of Rwanda. He received his Lic. Phil. et
Lettres from the University of Louvain (Belgium) in 1956, and has
carried out extensive anthropological research in Rwanda and
Burundi. He has also been African Studies Center Scholar in Resi-
dence at the African Studies Center, University of California, Los
Angeles. His published works include *Elections en Société Féodale*
(with J. J. Maquet, 1959), "Myth and Political Acculturation in
Rwanda" (1960), *Le Rwanda* (1962), and *La royauté sacrée de l'ancien
Rwanda: texte, traduction et commentaire de son rituel* (with A.
Coupez, 1964).

MARCEL d'HERTEFELT · *The Rwanda of Rwanda*

INTRODUCTION

LOCATION · Rwanda[1] lies in East Central Africa, bordering on Burundi, the Republic of Congo, Uganda, and Tanganyika. It stretches from lat. 1°04′ to 2°50′ S, and from lon. 28°50′ to 30°53′ E, with an area covering approximately 10,000 square miles. The longest distances in a straight line are about 100 miles from north to south, and about 150 miles from east to west. The present-day frontiers reflect only in part the conquests made by the ancient kings, as international arrangements concluded by the colonial powers when occupying East and Central Africa have modified the traditional boundaries. On the northern border, some districts were united to Uganda, but the Idjwi Island, in Lake Kivu, was joined to the (formerly Belgian) Congo.[2]

ECOLOGY · The topography of Rwanda is dominated by the mountain ridge that separates the Congo and Nile basins. This ridge stretches in a general north-south direction at a small distance from the eastern shore of Lake Kivu; its summits rise to about 10,000 feet above sea level. East of this ridge, Rwanda is a highland country the relief of which slopes down gently to the east. Hundreds of rivers and brooks cut deep, marshy valleys into the upland plain and wind round thousands of hills. Many small lakes are situated in the lower-lying eastern part of the country.

From a physical point of view, Rwanda may be divided into three relatively homogeneous regions: the eastern region, the altitude of which varies from 3900 to about 5100 feet; the central region, an upland plain at the mean altitude of some 5100 feet, and the northern and western region, at the altitude of about 6000 feet and above.

Most of Rwanda is characterized by a mean temperature of about 66°F., but the lower eastern region is warmer, whereas in the high western mountain ridge the thermometer may fall to the freezing point. The annual mean temperature is relatively constant, and the maximal variations between day and night are greater than those between the seasons. There are two rainy

405

seasons, from October to December and from March to May, and two intervening dry seasons, but these dates are subject to considerable variations
from one year to another. Moreover, the relative length of the wet and dry
seasons, as well as the average annual precipitation, varies among the three
areas. The mean precipitation amounts to fifty inches and more in the northern and western area but does not reach the forty-inch mark in the east.

Rwanda is characterized by a great many vegetation zones. The western
mountain ridge is forested, as are the northwestern volcanoes, which are also
covered with pseudo-alpine meadows, but forests are no longer to be found
under the 6000-foot line. Central Rwanda was almost entirely denuded at
the arrival of the Europeans, who have since applied a number of reforesta-
tion schemes. The eastern districts are characterized by wooded savanna with
Acacia, and herbaceous savanna. The overall scarcity of trees and the heavy
rains and steep relief have created very serious problems of soil erosion and
soil depletion.

Castes and ethnic composition

The population of Rwanda is composed of three castes: the Tutsi, the Hutu,
and the Twa.[3] The term "castes" refers to hereditary, occupational, and
endogamous groups that are arranged in a hierarchical, ranked pattern. The
recent social and political movements that have overthrown the traditional
caste structure will be discussed in the section devoted to social change.[4]

TWA • Traditionally, the Twa form the lower caste. Two subgroups may
be distinguished with respect to their occupational status: the hunters and
gatherers who inhabit the mountain forests of western and northern Rwanda,
and the potters who live scattered amid the other inhabitants of the country.

HUTU • The Hutu are agriculturalists. One cannot tell with certainty
whether they arrived in Rwanda at the same time as the Twa or later. As
long as the caste structure was in full swing, the production of the economic
surplus reserved for the Tutsi rulers devolved almost entirely on the Hutu.

TUTSI • The Tutsi are pastoralists; in the past, they were a warrior caste,
too. Their immigration into the country, which is attested by the oral traditions of Rwanda and of neighboring peoples, forms part of the great pastoral
migrations that resulted in the establishment of specific political units in the
interlacustrine region of East Africa. Various hypotheses have been set up
with respect to the former settlement of the Tutsi but the problem is as yet
unsolved. They may have inhabited the Nile Valley between Lake Albert
and the Bahr el Gazal, or the region situated to the east of this valley toward

the Ethiopian border. In any case, they arrived in the interlacustrine region about the thirteenth century or even earlier.

PHYSICAL APPEARANCE · Anthropology has shown that the Hutu, the Tutsi, and the Twa exhibit significant differences in their physical characteristics. The latter constitute a wide range of indices, some of which are given below.

	Tutsi	Hutu	Twa
Weight (in pounds)	126.6	131.2	106.7
Stature (in inches)	69.5	65.9	61.1
Total arm length (in inches)	30.9	30.	27.2
Nose width (in inches)	1.5	1.7	1.8

The Tutsi are Nilotes.[5] The Hutu are characterized by Negroid and Nilotic physical components. In addition, they have some characteristics of a proto-Rwanda population that mixed with the Hutu when they arrived in the area and whose type survives more or less in the Moso of southern Burundi. The Twa are pygmoids, akin to the Mbuti (Republic of Congo).

The total African population of Rwanda (1959) is estimated at 2,600,-000, of whom about 83 percent are Hutu, approximately 16 percent are Tutsi, and less than 1 percent are Twa. The three castes are unevenly distributed over the country: the Hutu outnumber the other castes everywhere, whereas the population of Tutsi varies from about 5 percent and less (for example, in northern Rwanda) to 40 percent and more in some central districts.[6] The Twa live in small residential groups scattered all over the country, but especially in central Rwanda and in the forest area. The demographic distribution pattern of Tutsi and Hutu stresses the pronounced heterogeneity of Rwanda society; it is functionally related to historical and ecological variables.

Population density is exceptionally high: about 220 inhabitants per square mile with variations from 75 (eastern region) to 450 (volcanic upland region in the northwest). Less than 1 percent of the African population are living in urban centers.

There are about 2000 non-Africans (1962), among whom were approximately 500 Belgians employed in the civil service or in missionary work, and Greek, Indian, Arab, or Pakistani traders.

INTRACULTURAL VARIATION · Although a general overall description of Rwanda society and culture is possible, the anthropologist should be very much aware of internal cultural variations, for they are very significant with reference to the process of social and political change that characterizes present-day Rwanda.

Tutsi Women Prominent Tutsi women attend a national celebration. (*IRSAC*)

Relevant variations in Rwanda are of two orders. There are the "vertical" variations referring to the cultural differences between the castes, and the "horizontal" variations that concern the differences between the regions. Those orders of variation are correlative and functionally related to history, to ecological variables, and to the demographic distribution of the traditionally dominant caste. Thus, in pastoralist central Rwanda, where the predominance of the Nilotic caste and of the central government is oldest and most influential, intercaste variations have been largely superseded by commonly shared patterns of attitudes and norms. On the contrary, where the Tutsi penetration has been slower, where the demographic importance of the Tutsi has been less significant, where the central administration has been weaker, or where the ecology has been of an almost exclusively agricultural type, the cultural variation between members of different castes is more pronounced and differs more from central Rwanda patterns.

Most analyses of Rwanda society and culture have overstressed the degree of cultural integration of ancient Rwanda by giving excessive prominence to the central districts and to the behavioral patterns, values, and

Tilling the Fields Hutu woman with her son and infant is shown tilling the fields. (*IRSAC*)

norms of the traditional rulers with whom investigators most frequently came in touch, a group that displays a great cultural homogeneity. But the actual enforcement of those patterns on the Hutu population that lived beyond the limits of central Rwanda was not examined very much. The regional differences between the northern districts (more than half a million people) and central Rwanda (about one million people) are especially important. They may be considered as a structural weakness of the traditional regime of which the recent political Hutu movements have taken advantage in order to destroy the established social system.

LANGUAGE · The language known as Kinyarwanda (*Ki-* is a Bantu prefix; *-nya* is an infix meaning language) is classed by Greenberg (1955) in the Bantu subgroup of the Central Branch of the Niger-Congo family. It is spoken by all three castes, with central Kinyarwanda providing the norms of speech for the entire country. It is not known whether the Nilotic immigrants and conquerors became Bantu speakers on their arrival in Rwanda or were already speaking a Bantu language.

ECONOMY

AGRICULTURE · Agriculture was, and still is, the basis of the Rwanda economy. Beans, peas, sorghum, millet, maize, sweet potatoes, and cassava (manioc) were the major crops. The dwellings were surrounded by vast banana plantations, whose yield was mainly used in making the beer that played an important part in all social relations.

An agricultural calendar, based on lunar months, set the rhythm of

Hutu life. Although it varied from one region to another, in central Rwanda its main divisions were the following.

In August and September, at the end of the long dry season, the soil was tilled and prepared for sowing. October and November were sowing or planting months, for beans, peas, pumpkins, millet, maize, and groundnuts. In January, beans and peas were gathered and sorghum was sown. Sweet potatoes and cassava were planted in the valleys during February and on the hills in March. Beans were also sown in March. Cassava was harvested in May; beans, sorghum, and maize matured in June and July. To prevent excessive impoverishment of the soil, a system of bush fallowing and crop rotation was followed, although fertilizers and irrigation were not used in the past.

The agricultural cycle was also marked by ritualistic observances. At the royal court, a first fruits celebration was held in June, with sorghum and millet coming from specified ritual fields in the northeastern part of central Rwanda. The autonomous Hutu lineages of northern Rwanda performed their first fruits ritual and a solemn ancestor cult rite in July.

ANIMAL HUSBANDRY · The Rwanda reared cattle, goats, woolless sheep, chickens, and dogs. Goat- and sheepskins provided wearing apparel for the Hutu, but goat flesh was considered impure except by Hutu men and Twa, who were allowed to eat it; only Twa ate mutton. The intestines of sheep and chickens were used as a divinatory substance. Dogs were used for hunting and as watchdogs.

As a rule, the long-horned Ankole cattle kept by the Tutsi pastoralists and their clients did not contribute much to the subsistence of the population. The milk production per cow did not exceed about a quart and a half a day in the good season. In general, only the Tutsi could afford enough cows to maintain a family on a balanced diet. Fresh or curdled milk formed the principal ingredient of the food of this wealthier pastoral minority. Meat was highly valued by Hutu and Tutsi alike but, since cattle were not slaughtered, meat was normally available only when a beast died from accidental causes.

Only the Hima, a very small Nilotic population of northeastern Rwanda, were nomads. However, herdboys hired by Tutsi pastoralists shifted the Tutsi herds seasonally according to the grazing possibilities. They drove the herds to pasture in the valleys during the dry seasons, on the hills during the wet seasons, or in the reaped fields in July. Each day they led them away from the byre in morning and back again in the evening.

The influence of the cattle on the social and political structure of ancient Rwanda will be discussed later. The major interest the people of Rwanda shared in cattle was reflected in the elaborate ritual that surrounded their raising, in the refresher rites at the royal court, in language, and in literature.

Thus, a very extensive vocabulary denoted the individual characteristics of cattle, numerous current metaphors and symbols were drawn from pastoralism, and the institutionalized pastoral literature exalted the beauty and virtues of the royal herds.

HUNTING, FISHING, AND GATHERING · The forest Twa and some Hutu lineages of eastern Rwanda hunted in order to live, whereas the Tutsi hunted as a sport in order to show their skill and their courage. The major implements used in hunting were bows, spears, javelins, and different kinds of traps. As a rule, fishing was not much practiced, since fish were not considered edible. Beekeeping was a fairly general subsidiary occupation, especially with the northern Hutu and Twa. Honey was used to brew hydromel, the favorite drink of prominent Tutsi.

DIET · The Twa were reputed to be greedy eaters and drinkers, but their diet was rather irregular: the hunters were dependent on the contingencies of their chase; others, frequently on the generosity of lords and people for whom they sang and danced on different occasions. Twa had fewer food taboos than the other castes, but they were not entirely without them. Their polygamists were not allowed to eat mutton; some kinds of game were forbidden to all of them; only children could eat eggs.

The diet of the Hutu was chiefly made up of beans, sweet potatoes, and banana or sorghum beer. The frequency of the meals depended on the amount of energy required by the work in the fields and so was rather irregular. In the evening, the Tutsi had a meal that did not differ essentially from that of the Hutu. But their attitude toward solid food was rather negative; they drank more (milk and hydromel) than they ate. This attitude has been interpreted as reflecting a tendency for the Tutsi to emphasize their independence from the agricultural production of the Hutu and to stress the fundamental and natural differences that were supposed to exist between them and the other castes.

Material culture and technology

HOUSE TYPE · Rwanda huts were beehive-shaped, the common type among the interlacustrine peoples. People built their huts with poles, branches, reeds, and grass. The circular base of a hut had a mean diameter of about fifteen feet. In the huts of rich Tutsi, artistically decorated folding screens separated the reception room from the rest of the hut. As a rule, the hut functioned at the same time as a place for sleeping, cooking, and eating, and, frequently, as a stable for goats and small cattle during the night.

Rwanda dwellings were scattered all over the countryside; the compact village was unknown, but a certain degree of residential concentration was

Inside a Rwanda Compound
(*IRSAC*)

typical for local kinship groups, especially among the northern Hutu. The huts were situated in a circular enclosure surrounded by a hedge that had only one gate. As a rule, a Hutu polygamist's married sons did not build their huts in their father's enclosure, but the father's wives lived in separate huts situated in his enclosure. As for the Tutsi, their sons dispersed more frequently than did the Hutu sons after their marriage, and their wives generally had their own enclosures at some distance from that of the husband.

CLOTHING · Boys and girls went naked up to the age of ten. Adolescent Tutsi girls and adult men wore girdles made of cowskin, whereas important Tutsi wore girdles of a lion's or a leopard's skin with fringes hanging nearly to the feet. Hutu girls wore girdles without fringes; Hutu men, bark skirts or goatskins; Twa, antelope skins or sheep- or goatskins. Married women were dressed in clothes made of cowskin. Before the arrival of the Europeans, the wealthy Tutsi, men and women alike, had adopted the brightly colored draped cloths imported by African merchants from the eastern coast. Married women and, as a rule, Hutu and Twa men shaved their heads, whereas girls and Tutsi men wore tufts, the pattern of which varied. Copper or iron armlets and thin rings made of copper wire or plant fibers as well as charms belonged to the attire of men and women alike.

Rwanda technology was not well developed. It included fire making (by gyration), the preparation of bark for the making of clothes, furriery, the fabrication of clay pots and pipes, utilitarian woodcarving, the smelting of iron ore, a slightly more developed metallurgy comprising a kind of soldering by means of quartz powder (especially in the north), and basketry. The latter is remarkable because of the wide range of its production, the fine geometric motives of its decoration, and the perfection of its techniques.

These small industries and crafts were considered specialties and were allocated—more or less—along caste and sex lines. Thus objects of wood and iron as well as large baskets were chiefly manufactured by Hutu men. Pots were made by Twa (sometimes by Hutu) men or women, but only men prepared bark clothes and skins. Hutu and Tutsi women wove mats, small baskets, and folding screens, but the more artistic items were made by Tutsi women. Twa manufactured a type of bow that differed from the common Tutsi and Hutu bow.

Agricultural work was not specialized along sex lines, although tasks that required much physical strength or considerable traveling were performed by men. Women were forbidden to take care of cattle; magic beliefs concerning the impurity of women justified this restriction, for the prohibition did not apply to females before puberty or after the menopause.

The nuclear family was the basic unit of economic cooperation and production; under the father's authority, the wife and children contributed to satisfy its subsistence needs. In fact, when the family was polygynous, each nuclear family formed an independent economic unit, but the husband could regulate the distribution of work and produce. With polygynous Tutsi, the wives were often in charge of political domains for whose good administration they were held responsible as genuine superintendents. In the northern districts, the patrilocal extended family was also important as a unit of economic cooperation; its members were mutually helpful in agricultural work under the direction of the family head.

When a hut was to be built, or at harvesting time, or on the occasion of other tasks that required much cooperation, a team of working bees of kinsmen or neighbors was often called for.

On the political level, the Tutsi regulated and controlled labor through the military, administrative, and clientship structures (see below). As members of the army, the Hutu had to keep the numerous royal residences in repair; as taxpayers, they were liable to statute labor at definite periods of the year, and as an overall rule, on two days of the five-day week; as clients, they were liable to numerous prestations, the nature and the amount of which were not specified by a genuine contract.

Trade and exchange

The principal mode of production exchange was significantly related to the social and political structure of ancient Rwanda, since the economic surplus was mainly distributed through the military, administrative, and clientship channels. On the administrative level, the Hutu contributed agricultural produce to the chiefs of the land, whereas minor Tutsi had to provide the chiefs of the cattle with milk. On the military level, the Hutu contributed victuals, sheep, and metallurgic objects; the Twa, game and pottery; the Tutsi, cattle. Clients had to provide their pastoral lords with food and other goods.

The economic products also circulated in kinship settings: on formal and informal occasions, such as the transfer of bridewealth and dowry, birth and burial gifts, the exchange of presents between lineage members and affinal kinsmen, between blood brothers and, in the north, between members of two joking clans.

There were markets in the western and northwestern border regions, but they probably did not date back very far. Itinerant merchants hawked the local products through the country, and imported foreign commodities, such as salt from Lake Edward, rings of plant fibers from the region situated to the northwest of Lake Kivu, and beads from the East African coastal areas. All trade was by barter or "money barter" where hoes functioned as common standards for the conversion of exchange values.

SOCIAL ORGANIZATION

Kinship groupings

Descent was reckoned patrilineally. Three (in the northern districts, four) groups were based on the agnatic principle: the *inzu* (house), the least comprehensive grouping; the *umuryango* (lineage); the *ishanga* (subclan of the northern Hutu); and the *ubwoko* (patriclan).

A lineage included all consanguines who could actually trace their relationship to a common ancestor. Lineages were exogamous and lineage depth often exceeded six generations, at least with prominent Tutsi. The numerical growth of the group, the presence of a wealthy, famous, or powerful man, as well as a change of residence could all cause the splitting up of a lineage into two or more new lineages. In the less centralized north, the lineage was given paramount importance. There, up to the end of the nineteenth century, it constituted a residential, politically autonomous group that owned a collective estate. Among these northern Hutu, a lineage head, assisted by a council of some important members, looked after the exploitation of the collective estate and, in the last resort, dealt with disputes among lineage members. Lineage loyalty expressed itself mainly through the blood feud that commonly developed into small local wars.

In central Rwanda, as a result of the parceling out of the collective domain, the lineage was no longer an important social group with the Hutu. There, Hutu lineages generally had no heads, whereas Tutsi lineages had chiefs who were often very powerful; the king, however absolute theoretically he might be, had to take into account their vested political interests. The prominence of a dozen Tutsi lineages also expressed itself on the religious level by their participation in the rituals of kingship performed at the court. With both Hutu and Tutsi, the blood feud was still being considered a sacred duty; however, where Tutsi were concerned, it was not infrequently superseded by the king's arbitration.

THE HOUSE • The relative importance of the lineage and the house varied as a function of political variables. In the more centralized districts, the lineage was generally considered much less momentous because the rulers dealt exclusively with the "house" as the base of the administrative and military structure. A house was here defined as a consanguineal descent group (four to six generations in depth) with the additional qualification that it be a unit liable to a set of prestations and rents. A lineage included several of these houses, groups of shallower generational depth than a lineage.

The house group provided the common overall framework within which the Rwanda carried out the roles they occupied in the kinship system. The *inzu* heads, who were more or less hereditary, were assisted by a council. They discussed all the important matters pertaining to the group as a whole, such as marriage proposals, mutual help, and the distribution of the prestations imposed by the political chiefs. They could also try cases arising among *inzu* members.

THE PATRICLAN • A patriclan was a nonresidential group whose members recognized a vague kinship bond among themselves without being able to trace their descent back to a common ancestor. It was actually not a pure descent group, for it included Tutsi, Hutu, and Twa simultaneously. This fact may be explained by the protective identification of clients with their lords and, possibly, by the impoverishment of some Tutsi who came to be classified socially as Hutu. The proportion of members belonging to different castes was variable from one patriclan to another, and members of the same patriclan who belonged to different castes behaved as strangers toward each other.

There were some fifteen patriclans, each of them connected with a particular animal that functioned as a kind of group symbol, but from which no special prohibitions or injunctions derived. Moreover, certain patriclans happened to be associated with different animals in different regions, whereas groups claiming the same animal association were sometimes considered as different patriclans or as subclans (clusters of lineages).

Patriclans or subclans had no chiefs, nor did their members share in collective activities. As a rule, they were agamous. However, some patriclans were endowed with special functions. For example, any member of the *gesera* and *zigaaba* patriclans could perform ritual duties when a house was building or when a kinship group ("house") was to be purged of the impurity caused by a co-member's death. In the north, clans and subclans were linked together dually by joking relationships.

Marriage

The legality of a marriage depended on the handing over of a brideprice by the groom's father to the bride's father. The mere performance of the marriage rites did not constitute a legal union. The transfer of bridewealth caused the husband—and subject to his higher priority, also his *inzu*—to acquire an exclusive right on his wife's reproductive power so as to make him stand out as the legal father (*pater*) of all children born to the woman, either begotten by himself or by another man.

Brideprice consisted of a principal contribution, which was ideally one cow, and numerous subsidiary gifts reserved for the bride's kinsmen, especially beer. In the northern regions, the presents of beer amounted to about 50 percent of the total brideprice. Among the Hutu goats and hoes often replaced the normative cow as a brideprice; a very poor man would perform bride service at his father-in-law's for a year or two in order to get a spouse. In central Rwanda, Tutsi grooms were frequently exempted from giving bridewealth; this was regarded as a proof of particular esteem and goodwill.

After the marriage celebration, the bride's father sent a dowry to the husband and his kin; the dowry, which consisted of cattle, equipment, wearing apparel, provisions, and beer, often outweighed the value of the bridewealth even though this was not considered polite.

The marriage was normally negotiated between the kinship groups concerned. The advice of the groom's and the bride's mothers was always taken into account. Generally, the young people did not refuse their assent; they preferred to agree (and occasionally divorce afterward) in order not to destroy the good relations between the two groups. Two young people whose love was thwarted by their kinsmen had recourse to means to secure their kinsmen's consent. The girl could deliberately move to her lover's, or be taken by force, or be subjected by surprise to part of the marriage ritual. But none of those proceedings could bring about a legal marriage unless a brideprice was subsequently paid.

The marriage rites, of which there were a great many local variations, were celebrated at the residence of the groom's father. The ceremony stressed the alliance between the two kin groups, the social value attributed to the girl's virginity and fecundity, and the transition—especially the woman's—from one social status to another. The significance of the latter was particularly prominent in the north, where the marriage celebration was more clearly a *rite de passage*. (However, proper initiations were unknown in Rwanda except in the religious sphere.)

Intercaste marriages were not formally forbidden, but they were rather uncommon. Tutsi men, however, frequently had Hutu concubines. For a Hutu man to marry a Tutsi girl was quite exceptional; when such a marriage occurred, it validated a Hutu's political rise. The marriage of a Twa to a member of another caste was inconceivable.

The marriage prohibitions deriving from kinship ties were also general sexual prohibitions; transgressing them was considered incestuous.[7]

Cross-cousin marriages were not properly preferential (that is, obligatory) in central Rwanda, but nevertheless socially much approved. Among the northern Hutu, it was strictly forbidden for a man to marry a patrilateral cross-cousin, whereas the matrilateral cross-cousin was definitely a preferential mate as well as the first wife's brother's daughter, for a second and polygynous union. Sororal polygyny was not popular in any area.

A divorce was discussed by the two affinal kin groups concerned; they exerted considerable pressure on the unwilling partners so as to maintain the established alliance. As a rule, temporary separations and reconciliations preceded the final rupture. Although husband and the wife alike could initiate the divorce procedure, the wife always left the common residence. A man could divorce a woman for repeated unfaithfulness or for carelessness in running the affairs of the home; a woman would seek a divorce for her husband's refusal to cohabit, or for ill-usage or for inability to provide her a living. A man's impotency or a woman's sterility was not socially recognized as a reason for divorce. The brideprice was returned if the woman had not borne children to her husband or if the dowry had not been given. Indications are that marriages were fairly stable although estimates of divorce rates are not available.

The family

The legal family took various forms. The nuclear family was composed of a husband, his wife, and their unmarried children; the polygynous family, of a husband, his wives, and their unmarried children. A family type not socially sanctioned was exemplified by a girl or a married woman living in concubinage. In the first case, the children belonged to the girl's father; in the second case, to the woman's husband. The above types made up the vast majority of conjugal unions. Their residence pattern was commonly patrilocal (virilocal) with the Hutu and the Twa, and often neolocal with the Tutsi.

Polygyny was culturally preferred. As a rule, ordinary polygynous Tutsi had two wives; Hutu, three or four. A polygynous family must not be regarded as a simple aggregate of various nuclear families, for it possessed a different kind of integration, sexually and economically. As noted earlier, each of the wives had (at least ideally) her own hut, which the husband visited in rotation. None of them could give orders to another, but the wife who had been married first—or a younger favorite—often tried to dominate the others. Rivalries and disputes are said to have been very frequent.

The wives were responsible to the husband for the cleanliness of their huts, the food and beer supplies, and the upkeep of their fields. In the northern regions, the husband merely enjoyed the usufruct of what his wife (or wives) had got as a dowry. A wife had to submit to her husband's authority, but he was expected to take her advice in important matters regarding the family. A husband's power, within the nuclear or polygynous domestic unit, was not absolute. Especially within the patrilocal extended family unit of the northern Hutu, it was balanced by his father's authority—as long as the latter lived—and by the authority of the *inzu* and lineage heads.

The possibility of the existence of ghost marriage and the levirate followed from the transfer of brideprice by which a man's kin acquired a right to his widow's fertility. Ghost marriage was found among the Tutsi and the northern Hutu. The new husband, who was a member of the deceased husband's *inzu* and generally belonging to his generation, could cohabit with the widow and beget children who would be considered as the deceased's offspring, the new husband being only their genitor and the widow's acting husband. The levirate was found, it is said, with the central Hutu; here, the husband's kinsman who took care of the widow was considered as the latter's real husband and as the pater of the children he begot with her.

Behavior within the kinship and affinity system was differentiated according to the sex, the age, the generational position (alternate or proximate generation), and the type (consanguineal, affinal) of the relationship existing between the persons involved. Only the most important roles can be mentioned here.

Consanguines of the same generation were expected to behave toward each other on equal and fraternal terms; however, a shade of reverence and respect colored the attitude of younger toward elder members, and of girls toward boys. In fact, jealousy between brothers was proverbial, and half-siblings often shared in the rivalries that existed among their mothers. One was expected to be very respectful toward members of the first ascending generation, especially toward paternal aunts, but joking relationships existed between cognates of alternate generations.

Joking was also allowed in central Rwanda between cross-cousins, either of the same or of opposite sex. With the northern Hutu, a joking relationship existed between a man and his matrilateral cross-cousins, male or female, whereas his behavior toward his female patrilateral cross-cousins had to be kept discreet. A man's attitude toward his maternal uncle was quite strained.[8]

Two types of behavior characterized the relationship between cognates and "entering members."[9] For those one generation apart, avoidance and restraint were the normative attitudes on both sides; sexual relations were deemed incestuous except between daughters-in-law and fathers-in-law. Within the same generation, however, joking relationships were typical be-

Tutsi Girls Carrying Milk Pots (*IRSAC*)

tween partners of the same sex and a broad sexual privilege was tolerated between male *inzu* members and each other's wives. This behavior was rooted in the transfer of brideprice, but it caused considerable tensions within the extended family.

CHILD TRAINING AND SOCIALIZATION

Although the socialization process went beyond the framework of the domestic unit, it was based on the family. Initially, the solicitous role of the mother was predominant, although among wealthier Tutsi she often shared baby nursing with a nursemaid. Babies were washed and smeared with butter two or three times a day. During the night, they slept in their parents' bed. A baby was given some solid food from the sixth month on and weaning took place at the age of about one year, but might occur later. As a rule, a new pregnancy put an end to breast feeding.

Until the age of four or five, children were not allowed to stroll outside their mother's enclosure and they were told to be clean. From that age on, the father's influence was more felt, especially by boys. Between five and ten, they were taught to look after goats, sheep, and calves, and were assigned household tasks such as carrying water or gathering wood. Girls learned to sweep and to cook. Boys between ten and fifteen drove the cattle to pasture and were instructed in agricultural work.

Parents were forbidden to instruct their children in sexual matters; male youngsters learned a lot about such things from the herdboys, while girls between fifteen and eighteen formed an informal age group that, besides making mats and basketry and dancing and singing, provided an opportunity for self-taught elongation of their *labia minora* and widening of their genital parts. It was considered that the success of their marriage depended on this preparation. From the *inzu* elders, boys and girls learned their people's traditions, myths, and ritual; Tutsi boys were taught the frequently changing constellation of the various important lineages and were encouraged to conduct mock trials in order to acquire astuteness and to improve their speaking ability. Their socialization was continued at the king's and the chiefs' courts and in the course of their military training.

Such events as birth, marriage, and death gave rise to a number of dramatic rituals in which not merely kinsmen but, to a certain extent, the local population also participated. The mother and her newborn baby as well as the young bride had to pass through a period of seclusion during which they were believed to be particularly susceptible to magical spells. In either case, this period was brought to an end by a public celebration in which friends and neighbors joined freely. In the first case, the baby's paternal grandmother called together the young children of the neighborhood, who would represent the newborn member of the society in a meaningful mimed scene. If the baby was a boy, the young guests tilled the soil with forked branches as hoes; if the baby was a girl, they cut the grass and swept the enclosure. The actual work setting was depicted by an adult sprinkling the children with water, shouting that there was a shower and that it was time to come home. The children then had a meal. This celebration was to demonstrate that a new member had entered society; it was common to Tutsi and Hutu. With the northern Hutu, it was repeated at a grandparent's death to display that the deceased's generation was replaced by the grandchildren.

On the termination of a bride's seclusion, a public feast was held to recognize her transition to full married status. On that occasion, her tufts, the hairdress symbolizing her maiden status, were shaved.

The time of mourning after the death of an *inzu* member was brought to a close by a big celebration. It consisted of a great many ritual purifications, the resumption of sexual relations, definite rites to terminate the interruption of the work in the fields, and a common meal.

BLOOD BROTHERHOOD · Blood brotherhood pacts were very frequently concluded between men belonging to different lineages that were not already linked by affinal bonds. Blood brotherhood was not caste-bound; Tutsi men often had Hutu blood brothers, but rarely did a Tutsi or a Hutu conclude such a pact with a Twa. Blood brotherhood compelled the partners to help each other unconditionally. It was often entered into with a view toward making sure of a set of witnesses to be used in the judicial affairs in which men were frequently engaged. Thus blood pacts were often kept secret in order to prevent the blood brother from being challenged as a witness.

POLITICAL ORGANIZATION

PRE-NILOTIC ORGANIZATION • Not much, if anything, is known about the political structure of Rwanda before the Nilotic expansion. But this expansion introduced a long historic process that is well substantiated by oral sources and its final phase was still in progress when the first Europeans arrived in the country. It thus becomes possible to make some statements about the political organization in several regions before the Tutsi centralization and about the lines along which the latter developed.

Something has already been said about the political organization along lineage lines in the north. Other Hutu collectivities in northern and western Rwanda were organized on a larger territorial base (small chiefdoms) and headed by hereditary *abahinza* (agricultural chiefs) endowed with magical powers for rainmaking and the preservation of crops. Up to the 1920s, there were two small hereditary Hutu kingdoms in southwestern Rwanda. The power of the king (*umwami*) was considered as being of divine origin; the monarchs were surrounded with a complex ritual; the country was governed jointly by the king and the queen mother.

The conquest and centralization of the country by the Nilotic kings were facilitated, and succeeded best, in those regions where pioneer lineages of Tutsi colonists had previously established a clientship and caste structure, although the subsidiary problem of bringing the pioneers under the king's power could arise. Elsewhere, the conquerors tried to impose a Tutsi protectorate upon the *abahinza* and the Hutu kings so as later to absorb them completely. The northern regions were actually incorporated into the structure of the Rwanda kingdom only through the efforts of German and Belgian expeditions.

The traditional centralized kingdom

The political organization that will be described below existed in central and eastern Rwanda at the end of the nineteenth century; its main patterns dated back to King Yuhi IV Gahindiro, who reorganized the political structure toward the beginning of the nineteenth century.

THE KING AND DYNASTIC OFFICIALS • The king's power was theoretically absolute. He possessed a pre-eminent right over all the land and cattle, and even over his subjects. He was considered a sacred being of divine origin. Consequently, traditional political ideology that was expressed in court ritual and poetry raised him above the caste structure. Numerous ritualistic observances and interdictions stressed his separateness from the secular sphere. A set of sacred insignia—especially drums—functioned as mediating symbols between the king and the divine source of his power. As a symbol of victory, the genitals of the foreign kings and the *abahinza* killed by the king's warriors were attached to the royal drums.

The king appointed his successor from among his younger sons, but the nominee was not aware of his selection until his father's choice was proclaimed by the court ritualists after the king's decease. Thus, political unrest often marked a king's accession to power, since the other possible candidates not infrequently opposed their brother's elevation to power. Although wars of accession were not institutionalized as they were in Ankole (Uganda), the court ritual provided a set of magical procedures to put an end to a struggle among pretenders.

At his accession, the king received a royal name. The royal names of the last fifteen kings show—with one exception—the following cyclical sequence: Mutara (or Cyirima), Kigeri, Mibambwe, and Yuhi. The court ritual defined a specific type of ideal behavior for the kings according to their names. Thus kings called Mutara or Cyirima were "kings of the cows"; they had to be pacific rulers and were not allowed to pass beyond the borders of the well-controlled central districts. Kings called Kigeri or Mibambwe had to be warrior kings and could conduct military expeditions everywhere. A king called Yuhi was a "king of the fire"; the symbolic meaning of this appellation was the generation of prosperity throughout the country. The ideal patterns of behavior that were ascribed to the kings were dramatically expressed in the court ritual, especially in the periodical refresher rites. The cyclical conception of royal behavior that underlay the court ritual conveyed the idea of a certain predestination of the kings' careers and diminished their political responsibility on the ideological level.

A queen mother shared the royal prerogatives; she was either the king's own mother or, after her death, a woman chosen according to the provisions of the sacred ritual code. Queen mothers, like kings, had royal names.

Although the king was theoretically absolute, there were some structural checks and controls on his power. Thus royal power was somewhat limited by the pressures that the influential Nilotic lineages—often holding hereditary offices—were able to exert on the central government. The association, within the royal institution itself, of two equally assertive Tutsi groups, the royal *nyiginya* and a matridynastic patriclan (most often *eega*), also kept a certain precarious balance.[10] The distribution of political influence over the prominent Nilotic kin groups was regulated to a certain extent by the secret ritual code known as *ubwiru*. The latter was learned by heart by a dozen *abiiru* (high dignitaries), who were in charge of performing the rites, which were held to be of fundamental importance to the existence and continuation of the established social and political order. The most important—and probably the oldest—ritual offices were allocated to three *reges sacrorum*; these ritual kings, whose office was hereditary, governed freeholds and had drums and cyclical royal names.

Thus the structure of "divine kingship" in ancient Rwanda was a bipolar one in the sense that there was a sectional, but complementary, allocation of political and ritual functions. Although the king was considered as a sacred person, and played a role in the court rites, he was not a Pontifex Maximus nor a rainmaker. The Nilotic king's office, unlike that of his Hutu predecessors, the *abahinza*, was essentially political. The ritual attributes of Nilotic kingship, some of which seem to derive from the former Hutu polities, were handed over to specialized high-ranking dignitaries.[11]

CLIENTSHIP • The institution of clientship is rooted in Rwanda customs of ownership of land and cattle. Ultimate proprietary rights in both land and cattle were vested in the king, who had the power to transfer the right to their use (usufruct) to other individuals who would become his clients. The king's clients, who were often appointed to administrative and military offices, could acquire clients of their own by passing on to others their usufructuary rights in land or cattle that they had received from the king.

When a lower-ranking individual wished to have the prestige resulting from cattle wealth, or to acquire more cattle, he offered his services to a higher-ranking man. If the latter was prepared to receive the applicant as an *umugaragu* (client), he would entrust him with one or several cows and thus become his *sheebuja* (pastoral lord). The pastoral lord who granted cows to his client kept proprietary rights over the cattle and could reclaim them at any time. The client possessed the usufruct, which meant that he was allowed to retain the milk products and the young bulls, to slaughter sterile or sick cattle, to set apart a cow as the bridewealth for a son's marriage, and to sublet livestock to his own clients if he were granted enough cattle to do so. (Ordinary Rwanda were not forbidden to own cattle that they had acquired by their own work and the exclusive possession of which they could legitimately claim, subject to the king's pre-eminent rights. But such cattle were not numerous and were always liable to seizure by the administrative and military heads or by the pastoral lords.)

Clients were expected to perform whatever services their lords asked for. A Hutu had to work in his lord's fields, to keep his huts and byres in repair, to provide him with agricultural products, to carry him in a litter when he traveled, and to attend him at night. Tutsi clients accompanied their lord when he visited his friends and kinsmen and gave him advice in his political intrigues. In return, Hutu clients counted on the economic profit of possessing cattle, relied on their lord's help when in distress, and, particularly, were confident of being protected by a powerful man in all the spheres of their life, especially when they became involved in lawsuits. Tutsi lords and clients alike sought to extend the network of their political alliances to lineages influential in the prevailing power constellation.

The *ubuhake* (clientship) agreement did not constitute a proper contract since the mutual duties of the client and the lord were not exactly determined and the settlement was skewed by the lord's pervasive social superiority. This was clearly demonstrated when the agreement came to an end. Either the client or the lord could demand the termination of the *ubuhake* but, in either case, in addition to the normal restitution of cattle, the client was liable to have some of his own cows seized. A clientship agreement was not canceled by the death of the persons who initiated it; the resulting obligations were patrilineally inherited.

The clientship structure played an essential role in traditional Rwanda society. The Tutsi conquest had created a situation in which it became necessary for the Hutu, as members of a socially inferior group, to be protected against their rulers' sternness. This was achieved by asking for personal assimilation with a member of the conquering caste, and for some share in the latter's prestige symbols, thus balancing the austerity of the Nilotic domination with a system of institutionalized protection.

But this represented only one moment of the dialectic reality of the *ubuhake*. Since all Tutsi were also tied up by clientship agreements, their reciprocal links of personal fidelity and patronage increased the unity and the homogeneity of the dominant caste, and as a rule provided the appropriate mechanisms to prevent its members from moving down the social scale. Moreover, since the Tutsi never relinquished their proprietary rights over cattle in granting the Hutu a precarious usufruct, the clientship structure was a bar to the impairment of their dominance by members of the lower caste. Lastly, the political structures (administration and army) correlated with the clientship system in the sense that political offices helped the rulers to increase the number of their clients, and the possession of cattle made it possible for them to acquire and maintain political functions. The interpenetration of the clientship structure with the military organization was particularly marked since the warriors' section of the army was composed of the king's direct clients. A "feudal" type of human relations pervaded the whole structure of roles existing between rulers and subjects. Thus the mechanisms of internal compensation that were built into traditional Rwanda political structures, and provided some degree of protection for the Hutu, were operative within the general framework of the conditions that made possible the continuation of their very dependence as a sociological minority.

The central Rwanda clientship pattern, with its concept of land tenure, was not successfully imposed by the Tutsi in the northern and northwestern districts until the beginning of the twentieth century. Until then, those districts were characterized by the system of *ubukonde* (cleared forest land) held by Hutu lineages, whereas central Rwanda was characterized by the

A Twa Man *(IRSAC)*

system of *isambu* (individual holdings) controlled by the political authorities. Forest land was opened up for cultivation by Hutu lineages, who paid a small indemnification to the Twa. It was exploited under the supervision of the lineage head. A member's escheated portion returned to the common lineage estate.

Twa, for the most part, were not highly involved in the clientship system nor was their concept of land rights infused with notions of the clientship ideal. However, in central Rwanda, several Twa lineages depended directly on the king, for whom they acted as political spies, court buffoons, and executioners. Each of the residential Twa groups possessed a preserve for hunting, but its rights were more related to the game than to the estate so that an animal the hunters were pursuing could be tracked down in the preserve of another group. Deposits of iron and clay and the cutting of wood, grass, and reeds were not subject to exclusive rights.

ADMINISTRATIVE STRUCTURE • Central Rwanda was divided into a frequently changing number of provinces and districts that in turn were split into a great number of administrative hills or subchiefdoms. The provinces were ruled by paramount chiefs who were generally military chiefs (see below) and direct clients of the king. Paramount chiefs and district chiefs were appointed by the king and subject to dismissal by him at any time. As a rule, the administration of an individual district was committed to two officials, independent of each other: the "chief of the land," who was in charge of the taxes payable by the agriculturalists; and the "chief of the cattle," who was in charge of the pastoralists. This administrative dualism increased the king's control over his officials and prevented them from becoming too powerful. However, this rule was less general than some authors have claimed. In fact, a single individual not infrequently happened to be at the same time chief

of the land and chief of the cattle. The district chiefs had only one subordinate per subchiefdom. Since the latter was appointed by the paramount
chief of the province, this system provided another check on the power of the
district chiefs.

These common divisions, run by the ordinary administrative officers,
were crosscut by other lines of cleavage that entailed a much more direct control by the king and his inner circle of favorites.

As a rule, a royal residence surrounded by an autonomous zone was
fixed in each district; it functioned as a centralized agency for collecting and
transmitting taxes but was not integrated into the common territorial structure. It could be a queen's fief when it was managed by a wife of the king's,
or a royal freehold when a concubine was put in charge of it. The king was
inclined to establish other free zones in each district, the management of
which was conferred upon intimates who were accountable to him alone.
Thus, hills on which royal burial sites were situated did not come under
ordinary jurisdiction; neither did the autonomous enclaves of the prominent
royal ritualists. The southern and western border districts were administered
by military chiefs.

The administrative (and military) chiefs belonged almost exclusively to
the Tutsi caste. Hutu could become chiefs of the land, but there is little
evidence that they frequently did, except in some mountainous areas un-
suited for pastoralism. A Twa could be appointed as a subchief—especially in
the vicinity of a royal residence—but rarely did he climb to higher office unless he belonged to an ennobled lineage, in which case he would be considered a Tutsi. All this, however, is not to mean that all Tutsi were rulers.
The latter were recruited within a relatively small number of Nilotic lineages that constituted a mobile, ubiquitous and, in that sense, national elite,
the hierarchy of which varied from reign to reign. Yet kinship principles as
a basis of selection were important, first, in the sense that officers drawn from
the king's consanguineal and affinal kin made up more than half of the administration, and, second, in that major offices were, in fact, very often
hereditary.

One of the major functions of the administrative officials was the levy-
ing of taxes. This function stems from the vesting of pre-eminent property
rights in the king and the resulting clientship system described above. A man
appointed to an administrative office by the king would, in turn, allocate individual holdings of land and/or cattle to others who, in exchange for corvée
labor and rents, became his clients.

A chief of the land and a subchief would collect agricultural products
from their subjects as taxes, each keeping approximately one third for himself and forwarding the remainder to the royal residence of their district.
Similarly, the chief of the cattle and the subchief were allowed to retain a

portion of the pastoralists' contributions. Labor prestations were required from every family, while other taxes were applied to the *inzu* grouping.

One should not overrate the degree to which taxes were fixed, for they were also considered as "presents" to the king. A chief had to be agreeable to the monarch, but not overburden his people with taxes. How to balance these imperatives was left to his discretion.

MILITARY STRUCTURE • All male Rwanda were subject to the authority of a military chief, who was frequently a paramount chief. The military organization was closely related to the structure of property rights on cattle. It constituted a privileged channel through which the king was able to control his subordinates' ownership of the symbols of social prestige; on the other hand, it provided some checks and balances to possible exactions by the administrative officers.

At a king's accession to the drum, a new army was formed. It consisted of two sections: the warriors and the herdsmen. The martial section comprised several hundred young Tutsi who were chosen from among the sons of the king's clients. They received an intensive military and athletic training and were also instructed in the major modes of artistic expression of the superior caste: poetry making, declamation, debating, and dancing. Thus, the Tutsi elite was the exclusive holder of the organized physical force and the privileged repository of a refined way of life. The other part of the army consisted of *inzu* groups that were detached from previously existing military formations and collectively joined to the newly raised one. Most *inzu* groups were in charge of the "army" cattle, which included the royal cattle entrusted to the army, the military chief's cattle, the cattle that *inzu* members had acquired as gifts by exchange, or as bridewealth, and the warriors' cattle. The cattle that a man possessed as a client belonged to his lord's army. Thus, all cattle on whatever grounds they were owned belonged to a definite military unit.

The military organization performed an economic function in allocating and circulating cattle and in ensuring corvée labor for the king and his family. In that sense, the military structure had a fiscal function too.

But it appears that its main benefit was to enable the king and the top Tutsi chiefs to increase their control over cattle prestige symbols and power instruments, and to redistribute them as they pleased. At his accession to power, the king took the census of all army cattle and appropriated a portion of the herds that were paraded in front of him. Moreover, at the same occasion every cattle-owning *inzu* had to make a present of one cow to the monarch as a token of homage. A similar presentation was made to an army chief at his appointment. Cattle taken as booty also belonged to the king, but a military chief was entitled to set a portion apart for himself. In that way, the king and his favorites were able to increase considerably the number of clients who would be personally bound to them.

On the other hand, the military structure provided certain checks against arbitrariness on the part of the administrative officers. As a member of the army, any man could appeal to the king's justice if he felt wronged by the lower courts. It was recognized that an army chief should intercede on behalf of his subjects when necessary. This role expectation followed naturally from the frequently existing clientship relation between a military chief and a great many of his subjects, but also from the prevailing notion that a highly placed individual should be a strong protector. Yet however effective the protection of a military chief might be, this assistance was not automatically granted to a subject; it depended on the latter's political loyalty and submissiveness that the army chief assessed without appeal.

Law

Almost any individual invested with authority could dispense justice to persons dependent upon him. Thus *inzu* and lineage heads settled disputes that arose among the members of their group. Matters that pertained to two kinship groups, such as divorce, elopement, legitimization of children, were discussed by the group heads, generally assisted by a council of elders. Until the Tutsi penetration, the kinship structure provided the sole judicial framework in the northern districts.

In central Rwanda, the clientship and political structures largely superseded the kinship groups as loci of adjudicatory functions, although internal familial affairs were generally dealt with by the group heads. Pastoral lords tried cases regarding their clients, particularly—but not exclusively—cattle affairs. As a rule, any suit could be referred to any official for judgment, at least in the latter's territorial division.

However, there was a certain degree of specialization, according to the nature of the case. Disputes among Hutu over land rights were settled by the district chief of the land; the chief of the cattle was *not* competent in affairs concerning cattle or grazing grounds, for those matters were under the jurisdiction of the military chiefs; high-treason trials were judged by a paramount chief or the king himself. The hierarchy of the courts ran parallel with the ranking of the officials. However, because they could directly appeal from any inferior to any superior court, even the king's, it was not necessary for unsatisfied plaintiffs to pass through all the courts from the lowest (the subchief's) to the highest. In fact, an affair could be laid before the king's court without having been tried by an inferior court.

The extent to which appeal to a higher court was made was closely related to the social and political status of the persons concerned. Hutu rarely went beyond their land chief's court; only wealthier Tutsi endeavored to obtain a paramount chief's or the king's sentence. At a subchief's or a land chief's court, the plaintiff and the defendant were expected to be assisted by their *inzu* or lineage heads; in the superior tribunals, they had to be accompanied by their army chiefs. This was to show that they were submissive and politically reliable men. Should they not have been such, there would have been no justice for them but death.

The composition of a court was highly informal. On any level, a judge could deliver judgment himself without taking advice from anyone; but since an important Tutsi was always surrounded with a train of friends and confidants, he very frequently discussed the affair with them or allowed one of his advisers to pass sentence. When the case was between members of different armies and was to be tried on the military chiefs' level, the latter —if they were on good terms with each other—made arrangements to compose a court they would preside over jointly. If they disliked each other, the matter was deferred to the king's tribunal, which would be more interested in the chiefs' problem than in the case.

Hearings were held in the open air. Sentences by default were rarely passed, except at the king's court in high-treason trials. The complainant aired his grievances first; then it was the defendant's turn. Their respective witnesses and supporters spoke in the same sequence. At last, the judge or his associates repeated the main arguments and tried to find inconsistencies in the opponents' statements. The judgment might be delivered at once or the case might be heard several times.

Judicial inquiry was nonexistent. The opponents had to collect and exhibit proofs they considered convincing: a piece of cloth they said had covered the hoofs of a stolen cow to disguise its footprints, or a herdboy's stick. But this was less important than the testimony of witnesses and litigants. Witnesses would be challenged by the adversary if they were supposed to be likely to give evidence on behalf of the opponent.

The hearing of litigants was most important, for the judicial procedures operated within the overall framework of dependence and protection. When influential persons interfered, lawsuits were decided more on the basis of the social position of the protector than on the rights of the case.

Murder and homicide were not court matters since they were dealt with by regulated vengeance; however, the king could suspend the feud and inflict a reparation (eight cows or more) on the murderer's kinsmen. People were allowed to kill a cattle thief caught *in flagrante delicto*. The most typical law cases involved high treason, cattle and petty thefts, disputes over land or cattle rights, rape, assault and battery, black magic, and the failure of rainmakers.

High treason (failure to succeed in a mission, being suspected of intending to poison the king or a chief, plotting against the established rulers, the mere fact of displeasing the king) was punished by emasculation and

death, or banishment. Cattle thieves were subjected to the bastinado and to
a very painful kind of binding, but if the wronged person were a powerful
individual the punishment would be death by impalement. The punishment
of rape depended on the social status of the persons involved. Thus if a Hutu
raped a Tutsi woman, he was put to death; if a Hutu woman was raped by
a Tutsi, the matter would be settled by compensation. Such distinctions also
applied to the repression of other torts. Besides a physical punishment in-
flicted on the persons found guilty, the judges always allocated compensation
to the wronged individuals. It consisted of cows, goats, or hoes. But because
courts were not interested in the actual enforcement of their decisions, new
disputes arose that could last for years.

RELIGION

The most significant religious term of ancient
Rwanda culture was *imaana*, a polyvalent and extremely complex notion. It
referred to a general quality of being removed from the secular sphere and
thus might be best translated by the word "sacred."[12] It applied to the Hutu
abahinza and later to the Nilotic king, who was thought to be or to have
more *imaana* than any other being; to the divining animals and their viscera;
to charms and sacred trees; and, less frequently, to the spirits of the dead
taken collectively. It had the general connotation of "chance, good or bad
luck." The basic ambivalence of the term *imaana* was especially perceptible
when it was used in the situational context of divination, when objects, called
imaana, happened to be "white" (or predicting good luck) or "black" (or
predicting bad luck). However, it seems that in the course of time much of
this ambiguity was expelled from the semantic field of the notion, and the
term was skewed in favor of the "good" side of the original dichotomy. Thus,
the predominant connotation associated with *imaana* was rather that of being
infused with a pervasive, still fortuitous, force causing fecundity and prosperity, joy and peace.

THE CREATOR GOD • It was in this sense that the term *imaana* referred
to a remote creator god who was believed to be essentially good-natured and
liberal. The creator god was represented anthropomorphically: he was believed to walk, to work, to get tired, to rest, and so on; but he was also conceived of as the powerful Producer of all things and mankind. Although a
great number of popular sayings and anthroponyms contained references to
the creator god, there were no rites to worship him. He was a *deus otiosus*
who did not trouble too much about the world he had created in the beginning of time. Nevertheless, he was said to sanction disobedience and revolt against the king, the political authorities, and the kinship heads. Al-

though he favored the country of Rwanda particularly, he was not properly thought of as a national deity.

ANCESTRAL SPIRITS • The major concern of the Rwanda was with the *abazimu* (spirits of the dead), which were conceived of as jealous and ill-natured beings, holding all the grudges of their lifetime against the living and constantly seeking to do wrong. The creator god was said to be the king of the spirits, but he did not seem to control the ancestors. However, he helped the diviners interpret the wishes of the ancestors and thus provided mankind with a means to hold themselves harmless against the ancestors' ill will.

The actions of the ancestors were unsystematic; so was the cult meant to appease them. When an unlucky event occurred, a diviner's advice was taken. He would find out which ancestral spirit had caused harm and what was to be done in order to still the wrongdoer. Generally, a very small abode would have to be built for the identified spirit and some offerings made to him or her (some drops of milk or beer, some beans or peas, a small piece of meat). The offerings were symbolic; filial devotion was more important than what was offered. As a rule, the cult applied only to patrilateral and matri-lateral ancestors of three ascending generations, particularly to those an-cestors who died without leaving male descendants, since they were con-sidered most dangerous. Women rarely performed the spirit worship.

The ancestor cult increased the cohesion of the kinship groups, especially the *inzu*, stressed the social ideal of enjoying a numerous posterity, and sanc-tioned the rules of social life of which the *abazimu* were said to be the implacable guardians.

CULT GROUPS • In the southern half of the country, some thirty widely known and powerful spirits—called *imandwa* (heroes)—were honored in a special cult reserved for the initiates. Tutsi (except the king), Hutu, and Twa alike could be initiated, but prominent Tutsi were not members: there hung about the cult a definite popular, even licentious flavor that scarcely squared with the Tutsi ideal of dignified and respectable behavior. How-ever, the cult was introduced at the royal court during the reign of King Cyirima II Rujugira (middle of the eighteenth century) and the *imandwa* cult group began to play an important part in the rituals of kingship.

There were two initiation grades. The initiation ritual stressed the idea that an initiate was separated from the *inzigo* (profane outsiders) (which was symbolized by heaping coarse insults on the initiate, then placing the naked candidate under a filth heap and asking him or her to commit incest) and that he or she consequently shared in a new way of life and was part of a new family. Initiations were expensive. They were taken on a diviner's ad-vice in order to be secure from unhappy events. The cult had a developed

Man Consulting a Diviner
(*IRSAC*)

mythology that told the heroic achievements of the *imandwa*, and the initiates translated this mythology into ritual action.

In northern Rwanda, the cult of Nyabingi, a famous and possibly historical woman, was prominent. It differed from the *imandwa* cult by the absence of any initiation rites, by the fact that it had priests and priestesses, and by the political overtones it had acquired toward the beginning of the twentieth century. At that time, some priests began to display chieflike—even royal—behavior, maintaining courts with numerous attendants and making a show of royal insignia, such as drums. Some ten years later, they aroused the local population to open revolt against the Rwanda kingdom. This was a moment of a more general revolt in the northern districts instigated by a pretender who promised to abolish the prestations imposed on the Hutu by the comparatively recent Nilotic penetration.

To become a follower of Nyabingi, a diviner's advice was required. The purpose was to be protected against the mishaps of life. Offerings generally made to Nyabingi's priests consisted of victuals, goats, and sheep. In conducting their audiences, the priests behaved, it is said, under the influence of Nyabingi's possession.

RELIGIOUS PRACTITIONERS · There were numerous specialists of the invisible world. One might conveniently distinguish between the "good" specialists whose actions were conceived of as beneficial to mankind, and the detrimental sorcerers. The former (diviners, charm makers, ritual purifiers, rainmakers, exorcists) were believed to practice their profession in cooperation with the benevolent creator god, whereas the latter were moved by jealousy and love of profit. The fear that they might be poisoned by a sorcerer or that a spell might be cast on them was a source of constant anxiety to all Rwanda.

Rwanda: An interpretive summary

Apart from its less integrated northern districts and some other areas in the southwest, ancient Rwanda was characterized by a social and political system that stabilized the power situation resulting from the Nilotic conquest. The Tutsi elite preserved its preponderance by maintaining the ultimate control over what was culturally considered economic wealth—cattle—which made it possible to regulate the people's labor and land tenure, as well as by exclusively possessing physical force through the administrative and military structures.

In this respect, ancient Rwanda constitutes an almost perfect actualization of the interlacustrine type of "conquest state," the essential problem of which was to balance the mechanisms that would maintain social stratification and the rule of privilege, and those that would prevent the political collectivity from dissolving. It should here be emphasized again that, unlike what happened in Ankole, for example, cattle, which supported the caste cleavage economically, also provided a means by which the Hutu could share the ideals of their lords and be protected by them. On the other hand, where "feudal" institutions develop, the central government is threatened by powerlessness when attempting to enforce its decisions. This was notably the case in ancient Burundi. The Rwanda system met this menace by distributing the administration and royal treasury over various officials, and by encouraging distrust, suspicion, and intrigues among the chiefs.

Traditional Rwanda was also typical with respect to the development of an ideological superstructure that rationalized the social and political inequalities in terms of divine sanctions threatening those who would rebel against the established order, and in terms of essential differences in human nature and rights among the various castes. Inegalitarian behavior pervaded all interpersonal relations. From the intercaste contacts, this behavior stretched to any interpersonal situation, the most momentous variable of which would always be the ranking position of the persons concerned. Much of this ethos was embodied in the copious official literature composed by court poets, chroniclers, and genealogists, and which, as far as the author knows, is not equaled by any of the other interlacustrine peoples.

CHANGE

Rwanda formally became a German protectorate in 1899. After World War I, Belgium was entrusted by the League of Nations with the Type B Mandate of Rwanda-Burundi,[13] a political and administrative merger entity of colonial origin that was maintained by the United Nations as a trust territory under the administration of the same power. The territory acquired independence on July 1, 1962. What are the major sociocultural changes resulting from sixty years of sustained European contact, almost totally governmental and missionary?

Economic changes have involved the attempt to reduce the problems caused by the irregularity of the rains, erosion, overstocking, demographic pressure stemming from population increases, and recurrent famine. Colonial authorities introduced new subsistence crops, soil conservation, and new forms of stock control. Coffee has been introduced as the major cash crop, making external trade particularly dependent on world market prices. The success of these schemes has been hampered by the fact that they were applied within the framework of a colonial paternalism that strengthened paternalistic authoritarianism rather than attempting a broad educational re-patterning of the rural society. The persistence of traditional dependence structures within the system of indirect rule limited the growth of both economic and personal incentives in the peasant society to a still greater extent.

Major changes have taken place in the field of religion and education. Christians now number about 45 percent of the population of Rwanda; most of them are Roman Catholics. There are several thousand Muslims, called "Swahili," living mostly in the small African cities and commercial centers. Education is almost entirely in the hands of state-aided Catholic and Protestant mission schools. There are no reliable statistics on literacy, but it is generally assumed that the illiteracy rate is about 60 percent. (The author's recent survey of Astrida Township and the neighboring area supports this conclusion.) The degree of educational attainment is correlated with caste membership; hence the Tutsi heavily outweigh the Hutu in education. This is to be expected, for the whole system of indirect rule favored the traditional elite.

YEARS OF SCHOOLING IN ASTRIDA TOWNSHIP BY CASTE[14]

Township proper	Tutsi (%)	Hutu (%)
Illiterate	17	58
Up to 5 years	37	29
More than 5 years	46	13
Rural area:		
Illiterate	69	82
Up to 5 years	21	16
More than 5 years	10	2

No more than 22 percent of school-age children are receiving a primary education; however, since 1961, the proportion rose to approximately 75 percent in the first form. About 20 Rwanda have qualified for degrees in European universities and approximately 150 are preparing for them (1962).

By far the deepest changes have occurred on the sociopolitical level during the revolutionary process of the last few years that resulted in the thorough upset of the established regime. This process is intelligible in terms of the dialectic interplay of three variables: the methods of European administration, the predominantly bipolar social stratification, and African nationalism.

The system of indirect administration applied by the German and Belgian governments rested on certain structural patterns: on the one hand, the European trustees were linked with the Tutsi elite, and this relationship was rooted partly in the force of the colonial power and the corresponding resignation of the traditional rulers, partly also in some measure of consent. On the other hand, the majority of the African population continued to be linked with their historic rulers by the established patterns of political consent or resignation. Thus the maintenance of the traditional balance between the two major castes appeared a necessary prerequisite to the very existence of indirect rule. The small number of Germans precluded their tackling administrative problems along any other lines.

Under the Belgians, the pure, structural model of indirect rule was modified by a humanitarian, paternalistic reformism aimed at introducing the rulers to Western bureaucratic standards of probity and efficiency and securing for the majority of the population personal liberty from the rulers' abuse. This led to some reforms more of a judicial or administrative nature than of a political character: the abolishment of the traditional military structure, the reorganization of territorial divisions so as to leave only one chief per district, and the institution of (at least the ideal of) double restitution for a Hutu despoiled by a Tutsi.

The deeper question whether or not power should be redistributed in a way that would better fit Western notions was kept in the background for almost forty years. Even the relatively recent reforms, such as the 1952 decree setting up councils, did not go as far as organizing truly representative assemblies but diffused political power more widely over the caste that already held it. On the other hand, the 1952 decree increased the king's control over the appointment of chiefs and subchiefs.

The clientship structure was progressively abolished from 1954 on, but the fact that the related system of land tenure (especially the holding of grazing grounds) was not, created a critical imbalance in the process of change. The Hutu peasants were freed from their *ubuhake* obligations but they encountered a much sterner Tutsi attitude when it came to finding pasture for their cattle.

The election of 1956 showed growing dissatisfaction among the Hutu and in 1957 the small Hutu counterelite issued a manifesto in which its members indicted the inequality they felt to be characteristic of Tutsi and Hutu in political power, social prestige, and economic and social opportunities. They noted that the ruling methods of the trusteeship administration were as accountable for the persisting caste inequality as was the traditional sociopolitical system. The caste "problem" would have to be solved, it was held, if the independence that was to come was to bring political stability. Two Hutu parties were formed: the *Aprosoma*, a reformist movement operating in the south, and the *Parmehutu*, a revolutionary and almost clandestine mass party, especially powerful in the northern districts but rapidly expanding all over the country.

The Tutsi rulers reacted by viewing the social unrest as due to a policy of division plotted by the European administration rather than due to any inequities in the traditional social order. Their nationalism was thus made to square with the structure of vested interests. They, too, formed a party, the *Rwanda National Union* (U.Na.R.), whose executive board consisted of the king's private councilors. It was soon regarded as a union of loyalists bound in the king's name to reduce the deviant Hutu movements through the application of the old patterns of pressure that, it was assumed, would produce the familiar, predictable responses.

But a Hutu revolution broke out in November 1959. It expressed the Hutu drive for emancipation as well as the cultural variations of northwestern Rwanda, where its success was complete. To keep pace with modified sociological conditions, the trusteeship administration appointed a large number of Hutu chiefs and subchiefs. In local elections organized for the newly established "communes" in June 1960, the two Hutu parties polled 77 percent of the seats. The king and some of his councilors, followed by a large number of Tutsi, then fled into exile. A provisional cabinet with a Hutu majority was established in October 1960.

General elections were postponed from January 1961 to a later date after a resolution to this effect had been passed by the United Nations General Assembly, largely in response to entreaties from an U.Na.R. delegation. As a reaction to this, the *Parmehutu* Minister of the Interior called together a national convention of mayors and councilors, which abolished the monarchy, its regalia (the sacred drums), and the *abiiru*, and elected a President of the Republic, a Legislative Council, and a fully Hutu government. These measures, although temporarily suspended by the Belgian government, were confirmed by general elections supervised by the United Nations in September 1961. Approximately 80 percent of the voters rejected the monarchy; *Parmehutu* won 35 seats in the National Assembly, U.Na.R. won 7, and *Aprosoma* won 2.

Rwanda is now a social democratic republic with a presidential regime.

In Africa today, Rwanda is significant for the thorough *dissociation* of two emancipation movements (at least for the time being): the one nationalist and based on the current anticolonialist themes, the other socialist-revolutionary in the sense that it aimed at—and succeeded in—overthrowing the established system of social stratification. In terms of the social background of Rwanda, the parties that support those movements are caste-bound. However, a new dimension has been added to this feature with special reference to the Hutu: the self-consciousness that led them to make up a political group that, on a nation-wide base, is determined by ethnic, economic, and cultural variables, as against another national group equally determined by such variables. This awareness was completely lacking in the past, since the Hutu were parceled out into small parochial communities lacking any group cohesion on a wider basis or any agency for the articulation of their collective interests. Rwanda parties, thus, might be considered as true class parties, and not as ethnic parties. This might lead to some corrections of the prevailing typology of African political movements. There is another approach to African politics to which the Rwanda case constitutes a challenge: the widely accepted simplistic evaluation of African nationalism through the mere cleavage between Europeans and Africans. A substantial sociological insight would be won by testing hypotheses as to the correlation between nationalism and properly African intergroup politics, and particularly the correlation between the adoption of African nationalist ideologies and the structure of vested interests of the group that does so.

NOTES

(1) This is the correct spelling of the country's name. The Swahili form "Ruanda," which was accredited by the German administration, has been dropped from internal official usage since 1960; United Nations papers continued to use it until independence.

(2) It is important to qualify the last two sentences. Actually, the Rwanda kings failed to implant their domination firmly, not only in the areas joined to Uganda or the Congo but also in the northern part of what is Rwanda today. Vansina (1962) has shown that ancient Rwanda consisted of a very well controlled central part (about one half of the country), of a zone in which the king exerted some measure of influence over the local peasant polities, and of an area exposed to military operations. The "lost" districts belonged to the latter category.

(3) These names are sometimes given with their Bantu (plural) prefixes as Batutsi, Bahutu, and Batwa. All three groups taken together are sometimes known as the Banyarwanda (or Banyaruanda). Here, Rwanda, the Anglicized form without the prefix or infix, which is conventional in scientific works, will be used as a noun to refer to the people and also as an adjective.

(4) Because of the profound nature of these changes, d'Hertefelt describes the only recently modified traditional institutions of Rwanda in the past tense and the contemporary patterns in the present tense.—ED.

(5) Their physical characteristics have been termed "éthiopide" by Hiernaux (1954). This term, which is much more specific than the vague "Nilotic," is not used in current British or American writings on Africa. The author conforms to the common English terminology but considers it less appropriate.

(6) This was the situation before the Hutu revolution; since that time approximately 120,000 Tutsi have left the country and the geographical distribution of the remaining Nilotes over the various districts is not known.

(7) There were local variations in the marriage prohibitions along the lines of the overall north-south distinction, but in central Rwanda these were the main rules: marriage is forbidden between lineage members, between *inzu* members, between "outgoing members" as long as people remember their links with the original lineage, and between members and outgoing members of the first and second descending generation, but not between a member and a first outgoing member of the same generation. Thus, a man was allowed to marry his matrilateral and patrilateral cross-cousins. *Terminology*: An "outgoing member" is an individual who is connected with a lineage through a woman; a "first outgoing member" is an individual who is connected with a lineage through his mother. *Example*: A (man) and B (woman) belong to Lineage I; so do A's children. B's children belong to Lineage II (that is, the lineage of B's husband): they are first outgoing members with respect to Lineage I. Similarly, the children of B's children are outgoing members with respect to Lineage I.

(8) This behavior was structurally not quite intelligible in central Rwanda, whereas it fell into pattern in the northern regions since a maternal uncle was a man's potential father-in-law: the respectful attitude, normative in the relationship toward affinal kin of the ascending generation, was imperative, even if the preferential marriage that supported the relation was not actually achieved.

(9) *Terminology*: An "entering member" is an individual, male or female, who has been married to an *inzu* member. He or she is an affine who enters a kinship group by marriage.

(10) The king belonged to the dynastic *sindi-nyiginya* patriclan; the office of queen mother circulated through four lineages belonging to the matridynastic *eega, kono, ha,* and *gesera* clans. Twelve out of nineteen historic queen mothers since the beginning of the sixteenth century were *eega*.

(11) This conclusion on "divine kingship" in Rwanda is based on material in d'Hertefelt and Coupez (1964).

(12) Many English writers are reluctant to use the word "sacred" in the sense of the French *sacré*; an alternative wording would be "having ritual value" (proposed by A. R. Radcliffe-Brown).

(13) Ruanda-Urundi in old Swahili spelling.

(14) Twa are disregarded in these figures since they number only 0.1 percent of

the population of the area considered; moreover, modern educational attainments are almost nonexistent among Twa.

Bibliography

With a few exceptions the following bibliography emphasizes contemporary work. Daggered items (†) are cited as references in the text of the chapter. Asterisks (*) indicate items that include significant bibliographies.

Albert, Ethel M. (1960). "Socio-political Organization and Receptivity to Change: Some Differences between Ruanda and Urundi," *Southwestern Journal of Anthropology*, Vol. 16, No. 1, pp. 46–74.

Centre de Recherche et d'Information Socio-politiques (1961). *Rwanda politique 1958–1960*. Brussels.
A very useful selection of political texts.

Codère, Helen (1962). "Power in Ruanda," *Anthropologica*, n. s. Vol. 4, No. 1, pp. 45–85.
Stresses the power aspect of traditional Rwanda society but tends to disregard the functional significance of ideological superstructures.

Coupez, André (1962). *Grammaire rwanda simplifiée*. Usumbura, Rwanda: Service de l'Information.
The only fully scientific introduction to the language of Rwanda.

Czekanowski, J. (1917). *Forschungen im Nil-Kongo-Zwischengebiet*, I, *Ethnographie* (Mpororo, Rwanda). Leipzig.
Excellent record of a German scientific expedition with ample material, especially in the technological sphere.

d'Hertefelt, Marcel (1960). "Myth and Political Acculturation in Rwanda," in A. Dubb (ed.), *Myth in Modern Africa*. Lusaka, Northern Rhodesia: Rhodes-Livingstone Institute for Social Research, pp. 114–135.
Discusses the reinterpretation of traditional myth in the new sociopolitical setting.

———— (1962*). "Rwanda," in M. d'Hertefelt, A. A. Trouwborst, and J. H. Scherer, *Les anciens royaumes de la zone interlacustre méridionale: Rwanda, Burundi, Buha*. Tervuren, Belgium: Musée Royal de l'Afrique Centrale, pp. 9–116.
A survey of Rwanda culture; stresses cultural diversity.

———— and André Coupez (1964†). *La royauté sacrée de l'ancien Rwanda: texte, traduction et commentaire de son rituel*. Tervuren, Belgium: Musée Royal de l'Afrique Centrale.
Contains the Kinyarwanda text, the French translation, and an abundant

commentary of the secret royal ritual. First edition of this type of text for the whole of Africa.

de Lacger, L. (1961). *Ruanda*, Kabgayi (augmented revised edition). Rwanda: Presses de l'Archevêché.
    Good introduction to Rwanda history.

Edel, May Mandelbaum (1957). *The Chiga of Western Uganda*. New York: Oxford University Press.
    Analyzes a society of southwestern Uganda whose culture is closely related to that of the northern Hutu of Rwanda.

Greenberg, Joseph H. (1955†). *Studies in African Linguistic Classification*. New Haven, Conn.: The Compass Publishing Co.

Hiernaux, Jean (1954†). *Les caractères physiques des populations du Ruanda et de l'Urundi*. Brussels: Institut Royal des Sciences Naturelles de Belgique.
    The best analysis in the field of physical anthropology.

Kandt, Richard (1921). *Caput Nili. Eine empfindsame Reise zu den Quellen des Nils*. 5th ed. Berlin: Dietrich Reimer.
    Especially interesting for consideration of the method of indirect rule.

Leurquin, Phillippe (1960). *Le niveau de vie des populations rurales du Ruanda-Urundi*. Louvain: Nauwelaerts.
    Excellent economic analysis; plentiful statistical material.

Maquet, J. J. (1960*). *The Premise of Inequality* (translation of *Le système des relations sociales dans le Ruanda ancien* [1954]). London: Oxford University Press for the International African Institute.
    Analysis of ancient central Rwanda political structures; shows a tendency to overstress the degree of consent given by the Hutu to their rulers.

Maquet, J. J., and Marcel d'Hertefelt (1959). *Elections en société féodale. Une étude sur l'introduction du vote populaire au Ruanda-Urundi*. Brussels: Académie Royale des Sciences Coloniales.
    The cultural variation is seen as a basic variable to explain the electoral geography of Rwanda.

Vansina, Jan (1962†*). *L'evolution du royaume rwanda des origines à 1900*. Brussels: Académie Royale des Sciences d'Outre-Mer.
    An evaluation of Rwanda oral traditions and outline of the country's institutional development and of the expansion of the ancient kingdom.

12

THE SUKU
OF SOUTHWESTERN CONGO

about the chapter

The Suku live in the Congo, a geographical region and culture area which, along with the Guinea Coast, probably typifies Africa for the nonspecialist. Because these are areas of tropical rain forest, the material culture, technology, and some social institutions of the Suku, like those of the Ibo, the Kpelle, the Tiv, and the Yoruba, reflect the influence of the habitat. In activities such as growing root crops, making palm wine, weaving raffia, smelting iron, and preparing magical medicines, the Suku are typical of equatorial Africa.

Yet for the specialist the Congo region is not "typical" of sub-Saharan Africa but indicates the degree of diversity among African cultures. The region in which the Suku live is the broad band bisecting south central Africa that has been referred to as the "matrilineal belt." One of the variations of matrilineal social structure found among the Suku offers a counterpoint to the basic patrilineality of sub-Saharan Africa. Their kinship organization presents a structural problem in that matrilineal descent is combined with patrilocal residence. However, the Suku have developed a series of cultural patterns which minimize and mitigate the conflicts between these virtually incompatible norms.

Another pair of principles sometimes in conflict are also combined in Suku society: centralization of political authority and the segmentary principle. In contrast to two of the societies described in this volume—Tiv and Somali—in which the segmentary principle is especially strong, the Suku are centralized; they have a monarchy. Viewing the Suku material, we see that the two principles are not completely incompatible, as they have sometimes been asserted to be, but complementary. The segmentary principle seems to come into play when the authority of the kingship is weak or cannot assert itself.

The Suku have one dramatic ceremony that is not common in sub-Saharan Africa. This is a periodic initiation of males *and* females of different ages and kin groups which is based partly on territorial ties. It is the crossing of sex and age lines in such a ceremony that is unusual. Such a ceremony is obviously integrative in function, and counteracts the cumulative effect of the strains and cleavages inherent in some of the numerous contending structural principles of Suku society.

Kopytoff describes the Suku religion "from the inside out," as it appears to a Suku, and demonstrates that all the institutions of Suku society are connected with the religious belief system. In its logical interrelating of diverse and disparate elements the system is typical of the Congo region. A comparison of the Suku religion with that of the Tiv of the Guinea Coast reveals striking similarities, especially in the way in which lineage elderhood, witchcraft, and the manipulation of medicines are interrelated. Both the logic of their religion and its connection with so many features of their society and culture permit it to serve as an explanatory mechanism for the Suku.

about the author

Igor Kopytoff, Assistant Professor of Anthropology at the University of Pennsylvania, received his Ph.D. from Northwestern University in 1960, and has taught also at Brown University. His field research among the Suku of the Congo Republic was carried out in 1958 and 1959 as a Ford Foundation Fellow and under the sponsorship of the Program of African Studies at Northwestern University. His writings include *The Samoyed* (1955), "Extension of Conflict as a Method of Conflict Resolution among the Suku of the Congo" (1961), "Socialism and Traditional African Societies" (1964), and "Family and Lineage among the Suku of the Congo" (1964).

IGOR KOPYTOFF · *The Suku of Southwestern Congo*[1]

INTRODUCTION

LOCATION · South of the equatorial forest that dominates most of the Congo River Basin, a wide band of savanna, sometimes open, sometimes lightly forested, stretches from the Atlantic coast to the area south of the great lakes of central Africa. In the centuries before the establishment of European control, the history of this region was no less eventful than that of the Sudan, although its details are, for the present, less well known. When the Portuguese, in 1482, reached the mouth of the Congo River, they found that the hinterland was controlled by three states, the best known of these being that of the Kongo. After they had rounded the Cape and touched the east coast, they heard of a kingdom in the interior, called Monomotapa. In the following centuries, other names, such as Luba, Lunda, and Kuba, became known, together with those of a number of smaller and often transient states.

One of these petty states is represented by the Suku, some 80,000 people who live in the Kwango district of the province of Léopoldville in the Republic of the Congo. Linguistically, they belong to the Bantu subgroup of the Central Branch of the Niger-Congo family of languages (Greenberg 1955). In the more local setting, their speech is closely related, to the point of mutual intelligibility, to the languages of the Kongo and Yaka groups to the west and south. This close linguistic relationship parallels presumed historical connections. Suku legends contain ambiguous memories of the Kongo kingdom and reflect the welter of conflicts and migrations that accompanied its disintegration and the subsequent establishment over the Kwango area of the hegemony of the expanding Lunda empire. The Suku appear to have emerged as a political entity around the early nineteenth century, when they escaped Lunda domination by moving into the largely empty lands to the east of the Kwango Valley, lands that they presently occupy.[2]

There are strong indications that periodically, over the last century and a half, the region has drawn in additional refugee lineages from surrounding ethnic groups. Thus the origins of the Suku must not be viewed as homogeneous; their present cultural uniformity is probably as much a matter of interassimilation as it is of the pre-existing cultural similarities of the Kwango groups on which the present Suku population drew. What gives the Suku their unity is, above all, their recognition of the political paramountcy of their king, the *MeniKongo*. Ideologically, the group is conceived of as a state, a territorial and political *dominium*, rather than as a tribe of single origin or one whose customs are alike in every detail.

PHYSICAL APPEARANCE ·· In their physical appearance, the Suku differ little from the general population of central Africa. Although the range of individual variation is considerable, one may say that generally the Suku, like their neighbors, tend to be lighter in complexion than the Africans who live in West Africa and in the central African forest. One of the more striking Suku features is their rather short stature, the mean being five feet two inches, and their light weight, the average for male adults being slightly over ninety pounds. However, the extent to which these last two figures are genetically significant may be questioned; protein deficiency in the present Suku diet must be taken into account before any simple hypotheses of "racial" origins or mixtures are advanced.[3]

HABITAT AND CLIMATE · The Suku occupy an area of rolling savanna, with occasional stretches of light woods; the soil is sandy and, when compared with neighboring regions, relatively poor for agriculture, but until recent times the area has been rather rich in game. The land is cut by several swift, northward-flowing rivers with numerous cataracts: the Bakali, the Inzia, the Luie, and the Lukula; smaller streams feed into these rivers from the east and west. The waters are usually fringed by heavy gallery forests and swamps over a distance rarely exceeding a few hundred yards.

Although only six degrees south of the equator, the region is about 2500 feet above sea level and the climate is by no means unpleasantly hot. There are two main seasons in the year. The dry, cool season begins in May and ends in September. At this time, the sky is gray, dusty winds blow during the day, and the nights are uncomfortably cold; the landscape is yellow, dotted with dark stretches of burned grass. As the rains begin in September, the countryside seems to rejuvenate, the dust vanishes from the air, the skies become blue and clear, and tall new grass pushes up. This wet season is not one of continuous rains; rain falls intermittently, and dry spells may last several days.

ECONOMY

The yearly cycle of subsistence activities is related to the alternation between wet and dry seasons. Agricultural work is most active during the rainy season; with the onset of the dry period, large cooperative hunts dominate the scene. These two principal phases of the subsistence economy also correspond to the division of labor between the sexes. The bulk of the subsistence is provided by hoe agriculture, which is entirely the work of women, who plant their fields in the open grassland; hunting, on the other hand, is done exclusively by men. Fishing is engaged in separately by both sexes.

CROPS • The agricultural staple is cassava (manioc); at present, with the diminution of meat from hunting, it provides the overwhelming portion of the Suku diet, as much as 90 percent of the total calories (Holemans 1959). Planted among the cassava are sweet potatoes, pumpkins, beans, and peas; these are harvested first, the cassava being left for at least twelve months. Thereafter, the tubers remain in what may be called an underground storage, to be dug up when needed. For peanuts, separate fields are kept, usually on the sites of abandoned villages, where the soil is more fertile. During the rainy season, every adult woman plants three and sometimes four fields in succession, so that new crops are available from the previous fields while a new one is being prepared. With the end of the wet season, however, no new fields are made and a shortage of vegetables, though not of cassava, sets in by the middle of the dry season. Cultivation is necessarily of the shifting type because the soil, once used, requires fifteen to twenty years to recover its fertility. The fields are always small, a little over an acre a year being sufficient to feed a family of four or five persons. Population density being low (some fifteen persons per square mile), land is more than abundant, and is, in fact, treated as a free economic good.

In addition to what is grown in the fields, minuscule gardens are made inside the villages, sometimes by men. Here bananas, tobacco, and the more recently introduced vegetables, such as tomatoes and radishes, are grown. Palm trees and small bamboo groves constitute another important resource; the men tap them for the "wine" that is a necessary accompaniment of all social occasions.

Cultivated crops are supplemented by collections of wild fruits, berries, mushrooms, and various roots of bush and forest. The delicacies include caterpillars, small types of mudfish, flying ants, palm-tree grubs, and wild honey.

HUNTING AND ANIMAL HUSBANDRY • Hunting, the primary male occupation in the productive economy, is of more than mere economic importance. A man must provide meat for the family, and prowess as a hunter is greatly valued and boasted about. The introduction of firearms has depleted the game considerably, but hunting is still pursued with undiminished enthusiasm even though, from the purely economic point of view, it represents

Making Pottery

one of the least productive investments of labor. Among the principal animals that are hunted are the various kinds of antelopes, wild hogs, leopards and several varieties of wild cats, buffalo, monkeys, birds, rodents of different types, and a few species of lizards. Hyenas and jackals are considered inedible. The hippopotamus and the crocodile are rarely hunted; the elephant, though prized, makes only a very occasional appearance in the region; lions, although remembered from the past, are at present entirely lacking. The traditional weapon, the bow, is extensively used, but firearms have become rather common in recent years. Hunting methods also involve the use of pits, net-drives, and traps.

Domesticated animals include dogs, goats, pigs, and chickens; and, since European contact, pigeons, ducks, guinea pigs, turkeys, and rabbits. No special care is given to the first group of animals which are by far the more numerous, and they are expected, on the whole, to fend for themselves.

CRAFT SPECIALIZATION · In addition to these subsistence activities, the Suku engage in crafts, and here the division of labor between the sexes is also clearly pronounced. Pottery is made exclusively by women. The men weave baskets, mats, raffia cloth, fishing nets and weirs, and carve wooden objects, such as drums, household utensils, mortars, and statues used in religious ceremonies. Blacksmithing is an important and respected occupation, surrounded with taboos and requiring a special initiation; the smith produces hoes, knives, arrowpoints, and axes. To some extent, all male adults are craftsmen in a general sense, for all men can build houses, make a bow, weave a simple mat, and hammer out a crude arrowpoint. At the same time, those knowledgeable in more specialized crafts never make them a full-time occupation, and every craftsman is also engaged in the more ordinary activities, such as hunting and fishing. Many craftsmen tend to specialize in making particular objects of their trade; for example, most basketmakers weave only one or two types of baskets. There is also some tendency to regional specialization, certain villages producing particular kinds of baskets or mats.

Other part-time specialists to be mentioned may be classified as "professionals." These are the medical practitioners who engage in curing; dancers and musicians who, at the time of ceremonies, travel from village to village and perform for money; circumcision specialists; diviners; and judges who settle disputes for a fee.

MARKETS AND EXCHANGE • The Suku and surrounding regions are not famous for large markets, and the Suku are in no sense inveterate traders. But economic exchange does take place by means of individual trading and small-scale markets, and money as well as barter was an integral part of this exchange system long before European contact. At present, the unit used is the Congolese franc; as recently as the middle 1930s, shell money was used.

One of the striking characteristics of the Suku productive economy is its individual orientation. Trading, engaging in craft production, and animal breeding are done individually; women farm individually, houses are individually built, fishing weirs are individually exploited. Even in the large communal hunts of the dry season, involving as many as five hundred hunters, every man hunts for himself, and the game is never divided among all the participants. This pattern contrasts sharply with the system of ownership, distribution, and consumption, where the lineage and not the individual is the relevant unit. This point will emerge clearly when Suku social organization is examined.

SOCIAL ORGANIZATION

THE VILLAGE • When Belgian administration became firmly established in the Suku area in the middle 1920s, most Suku villages varied in size between fifteen and seventy-five persons. The administration pursued a policy of amalgamating the many small villages into larger settlements; at present, a few of these contain as many as five hundred persons. Within these amalgamated settlements, however, the Suku view the old villages as separate entities.

The distance between neighboring settlements is seldom less than two miles and ordinarily is more. This is to be expected, given the low density of population. Villages are relatively stable; those that move usually resettle in toto within a short distance of the old location. An entire village is moved when it is decided that the existing site is "unlucky" after a chief dies, or an epidemic breaks out, or an unusual series of misfortunes occurs. Shifting cultivation is not a factor in the displacement of villages. Planting

A Village Compound

is always done half a mile or more from a village to keep it out of reach of domestic animals; this provides a large area of cultivable land around each village, within which shifting cultivation is carried on.

THE COMPOUND · At present, under Belgian influence, the compounds in most villages are set on both sides of a central street. Traditionally, however, settlement was more haphazard, with irregularly shaped spaces separating clusters of compounds. A compound consists of a roughly circular or square area, about a hundred feet across, whose boundaries are marked by a row of low bushes. The Suku house is rectangular in shape, with a gable roof; it consists of a skeleton of piles driven into the ground and reinforced by a framework of light strips of branches and bamboo, the whole covered with thick, even layers of grass. The typical house measures roughly eight by fifteen feet; houses of chiefs may be larger, the upper limit being about ten by twenty feet. As a rule, the house is divided into two communicating rooms, the inner room serving for sleeping and the outer for storage and sitting.

Every compound lodges a husband, his wife or wives, and their unmarried children. A son, at his marriage, starts his own compound in the vicinity of his father's. There are several houses in a compound. In his own house, the husband receives visitors, eats by himself or in male company, and keeps his personal belongings. Every wife has her own house, which she occupies with her small children. Adolescents rarely have a specified house to sleep in; they find their quarters wherever they can around the village, usually staying with their friends of the same sex in whatever empty house is available; such houses are found in every village and are used for storage and for putting up visitors.

Lineages

Although a Suku village is the area where most of the face-to-face social relationships take place, the residents of a village do not represent the fundamental unit of Suku social organization, that unit being the matrilineage. The Suku are an example of a society that follows matrilineal descent but patrilocal residence at marriage, with adult sons continuing to reside in their own father's village. Therefore, while the village itself is said to "belong" to a particular lineage (the one that first established it), about half its residents are not members of that lineage. Thus the grown sons who build their compounds near their father's belong not to his lineage but to their mother's, which is usually (but not always, since lineages are not exogamous) different from their father's. At the same time, every married daughter of the family lives with her husband, who is usually a resident of some other village, and raises her children there.

Every Suku belongs to several matrilineally based groups, all of which are known by the same term—*kikanda*. At its widest, *kikanda* may be called the clan; its members recognize their common descent but ignore the genealogical details of the relationship. Clans, however, are widely dispersed territorially and there is little persistent interaction among their members. Functionally, the fundamental unit of Suku social organization is the *kikanda* in its narrowest sense, to be referred to here as the "autonomous lineage" or simply as "the lineage." On the average, such lineages number about thirty persons. Several such lineages further combine into a group of the somewhat less immediate importance, the "major lineage."

CORPORATE NATURE • An autonomous matrilineage is a *corporate* group in that it has a name and a formal head, in that it possesses continuity through time even while its membership changes, and in that it acts as a single unit in a variety of economic, social, jural, political, and religious contexts. Formally, the headship of the lineage belongs to the oldest male member, but in fact authority rests with the entire group of elders; no decision of importance is taken and no negotiations affecting lineage interests are held without consultations among this group. As this oldest generation begins to die out, the next one, containing by then several middle-aged adults, becomes involved in making decisions and, in time, becomes the generation of elders.

Lineages, as corporate groups, own certain resources. As has already been stated, land for agricultural uses is regarded as a free good. But ownership of land in the sense of hunting rights over determined stretches of bush is in the hands of specific lineages. Through prior occupation or later purchase from the first owners, a lineage acquires the exclusive right to burn its land during the communal hunts of the dry season, to hunt freely in this land, and to collect a portion of all the game killed by other hunters. Similar rights are exercised by lineages over fishing sites and small streams, and over palm and bamboo groves.

The Suku say that when a person acquires any property, he does so because of the supernatural and physical protection of his lineage. Thus all individual domestic property is viewed as ultimately belonging to the lineage as a whole and there is a continuous circulation of household goods and money among members. Such sharing is especially pronounced at times of collective lineage needs, when legal fines or taxes are to be paid or when bridewealth for a lineage member is to be assembled. Conversely, when a legal compensation or bridewealth is received, every adult member claims a share.

All this does not mean that everything in the lineage is continuously and meticulously redistributed. Individuals do manage to accumulate money, domestic animals, and household goods. What counts, and this no Suku questions in principle, is that the rights to these possessions are ultimately held by the lineage, which may exercise them in times of need and that upon a person's death all his property actively reverts to the lineage as a corporate body. Since it is the elders' responsibility to look after lineage interests and to manage its affairs, they must of necessity control greater means than the younger men. This they usually do, first, because they have had some time in which to accumulate wealth, and, second, because they can use their authority to channel much of the lineage wealth into their own hands by claiming a greater share when subdivisions are made. Thus, although wealth is distributed throughout the lineage, it is concentrated in the group of elders.

THE LINEAGE CENTER · Every Suku lineage has a center, which is the village originally built by its founders and bearing its name. Here the head of the lineage resides and sacrifices; here ceremonies are performed, marriages are celebrated, and lineage members are preferably buried. The functioning of an autonomous lineage around this center, given its strongly corporate organization, presupposes relative ease of communication among members; in this society, as in most, this requires geographical proximity. Yet as has already been pointed out, the lineage cannot ever be strictly localized, since patrilocal residence results in scattering the membership among several villages.

FISSION AND FUSION · As long as marriages are contracted with close neighbors, this dispersal does not greatly affect communication among lineage members. When, however, a woman of the lineage marries a man from a distant village, and bears children who remain in their father's region, the effect is to produce a lineage offshoot which, in time, may grow in number. Given Suku conceptions of lineage unity in economic, legal, and ritual matters, this offshoot must of necessity possess a certain degree of autonomy in its dealings with its own neighbors. This factual autonomy, if it persists, is confirmed in time by a formal separation of ritual paraphernalia from the original lineage. Thus what before was one lineage now becomes two. Another way in which lineages segment is through quarrels: an elder may be accused of cupidity, of witchcraft, or of favoritism to those members who are closest to him, and a formal separation between two lineage segments may follow.

Such separations, however, are never viewed as final and irrevocable. Blood ties, the *raison d'être* of lineage unity, are seen as indissoluble; segmentation resulting from quarrels is always viewed by the Suku as a temporary aberration, and segmentation caused by geographical distance as a necessary concession to the reality of difficulties in communication. At certain levels, the old lineage continues to be a corporate body, and we shall refer to it as the "major lineage." Thus hunting lands and political offices, when such were held by the previously unified lineage, still belong to the major lineage as a whole. When one autonomous lineage lacks any mature adults to head it, it will call upon another related lineage to supply it with a head. Finally, an autonomous lineage may move back into the territory of its parent-lineage and the two segments become reunited. Suku lineage structure thus allows for re-fusion as well as separation. But in the flow of everyday life, each lineage acts as a corporate body, installs its own head, and controls de facto the lineage property that is in its vicinity while holding it in trust for the entire major lineage.[4]

MAINTENANCE OF THE LINEAGE CENTER • We have said that as long as the women of a lineage marry men within a relatively short distance from the lineage center, the dispersal of lineage membership, resulting from patrilocal residence, need not vitiate communication among the members and the smooth functioning of the lineage as a corporate group. Even under these conditions, however, patrilocal residence poses a problem as far as the maintenance of the lineage center is concerned. At first glance it would appear that such a village will lose all members of its founding lineage within a generation because the women leave to reside with their husbands and produce children who will live elsewhere, while at the same time the lineage members living in the center bring in wives from outside and thus populate the village with children who are members of other lineages.[5]

This trend, among the Suku, is countered by several mechanisms. As a rule, the lineage head resides in the center; if he lives elsewhere at the time of his accession, he changes his residence. Other members, with advancing age, also tend to drift into the lineage center. Ideally a man is expected to reside with his father and, after the latter's death, with his father's lineage, but in fact a few men move to their own lineage center at their father's death and even more men do so once all their classificatory "fathers" (that is, their father's lineage members of his generation) have died. A certain proportion of men do follow the ideal rule and live with their father's relatives to the end, but enough people do not, and thus repopulate the center with lineage members.

There are ways in which marriages may be arranged to bring about the same result. Some women marry men who already live in their (the women's) lineage center. It is in this connection that the Suku express some preference for patrilateral cross-cousin marriage, that is, the marriage of a man with his father's sister's daughter. An elder living in his lineage center may arrange such a marriage for his son who lives with him and thus bring a woman member of the elder's lineage (his sister's daughter) and her future children into the center. Finally, Suku lineages are not exogamous, and incest prohibitions preclude marriages only between lineage members of the same generation (for they are regarded as siblings). But a man may marry a daughter of his classificatory sister and even that of his true sister, although the latter match is not generally approved. In such a marriage, a man living in his lineage center brings in a wife of his own lineage and thus assures that their children will also reside there.

Through a combination of these various patterns, the centrifugal forces of lineage dispersal are counteracted and the lineage center continues to hold a core of members in residence, giving the entire lineage organization a fixed point of reference in space and over time.

Marriage

Polygyny is an accepted pattern among the Suku, but the majority of married men (some 80 percent) are in fact monogamous. There is no culturally defined limit to the number of wives a man may have but only a few can afford to pay the bridewealth for many. The majority of polygynous marriages (about 70 percent) involve only two wives, but there are individual cases on record, particularly in the past, when important chiefs had as many as ten or more, and one of the Suku kings had close to forty.

As in every society, there is a formal, legal side to marriage as well as a personal one. Choosing one's mate is primarily a personal matter. To be sure, a certain number of marriages are prearranged by relatives, but it is rare for such a marriage to be forced on a person who strongly objects, for the Suku know that it will not last. Most marriages are initiated by the young people themselves and acceptance by a girl is preceded by a period of courtship. However, once the girl has agreed, the arrangement of the legal side of marriage is a matter between the lineages concerned.

First, the groom must secure the consent of the girl's father, to whom he comes with a gift of palm wine, and of her mother, to whom etiquette requires a small present, such as a handkerchief. Acceptance of these gifts signifies that the parents have no objections. The next visit, also accompanied by a gift of palm wine, is to the head of the girl's lineage or her mother's brother (true or classificatory). The young man is accompanied by the head or an elder of his own lineage. At the meeting, lineage genealogies and histories are reviewed and any past quarrels between the two lineages discovered; if there are outstanding claims, arrangements are made for their settlement before the marriage. At this time the amount to be paid as bridewealth is agreed upon.[6] The groom is allowed a period of several months to assemble it.

At the time of its payment, the bridewealth is formally handed to the head of the bride's lineage, who immediately gives the greater portion of it (between two thirds and three quarters) to the bride's father. The Suku regard this as payment to the father for his care and trouble in bringing up his daughter for her lineage; once the sum is paid, her lineage assumes the legal responsibility for the woman in any future matters connected with the marriage. The groom's lineage considers that the payment has been made to the woman's lineage and should there be a divorce it will claim reimbursement from the woman's lineage and not from her father. If the woman later remarries, the new bridewealth will go entirely to her own lineage.

If the wife dies, her lineage must either return the bridewealth or provide another wife. Should the husband die, the bridewealth must similarly be reimbursed or the widow must remarry another member of her husband's lineage, his true or classificatory brother.

The return of bridewealth in case of divorce or death represents a readjustment in the balance of reciprocity between the lineages involved. When the marriage has produced children, new factors enter into this balance. Since the husband has the right to collect the greater part of his daughter's future bridewealth and since his sons will live with him and help him, these advantages are taken into account. The presence of a daughter reduces the amount of the reimbursed bridewealth by a half; that of each son, by a quarter.

In effect, then, bridewealth is exchanged, and may be re-exchanged in the future, for certain rights in a woman that are acquired by the husband and his lineage. The most important of these rights are those to her domestic labor and exclusive sexual rights. For the actual exercise of the right of sexual possession, however, a ceremony must be performed in which a goat is sacrificed. Until this is done, sexual intercourse is punished by fines levied on the groom, fines that are the same as those collected in any case of fornication.

The goat is supplied by the groom, and it is the only transfer in marriage that is not reimbursable. The sacrifice is performed at a crossroads by the head of the bride's lineage. Sexual intercourse between members of different lineages is viewed as a "mixing" of different "bloods"—a dangerous thing, potentially threatening the life of any member of the woman's lineage unless the danger is removed by sacrifice.[7]

The interweaving of the personal and the legal elements in marriage appears clearly in the relations between the spouses. Love, warmth, and affection exist, as do indifference, distrust, and rancor. But this natural play of personalities and individual feelings takes place within a given family structure in which the principle of lineage unity is dominant. When the spouses belong to different lineages, they have no rights to each other's property; for example, the husband cannot use his wife's food without her permission. It is her duty to plant fields so that the family may be fed, as it is his duty to provide her with meat, clothing, and household utensils. Whatever a wife earns by selling the produce of her fields, she shares half with her husband; what she earns from making pottery or breeding livestock, she keeps as her own. This arrangement reflects the Suku woman's relative independence of her husband, for she remains throughout her life a full-fledged member of her own lineage and is never incorporated into that of her husband. One consequence of this is that divorce is rather easily resorted to. Roughly half of the Suku women in their late middle age have been married at least twice. When an old woman becomes widowed, her life in her husband's village is often a lonely one, and she will usually move to her lineage center, where she can be among her own and where some of her middle-aged sons may also be moving.

THE PATRILOCAL RESIDENTIAL UNIT • Matrilineal descent divides the Suku family into two subunits—the father as opposed to the mother and her children—each of which owes its primary loyalty to its own matrilineage. Although the father is not interfered with in the day-to-day task of educating the child, he always consults his wife's lineage about serious matters affecting the child. Legally, it is the matrilineage that is responsible for a child's misdemeanors, and it pays the fines in cases of theft or homicide. In contrast to this division of lineage affiliation within the family, however, is the residential unit composed of a father and his adult sons; the father, in turn, together with his brothers, lives by the side of *his* father, and the latter's other sons, by his other wives, also live in the same village. Hence there may emerge a residential group that is a patrilocal extended family with a depth of three and even four (if small children are included) generations. Such a group, however, does not last. It begins to break up at the death of the oldest man (that is, the grandfather) around whom it was organized, when each group of brothers by the same mother begin to drift away toward its own lineage center. The transient nature of this patrilocal group appears to be related to the recognition of a transient patrilineage of a depth of only two generations, called *kitaata kya mukongu* (literally, fathership of the hunting "medicine"), whose functions are primarily related to the maintenance of the hunting luck of its members. Such a patrilineage includes a person's siblings by the same father, the father himself and his siblings by the same father, and the children of the father's brothers, but it specifically excludes the father's father.

LIFE CYCLE

CHILD TRAINING AND SOCIALIZATION • Children are very much valued among the Suku, who have a strong and realistic belief that a lineage derives strength from large membership. An expectant mother continues with her household duties right until childbirth and goes back to work a few days after. Difficulties at delivery are far from rare, and, before the establishment of the relatively extensive medical network of recent years, death of women in childbirth was not infrequent. In the early 1940s, infant mortality was high, hovering in the vicinity of 20 percent in the first year (Lamal 1949:68); since then it has been reduced roughly by half.

A few weeks after birth there is a "coming out" and a "naming" ceremony for the child, when it leaves the inside of its mother's house for the first time. Exclusive breast feeding lasts for about six months, after which time solid foods are added to the diet. But breast feeding continues, though gradually waning in frequency, until the child is at least two and sometimes three years old; occasionally even four-year-olds may be given the breast. As long as breast feeding is regular, sexual intercourse on the part of the mother is believed to be dangerous to the child's health.

Young boys enjoy considerable freedom from household tasks. The learning of adult occupations takes place gradually, without compulsion, and largely through participation and imitation. As a result, by late adolescence, boys control the ordinary skills that every Suku male does, and many of them begin to concentrate on some specialty they find attractive. Sometimes, this involves a period of apprenticeship and a payment to the teacher. Traditionally, this was the case with professional dancers, blacksmiths, diviners, and specialized curers; at present, apprenticeships are served by tailors, carpenters, mechanics, drivers, and sometimes even by those who wish to become domestic servants to Europeans and the wealthier Congolese.

In contrast to the boys, the girls are expected to help their mothers with household tasks almost as soon as they have learned to walk. At first,

Circumcised Boys This is during the period of seclusion. The boys live in the hut in the background at this time.

they are charged with carrying water from the river; as they grow older, they take care of younger children, bring firewood, and help their mothers in the fields, in the house, and in pounding cassava into flour. By the time a girl reaches marriageable age, which is normally about eighteen or twenty, she has not only learned all the tasks required of a wife but has been practicing them for some time.

MALE CIRCUMCISION · Though a boy's journey into manhood is gradual and without definite landmarks as far as the learning of tasks is concerned, there is one point in it that represents a definite psychological and social break with the past. This is the circumcision ceremony, which at present normally takes place between the ages of ten and fifteen and, in the old days, at eighteen or even later. For the girls, there is no comparable ceremonial.

A lineage chief in a given region takes the initiative in organizing the ceremony when he feels that there are enough boys of the right age in the area. Participation is entirely unrelated to lineage, clan, or political ties. The ceremony occurs in the dry season, partly for hygienic reasons. The organizer secures the services of a professional circumciser, who must also be knowledgeable in the details of the ceremonial because mistakes are considered to expose the children to witchcraft. The organizer is paid a fee by the parents of each child; out of this money he must pay the circumciser and the professional dancers who provide both entertainment and ritual protection against supernatural dangers for the children.

Circumcision takes place at early dawn, and the children immediately move to a special hut that has been previously erected outside the village. At present, they reside there only a few weeks, since most of them have to return to school in early September; traditionally, the period lasted for several

Masked Dancer This masked, costumed dancer is performing in a village in which a circumcision ceremony has taken place.

months. During their residence, they learn various dances and songs (most of which are derisive of women) and they are exposed to systematic hazing by their elders. Some of this hazing may border on physical cruelty; much of it consists in forcing the boys into admitting imaginary incestuous relations and making sexual jokes about their parents—behavior that would be unthinkable under normal circumstances. The entire ceremony is believed to ensure the boys' virility. Throughout the period of seclusion, women are strictly forbidden to approach them; those that do so by mistake are fined by the boys. At the end of the period, the boys go to the river, wash themselves, put on new clothing, and return to the village amid dancing and singing. They have now acquired new names and may collect a fine from anyone using their old ones.

One of the most apparent effects of the ceremony is psychological: the boys feel that they have become adults, superior to all females and uncircumcised children, and that this superiority is based on the fact that they have "suffered" as the others have not. There is a rather vague feeling of solidarity among the men who went through the same circumcision ceremony together, but it is neither obligatory nor institutionalized in any way.

THE KITA CEREMONY · Another ceremony, called *Kita*, crosscuts lineage ties and, this time, involves both males and females of different ages. Periodically, and usually after the death of a regional chief, it is felt that the land and the society require a kind of renewal, particularly if there has been what is regarded as an unusual number of abnormal births, of albinos and of twins (the latter, though not welcome, are both allowed to live). The ceremony is directed by a man and a woman who possess a special ritual medicine concerned with abnormal births. The initiates are all those in the region who have not previously been through *Kita*; since *Kita* occurs at long intervals of time—at least a decade and often longer—the initiates vary greatly in age.

The ritual itself consists of the symbolic killing of the initiates, a residence of some weeks in a specially built large house in which the initiates literally "play dead" during the daytime, and, finally, a coming-out ceremony, with special songs and dances, after which the initiates are known by their new names. As is true of the circumcision ritual, *Kita* is viewed in personal terms and does not give rise to any kind of society nor to any feeling of commonality among the initiates.

Stratification and slavery

The absence of age grades and of secret societies that would introduce ties other than those of kinship and residence points up once again the pervasive functions of the corporate lineage. Solidarity based on lineage affiliation similarly eliminates individual differences in wealth. To be sure, some lineages own hunting lands whereas others do not. A few lineages control the offices of regional chiefs and profit from the tribute they collect in the king's name. But the resulting differences in wealth are, on the whole, slight, and the successful pursuit of hunting, animal breeding, or trade, or of a profession, such as blacksmithing or divining, easily offsets such differences.

One Suku institution, slavery, may lead to the conclusion—it has, in fact, been so interpreted by some travelers in this region—that the society is at the very least divided into two classes, the "slaves" and the "free." The way the institution functioned in the past (at present it is illegal) indicates that such a description does violence to reality.

Among the Suku, homicide was compensated for by the guilty lineage by substituting for the dead person two persons of the same sex, or by paying the price of two slaves. A lineage without money was therefore forced to give up two of its members. Also, persistent thieves and adulterers, whose behavior cost the lineage numerous fines or exposed it to supernatural dangers, were sold after several warnings. On the other hand, the desire to increase lineage membership always made it easy to find a willing buyer who would not always be informed about the true reasons for the sale. The people bought were usually children and adolescents, and sometimes young women; these could be expected to adapt to their new environment and, above all, to find it harder than would a mature male to escape back to their original lineage.

The Suku are too far east to have been directly touched by the large-scale slaving activities on the Portuguese-held west coast, and too far west to have been reached by the Arab slavers operating in central Africa. Slave raiding appears to have been unknown, and the buying and selling within the Suku region was done on an individual basis. Suku slavery cannot even be called "domestic slavery"; perhaps the term "adoption" is closest to the truth. A slave was, for all practical purposes, a full fledged member of the lineage, living the same life as the other members and engaging in the same occupations. What he accumulated as property was his in the same limited sense that any Suku property is ever personal. In conformity with matrilineal descent, the children of a female slave became members of their mother's adoptive lineage, and the children of a male slave belonged to that of their mother. Marriage with a slave was neither more nor less desirable, the amount of bridewealth was the same, and elders descended from female slaves could become lineage heads. Nevertheless, a subtle difference in treatment did exist. If the lineage was faced with the necessity of selling one of its members, it was more willing to select a slave member, all other things being equal; similarly, less patience was shown a slave thief or adulterer. But an undesirable true member would still be sold before a good slave member.

Slaves, then, did not represent a "class" in Suku society. Such a term emphasizes a horizontal division over the far more significant vertical one separating the different lineages. The importance of the cultural context of slavery may be clearly seen in the fact that in some lineages all the members are "slaves" in the sense that true blood membership has entirely died out and only the descendants of slaves are present; such a lineage continues to operate in the same way as before vis-à-vis the lineages and the clan to which it was originally related.

POLITICAL ORGANIZATION

At the present time, the Suku are a part of the political organization of the Republic of the Congo, an organization that has been largely inherited from the Belgian colonial system. The changes the colonial administration brought about will be touched on later. For the moment, the traditional political system will be discussed and, consequently, the past tense is necessarily used.

Traditional kingship

Upon the arrival of the Suku in the north of their present area, after their exodus from the Kwango Valley, the *MeniKongo,* as the king is called, established his village at its very border, in the northeastern corner, and it is here that his successors, including the present and powerless one, have lived. The king's village was large by the usual standards; comparisons made by informants with modern villages suggest a population in the neighborhood of three hundred persons. It accommodated most of the members of the royal lineage and the numerous wives of the king and of his brothers and sororal nephews. The women of the royal lineage were preferably married to its slaves so that they would remain in the capital and there bring up their children (some of whom would succeed to the kingship) while conforming to the rule of virilocal residence. In addition to a considerable number of slaves of the royal lineage, the village also housed many sons and grandsons of former kings, who, rather than join their own lineages, preferred to remain at the capital and enjoy the advantages of their kinship ties.

The king's compound was surrounded by a fence of bamboo and visitors had to be admitted by a guard. The compound contained the king's own house, those of his wives, and a small hut containing the ritual paraphernalia of kingship. These consisted of several kinds of magical medicines that had the power to injure enemies and to maintain the well-being of the people as a whole; there were also bracelets that had belonged to previous kings, the king's stools dating back to the time of the exodus, and the skull and jawbone of a Lunda chief killed in the war. The paraphernalia were in the charge of one of the king's specially initiated wives, and of a male guardian with his boy assistant. The male guardian was, in effect, a kind of priest of the royal cult; he performed the main sacrifices to the royal ancestors, buried dead kings, and initiated their successors. He was always chosen from among the slave members of the royal lineage.

The king's person was surrounded by a number of taboos. No one could see him eat; he could not walk in cultivated fields for fear of affecting the fertility of the soil; he could not see a corpse nor cry over the dead, for that, too, would spoil the land. He could not die a natural death, for that would affect the power of his sacred "medicines;" it was the duty of the male guardian to smother him when he was about to expire. When the king drank, those present had to cover their faces while one of the attendants recited proverbs and sayings recapitulating historic events, praising the king for his good deeds and also hinting at those where he had shown himself unjust.

The symbolic association between the king and the political order in the society was clearly revealed during the interregnum after his death. The Suku say that when the king dies, "the land also dies." As the news of the king's demise spread through the country, a period of institutionalized anarchy would set in: strangers were attacked, animals and crops were openly stolen, warfare would break out, and the authority of the regional chiefs was defied. With the installation of the new king, these eruptions of violence ceased, and the "land," meaning social order and political authority, was considered restored.

The king had no formally constituted council nor assistants with highly specific functions. One cannot, without forcing facts, speak of a "court" or of "ministers." The guardian of the king's paraphernalia sometimes handled political matters, such as settling disputes between regional chiefs, but at other times this was done by the king or by any of his brothers. Similarly, the king's sisters, when they were old and respected, could play an important part in the deliberations of the royal lineage, but there was no formal office of "Queen Sister" or "Queen Mother" that is often found in other African groups.[8]

In any immediate sense, the king actively ruled only over some twenty or thirty villages surrounding the capital, and for this purpose no elaborate organization was necessary. The principal problem in the political organization was that of administering the rest of the Suku state, of keeping as a political unit a population divided into strongly autonomous lineages, numbering probably less than the present figure of 80,000, and scattered over an area of some fifty by one hundred miles (roughly the size of Connecticut). Given the limited means of communication imposed by the existing technology, the problem of organization required special techniques of political control.

Regional organization

The model that was followed was, in general, typical of the kingdoms of the savanna belt of central Africa; more specifically, it appears to be Lunda, for much of the terminology is of Lunda origin. The kingdom was divided into several major regions of unequal size (before European occupation, there were about a dozen such regions). Ideally, the structure was pyramidal: the king at the apex delegated his powers to these regional chiefs; each of them, in turn, stood over several local chiefs who themselves had authority over groups of villages. Just as political power extended downward, step by step, from the king, so tribute, the visible expression of this power, flowed upward from the local level and by way of each successive link to the king.

The position of regional chiefs duplicated that of the king, but on a smaller scale. They were surrounded by the same kind of ritual and constrained by the same taboos. Like the king, they could act as judges in any matters brought before them, and they similarly lacked any well-defined council but relied on informal consultations with the elders of their village. There were no formal and continuous lines of communication between the king and his subordinate chiefs, and the latter had no representatives at the king's village.

The king's position as the center of the system was reasserted periodically and forcefully by his travels around the kingdom every few years for the purpose of collecting the tribute that the regional chiefs had previously gathered in his name. At this time, too, unresolved quarrels and complaints against local chiefs would be brought to the king and, conversely, a regional chief could inform the king of cases of insubordination. The king had no professional standing army, but his judgment could be swiftly enforced by his retinue, much of it consisting of hangers-on amassed during the trip and only too eager to burn and loot a designated village.

The above description represents what is more or less an ideal conception of the political organization. In reality, the political system appears to have been more successful in providing a tribute-gathering network than in regulating conflicts and maintaining order. This vitiation of the ideal is understandable when the position of the regional chiefs is examined. Their authority was maintained by their prestige as the king's representatives and by the fear that recalcitrance would bring retribution during the king's next visit; this ensured a more or less successful collection of tribute. But positive interference with quarrels between lineages was more difficult and brought no visible rewards. If a war broke out between two lineages, the regional chief could mediate and try to stop it, and in this his person was inviolate. But if passions were running high, it was not easy to enforce his decision, since all he could rely on was his prestige and the support of the membership of his own lineage whose strength was no greater than that of any other. Even such factors as the chief's age, energy, and physical strength influenced the operation of the political system. It is not surprising that there were always some chiefs who restricted themselves to collecting tribute (a right seldom disputed them) and avoided the discomforts of keeping the peace. The political vacuum that resulted was filled by other mechanisms outside the formal political system; some of them may be viewed as extralegal even though institutionalized. Their importance will be seen presently, when Suku law is examined.

Law

Any disputes inside the lineage were within the exclusive jurisdiction of the lineage itself, that is, of its elders; no other authority, not even that of the king, interfered with this lineage autonomy. As a result, such internal conflicts either were settled or remained unresolved, to be eventually outlived or forgotten or, if very serious, to bring about a division of the lineage into two autonomous segments.

One of the correlates of the strongly corporate organization of the lineage was that conflicts between persons of different lineages automatically pitted one lineage against another. Correct relations between lineages were conceived of in terms of strict reciprocity, and Suku traditional law made no allowances for intent or accident when someone's interests had been infringed upon. A theft demanded the return of an equivalent object and a fine, or a reciprocal theft. Homicide, accidental or not, was erased only by furnishing two persons to the wronged lineage, or their equivalent in money, or, finally, through the reciprocal murder of a member of the lineage at fault.

When a lineage felt that it had been wronged, the initiative of obtaining restitution belonged entirely to it. A moot could be called, in which neighbors and friends of both sides were free to participate and argue and thus to put some public pressure on the recalcitrant. If the moot were not successful, several other approaches remained. The case could be taken to the regional chief when both parties were of the same region; if they were not, this procedure, involving two different chiefs, became cumbersome. Also, as has already been shown, enforcement of the law by regional chiefs could not always be relied upon.

Another possibility was for both parties to take the case to a judge who specialized in settling disputes but worked entirely on his own, without any relation to the formal political organization. Such judges had no power to enforce their decisions; hence they demanded in advance from each side a fee and a deposit of money equivalent to the amount at stake in the dispute, the total of the two deposits being awarded to the party judged to be in the right. A judge's reputation rested on knowledge of custom and precedent, adroitness at questioning witnesses, and impartiality.

The procedure at the trial was well defined. Each side, represented not only by the person directly involved but also by an elder of his lineage, ordinarily chose a friend, talented at pleading, as an advocate. Each advocate stated his case; the judge summarized it, emphasized the main points at issue, and allowed the advocate to correct his summation. If necessary, additional arguments and questioning by the judge would follow. Although witnesses were used, little stock was put in their testimony: they were by definition biased and acted, in effect, as minor advocates for the side they favored. There was always a crowd of onlookers during the trial; they could contribute to the arguments, make additional points, and remind the audience of precedents. At the end of the trial, the judge retired to his house to think and to "sleep" over the decision and also, secretly, to consult various elders of his village. When the final decision was to be given, the judge emerged dancing and singing out various proverbs whose meaning favored now one side and now the other, thus keeping the audience and the litigants in suspense. Once again, the cases were summarized, first on their merits, and then, slowly, by allusion and proverb, the summary would begin to favor one party as the inconsistencies of the other became crystallized. By the time the decision was given, the outcome had been clear to all for some time. The entire deposit was then handed to the winner. If he had been the wronged party, he was thereby compensated for his original loss; if he had been unjustly accused, the extra amount he received was seen as compensation for libel.

If the parties to a dispute could not agree on a judge, the remaining possibility for the claimant was to take direct action. For example, in case of theft, one simply took one or several animals belonging to the other lineage or one captured a member of the other lineage as hostage to force it to come to terms. There was one interesting variant of self-help. Since the other side was usually on guard against direct action, the wronged lineage would resort to self-help against any third lineage that had nothing to do with the quarrel, telling it to lay its claims against the people responsible for the quarrel in the first place. The effect here was to involve forcibly a third lineage in a matter that had reached an impasse and thus to ensure that a third party, impartial yet actively concerned about having the issue settled, would act as a mediator.[9]

Another method of direct action was warfare. The wronged lineage invited the people of neighboring villages, particularly of those where there were relatives, to join in the coming battle; the other side similarly asked its neighbors for help. After a night of drumming and dancing, the first party would begin the attack on the village of the enemy. The goal was to put the enemy to flight, loot the village, and burn it. Few people were killed in these skirmishes, which, more often than not, were stopped by the elders of both sides as soon as any person was killed or even seriously wounded. The main purpose was to frighten the opponent into settling the dispute, and the warfare itself had some of the character of a mock battle in which more insults than arrows were traded.

It has been said that, in general, any violation of the principle of reciprocity in the relations between lineages held in it the potential for overt conflict. The strength of this principle is seen in quarrels over such apparently inconsequential matters as a borrowed basket of peanuts. At present, in the tribunals established by the administration, in which a fee must be paid before any matter is examined, one sometimes sees cases brought for judgment where the stakes are no higher than the fee itself. Such behavior, however, is not illogical, for the problem of an unsettled dispute is a moral one. The defense of its interests, no matter how small, is a duty to the lineage and to the community of blood that it stands for; lack of such defense is a betrayal. Hence the persistence with which justice in these terms is pursued.

Most of the conflicts among lineages may be grouped into a few categories recognized by the Suku themselves. The most inclusive of these is theft, which covers any infringement on lineage property in the widest sense, such as refusal to reimburse the full bridewealth upon divorce, evasion of the customary hunting tribute, any destruction of property (accidental or willful), or loss of a borrowed object. Another broad category is that of tribute related to political subordination or to kinship ties, such as the failure to present regular gifts to one's father or, if he is dead, to his lineage. A great number of cases falls under the rubric of illicit sexual relations. Insults, libel, and injuries that draw blood may also lead to a court case. Finally, homicide is an important but rare cause of serious conflict.

Traditionally, minor claims, such as insults, were rarely taken to court. In the recital of conflicts in the past, what stands out most is theft, the enslavement of strangers, adultery, failure to pay the hunting tribute, accidental homicide, and arguments over the ownership of hunting lands. Argu-

Tribunal in Session The judges are sitting at the far left. They are addressed by the pleader (standing at left with raised arm). His opponent is in the foreground. The others are spectators or pleaders waiting their turn.

ments over hunting lands and the occasional quarrels over the chieftaincy and political tribute were settled in the framework of the formal political organization, that is, through the chief's and the king's court. By contrast, moots, independent judges, and extralegal self-help were more prominent in matters involving the reciprocal relations among individuals and their lineages.

Political organization and law: An interpretive summary

If one considers traditional Suku political organization in all its manifestations, two seemingly contradictory features emerge. On the one hand, there were the politically quasi-independent lineages, maintaining relations among themselves by means of techniques that are generally associated with stateless societies. On the other hand, there was the formal political organization, built on a hierarchical model and imposed from the top, which functioned successfully within certain limits. The two systems are not so much contradictory as they are complementary. Historically, when the power of the formal political organization weakened, the political mechanisms based on the segmentary principle rose in importance in maintaining the balance of political relations. This happened regionally when chiefs lacked energy and in the entire Suku kingdom, about 1920, when the *MeniKongo's* own area in the north came under colonial control while the south still remained largely untouched by the administration. Thus Suku society may be said to have possessed the characteristics of both the principal types that have been proposed to classify African political systems (Fortes and Evans-Pritchard 1940).

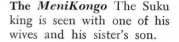

The *MeniKongo* The Suku
king is seen with one of his
wives and his sister's son.

THE COLONIAL ADMINISTRATION • In the sphere of political organization, the impact of colonial rule was to destroy, for all practical purposes, the powers of the king and the regional chiefs, although they continued to hold their offices in an essentially honorary capacity and were paid a salary by the administration. Effective administrative work was vested in the so-called sectors organization, each with a head, clerks, and policemen, selected by the colonial officers without regard to traditional position and on the basis of literacy and bureaucratic competence. These authorities were concerned with such matters as collection of taxes, maintenance of roads, supervision of sanitary measures in villages, census, and the registry of births, marriages, and deaths. Attached to each sector was a customary court whose members were selected from among those versed in traditional law. These courts dealt with all civil cases, such as divorces, debts, thefts and injuries, and breaches of administrative regulations. Their decision could be appealed to the colonial officer who also handled the more serious criminal cases and arbitrated disputes involving such important matters as ownership of hunting lands or arguments over chieftaincies, in consultation with an appointed body of traditional judges. This overall administrative structure has been retained after independence, the higher offices of the local administration being now occupied by Congolese nationals.

RELIGION

Any description of the total environment in which the Suku live would be incomplete without treating that part of it which, in the rationalist tradition of Western culture, is usually segregated under the rubric of the supernatural. To the Suku themselves, however, the concepts about to be described stand for a reality as natural, as mundane even, as the growing of crops or the everyday relations among people. In addition to their psychological reality, these concepts must be viewed as part of social reality as well, for their effects on behavior are no less observable and concrete than those of economic or political factors.

The system of ideas with which we are dealing is organized around several key concepts: the Creator, medicines, witchcraft, the powers of eldership, and, finally, divination.

THE CREATOR GOD • Of the concepts listed, that of *Nzambi* (the Creator) has the least functional importance, for it scarcely affects behavior, is not integrated with the other concepts, and remains a necessary but essentially isolated logical axiom. The nature of *Nzambi* is regarded as unknown and largely unknowable. The Creator is not anthropomorphized in any way. He ("it" would perhaps be a better pronoun) is by no means a distant god; on the contrary, his presence is seen everywhere and serves as the ultimate explanation of all things, but precisely because he is so pervasive, because everything is attributable to him, the concept has no practical utility in understanding or influencing specific events. No appeal is ever made to *Nzambi*, no prayer or sacrifice is ever addressed to him. In the causative chain explaining any phenomenon, he is the ultimate link, accounting for the inexplicable.

MEDICINES • The generic term *mukisi* (plural, *mikisi*) is applied to a whole range of objects and special preparations, and is best translated by the term "medicine." Within this category, more specific words exist to indicate the different kinds of *mikisi*. The simplest, the *miemu*, are what we would call herbs and are used for treating wounds, coughs, and aches, and for curing sterility or for setting broken limbs. What distinguishes these herbs from the other medicines is that they cure but cannot harm, and they act directly upon an individual through physical application. The other medicines, by contrast, can act at a distance, can harm as well as cure, and belong more clearly in the realm usually called magical.

These magical medicines are of two types: those held by and acting on individuals, and those whose field of action is the lineage as a unit. The first, called *bunganga*, include such things as good-luck charms, love potions, preparations that help their owners to find lost objects and ensure their success in hunting or trade, harmful magic used against enemies (including poisons), as well as ways to counteract such harm. These preparations are kept secret and may be acquired only by purchase. As a rule, the recipes consist of various herbs but also involve the sacrifice of an animal (a chicken or a goat) and the use of the animal's blood; it is this that gives them their special strength and clearly differentiates them from the more ordinary herbal medicines. At present, many such new magical preparations have come from the urban centers, where a brisk trade in such things takes place among members of different ethnic groups.

The medicines in which the lineage and not the individual is the relevant unit are called *bisungu* (the "great medicines"). Every lineage possesses a certain number of these, many of them dating back to the time when the Suku lived by the Kwango River. Whereas the individual magical medicines are taken voluntarily and lose their power at their owner's death, the lineage medicines are acquired because of necessity and, once obtained, can never be given up by the lineage. The reason for taking a lineage medicine is always associated with some transgression against such a medicine held by some other lineage. For example, a member of the lineage steals some object that has been put under the protection of a lineage medicine by its owners; or a person, accused of some misdemeanor, falsely swears over a medicine that he is innocent. In such cases, the medicine is believed to "enter the blood" of the guilty person; since all members of a lineage share their blood, it also "enters the blood" of the lineage as a whole, with the result that any member of the lineage, and not necessarily the culprit himself, may fall sick.

The explanation for the sickness is sought from a diviner, who will indicate its cause. Once the medicine has entered the lineage, it can never be disposed of again; all that can be done is to "calm" it, that is, to prevent it from generating more disease. This is accomplished by a ceremonial in which the medicine is formally taken by the lineage. One of its members is initiated into it in a ceremony in which animals are sacrificed and their blood is "fed" to the medicine in place of the lineage blood that it would otherwise take; the initiate learns the taboos associated with it and the ways in which it must be kept quiescent, and he becomes its guardian for the lineage, maintaining the paraphernalia (which usually include a carved statue) in his house or in a special little hut. The initiation is done for a fee by the guardian of a similar medicine from some other lineage. But once the medicine is taken by the lineage, its misuse, loss, lack of proper attention and treatment, the breaking of its taboos, or illicit sexual relations by its guardian—all these cause the medicine to break out again, causing disease in the lineage and requiring a new ceremony to "calm" it.

As conceived by the Suku, these medicines cause illness and death in an entirely mechanistic way. They have no volition of their own and they are not animated by anything like a spirit; they act automatically under precisely given conditions, and affect not simply the transgressor but anyone in his lineage. Thus they are not ethical agents in themselves. Nevertheless, their existence does support, although indirectly, the Suku ethical code. For example, an object put under the protection of a medicine is dangerous to anyone who touches it inadvertently; by this very fact, it is dangerous to a potential thief and, as a result, indiscriminate stealing is discouraged.

WITCHCRAFT · The other major source of illness and death in Suku belief is *kiloki* (witchcraft). The Suku say that a witch is a person who has been fed human flesh shortly after birth by another witch and who, from adolescence on, must "eat" human flesh to survive and for this purpose periodically kills others by magical means. Witches are believed to control various kinds of secret knowledge and to possess numerous and wondrous magical medicines of their own that they buy from other witches by giving them the lives of junior members of their lineage. It is said that witches can become invisible, fly through the air, and, while going about their nefarious business, disguise themselves as leopards, jackals, mosquitoes, and owls. Witches are believed to be in contact with each other; when one of them procures a victim, others will share in consuming it and thereby will contract a flesh-debt to be repaid in kind at some future date.

One important point must be kept in mind: a witch is not a being living and operating in some nether world separated from everyday life. Witches are, above all, living people and witchcraft is simply an attribute of persons who simultaneously play normal social roles and have their own unique personalities. Although witchcraft is itself by definition evil, a person who has it is not necessarily and entirely so. To a Suku, a witch may also be a friend, a father, a sister, or a respected and liked head of the lineage who has fulfilled well his obligations to it and has worked hard for its interests.

That witchcraft is viewed with some ambivalence can be understood from the fact that it is dangerous for a lineage to be without any witches; such a lineage would be immediately exposed to the depredations by witches from other lineages. On the other hand, an elder who is himself a witch but who, like any other elder, defends the interests of the lineage against outsiders, is an asset, for he is capable of knowing what other witches are doing and of insisting that some reciprocity be maintained, as it should be in any relations between different lineages. Since the world of witches exists, this means that it is best to have someone who can operate in it, and that someone must, of necessity, be a witch himself. For this protection, to be sure, a price must be paid. When deaths in the lineage are few, some of them will be attributed to a suspected member, but little is said about it if the suspect is regarded in other respects as a good person. But if deaths become numerous, this in itself soon becomes proof that the witches of the lineage, by their excesses, show that they are indifferent to lineage interests; hence an ordeal by poison is justified. This test for witchcraft involves the administration of a specially prepared drink to the suspected witch; death from the poison establishes guilt and survival indicates innocence.

Within the lineage, belief in witchcraft tends to maintain a balance between the authority of the elders and the natural resentment of it by the junior members. The latter often fear that disobedience of an elder, who may be a witch, may result in his avenging himself by witchcraft (generally, it is the elders who are thought to be witches because they have outlived others). At the same time, the elders are also careful not to tyrannize the young, for misuse of their authority leads to suspicions that may culminate, at someone's death, in outright accusations and a demand for an ordeal by poison. Although poison is believed to act only on witches, unpopular elders have at times been killed under the guise of such a test.

POWERS OF ELDERSHIP • There is for the Suku a third possible explanation of misfortune, and it is related to the conception of supernatural powers inherent in lineage eldership. There is a belief that lineage membership offers supernatural protection against misfortune and that this protection may be withdrawn. Thus, disobedience or refusal to meet one's obligations as a lineage member may be punished by a curse, formal or secret, of the elders; this "opens the road" to misfortune, failure, poverty, and disease.

For an individual, the class of elders includes all those who are in the generations above his or who are considerably older than he is—living as well as dead. Thus when he is sick or when he is preparing for an important hunt, a young man will ask his living elders for assurances of their goodwill. Old men, on the other hand, to ensure the benevolence of their lineage, must go to *their* elders, and these are dead. They therefore visit the lineage cemetery and at the graves of the dead ask for prosperity for themselves and their lineage. Although this accords with what is usually called the "ancestral cult," it must be stressed that this cult is but a part of a wider and more fundamental idea about the powers of eldership.

DIVINATION • Medicines, witchcraft, withdrawal of protection by the elders—these three conceptions are the key points in the traditional belief system that, to the Suku, gives meaning to those events in life men everywhere have sought to understand—misfortune, illness, and death. Each of these, by itself, may be a cause of sickness. They are further integrated into a wider system of multiple causation, in which two or even three of them may be simultaneously active. Thus when a medicine is the initial cause of sickness, it is believed that witches often attempt to "hide behind" medicines, contributing their power to make a sick person worse and hoping that they may thus obtain a victim whose death the people will blame on the medicine. In the same way, witches may attempt to "hide behind" an elder's curse. In short, the entire causative system is such that varied factors may converge to produce one and the same visible result, which is sickness. One is never sure, however, which causes and in what combination are relevant in any specific case. The causative system is a closed one, but the Suku demand from it more than the satisfaction of the need for explanation. It must also be a guide to counteracting the illness and it must indicate which specific factors are responsible so that they may be eliminated.

It is at this point that the role of the diviner is crucial. A diviner is a person, male or female, who possesses his own special medicines that allow him to see what is hidden from others. In a sense, his is the capacity to enter inside the system of causation, to sort out the specific causes of an illness or a death, and to indicate them to his clients. Consequently, the viability of the belief system as a guide to empirical action rests squarely on the success of the diviner.

When a person falls ill, the Suku will not immediately resort to divination. It is accepted that illness may be "natural," and the patient will at first be given the ordinary herbal medicines. If he recovers, nothing more is thought of it, and whatever latent suspicions of witchcraft there may have been are abandoned. But if the patient grows worse, suspicions that other causes are at play come to the surface. A public warning may be given to unnamed witches to desist, and people begin to speculate about the possible taboos that may have been broken, inducing a medicine to react. The goodwill of living elders is secured for the patient by having them express it publicly. Should all these steps fail, divination becomes necessary. A professional diviner is selected and his diagnosis is acted on; for example, a new medicine may be taken by the lineage, or witches are told once again to desist and are threatened with a poison ordeal, or a specified ancestor is placated through a sacrifice. If all these attempts fail, another diviner may be tried, and sometimes a third. If in the end the patient dies, it is said that the cause is beyond the ken of anyone, and it is referred to the unknowable *Nzambi* as the ultimate source of all things.

In Western culture the belief in the fundamental validity of the scientific method does not preclude the acceptance of failure in specific cases; so with the Suku the total belief system is viewed only as an overall guide to understanding and action. The failure of a diviner to reveal the truth may be attributed to his relative lack of ability or even to his lying. Hence the system contains within itself the explanation for its failures and it is not expected to be successful in every single case.

CHANGE

Occasional explorers aside,[10] the first impact of European activity in the Suku area dates back to the first decade of this century, when one or two representatives of rubber companies collected a rather inferior latex produced from ground vines (the soil is too poor for ordinary rubber trees). These rubber operations were, however, peripheral to the more intensive and notorious ones in other parts of the Congo, and they steadily declined in importance, disappearing by the early 1930s, to be revived again for a short time during World War II. These periods of rubber collection were the only ones when the Suku had any cash crops to sell. At

present, the region is both too poor and too far from the centers to export
a commercially feasible product of any kind.

It was only by the late 1920s that an effective colonial administration
began to be installed in most of the Suku region. It was also at this time that
Catholic and Protestant missions commenced their work in earnest, with the
attendant introduction of more than sporadic schooling and of a modicum of
medical facilities. One result of their activities is that nearly all Suku under
the age of forty are nominally Christian.

In the absence of cash crops, whatever money flows into the Suku
economic system from the outside does so primarily through the various employees of the administration (clerks, policemen, and workers) and through
migrant laborers. To the north and east of the Suku, where the soil is richer,
a few commercial plantations are established, and these employ a certain
number of Suku workers. Some Suku also periodically leave to work in
Léopoldville and a few other smaller towns. These migrant laborers retain
their ties with the village; those in Léopoldville return for visits at least every
few years, and those working on the plantations far more often. Many do
not spend more than a few years away and all of them, on return, are immediately reintegrated into their villages and lineages. Thus, although at
times half or even more of the youths and the younger males have been absent from their villages, this has not had the kind of disruptive effects on the
society and culture as may be imagined a priori. It must be remembered that
cultivation has always traditionally been in the hands of women and, in the
absence of cash crops and the decline in the importance of hunting, the removal of a part of the male labor force has not had any significant effect on
the internal economic balance. At the same time, the products of traditional
craftsmanship, where males predominated, have been to a considerable extent
replaced by more durable goods now bought in the stores for money.

It may be noted that the traditional Suku family was never very stable.
There is no indication that the number of divorces at present is greater than
in precolonial times. The lineage remains the main point of orientation for
each spouse and the traditional independence of the wife has certainly contributed to the elasticity of the response to those situations when the husband
is absent at work elsewhere.

One of the consequences of the introduction of larger amounts of money
has been the strengthening of the matrilineage. Now that there is more
wealth to be had and more situations in which it is important, the lineage is
more jealously on guard to maintain its rights over the property of its members. The stringent application of traditional rules of lineage ownership in a
variety of new situations is supported by the customary tribunals, which, in
contrast to those in precolonial times, have effective means with which to enforce their decisions. (See page 466.)

Some of the most important social changes have taken place since World

War II, with the consistent expansion of educational and medical facilities. By the late 1950s, almost every male child was enrolled in a three-year elementary village school, a somewhat smaller number going on to the end of elementary education. On the other hand, only a few Suku have had the opportunity to go to secondary or trade schools, and, with the exception of several priests, none has had the equivalent of a university training. It is difficult to determine the literacy for the entire population; for youths and adult males up to the age of thirty, it may be roughly estimated to be over 50 percent. Among women, on the other hand, it is much lower.

The introduction of Western medicine has had a great demographic effect. In the 1930s and 1940s, the population was either stable or even, in some years, declining, but at present it is increasing at a rate that should double it in some twenty-five or thirty years. After an initial lack of interest, the Suku have taken with great enthusiasm to the two hospitals and the numerous dispensaries scattered through the area. It will be remembered that traditional Suku religion was focused to a large extent on disease and its cure. The wide acceptance of modern medicine did not undermine significantly the traditional conceptions; rather, the two have been integrated into a wider system. It is the successful treatment of disease viewed as symptom that the imported medicine is readily credited with, just as traditional herbs are regarded as a somewhat less efficient way of accomplishing the same end. But neither is seen as removing the underlying causes (such as witchcraft or the curse of elders) and with these only traditional methods can cope.

Anti-acculturative feeling and conscious generalized reaction against the colonial authorities (as opposed to particularistic resentment of its various features or its individual representatives) began among the Suku after the first independence riots in Léopoldville in January 1959. These were expressed in local political activity among the literate administrative employees and, among the villagers, in a spontaneous movement of sullen noncooperation with the colonial administration. As a group, the Suku are too small in numbers and occupy too unimportant and peripheral a region to have figured significantly in the political evolution of the Congo or even of their own province in which there are more powerful ethnic groups. Yet, unspectacularly, with little political articulation and with the larger goal but dimly perceived, the Suku have nevertheless effectively added to the spontaneous movement that rapidly swept the Congo into independence.

Notes

(1) I did fieldwork among the Suku during 1958 and the first half of 1959. The research was supported by a fellowship grant from the Ford Foundation and was conducted under the auspices of the Program of African Studies, North-

western University. Certain ethnographic material used in this chapter appears in a selection I contributed to *The Family Estate in Africa* edited by Philip H. Gulliver and Robert Gray (London: Routledge & Kegan Paul Ltd., 1964), to be published in the United States by Boston University Press.

In accordance with the standard practice of dropping the Bantu prefixes in ethnic names, the term Suku is used throughout this paper, in place of MuSuku (singular) and BaSuku (plural).

(2) Another group of Suku, according to tradition, moved south and gave rise to the present Suku enclave, numbering some thirty thousand people, that straddles the Congo-Angola border a little east of the Kwango River. I did not visit this group. According to reports, it has been heavily influenced, both culturally and linguistically, by its western neighbors, the Holo.

(3) For technical information on nutritional problems among the Suku, the reader is referred to the publications of Holemans (see bibliography). The mean stature among the Suku falls below the usual figures for central Africa and approaches that of the Bushmen. However, the temptation to see a Bushmanoid genetic component must be resisted for want of any objective support in the present data on the Suku specifically, who would have to be treated, for no discernible reason, in isolation from their relatives and neighbors who live in a more favored environment and are taller.

(4) An analogy may perhaps be helpful. The structure is comparable in certain respects to that of American collegiate social fraternities. Although the national organization formally owns the property of the local chapters, it is the latter that actively control it, elect their own presidents from among local members, operate as independent corporate bodies in their relations with the rest of the society, and have provisions for incorporating members of other chapters when these members change their college residence.

(5) This is an example of the apparent structural contradictions inherent in matrilineal societies. Other examples to be found in central Africa are discussed and analyzed by Richards (1950).

(6) Bridewealth fluctuated, in the late 1950s, between the equivalents in Congolese francs of thirty and forty dollars—roughly the price of five goats or the pay for three or four months' work as an unskilled laborer. In addition to this money, various presents are given to the bride's relatives, such as cloth, clothing, glasses, bottles, soap, and lamps.

(7) The described pattern of exchange and sacrifice varies with the type of marriage contracted. If both the groom and the bride are members of the same lineage, a slightly reduced bridewealth must still be paid to the bride's father (if the latter is of another lineage), but the sacrifice need not be made since different "bloods" are not mixed. On the other hand, if the bride herself is the daughter of such an intralineage marriage (that is, when she belongs to her father's lineage) and the groom is of another lineage, the goat is sacrificed

and the entire bridewealth goes to and, in case of divorce, is owed by one and the same lineage. In line with these principles, the reader may examine other possibilities for himself.

(8) The Suku claim that before the exodus from the Kwango Valley there was indeed, at that time, a king's "sister" who lived in her own village, had her own ritual paraphernalia, and ruled over several chiefs in her own right. During the war with the Lunda, she led her group southward and founded the Suku enclave referred to in note 2, which is the explanation given for the fact that this latter group is under a chieftainess. If this tradition is taken to be valid, then the Suku conformed at one time to a widespread African pattern and its abandonment by them is the result of a historic accident.

(9) For a detailed discussion of this pattern, see Kopytoff (1961).

(10) To one of these, Torday, we owe the first detailed ethnography of the Suku (see bibliography).

BIBLIOGRAPHY

Works dealing with the Suku are marked with an asterisk (*) and annotated. Reference is made in the text to the daggered (†) items.

Fortes, M., and E. E. Evans-Pritchard (1940†). "Introduction," *African Political Systems*. London: Oxford University Press.

Greenberg, Joseph (1955†). *Studies in African Linguistic Classification*. New Haven, Conn.: Compass Publishing Co.

Holemans, K. (1959*†). "Études sur l'alimentation en milieu coutumier du Kwango: II—L'Enquête familiale directe," *Annales de la Société Belge de Médecine Tropicale*, Vol. 39, No. 4, pp. 361–374.
This article, one of a series, derives from a carefully controlled study of the nutrition of the Suku and their immediate neighbors, the Sonde. It shows the extremely high proportion of carbohydrates, mainly in the form of cassava, in the diet (about 90 percent of the calories consumed). Dr. Holemans conducted nutritional research in the area for almost a decade; the results of these investigations (some forty articles) may be found in the above journal and in the *Revue Médicale de Liège*, *Mémoires de l'Académie Royale des Sciences Coloniales*, *Journal of Nutrition*, and *Journal of Tropical Pediatrics*.

Kopytoff, Igor (1961*†). "Extension of Conflict as a Method of Conflict Resolution among the Suku of the Congo," *Journal of Conflict Resolution*, Vol. 5, No. 1, pp. 61–69.
An analysis of some of the principles of conflict resolution among Suku lineages.

———— (1964*). "Family and Lineage among the Suku of the Congo," in *The Family Estate in Africa*, Robert F. Gray and P. H. Gulliver (eds.).

London: Routledge and Kegan Paul Ltd., pp. 83–116, and Boston: Boston University Press (in press).
An analysis of family structure, property, and lineage continuity.

Lamal, Fr. (1949*†). "Essai d'étude démographique d'une population du Kwango: Les Basuku du Territoire de Feshi," *Mémoires, Institut Royal Colonial Belge, Section des Sciences Morales et Politiques*, Vol. 15, No. 4.

———— (1954*). "L'Exode massif des hommes adultes vèrs Léopoldville (Les Basuku du Territoire de Feshi)," *Zaïre*, Vol. 8, pp. 365–377.
The first item is a monograph concerned with the vital statistics of the Suku, relating them to cultural and social factors, administrative policies, and labor recruitment; the latter is largely blamed by the author for the population decline of the 1930s and 1940s. The picture presented is overly pessimistic. The thesis that population decline is due to social dislocation and a concomitant decrease in the birth rate may be questioned, since the birth rate was already among the highest in the world, but did not always keep up with the death rate. With the increase in medical facilities through the 1950s, mortality declined; the result has been something of a "population explosion." The interpretation does not detract from the value of the carefully compiled data. Father Lamal is a Catholic missionary who has lived in the area since the early 1930s and is intimately acquainted with Suku life.

Plancquaert, M. (1932*). "Les Jaga et les Bayaka du Kwango. Contribution historico-ethnographique," *Mémoires, Institut Royal Colonial Belge, Section des Sciences Morales et Politiques*, Vol. 3, No. 1.
This monograph is primarily concerned with validating the hypothesis that the Jaga, who invaded and nearly destroyed the Kongo Empire in the sixteenth century, are the ancestors of the present-day Yaka and related peoples. This is the best historical introduction to the region available at present, combining documentary evidence with local traditions, among them those of the Suku. Father Plancquaert, a Catholic missionary, has spent several decades among the Yaka.

Richards, A. I. (1950†). "Some Types of Family Structure amongst the Central Bantu," in *African Systems of Kinship and Marriage*, A. R. Radcliffe-Brown and Daryll Forde (eds.). London: Oxford University Press, pp. 206–251.

Torday, E., and T. A. Joyce (1906*). "Notes on the Ethnography of the Ba-Yaka," *Journal of the Royal Anthropological Institute*, Vol. 36, pp. 39–58.

———— (1922*). "Notes ethnographiques sur des populations habitant les bassins du Kasai et du Kwango Oriental," *Annales du Musée du Congo Belge*, Ser. 3, Vol. 2, No. 2.
Most of the "Yaka" referred to in these works are the Suku; the authors apparently followed the usage of some of the neighboring groups. The second work deals with all the ethnic groups of the eastern Kwango region and, together with the first, represents the first systematic ethnographic report on the Suku. The descriptions of the material culture are excellent, but the data

on social and political organization and on religion must be interpreted with great care.

Van de Ginste, Fernand (1946*). "Anthropometric Study of the Bapende and Basuku of the Belgian Congo," *American Journal of Physical Anthropology*, N.S., Vol. 4, pp. 125–152.

———— (1947*). "Le Lupambula chez les Basuku," *Bulletin des Juridictions Indigènes et du Droit Coutumier Congolais*, No. 1.

———— (1947*). "Le Mariage chez les Basuku," *Bulletin des Juridictions Indigènes et du Droit Coutumier Congolais*, Nos. 1–2.
The late Fernand Van de Ginste was a colonial administrator in the Suku area through most of the 1940s. Although without anthropological training, he possessed great curiosity and was well acquainted with Suku life; in addition to the articles listed here he left numerous unpublished papers recording his observations, which are deposited in the Feshi territorial archives. The second article describes the *Lupambula*, an antiwitchcraft movement that arose in the early 1940s and was accompanied by the rejection of traditional magical medicines and the taking of a new protective medicine.

13

THE SWAZI OF SWAZILAND

about the chapter

Because of the wide area in Africa over which the Bantu languages are spread, Bantu-speaking peoples are found in many different ecological areas and as neighbors of peoples of many varied stocks. It is not surprising, then, that in the 2000 or so years since they spread out of their Cameroonian highland homeland the Bantu have developed many different types of social and political organization. A sense of the diversity among the Bantu emerges when one compares the Swazi with the four other Bantu-speaking groups described in this volume.

The southeastern Bantu include the Nguni-speaking subgroup of which the Swazi and the famed Zulu are a part. This cluster of peoples is of special interest to the anthropologist and the political scientist because of the type of centralized state they created. More than Rwanda, the other Bantu conquest state represented here, the Nguni state is an absorptive state, which continually welds into a single political structure peoples of diverse languages and customs. This is remarkable when one considers that the Swazi and other Nguni do not live in towns, but in scattered homesteads, which makes the matter of political and military control somewhat difficult. Kuper's analysis indicates that the primary features of the Swazi kingdom facilitate the political integration and absorption of new peoples.

A unique feature of the Swazi state is the institution of a dual monarchy with "twin rulers," a king and a queen mother. Allegiance to these dual monarchs and participation in rites of kingship are the strongest factors linking the various peoples absorbed into the Swazi state. The state employs what Kuper isolates as the major structural principle of rank by descent. The Swazi have a series of ranked clans, composed of constituent lineages. Individuals from specific lineages within each rank perform different political tasks. This same principle is expressed in the dual nature of the monarchy. The prince to become king is chosen by the rank of his mother among his father's wives. She, as queen mother, exercises complementary rights almost as important as his, and has equal honors. The vesting of certain powers in a royal woman is carried further in the Swazi kingdom than in most other sub-Saharan monarchies. A system of two councils of advisers represents another device for dividing political authority which is similar to that of other African kingdoms, as among the Yoruba.

Men's and women's age grades are an important institution. The men's age grades, the more important among the Nguni, formed regiments under the dual command of a royal prince and a commoner. While carrying out public works is the regiments' major duty nowadays, the age grade activities, especially participation in state rituals, and their regalia and insignia act as common symbols that facilitate monarchal support and social integration, and increase the Swazi state's absorptive qualities.

Although the Swazi are primarily agriculturalists, cattle keeping is valued more highly than agriculture, and the ritual, wealth, and power of kingship are all connected with the role of cattle. As in Rwanda, lending cattle is a way of attracting clients and using royal power, but cattle in Swazi are also transferred as bridewealth in marriage and sacrificed in ritual. In sub-Saharan Africa, the uses of animals and the social structure are linked in agricultural as well as in herding societies.

about the author

Hilda Kuper, who is Professor of Anthropology at the University of California, Los Angeles, received her Ph.D. from the London School of Economics in 1942. In 1961 she was awarded the Rivers Memorial Medal of the Royal Anthropological Institute of Great Britain and Ireland for her research in Natal and in Swaziland. She has been a research fellow at the International African Institute and at the University of Manchester and has taught in South Africa at the University of the Witwatersrand and the University of Natal. Dr. Kuper carried out field research in Johannesburg (1940–1945) as well as in Natal (1952) and Swaziland (1934–1940). Her published works include *An African Aristocracy* (1947), *The Uniform of Colour* (1947), *The Swazi* (1952), *The Shona* (1955), *Indian People in Natal* (1960), and *The Swazi: A South African Kingdom* (1963).

HILDA KUPER · *The Swazi of Swaziland*[1]

INTRODUCTION

LOCATION · The Swazi, a Bantu-speaking people living in southeast Africa, are characterized by a highly developed dual monarchy, a hereditary aristocracy, elaborate rituals of kingship and state-wide age groups. Over 180,000 Swazi are settled in the British High Commission Territory of Swaziland, and some 40,000 in the adjacent territories of the Republic (formerly Union) of South Africa and the Portuguese province of Mozambique. This chapter deals with the Swazi of Swaziland, and unless specifically stated to the contrary, the data described in the present tense were collected between 1934 and 1940, when I did my most intensive fieldwork.

PHYSICAL APPEARANCE · The Swazi appear to be predominantly of Negro stock with some Bushman and Caucasoid admixture. People range in skin color from almost black to light brown. The majority are of medium height, well built and long-headed. Flat noses are usual but one also sees many Swazi with thin, aquiline features. Bodies are virtually hairless but head hair is thick and tightly curled and may grow to shoulder length and be worn in many decorative styles. Swazi have no specific tribal scarification or mutilation but it is customary for a slit to be made in the lobe of each ear. Men and women are very interested in personal appearance and give a general impression of good looks and strong physique.

LANGUAGE · SiSwati is a click language of the Nguni group of the Bantu subgroup of the central branch of the Niger-Congo family (Greenberg 1955).

HABITAT · Swaziland is a beautiful little country, 6704 square miles in area (about the size of Connecticut and Rhode Island combined) with a rich diversity of climate and natural resources. From the west, the territory falls roughly into three north-to-south belts, known locally as the highveld, middleveld, and lowveld; flanking them on the east is a fourth, the Lebombo

481

Topographical View of Swaziland (*British Information Service*)

Mountains. The highveld, 3500 to 6000 feet above sea level, is part of the Drakensberg Range and has cold, frosty winters and an annual rainfall of 45 to 75 inches. Rugged and broken, the mountain slopes are covered with sparse, sour grass, and the gorges are vivid with indigenous shrubs. The more gently undulating middleveld, separated from the highveld by a marked escarpment, is characterized by a warmer climate, less rain, taller grass, and mixed parkland. It merges with the bush and sweet grass of the lowveld, 500 to 1000 feet above sea level, where the intense summer heat is shattered by occasional torrential storms, and the rain averages only 20 to 30 inches a year. From the bush, where cattle thrive, the narrow Lebombo Mountains rise to a height of 2700 feet before they descend to the seaboard in Mozambique. Four large rivers and many tributaries flow through Swaziland, and the overall adequacy of water is taken as evidence of the rainmaking powers of the traditional rulers, a king titled *Ingwenyama* (Lion) and a queen mother titled *Indlovukati* (Lady Elephant).

HISTORICAL BACKGROUND · The Swazi were never conquered by armed force, and the traditional political authorities continue to be recognized in British territory, where the *ingwenyama* is described by the white administration as the paramount chief, and the *indlovukati* as the queen mother. The ruling *ingwenyama* is Sobhuza II, and at the time of my arrival the *indlovukati* was his own mother, Lomawa.

Kingship is hereditary in the proud Nkosi Dlamini clan, and Swazi historians recall the names of some twenty-five kings, though there is agreement on only the last eight, beginning with Ngwane II, the first king commemorated in modern ritual. The Nkosi Dlamini are of Embo Nguni stock, closely related to the Zulu, and over a period of some two hundred years

Dlamini kings extended their rule by conquest and strategy over several Sotho clans as well as over other Nguni, welding them into a single state. The Nkosi did not attempt to enforce their culture, and even today there are local differences in dialect, architectural style, dress, food, utensils, and ritual. But considerable uniformity resulted from the method of absorption and the participation in national affairs granted to all subjects. The groups have intermarried; all are entitled to be protected, to own land, to bear the national mark—a slit in the lobes of the ears—to wear Swazi costume on state occasions, to serve together in the age regiments, and to speak in the council. These privileges and responsibilities of citizenship are conferred on everyone owing allegiance to the "twin" rulers—mother and son, but the cultural homogeneity is greatest in the areas closest to these central authorities.

The Swazi have for themselves as many names as they have had rulers, but most frequently they speak of themselves as "People of Ngwane," founder of the modern Swazi, or "People of Sobhuza," the first king to settle in the midlands, the area of subsequent royal villages. The name "Swazi" was popularized by whites who entered the country in the reign of Mswati, in the latter half of the nineteenth century.

The area's favorable climate and good agricultural possibilities, the discovery of gold in 1872, and the indication of other mineral potentialities attracted white speculators and settlers. This was the period of colonial expansion in which concessions, backed if necessary by physical force, were used as a technique of acquiring possession of land and mineral rights from preliterate—and technologically more simple—people. In Swaziland, concessions reached a climax of ironical absurdity.[2] Although the validity of the concessions made during this period was contested, they were recognized by the white man's court, and in 1907 the British government which had reluctantly taken over the country from the Boers after the Anglo-Boer war issued the Concession Partition Proclamation. The Swazi received one third of the country for their "sole" and exclusive use, and the rights of concessionaires to the remaining two thirds were confirmed. The Swazi portion was not in a single stretch, but in twenty-five blocks or reservations within larger white areas. The white population numbered less than 3000, many of whom became absentee landlords. The first public duty given by the Swazi to Sobhuza II when, at the age of twenty-one, he was installed as king, was to challenge the basic validity of these concessions. The Swazi lost the case on a technicality. This brief mention of a most complicated historical background explains the present patchwork distribution of land in Swaziland and its pattern of economic development.

In "Native areas," Swazi live in *imiti* (singular, *umuti*), which I shall translate as "homesteads," dotted at irregular intervals over the countryside, and linked by narrow winding footpaths. Swazi have no traditional towns and the largest concentration of population is the tribal capital of Lobamba, with a permanent population of some 400 men, women, and children. The majority of whites are concentrated in a few major administrative and industrial centers, and these have become the foci of a newly developing urban and peri-urban Swazi population.

SOCIAL ORGANIZATION

THE HOMESTEAD • The homestead is the basic economic and domestic unit. In charge is an *umnumzana* (a headman), and the pattern of behavior between him and other occupants is the model of relationships in wider political units. There is a patriarchal, rather Old-Testament quality running through Swazi social organization, with a higher value placed on men than on women, and with deference demanded from the young by their seniors. Polygyny is a social ideal, and women, who usually marry men ten or more years their seniors, outnumber the men in all but the juvenile age groups. Women are legally married by *ukulubola* (the passing of brideprice); generally only the nobles and the wealthy, elderly commoners are able to support several wives. The king has the right to *qoma* (take by force) girls not already betrothed and he need not give cattle to their parents. Sobhuza was the first king to give *lobola* (bridewealth) and in 1936, when he was thirty-five years old, he had over forty queens and some seventy children. It is seldom that any other man, even a senior Dlamini prince, has more than ten wives. The extensive polygyny of the ruler is considered a political mechanism linking him with different sections of his people, his wives being placed in several villages throughout the country at strategic points in the administration.

The core members of a homestead are the headman's wives and children, but since marriage is patrilocal, sons bring their own wives to their father's home whereas daughters go to live with their in-laws. In addition to the headman's immediate family, it is customary for young men to build in the vicinity of older brothers, and the occupants of many homesteads also include more distant relatives and nonrelated dependents. The number of people for whom the headman is responsible, legally, economically, and ritually, therefore depends on his wealth and status; in a sample area the inhabitants averaged seven in commoners' homes and twenty-two in aristocrats'. Headmen frequently subdivide very large homesteads in order to gain access to a wider area of cultivable land or to separate quarrelsome wives, and the size of homesteads in general is said to be decreasing since there is no longer need for defense against the attacks of man or beast.

Homesteads are built according to a definite plan that reflects the interests and relationships of the inhabitants. In the center is an unroofed enclosure where the cattle are kept at night and grain may be stored in underground flask-shaped pits. Only the men have free access to the cattle pen, and

Strengthening a Reed Fence

go there even to urinate; women are permitted into the enclosure only on ritual occasions. Grouped in a semicircle at the western end are the living quarters, with the *indlunkulu* (great hut), associated with the ancestral spirits, as the pivot. In charge of the "great hut" is the most important woman of the household, the mother of the headman, or, if she is dead, a substitute "mother." On either side are the wives, each with her own sleeping, cooking, and storage huts generally enclosed for privacy, and protected from the wind by a high reed fence. Wives are not as rigidly organized into ranked units as they are among the typical Nguni, their placement depending largely on the whim of the headman and the personal preference of the women. The clear demarcation of each wife's huts, coupled with the fact that she receives her own garden lands and cattle, facilitates her establishing a separate home with her own children when her oldest son marries, but the section with the great hut of the headman's "mother" remains the "capital."

Children sleep with their mothers until they are weaned; then they generally move to the "great hut" of the paternal grandmother and stay with her until they are considered old enough to be separated by sex. Growing girls have huts close to their mothers; boys and unmarried men live in huts in barracks at the tips of the semicircle.

THE KING'S HOMESTEAD · The homestead of the *ingwenyama* is organized on principles similar to those of other polygynists, but has certain significant additions reflecting the main stages of his social growth. If he is a minor at the time of his selection (as frequently happened) he must live in the same homestead as his mother, the future *indlovukati*, while the queen regent (the "mother" for the deceased king) maintains the old capital. After he is installed, he and his mother establish the new capital, sanctified with material from the old. The rulers remain together until the king takes his first ten queens, when he builds his own residence some distance away. His mother remains in charge of the capital, the largest homestead in the country; his homestead is second in size. As the number of queens increases, he settles some in the old capital, and also "wakens" other royal homesteads of his predecessors. In the royal homesteads, the king's wives do not each have separate enclosures; a group of four or five share the same huts, recognizing one queen in each group as senior. The queens and their children are fenced in a single enclosure, conspicuously separated from other inhabitants. Royal homesteads also include huts of a number of trusted officials and unrelated dependents, and permanent regiments are stationed in barracks to protect the royal women.

SUCCESSION AND INHERITANCE • In every society, continuity between past, present, and future is ensured by various social mechanisms. Names of important homesteads, and the names of key ancestors are repeated periodically, and succession to their positions and the inheritance of wealth are never left to chance. In simple monogamous families primogeniture is the rule, but in polygynous families the eldest son is specifically debarred, and the successor is not publicly known during the father's lifetime. On his death the family council "sifts out" the claims of the widows and the sons.

Power and property are inherited from men, but are transmitted through women whose rank more than any other factor determines who will be chosen as the main wife, that is, mother of the heir. Dlamini princesses are rated more highly than wives of less noble pedigree, and if an important man marries a woman who will obviously be his main wife, he does so only when he is well on in years, so that the heir presumptive will be too young to threaten his position. Guardianship is thus a recognized part of the Swazi system of succession, and the institution of regency is a stereotyped stage in the transmission of royal authority.

The first wife has special privileges during her husband's lifetime, and her son (titled First Circumcised) is entrusted with important duties by his father and becomes adviser to the main heir (Eater of the Inheritance), but their roles are complementary and should not be combined in the same person. The first queen of the ingwenyama, described as "Wiper away of his (boyhood) dirt," is his main partner in ritual and is specially debarred from the position of main wife. There are also certain preferential marriages with women in particular kinship categories; thus any woman called "grandmother" because she has the same clan name as the headman's paternal grandmother has a recognized lead over most wives.

Each case, however, is seen to some extent as unique, and on rare occasions character has overridden all other considerations.[3] The successor must be the full son of his father, but so much emphasis is also placed on the rank of the mother that if the woman chosen as main wife has no male child, a son by a junior co-wife (preferably her own full sister) is "put into her womb." Once the heir is appointed, he keeps his position till her death; if his mother dies before him, a suitable substitute "mother" must be appointed.

Marriage

Marriage among the Swazi is essentially a bond between two lineages, rather than two individuals, and arranged marriages were formerly the norm. They have become less frequent and acceptable with the growing independence of women (which is backed by mission influence and Western law). However, individual choice must still be publicly confirmed and a Swazi marriage is generally still a most elaborate affair.[4]

After long formal negotiations between representatives of the two families, the girl, accompanied by her bridal party, is sent from her home with the blessing of her ancestors and gifts for her in-laws. Initially, she must appear reluctant to leave her own group, and must reject the demonstrations of welcome made by her future in-laws. In a dramatic scene in the ritual, she stands in the cattle pen of the groom's home, lamenting her plight and appealing to her brothers to rescue her. They have been waiting in hiding, and rush to her assistance. But, in the end, she accepts her fate and her future mother-in-law smears her with red clay, symbolizing the loss of virginity, and puts a baby on her lap to demonstrate her role as wife and mother. The transfer of *lobola* in the following winter formalizes the change in her legal status. The number of cattle varies with the girl's rank: twelve head is the current rate for commoners, princesses command fifteen and more. A boy's father should provide the animals for his son's first wife, and subjects contribute for their chief's main wife. Chiefs and important headmen throughout Swaziland contribute the several hundred cattle ratifying the choice of the future queen mother, who is in this way made "Mother of the Country," and her son the "Child of the People."

Patrilocal marriage, patrilineal descent, and a high brideprice combine to stabilize Swazi marriage, and the interests of the interlocking lineage override personal emotions. A woman's primary role in marriage is the production of children, and once the *lobola* has been given, the husband's group may claim any children she bears, irrespective of their genitor (biological father). If she is barren, provision is made in the marriage ritual for a sister to be sent to "bear for her" and her people may demand no additional cattle. Should the man die, his widows are "entered" by a male kinsman under the custom of the levirate, and the children are regarded as belonging to the deceased, while the genitor may be rewarded with a "beast of the thighs." Divorce is recognized in Swazi traditional law, but is rare. A man may send away his wife for continued misbehavior or sorcery; a woman may divorce her husband only for brutal treatment. As a rule, the elders of both families do their utmost to maintain the union: the man's lineage desires the woman's children, and her lineage does not want to return the *lobola*. Fewer cattle are given for a woman at her second marriage, and in a polygynous homestead a divorcée will never be appointed main wife.

Kinship

KINSHIP BEHAVIOR · Swazi classify kin into a limited number of broad categories, embracing in a single term relatives who in more specialized and isolating societies are kept distinct. Thus the term "father" is extended from ego's own father to his father's brothers and half brothers and sons of his father's brothers. Similarly "mother" embraces ego's own mother, her sisters, her co-wives, and wives of the father's brothers. The children of these "fathers" and "mothers" are his "brothers" and "sisters" and their children are grouped in the same category as his own grandchildren. The use of a common term does not mean that a particular key relationship is ignored. Within the category there are usually accurate descriptions of degrees of closeness. "The father who bore me" is distinguished from "my big father" (my father's older brother) or "my little father" (father's younger brother) but my behavior toward all "fathers" is modeled on a single pattern.

A Swazi soon learns to separate in word and action relatives of the father from those of the mother. They are distinct legal groups, and so strong is the identification through one or other parent that the word for father's sister is literally "female father" and the mother's brother is "male mother." Toward the "female father," a Swazi behaves with the respect and obedience associated with the word "father," and toward the "male mother" with the affection and familiarity evoked by the "mother." The children of my "female father" and "male mother" are included in a single term that can be translated as "cousins" and they are treated differently from "brothers" and "sisters."

Behavior is patterned by the kinship system. The headman as "father" exercises legal authority in the homestead, but much of the responsibility for maintaining harmony rests with the "mother." She intervenes in the more intimate and personal situations; the father remains aloof. She acts as intermediary between him and her sons, and supervises the behavior of the daughters-in-law. He is avoided by his son's wives, who may not speak his name or any word with the first syllable of his name, and must in their general behavior demonstrate the social distance between them. Swazi describe this as *inhloni* (shame, respect) and illiterate informants volunteered the direct Freudian explanation that if a man "saw" his daughters-in-law, his sexual desire might be stirred and rouse the deepest jealousy in the son-cum-husband. Patrilocal marriage separates a man from his wife's relatives, but toward his senior in-laws, more particularly his mother-in-law, he must show restraint comparable to that imposed on the young daughters-in-law. Women retain their own clan names on marriage, and remain conspicuous outsiders among the husband's agnates. Between the women there are both cooperation and hostility—and a special word to describe the jealousy of co-wives.

Certain tensions in the homestead that are expressed in personal terms are rooted in institutionalized conflicts, such as the conflicts between proximate generations for women or power, or between half brothers for succession to the position of father, or between co-wives battling for the favors of a single husband and privileges for their own sons.

The strongest, "sweetest," and most enduring bond is expressed with the real mother. A married woman bears her children in her husband's home, under the harsh care of the mother-in-law, who is ready to attribute any weakness or difficulty in labor to the daughter-in-law's infidelity. The girl's own mother may never be present, lest her sympathy lessen her daughter's self-control. If the young mother dies, the maternal grandmother, never a co-wife, and only occasionally the paternal grandmother, may act as foster mother. Suckling is the basic and privileged demonstration of maternity.

CHILD TRAINING AND SOCIALIZATION

Children are precious. They are recognized as weak and vulnerable and their death rate is tragically high. Mother and child remain secluded in the birth hut for a week to a month, depending on the husband's rank, and numerous rituals are performed to protect them from dangers believed to emanate from hostile men, animals, and nature. Food is recognized as important; and the baby's first food, dictated by the paternal clan, is a thin gruel of special cereal. The mother may suckle the baby only on the fourth or fifth day, when the baby's umbilical cord withers and the mother's milk flows freely, but the gruel is still continued. At the same time, regular daily enemas are administered, and the baby is periodically "smoked" over special potent-smelling medicines. Only certain women—and no man other than the ritual specialist—may hold the baby. It sleeps beside the mother on her mat and when the mother resumes normal activities, she carries it snugly on her back in a goatskin sling provided by the maternal grandparents. When it is three months old it is given a name, signifying that it has changed from a "thing" to a "person," and is symbolically "shown" to the world of living nature. After that, it can be more freely handled and played with, and is deliberately introduced to language and "right" behavior. But it remains in close body contact with the mother, who feeds it when it cries and should not wean it until it has "teeth to chew" and "legs to run."

Weaning, frequently enforced by the mother's rubbing an unpleasant-tasting substance on her nipples, is a symbolic as well as a real departure

Children Imitating Adult Activities

from constant maternal care. The toddler must begin to associate with his peers. When the mother goes to work in the fields she leaves him behind in charge of little nursegirls, often not much bigger than himself, who spend hours singing and dancing, joking, "playing house," and imitating the activities of the adults.

By the time a Swazi child can run, he is generally also toilet-trained, an achievement reached without much apparent conflict; occasional lapses are treated with tolerance. The threat of a beating is constantly uttered by both adults and older children for various "mistakes," but the threat is seldom executed. Discipline becomes more strict, and punishment more physical, as the child grows older, but the overall impression is that Swazi children are reared with unself-conscious indulgence.

At about the age of six Swazi infants have a small slit made in the lobe of each ear; thereafter they are held more responsible for their actions. Sex differences are emphasized and are related to different activities. Boys go in small neighborhood gangs to herd the calves, and are later promoted to care for the cattle; the girls accompany their mother to the fields, draw the water and learn "woman's work."

PUBERTY · Puberty is recognized today as a private family matter, but in the past, group circumcision of boys was an essential preliminary to marriage. Circumcision was abandoned in the reign of Mbandzeni; it is, however, still recorded in song and performed symbolically at the installation of a king. Swazi have no tradition of any operation on girls; but menstruation is regularly marked by conspicuous taboos on normal behavior. After puberty, boys and girls are expected to find lovers with whom to indulge in a stereotyped sex play, stopping short of full intercourse. Formerly, a girl who became pregnant before marriage was mocked, and the boy was beaten and fined, but the occurrence has become too frequent to evoke strong social reactions.

Age groups

The age of marriage is always socially regulated, and among the Swazi a man was not allowed to marry until his entire age group (*libutfo*, plural, *emabutfo*) received permission from the king in council. Men's age groups were formed roughly every five to seven years, the determining factor being the need to have a group of immature youths available for specific state rituals. In 1936, the last *libutfo* was inaugurated by the king at a representative gathering at the capital and it was the duty of each chief who was present to inform the people in his area. Each *libutfo* had its own name, insignia, songs, barracks, and officials. Every Swazi male was automatically enrolled and remained a member of the same *libutfo* from its inception until his own death, but membership did not involve all men to the same extent. Some resided more or less permanently in the barracks at the main royal village, others stayed in barracks of local chiefs, and the rest lived in their own homesteads and performed temporary and spasmodic service. Those at the homestead of the king or his mother had the highest status, distinctive costumes, titles, and songs and received special considerations (for example, they might be assisted with cattle for marriage or money for tax) and though they were responsible for their own subsistence, the rulers frequently provided them with meat and beer.

At the head of the age groups was a commander in chief officially appointed by the king, and chosen from among the commoners for his ability to maintain discipline, his military knowledge, trustworthiness, and loyalty. He worked together with a Dlamini prince, appointed as the king's representative, several junior officers, and a few "old persons" selected as tutors in tradition. Each regiment was divided into units that were the parallel of squads and platoons, the smallest social group being composed of men who shared the same hut.

Age groups cut across the boundaries of local chiefs and the bonds of kinship, and incorporated individuals into a wider state unity. A man did not need to obtain permission from his chief or his father to become a permanent royal warrior, for no one could stop another from working for the king, the "Father of the People." Warfare was formerly a major activity of the age groups, but wars were intermittent. When not engaged in battle,

Age Group in Ritual Clothing

the regiments served as labor battalions on public works and took part in the annual ceremony of kingship in which certain functions could be performed by the unmarried, and others by the married. The regiments were the main nonkinship associations maintaining and enforcing morality; and between members of the same age groups, particularly those in royal residence, there was the greatest camaraderie and spirit of mutual help.

The age groups survive today in attenuated form; they have lost much of their vitality and their official membership is less specific. Intertribal fighting has been prohibited, and the traditional regiments are not organized or equipped for modern warfare.[5] Age groups continue to render periodic labor, but the majority of adult men are absent for long periods in wage employment. The ritual and morality associated with the traditional *libutfo* runs counter to the teachings of Christian missionaries, and the tribal authorities no longer have the power to enforce control over the age of marriage.

Swazi women are also organized into age groups but these are less formal than the men's. They do not extend under a common name throughout the country, their membership is less rigid, and their functions are less precise. They are essentially work teams, in which unmarried girls and/or married women are called by the rulers for specific temporary tasks. The age of marriage of Swazi girls has always been controlled by their own parents, not by the rulers of age groups.

ECONOMY

Agriculture

Swazi peasants cultivate crops, keep cattle and other domestic animals, hunt, and gather numerous wild fruits and vegetables. The main crops are maize and millet; every Swazi homestead produces subsidiary foods: peanuts, beans, gourds, sweet reed, and pumpkins. Economic activities follow the rhythm of the seasons. The women begin by hoeing and sowing small plots along the river banks, where the soil is generally moist and seeds germinate quickly. With the coming of the rains in September, men and women cultivate the larger inland fields; heavier rains are expected in summer—November to January—when the last gardens must be planted. Agricultural work is intensified and communal work parties, especially for weeding, are frequent The homesteads are emptied of able-bodied adults and even the young chil dren toil in the fields. In autumn—February to April—the crops are harvested and activity shifts back from the fields to the homesteads. Once the grain is stored, sociability increases. Beer-drinking parties are frequent and the hunting season is opened. Winter is also the time for cutting thatching grass and repairing and building huts. Despite their wide range of resources, Swazi live at a precarious subsistence level, their food fluctuating annually between plenty and a scarcity bordering on famine. In summer before the new crops ripen, comes the moon named "to swallow the pickings of the teeth," whereas winter is the time of satisfaction and physical well-being.

LAND TENURE · Swazi say that land, the basis of subsistence, is "served" to the people by their political overlords. Individual ownership through freehold and leasehold are alien concepts; rights are secured by allegiance and usage, not by purchase or rental.

Tribal land is vested in the rulers and divided into districts, each controlled by princes, chiefs, or governors, who are in turn responsible for allotting land for building and cultivation to ordinary headmen. Swazi have no objective measure of area, and the size of plots attached to each homestead depends primarily on the supply of resident labor. Women, who are the main cultivators, receive gardens from their husbands on marriage, and may obtain occasional assistance from work parties of kin and neighbors. The rulers have several "gardens of kingship" in different localities, cultivated for them by chiefs in the area; and they are also able to command the service of regimental age groups stationed at royal homesteads, a privilege shared by district chiefs over local contingents. A headman's rights to land are secure as long as he fulfills his political obligations, in the form of occasional service and occasional gifts, and is generally law-abiding; if he moves from the area, his land reverts to the chief.

Although sites for building and for cultivation are individually allocated, grazing lands are communally used. The general approach of conservatives is that land not specifically altered by the efforts of man remains under the control of the political authority for the use of his people as a whole. Hence such materials as reeds for fencing, grass for thatching, and indigenous trees for firewood are available to all people in the district. Hunting lands are similarly controlled by chiefs, who organize communal hunts.

Swazi move their homesteads periodically from one part of a district to another and, less frequently, from one district to another. These moves, involving an assessment of status obligations and economic interests, reveal the complexities underlying traditional laws of land tenure. The head of the family looks for a site with good arable land, and near wood and water; but he also seeks friends, preferably kinsmen, as neighbors and a chief respected for his consideration. Non-Swazi must be accepted by the *ingwenyama* before they may settle in his country and cultivate the land.

Stock keeping: The cattle complex

Cultivation provides the staple food of the Swazi, but pastoralism is more highly rated. Swazi have the so-called cattle complex typical of many tribes in eastern Africa: cattle, in addition to their direct value as a source of food and clothing, serve as potent symbols in a wider range of situations both economic and ritual. They are the conservative's closest approximation to currency, his highest reward for service, his means of ratifying marriage, the medium of sacrifice to the ancestors, and an essential requirement in nearly all "treatments" to ensure health and prosperity. Their importance is reflected in the language, rich in terms for hides of different colors, horns of many shapes, and organs of animal anatomy. Men are referred to in terms of cattle and cattle are praised with the praises of men. The king is "the Bull" of the nation.

Cattle are unevenly distributed and the "cattle of kingship" exceed the herds of any single individual. They are kept at cattle posts in different parts of the country, and represent capital investment of a premonetary period. Some outposts were started from cattle looted in intertribal war, some from herds of too wealthy and ambitious men executed on charges of witchcraft, and there is a sacred herd, used only for anointing the body of the king, his mother, and his main ritual wife. The present sources of tribal revenue in cattle are fines from court cases, death dues for important headmen, gifts accompanying requests to make rain, "thanks" for favors received, and, more especially, the brideprice of royal women, who are more highly rated on the marriage market than any commoner. I calculated (in 1936) that the royal cattle numbered over 3000; the total cattle owned by Swazi was counted as 334,000, of which some individuals owned several hundred. The white administration keeps accurate vital statistics of cattle (more accurate than the statistics of the human population), but the records do not reflect actual ownership; cattle of kingship are often registered in the names of the keepers of the ranch; rich men "lend" out beasts to poorer families; and men without sons of herding age may be forced to leave their cattle with kin or friends. A headman without claims to any cattle is considered poor and insignificant.

Cattle circulate primarily through marriage, and cattle and wives together are the traditional hallmarks of status and the indices of wealth. In

Swazi society, wealth may fluctuate considerably in a man's lifetime, not through the artificial manipulation of the exchange nor as a result of training, concentration, thrift, and industry, but through "good luck" or "bad luck." Death and sterility are economic as well as social threats. Swazi political leaders, because of their favored position in a polygynous society, have more opportunities than their subjects to recuperate from misfortunes.

In addition to cattle, Swazi also keep sheep, goats, dogs, chickens, and, in some areas, horses, but these have not the same importance in the ritual or economy.

Division of labor and material culture

Tribal economy has little room for specialists, and the main criteria for division of labor are sex, age, and rank. Swazi attach value judgments to activities monopolized by either sex on psychophysical grounds. Men have a higher status than women, and specific "masculine" tasks include warfare, animal husbandry, and hunting. The men are also the important public figures, the orators and councilors and family priests. A woman's life is more restricted by domestic activities—the rearing of children and the regular chores of grinding grain, carrying water, cooking foods, smearing the floors with cow dung. Men and women cooperate in agriculture and building, but the man's share is more spasmodic and energetic, the woman's more monotonous and continuous.

Age has a less defined influence on the division of labor. Children are encouraged to do the same work as the adults and relieve their mothers of certain tasks in the home, but it is only in relation to rituals that age becomes a primary qualification. Thus immature girls are required to help in the national rain rites and in ceremonies periodically organized to drive off pests from the crops; similarly, old women are considered ritually pure and are given specific tasks.

Every Swazi does not participate to the same extent in manual labor. Aristocrats and leading councilors are more responsible for providing suitable conditions for successful efforts than for contributing their own labor. They arrange that specialists treat the land and seed, they summon men and women for work parties in district and national enterprises, and they supervise the feeding and entertainment of workers when a task is complete. They are not, however, exempt from working with their subjects, and most of them perform certain services for the rulers. Only the school-educated tend to despise the heavier physical tasks, but even the most privileged women, including the queen mother, are praised for diligence in cultivation.

As a result of the economic homogeneity of traditional Swazi society, each individual plies a number of crafts, but recognition of individual aptitude has led to a limited specialization within the general skills expected of each person. Some men are better than others at tanning the hides used for shields and for the skirts and aprons worn by conservative married women, and some women are more skilled than others at beadwork, basketwork, and mat plaiting, and so they are asked to produce these, at a price, for the less skilled. There is a marked tendency for all goods to be commercialized at the present time. The main source of income for women who have no special skill and do not have outside employment is the sale of home-brewed beer. The profit may be as high as 100 percent, but the total amount involved is seldom more than ten dollars!

The term *inyanga* (specialist) is applied specifically to medicine men and diviners, but may be extended to smiths and woodcarvers, who are always men, and to potters, who are always women. These crafts tend to be hereditary and are believed to involve unusual "power" and require ritual protection. Carving is limited to headrests, milk pails, meat dishes, and spoons; there are no masks or sculptured figures. Pottery is restricted to different-sized cooking pots with simple geometrical designs. Smithing, which included both smelting iron from the rock and forging it into shape, was the most exacting and remunerative craft. The finished articles, especially iron hoes and different kind of spears (the main weapons of war), were in great demand and in the past were in short supply. Only one smith survives in modern Swaziland, and he makes spears from old scrap iron; imported manufactured goods have replaced most of the indigenous ironware.

The most exclusive and resistant specializations are practiced by specialists in rituals. Medicines are either learned or inherited, and men are the main practitioners, women being restrained by their domestic obligations. Divination, a calling beyond personal volition, is acquired through possession by an ancestral spirit, and is open to both sexes. However, women diviners appear to outnumber men. The *tinyanga* (diviners) have the opportunity to acquire cattle and cash by individual achievement, and are often wealthy and influential. The time they devote to their work depends on personal interest, but most people do not regard even these occupations as substitutes for peasant farming.

Swazi craftsmen had no rigid price for their goods or services, which were exchanged for grain or livestock. There was no organized interdistrict exchange, comparable with that found in east or west Africa, though a certain amount of internal trade followed from the irregular distribution of raw material.

With Westernization, a range of new full-time occupations came into being. Some 12,000 Swazi males are employed each year as unskilled laborers in farming, mining, building, and transport, and some 1000 women in farming and domestic service. There are also teachers, clerks, and messengers, and there is a growing number of Swazi, mostly men, in self-employment as shopkeepers, butchers, and "agents."

New jobs that are associated with "school" education carry a higher prestige and make possible a more comfortable standard of living than do those that do not require "writing." But as yet there is no economic class division, and the few educated men and women in financially good positions have not cut adrift from the extended family; the majority of their kin are both uneducated peasants and unskilled laborers.

WEALTH DIFFERENCES · Accumulation of wealth is not conspicuous in traditional society, where rulers and subjects live in the same type of home, eat the same kind of foods, and use the same limited range of utensils and implements. The emphasis is thus placed on generosity, not hoarding and display. "Begging" from the rich enhances their status, and expresses the deference of the poor. The rulers, who control most wealth as representatives of the people, are expected to help their subjects in times of need.

The introduction of new goods has to some extent changed the attitude to wealth, and bicycles, gramophones, sewing machines, and, among converts, smart clothing are among the most prized possessions. But the limits of wealth are still defined largely by status, and commoners are socially controlled from boasting of their wealth or exhibiting it too blatantly.

POLITICAL ORGANIZATION

The ranking of clans

Differences in wealth bolster the traditional political structure with its hierarchy of rank by descent. The centralized monarchy is built on a network of ties between the royal Nkosi Dlamini and commoners. The clans, over seventy in number, fall roughly into four major grades. At the apex is the Nkosi Dlamini in which the lineage of the king, known as the *Malangeni* ("Children of the Sun") is pre-eminent; then come clans known as "Bearers of the Kings," which overlap with other clans that predominate in certain local centers and retain minor roles of chieftainship. Third come clans whose members hold hereditary official positions (for example, specialists for state rituals, governors of royal homesteads) and, finally, clans between whose members there is a minimum of social interaction. The division between the grades is not sharp or permanent, and some clans have risen through diplomacy or the loyalty of specific individuals, whereas others have been deprived of their honors. However, achieved honors tend to be made hereditary, and an individual's misbehavior taints people of "the same blood."

In the past the clan was a local as well as an exogamous patrilineal kinship group, but as a result of warfare and internal migration, clansmen separated. At the present time the positions held by individuals and lineages, and not by clans as units, indicate the original clan position.

A Ritual of Kingship Senior wives of Sobhuza II are taking part in the annual ceremony of kingship.

The kingship and "twin" rulers

The king is the recognized lineal descendant of the first leader of the conquering Nkosi Dlamini; the closer a man is to the king, the greater are his privileges. The children of kings and the senior branches of their families are described as "Children of the Sun" and form a distinct social and political elite. More distant relatives merge with the "dogs" (commoners) but their social standing is always slightly higher, raised by their clan title "Nkosi." The king has the power to subdivide the Nkosi Dlamini in order to be able to marry clan sisters; thus by substituting another name for Dlamini he avoids too flagrant a violation of the rule of exogamy, and at the same time maintains the Dlamini section as an exclusive minority.

The king is chosen by the rank of his mother, and together they symbolize the Swazi state. They are addressed with a rich extravagance of titles and praises, have unique regalia, and may expect the utmost deference. Honors are fairly evenly distributed between them, and though the king, as the male, is dominant in legal and executive activities, she—the source of his selection—exercises complementary rights. His authority is validated by rituals performed at the capital, where the rain medicines are in her control, and though he is at the head of the state regiments, other leading military officials and at least as many royal guards are permanently with the queen mother.

Conflict between the two rulers is recognized as a potential threat to national security, and certain laws, not always obeyed, have been specifically formulated to guard against this. Ideally, the queen mother should have only one son to avoid any chance of preference, and no matter how young she may be when her husband the king dies, she alone of the widowed queens may not be taken by the levirate. Should the queen mother die, a classificatory mother is substituted. It is extremely irregular for a king to rule with one of his own wives.[6] The elimination of sexual intercourse is articulated as one of the deliberate constitutional attempts to ensure the smooth working of the dual monarchy.

The senior princes, particularly the king's uncles and half brothers, are his main advisers and supporters, but because they too are of royal blood, their ambitions for personal power must be kept in check. They should never be settled too close to the king, nor be given the opportunity to use the medicines essential for kingship. The more important princes are granted districts over which to rule, and formerly were used to extend state territory; at present they may be placed over minor chiefs or be allotted a section within a larger district.

Between the king and the princes stand two special, artificially created *tinsila* (blood brothers, literally, "body sweat" or "dirt") drawn from specified commoner clans. Blood from their bodies is transferred to the king and vice versa; thereby they act as his "shields," protecting him from evildoers and serving him in intimate personal situations from which the Dlamini princes are excluded. So close is the bond between the king and his first two *tinsila* that should they die before him, they may not be publicly mourned and even their widows may weep for them only when the king himself dies.

In addition to the ritual blood brothers, the king is guided by non-Dlamini *tindvuna* (councilors), both civil and military. The relationship between the king and his councilors is expressed in two frequently quoted axioms: "The king is king by the people" and "The king is ruled by his councilors." The chief civil councilors, who act as governors of royal homesteads, are chosen from a limited group of clans, but the positions need not be inherited by the main heir of the senior lineage. The emphasis is placed on ability and "respect for people" so that within the general structure recognition is accorded individual qualities.

The people voice their opinions through two councils. The *liqoqo* (inner, or privy council) is composed primarily of senior princes; merit is also a qualification. They rarely number over twenty, their discussions are private, and the rulers, as ex officio members, usually give their opinions at the close of the session. Rulers continue with the inner council of their predecessors, occasionally adding a member of their own choice and ignoring a man whom they find a constant obstruction.

Whenever the *liqoqo* thinks necessary, it reports its discussions to the second council, the *Libandla Laka Ngwane* (Council of the State) composed of chiefs and headmen and open to all adult males. Both councils are more in keeping with a slowly changing society than with the accelerated pace of modern times. The members hold no regular sessions, follow no clearly stated agenda, and as their guiding principle make every effort to achieve agreement before action is taken. Should consensus not be possible, the matter is generally shelved: organized opposition parties are not part of the traditional system. The *liqoqo* may never override the decision of the *libandla,* and the king, who is usually the last speaker, should try to reconcile the wishes of both councils.

LOCAL GOVERNMENT   ·   The organization of the districts is similar to that of the central government. The chief, whose position is either inherited or sanctioned by the king and his mother, appoints a number of *tindvuna* to assist him. He always has one main councilor to attend to cases, supervise labor, and represent the claims of subjects. His mother supervises his domestic arrangements, and is in charge of the main section of his homestead. His paternal kin constitute a *lusendvo* (family council) which takes the place of the *liqoqo.* Nonrelatives are represented by his leading councilor. The local *libandla* is constituted by headmen of the area, some of whom are consulted more frequently than others and form in effect a working committee.

Swazi officials normally hold their positions for life, and are dismissed only for treason or witchcraft. Incompetence, habitual drunkenness, stupidity, and weakness of character are criticized, but as long as a man is considered loyal he retains his post; the only way to offset his defects is to appoint younger, capable men as assistants. The *ingwenyama* may instruct a recalcitrant chief "to rest," but neither he nor the family council will appoint a son to assume the post while the father is still living.

The relationship between a chief and his subjects is essentially personal. He generally knows each family in his district: his female relatives and the other women work together; the headmen are his cronies and help him decide cases. His importance depends less on the size of his district than on the number of his followers, and the main check on his autocratic behavior and excessive demands is their ability to transfer their allegiance, expressed in service and tribute, to a more responsive chief.

A subject is not a slave. Formerly in a different category from *tikhonti* (ordinary subjects) who offer voluntary allegiance were *tigcili* (mainly children captured in war). *Tigcili* were taken into the homes of the rulers and leading subjects, who were described as their "owners," but *tigcili* could not be sold or killed. Chattel slavery of the plantation type was in fact unknown. Moreover, there was no barrier to intermarriage, and there is no section of the population today that bears any stigma of "slave descent." *Sigcili* (singular of *tigcili*) remains, however, as a term of contempt, indicating that a person is without the security of a kinship group and has limited independence.

LAW   ·   Swazi stress the importance of "the law" in regulating social relationships. Like all southeastern Bantu, they have a highly organized legal system and a graded hierarchy of courts coinciding roughly with the political structure. Private matters ("dirt of the home") are dealt with by the head-man, his mother, and his senior male kinsmen. Disputes between unrelated people are discussed in the first instance by the family councils of the litigants, but if they cannot reach a settlement, the complainant reports to his chief, who sends him with a representative to the chief of the defendant, where the case is tried in public. If this court does not settle the matter satisfactorily, either party may appeal to a higher political authority. Certain cases may go directly to the capital, others to the highest tribal court, presided over by the *ingwenyama*. There are no lawyers, and each man is his own advocate. Cases are discussed at length, and any male present may take an active part in cross-examination. Precedents are frequently quoted, but the main concern is to unravel the complicated interplay of interests involved in each specific dispute, and the chief or his leading councilors give judgment accordingly. Divination is sometimes resorted to in cases involving suspicion of witchcraft.

In their legal practice, Swazi distinguish between torts (that is, cases in which compensations must be given to the injured party as well as to the court), and cases "with blood" (criminal cases) in which reparation must be made to the king as representative of the state. Theft, adultery, and property disputes fall into the first category and are punished by fines; murder and witchcraft into the second, and for these death was the usual sentence, immediately executed.

Colonial administration

Within the broad framework of white control, the traditional authorities have been retained although their functions have been changed and tribal alignments thereby altered. Swaziland, together with Bechuanaland and Basutoland, is under the direct control of the British government. Policy directed from the Commonwealth Relations Office (formerly the Dominion Office) is channeled through a high commissioner, stationed in the Republic of South Africa, who occasionally visits the territories. He is assisted by a small, all-white staff on the administrative side, and a separate, all-white staff on the political side. The majority of Swazi discuss government in terms of officials with whom they have direct contact. In Swaziland itself, white and Swazi run parallel systems that interlock at certain levels. At the head of the local administration is the resident commissioner, who makes recommendations regarding policy and legislation, and is held responsible for their execution. His staff consisting of administrative officers and technical experts, is employing an increasing number of educated Africans.

"Native law" is respected except insofar as it may be "incompatible with the government's power and legislation or clearly injurious to the natives themselves." The powers of chiefs have been redefined, and Roman-Dutch law is applied in a wide range of new situations. Courts of the district commissioner exercise parallel jurisdiction with recognized courts of district chiefs; appeal in all cases lies with the High Court of Swaziland, presided over by a white judge who may be aided in certain cases by native assessors.

The position of Swazi chiefs is typical of the dilemma of many hereditary rulers in pre-independent Africa. On the one hand the powerful white administration, which sanctions their position and controls the country's economy, expects them to advocate certain fundamental changes, while their own conservative subjects regard them as their traditional representatives, preservers of the status quo. A new political group, moreover, is rising in Swaziland, as elsewhere, and is critical both of the traditional monarchy and of all forms of white control.

RELIGION

ANCESTRAL SPIRITS • Swazi traditional religion projects the world of the living into the world of spirits. The dominant belief is in *emadloti* (singular, *lidloli,* ancestral spirits) who perpetuate the status differences of their descendants. The greatest power is exerted by deceased rulers, to whom the king appeals on behalf of his subjects. The ghosts of women and children are less active than those of adult men, but may obtrude themselves unexpectedly. The more recent the death, the more frequently the ghost demands attention from the living.

Ancestors may appear in dreams or materialize in the form of snakes commensurate with their status—the king as the mamba, a woman as a harmless little green snake or lizard. Frequently the dead make their presence felt by sending illness or other misfortune, but Swazi believe that ancestors act in this way for the social good and are not motivated by malice. The mean husband, the adulterous wife, the disobedient son, the neglectful kinsman may all be punished, directly or vicariously, by the spiritual custodians of correct behavior and tribal ethics. Their anger stops short of the death sentence; death is the act of "evildoers" (sorcerers and witches) interested in destroying, not perpetuating, the lineage or the state. Ancestors represent the desire to live and multiply; evildoers, the fear of death and extinction.

Swazi have no class of ordained priests, and the privileged duty of appealing to the *emadloti* rests with the head of the family, the father acting on behalf of his sons, and, if he is dead, the older brother acting on behalf of the younger. In this patrilineal society, ancestors of a married woman remain at her natal home, approachable only by her senior male kinsman, but they retain a protective interest in the woman—who, in marriage, has brought in cattle—and in her children, who consolidated her position as wife. Contact is usually made through the medium of food, meat, or beer, and the dead, who are said to be often hungry, "lick" the essence of the offerings laid at dusk on a sacred place in the shrine hut and left overnight.

Each family propitiates its own ancestors at the specific domestic events of birth, marriage, and death and at the building and moving of huts. In addition there are state occasions when the royal ancestors receive public recognition. Every year cattle are sent from the capital to the caves in two tree-covered groves, where kings and leading princes lie buried in state. The officials in charge report the affairs of the country and ask for prosperity, health, and rain. Some of the animals are sacrificed at the graves. The remainder are identified with particular dead, and consumed on their return in a sacramental feast.

Approach to the ancestors need not be so direct; frequently their presence is accepted as self-evident, for it is to them that Swazi attribute their unique way of life. The most illuminating and dramatic state ritual is the *Incwala*, which centers in the king as descendant of all Swazi kings, and the ceremony requires participation, on the basis of rank, of all sections of the people. The *Incwala*, carefully timed by the position of sun and moon, lasts over three weeks and is divided into two major rituals, the little *Incwala*, which lasts two days, and the big *Incwala*, which lasts six. In the interim period sacred songs and dances are practiced at key villages in the country. The little *Incwala* symbolically breaks off the old year, the past; the big *Incwala* heralds the new, the future. The king is fortified and revitalized; he is bathed with potions of water fetched from the sea and from the main rivers of the country, mixed with plants symbolizing toughness, evergreen freshness, and quick growth; he is given doctored meat cut from a fierce black bull thrown and pummeled by unmarried warriors; he "bites" ritually of the new crops of the year, and his mother, the queens, the princes, the councilors, and the commoners follow his lead, their "medicines" graded by status. The rivalry between a king and princes of the blood, and the bond between him and the queen mother are dramatized in song and dance; at the climax of his "treatment" he is supported by his ordinary loyal commoners to whom he represents both child and father. On the final day, relics of the past year are burnt on a pyre in the great cattle pen of the capital, and rain (the "blessing of the ancestors") "must fall" to extinguish the flames and drench the rulers and their people. The ancestors are considered to be present and active at every stage, their praises are periodically recited, and the ceremony of kingship is a reaffirmation of their existence.

But Swazi ancestors are not worshiped. They are generally addressed in much the same way as if they were living, and prayers to them are spontaneous and conversational, interspersed with rebukes and generally devoid of gratitude. It is mainly the state rituals that are marked by awe and reverence, and recognition of the holy, remote from the profane, is frequently expressed in sacred songs, some of which are theme songs in several different situations. The song chanted when the cattle of the ancestors "return from the royal graves" is a theme song of the *Incwala*; it also marks the installation of each king, his marriage to his first ritual wife, and, finally, his burial. For the king, and the king alone, Swazi practice a primitive embalming; and his body is kept hidden while the council of princes decides on the successor to kingship. The theme of all monarchies—"The King is dead. Long live the King"—is thus developed in typical Swazi cultural idiom.

No ancestor reaches complete deification, and Swazi are not confronted by the conflict presented by belief in a God who is all-good, all-wise, and all-powerful and the evidence of a world of suffering and sin. There exists a concept of a heavenly being, The Great Great One, (whom many missionaries translate as God), but having created man and given him the message of death, he apparently retired from active interest in human affairs. There are also various other spirits who fit into a rather nebulous cosmology, for the Swazi view of the world is not embraced in a single closed and rigid system, but involves various, and at times conflicting, notions.

RAINMAKING · The ancestral cult is linked with the forces of nature, but Swazi do not worship any nature gods. There is a fascinating body of folklore relating various animals, mythological and actual, to the world of man.

Rain, as previously stated, is believed to be controlled by medicines associated with kingship, and is in a different category from most other natural phenomena. The queen mother carries some of the magic hidden on her person, and from her crown of wooden pegs and lucky beans rises the red feather of the flamingo, the Rain Bird. Knowledge of rainmaking is secret to the queen mother, her son, and three trusted assistants, but every subject is aware that at certain times the rulers are "working the sky for rain." The techniques they use increase in strength with the month and general climatic conditions, and move if necessary, and over a period of time, from minor to more elaborate rites. Failure has many explanations: disobedience and disloyalty of the people, anger of royal ancestors, breach of taboos, hostility between the rulers themselves. But the ultimate efficacy of the medicines is not doubted—rain eventually falls—and the belief in the rulers as rainmakers, held even by many Christians, remains one of the strongest sanctions of traditional power. Lightning, on the other hand, is associated with the Bird of the Sky, which lives in certain pools, and can be controlled by particularly powerful evildoers, and there are special lightning doctors to treat homesteads and people with anti-lightning medicines.

MEDICINE MEN AND DIVINERS · Interwoven with the ancestral cult, and the other notions of the nature of life and death, are medico-magical beliefs and practices. Swazi have two main categories of specialists able to tap "deep powers" by esoteric means: medicine men who work primarily with pieces of

A Famous Diviner

trees and roots and other natural substances, and diviners who rely mainly on inspiration and possession. The least influential medicine men are herbalists who have picked up a larger stock of remedies than their friends and are not prepared to distribute them without reward. They claim no inspiration from the ancestors and no tradition of belonging to a family of doctors. Far more respected are men who inherit "the bags," and claim the sanction of their ancestors in their use. Some may concentrate on specific situations or treat a single sickness; others have medicines for an extensive and varied range of symptoms. Some medicine men are more successful than others, and because there are numerous possible explanations for particular failures, the belief in medicines as such remains unshaken. Indeed, added tension and insecurity have extended the situations for which medicines are desired, and Swazi, like other Africans, now apply the same principles to get better jobs, make profitable beer sales, and "sweeten the mouths" of men brought before magistrates. Medicines controlled by state specialists are carefully guarded secrets, and for any subject to use the medicines of the king is regarded as treason. Swazi have a highly developed and graded personality magic to produce "the shadow" equal to a man's social substance.

Although medicine men enter the profession voluntarily, diviners are "possessed," even against their will either by ancestral spirits or, occasionally, by spirits of nonrelatives. The training of a diviner is lengthy and arduous; they experience suffering and solitude in their search for inspiration. Finally, they are "reborn" and able to demonstrate their powers in a public séance.

Swazi techniques of divination are varied. The most usual involves an interplay of statements with verbal responses by the audience. Emotional intensity indicates the extent to which the "findings" confirm their suspicions. "Bone throwing," ventriloquism, and similar devices are also used. The poison ordeal may be administered as the ultimate test: the innocent will not be affected but the guilty will writhe, vomit, and confess. The poison is collected in Portuguese Territory and as a rule diviners from that area are asked to assist in its preparation.

Swazi consult diviners in almost all situations of difficulty. Diviners interpret the wishes of the ancestors, direct people to particular medicine men for treatment, and detect thieves, sorcerers, and witches. Aristocrats and political leaders employ both herbalists and diviners to bolster their powers, but are themselves discouraged from entering this profession, since it might interfere with their administrative duties and not accord with their ascribed status. At the same time, the *ingwenyama* is believed to have "deeper" knowledge of medicines than any of his subjects and by virtue of his unique royal medicines be able to detect evildoers without preliminary training.

WITCHCRAFT AND SORCERY • Witchcraft and sorcery are effective social mechanisms for separating friends from enemies, and beliefs associated with "evildoers" provide a logical system of explanation for the misfortunes that beset all people, to a greater or lesser degree, in the course of life. Swazi distinguish roughly between the witch whose evil has a physiological basis, and the sorcerer who relies mainly on poisons. Though both types are described as *batsakatsi* (evildoers, singular, *umstakatsi*), the propensity to witchcraft is transmitted through a woman to her children, who, to become effective witches, must also be injected with "poison," and instructed in its use. Witches are believed to operate as a gang at night but to be conscious in the day of their nefarious achievements. A sorcerer obtains his poisons from outside, and acts individually in specific situations against personal enemies. To be effective, he may seek assistance from a medicine man who by collusion also becomes an evildoer, and the most powerful *tinyanga* (diviners) are sometimes feared as the greatest of the *batsakatsi*.

Witchcraft and sorcery emanate from hate, fear, jealousy, and thwarted ambition, and accusations of evil practices indicate lines of tensions in Swazi social structure. In a polygynous homestead, the *umstakatsi* is usually a jealous co-wife or half brother, ambitious for wealth and power; outside the homestead, suspected evildoers are blatantly successful and aggressive peers. Important men do not need to use sorcery against inferiors, nor are they suspected of doing so.

Included by Swazi in sorcery is "doctoring" with actual parts of the human body. This potent "medicine" may be demanded by an *inyanga* (specialist) called in to "doctor" seeds for improving crops, or to make a person more powerful and popular. The victim, referred to as a "buck," is innocent of any crime and killed with as much secrecy as possible. An analysis of cases revealed that the guilty have generally been important headmen, sometimes chiefs, and these "ritual murders" can be interpreted as signs of their economic or personal insecurity. The average Swazi condemn their actions as murder, and place them in a different moral and legal category from diviners who condemn evildoers to death. This distinction is, however, not drawn by the court presided over by a judge administering Western law, with the result that Swazi complain that "white man's law protects women and witches. Bad men flourish and those who smell them out are hanged."

CHRISTIANITY · Traditional Swazi religion is challenged by Christianity. In 1940 nearly 40 percent of Swazi were registered as "Christians," and more than twenty different sects were listed. In Swaziland, as in the Republic of South Africa, a growing number of converts belong to "Native Separatist Churches," which vary greatly in organization and credo but share one common characteristic—separation from white control. These churches offer new opportunities for self-expression and power; many of the founders are men of unusual personality and some are more highly educated than the average. Largely on account of tribal status, and a vested interest in polygyny, Swazi male aristocrats have tended to resist conversion from the ancestral cult, but their wives have been rather more responsive.

In the '40s, a group of Christian Swazi from different denominations, reacting against church rivalry, decided to form a Swazi National Church under the "Paramount Chief." The dogma was flexible, no one who wished to belong was excluded from membership, and the scheme advanced as far as the building of the walls; then friction, accentuated by lack of funds, stopped further construction. So it remains, a symbol of a unity that is desired but does not exist in modern Swaziland.

Informants frequently stated, "The world of today is upside down." Inevitably life has become more complex, and choice more difficult. On the whole, Swazi do not spend much time philosophizing; anecdotal illustration, not abstract speculation is the cultural idiom. Their approach to the supernatural is materialist: the ancestors are said to want what man himself desires; the dissident sects, with the largest membership, base their teachings on the Old Testament and interpret Jehovah as an all-powerful punishing patriarch. The orthodox churches that make meaningful conversions must make concessions to established rituals and beliefs.

CHANGE

Many changes in traditional society since contact with whites have been indicated. From the viewpoint of social history, these changes fall into three broad time periods: 1800–1900, 1900–1945, 1945–1963.

The first white men who arrived in Mswati's territory in the early nineteenth century were cordially received. They introduced a wide range of new material goods but did not oppose the Swazi's claims to internal sovereignty. Until the end of the century the political structure of the kingdom remained relatively stable, and the culture relatively integrated. There were no schools, missionaries were not obtrusive, and the "paper conquest" by concessions was not yet backed by military force.

The imposition of tax heralded the second phase of politico-economic interaction. Swazi objected to "paying money to keep white men in the country," and there were rumors of armed rebellion. A leading councilor, sympathetic to the whites, was murdered and the ruling king was summoned on a charge of murder by the Boer government that had assumed control. The British intervened, and the king was reinstated, but the powers of traditional rulers were drastically curtailed. Payment of taxes was enforced, driving men into wage employment. With the transfer of Swaziland to the British, after the Anglo-Boer War, Swaziland became a burden on British taxpayers and received the minimum of financial assistance. Schooling was undertaken mainly by missions, whose primary interest was conversion; but a nondenominational school was started by Queen Mother Gwamile, who taxed her people for financial support. The technical departments of the administration were understaffed and poorly equipped. In short, Swaziland was a typical underdeveloped African territory whose potentials were neglected.

Then came the third phase, the postwar, late colonial era, when the "Winds of Change" reached even the most isolated corners of Africa. Swaziland assumed a new economic significance: private enterprise made considerable capital investment in agriculture, forestry, and mining; the British government more than trebled its grants-in-aid, the local government raised its first general purpose loan, the World Bank responded. African taxes, which until 1946 had constituted over 40 percent of the total revenue, netted by 1956 only 5 percent. Income tax, paid by whites, rose correspondingly.

The geographical isolation, a crucial factor for conservatism, is rapidly and deliberately being broken down. New highways connect the homesteads with urban centers, small aircraft carry executives from the South African republic to expanding points in the territory, and, most important, a contract has been signed for the building of a railway through Swaziland, linking it with a port on the eastern seaboard.

Social and political developments have been less certain than economic growth. Increasing wealth brought an influx of white settlers, swelling their numbers from 3201 in 1946 to 5919 in 1956—an increase of 85 percent in ten years. Socially, there has been a deliberate effort by the administration to desegregate, but throughout southern Africa "desegregation" means meeting on the basis of Western, not African, cultural values. In Swaziland, the interaction is mainly between white officials and a small Swazi elite of Western-educated. These whites do not have the support of the majority of the white settlers, and the Swazi are only tenuously linked with white officialdom.

Influenced by dramatic events in other parts of Africa, Britain has directed that a new constitution be introduced in Swaziland, giving the Swazi a greater share of governmental control. A fundamental problem is how to adjust the claims of white settlers and African tribesmen, a problem complicated by growing cleavage within the tribe itself between conservative supporters of hereditary rulers and members of more modern political parties. None of the political groups, however, found the British Government's constitutional proposals acceptable. No date has been set for independence, but the 1963 constitution can, perhaps, be regarded as marking the end of one period of Swazi social history and the beginning of a period of independence.

Notes

(1) I should like to express my thanks to the African Studies Center, UCLA, for assistance in the preparation of this chapter.

Certain ethnographic material in this chapter has appeared in some of my previous works: *An African Aristocracy* (London: Oxford University Press for the International African Institute, 1947); *The Swazi* (London: International African Institute, 1952); and *The Swazi: A South African Kingdom* (New York: Holt, Rinehart and Winston, Inc., 1963). The material is used by permission of the International African Institute, Oxford University Press, and Holt, Rinehart and Winston, Inc.

(2) In return for guns, gewgaws, gin, money, and other objects of the "civilized" world Mswati, and later Mbandzeni, his successor, put their cross to hundreds of documents, granting land and mineral rights over the whole country as well as various monopolies over its future industrial and commercial developments. Swazi recall with bitterness that most of the monopoly concessions were granted when Mbandzeni, confused and increasingly aware of his own limitations, appointed and paid a trusted white man to act as "Resident Adviser and Agent of the Swazi nation."

(3) Indeed, it was on this qualification that Gwamile Mdluli, daughter of a commoner headman, was selected by the family Council of Princes from the wives of King Mbandzeni. Gwamile was the outstanding figure in Swazi politics for twenty-five years, first as queen mother with her older son Bunu, and then as queen regent, with Prince Malunge, during a twenty-year-long minority of the present king Sobhuza II, whose mother Lomawa was chosen as Bunu's main wife because she was from the same clan that had provided the main wife of Sobhuza I, three generations back.

(4) Apart from the full traditional marriage, Christianity and civil law introduced various forms.

(5) In World War II, Sobhuza recruited some 4000 Swazi in their age groups to serve with the Allied forces. They were trained as stevedores, stretcher bearers, drivers, mechanics, and gunners, but they were part of an entirely different political military machine.

(6) This is the present position—Sobhuza's own mother, Lomawa, died, her full sister and co-wife was then appointed in her place; then she died, and the Council appointed one of Sobhuza's most senior wives from the same clan as the deceased "mothers."

BIBLIOGRAPHY

With a few exceptions the following bibliography emphasizes contemporary work. Daggered items (†) are cited as references in the text of this chapter.

The Swazi

Cronin, A. M. D. (1941). "The Swazi," in *The Bantu Tribes of South Africa.* Cambridge, England: Cambridge University Press, Vol. VIII, Sec. 4.
   Fine photographic record with an introductory article by Hilda Beemer.

Kuper, Hilda (1947a†). *An African Aristocracy*. London: Oxford University Press for the International African Institute.
   A full study of the traditional Swazi political system, and its economic and religious institutions.

——— (1947b†). *The Uniform of Colour*. Johannesburg: Witwatersrand University Press.
   A continuation of *An African Aristocracy* analyzing the influence of Western civilization on the traditional society.

——— (1952). *The Swazi*. London: International African Institute. (Ethnographic Survey of Africa.)
   A concise survey of Swazi social conditions, political and economic structure, religious beliefs and practices, technology, and art.

——— (1963). *A South African Kingdom: The Swazi*. New York: Holt, Rinehart and Winston, Inc.

Marwick, B. A. (1940). *The Swazi*. Cambridge, England: Cambridge University Press.
   A useful ethnographic monograph.

The Culture Area

Barnes, John A. (1954). *Politics in a Changing Society*. London: Oxford University Press for the Rhodes-Livingstone Institute.
   An account of the Ngoni, a branch of the Swazi.

Bryant, A. T. (1929). *Olden Times in Zululand and Natal*. London: Longmans, Green & Co., Ltd.
A detailed historical description of the tribes of southwestern Africa.

Forde, Daryll, and A. R. Radcliffe-Brown (eds.) (1950). *African Systems of Kinship and Marriage*. London: Oxford University Press for the International African Institute.
A series of essays with a masterly introduction by Radcliffe-Brown, indicating the structure and variety of African kinship systems.

Fortes, M., and E. E. Evans-Pritchard (eds.) (1940). *African Political Systems*. London: Oxford University Press.
Describes the political structure of eight African tribal societies, of which five are Bantu. Of particular relevance is Gluckman's analysis of the Zulu, Swazi's powerful neighbors to the southeast.

Gluckman, M. (1952). *Rituals of Rebellion*. Manchester, England: Manchester University Press.
A stimulating interpretation of rituals including the Swazi ritual of Kingship.

Read, Margaret (1960). *Children of their Fathers*. New Haven, Conn.: Yale University Press.
Study of the Ngoni of Nyasaland, who retain many similarities with the Swazi despite separation in space and time.

Schapera, I. (ed.) (1937). *The Bantu-Speaking Tribes of South Africa*. London: Routledge & Kegan Paul, Ltd.
A useful introduction to the main tribal groups of southern Africa.

———— (1955). *Tswana Law and Custom*. London: Oxford University Press.
A lucid analysis of a tribal system in many respects similar to the Swazi.

Other

Greenberg, Joseph (1955†). *Studies in African Linguistic Classification*. New Haven, Conn.: Compass Publishing Co.

14

THE TIV OF NIGERIA

about the chapter

The Tiv of central Nigeria differ in many ways from their more populous Nigerian neighbors—the pastoral Fulani, the Hausa, the Ibo, and the Yoruba. In many respects they do not differ from other sub-Saharan peoples. But, like the Suku, they are basically very African, yet atypical in giving new emphases to principles common in sub-Saharan Africa or arranging them in original configurations.

The principle of patrilineal descent, for example, is the dominant principle in Tiv culture and permeates practically every cultural institution. The family and the compound are patrilineal, and both political organization and dispute settlement procedures are based on segmentary opposition of lineages, as among the Somali and the Suku.

What is unique among the Tiv is the *way* in which the patrilineal principle links political, judicial, and religious institutions. The ancestral cult, which is a significant aspect of religion in many African societies, plays only a minor role among the Tiv. The core of their religion is belief in a series of supernatural forces known as *akombo*, which most Tiv feel are activated by *tsav*, another force, which is an attribute of human beings, especially patrilineage elders. Such elders as a group should use their *tsav* to manipulate major *akombo* ritually so that fertility and other benefits flow to members of the patrilineage, and so that the members of their lineage may be protected from the supernatural activities of other elders—all of whom must obtain "metaphorical" human sacrifices (referred to as witchcraft) in order to maintain the *akombo*. Traditionally, the Tiv had no chiefs; it was the lineage elders who, by day, made—and make—secular political decisions. At night, in their role as manipulators of the supernatural, they can support these decisions by the way in which they use or fail to use *tsav*. Many judicial procedures are also cast in this idiom, for the airing of accumulated grievances may take place in a hearing that begins with accusing elders of failing to provide a lineage member with supernatural protection from other elders. Although fusion of political, judicial, and religious roles is found also among the Jie, the Kpelle, and the Suku, the pattern of interrelationships in Tivland is rather unique.

In his schematic analysis Bohannan connects separate aspects of Tiv culture, showing that men's age sets and the marketplaces both serve to give escape from the constriction of the patrilineal principle and soften the inequities that would result if it were to prevail completely. The roles of the marketplace, of land, of labor, are also briefly analyzed in economic terms, which can be applied to parallel features of the other cultures described in this volume.

The other traditional Tiv cultural institution that reminds us of the disparate ways in which the leitmotifs of African culture are expressed is marriage. Among the Tiv the principle of exchange at marriagé is focused on the exchange of women who were "marriage wards" rather than on the exchange of livestock or goods as bridewealth.

about the author

Paul Bohannan, Professor of Anthropology at Northwestern University, received his D.Phil. from Oxford University in 1951. He has also taught there and at Princeton University. He has served as president of the African Studies Association, and in 1960 received the August Volmer Research Award of the American Society for Criminology for his study *African Homicide and Suicide*. Dr. Bohannan has conducted field research among the Tiv, and among the Wanga of Kenya. His published works include *The Tiv of Central Nigeria* (with Laura Bohannan, 1953), *Tiv Farm and Settlement* (1954), *Justice and Judgement among the Tiv* (1957), *Markets in Africa* (co-editor with George Dalton, 1962), *Social Anthropology* (1963), and *Africa and Africans* (1964).

PAUL BOHANNAN · *The Tiv of Nigeria*[1]

INTRODUCTION

LOCATION AND HABITAT · The Tiv are the largest pagan group in the Northern Region of Nigeria. In the population census of 1952, they numbered about 800,000. Since their rate of increase is about 1.5 percent per annum it is likely that in 1962 they numbered nearly a million.

The Tiv, who came into their present location from the southeast, now live on a wide plain cut by the Benue River and the Katsina Ala River, its most important southern tributary. Only a few hundred feet above sea level at the river, the plain rises, both north and south, to several thousand feet (still within Tiv territory) almost to the escarpment of the Bauchi Plateau and to the foothills of the Cameroun Highlands. The country is covered by high grass and orchard bush, the elephant grass sometimes reaching as much as ten feet in height in the northern areas along the river. The trees are primarily deciduous varieties, such as the locust bean and the silk-cotton tree.

The year is divided into two distinct seasons: a wet season begins in the middle of March and reaches its climax in September, then tapers off quickly in October; a dry season begins sometime in November and is marked by the appearance of the dust-bearing harmattan wind from the Sahara, which reaches its height in January and February and is settled only by the rains beginning in March and early April.

LANGUAGE · The Tiv language is classified by Greenberg (1963) as an independent language of the Niger-Congo family of languages. It has a position precisely equivalent to that of the Bantu *group* of languages. Formerly it was called a semi-Bantu language, a term that has proved more or less meaningless. The Tiv language has three tones and uses them for grammatical purposes, especially for the conjugation of verbs (Arnott 1964). It resembles Bantu in that it has several classes of nouns, each of which has a different copula, and each of which takes its own pronouns and gives characteristic forms to modify adjectives.

PHYSICAL APPEARANCE • Tiv are a Negro people commonly said to be shorter and stockier than the peoples to their north. In fact, their range of height is about that of Americans. Skin color ranges from light café au lait to purplish black. Tiv classify people as "red" and "black"—light or dark— and have the same kind of preferences for people of different coloring that Americans or Europeans voice in expressing preferences for "blondes or brunettes."

CULTURAL PROFILE • The Tiv are not particularly typical of their area of Africa, although there are tribes, such as the Jar on the Bauchi Plateau, who resemble them. The most important areas of similarity are to be found to their southeast in Cameroun, where there are few small "Bush tribes," as they are called, who resemble the Tiv in language and culture. Much Tiv culture is of Congolese affinity. Particularly is this true of some of the drums and musical instruments, and obviously also of some of the religious beliefs and ideas that are very like the religious ideas of such Congolese tribes as the Suku and most unlike the religious ideas of the other Nigerian tribes of the so-called pagan belt or the Islamized peoples of the Sudan areas or the complex pantheons found in the coastal kingdoms.

Paradoxically, their chief significance for anthropology is perhaps to be found in the fact that they are atypical—especially in their religion and in some of their marriage customs—and yet basically so African. The lineage system, which provides the basis of their political organization, is more extended and more nearly perfect than that found in any other tribe save perhaps the Somali, their system of exchange marriage was far more intricate than any other that has been reported either in Africa or any place else. Their arrangement in space and land usage is among the most overt systems in Africa, and has led to the questioning of many of the ideas common in land-tenure studies. The Tiv provide, in short, a test case for the ideas of political organization and family organization, for ideas of property and legal development, and for one of the most highly developed sets of ideas of the sort commonly called witchcraft to be found on the continent.

The Tiv were characterized by Frobenius (1924:239) as the "most practical and unsuperstitious people I have found in Africa." The first European to be killed by them, for example, was first asked "Is it true what we are told, that all Europeans are immortal?" When the European answered "Yes, it is true," the questioner whipped out an arrow, shot him on the spot, and turned to the other European and to the Tiv present and said, "I didn't really believe it."

Tiv are of an independent turn of mind, and are almost surely one of the most ethnocentric people in the world. Their interests center in their farms, in the ceremonies involved in the curing of illness, in considerations of kinship and family, and in the complex ring of kinship relations created by exchange marriage and by a high rate of divorce.

ECONOMY

Agriculture

CROPS AND THE AGRICULTURAL CYCLE · Tiv are subsistence farmers in the sense of having the type of economy in which the same small group who are the consumers are also the producers, but they have a standard of living well above the subsistence level. Their country lies in the "middle belt" of Nigeria, where it is able to have both the subsistence economy of the north, based on grain, and that of the south, based on yams and other root crops. The Tiv thus have three staple crops, millet, sorghum, and yams, and garner many of the advantages that come from a widely diversified agriculture.

Yams, a major item in their diet, are prepared by being peeled and boiled, and then pounded in a mortar until they reach a thick consistency and can be patted into a loaf. A piece of the yam loaf is broken off by the diner, rolled into small balls of a size that can be swallowed; the balls are slightly flattened, depressed with the thumb on one side so as to form a sort of spoon, then dipped into a sauce, and swallowed whole. Both millet and sorghum are made into porridge and eaten in the same way.

The sauces into which this grain or yam porridge is dipped contain the vegetables, the meats, and the oils, although if there is any large quantity of meat present, Tiv will cook and eat it separately. Although there are some protein deficiencies and some mineral and vitamin deficiencies in Tiv diet, there is very little hunger in Tivland, and what little there is tends to be concentrated during the early rains just before the harvest. The harvest of millet begins in early June, of yams in August, and of sorghum in December.

Tiv have detailed knowledge of the botany and the animal life in their area. Every plant has a name and each is recognized by its leaves, but Tiv do not generally recognize the flowers of plants if they are picked off, unless the flower itself is put to some use.

Every year during the middle of the dry season the farmer and his brothers and all their wives select the site they will bring into cultivation for the next year. All of them proceed to pull the grass that has grown on it, and to prepare the field for mounding.

Like tropical soils everywhere, those of Tivland are thin because there is no winter period in which oxidation of humus ceases. In order to grow the large Indonesian type of yam in such soil, it must be stacked up and mounds up to two feet high must be created. This work is done with the short-handled hoe and is skilled as well as arduous.

Making Yam Mounds

As soon as the rains have come, the men begin making the mounds. The mounds are arranged in traditional geometrical patterns that are quite intricate. Tiv take great pride in the appearance of their farms and, on occasion, will move mounds in order to achieve symmetry.

As soon as the men's work of mounding is completed, women, sometimes with the aid of men, plant the seed yams in the top of the mound. Men do this work with a small hoe; women with a digging stick. In most areas of the country, the men plant cassava toward the bottom of the yam mounds. Women plant all manner of side crops on the sides of the mounds. Most contain a stalk of maize, at least one bean plant, various greens, such as sorrel, and perhaps cotton. As many as twenty-two different crops have been counted on a single mound.

It is up to the women to do the weeding of the yam fields, and when harvest is ready it is they who do the harvesting. Seed yams are usually left in the field (although in the south where seed yams are rare they may be taken to the compound), while the rest of the yams are taken into the compound and stored in granaries. In a few of the northernmost parts of Tivland, it is possible to store yams in the ground and dig them only as required. In these areas, too, there is sufficient food that there is only a minimal risk that such yams will be stolen.

The next year the mounds are leveled and the field is planted first to millet in the early rainy season and then, after the harvest of the millet, to Guinea corn or sorghum, which is harvested at the middle of December. In most areas of Tivland, the field produces a cash crop during its third year—either sesame (locally called benniseed) or soybeans, or, in a few cases, castor beans. After such crops have been removed, the land is allowed to revert to fallow until it regains its fertility. The fallow period may require two to twenty years. Tiv can tell by the combination of grasses, and by such other signs as the number of earthworms in the soil, when it is again sufficiently fertile to be used.

ANIMAL HUSBANDRY · Since Tiv live in an area of endemic sleeping sickness, ordinary cattle found farther north in Nigeria soon sicken and die there. The Tiv have a few small, dwarf type of cattle, which are sometimes called tsetse-resistant but which, in fact, often get sleeping sickness. Goats are plentiful and there are some sheep. Chickens are found everywhere and are the most common of the domestic animals. Ducks and some pigeons are kept.

Factors of production

As is true of any other economy, if that of the Tiv is to be understood it is necessary to see the ways in which the factors of production are moved into use and the way in which the product is distributed and utilized. Factors of production everywhere include land, labor, entrepreneurial activity, skill—what Americans call "know-how"—and accumulated capital.

LAND · Land among the Tiv is not a commodity in the sense it is in our own society, where land enters the same market as everything else. Among Tiv, as among most other subsistence farmers, it is not the land as a factor of production that is of primary importance but rather land as a spatial dimension of the community. The local group is a phenomenon of kinship; the exploitation of the land and land-tenure rules both follow.

A Tiv who is a member of a community has a right, because of his membership, to exploit sufficient farmland within the area dominated by the community. This right does not amount to "ownership" of specific land. It is, rather, a right to a *sufficient* amount of the land that is associated with the community. If the analogy is not carried too far, it can be seen to be rather like what biologists have called *territoriality* in birds. The English robin, for example, will not allow any members of his own species near the place he has chosen for his nest. He protects, likewise, a somewhat larger area as a feeding ground, but will allow other robins within his feeding ground under specific conditions. A balance, or distribution of robins on the land results from such activities. Land is systematically exploited by robins, but it can scarcely be said to be owned. In the same way, each Tiv lineage has an area it exploits. The important factor is not exactly where the boundaries are—although they may be known precisely at any given time, they change very rapidly—it is rather who one's neighbors are and how close they are allowed to come. The important point is the juxtaposition of the lineages, as we shall

House Building (*Donald Van Reken*)

see in the next section. The specific land on which a lineage finds itself and that it exploits changes more or less rapidly. The juxtaposition of lineages changes much more slowly, and Tiv say it should not change at all.

LABOR · Labor, too, is seen not primarily as an economic factor, but rather as part of the division of tasks within the household or compound group. Labor is no more an item for sale on the market and measurable in terms of money than is land: it is primarily a set of obligations that one owes to one's family or one's kinsmen.

Tiv work hard. They do not, however, work regular hours. Rather, their work is determined by the tasks that absolutely must be done. Tiv men work hardest during the time when new fields are being mounded and planted, and in which the second-year fields are being leveled and planted. A man working hard can mound about an acre and a half of yam fields during the season. During the dry season, before the time for mounding yams, he has probably been engaged in building houses and storehouses. During the wet season, when women's work is most arduous, men have somewhat less to do. In any case, like women everywhere, the work of Tiv women is never done. They work hard but not at such strenuous jobs as men, although they work at a much more steady rate than do the men. The men, who have been called lazy by superficial observers, actually work hard only during certain seasons, but at those times they are capable of almost unbelievable amounts of exertion. They then may take a period of days or even weeks off during which time they do comparatively little in the way of agricultural work—most of them are, at this time, occupied with the incessant court cases, marriage disputes, and other activities that are called "governing the country."

TECHNOLOGY OR "KNOW-HOW" • The technology or "know-how" of the Tiv is very simple. It has, however, developed a very efficient method for exploiting the land in their environment. The equipment consists primarily of the short-handled hoe, the long knife known as a "machete" in Nigerian English, and the digging stick, the latter used primarily by women. Tiv have a tradition that they once used wooden hoe blades, but no Tiv I could find was old enough ever to have seen one. The hoe blades are made by Tiv blacksmiths from imported iron (although Tiv also have a tradition that they once did their own smelting and there are ruins of smelting furnaces, similar to those in northern Cameroun, still to be found in Tiv country).

The hoe blade is about the size and more or less the shape of a Western type of shovel. It is mounted into a short, forked branch and used by grasping one fork to which the blade forms an angle of sixty degrees or so. With this instrument the major work of the farm is done. Such a hoe has the advantage that it does not cut too deep into the earth's surface and thereby lead to the rapid deterioration of the soil.

MARKETS • Certain amounts of Tiv produce enter the market, and marketplaces play a very important part in the lives of Tiv. They are from three to ten miles apart, and markets are held in each every five days. There is, thus, a market somewhere every day, and everybody is within range of a market at least two days during the five-day "week." Marketplaces range in size from a few square feet to several thousand square yards, and are attended by crowds of from fifty to over twenty thousand people.

The marketplace is always organized. It may be controlled by a local chief or by a committee of elders. There must always be someone on hand, however, to see that peace is maintained in the marketplace and that traders do not overstep or take needless advantage of one another. Prices are determined by higgling, although it is impossible to find a very great range of prices on any particular day.

However, Tiv do not get any major proportion of their subsistence from marketplaces. Thus the market as a principle for organizing social life has not penetrated much beyond a superficial level, whereas with ourselves it has become the most important single principle in the organization of our society as well as of our economy.

Markets serve as places for the exchange of goods, but they also may serve other important purposes. They are favorite centers at which the political leaders of the community meet to discuss their problems and make decisions. Very often these leaders even establish themselves as a court at the marketplace in order to settle the outstanding disputes of people who have come to the market as well as those commercial disputes that arise in the course of marketing. In the past, control of a marketplace was a legitimate goal for a man of political ambition. Since people met here, and since the

A Tiv Market (*Donald Van Recken*)

market therefore formed a hub in the communications network, to control a marketplace also implied a capacity to control people and their activities. Many Tiv wars have been fought over control of marketplaces.

The marketplace is also a place where people have fun. Beer and—in southern regions—palm wine are available in all of them, and in most there are dancing and perhaps other forms of celebration almost every market day. Tiv go to markets to meet their friends and to enjoy themselves, as well as to sell small portions of their produce and to buy such imported items as cloth, pencils and notebooks, hinges and nails, and perfume. Food for snacks is available, as well as most of the craft items.

Most subsistence items enter directly into the domestic economy without ever having passed through a market. Within the domestic economy, most of the items belong to the women. Except for compound heads, few men have food granaries and only a few husbands keep special farms for themselves with food whose distribution they control. Unlike many African polygynous societies, Tiv men do not control the food and they certainly do not have a daily distribution of it. Some Tiv men do claim to control the millet supplies and to hand them out to their wives during what would, without millet, be the hungry season. Such a practice is certainly not universal and in many areas not even common.

PART-TIME OCCUPATIONS · All Tiv men, and indeed all Tiv women, are farmers. No one is a full-time specialist at any other task except those who in recent times have received sufficient education to be clerks, traders, preachers, and politicians.

Among the special part-time occupations probably the most important for men are weaving and basketry, although some others do woodworking, such as making the mortars and pestles that are required by the women, making the pipes that all Tiv smoke, and creating a few figurines and other ceremonial objects. There are also a few master craftsmen who turn out chairs and sleeping platforms.

Tiv wear cloth and prize it highly. Young men wrap towellike cloths, tied at one side, around the loins; women wear rather wider cloths that are fastened by being overlapped in front and that fall to about the knees. Important elders wear cloths extending from their waists to their ankles, and may in addition have a toga that they hang across their shoulders. Traditionally, all this cloth had to be locally produced from locally grown and spun cotton. Today, shorts and skirts are common among men, and Manchester, Indian, and Japanese prints have all but replaced the cloth worn by women. The togas of the elders, however, are still all made locally because, in part at least, no satisfactory substitute for them has been imported.

A few men also specialize by becoming diviners, which is to say that they diagnose the spiritual ills of people who are unwell, so that these spiritual ills can first be put right and medicine effectively administered.

Although Tiv men set an important store by hunting, no one actually provides any major proportion of the food for his family in this way. Tiv live so close together that only a few small animals and birds can still live in the same area. Tiv either drove before them the herds of antelope on which the large game fed or else themselves decimated the game.

SOCIAL ORGANIZATION

THE LINEAGE SYSTEM · The social organization of the Tiv is simple. It is, in fact, so simple that it is difficult to understand. It utilizes a single principle of organization—the agnatic lineage structure, based on the principle of segmentary opposition. The meaning of these terms will become clear as the exposition proceeds. The family has at its core the agnatic lineage, the compound also has at its core the agnatic lineage, and the lineage is fundamental to the political and religious institutions.

A lineage is a group of people who are descended from a common ancestor or ancestress. An agnatic or patrilineal lineage is a group of people descended from a common ancestor through males only. It is a ubiquitous group among the Tiv. The matrilineal lineage is not recognized by the Tiv for any purposes whatever.

A lineage *system* comes into being when several lineages are grouped to form a single social unit. There are several principles on which such an organized agglomeration of lineages may be formed. The one used by the Tiv is the principle of segmental opposition. They, like some other African peoples, organize their lineages into such a system by citing genealogical associations. The lineages made up of the descendants of men who were brothers form an inclusive lineage in the name of their common "father," as opposed

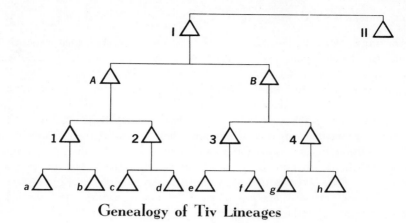

Genealogy of Tiv Lineages

to lineages descended from more distant kinsmen. Thus, as the diagram shows, all Tiv can be placed on a single agnatic genealogical chart and at every generation back in time a new and inclusive lineage is formed. Ultimately, all Tiv form a single lineage, descended from the original ancestor, "Tiv."

The principle of segmental opposition is expressed in Tiv terms by saying, "Would I take something away from my full brother when I can get it from my half brother?" In scientific terms we explain it by saying that two segments of any lineage, whether those segments be individual people or smaller lineages within larger lineages, are completely equal in all things. Two lineages opposed in one context may join forces in another as a single lineage against an external lineage or against foreigners.

To take an example, the diagram represents a genealogy in which only the males have been shown. Each symbol can represent either a living individual or a lineage of agnatically related individuals. Thus, if c were to argue with d, the two, be they lineages or individuals, are equivalent to one another; no one else is concerned in their dispute. However, if c were to have his dispute with b, then c and b are themselves not equivalent. Therefore, d is obliged to come to the assistance of c, and a is obliged to come to the assistance of b. In effect, the dispute then becomes one between the descendants of 1 and the descendants of 2. At that level, 1 and 2 are equivalent, and no one else is concerned. In the same way, if c were to be in dispute with f, c is part of Lineage 2, which is itself part of Lineage A, whereas f is a member of B. Therefore the dispute would be carried to the level of the opposed equivalents: Lineage A and Lineage B. In an ordinary situation, all the members of the two lineages would be opposed to one another over any dispute between their members. It is obvious that this principle can be carried all the way to the top of the genealogy, no matter how great its genealogical depth: the members of Lineage I are opposed to those of Lineage II, and so on.

The genealogies that support the Tiv lineage system are about seventeen generations in depth, and go back to a single ancestor. Every member of the tribal group can trace his descent, real or putative, from the founder of the entire group. He does so by tracing the relationship through males only.

This means of linking lineages into systems is remarkable in that it is such a simple mode of organizing the system at the same time that it disallows a highly developed institutionalized authority. If one person is given more authority than another, the lineage system ultimately breaks down and will not work: its segments are no longer equivalent. If authority is vested in a man from Lineage A, all others can ultimately dissociate themselves by invoking the fissions built into the system.

Such a lineage system forms the basis of the family and the household system of Tivland; it also forms the basis for the settlement pattern and the political system. We shall take these matters up in that order. Such a lineage system must occasionally be subverted, and we shall examine some of the recognized means for doing so.

The lineage among the Tiv forms the basis for all local groups. Tiv are largely patrilocal—a man lives with his father. In three samples taken from widely different parts of Tivland, 83 percent of males were living with their lineages. Some, however, did live with their mother's agnatic lineages, a few with their mother's mother's or father's mother's agnatic lineages, and 2 percent were in areas where they were considered "strangers"—areas to whose lineages they could trace no kinship at all. But residence is uncomprisingly virilocal. I discovered only three men who were living uxorilocally, and of these one was in the record of a murder trial of a man who had killed the person who taunted him for living uxorilocally.

The exogamic group is a lineage containing four or five hundred people. It is sometimes possible for Tiv to take lovers within this group so long as they do not contravene their society's definition of incest: anyone who shares a single grandparent is forbidden. There is another lineage, more inclusive than the first, beyond which it is possible to take a senior wife or one who can ritually be more fully honored (though she is no more legitimate).

MARRIAGE · Tiv practiced, until 1927, a form of exchange marriage based on simple premises that nevertheless led to arrangements that became extremely complex. A small lineage—almost always smaller than the smallest exogamic lineage—distributed its female members as wards to its male members, who were called their guardians. The guardian was then responsible for the marriage of his ward. In the simplest cases a man exchanged his ward for the ward of another and each married the ward of the other. Their children were thus double cousins.

Tiv, of course, recognized the fact that unless spouses are congenial, a marriage is not likely to be successful. The rigidities of exchange marriage therefore had to be softened by some device: elopements and a complex network of ensuing debts. If I elope with the ward of a man but do not have a ward to give him in return, I fall into debt to him. This debt is most commonly paid when my oldest daughter by this marriage is old enough to be married. However, my daughter cannot marry my wife's guardian because to do so would be incestuous—the guardian is her mother's brother. Therefore, instead of becoming his wife, she becomes his ward. He gives her in marriage either to pay some of his own marriage-ward debts or else in a new exchange with the lineage of the man with whom she elopes.

Obviously, such a system quickly becomes extremely complicated, even though its principles are simple. Most exchanges were two or three generations in arrears and the debt relationships reinforcing the kinship relationships created an extremely tight network.

Only an exchange marriage was considered to be the fully correct sort. The Tiv recognized other forms of marriage but these resulted in greater or lesser disadvantages either to the wife or to the children. The most common of these other forms of marriage was called *kem* marriage. The word *kem* means "to accumulate" in Tiv; in this type of marriage the husband makes a series of payments to his wife's guardian, mostly on demand of the guardian. Before about 1920, *kem* payments were made in brass rods. After that time, the payments were made in cash. There was always some doubt about the filiation of children of *kem* marriages. In the long run, however, they were usually filiated to the lineages of their mothers—that is, the agnatic lineage of their mother's father. Under some conditions, it was possible for a man to pay a fee to his mother's father's lineage so that he could be filiated to his natural father's lineage. Indeed, filiation of children even of exchange marriages was not known for certain until both women involved had passed the age of childbearing: children were then evened out. If one exchange marriage bore three living children and the complementary exchange marriage resulted in five living children, one child was taken from the family of the second and placed in the family of the first so that each lineage would gain equally in membership.

In 1927, after considerable agitation, the colonial government declared exchange marriage in the Tiv fashion illegal and replaced it with a form of bridewealth marriage. The bridewealth marriage resembled *kem* in some ways and came in some contexts to be called *kem*, but was very different in that *kem* marriage was actually considered to be a stage in an exchange marriage—an incompleted exchange marriage. Bridewealth marriage, after 1927, was considered to be the sole form of marriage.

Because Tiv did not traditionally pay bridewealth and because, in any case, cattle or other goods used in other areas for bridewealth payment were not to be found in very large quantities among Tiv, bridewealth payment was made in money. Moreover, in a polygynous society, the demand for wives is unlimited, and the supply of women is necessarily limited. Since it became possible for Tiv to sell subsistence goods or their labor on the market in order to earn the very money they could use for bridewealth, it follows from simple economic principles that the price of brides became inflated.

One of the most interesting institutions of the Tiv is the one they call "sister marriage." A young man makes a payment "to remove the shell" (a snail shell worn around the neck, a symbol of sexual inaccessibility, sometimes resumed after the menopause) of the unmarried girl to whom he is attracted. This girl usually is within his exogamic lineage but beyond the bounds of incest prohibitions. If the girl's mother accepts the gift (of course, with the girl's consent), the young man may sleep with his girl friend in her mother's hut until she is married—sometimes a period of as much as two years. If the girl becomes pregnant—and it seems that most of them do not—she is married and her husband becomes the legal father of the child. Such relationships should cease at the time of the girl's marriage, but actually they are sometimes resumed when she returns home for a visit.

The system of kinship terminology and many attitudes toward kinsmen underwent profound change in the period immediately following the changes of 1927. Thus, in the early 1950s Tiv were still more or less confused about what made a proper marriage and what role kinsmen should play vis-à-vis one another. The age of marriage for Tiv men, although it has been falling in recent years, is still some point in the early twenties, and was formerly much later. Thus the proportion of the female population that is marriageable is somewhat larger than the proportion of the eligible male population. It is therefore possible to have a considerable degree of polygyny present in the society, although most men have only one wife. Some 30 percent of Tiv men have more than one wife at any one time, but most of them have at one time or another been polygynous. Marriage is brittle, and often a woman will leave a husband whom she likes because she does not like her co-wives; if she has good and congenial co-wives she may also, of course, stay with a husband for whom she does not care much.

Most Tiv polygynists—at least those who have more than three wives—assign new junior wives to the living quarters and working groups of one of their senior wives. There is some degree of authority exercised by this senior wife over the work and the marketing activities of the junior wife. The relationship between senior wife and assigned junior co-wife is somewhat reminiscent of the relationship between a woman and her son's wife and is thought of in somewhat the same terms.

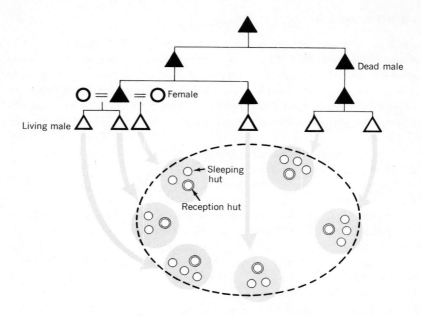

Living male, Female, Dead male, Sleeping hut, Reception hut

Map and Genealogy of a Tiv Compound[1]

THE FAMILY · The polygynous family lives in a cluster of round huts surrounding a reception hut called an *ate,* which is thought of as the sphere of the husband. Each wife has a hut a few yards away from the reception hut. Here she cooks and here she lives with her children. Junior wives' huts are usually placed next to and somewhat behind those of the senior wives to whom they are attached.

As soon as a man is old enough to marry, his wife is brought into his mother's hut. Within a few months—certainly by the time a child is born— a separate hut, close to his mother's hut, is built for the new wife. The living arrangements of the polygynous family thus reflects the central husband-father, and also the disparateness of each wife and her children. Finally, it reflects the fact that as a new generation comes of age, the lines of cleavage within the polygynous family (first between groups of full brothers and then between groups of half brothers) are accentuated.

The polygynous families of several brothers usually live next door to one another. They form a group—an incipient lineage—with regard to the polygynous families of the half brothers of the men. All of them together form a group with regard to their father's brothers' sons. Thus, as shown in the diagram, the position within the compound of the various members can be related directly to the genealogical positions they hold. The relationship of the men is in terms of lineage and descent; women live either with their fathers or with their husbands.

For all the overlap between the compound and the family, it is vital to keep in mind a very important distinction: the family is a kinship group based on descent, collaterality, and marriage. The compound is a local group based on contiguity—the fact that people live near one another. The overlap of personnel between family and compound must not be allowed to obscure this distinction—it has already been pointed out that 17 percent of the men who belong to the extended households are not members of the lineage. Therefore, although the agnatic lineage forms a core around which the family grows up, and the family in turn forms the core of the community, each must be kept analytically separate.

CHILD TRAINING AND SOCIALIZATION

Growing up in such a compound, in close association with a large extended family, is the experience of most Tiv. Most of the people a child meets during his early years are likely to be members of his extended family. He grows up with his immediate brothers and sisters, close beside his half brothers and half sisters. Just beyond him live his paternal cousins and then his more distant agnatic kinsmen. The important visitors to the house to whom he is introduced will probably be his non-agnatic kinsmen, particularly those on his mother's side. Therefore, except for the odd visitor who does not stay very long, a child grows up almost completely in a world of kinsmen.

The child's mother takes care of him during the first few months of his life, but by the time he is able to sit up sturdily and firmly he is handed over to an elder brother or sister who becomes his nurse. It is thought better that the nurse be the same sex as the baby, but such is not absolutely required. It is also advisable that the nurse be as closely related to the baby as possible. Sometimes, indeed, women prefer their own agnates to be nurse to their children, especially if there is no one available but the child's half sibling—who is no kin to the mother. In such a situation, a woman may send to her natal compound and ask to "borrow" a child—usually her younger half sibling or her brother's child.

It is the nurse who is responsible for the day-to-day tending of the baby. The result is a close and affectionate relationship that often lasts through life. "The brother you carried on your hip" or "the sister who carried you on her back" is the very closest of your kinsmen. Old men often introduce one another thus: "This is the brother who carried me on his back when I was a child."

There are some important things the older children are expected to teach their young charges. The first, in their own estimation, is that the baby must be silent on command. Nurses say that the main reason they teach babies to be quiet is that they are always made to take a crying child away from the places where the most interesting things are happening. A child is quieted by simple and effective means. The nostrils are pinched closed, which forces the mouth into use for breathing instead of merely for wailing. It is usually firmly accompanied by the equivalent of "Shut up!" The more polite phrase corresponding to our "Be quiet!" is never used in this situation. Another common phrase used with children, literally translated, means "I'll beat you," but really means "I shall take steps to discipline you," for the beating is usually merely verbal. Few Tiv actually beat their children. Although it is not considered the nurses' responsibility to wean babies, they nevertheless play an effective part in the process. It is largely at the insistence of nurses that toilet training is achieved.

Until they are eight years old or so, the nurses, and children in general, stay in the compound while their parents go to the farms or to their other duties. A nurse may, however, accompany his charge's mother to the fields and may even do some work if he likes. He may carry the child back and forth from the compound to the farm if the distance is not too great.

Weaning is a traumatic time that takes place at about two and a half years. It is not as sudden as it is among some peoples, but the fact remains that there is no satisfactory transitional food between mother's milk and the staples eaten by adults. Tiv furthermore have a notion that children can eat anything without harm, but that adults must be very careful of their diets in order to avoid illness. During weaning, even though they are not pushed forcibly away by their mothers as they are in some societies, children are usually peevish and often sick. It is at this period that disease takes its greatest toll.

Usually some time between three and six years old a child gets yaws. It is thought that everyone gets yaws some time during his life, although the number who actually do so was dramatically reduced by UNICEF's antibiotic campaign in the late 1950s. Yaws is one of the unpleasant things in the lives of most Tiv children, especially since their mothers wash the lesions with cold water, which is said to be very painful. The child's emotional support during the time of his weaning or the time of his treatment for yaws is his nurse.

A woman is usually married by the time she is sixteen; she has moved to her husband's compound and has begun the process of forming a satisfactory relationship with her mother-in-law—not as difficult among Tiv as it is said to be among other people, such as the Chinese, but nevertheless sometimes difficult.

Youths often form a labor force in the community—in the old days, they formed its warrior force—and are, in addition, still carrying on many of the crafts. Weaving, for example, is done entirely by young men. There does not seem to be a teen-age problem among the Tiv: the young people are given very grave responsibilities for the production of agricultural goods and craft goods, and they are allowed many cultural rewards, although the major cultural rewards of the society—status and the knowledge of occult affairs—are not vouchsafed them until they become "elders," at forty-five or so.

There are no formal initiation ceremonies among Tiv. Men are formed into age sets, but no ceremony accompanies the recognition of the set, which is described later in the chapter. Men are circumcised, but the age at the time of the operation ranges from as early as seven to as late as eighteen. Circumcision must, by Tiv definition, precede adult status, but does not thereby create it. Tiv of both sexes are scarified on face and shoulders. Women often have complex scars on their abdomens; this scarification is an ordeal that is sometimes compared to circumcision of males, but it is by no means required and many Tiv girls choose not to undergo it. Scarification is done primarily for cosmetic purposes and has nothing to do with status. Styles in scars change, and it is possible to tell roughly the age of a man by the type of his scars—although some men have old-fashioned scars put on them in order that they may appear older.

POLITICAL ORGANIZATION

The lineage system is the basis not only of the family system but also of the geographical and political organization. The geographical organization is a simple one. At one level in the lineage structure there is associated with each lineage a territory within which, as we noted, 83 percent of the males are agnatic members of the lineage.

As the diagram shows, if the territory of Lineage *a* is beside that of *b*, in combination they form the territory of Lineage 1. In the same way, if Lineage 1 has its territory beside that of Lineage 2, made up in its turn of Lineages *c* and *d*, then Lineages 1 and 2 form the lineage, and the lineage area, of Lineage and Area A, and so on. Therefore, the geography of the country is seen in accordance with the same pattern or model as is used for the social organization of the people themselves in other contexts. Tiv have place names for streams and for the highest hills. Aside from this, all place names are referred to in terms of the lineages of the people who occupy them.

The individual's geography becomes an integral part of his kinship system. One's agnatic lineage, of whatever depth, is called his *ityô*. My mother's *ityô* is my *igba*. My mother's mother's people are my *igba ngô*, and my father's mother's *ityô* are my *igba ter*. During the early stages of my life, my geographical world is limited by my various *igba*, and by my *ityô*. Every lineage to which I belong right up the scale of lineages is my *ityô* until I come to a point at which my *igba* and my *ityô* are structurally opposed segments. Therefore, if I am a member of Lineage *b*, and mother has her *ityô* in Lineage 4, then my *ityô* is Lineage A and my *igba* is Lineage B. However,

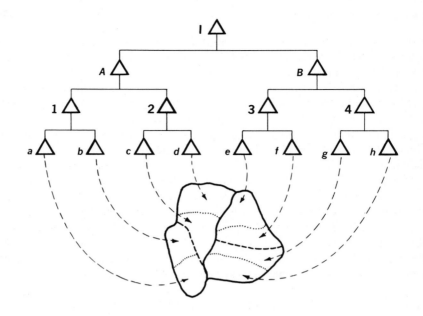

Map and Genealogy of Tiv Political Divisions[1]

if my mother comes from Lineage 2, then that is my *igba* and Lineage 1 is my *ityô*. In this way, the entire world with which I am acquainted as a youngster can be turned into a series of kinship areas.

The function of a political system is to control law and warfare—the exercise of power—within a territorial framework. Since the territorial framework is conceived in lineage terms, the control of power must also take these terms into consideration.

The nature of the lineage system based on the principle of segmental opposition is probably nowhere better shown than in the way in which it deals with the problem of warfare. It acts as a system of built-in checks and balances that generally allows warfare to take place without getting out of hand. In theory—and usually in fact—fighting is stopped short when it embroils two equal and opposed lineage segments. When Lineage *b* fights with Lineage *c* all of Lineage 1 and Lineage 2 may become involved, but Lineage *B* will not because the members are not more closely related to one of the combatants than they are to the other. Individual people of Lineage *B* may, however, go to their matrilateral kinsmen in either Lineage 1 or Lineage 2 and join, as kinsmen, with the combatants. Such a situation does not count as the official entry of Lineage *B* into the fray, and, indeed, if individuals from Lineage B do join there are likely to be as many on one side as there are on the other. Thus, by means of the lineage principle, wars are localized.

Close kinsmen and even lineage mates may be fighting on opposite sides in any given fray. When asked what they do if brought face to face with their lineage brothers in the fighting, Tiv reply that they see one another and shout "Hey look, it's me. I'm your brother. You go that way, and I'll go this way." So that although they are fighting on different sides, they do not engage one another in hand-to-hand combat.

Law

Like warfare, law was also institutionalized within the limitations imposed by the lineage system. The two most important characteristics of the legal practices are both imposed by the lineage system: the absence of offices and officeholders, and the fundamental equality of opposed lineages.

In the indigenous political system, there is no role above the level of compound head that can be called by a title to which authority in any sense may inhere. Political leaders can be described, and the functions of leadership discussed—but any man who performs the tasks of leadership can be described with the words. The words describe acts, not roles. During the colonial era, one of the difficulties was a constant misunderstanding on the part of the British administrative officials, who kept assuming that these descriptive words were in fact names for official positions. The British then tried to tie down each of these "positions" to a given individual, thereby creating a static system of the sort to which they were accustomed. Tiv refused to have power concentrated in the hands of any given individuals, with or without offices. The few exceptions to these generalizations were ritual offices that Tiv bought from the Jukun tribe nearby, and in which little or no political authority inhered.

In the absence of officials, law was maintained by a series of meetings of the elders of lineages of various depths. The lineage involved in the settlement of a dispute was determined in precisely the same way as was the lineage involved in fighting. The dispute settlement also became a general airing of grievances between the two contending groups, not merely the particular difficulty that was instrumental in bringing the elders of the two groups together. These sessions, which can be called moots, were a device by means of which all the difficulties involved in the community could eventually be brought into the open so that, at least, a general awareness of them could be had and, at best, practical solutions found. All of the elders of the community participated in these moots. There was no specialized personnel such as there is in a court.

The British established a system of courts among the Tiv soon after World War I. They took lineages that contained about 8000 people and gave them, quite arbitrarily, the term *clan*—this term is not used in accordance with any anthropological definition. Each clan, they said, was to have a "chief," who later came to be called a *ter* (father). He was to be assisted

Chiefs at Work Government chiefs dictate a decision to a scribe.

by three or four judges; again the British administration took a Tiv word, *mbatarev*, which described men who were influential in settling disputes within their community, and made of it a title for the officials concerned. Each of the *mbatarev* (chief and judges) was given two or three Native Authority policemen, armed only with nightsticks. There was also a scribe attached to the chief, both to write letters for him and to keep rudimentary court records. Such an organization was called a Grade D court.

There was another court, made up of from four to as many as a dozen combined Grade D courts. They were called Grade C courts, and acted on appeals from the Grade D courts. They also acted as courts of first instance in civil cases involving over £25 and criminal actions which bore prison sentences of between three and six months. The combination of all the Grade C courts of Tiv Division (this obviously is also the collection of all the Grade D courts) was called the *jir tamen* (big court). It acted as a Grade B court and was the appeal from the Grade C court. There was no Grade A court among the Tiv—there were only a few in all of northern Nigeria. Appeal from the Grade B court was to the magistrate's courts in the system of law imposed by the British on the Northern Region of Nigeria.

The judges of a Tiv court all sit together to form the bench. The complainant is allowed to recite his complaint—he may go on at any length so long as he can convince the judges that what he is saying is relevant.

The defendant is then allowed to tell his side of the story. Neither of the principals is sworn, or allowed to take an oath. Witnesses, however, may be sworn, but often are not. They are called by the judges, and although a principal can suggest witnesses, he cannot call them. After the stories of principals and the evidence of witnesses are all in, the judges announce a decision. They do not speak in any particular order, and they may disagree with one another, though disagreement will be overcome before a final decision is announced. The decision must meet the concurrence of the principals and of the community—community pressure can make a recalcitrant litigant accept a decision, and there is no other sanction that is fully effective. Decisions are ad hoc, with minimal reference to legal precedent or to any body of laws, although the ethnographer can elicit both precedents and laws.

The major work of any Tiv tribunal is made up of the settlement of marriage disputes, the filiation of children, and disputes over land and farming rights. Tiv are a litigious people and enjoy court cases; they also get a great deal of satisfaction from having their difficulties arbitrated in this way. The judges, who have considerable leeway to make compromises, give moral lectures and ethical advice. Although they are not always orderly, Tiv are fundamentally a law-abiding people.

It can be seen that the administrative courts follow the hierarchy of the Tiv lineage system. At the same time, however, the courts allow an individual some degree of escape from the dominating principle of the lineage. Two other institutions provide an even better means of escape if the lineage principle becomes too confining. One of these is the age set; the other is the marketplace.

AGE SETS · Tiv are organized into age sets called *kwagh*. Each set includes men born in a period of about three years, but full brothers—even twins— cannot belong to the same age set. Like most other Tiv institutions, the age set does not originate formally, but rather drifts into existence as it is required by members of the group who will be its adherents. By the time that men reach the age of seventeen or eighteen, they know who are going to be in their age set; the group of young men is taken in hand by men from an older age set—but younger than that of their fathers—who are called *igba* to the younger age set. The *igba* instructs the members in their duties to one another. These duties involve mutual assistance in work and in financial matters, but, more important, they involve the capacity to treat with diviners, doctors, and other ritual specialists. The age set is a man's primary ally should the members of his lineage withdraw supernatural protection, which is evident to Tiv whenever a person falls seriously ill. The age set, which includes all of one's age mates among one's lineage of whatever depth, can convene all of the lineage members who belong to older

A Hoeing Party

age sets to inquire into the ill health or discomfiture of one of its members. Therefore, if the members of the lineage become too pressing and do not allow a person full rights or if they threaten him, it is to his age set that he turns. The age set is thus one of the chief alleviants of lineage pressure.

Age sets are of greatest importance to young men in their early twenties, who are doing a major part of the physical work of farming. Age mates very often work together on the farms first of one, and then another of their members. The recipient of the labor for the day provides food and beer and is, of course, obliged himself to work for another member of the age set on another day.

The primary function of the age set changes when men reach the age of about forty. At that time, when the members are passing into elderhood, the age set is used most to maintain rights and to stave off the pressures of other members of the lineage who may be jealous, or who may resist the advancement or the wealth of the incoming group of elders. After its members reach the age of about fifty, their age set becomes very little more than a sentimental association.

OTHER COUNTER-LINEAGE FACTORS · It is readily seen that Tiv social organization gives little opportunity for men to achieve legitimate power positions. There are several avenues, however, by which some power and prestige may be gained. One of these is to become the most important man in the age set; another is to become an important ritual specialist; and still another is to gain control of a market. In order to maintain one's position in a marketplace, it is necessary to be able to assure those who come to trade that they will be safe and that their rights and goods will be respected. In order to make such assurances, it is necessary to have fairly large and fairly strong followings. These two factors interplay, and if a man is canny enough to do so, he can become a power in the land by controlling a point of trade and communication. He can, in this way, even stand out against his own lineage. Hence the market becomes one of the most important of the alleviating factors for the force of the lineage principle.

The absence of offices is paralleled by the fact that Tiv is a classless society. Although traditionally there was a group of slaves, the slaves themselves were kinless persons attached into a lineage and into a family by a slave-master relationship instead of by a kinship relationship. Within the family, they suffered an inferior status, but before members of other families, or before members of other lineages, they were considered as equal to lineage members by birth. Slaves, if they were the the oldest men in the compound, could inherit the compound headship, although such an arrangement usually was not stable and led to a breaking up of the compound at a relatively early stage. Slavery in Tivland was never, even secondarily, an economic institution, and was never widespread.

The only hierarchical social relationships are those that involve kinsmen and most specifically those that involve older and younger persons. Older men are always right by virtue of their seniority, and when strange Tiv meet, they must soon decide which is senior.

Friendship between unrelated men may be institutionalized and they may or may not become blood brothers. These special friends have specific obligations and rights, some of which can be enforced in a court or a moot. They include financial assistance and assistance in labor; perhaps most important of all, the best friend is a sanctuary if one must escape the machinations of one's lineage. It is a fact that friendship in Western society is an extremely personalized relationship with a minimum of formal content. For this reason, Western social scientists have given little regard to the institutions of friendship in other societies. Although best friends among the Tiv like each other and do personalize their relationship, the formal element of mutual assistance and protection is considered to be the more important aspect.

We have seen that Tiv political organization is oriented about the lineage principle. It is inevitable that whenever a single principle of social organization emerges so strongly, difficulties emerge. As we observed above, Tiv have several means of getting around such problems: the market itself is one such organization that can be used to control the inexorability of the lineage principle. The age set is another. Various kinds of cooperating groups or "friendly societies" and several types of institutionalized friendship also ameliorate the force of the lineage principle, thus, in fact, making it possible for the principle to work.

RELIGION

Probably the most important single fact about Tiv religion is that it does not form a single system of thought. As in many another African religion, there are several ways of accomplishing the same religious ends, and several means of explaining the same misfortunes. Having more than one string to their bows, Tiv are able to make their religious practices more satisfactory to themselves. Such a state of affairs may simplify Tiv religion for them, but it complicates an anthropologist's attempt to describe it in narrow compass.

Investigation of Tiv religion leads first into ideas of the nonmoral aspects of the human being; second, into ideas of special capacities for actions that would be considered supernatural in a non-Tiv context; third, to the forces called *akombo*, which figure in the rituals and provide the avenues to God; and, finally, to the place of religion in social life.

SOULS AND ANCESTORS • Every man has a *jijingi* that is manifest in his shadow and in his reflection in water or a mirror, but departs at death. Tiv say that dead men cast no shadows. If the shadow of a corpse is pointed out to them, they say solemnly that this is not a *jijingi* any longer, it is merely his *mure,* which is the word for the shadow of a tree or an inanimate object. During life, the *jijingi* is the agent by which dreams are received. Most Tiv agree that the *jijingi* does not leave the body when it dreams, but rather that the perceptions of dreams are brought to it, usually by nefarious human means.

Jijingi is to be distinguished from two other human characteristics. The first is the *ikpa or* ("human bag"), by which the Tiv mean the superficial physical characteristics; the second is what they call the *or iyor na* ("real self," literally, "person his body"), which is the personality.

The *jijingi* is said to go to *Aondo* (the heavens) at the time of death, but almost everyone claims ignorance in the matter and says that they have taken the missionaries' word for it. Tiv themselves are only minimally interested in what happens to the *jijingi.* Another form of the belief—and although the two may seem to be contradictory, both can be held without contradiction—is that the *jijingi* goes to the land of the *mbakuv.* This word literally means "the dead" in the plural. However, it also means a type of sprite. When a *jijingi* goes to the *mbakuv* it undergoes a fundamental change, and loses any human characteristics. These sprites are important in folklore, but not in religion.

Tiv religion, unlike that of much of the continent, does not include an ancestral cult. Tiv remember their ancestors and use devices by which they can make offerings to them. But their attitudes are more like those of

modern Westerners who pay special respect to their forebears on Mem
Day than like the ancestral cults of much of the rest of Africa.

The *jijingi* is said to lodge permanently in oneself, and also to be heritable by one's child. A child may inherit the *jijingi* of either parent, but not of both. Being heritable, it is divisible. These various beliefs are not contradictory. The important point is that the *jijingi* of the dead have little or no effect on the rest of Tiv life. There is a recognized means of getting in touch with them to honor them and to get their concurrence in the settlement of disputes that were outstanding at the time of their deaths. However, there is no idea that dead men per se, or the *jijingi* of dead men, can cause any difficulties or need be propitiated. There is one exception: if a dispute was unsettled at the time of death it may have to be settled later, with the heirs of the dead man, in which case the sacrifice of a chick notifies the dead man that settlement has finally been achieved. Such beliefs about the *jijingi* and about the dead are more or less effectively sealed off from the rest of Tiv religious beliefs.

"RELIGION" AND "WITCHCRAFT" · The major components of Tiv religion can best be set forth in the form of a myth. Myth is a narrative that organizes data for some purpose. The following myth is an anthropologist's myth that organizes the data of Tiv religion. It does not do violence to Tiv concepts or dogma, but it is more organized than any statement that can be collected from them. There is a constant danger that an anthropologist will "write scripture" for a tribal religion merely in explaining it—such a charge can be countered only with the firm insistence by the anthropologist that a religion like that of the Tiv gains its very strength from being diffuse, but that such diffuseness must be reduced for purposes of explanation.

In the beginning, the myth of Tiv religion might commence, all the world and all the heavens were created by God. The word for God and that for heavens—as well as the ordinary word for sky are the same: *Aondo*. *Aondo* is what the theologians call an otiose god—a god who created the world and then withdrew and left it to be run by persons, spirits, and forces that he created but that are other than himself. It is not quite true to say that Tiv never pray to God or that they never get in touch with God. The recognized way to do so is to cut the throat of a baby chick and throw it into the bush, a practice that can be used both to put the sacrificer in touch with God as in prayer, or (as we have seen) to symbolize the concurrence of a dead person to an arrangement made subsequent to his death.

In the process of creating the world, God made a series of forces that the Tiv call *akombo*. *Akombo* forces are manifest in the emblems that represent or symbolize each force and also in the diseases that each creates. The number of *akombo* runs to several hundred, although the important ones do not exceed three dozen. Specific *akombo* are probably fairly short-lived. New ones are "discovered" and old ones that prove ineffective are dropped. Tiv explain this fact by saying that there is no way that they can ever know all of them, and that some may occasionally lose their power. The universe, that is to say, is undergoing constant change and re-creation.

Although some Tiv would say that *akombo* can work with almost a mechanical causation, most of them claim that *akombo* must be activated by another kind of force that is an attribute of human beings and that was also created by God—*tsav*. *Tsav* is the word for a substance that Tiv claim grows on the hearts of people with any special power, talent, or ability. It also grows on the hearts of some animals. *Tsav* is itself morally neutral, to be used either for good or for evil. It becomes good if the person is good and nurtures it through good deeds—what we in the West would call "public service." It becomes bad if the person is disliked, distrusted, and self-seeking; Tiv say that such a man has nurtured his *tsav* by a diet of human flesh.

People with *tsav* are said to "know things" about activating *akombo*, of which most Tiv claim to be ignorant. Therefore, when the *akombo* (in the form of disease, such as tuberculosis) "touches" a man, the assumption is that some person of evil *tsav* has activated the *akombo* through nefarious ritual. The first step toward counteracting the *akombo* is to find the person whose *tsav* has activated it, get him to withdraw the power at work, and then to apply the specific medicines for that *akombo*.

The supposed use of *tsav* to explain misfortune is usually expressed by saying that a person has been *tambe* (bewitched). The use of English witchcraft terminology must be circumspect, however, for it may hide more than it reveals. Tiv most readily suspect that it is their own agnatic kinsmen, those within their fairly small lineages, who bring the power of *akombo* to bear through the magical use of *tsav*—that is, who "bewitch" them. Their opinions are reinforced by diviners who, by using their special, consecrated equipment, may discern the lineage area in which the attacking *akombo* was activated. Some diviners, if pressed and adequately paid, will "reveal" the person whose *tsav* was primarily responsible.

When a man becomes ill, his age set will go to a diviner to determine what *akombo* has attacked him and where it is located. They will then call up the elders or other members of his lineage and ask why they have not protected him—it is up to the elders to protect a man from one of their number. Yet Tiv all say that it is up to these elders also to make occasional sacrifices—human sacrifices—so that the community can prosper. Such sacrifices are, in fact, mystical sacrifices, for death occurs by what Westerners would consider to be natural means. The corpse is then said to be brought back to life by a group of persons with *tsav*, acting at night. It is the "reactivated" corpse that is sacrificed "at night" on emblems of "the great *akombo*." The human sacrifice metaphor is one with which Christians are familiar: it is necessary for one man to give his life for the salvation of the community, and for the guardians of the community to take it for that purpose.

To sum up, God made the world and everything in it before He withdrew. He created forces, called *akombo*, that were to be manipulated by the responsible members of the community for the good of the community. He also created the capacity, *tsav*, to manipulate the forces. As God made them, these things were good. Both *akombo* and *tsav*, however, can be perverted to selfish ends. Used selfishly, the forces for good are turned into the sources of evil: illness, death, and calamity.

So summed up, Tiv religion appears simple—so would any other religion stated so succinctly. In its practical detail, however, it is complex and satisfying both intellectually and emotionally.

THE *akombo* • *Akombo*—magical emblems *are* the forces they represent— are divided into two sorts: the great and the small. Great *akombo* have human sacrifice (or its metaphorical substitutes) associated with them. Small *akombo* do not; the sacrificial animal is of lesser size and value—from a mouse to a sheep, although the usual sacrificial animals are chickens and goats.

To describe an *akombo*, one must state (1) what it is, (2) what it has, (3) what it does, and (4) what it undergoes.

An *akombo* is a symptom of disease and also is the emblem or symbol on which sacrifice to it is made. Thus, the *akombo-iwa* is a back pain that, in men, may be associated with impotence; it is also a potsherd hung on a stick at the edge of a yam field.

An *akombo* has ritual regulations of several sorts and it has medicines. If a person disregards or accidentally infringes these regulations, he is said to have "pierced" the *akombo*. The acts that are ritual transgressions may be considered either immoral or amoral—it is not the task of *akombo* to protect the morals of the community, although some immoral acts do pierce *akombo*. If a symptom strikes a person, he is not necessarily believed to have committed an immoral act, because many amoral acts could have brought about the same result. There are other types of ritual regulation that must be observed when setting the *akombo* right again. There are plant and animal medicines associated with each *akombo*; some of these medicines are therapeutically effective. Tiv claim, however, that no medicine can be effective until the volition (expressed in terms of *tsav*) that activated the *akombo* has been countered.

An *akombo* does only one thing: it "seizes" people. If a man transgresses an *akombo* regulation, he has "touched" the *akombo*; if the *akombo* has been activated by *tsav*, it "seizes" him. The illness or misfortune is direct evidence of *tsav*, because (Tiv reason) the *akombo* seized when it was touched.

An *akombo* undergoes—besides being "touched" or "pierced"—a series of ritual manipulations. It can be "washed," which renders the victim amenable to proper medical treatment if the volition is no longer operative. An *akombo* can itself be "seized," which means that someone performs a ceremony, after which he is allowed to "wash" it for someone else. An *akombo* can be "rejoiced," which has many meanings but is basically a reaffirmation of a former positive relationship with the *akombo*. Finally, it can be "repaired," which is a generic term for any of the three operations already mentioned. It can be "finished," which makes a person its master in all situations. The rituals for washing, seizing, and rejoicing the *akombo* are all much the same: each *akombo* has slightly different regulations that must be observed, but the climactic rite in each is the sacrifice of an animal and the creation of a relationship between a person and the *akombo* by smearing blood (and usually feathers as well) on both the emblems and some specific part of the human body (which part changes with the *akombo*). The sacrificial animal is then cooked and eaten by all those present who have ever been beneficiaries of a ritual for this *akombo*, thus creating a further ingestion of the life and health that the sacrificial animal symbolizes.

Small *akombo*, discussed above, affect only individuals. Great *akombo* can strike social groups as well as individuals. They demand either a specific (but varying) piece of human body as an emblem, or the sacrifice of a human victim when they are repaired. Human sacrifice may be metaphorical. The great *akombo* affect crops rather than individuals; they are epidemics rather than individual symptoms. They are "touched" by individuals who perform gross antisocial acts such as homicide or witchcraft, or by lineages that have, as groups, failed in their social obligations.

It is of the great *akombo* that Tiv stand in a certain awe: they are necessary if crops and people are to be fertile. But they also, eventually at least, require the ultimate sacrifice from some member of the community. A decidedly ambivalent attitude results: they are both necessary and fearful. They bring ultimate good but demand immediate acts that, in any other context, would be evil.

THE *mbatsav* · This dilemma of the great *akombo* is solved by postulating an organization of all the elders of the community who have *tsav*. This organization, called the *mbatsav,* meets and does its work at night. The proper work of the *mbatsav* is the reparation of the great *akombo*. The human sacrifice involved is thought to be performed first by the activation of a small *akombo* that will cause the death (by what Westerners would consider "natural" means) of the victim. It is said that, as a group, they revive the buried corpse—though only one of the three "souls" returns to it— and then sacrifice (by cutting its throat) the "zombie" on the emblems of the great *akombo* in question. The story continues that such sacrifices are "eaten" by the *mbatsav* just as the chickens and goats sacrificed on t small *akombo* are eaten by practitioners.

Tiv doubt that elders, given such power, always use it to the socially approved ends it is meant to serve. The *mbatsav*, besides being the protectors of the Tiv, are also the bogeymen. Using a series of vivid metaphors, Tiv claim that men of power demand more power—that they begin to hunger for the flesh of their neighbors. Selfishness can create in the individual the perniciousness that will lead him to aggrandize himself at the cost of his brothers. He strikes them because of his meat hunger as well as because of his desire to succeed to their wives and their positions. As he does so, the metaphor continues, the *tsav* on his heart grows to grotesque proportions and shapes and, in the last stages of depravity, may grow claws. When such a state is reached, the *mbatsav* have "spoiled the land," when it should be they who "repair the land" by performing "at night" only the necessary sacrifices and by governing intelligently and altruistically "by day."

In such a situation, the community can turn to the greatest *akombo*, *swem*. *Swem* is also the hill from which the original Tiv and his descendants are said to have sprung. *Swem* is, to put it so, the totality of Tiv society and culture in all its sacredness. People swear on *swem*—this is the main *akombo* used in Tiv courts to swear witnesses; it is also the *akombo* used as an ordeal for innocence. In the traditional system, *swem* sometimes took the form of sasswood, a poisonous bark from which an infusion was made, administered to suspects to see whether they vomited it (indicating innocence) or died (combining indication of guilt and punishment therefor). More often, however—and in all cases after about 1920—*swem* is prepared magically of ashes, ground camwood, and leaves that signify male and female principles. The *swem*, so "dressed," is then broken, and the ashes scatter in the wind. When *swem* is thus broken, justice is loose in the land; the evil use of *tsav* will be apprehended and punished by illness and death. *Swem* is absolute justice; it can also be seen, by the analyst, as the epitome of the value Tiv place on their own culture. When *swem* is no longer effective, the Tiv, by their own criteria, will have changed out of all recognition.

CHANGE

The major impact of European civilization on the Tiv has come with increasing intensity in the years following World War I. Cash crops (benniseed, soybeans) have been added; food crops are exported to the southern part of Nigeria in vast quantities. A "Native Administration" has overhauled Tiv political institutions by introducing the notion of roles with inherent authority. Tiv mistrust authority and reacted to the new system with a series of counteractive cults and movements that led to their being artificially cut off from the rest of Nigeria. "Tiv specialists" were created among the British administrative officers, and special regulations denied rights of trading, building, and residence to non-Tiv. Such special treatment meant that the Tiv remained more "backward" than their neighbors, for they were protected for some years from many of the agents of social and cultural change that were at work in the rest of Nigeria.

Missionary activity began among the Tiv in 1911, when the Dutch Reformed Church of South Africa established its first mission. It was the policy of this mission to teach the Tiv to read and write their own language and to teach some Hausa; English was added only at a late date. The Roman Catholic missions were established in the 1930s and were not manned during World War II, which further delayed the Tiv in achieving the sort of educational standards that were reached in the southern part of Nigeria. In the 1950s, the Dutch Reformed Church was replaced by American missionaries of fundamentalist faiths, and the processes of education and conversion speeded up. A few Tiv have professed Islam, but for most of that group it is no more than a handy device to be used on trading expeditions and given up on return home—a few Tiv Muslims are, of course, devout.

It is difficult to distinguish nativistic cults among Tiv—although there have been some—from the renovation movements that were normal in their society (even before European contact) whenever the authority situation became too rigid. During the celebrations of the independence of Nigeria in October 1960, Tiv rioted—not about independence, but in order to uproot those in authority in their local administration. They rioted again in 1964.

The Tiv are an independent, ethnocentric people who are just beginning to "open their eyes" (their own idiom for social and economic development and change). They arrived late on the scene, being among the last Nigerians to come under British administration and among those most carefully protected from the forces of modernization. Their task in becoming citizens of a new, independent nation is a tremendous one. The success with which they will be able to carry it out will depend on the clarity with which they understand their position. They are a strong and vital people; they are also stubborn. They will add much to Nigeria, but they may have to endure much before they see their way clear to doing so.

Notes

(1) Certain ethnographic material in this chapter appeared previously in *The Tiv of Central Nigeria* (London: International African Institute, 1953) which I co-authored with my wife Laura Bohannan; and in my *Justice and Judgement among the Tiv* (London: Oxford University Press for the International

African Institute, 1957). This material is used here by permission of the International African Institute and Oxford University Press.

The diagram "Map and Genealogy of a Tiv Compound" is reproduced from my *Tiv Farm and Settlement,* Colonial Research Study No. 15 (London: H. M. Stationary Office, 1954), by permission of the Controller of Her Britannic Majesty's Stationery Office.

The diagram "Map and Genealogy of Tiv Political Divisions" is reprinted from my paper "Migration and Expansion among the Tiv" (*Africa,* vol. 24, 1954) by permission of the International African Institute.

BIBLIOGRAPHY

With a few exceptions the following bibliography emphasizes contemporary work. Daggered items (†) are cited as references in the text of the chapter.

Abraham, R. C. (1940). *The Tiv People.* London: Crown Agents for the Colonies.
An account by an administrative officer, on conditions in the early 1930s.

Akiga (Benjamin Akighirga Sai) (1939). *Akiga's Story,* Rupert East (tr.). London: International African Institute.

———— (1954). "Descent of the Tiv from Ibenda Hill," *Africa,* Vol. 24, pp. 295–310.
Akiga, himself a Tiv, collected his material during years of travel in Tiv country as a catechist for the Dutch Reformed Church Mission. The original, written in Tiv, has never been fully translated. Akiga was a delegate to the Northern Region House of Assembly for Benue Division until his death in the late 1950s, and was the first editor of the Tiv newspaper, *Mwanger u Tiv.*

Arnott, D. W. (1964). "Downstep in the Tiv Verbal System" *African Language Studies,* Vol. 5, pp. 34–51.

Bohannan, Laura (1952). "A Geneological Charter," *Africa,* Vol. 22, pp. 301–315.

———— (1958). "Political Aspects of Tiv Social Organization," pp. 33–66 in *Tribes without Rulers,* John Middleton and David Tait (eds.). London: Routledge & Kegan Paul, Ltd.

————, and Paul (1953). *The Tiv of Central Nigeria.* London: International Institute. (Western Africa, Part 8, in the Ethnographic Survey of Africa.)

Bohannan, Paul (1953). "Concepts of Time among the Tiv of Nigeria," *Southwestern Journal of Anthropology,* Vol. 9, No. 3, pp. 251–262.

———— (1954a). *Tiv Farm and Settlement.* London: H. M. Stationery Office.

———— (1954b). "The Migration and Expansion of the Tiv," *Africa,* Vol. 24, pp. 2–16.

———— (1955). "Some Principles of Exchange and Investment among the Tiv," *American Anthropologist,* Vol. 57, No. 1, pp. 60–70.

———— (1956). "Beauty and Scarification among the Tiv," *Man,* Vol. 56, pp. 117–121.

———— (1957). *Justice and Judgement among the Tiv.* London: Oxford University Press.

———— (1960). "Homicide among the Tiv of Central Nigeria," in *Homicide and Suicide in Africa,* Paul Bohannan (ed.). Princeton, N. J.: Princeton University Press.

————, and Laura (1958). *Three Source Notebooks in Tiv Ethnography.* New Haven, Conn.: Human Relations Area Files.

Bowen, Elenore Smith (1955). *Return to Laughter.* New York: Harper & Row; and New York: Doubleday Anchor Books, 1964.
The novel of an anthropologist and her adjustment to working among the Tiv.

Downes, R. M. (1933). *The Tiv Tribe.* Kaduna, Nigeria: Nigerian Government Printer.
A report by a government officer, published (he claimed in 1954) against his wishes.

Frobenius, Leo (1924†). "Die Muntschi, ein Urwaldvolk in der Nachbarschaft der Sudanischen Kulturvölker," Part 3 of *Volksdichtungen aus Oberguinea,* Atlantis, Band XI, München.

Greenberg, Joseph (1963†). *The Languages of Africa.* Bloomington, Ind.: Indiana University Research Center in Anthropology, Folklore, and Linguistics (Publication 25).

Murray, K. C. (1951). "The Decoration of Calabashes by Tiv (Benue Province)," *Nigeria,* No. 36, pp. 469–474.

———— (1949). "Tiv Pattern Dyeing," *Nigeria,* No. 32, pp. 41-47.

15

THE YORUBA OF NIGERIA

about the chapter

Like many of the larger African societies, such as the Swazi, the Yoruba of the Guinea Coast are not really a single "tribe." Rather, they are a series of diverse peoples bound together by common language, dress, symbolism in chieftaincy and ritual, as well as mythology and history.

Lloyd writes: "One could, I think, write a textbook on comparative political systems, drawing almost all one's examples from the Yoruba!" Yet the political organization of each of the Yoruba peoples has one thing in common: the political structure, or "constitution," shows a combination of several different principles of representation. This makes possible the operation of checks and balances on the use of political power, a process found in Rwanda, Swaziland, and most of the indigenous African states.

One of the elements that unite the various Yoruba peoples is their history and their awareness of this history. Lloyd shows some of the ways in which this history was shaped by external forces, such as trade and slaving, as well as by internal forces, and how these historical factors partially explain the variation in political institutions from kingdom to kingdom. The realization that a given African society may vary internally in content and form from area to area is gained also from a study of the Rwanda.

Yoruba history helped to shape another cultural institution that has a unique development among the Yoruba: the Yoruba city. The Hausa, too, have large cities, but the Yoruba were the most urbanized people in precolonial Africa. Their cities differ from the metropolises of Europe in being primarily communities of farmers and of

547

large aggregates of people linked by ties of kinship. These areas are urban in population size and density, and as occupational and social differentiation proceed and kinship ties weaken, they are acquiring the urban social features of Western cities.

An interesting parallel change is the development by more educated Yoruba of a "basic Yoruba culture" devoid of local peculiarities. The features of this core culture, summarized in Lloyd's structural analysis, are in some ways typical of the more complex Guinea Coast societies. They include the role of markets, the role of religious cult groups, and the role of women. The role of Yoruba women has captured the attention of Western observers because they appear so "emancipated," contrary to stereotypes about nonliterate societies. The Yoruba have a complex economy and market system with much of the marketing in the hands of women, for whom trading is virtually a full-time occupation from which they often become independently wealthy. Unlike women in most African societies, they do no farm work, and take their status more from their standing as market women than from their husband's status. This economic and social independence apparently undermines marriage; divorce is frequent among the Yoruba. It is interesting to compare the position of Yoruba women with both that of Kpelle women, who work household farms for the ultimate enhancement of their *husband's* status and commonly face divorce; and that of Swazi women, who are economically dependent but, in the role of queen mother or queen, have significant political powers.

about the author

P. C. Lloyd, Senior Lecturer and member of the Centre for West African Studies at the University of Birmingham, England, received his D.Phil. from Oxford University in 1958. He has been head of the Department of Sociology at the University of Ibadan in Nigeria and has carried out fieldwork among the Yoruba (1949–1959) and the Itsekiri (1955–56). He has written *Yoruba Land Law* (1962) and numerous journal articles on both peoples.

P. C. LLOYD · *The Yoruba of Nigeria*

INTRODUCTION

In the savannas and forests that lie between the lower Niger and the Gulf of Guinea live the Yoruba, a people whose kingdoms are among the oldest in Africa, whose art treasures—the brasses and terra-cottas of Ife—are world-famous, a people whose traditional flowing robes, still cherished, make them so prominent in any international gathering.

Today the land of the Yoruba embraces the Western Region of Nigeria, where they form the dominant stock; the Yoruba emirate of Ilorin, together with the Kabba groups, are within the Northern Region, while scattered groups of Yoruba are found through Dahomey, even to northern Togo. It is, however, the Yoruba of Nigeria whom I shall describe in this chapter.

ECOLOGY · The ruined capital of the former empire of the Oyo Yoruba— Oyo Ile—lies nearly two hundred miles from the sea, far into the savanna region, in a countryside ecologically similar to that of the Hausa-Fulani emirate of Zaria. At the other extreme, Ode Ondo lies amid the tropical rain forests. Today the Yoruba live along the lagoons; they travel by canoe but are little interested in fishing. Lagos, the present federal capital of Nigeria—two thirds of whose people are Yoruba—has an annual rainfall of seventy-two inches; Ibadan, the regional capital, forty-eight inches; and Shaki, forty inches. The beginning of the rains, in March in Lagos and in April or May farther north, is heralded by terrific thunderstorms. Then follows a period of lighter rains and cool, cloudy months when the day temperatures do not exceed 83°F. Thunderstorms again mark the retreat of the rains in September–November. In the north of Yorubaland the dry season lasts for four months or more, with afternoon temperatures reaching 95°F. and night temperatures falling toward 50°F. only during the harmattan. The dry season is shorter nearer the coast. It is this climatic difference, together with the intensity of cultivation and the practice of firing the bush in the savanna areas, that determines the rather sharp transition from savanna to forest.

Most of Yoruba country lies on a denuded peneplain of ancient crystal-

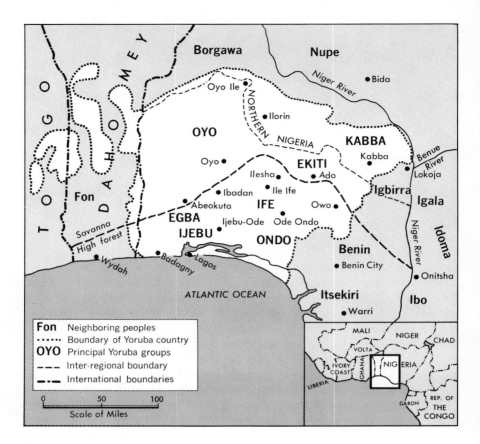

Sketch Map of Yoruba Tribal Distribution

line rocks. In the southwest, between Abeokuta and Ijebu Ode and the sea, run a series of sedimentary escarpments. Geological differences seem to have little influence on the natural vegetation, but cocoa and yams thrive only on soils derived from crystalline rocks. The country is gently undulating and, in the south, the forest restricts the view. From Shaki to the north of Ekiti, at a height of 1500–2000 feet, runs the watershed between the Niger and the seaward-flowing rivers, and here one finds a more striking scenery as huge bare granite inselbergs dominate the countryside. In the shelter of these hills are often found the most secure town sites.

In the crystalline country the rivers are choked with boulders and are quite unnavigable. Thus although there has been, for centuries, a considerable east-west movement along the shallow coastal lagoon, penetration of Yoruba country by canoe has been impossible. Sandbars occlude the only openings of the lagoon to the sea—at Lagos and Mahin—and the absence of any good natural harbor undoubtedly contributed to the lateness of European exploration of Yorubaland.

CULTURAL DIVERSITY AND LANGUAGE · The 6,000,000 Yoruba of Nigeria are divided among over fifty kingdoms, some twenty-two of which have a population exceeding 25,000. But, save in the myths of origin, there has been no time at which all the Yoruba are believed to have lived within a single political unit. The term "Yoruba," now used to describe all those who speak a common language, originally applied only to the people of the Oyo king-dom. There seems to have been no term used in the past by the Yoruba to designate themselves. Yoruba in Dahomey are sometimes called "Anago" and I have heard this word used in Ondo to describe the Yoruba language. The original use of other words designating Yoruba groups, such as Ulkami, is obscure. It seems likely that people were formerly designated, as they still are, by the name of their kingdom—Oyo, Ijebu, Ife, Ijesha, and so on.

The Yoruba language belongs to the Kwa group of Greenberg's Niger-Congo family (Greenberg 1955:10). The languages most nearly related are those of the Igala and Idoma, south of the Benue River.[1] In the past, dialects within Yoruba country were more marked; Bishop Samuel Crowther, native of Oyo, could scarcely understand the Lagos dialect in the 1820s and found difficulty in understanding the speech of the Egba and the Ijebu.

We have, in the Yoruba, an ancient people moving southward from the savanna into the forest. Immigrant groups and conquerors from without and interkingdom wars within have all contributed to produce a kaleido-scopic pattern of culture and structure, that seems to defy classification into three or four basic types. There are some very marked differences in the social and political structure of the various kingdoms. One could, I think, write a textbook on comparative political systems, drawing almost all one's examples from the Yoruba!

Yet there is a cultural uniformity among the various Yoruba groups that clearly differentiates them from their neighbors. Common language, dress, symbolism in chieftancy, and ritual unite them. This is even more evi-dent at the present time, when the educated have adopted a "basic Yoruba culture" devoid of most of its local peculiarities. This culture, together with legislation purporting to define a traditional social or political structure com-mon to all Yoruba, is creating a greater uniformity—paralleled by a similar process among some neighboring peoples. Thus the differences among neigh-boring peoples and the boundaries separating them are probably more starkly defined now than at any time in the past.

HISTORY

The Yoruba are a history-conscious people. At major festivals they chant the praises of their past kings, ascribing to their reigns events that are the charters for much of present-day behavior.

The creation myth describes how God let down a chain at Ile Ife by which Oduduwa—the ancestor of the Yoruba, and, indeed, of all men—descended, carrying a cock, some earth, and a palm kernel. He threw the earth into the waters, the cock scratched it to become land, and the palm grew with sixteen branches—representing the sixteen original kingdoms. An Oyo version describes Oduduwa as coming from the east and settling at Ile Ife, where he sired seven sons. To this, one must add Ife legends of an indigenous people being subdued or driven out by invaders. Thus in the several versions of this general origin myth one finds themes of creation and conquest. But every town and lineage and every deity has its own origin myth in which the legendary heroes appear and reappear in various roles. Nevertheless, in all of them, Ile Ife is regarded as the center from which all Yoruba dispersed to their present abodes, for the myths state that the town soon became so overcrowded with princes that on a given day all were dispatched to found their own kingdoms.

How kingship first came to the Yoruba we cannot tell—it may well have developed, as has been recorded among the northern Ibo in more recent centuries, with petty priest-rulers holding ritual sway over contiguous village groups. Artistic similarities seem to link the early Yoruba with the people of the iron age Nok culture—found between Jos and the Benue River and dated 900 B.C.–A.D. 200. Ile Ife seems to have become a very important center, with, at this time, perhaps, a highly developed art in terra-cotta and stone. Myths then suggest a later conquest of Ife—possibly in the thirteenth century—by men who established dynasties at Oyo and Benin. At the same time, perhaps, the art of brass casting by the *cire perdue* method was introduced, leading to the manufacture of the famous Ife brass heads in the same naturalistic style as contemporaneous terra-cotta heads. But these events are still largely speculation, for in the lateritic soils the archaeologist gets little stratification to help him date his finds.

We are on safer ground when we describe the rise of the empires of Benin and Oyo. Aided by guns brought by the Portuguese at the end of the fifteenth century, the Benin armies conquered as far afield as Idah on the Niger, and Ekiti. It seems possible that the present dynasties in Lagos, Ijebu, and Ondo derive from Benin princes or warriors. The empire went through alternate periods of expansion and quiescence, and the conquered territory seems never to have been closely or systematically administered.

Based on Oyo Ile, the Oyo empire quickly expanded when its rulers acquired the horse. It grew to control the major slave-trading route from the Niger to the coast at Badagry and Wydah, a route that avoided the dense forests. At the height of its power Oyo held the neighboring kingdoms as vassals. Today the Oyo people (found mainly in Ibadan and the large towns to the northeast, and in the Ilorin emirate) number over two million.

Between these two great empires lay a zone of small kingdoms, many numbering only a few thousand people. Some of these were of ancient foundation; others seem to have been created by rebels fleeing from the great kingdoms into the regions at their peripheries. The kingdom of Ijebu, however, whose present ruler is the fifty-second in succession from the founder of the dynasty (who himself supplanted earlier crowned rulers) seems to have remained isolated, protected on its north side from Oyo by the many little Egba kingdoms, and from Benin to the east by vast and almost uninhabited forests.

Imperial expansion led to the development of a complex system of government at Oyo. But it seems to have been an unstable one, perhaps because the traditional balance between king and chief was upset by the possession by one group or the other of large forces of slaves. At the end of the eighteenth century civil war broke out, Oyo rebels at Ilorin called on the Fulani for aid but the latter not only took control of Ilorin but steadily picked off all the other Oyo towns (seizing Oyo Ile in the mid-1830s), forcing the peoples southward into the towns along the forest margins—Iwo, Ede, Oshogbo and Ogbomosho, a new Oyo, and others. Ibadan was founded at this period; the indigenous Egba, whose kingdoms fought each other instead of cooperating, were pushed southwestward and they founded, at Abeokuta, a single kingdom whose peculiar federal system of government bears witness to the town's origin in the scores of little kingdoms.

The Ibadan armies, protected by the forest, held off further Fulani advance; in turn, they raided eastward for slaves that were absorbed into their own domestic economy. Intermittently they fought the Egba and the Ijebu, who controlled their routes to Lagos by which guns and gunpowder were imported. Finally, in the late 1880s, the various Yoruba kingdoms, through the mediation of consular officials and mission priests, signed treaties of peace with the British government, and the tribal wars were ended.

Legends say that the Portuguese once lived in Ijebu Ode but there is no documentary corroboration of this story. Clapperton and Lander were probably the first white men to penetrate Yoruba country when they traveled from Badagry to Oyo Ile in 1826. In the early 1840s Christian missionaries began to arrive, settling first at Badagry, then at Abeokuta, and later at Ibadan in the 1850s. But Islam had begun to gain a foothold in this area some decades earlier, especially in the Oyo kingdom and along the routes to the coast. It was not until the last decade of the century, however, that Christian mission activity reached Ijebu or Ekiti.

Lagos became a colony in 1861 as the British tried to stop the export of slaves. The hinterland was an area of British influence but it was not until 1901—after a flurry of treaty making in 1893—that Yoruba country became a British protectorate. In the administrative system imposed on the country British officials retained with remarkable exactitude the traditional boundaries

View of Ibadan (*Western Nigeria Information Service*)

of the Yoruba kingdoms, and, following Lugard's concepts of Indirect Rule, endeavored to give recognition to all indigenous rulers and their most important chiefs.

The Yoruba town

Yoruba towns are among Africa's curiosities, and have a long history. Ibadan has a population of 750,000 and seven others (excluding Lagos) have populations exceeding 100,000. The Yoruba have lived in towns as long as they can remember and despise their townless and kingless neighbors. The Portuguese mention Ijebu Ode as being a big town in the year 1505. It would seem probable that the metropolitan towns of the various kingdoms at this period were towns of 20,000–50,000 people. The vast size of Ibadan and its neighbors is the result of the nineteenth-century tribal wars that denuded the savannas of the old Oyo kingdom (where the present density of population is 50 per square mile) driving the refugees to the forest margins. Here, in Ibadan Province, 60 percent of the people live in towns of over 20,000 inhabitants; the density of population exceeds 350 persons per square mile.

These towns are not agglomerations of rural compounds, each surrounded by kitchen gardens, but dense aggregates of buildings housing 75 persons to the acre in the built-up areas. But within the old walls are vast open spaces; the town occupied but a fraction of the area so enclosed.

In the center of the town lies the palace, usually covering several acres. Within its large entrance courtyard are held many of the town's major ceremonies. The *oba* (king) and his family live in the small inner courtyards and here he sits with his chiefs. (Many rulers now have very modern palaces.) Behind the palace, enclosed by its walls, is an area of bush, the

Compounds in Igbetti

site of numerous shrines and royal graves. In front of the palace is the main marketplace from which roads once radiated through the town gates to the very much smaller subordinate towns of the kingdom.

Grouped around the palace are the compounds of the constituent patri-lineages of the town. In the past these were vast structures of rectangular courtyards, each with but a single entrance. Around each courtyard ran an open or a semienclosed porch where the women would sit, weave, and cook; behind this were the rooms of each adult. Facing the main gate was the porch of the compound head, often a titled chief. Today the old com-pounds are rapidly being replaced by modern cement-plastered bungalows with corrugated iron roofs, and two-story houses that tend to face the modern roads.

The Yoruba town had few public buildings in the past—some shrines and, among the Egba and the Ijebu, the meeting house of the *ogboni*, a political association. Today there are churches, mosques, the courthouse, and many local government offices.

Yet the Yoruba are predominantly farmers, and their towns are rural settlements. Ibadan was once termed a "city-village," for it has the size of a city but the structure of a village. A typical Yoruba town has 70 percent of its adult men engaged in farming, and 10 percent each as craftsmen and traders. The smaller subordinate towns of a kingdom usually have a slightly lower proportion of craftsmen and traders than has the metropolitan town. The farmlands of Ibadan extend for twenty miles from the town; those of a smaller town, say of 20,000 inhabitants, probably four or five miles. When the farm is so far from the town compound, a small hamlet is built at the farm; the houses there are never as well constructed as the town home. The farming population commutes between town and farm: some men come to the town only for major religious festivals; others go to the farm for the weekend. Chiefs must live in the town, and all marriages and funerals take place in the town compound. A man often has one wife with him at the farm, and another in the town. With the erection of schools and churches at the hamlets and the improvement of roads, many people now tend to live more at their farms.

Ibadan and Abeokuta each have over 3000 hamlets, but these towns are exceptional. Again the foregoing description is only partially true for Ijebu Ode and Ode Ondo. Rights to land in Ijebu and Ondo pass both in the male and the female line. The two capitals are surrounded by villages that are settlements of permanent residence (though not universally so in the latter kingdom). The towns are built on a grid pattern reminiscent of that of Benin, each compound being somewhat smaller and containing an extended family or a cognatic descent group.

ECONOMY

AGRICULTURE · Almost three quarters of the Yoruba men are farmers producing food crops for their domestic needs. In the forested areas, on soils derived from crystalline rocks, most farmers have some cocoa trees—most of the crop is produced by men with less than an acre of cocoa. The remaining Yoruba are traders, craftsmen, or men engaged in administration and the services, such as chiefs, teachers, clerks; most of these will have a small farm on their lineage land.

In farming, crafts, and trading, two features are pre-eminent: the differentiation of economic roles between the women and the men, and the lack of any large-scale economic units. With his unmarried sons, a farmer can cultivate about three acres of land annually. His tools are the simplest: the short-handled hoe, the ax (the former invariably and the latter usually made locally), and the imported machete.

In the beginning of the dry season the farmer clears the bush, lopping the branches of the smaller trees and burning them. He then makes heaps a yard apart and plants his yam sets. When the rains begin, he interplants early maize at the sides of the heaps, harvests it in June and plants late maize. The yams are harvested in October. In the second year he interplants a variety of crops: maize, peanuts, cotton, beans, cowpeas; and, in the third year, cassava (manioc). Each year, weeding is a major task in the wet season, although a cassava crop gets little attention.

After the cassava is harvested, the land reverts to fallow. The trees left on the land to support the yam vines soon branch out again and in a minimum of three years (but more often seven to ten in less densely farmed areas) the land is ready to cultivate again. The farmer is thus following a bush fallow rotation. The details naturally vary from one area to another; for instance, Guinea corn replaces maize in the savanna, and cassava is more important in the south.

A number of other crops grow without much attention: peppers, plantains, citrus fruits, kola nuts (especially south of Abeokuta, where they replace cocoa as the main export crop), and the oil palm, which is protected but almost never deliberately planted. The Yoruba farm is a tangled growth of crops and fallow!

Young men sometimes form a small group and work on each other's farms in turn. Wealthy men can call their friends together, provide drummers and a big feast, and set them all to work for a day, but there are no landless men obliged to hire themselves out for wages. Some casual labor is done by young Yoruba needing a little ready cash, but most of the laborers employed on Yoruba farms are men from Sokoto or Igbirra country.

Women do no farm work at all. As housewives they visit their husband's farms to collect firewood and wild fruits and leaves and perhaps to help to harvest the maize. If they help to harvest a crop that is not for domestic consumption—cotton, for instance—they will be given a proportion of it as their wages. The women are usually responsible for the livestock that run in the compound; most of them have poultry and a few sheep and goats. The latter are bought and sold as a form of savings. In the hamlets women make gari (a flour prepared from cassava) and palm oil, or they crack palm kernels, selling the greater part of the produce. If a woman uses her husband's crop she buys it from him; the men do not like their wives to market their surplus: "They would cheat us," they say.

CRAFTS · The traditional crafts of the men include weaving on the horizontal loom (found in Oyo), blacksmithing, and woodcarving. Modern crafts include tailoring of men's garments (with treadle sewing machines), shoemaking, carpentry, and building. In each case, the tools are simple enough for each man to own a set. The traditional crafts are hereditary within the lineage, a father teaching his sons. All members shared a common workplace; the lineage meeting regulated prices and the terms of work. The modern craftsman, who is usually illiterate or semiliterate, learned his craft as an apprentice to a master unrelated to him. The organization of these crafts resembles that of medieval guilds. Most of these craftsmen make goods to their customers' orders.

There is little entrepreneurial activity to be found among the Yoruba. The modern building contractor employs carpenters and mudwall builders to work with him on a specific building. At Iseyin, a town with 2000 weavers, wealthy traders supply the weavers with yarn, paying them piece rates, then

A Market Scene (*Western Nigerian Information Service*)

hand the cloth to traditional tailors and embroiderers, and finally market the finished gowns in Ibadan or Lagos. But this economic organization seems to be unique.

The traditional crafts for a woman are pottery, spinning, dyeing, and weaving—on the vertical loom—cloth that is twenty inches wide and is made into women's wrappers, men's covering cloths, and farming tunics. A woman's pots and cloths are usually sold in the market. Today, the educated women sew (with a hand sewing machine) dresses for members of their own sex and for children.

MARKETS • The Yoruba enjoy trading, and huge markets with over a thousand sellers are a common sight. Yoruba traders are conspicuous as far afield as Accra and Abidjan, Bamako and Ouagadougou. The nineteenth-century travelers reported meeting large caravans of traders passing from one region of Nigeria to another; today, the collection of the export crops and the distribution of goods imported by sea are both important. There is also an extensive trade in local foodstuffs: men who do not farm must buy all such food in the markets; other families in the town usually have to buy some to offset the irregular supply from the farm.

The marketing process is complex. One woman visits a farmer on his land and buys a headload of yams; she sells these to a second woman in a small rural market. Then, at a larger rural market—held every four days—the latter sells to a woman wholesaler from the town, who later resells to women who will sit in the town's night market (among the Oyo) and sell to the consumers. In a similar manner, imported goods travel from the warehouses of the expatriate firm to the rural consumer. Most four- or eight-day markets are held in cycles, the women visiting each in turn. Trade in food-stuffs and in cloth is confined to women; meat selling and produce buying (the purchasing of export crops—cocoa and oil palm kernels) are the province of men. The traders in each commodity are organized in an association very similar to the craft guild.

A farmer can become prosperous by working hard, by enjoying good health, and by being blessed with many sons. Today only a few men have enough capital to establish large cocoa farms worked by hired labor. But by trading an astute man can become very rich. In the past there were noted traders; today the produce buyers, the building contractors, and the truck owners are a town's wealthiest men, enjoying the highest prestige. In the past, this wealth was spent on luxuries—houses, clothing, and the acquisition of wives who, by bearing many children, ensured the extreme fragmentation of the deceased trader's estate. Today modern houses and cars are in vogue, and every man hopes to send a son to study in England. Business profits are rarely invested in manufacturing industry. There seems to be a limit to the business capacity of a simple trader, and partnerships among the Yoruba are uncommon.

The less wealthy save money through the *esusu* club, in which each member pays a fixed sum each week or month, taking the whole sum collected, in his turn. Loans are freely given and men are beginning to pledge their houses as security, though this practice raises a number of legal issues. The pawning of cocoa farms is common. Thus it is fairly easy for all but the few desperately poor to raise a small capital sum.

Wealth confers great prestige on a man, and popularity if he is generous to his friends and relatives. In fact, where trader and customer enjoy a face-to-face relationship, popularity is essential to business success. The wealthy man usually aspires to political office—to take the highest chieftaincy title open to him—and, today, he is generally successful. The asceticism characterized in the Protestant ethic is conspicuously absent in most Yoruba traders.

SOCIAL ORGANIZATION

I have already mentioned the diversity in the social and political structure of the Yoruba kingdom and it seems appropriate that, at this point, I should confine my description to a single kingdom. I have selected Ado, one of the twenty independent kingdoms in the eastern part of Yorubaland, known collectively as Ekiti.

The agnatic lineages of Ado are structurally similar to those of most of the northern Yoruba kingdoms; Ijebu and Ondo, with their cognatic descent groups, are distinctive. Chieftaincy titles are gained in a number of ways. In Ado, as in most northern Yoruba kingdoms, they tend to be hereditary within the lineage. Elsewhere they are gained through title associations, such as the

Egba *ogboni*, or chiefs are selected by the *oba*, as in Ondo. Ibadan, with its system of ladder promotion to the highest titles, Abeokuta with its federal constitution, Oyo with its highly developed palace organization, and the Kabba groups without kingship are all variants.

Ado is a town of 25,000 people; rather, it is three towns acknowledging a single ruler. I shall describe only the largest of these—Oke Ewi, with 16,000 inhabitants. Today Ado is an administrative and commercial center, but 65 percent of its men are still farmers. Two thirds of its people are Christians, one fifth are Muslims. In the nineteenth century the town was raided by Ibadan for slaves. Today it is anxious to shake off the stigma of inferiority. Cocoa was first extensively grown in the 1930s and the high prices after the war brought prosperity. Even before the introduction of free primary education in 1954, 70 percent of the Ado children attended school. However, this wealth and "enlightenment" is of very recent growth.

A visitor to the town half a century ago would have found the large rambling compounds grouped around the palace. Today few of these remain, but the modern houses replacing them are nearly all built on the land of the owner's lineage. Thus, although the buildings continually change, the compound still remains as a territorial and social unit.

The lineage

In the compound live the men who are descended in the male line from the lineage founder, together with their wives and children. There are usually also some unrelated strangers. Oke Ewi has nearly twenty such lineages, some of them numbering over 1000 persons.

The corporate identity of the lineage is instanced in a number of ways. First, the members live together. The lineage myths tell how the founder— who is usually placed in the current and foreshortened genealogies about four generations above living elders—left his home town; a dispute over a title is often cited, the founder being the loser. Founders of many Ado lineages seem to have come from the east in what is now Akoko District, probably in the eighteenth century. Arriving in Ado, the immigrant and his group of kin were welcomed by the *Ewi*, the king of Ado, and, say the myths, were granted land in the town for their compound and outside for their farms. The *Ewi* also bestowed a chieftaincy title on the head of the group—the lineage founder. In their new home the immigrants continued to worship a deity from their original home, a deity thus peculiar (in the new home) to the lineage. All the lineages in Ado (except the royal lineage) are equal in status, though those with the more senior chieftaincy titles carry greater prestige. The myths thus serve as a charter for each lineage, defining its position in the town.

Lineage members in Ado cannot be identified by any facial marks peculiar to them (as in Oyo), though the royal lineage has exclusive body marking. Each lineage has a pair of names, one for each sex, by which its members are addressed or hailed in the street. Lineage members share a common food taboo; the myths sometimes ascribe this taboo to the worship of a particular deity, at other times to a historical event—the animal concerned is said to have once saved the lineage. The Ado lineage is usually named after the chieftaincy title it holds.

It is, perhaps, easier to understand the structure of the lineage if we look first at the patterns of inheritance. When a man dies, his statuses and rights in respect to his property pass to his heirs. Some of these rights he will have acquired in his own lifetime: rights in wives, in land purchased, or in a house built by himself. Other rights will have been inherited: rights in lineage land in general, in a part of the traditional compound, or in a chieftaincy title. Some property, money for instance, may be divided among the heirs—though the Ekiti do not often partition land, for it has no scarcity or market value; other types of property may be held corporately, such as the deceased's cocoa farm worked by all his sons; others, such as a title, can be held only by a number of persons in turn.

At a man's death his nearest elder relative—an elder brother or the father's brother, or, failing these, his eldest son—acts as executor, arranging the funeral and distributing the property. But the Yoruba are adamant that no man can ever inherit from a person younger than himself. The heirs thus fall into two groups—the deceased's younger brothers, led by the most senior among them, and his sons, led by the eldest. The eldest son becomes head of the new segment of the lineage—the issue of the deceased; the junior brother takes the place of the deceased in the next ascending segment, acting *in loco patris* to the deceased's children. The differentiation of these two statuses does not clarify all the problems of inheritance. Broadly, a man's self-acquired land or house passes to his sons. But his status with respect to property he has inherited from his own father passes to his junior brother. A man's sons will continue to farm where their father did; as they married, he gave them part of his own land until, in his old age, none remained. But part of the deceased's assets in cash and clothing are given to his junior brothers and, perhaps, sisters.

That property which passes to the children is divided into as many equal parts as the man had wives with children. Nothing may pass to the wife herself, though mothers are vigilant on their children's behalf. *Omoiya* (children of the same mother) share equally irrespective of their number; the children of a concubine receive as if their mother were a wife. Some property can be equally divided, other types, such as the house, are held corporately, and a hereditary chieftaincy title bestowed on the deceased is held by one son from each *omoiya* in turn. Children of the same mother are supposed to cooperate closely and not divide property rigidly among themselves, but competition and rivalry exist among *omoiya*.

This short analysis brings out two important concepts: first, corporate or, as the Yoruba call it, family property. Just as a man's self-acquired land and house become the corporate property of his sons and all subsequent agnatic descendants from the time of their birth, so are the rights held to have been granted to the lineage founder held to be the corporate property of all lineage members. Second, although the segmentation of the polygynous family is overtly not repeated in each ascending generation (for there is no division of property at these levels) it is seen again at the apex of the lineage genealogy. The lineage founder is said to have had sons by two, three, four, or five wives, one of each group being the founder of the major segments into which the lineage is divided. Each segment ought to hold the chieftaincy title in turn; and if usufruct or ownership of lineage land is ever divided, it is between these segments that the partition is made. It seems that genealogies can be adjusted, probably during the foreshortening process, so that each segment has approximately equal membership, thus giving each member a similar opportunity to hold the title or land.

Let us return to the structure of the lineage. All members are ranked strictly according to age. A man terms his elder siblings and collaterals, irrespective of sex, *egbon*; his juniors, *aburo*. Father and mother are *baba* and *iya*, respectively; the same terms are used, according to sex, for one's parents' siblings, who can be further distinguished according to whether they are senior or junior to one's parent. Grandparents are *baba'gba* and *iya'gba;* children are *omo*. The Yoruba kinship terminology is extraordinarily simple, being based on relative age in one's own generation, on sex and age in ascending generations. The terms used for near kin are used alike for lineage and nonlineage members; thus any man of one's father's age is addressed as *baba*, an older member of one's own age group as *egbon*, any child as *omo*.

The Ado lineage is a corporate body because its members have certain interests in common. And it is these interests that the lineage meets to discuss: to settle disputes among competing groups within the lineage, to preserve the rights of the lineage from encroachment by other lineages. Lineage members meet regularly, often after Sunday church service in Ado, in the house of the oldest male member, the lineage head. Members speak, generally, in ascending order of their age, the lineage head announcing the conclusions of the group.

Domestic issues are prominent: the settlement of family quarrels, the arrangement of marriages and funerals. All lineage members have, by virtue of their birth, a general right to as much farm and house land as they need, and a specific right to undisturbed occupation of that already allocated to them. The lineage meeting allocates land to members, and, today, often alienates it to nonmembers. Certain usufructuary rights, to the oil palms, for instance, are often reserved to the lineage head. But in matters of allocation and alienation, the lineage head can act only with the authority of the whole lineage; unanimity is presumed in all decisions. The lineage meeting hears disputes among lineage members over the areas of land allocated to them, and takes legal action when members of other lineages holding adjacent land trespass and claim the land that they clear as being that of their own lineage. The lineage is also the electoral body for its hereditary chieftaincy title, as we shall see below.

Associations

In the past, a system of age grades and sets flourished in Ekiti towns. Sets were formed at three-year intervals and continued in existence from adolescence until the death of all members. Full brothers could not belong to the same set. Membership was automatic and universal throughout the town. Meetings were held weekly and were similar in nature to those of the modern *egbe* (see below). The five age grades were of nine-year intervals and designated a young man's public duties in the town. The youngest grade, 0–9 years, did no work. The next grade weeded the roads, and the two highest grades provided the warriors. At the age of forty-five a man became an elder and was exempt from manual public work. These traditional duties are now obsolete and the grades are becoming forgotten in Ado and most other towns. The age sets are replaced by the modern *egbe*.

The *egbe* is a group of men of approximately the same age, probably from the same quarter of the town, who decided voluntarily, at adolescence, to form an association. Most youths do join an *egbe*. Membership continues for life but, once the members become middle-aged, the intensity of their participation often declines and they may form new groups with more recently won friends. A respected elder is invited to be the patron of the *egbe*, but other offices are filled by election among the members. The *egbe* gives a young man a good opportunity to demonstrate his qualities of leadership long before he seeks political office.

At their weekly meetings the *egbe* members drink and discuss their personal problems. For example, a youth will take his troubles over a girl to his *egbe* rather than to his parents or his lineage meeting. Indeed, at this age, a youth will usually give attendance at a meeting of his *egbe* priority over a lineage meeting. Absence or lateness is often punished by a fine. Annually the *egbe* holds a dance, all the members wearing identical cloth; members also attend each other's personal ceremonies: a funeral of near kin, marriage, the naming ceremony of a child.

The *egbe* upholds the norms of society by sitting in judgment on any member who has erred; the castigation of one's fellows and possible expulsion from the *egbe* is usually feared more than the punishment of parents or the customary court. The *egbe* is thus an important instrument of social control during that period when a youth has ceased to be a child, closely subject to parental control, but has not reached full maturity as a married and responsible member of his lineage.

In addition to the strictly secular *egbe*, the congregations of the several churches in Ado are also divided into associations based on age, sex, and marital status, on residence, and sometimes on wealth. Members of these associations meet for Bible study; they also collect contributions for the harvest festival, when the group decides on the sum to be raised and then allocates a share to each member. These church associations also fulfill many of the purposes of the *egbe* in maintaining the social norms of the society.

Credit organizations, such as the *esusu*, were described above (see p. 559).

Marriage

A man may not marry any woman of his own lineage, nor of the lineages of any of his great-grandparents. In the past, he could not marry from a lineage bearing the same taboos or appellations as his own, for such implied descent from a common, if forgotten, ancestor. Today, however, relationship is held proved only by the current genealogies. There are no forms of preferred cousin marriage among any Yoruba. Most men find their wives from their own town, or from neighboring towns within their kingdom.

Parents are deeply involved in a man's first marriage. It is becoming less common for a male to be betrothed to a young girl while both are children, but a man still expects his father to help him to find the money for the marriage payment. Parental views on the suitability of the chosen girl, expressed in terms of the health and moral character of her own family, still tend to outweigh the selection of the young man based, perhaps, on physical attraction. After betrothal a man must not only give presents to his future wife, but also help her father on his farm or when he builds a house, and contribute to any important funeral of the future wife's near kin.

The wedding ceremony usually takes place when the girl is from sixteen to eighteen years old, and the man in his middle or late twenties. At this point, the man makes a payment, now in cash, to the girl's parents. There is no fixed amount, and from £10 to £30 is common. Part of this sum is kept by the mother to buy pots and utensils for the new home. The rest is shared among the members of the girl's lineage.

Marriage gives the man a right to his wife's domestic labor, to sole sexual access to her (a husband can claim damages from an adulterer), and rights to all children born to her during the marriage. The man, of course, is sexually free and may contract other marriages; children born to concubines may inherit from him if he recognizes them as his own and if they act as sons at his funeral. No reliable figures exist of the degree of polygyny among the Yoruba; most men aspire to have several wives. One survey, however, suggests that Yoruba men who have reached the state of marriage have an average of two wives each; one third have only one wife at any given time, one third have two and one third have three or more wives. The disparity in the age of marriage of men and women produces a greater number of adult women than of men who are of marriageable age, thus facilitating polygyny.

Today, divorce is frequent, though the Yoruba say that it was rare in the past (perhaps because it was easier then than now for a powerful and wealthy polygynist to victimize the seducer of one of his wives). In Ekiti, 3.5 percent of extant marriages seem to be broken in any one year; but many divorces seem to involve young, childless women, a corollary perhaps of the extreme stigma attaching to barrenness. When a divorce is imminent, the woman secretly moves to her lover's home and immediately sues her husband for divorce. This the customary court almost invariably grants (for she will have been living with her lover for several weeks or months before the case is heard). The woman must repay all or a portion of the marriage payment, depending on its amount and the length of her marriage, together with the cost of all such substantial gifts from the husband and his various contributions to her parents as he can prove before the court. Little stigma attaches to divorce, and it is not uncommon for a man to seduce his childhood sweetheart after she has been married to the man of her parents' choice. He repays to the husband whatever sum the court orders. A woman is allowed to keep her small children with her after her divorce, but after they are seven years old the father may claim them; at this age a boy begins to accompany his father to the farm. A child conceived for the lover, before the divorce action is taken, is held to belong to the lineage of the husband, though most lovers seek custody of their own offspring and husbands are reluctant to care for the children of other men.

Death of the husband does not end the marriage. His marital rights over his wife pass to a junior brother or to a son, other than her own, who can maintain her together with her children. If she does not like the heir she must divorce him. Women who are past childbearing are usually maintained by their own children and the heir's duties are nominal; often such women return to their own compound to live.

The Yoruba wife's status is characterized by great overt submission to her husband together with considerable economic independence. Her seniority in her husband's compound is determined by the date of her marriage. She is junior to all men born before this date and calls them "Husband" if they are her husband's collaterals, or calls them by a nickname if they are small; they reciprocally call her "Wife" or address her by the name of her children, for example, "Mother of ———." Each wife has her own room in the compound, where she sleeps with her young children and keeps her private property. The husband has his own room, where the wives visit him. Husband and wife do not eat together; she serves his food on bended knee. Most domestic roles are strictly segregated.

A wife participates in the meetings and rituals of her husband's lineage and observes his food taboos while pregnant. But she retains her membership in her own lineage and often takes her children to its meetings. A husband's behavior toward his in-laws is very formal. He prefers not to sleep at his wife's home. Although he uses the normal kin terms in addressing the members of his wife's lineage, he raises their seniority; thus any brother-in-law is an "elder brother."

As we have already seen, the woman works independently of her husband, though she expects him to give her an initial sum to start her trade or craft; her profits, however, are her own. Most women earn enough to buy their own clothes, although they expect presents from their husbands. Very many provide from their own money some of the food used in the household and a good proportion—perhaps a fifth—are financially independent of their husbands, buying all their own food and clothing. On her death, a woman's children inherit from her, or if she has no children, the nearest relatives in her own lineage. Husband and wife can never inherit from each other. Many women are wealthier than their husbands—though the men do not like to be told so. Women are more likely to invest their profits in house property or further trading, whereas a man spends his in achieving political office. A woman's public status is determined not so much by that of her husband as by her own position in her market guild or social club.

Many writers describe the African marriage payment as creating for the wife a status of near slavery, and literate Yoruba sometimes adopt the same usage. Yet the overt submissiveness of the Yoruba wife to her husband is perhaps the corollary of her great economic independence and her freedom to secure divorce.

CHILD TRAINING AND SOCIALIZATION

Every wife expects her husband to sleep with her frequently so that she may conceive. But once she knows that she is pregnant she will not have sexual intercourse until her child is weaned, that is, for a period of two or three years. A woman may go to her mother to deliver her child and stay there for several months. The child is named on the eighth day after its birth; the umbilical cord is buried in the father's compound (and in Oyo the father arranges to have his own facial marks cut on the child's cheeks). Circumcision and clitoridectomy are simple surgical operations performed in youth without any ritual.

In the polygynous home, ties of close affection bind mother and child.

Each wife cooks for her own children, though co-wives take turns cooking for their husband. Mothers indulge the children with delicacies. A man is expected to treat each wife equally and not according to the number of her children; each wife expects to clothe and educate at least some of her children. The mothers compete to gain additional favors for their own children, and to protect them from undue punishment. The father is distant and authoritarian, often seeing little of his children if he is at the farm and they are at school. Wishing that his sons should achieve at least the same status as his, and believing that such a status is the result of obedience to norms and hard work, he flogs his children, often viciously, for their misdeeds. Older siblings similarly discipline the younger ones. Thus a youth often stands in as much awe of a much older brother as of his father.

Grandparents are indulgent and the mother's kin are kindly disposed toward the children, but there seem to be (outside the polygynous family) no relationships of excessive affection or hostility, no joking relationships or special attachments, as, for instance, to the mother's brother.

POLITICAL ORGANIZATION

THE KINGSHIP • Ado is governed by the *Ewi*, the *oba* or king, and his councils of chiefs. Myths tell how the first *Ewi* left Ile Ife at the time of the dispersion of the princes and traveled to Benin with his elder brother, the *oba* of Benin; here the brothers quarreled, so the *Ewi* retraced his steps, settling at Ado, where he met some indigenous people who, because of his royal origin, accepted him as their ruler. Myths of some neighboring towns, however, suggest that the first *Ewi* in Ado was a prince of Idoani, a town on the marches of the Benin kingdom, who had unsuccessfully contested the throne. The essence of the myth is that the *Ewi* "founded" Ado; the other lineages in the town came later. Since all Yoruba believe themselves to be descended from Oduduwa, there is no royal clan, but in each town the descendants of the founder *oba* constitute the royal lineage of that town, being described as *omo oba*—children of the king.

The *Ewi* is the personification of his town; the Yoruba say that no town could exist without its *oba*, for the lineages would start fighting among themselves and so destroy the unity of the settlement. The wealth of the *oba* and his palace symbolize the prosperity of the town. And this prosperity was, in the past, thought to be due to the *Ewi*'s proper attention to the ritual.

Many attributes of divine or sacred kingship are held by the Yoruba *oba*. In the past the *Ewi*'s wives worked naked to prepare his food; he is never seen eating in public. He might seize any woman as wife, and adultery with such a woman was treason. He appeared in public on very few occasions, usually on the days of the town's major ceremonies. Then he was heavily veiled by his conical beaded crown and surrounded by his servants

A Yoruba *Oba* (Western
Nigerian Information Service)

holding fans and umbrellas. The present *Ewi* is, however, a comparatively
highly educated man and a prominent member of the Western Region House
of Chiefs. He travels widely. But he appears in public only in the most
voluminous gowns and his people still prostrate themselves before him as he
moves with the dignity of a ruler.

The right to the throne is held corporately by the royal lineage—that is,
the agnatic descendants of the first *Ewi*, but only few members are eligible for
the kingship. The royal lineage is now segmented into two ruling houses
that alternately provide the *Ewi*. On the death of one *oba*, the elders of the
other ruling house put forward as candidates men who were born to a
previous *Ewi* of their own house during his reign (that is, born on the
throne), have free-born mothers, and are free from physical blemish. These
names are submitted to the *Ihare* (the senior chiefs), who consult the *ifa*
oracle as to the nature of the reign of each man, should he be selected. They
also use their personal judgment about the character of each man, and perhaps, heed popular opinion (though in the past this was rarely expressed
overtly). Making their selection, the chiefs set in train the long and complex
installation ceremonies.

The installation and the burial of an *oba* both involve most of the
lineages of the town, each of which has a jealously guarded rite to perform
that symbolizes the participation of the lineage in the kingship of the town.

The Ado installation ceremonies follow a general pattern common to
most Yoruba kingdoms. The *Ewi* is seized by a group of young men and taken
to the bush, where he is taught how to rule his town. He travels back to
Ado along the route taken by the first *Ewi*, and to the compound of the
original inhabitants, where he promises to rule well. He is clad in rags,
beaten, and then robed in white and given a new name. He remains secluded

in a compound opposite the palace gates for three months before his corona-
tion and entry into the palace. In the past the Yoruba *oba* ate the excised
heart of his predecessor, thus assuming all his mystic strength; this seems to
have represented the consecration of the ruler. It was believed that a man
who was not a legitimate candidate for the throne would die if he underwent these rites, but proper installation enabled the new *oba* to withstand
the potency of all the magic charms incorporated in the royal regalia from
past ages.

The royal lineage is ranked, in prestige, *below* all the other lineages of the
town. Its members may hold no chieftaincy title giving political power. They
have no privileged access to the *oba*—not even his brothers may freely visit
him. No large tracts of land are the corporate property of the lineage—most
land is held by the nonroyal lineages. The new *oba* takes no wealth to the
throne with him—his property rights pass to his brothers; but everything acquired during his reign passes intact on his death to his successor in office.
By customary law nothing may be distributed among the children of the
oba, though educated rulers today do find means to provide for their own
issue by investing privately in house building.

The *oba* always has more wives than any other man in the town, and
a correspondingly greater number of children. Why, then, does the royal
lineage not outnumber the rest of the town, for we presume it to have
existed for three centuries? It is noticeable in Ado that few men claim
descent from early *Ewis*—and these tend to be members of lineages now
considered independent; most of those claiming to be *omo oba* trace their
descent from recent rulers. Where are the descendants of the earlier *obas*?
It would seem that in the past, influential princes were sent to rule subordinate towns in the kingdom or to found their own little settlements that
might later grow into towns. Less important men became absorbed into
their mother's lineages, for a royal wife could not deliver her child in the
palace and so usually went to her father's compound. Here her sons grew
up and often continued to live, being granted land by the lineage elders.
It seems likely that in four or five generations their royal birth was forgotten
and that they henceforth appeared in the genealogies as the children of the
father of the royal wife. This, of course, applies only to those who did not
ascend the throne. Each Ado lineage relates with pride the names of its
female members who bore an *Ewi*. Ado has no institutionalized office of
queen mother.

THE CHIEFS · There are three grades of chief in Oke Ewi—the *Ihare,
Ijoye,* and *Elegbe* title holders. Of the *Ihare* chiefs the most senior are the
olori marun (five heads), each of whose titles is hereditary in one of the
largest lineages of the town. Some of the lower *Ihare* titles are held by the
smaller lineages; others may be bestowed on any person by the *oba* and

the chiefs. In less structurally complex Ekiti towns, each lineage holds a major hereditary title, the minor titles being distributed among the lineages equitably.

Titles that are hereditary are the corporate property of the lineage members, who elect the new chief. The title should be held by a member of each segment in turn. Although a son of a previous chief is often a prominent candidate through his association with his father during the latter's period of office, the title is open to all lineage members and—failing a suitable candidate—to sons of women of the lineage. The *oba* and other chiefs may interfere in this election only to ensure that the new chief is the unanimous choice of the lineage. The *oba* accepts the victorious candidate and, with considerable ceremony, bestows the title upon him.

Of the *Ijoye* titles, only the most senior is hereditary within a lineage; most of the twenty-two titles remembered are now vacant. Similarly, most titles in the *Elegbe* grade are also vacant. It seems probable that in the past each lineage held one or two of these titles, some in fact being reserved for members of the royal lineage. These *Elegbe* chiefs seem to have been associated with the administrative organization of the age grades.

These are the personnel of the government of Ado.

THE PROCESS OF GOVERNMENT • The government of the *Ewi* and his chiefs is sovereign: it is concerned with the public affairs of the people of the town. We may describe its duties as the maintenance of peace and order within Ado and the preservation of the integrity of the town and kingdom against its neighbors. Within Ado disputes among lineages over rights in land or over titles are brought to the *oba* and the chiefs. Usufructuary rights in farm land are allocated within the lineage, but the *oba* may control the use of land, such as the firing of the bush. In the nineteenth century, the *Ewi* and the chiefs made war on neighboring towns, and defended their own town from invasion. Today they protect the boundaries of their territory against trespassing farmers from adjoining kingdoms.

In the past the political opinions of the mass of the people were expressed in the meetings of their age sets and lineages and transmitted by the more junior chiefs to the senior *Ihare*. These men, sitting on the palace veranda and speaking in order of seniority, made the ultimate decisions, and one of their number, entitled to enter the private apartments of the palace, would convey them to the *oba*, who ordained these decisions, his royal "ban" giving them the highest authority and attaching to their violation the most severe penalties.

The royal commands were announced in the streets by the palace messengers and to the lineages by their chiefs. Execution of the decisions rested with these junior chiefs—the *Ijoye* organizing activities on a lineage basis, the *Elegbe* those that were carried out by the age grades.

In Ado, public work was performed by the age grades, the more senior of which also provided the warriors. But an army organized in this way seems to have been effective only in defense. In the nineteenth century Ado's offensive campaigns were usually led by self-styled war leaders, with armies composed often of refugees from intertribal fighting who owed but slight obedience to the *Ewi* and his chiefs and constituted, in fact, a threat to their rule.

The costs of government were borne, in the past, by levies and tribute, by judicial fines and fees, and by war booty. Tribute, usually in the form of yams and other foodstuffs, was payable annually by every man at one of the major religious festivals. It was collected by the lineage head and trans-mitted to the chief of the lineage and thus to the *oba*. Levies for special purposes—to buy firearms, for instance (or, today, to fight a land dispute) —were similarly collected. Lineage heads and chiefs each kept a fraction of what they collected as their own perquisite. Any man who had a problem to raise with the *oba* could not visit him directly but had to seek the media-tion of junior and senior chiefs, who would take a part of the gift destined for the *oba*. Of slaves and other booty seized in war the captor might keep one third, giving one third to his chief and one third to the *oba*.

The net result of this flow of tribute and booty was that the *oba* was approximately equal in wealth to all his chiefs together. But the wealth of the *oba* remained intact at his death, passing entirely to his successor on the throne. The wealth of a chief, on the other hand, was distributed among his heirs—his junior brothers and children—according to the customary rules of inheritance. The wealth thus benefited the lineage as a whole but no particular member of it; each segment benefited when it held the title. Similarly, the numerous wives of the senior chief were distributed among the heirs, while those of the *Ewi* passed to his successor. This system thus enhanced the wealth of the throne against that of the chiefs as individuals; it also contributed to the growth in size and power of those lineages having the most senior titles at the expense of the smaller lineages and, probably, the royal lineage.

Government in Ado was, in the past, characterized by the conflicts and rivalry among the constituent lineages of the town, expressed in the context of land, titles, and wealth; but there was also a conflict between the *oba* and his chiefs—the royal and the nonroyal lineages. The Yóruba believe that government is vested in the chiefs, representing the nonroyal lineages of the town; the *oba* should accept the decisions of the chiefs who have selected him to reign. But many an *oba* was not content to assume such a passive role. The *oba* had no control of an army and no police force (except a few palace servants) by which he could coerce the chiefs. But he could easily divide his chiefs against each other. For example, he could decree that one title should become hereditary within a lineage, or abolish another title.

He might forbid a chief to enter the palace, thus preventing him from participating in the government of the town. Often, when the chiefs conspired against their *oba*, one or more would secretly betray the plot to the *oba*, hoping that they would gain greater favors from him than they would receive as the result of a successful rebellion.

The chiefs, for their part, were better able to coerce their *oba* if they could but combine. They could boycott the palace, thus governing without the *oba*. And as a last resort they could ask their *oba* to die; he would then take poison. Yet, although this is recognized as a legitimate procedure by the Yoruba, deposition seems to have remained a rare occurrence in most towns; and there is no record that any *Ewi* of Ado was ever deposed. For, though the *oba* alone lacked the physical force to ensure obedience to his commands, his power lay in his sacred right to rule: he was the "consecrated" *oba*. The Yoruba believe that the *oba*, legitimate and properly installed, would almost inevitably rule to the benefit of his people, and rebellion by the chiefs could often be interpreted not as an action in the interest of the lineages but as a move for the personal aggrandizement of the chiefs. The *oba* could thus speak for his people against their own chiefs.

THE KINGDOM • Ado is the metropolitan town of the kingdom; subordinate to the *Ewi* are seventeen smaller towns. Their total population—35,000— exceeds that of Ado, but the largest of them has only 6000 inhabitants. This great disparity in size seems to be typical of Yoruba kingdoms; the capital maintains its position by sheer weight of numbers. The farthest of these towns is twenty-five miles from Ado.

The structure of each of these subordinate towns is quite similar to that of the capital. Each has its own ruler whose position vis-à-vis his own people is similar to that of the *Ewi* in Ado. But the subordinate ruler may not be termed an *oba* nor wear a beaded crown or other paraphernalia of royalty, and his appointment (by his own chiefs) must be ratified by the *Ewi*.

Each town has its own myths of origin similar to those of Ado. In some cases the town claims to antedate Ado and in these there are persistent attempts at secession, with the ruler surreptitiously—and indeed openly on occasions—wearing a beaded crown. Such attempts, of course, are bitterly resented in Ado; yet some towns won their independence during the period of colonial rule, and the towns at the eastern end of the kingdom have recently gained a district council of their own, separate from that of the rest of the kingdom. However, other towns are ruled by men claiming descent from Ado princes. In the past a Yoruba *oba* never left his own town and when a prince was installed as ruler in a subordinate town, he was not allowed to revisit the capital. He founded a new lineage and never claimed any political rights in the town of his origin. It was, in fact, rare in the past for the rulers of the subordinate Ado towns to visit the *Ewi*, though now the more educated officeholders do so. Some of these men have important rites to perform at the installation or the burial of an *oba* (thus symbolically linking their towns to Ado). In one case, the ruler may never see the *Ewi* face to face, a rule still upheld today in Ado, with the result that the subordinate ruler cannot play his role in the local government council.

Each subordinate town has a large measure of internal independence. In the past its rulers could not punish a man with death. The foreign policy of the kingdom was controlled by the *Ewi* and his chiefs of the capital. Even today the *Ewi* expects to be notified of grants of land in subordinate towns to men of neighboring kingdoms: if the boundary of the kingdom is disputed, it is the *Ewi* who must contest the suit, though the people of the subordinate town will be expected to be active in the defense of their land.

There is no supreme council of the *Ewi* and the rulers, or their representatives, of the subordinate towns. Each of the five senior *Ihare* chiefs of Ado is responsible for a number of towns—usually those along the road leading out of Ado past his own compound. Tribute was brought to this chief, who carried it to the palace (minus his own perquisite). Any dispute in the subordinate town is brought before the overlord chief who, if he cannot settle it himself, raises it in the palace with his co-chiefs. The subordinate towns have no part in the selection of their overlord chief nor, of course, of the *Ewi*.

In this section I have discussed the traditional government of the Ado. In the present century two new structures have been superimposed—first the Native Authority and later the local government council—in both of which the *Ewi* and his more senior chiefs have held offices. In a later section I shall describe the changing roles of these traditional officeholders at the present time. Yet, inasmuch as the colonial system of native administration endeavored to preserve the traditional patterns of government, and economic changes have not destroyed the Yoruba lineage, much of the traditional government of Ado continues to the present day. The age grades are now defunct: they have no duties to perform. Most of those chieftaincy titles, the role of which was largely administrative in character, are now vacant. But the senior chiefs, holding salaried offices in local government council or customary court, still sit in the palace to advise the *Ewi*.

RELIGION

The Yoruba say that they have 401 deities; this is certainly an understatement. Such is the complexity of their cosmology that scholars have tended to avoid the analyses of Yoruba rites and beliefs, preferring the search for origins in ancient Egypt or the study of Yoruba art: most of the carved wood figures made by the Yoruba are destined for the shrines of their deities.

In the last census the number of Yoruba who admitted to being devotees of the traditional cults, rather than being Christians or Muslims, varied from 20 percent of the population in Oyo or Ekiti (presumably mostly elderly people) to only 6 percent in Ijebu. However, most people continue to participate in the annual festivals of their town, though Muslims are probably a little more rigid than Christians in the nonobservance of certain rites. In this section I can but briefly outline the traditional religions, omitting all reference to Islam and Christianity, save perhaps to add here that in most Yoruba towns (the emirate of Ilorin being, of course, an exception) Islam is a personal and not a state religion and that Muslim law is not followed by the people, being indeed unknown to most of them.

Cults concerned with propitiation of the myriad Yoruba *orisha* (deities) are a prominent feature of Yoruba religion. Most Yoruba deities are anthropomorphic, but frequently these mythical figures are also associated with natural features, especially with rivers. The kaleidoscopic pattern of cults is due, of course, to the movement of people and ideas within Yoruba country in past centuries. There is perhaps an analogy in the Greek pantheon of deities that developed from local to national cults.

The priests of Yoruba cults usually hold no political office; they do not sit among the chiefs. They are usually—and especially so today—men of little wealth; their prestige in the community tends to be low though their sacred powers are feared. Thus, inasmuch as they may refuse to perform the expected rituals for the *oba* and the chiefs, they can be credited with some political influence.

Olorun (literally, owner of the sky) is the high god. He is the creator. But no shrines exist to him, no organized priesthood. He is invoked in blessings or in thanks, and one may call on him with prayers or by pouring water on kola nuts on the ground.

Next one must mention the *ifa* divination; this is believed to have been founded by Orunmila at Ile Ife; a similar system exists not only throughout the Yoruba country but also in the Benue Valley and among the Nupe and the Benin. The *babalawo*, the diviner, casts down onto his *ifa* board two chains of four palm kernels, cowries, or similar objects, some falling face up, others face down. For each of the 256 possible positions there is a lengthy verse, which is interpreted by the supplicant seeking to know the cause of illness or bad luck, the relative merits of candidates for a title, the fortune of war, the deity whom he has offended or ought to serve.

The Yoruba believe that, at their death, they go to live in a world beyond, where they can still influence and interfere in daily events on earth. A man thus makes annual sacrifices at the graves of his own immediate forebears on the same day that the lineage head and all lineage members sacrifice to the founder of the lineage. The *egungun*, masked dancers, in

Egungun **Dancers** (*Western Nigerian Information Service*)

whom the spirit of a deceased person is thought to reside temporarily, appear at funeral ceremonies. In Ado, as in most northern Yoruba towns, a festival is held in which each *egungun* dances through the town on a certain day, and on a final day all dance to the palace to greet the *oba*. It is these *egungun* who carry the carved wooden masks, the whole of their bodies being covered with cloth, raffia, or feathers.

The annual sacrifices to the royal ancestors are important, for the founder of the town will exercise his influence for the benefit of the whole town; however, in Ado these rites were carried out only perfunctorily.

In most Yoruba towns spirits said to be residing in a nearby hill or river are considered to be protecting the town. These spirits are not ancestors, but are sometimes more akin to "little people," perhaps representing earlier inhabitants of the area. Nobody would venture onto the hill at Ado where they reside. Annually the priests dance to the palace, where they convey their blessings to the *Ewi*, ceremoniously arrayed. In a sequence of later festivals, the junior and senior chiefs dance before the *Ewi*, making their obeisance to him and receiving in turn his blessing. In most Yoruba towns similar ceremonies of political allegiance are incorporated in religious festivals.

In only a few towns does there seem to be a specific harvest festival; but in all, the eating of new yams is associated with one or another festival held in September or October. Nor is there, today, any earth cult, although some writers see in the rites of the *ogboni* association the vestiges of such beliefs. Many of the deities peculiar to individual lineages represent, perhaps, the hill or river spirits of their town of origin.

Of the numerous Yoruba cults, I can give but a few examples. Shango is an early mythical *Alafin* (*oba*) of Oyo who hanged himself; he is god of thunder. The cult is important in Oyo, but is found in Ado too. The shrine in the compound of the hereditary priest contains the "thunderbolts" (often neolithic axes), carvings with the double-headed ax symbol, and the priests' paraphernalia. Lightning strikes thieves, and the priests appropriate all the deceased's property. When lightning in Ado killed a woman and her goat (but not the child on her back) the explanation was immediate: Lightning had killed her mother some years earlier but the daughter had withheld the goat from the priests; they were now taking their revenge.

Ogun, the god of iron and war throughout Yoruba country, is associated with Ire, an Ekiti town. At Ile Ife and neighboring towns the shrine of Ogun is a group of phallic-shaped granite monoliths. The annual festival of Ogun is usually one in which most of the townspeople participate; a dog is always sacrificed.

Orisha Oko, the farm deity, is associated with Irawo, a town near Shaki; the cult is found in most Oyo towns. Oya, the mythical wife of Shango, is also identified with the Niger River; several other mythical hero-deities are associated with the Oshun River. The myths describing the earthly activities of these gods vary widely from one town to another.

Most of these cults are held by individual lineages whose members participate, especially, in the annual festivals performed for the spiritual benefit of the whole town. Other men and women may be directed to the worship of a particular deity by *ifa*.

Although one group of *babalawo* consists primarily of diviners, others are doctors with considerable skill in treating physical and mental illness. Most of the latter tend to be specialists in one or more types of disease; they treat their patients on the basis of symptoms observed. Some of the treatments are prescribed in the *ifa* verses—one cites the use of the tranquilizer rauwolfia in treatment of mental illness. Yet with all this technical knowledge, the Yoruba believe that most disease and death is caused supernaturally —by witchcraft, by curses or charms. The witches are women, usually elderly, thought to possess some immaterial or concrete witchcraft substance; their powers are usually directed, either by design or otherwise, against those nearest to them—their husbands, co-wives, or children. Protection against witchcraft can be given by the doctors and by membership of certain cults.

The fear that one's rival is endeavoring to harm one is widespread among the Yoruba. Yet they are not a violent people. Their suicide rate is among the lowest in the world—probably less than five persons in a million dying annually in this way. Deliberate murder (outside modern urban situations where housebreaking is involved) is also rare; hunting accidents form a high percentage of the homicide cases brought before the courts.

CHANGE

Technological and social changes are taking place in West African society at a faster rate than the world has ever known; a boy born to an illiterate farmer becomes a brilliant surgeon or an atomic physicist. Yet these changes seem to be occurring among the Yoruba in such a way as to preserve much of the traditional social structure of the people.

Yoruba society is still a peasant society. The wealth gained from export crops gives employment to increasing numbers of craftsmen, usually local men. Yoruba country has no towns that are twentieth-century creations, though Ibadan has a large population of strangers, and Lagos is peopled almost entirely by immigrants of the past century. Government offices, schools, and hospitals are all built in the ancient Yoruba towns. There is, as yet, little industrialization and the few factories in Ibadan and Lagos are so highly capitalized as to employ a very small proportion of the total population. Free primary education results in greater population movement as those who leave school drift to the more commercial towns to seek work. This is a major social problem, and the government is endeavoring to get these boys to stay in the more rural areas by establishing collective farm settlements, and supplying provincial towns with piped water, electricity, and radio in order to make life there more attractive. But although agricultural research has produced new varieties of the staple food crops, it has discovered no new techniques that would revolutionize the traditional methods of growing them.

As a result, the traditional social structure is being largely maintained. Most men still live in the compounds of their own lineage. In some towns, where building land has a high market value, the lineage has become an agency for controlling the use and sale of land, its literate members keeping accounts and regular minutes of meetings.

The stranger in a Yoruba town—that is, any person not a member of one of its constituent descent groups—is not assimilated. He plans to return to his hometown eventually. In the town of temporary sojourn he joins the tribal union or improvement society—an association of his own townspeople. These associations provide recreation and security for their members and spend much time in discussing the affairs of their hometown, sending deputations to advise the chiefs and money to establish new schools or roads. Membership in the association is almost obligatory; a man who dissociates himself from his hometown is ostracized. The Yoruba town offers few opportunities to wealthy or educated strangers to achieve high prestige or political power; hence the desire of each man to retire to his hometown, where he is probably eligible for a chieftaincy title and will, at least, be a highly respected elder of his own large descent group. However, this attachment to the hometown may well be less strong among members of the rising generation who were born and are growing up in the distant places to which their parents had migrated.

Perhaps the most striking feature of the past three decades is the growth of a wealthy and educated elite. Yet the elite is a small group; only a half of 1 percent of the population earns more than £500 a year, and a half of these are employed by the government, public corporations, missions, or large commercial firms. A disproportionate number, nearly half of them, live in Ibadan. Here new associations develop that enhance feelings of corporateness among the elite and their wives—Freemasonry, charitable organizations such as the Red Cross, the Rotary club.

New family patterns emerge. Husband and wife both live in a European style of house, far from their parents and near kin, but each has numerous friends close by. The wife tends to take her husband's status, which is determined by the rank of his office or position; however, most wives expect to follow their own careers as teachers or nurses. The modern wife looks more to her husband for affection and companionship; yet he, as we have seen, is still closely tied to his own family. He is expected to educate a number of junior relatives. All but the most sophisticated men regard their mothers as being more closely related to them than their wives. Domestic roles are still segregated, and it is uncommon for men and women to interact freely in social gatherings. The absence of shared companionship in marriage, together with the economic independence of the wife, the relative ease of divorce and the lack of stigma attaching to it, and the suspicion of many men that women are primarily interested in winning the richest man possible—all these contribute to create tensions in marriage. Most educated Yoruba prefer a wife with a lower level of education than theirs—they do, of course, have little other choice—expecting her to be dutiful and subordinate to her husband.

A few men, usually with well-educated wives, do achieve a family relationship and household pattern not unlike that of the professional middle classes of England, whence comes their point of reference. And it is these few men who seem most concerned with theories of *Negritude* and the development of African culture. Most educated men wear Yoruba dress and speak Yoruba at home; yet they seem slow in actively supporting indigenous art, literature, and music. They incorporate European techniques and ideas into their own life without producing that feeling of alienation from their own culture that would lead them into conscious attempts to revive and preserve it.

There have been far greater changes in the government of the Yoruba town. The colonial administration tried conscientiously to preserve to the *obas* and chiefs their traditional authority. Yet inasmuch as the *oba*'s power derived, in fact, from the British, the relationship between the *oba* and his chiefs was reversed. The latter could no longer dethrone him, and he became an autocrat. This autocracy was increased when young men, such as the present *Ewi* of Ado, came to the throne. These men, correctly appointed according to customary law, were often the best-educated men living in their towns, while their chiefs remained elderly and illiterate.

The young *obas*, active in bringing new social services to the towns, became popular with their people. But most of them experienced periods of tense relationships with their chiefs as the power and prestige of the latter declined.

Between 1953 and 1955 local government councils were introduced into Yorubaland by the Action Group government of the Western Region. The elected councilors, predominantly young, literate men, have tended to become the local agents of their party. The region's legislators have endeavored to avoid any direct clash with the *obas*, claiming on one hand to support the traditional institution of kingship while on the other subjecting it to a control stronger than that in colonial times. In openly supporting the regional government the *obas* risk their popularity in their own towns. It seems probable that the *obas* will fail to find a new role that satisfies the expectations both of their people and of the government and that kingship will very slowly degenerate into an archaic survival.

Yoruba society provides a number of fascinating problems for the social scientist. The size and the antiquity of the towns are striking; yet these have been primarily rural settlements, characterized by groups based on descent and age. Today they are becoming urbanized *in situ*. The Yoruba kingdom, in which the sacred *oba* is elected by and is responsible to a council of titled chiefs, often themselves elected by lineage members, typifies a political structure that has hitherto received little attention. The status of Yoruba women, economically independent of their husbands while remaining overtly submissive, is another unusual feature.

The present century has wrought great changes in Yoruba society. The people have become among the wealthiest of African peasants and have eagerly adopted much of European technology. In a century the Yoruba kingdoms have passed from a period of internecine local wars, through a period of colonial rule, to become local government units in a modern independent state. Traditional roles are everywhere being modified and altered to meet the demands of modern society. But while social relationships change, much of Yoruba culture remains. The nationalism of the young, educated elite preserves the loyalty of the Yoruba to their own indigenous gowns and music, and reawakens their interest in their historical past. In the modern world the Yoruba will maintain their cultural identity for decades to come.

Note

(1) Lexico-statisticians describe the distance between the language of the Yoruba and those of the neighboring Edo, Nupe, or Fon, as being several thousand years; crudely, they are as remote as English and Russian. The marked differences between languages of neighboring peoples of the west African coast contrast strikingly with the close relationships among the languages of the Bantu-speaking peoples.

Bibliography

Daggered items (†) are cited as references in the text of the chapter.

History

Biobaku, S. O. (1957).   *The Egba and Their Neighbours, 1842–1872.* London: Oxford University Press.
The history of the growth and political development of the Egba Kingdom.

Fagg, William, and Frank Willett (1960).   "Ancient Ife, an Ethnological Summary," *Odu,* No. 8, pp. 21–35.
This and Willett (1960) summarize all that can be confidently stated about Ile Ife and its traditional art.

Greenberg, Joseph H. (1955†).   *Studies in Linguistic Classification.* New Haven, Conn.: The Compass Publishing Co.

Willett, Frank (1960).   "Ife and Its Archaeology," *Journal of African History,* Vol. 1, No. 2, pp. 231–248.

The Economy

Bascom, W. R. (1952).   "The Esusu: A Credit Institution of the Yoruba," *Journal of the Royal Anthropological Institute,* Vol. 53, pp. 63–69.

Galetti, R., K. D. S. Baldwin, and I. O. Dina (1956).   *Nigerian Cocoa Farmers.* London: Oxford University Press.
A very detailed account of the economy of the cocoa farmer, with a long introduction to Yoruba society.

Hodder, B. W. (1961).   "Rural Periodic Day Markets in Parts of Yorubaland," *Transactions and Papers of the Institute of British Geographers,* Vol. 29, pp. 149–159. (Cf. by the same author "The Yoruba Rural Market," pp. 103–117 in Paul Bohannan and G. Dalton, eds., *Markets in Africa,* Evanston, Ill.: Northwestern University Press, 1962.)

Lloyd, P. C. (1953).   "Craft Organisation in Yoruba Towns," *Africa,* Vol. 23, pp. 30–44.

Social Structure

Bascom, W. R. (1942). "The Principle of Seniority in the Social Structure of the Yoruba," *American Anthropologist,* Vol. 44, pp. 37–46.

Izzett, A. (1961). "Family Life among the Yoruba, in Lagos, Nigeria," in Aidan Southall (ed.), *Social Change in Modern Africa.* London: Oxford University Press for the International African Institute.

Lloyd, P. C. (1952). *Yoruba Land Law.* London: Oxford University Press for the Nigerian Institute of Social and Economic Research.
Land law is studied in relation to the social and political structure of four kingdoms—Ijebu, Ondo, Ado Ekiti, and Egba.

——— (1953). "Craft Organisation in Yoruba Towns," *Africa,* Vol. 23, pp. 30–44.

——— (1955). "The Yoruba Lineage," *Africa,* Vol. 25, pp. 235–251.

Schwab, W. B. (1958). "The Terminology of Kinship and Marriage among the Yoruba," *Africa,* Vol. 28, pp. 301–313.

Political Structure

Lloyd, P. C. (1960). "Sacred Kingship and Government among the Yoruba," *Africa,* Vol. 30, pp. 221–237.

Morton-Williams, P. (1960). "The Yoruba Ogboni Cult in Oyo," *Africa,* Vol. 30, pp. 362–374.

Religion

Bascom, W. R. (1944). "The Sociological Role of the Yoruba Cult Group," *Memoirs of the American Anthropological Association,* No. 63.

Idowu, E. Bolaji (1962). *Olodumare, God in Yoruba Belief.* London: Longmans, Green & Co., Ltd.

Morton-Williams, P. (1954). "The Atinga Cult among the South Western Yoruba: a Sociological Analysis of a Witch Finding Movement," in *Bulletin de l'Institut Français d'Afrique Noire,* Vol. 18, Ser. B., pp. 315–334.

Parrinder, G. (1963). *Religion in an African City.* London: Oxford University Press.
A survey of churches and sects in Ibadan.

Prince, R. (1961). "The Yoruba Image of the Witch," *The Journal of Mental Science,* Vol. 107, No. 449, pp. 795–805.

——— (1962). "Some Notes on Yoruba Native Doctors and Their Management of Mental Illness," T. Adeoye Lambo (ed.), *Report of the First Pan-African Psychiatric Conference, Abeokuta, Nigeria, November 1961,* pp. 279–288. Ibadan: Government Printer.

Twentieth-century Change

Leighton, Alexander H., T. Adeoye Lambo, Charles C. Hughes, Dorothea C.

Leighton, Jane M. Murphy, and David B. Macklin (1963). *Psychiatric Disorder among the Yoruba: A Report from the Cornell-Aro Mental Health Research Project in the Western Region, Nigeria.* Ithaca, N.Y.: Cornell University Press.

Lloyd, P. C. (1955). "The Development of Political Parties in Western Nigeria," *American Political Science Review,* Vol. 49, pp. 693–707.

———— (1959). "The Yoruba Town Today," *Sociological Review,* Vol. 7, No. 1, pp. 45–63.

PRONUNCIATION GUIDE

FOR AFRICAN WORDS

Some of the African languages are conventionally written with the Roman alphabet and others with the more phonetic International African Alphabet (IAA), an orthography developed by the International African Institute and widely adopted in sub-Saharan Africa [cf. "Practical Orthography of African Languages," Memorandum I (revised edition). London: International African Institute, 1930]. The following general guide indicates the usual phonetic values (sound equivalents) of the relevant symbols of both the Roman alphabet and the IAA when used in writing African languages. It is intended as an aid in pronouncing the terms and names from African languages that occur in the selections.

The standard African orthographies have not been used in this book for place names. These follow current usage, which often gives a Europeanized spelling that does not follow the phonetic principles outlined below. For example, Wagadugu, capital of the Republic of Upper Volta, is customarily written in French orthography, as Ouagadougou.

CONSONANTS

1. *p, t, k, b, d, w, f, v, s, z, l, h, m,* and *n* generally are pronounced as in English.
2. Ɓ is an implosive *b*, created by making a slight sucking in of air as *b* is pronounced.
3. ḍ is used for a retroflex *d*, which is pronounced with the tip of the tongue further back than when pronouncing *d* and sometimes with the underside of the tip of the tongue.
4. *g* is pronounced as a hard *g*, as in *got* or *gone.*
5. *r* has the sound of the rolled lingual (tip of the tongue) *r* of Scottish or Spanish.
6. *x* is pronounced as the *ch* in the German *ach* or Scottish *loch.*
7. *y* is pronounced as in *yet* or *your.*
8. *ty, dy, ny, ly, sy,* and *zy* represent palatal *t, d, n, l, s,* and *z.* For example, *ny* has the sound of *n* in *senior.*
9. *kp* and *gb* are pronounced as one sound, known technically as a labiovelar. For *kp* the sound is produced by making a "guck" or clucking sound with the velum (the soft palate which is behind the palate) and simultaneously opening the lips. For *gb,* the "guck" sound is made lower in the velar region

583

as the lips are opened. The two letters are never pronounced separately. For example, *Afikpo* is divided *A-fi-kpo,* never *A-fik-po:*

10. ŋ or *ng* is pronounced as *ng* in *sing.*
11. ɣ is a voiced velar fricative and is the voiced version (equivalent) of the unvoiced *ch* sound in the German *ach.*
12. ' is a glottal stop as in the *t* sound in *bottle* in the Brooklynese variant of American English.
13. Where *m, n, b,* or *h* precede *w,* they are pronounced together.
14. Where *m* or *n* precede any other consonant, the two consonants are sounded separately. The *m* or *n* is sounded as *mm* or *nn,* that is, with a slight hum, as in the African *Mboya* or *ndɛbu.*
15. Clicks, characteristic of the Khoisan languages, are made by closing the oral passage front and back, drawing the tongue downward to produce a vacuum, and releasing it at some point. The clicks are named in terms of where the tongue is released. / is a dental click; // is a lateral click; ! is an alveolar (gum-ridge) click; and ≠ is a palatal click.

VOWELS

16. *a, e, i, o,* and *u* are given their Italian values; that is, *a* is pronounced as in *alms, e* as the *a* in *ale, i* as the *ee* in *bee, o* as in *old,* and *u* as the *oo* in *loose.*
17. ɛ is pronounced as the *e* in *bet.*
18. ɔ is an open *o* with the sound of *ou* as in *ought.*
19. θ represents a middle *o* between the close *o* of *o* and the open *o* of ɔ.
20. ~ indicates nasalization.

LENGTH

21. Double letters indicate length (either for vowels or for consonants).

TONES

While many African languages are tonal, neither tones nor stresses are indicated here, as is conventional except in books written in African languages.

INDEX